HENDRIKUS BERKHOF

CHRISTIAN FAITH

An Introduction to the Study of the Faith

translated by
SIERD WOUDSTRA

REVISED EDITION

WILLIAM B. EERDMANS PUBLISHING COMPANY
GRAND RAPIDS, MICHIGAN

255 Jefferson Ave. S.E., Grand Rapids, Mich. 49503
Printed in the United States of America

Translated from the Dutch edition, *Christelijk Geloof,* © 1985
by Uitgeverij G. F. Callenbach B. V., Nijkerk, the Netherlands

Reprinted, November 1990

Library of Congress Cataloging in Publication Data

Berkhof, Hendrikus.
Christian faith.

Translation of Christelijk geloof.
Includes indexes.
1. Theology, Doctrinal. I. Title.
BT75.2.B4713 230 79-12673
ISBN 0-8028-3521-X

To my wife

To the University of Bern
In appreciation for the honorary
degree of Doctor of Divinity

Contents

CREATION

ISRAEL

JESUS THE SON

THE NEW COMMUNITY

THE RENEWAL OF MAN

THE RENEWAL OF THE WORLD

Why This Book?

IN 1 PETER 3:15 we are challenged to be ready at all times to give an answer to everyone who asks us to give the reason for the hope we have. That challenge comes to all Christians. Yet it puts theologians under a unique obligation. Much of systematic theology since the Enlightenment may be regarded as taking on that task in a secularized culture. But the theologian also hears a call in the confusion and polarization that disturb most major denominations.

These were the major considerations that prompted me to write this book. Relative to our secularized age, my aim was to present a restatement of the gospel which is as up-to-date and lucid as possible, stripped of all the ingrained misconceptions which obscure it for so many. Relative to the church, this book aims to articulate the gospel in such away that the reader will see how it goes its own way between rigid traditionalism on the one side and rudderless modernism on the other.

With this book I would like in the first place to help those who have been theologically trained for a special role in the interpretation and transmission of the gospel: preachers and pastors and, seeing how much all of us share the same questions, also priests. Secondly, I have in mind theological students. In my judgment they can use a one-volume survey of the whole of theology, a book that stands midway between Karl Barth's monumental *Church Dogmatics* and the hundreds of monographs on theological topics. Yet as with my earlier books—several of which have also appeared in English—I could not forget the many "ordinary" church members, who face in all kinds of ways the mandate of 1 Peter 3:15. They have a tougher time than ever before. They look to the theologians for help. And of what value is our theology if it is not also meant to equip the saints for service?

But that does give this book a dual character. I want it to be both informative and inspirational, to serve professionals as well as a larger public. To help accomplish this in one book I have used two type sizes in the text. Sections printed in the larger type are meant for all readers. These sections together form a coherent whole which can be understood apart from the sections in smaller type. The latter, meant specifically for theologians, indicate links with other theological disciplines, draw lines through history, mention important controversies, cite literature, and offer further argumentation and elucidation.

Trying to do both in one book is a tall order. What one reader might regard as superficial and too general would seem to another profound and overly detailed; what is to the one traditional Christian jargon may sound like heresy to the other. Those were some of the uncertainties I faced when this book was first published in the Netherlands in 1973. I am deeply grateful for the welcome the book received; the Dutch version is now in its fifth (revised) edition. Evidently, as regards my own country, my fears were ungrounded. Now I face the same uncertainties about this English edition. Besides, ecclesiastically and theologically the English-speaking world is not the same as the Netherlands or continental Europe. Moreover, because my original audience was Dutch, the references to English literature are not nearly as extensive as they would have been if the book had also been designed with English-speaking readers in mind.

The title of this book bears on these considerations. The concern of this book is not just *my* faith, or *our* faith, but *Christian* faith. Yet the title of the book is not "*The* Christian Faith." Such a claim would be presumptuous. What God has given us is inexhaustible, but we are only little people, still on the way toward fully understanding everything, while the gospel needs restating in ever new situations. There are bound to be many theological articulations of the faith, all of them pointing to the same thing and by their multiplicity relativizing and complementing each other. All of us write "according to the grace given to us," "in proportion to our faith." This book is one articulation among many. To some people it may not mean anything, even though—or because—they are just as good or better believers than the writer of this book. To many others, I hope it will be a welcome help for their faith and witness.

The subtitle is "An Introduction to the Study of the Faith." The size of this book may make the word "introduction" seem like false humility. I mean it in all seriousness, however. The study of the faith may be a scientific discipline, yet it is first and foremost an art. In the study of the faith one ventures, after having listened to others, to express God's truth oneself. The study of the faith—or, as it is better known in the English-speaking world, the pursuit of systematic theology—is thus not something to learn so much as something to do and practice. A book can do no more than help us to get started and stimulate us to try to do it on our own.

Keep this in mind in the large-type sections, where I try to put into words how I understand the truth of God. However, any reader should feel free to come up with better formulations. In the small-type sections I give readers the opportunity to see how I arrived at my formulations, and in particular I nudge them to move beyond what I have said with the use of the informal directions provided there. I introduce readers to the subject; from there they are to go on by themselves. As a matter of fact, that is what I am doing myself. More than anyone else I am aware how much I had to leave unsaid. All too often I had to break off what seemed like a promising line of thought before I could develop it fully, so that an already long book would not get any longer.

But in the small-type sections as well I have kept in mind this introductory character. All sorts of terms, problems, and controversies which once played a role in theological history and which most dogmatic handbooks now dutifully pass on, are left out. The history of theology frankly includes a lot that is useless to the modern believer reflecting on the faith. However, in cases of disagreement, the literature I have cited can help correct my judgment.

The choice of a limited but suitable bibliography was a mind-boggling task. The mere listing of titles is easy enough, but equally meaningless. I have tried to restrict myself to books which competently explicate a distinctive point of view or give one a useful overview of particular themes. In this second category Dutch literature takes priority. As I wrote in the preface to the first Dutch edition, "It always strikes me how much fine Dutch material is available on many themes." To substitute English works for these would have meant a major overhaul—if not more. Of course, I do not always agree with the publications I have cited: occasionally—but not always—I have put my own viewpoint over against them. While writing this book I also became aware how much my own earlier books proved to be building blocks for this more comprehensive volume. More than once I had to refer to these—for which reason I am grateful for the translation of several of these into English—because there I give a more detailed argumentation of what is more succinctly stated here.

Particularly from the classical writers I have occasionally culled representative quotations to indicate their point of view. Nevertheless, however judiciously selected, these are only references, no more. Let no one get the idea that he now knows where such a writer stands. These quotations are only meant to arouse the reader's theological curiosity and desire to search for more.

To assist readers, I decided to use a number of older and more recent systematic theologies as fixed points of orientation and to consult these regularly. These works are mentioned in the list of abbreviations.* It is a

---

*To the list of regularly consulted works should be added R. Prenter, *Creation and Redemption,* E.T. by Theodor I. Jensen from the second Danish edition (Philadelphia: Fortress

series that starts with Irenaeus and ends with Ott, though the latter work appeared too late for extensive consultation.

Since this book is written in such a way that each paragraph can be read separately, it can be used as a reference work, though that is not its primary intention. For that reason bibliographical references cited earlier may be mentioned in full in succeeding paragraphs. Normally, the year mentioned in a bibliographical reference is that of the first edition.

In the main text quotations from languages other than Dutch are only from German, English, and French sources. In the small-type sections I have also used Hebrew, Greek, and Latin. Yet there, too, I have severely restricted myself, lest many long quotations disrupt the flow of thought. Still, for centuries, Latin has played a large role in theology, and anyone who wishes to study the subject in depth should master that language. To make this English-language edition even more accessible to the reader, the translator has seen to it that most of these classical and foreign language quotations are here in English.

At this point I want to express my gratitude to and admiration of Dr. Sierd Woudstra, who translated this book so meticulously and with such a deep understanding of its content. He also discovered a number of mistakes and infelicities which have been corrected in the most recent Dutch edition.

This book has a dual dedication, to a person and an institution. Together they symbolize the two worlds that have made this theological volume possible. Bern symbolizes the diligent pursuit of theology everywhere in university faculties, theological schools, and seminaries, in Europe and North America. And my wife—well, she is no symbol. Fortunately not! She typed the entire manuscript and did much more besides. But that is not the most important. She has contributed more than anyone else to the calm and happy atmosphere within which this book could be written.

Leiden, summers of 1973 and 1979 —HENDRIKUS BERKHOF

Press, 1967). Because in this English edition of *Christian Faith* the full title of Prenter's work is always cited, it has been dropped from the list of abbreviations. [Translator's note.]

A Word from the Translator

MY FIRST EXPOSURE to the theology of Professor Hendrikus Berkhof was through his book *Well-Founded Hope.* I still remember the questioning excitement with which I read those lectures many years ago. Little could I have surmised at the time that some day I would have the opportunity to translate his major comprehensive volume on what in the English-speaking world is usually called Systematic Theology.

From a technical point of view, translating this book has caused me a number of difficulties, not all of which could be satisfactorily solved. Not only does Professor Berkhof write with great economy, but he is also most careful in his choice of words and does not hesitate to depart from traditional terminology. I am deeply grateful for his unfailing promptness in responding to my queries about such matters. If the translation has retained some of its original Dutch flavor, I ask the reader's indulgence. The book is tightly reasoned and a more or less free translation might have detracted from its theological precision.

In paragraph 5 of the opening chapter, Professor Berkhof explains why he has avoided—though not entirely—the traditional "dogmatics" and chosen instead *Geloofsleer* (German *Glaubenslehre*). Although this term has no specific English equivalent, I believe that "study of the faith" is unpretentious enough and at the same time sufficiently expressive of what this book is all about to serve as a substitute. The reader not accustomed to the term "study of the faith" should at first bear in mind that what this book offers is in effect a systematic theology.

Christian Faith first appeared in 1973, with a second edition following within a year. Not until the third edition (1975) could the author introduce a limited number of more substantial changes, primarily in response to significant comments from other theologians. Many of these reactions are published in a 1974 volume entitled *Weerwoord. Reacties op Dr. H. Berkhof's "Christelijk Geloof"* ("Reply. Reactions to Dr. H. Berkhof's 'Christian Faith'"), which 25 contributors presented to Professor Berkhof on his sixtieth birthday—another demonstration of the intense interest with which *Christian Faith* has been received and studied in the Netherlands. These few changes have in no way altered the basic design of the book. Late in 1978 the Dutch publisher requested a fourth edition, which allowed room for still more changes, primarily in the area of clarifying the author's Christology and updating the bibliographic references. All these changes have been incorporated into the present English edition. My own editorial changes are, with few minor exceptions, limited to the pruning of some Dutch periodical articles and book titles from the bibliography.

This is the fifth of Professor Berkhof's books to appear in English. His earlier books are *Christ and the Powers* (1962, 2nd ed. 1978), *The Doctrine of the Holy Spirit* (1964, 1976), *Christ the Meaning of History* (1966, 1979), and *Well-founded Hope* (1969). It is by far his most ambitious undertaking, although (as he reminds us in his foreword) these earlier publications have led up to this book.

Needless to say, a translator is neither responsible for nor necessarily in full agreement with what he translates. Often I have found myself silently entering into discussion with the author—though always driven by the same questioning excitement I felt when I read *Well-founded Hope.* Surely the ability of a theology book to stimulate reflection and discussion is precisely a great strength.

This book is not meant to be the final word. As Professor Berkhof is the first to say, all our theology, all our attempts to articulate in more or less precise concepts our Spirit-given faith, are but first words. God and our faith in him are always more than our systems. Yet notwithstanding their obvious limitations, the words must be spoken. The Christian faith seeks and demands the response of the study of the faith. Professor Berkhof has given us his response, one by which he has tried to help others as they believe and try to give their response. I believe he has given us a fine book, thoughtful and thought provoking, as well as an outstanding example of genuinely ecumenical theology. I consider it a privilege to have had a share in making this work available to the English-speaking world. Here the theologian will find something to chew on, the person in the pulpit a theology that is preachable and vitally related to life and its perplexing questions, and ordinary believers a theological perspective that can deepen faith and thereby establish them more firmly in that faith.

No one writes or translates a book in complete independence of other people. It is my pleasant duty to say how much I have appreciated the suggestions and advice I have received along the way. I also owe a word of thanks to the people at Eerdmans Publishing Company for much work behind the scenes; I appreciate their willingness for regularly extending deadlines. In particular I wish warmly to thank Professor Berkhof for his promptness in doing his homework whenever I sent him another letter with questions. It has also been a delight to come to know him and his gracious wife more personally.

Grand Rapids, summer 1979 —SIERD WOUDSTRA

List of Abbreviations

Althaus, *CW*	Paul Althaus, *Die christliche Wahrheit.* Gütersloh: Bertelsmann, I (1947), II (1948)
Barth, *CD*	Karl Barth, *Church Dogmatics.* Edinburgh: T. & T. Clark, E. T. 1955ff., Vols. I-IV
Bavinck, *GD*	Herman Bavinck, *Gereformeerde Dogmatiek,* quoted from the second revised and enlarged edition, Kampen, I (1906)–IV (1911). Because later editions have a different pagination, reference is made only to the paragraph and the number of the 580 subdivisions (indicated with *no.*).
Beker-Hasselaar, *WK*	Dr. E. J. Beker and Dr. J. M. Hasselaar, *Wegen en Kruispunten in de dogmatiek,* Kampen, I (1978), II (1979), III (1981)
Brunner, *Dg*	Heinrich Emil Brunner, *Dogmatics.* London: Lutterworth, 1950ff., Vols. I-III
Calvin, *Inst*	John Calvin, *Institutes of the Christian Religion.* Edited by John T. McNeill. Translated by Ford Lewis Battles. Philadelphia: Westminster Press, 1960
D	Henricus Denzinger, *Enchiridion symbolorum, definitionem de rebus fidei et morum,* in the revised edition of Adolfus Schönmetzer, S.I. All quotations from the 33rd edition, Freiburg, 1965, and rendered into English by the translator of this book *(Christian Faith)*
H	Heinrich Heppe, *Reformed Dogmatics.* Set out and illustrated from the sources. Revised and edited by Ernst Bizer. English translation by G. T. Thomson. London: George Allen and Unwin, 1950; Grand Rapids: Baker, 1978
Irenaeus, *AH*	Irenaeus, *Against Heresies,*, quoted from *The Ante-Nicene Fathers.* Grand Rapids: Eerdmans, 1953, Vol. I
MS	*Mysterium salutis. Grundriss heilsgeschichtlicher Dogmatik.* Edited by Johannes Feiner and Magnus Löhrer. Einsiedeln, I (1965)–IV/2 (1973)
Ott, *AG*	Heinrich Ott, *Die Antwort des Glaubens. Systematische Theologie in 50 Artikeln.* Stuttgart-Berlin, 1972
R	Carl Heinz Ratschow, *Lutherische Dogmatik zwischen Reformation und Aufklärung.* Gütersloh, I (1964), II (1966)
RGG	*Die Religion in Geschichte und Gegenwart,* 3. Auflage. Tübingen, I (1957)–VI (1962)

S	Heinrich Schmid, *Die Dogmatik der evangelisch-lutherischen Kirche dargestellt und aus den Quellen belegt,* 7. Auflage. Gütersloh, 1893
Schleiermacher, *CF*	Friedrich Schleiermacher, *The Christian Faith.* English translation of the second German edition. Edinburgh: T. & T. Clark, 1928
Thomas, *ST*	Thomas Aquinas, *Summa Theologiae,* left unfinished because of his death in 1274, divided into Books (I, etc.) and Questions (indicated by q.), which are again subdivided into articles (indicated by art.)
Tillich, *ST*	Paul Tillich, *Systematic Theology.* Chicago: University of Chicago Press, I (1951)–III (1963). The pagination is that of the American edition.
Trillhaas, *Dg*	Wolfgang Trillhaas, *Dogmatik.* Berlin, 1962, quoted from the 2. verbesserte Auflage of 1967
TDNT	*Theological Dictionary of the New Testament.* Translated and edited by Geoffrey W. Bromiley. Grand Rapids: Eerdmans, 1964–76, Vols. I-X
Weber, *Gl*	Otto Weber, *Grundlagen der Dogmatik.* Neukirchen: Kreis Moers, I (1955), II (1962)

Scripture quotations are as a rule from the *Revised Standard Version.* Where a different version has been used, this has been indicated.

Preface to the Revised Edition

The idea of writing a Systematic Theology occurred to me one evening in May 1969. I was riding home on my bike, having just attended one of the large meetings at which the future of the university was being examined and discussed. It was thus the time of the so-called "student revolts." Pedalling home I had a sudden "inspiration" (I know of no other word for it) to write a Dogmatics now. Why now? At the time I did not know. In retrospect I would say that the farther we want to venture in bringing about greater freedom, equality, and brotherhood in our society, the more we need to go back to what is firm and unchangeable, to the God who makes history with his covenant and wants to involve our history in his covenant.

In referring to "our society" I was thinking first of all of our Western society as it revolves more and more around autonomous man and considers God a superfluous hypothesis. But I was also thinking of Christianity, which everywhere comes up with contradictory answers to the question how the gospel can best be articulated in word and deed in this society. I wrote thus against the backdrop of secularization and polarization. But of course the turbulent period of the sixties continued to make its impact. Readers will notice this especially in the part "The Renewal of the World," a theme which to the best of my knowledge is not discussed in any of the other dogmatics textbooks, and which in the present egocentric age is all too quickly forgotten.

I can summarize all these motives as concern for a world which is losing its cohesive power, which is pluralistically and permissively falling apart, and which is losing its sense of meaning, purpose, and direction. Yet I am not a prophet of doom. If it is true that God watches over his world, the counterforces are also bound to be there. We see these forces in a widespread quest for the *meaning of life.* Precisely in our culture this is a question which consciously or unconsciously occupies the minds of many. Other concerns, such as those about food, medical care, education, recreation, and political and social rights, have to a great degree been met. But the solution to the so-called "ultimate questions," which for centuries seemed more or less self-evident, threatens to elude us.

As a human being who himself struggles in this Western world, I have looked at the Christian faith especially from this angle. Such a stance both sharpens and restricts our view. Many believe that it is better to do without such a stance because of its restrictive character. But no one escapes having a perspective from which to operate. All the giants in theology have worked that way. The keener the awareness that one writes from a certain angle, the more one will try to push back the boundaries. And anyone who is not aware of this state of affairs, presuming to be articulating the truth of God in its fullness, more than anyone else becomes the victim of this narrowing of his or her perspective.

Just when the first edition of my book came out (December 1973), the term *contextuality* came into vogue. In the Third World the attempt was made to study the faith entirely in the context of one's own socioeconomic, historical, or cultural problematics. Western theology was therefore rejected as being "academic." At the same time some scholars tried to unmask this being academic as disguised contextuality. But the results ("imperialistic," "capitalistic") were meager and not very convincing, because the attempt was made from too narrow a political and economic perspective. Of course in principle our colleagues in the Third World are right: we, too, theologize contextually, but then in an altogether different context from, for example, that in Latin America (poverty and exploitation), in Africa (tribal cultures and religions), or in Asia (the individual in relation to the All). Our context is determined by the questions concerning meaning: What do we live for? What is the purpose of this world? Is there progress in society and culture? Is there a future for my life beyond death?

From the Third World we must learn to be willing to theologize contextually, because only thus will we be able to serve our ecclesiastical and sociocultural neighbors with our work. Western theology must articulate the Word in such a way that it comes through especially as the answer to our anxious questions concerning meaning. That is how I intended my book when I first wrote it, and that is how I still intend it. No one is served if we step outside our context and, for example, develop a "theology of the poor"—any more than if, for example, the Koreans would annex Pannenberg. We should both gratefully accept the contextualities of others and use our own contextualities to reach our regional neighbors with the gospel. The conditions, however, are a mutual awareness of the limiting significance of our stances, regular attempts to go beyond the boundaries this imposes upon us, and striving for greater universality and catholicity. Exactly for such overstepping we need the accents provided by theologies from other contexts. The gospel is both one and universal, and the evangelical legitimacy of our contextuality can only lie in its complementary character. That is how I intended my design of the study of the faith. In a particular time and in a particular locality (secular 20th-century Europe [or America]) it seeks to articulate the Good News which is an answer to our questions, precisely because it goes far beyond our boundaries in terms of its origin, content, and purpose. The tension in this last sentence (between contextuality and universality), which is also heard in the motto of Tennyson on p. ii, should, if what I write is to the point, constantly be felt in this book.

Having thus stated the purpose of this book in general, I must now try to point out what is special about this new edition. Exactly ten years after the appearance of the first edition, the publisher informed me that I should prepare the text of the fifth edition [the source of the present revision] and that I would be free to make whatever changes I felt were necessary. I was even happier with the second half of that notice than with the first. To be sure, numerous larger or smaller changes had been made in the third edition (1975), as well as in the fourth (1979 [the source of the original English translation]). But I and the publisher regarded it as absolutely necessary that it be possible to use the old and new editions side by side in classes, courses, and study groups without undue difficulty, which also meant that the pagination had to remain pretty much the same.

After ten years this is no longer possible. Like other disciplines, dogmatics does not stand still. That is not the same as "making progress." But it does mean that new angles regularly present themselves beside the earlier ones, or even dislodge them. That may happen through the appearance of different contexts, through shifts within one's own context, or simply on account of the ongoing thinking in a certain segment of one's context. Life is fast, and much can happen in a decade. If this book is to be of service for another ten years to an apparently still growing number of users who seek theological instruction, it may not remain tied to the iron leash of its first size and contents. Both I and the publisher have tried to keep the size and thus also the price down while meeting the goal of bringing the book up to date (in more than one respect).

Most users will undoubtedly appreciate specific indications of drastic changes in size or content. Therefore I list here a number of changes which I consider important, following the paragraphing and pagination of this revised edition.

par. 3, p. 19—more material on religion and faith;
par. 4, pp. 22–23—greater precision on Islam;
par. 6, pp. 36–37—more up-to-date information on systematic theology as a science;
par. 7, p. 47—new and added material on "revelation" as prolegomenon;
par. 10—an entirely new paragraph on "Revelation and Experience"!
pars. 11–59—the numbering of all paragraphs has moved up by one from the old edition (from pars. 10–58).
par. 13, pp. 71–72—a new discussion of the concept of history in theology;
par. 17, pp. 94, 96–97—changes and additions with respect to the authority of Scripture;
pars. 19–25—scattered additions on the position of process theology (see also the new entry in the subject index);
par. 30, pp. 234, 237–238, 239–240, 245—changes in the discussion of the covenant and covenant history;
par. 31, p. 258—an addition in the section on the titles of Jesus; pp. 258–260—the section "The rejection" entirely rewritten; p. 270—the section on the promise of the land also rewritten;
par. 33, pp. 294–297—the section in small type rewritten with an eye to the

more complete discussion and evaluation of Arius later in the book;
par. 35, pp. 308–310—changes in the presentation of the doctrine of reconciliation;
par. 37, pp. 332–333—replaced by a hopefully better constructed text;
par. 38, pp. 338–339—additions on the "filioque";
par. 40—additions to the discussion of baptism, the meal, and office because of the Lima reports; pp. 390–392—added material on the basic difference between the Roman Catholic and Protestant views of office;
par. 41, pp. 408 and 410—clarification of the ecumenical problematic;
par. 43, pp. 429–430—more on the difference between Roman Catholicism and Protestantism in the appropriation of salvation;
par. 45, p. 441—agreement with present Roman Catholic theology on the doctrine of justification;
par. 48, pp. 464–466—addition on the poor as a theological concept;
par. 51, p. 489—addition on current views of the hereafter;
par. 54, pp. 513–514—more restrained and mondial on the European model;
par. 58, pp. 529–531—changes on the relationship of the individual and humanity in the consummation;
par. 59, p. 545—the same, but now in the form of asking questions.

In my judgment these are the most important changes. But this is by no means all. In the subject index one should consult such concepts as Auschwitz, liberation theology, experience, feminist theology, and Pneuma-Christology. Note, too, how often the term "Scripture" has been replaced by "Bible" (whenever the discussion was not about the theological status). Changes have also been made on a number of pages where the reader might be offended by a sexist use of language.

Particularly time consuming was the striking and adding of items in the literature. Was it really worth all the effort that went into it? However, precisely in the small-type sections I have kept in mind future dogmaticians. Dogmatics is not repeating or explaining what others have said, but after much listening and weighing expressing the truth oneself as one sees it. For this search for answers of one's own it is necessary to study views with which one is not familiar, views that often contradict each other. The citation of books is no indication of agreement on my part, but simply an offer to help others learn to think along different lines and so to arrive at a position of their own.

I had thought that the reworking of the text and the updating of the literature would take a little over two months. As it turned out, it took over half a year. But it was an exciting and beautiful time, in which I was forced as well as privileged to reexamine in many directions the whole territory of the study of the faith. I hope that the reading and study of this book will give many readers some of the inspiration and information, of the spiritual deepening and the intellectual clarification, that the reworking of the book gave to me.

Leiden, August 1, 1984 HENDRIKUS BERKHOF

Introduction

1. PROLEGOMENA

IT IS CUSTOMARY to begin this kind of work, which seeks to penetrate a particular area of reality, by showing how that area relates to adjoining areas. With a few rough lines the writer quickly outlines a map of that wider field, and then goes on to point out where his specific subject is located on that map, together with the roads that lead to it from the surrounding territory. There seems to be no good reason not to follow the same procedure when we deal with the Christian faith. We would thus have to begin by making a general sketch of the wider area of religion and faith, and then within those contours indicate the place of the Christian faith.

The matter is, however, not quite as simple as that. Already at such a seemingly innocent point as methodology, the specific character of the area of reality we wish to enter makes itself strongly felt. For assuming that the Christian faith expresses itself normatively in the New Testament, we face the fact that from the very outset this faith is opposed to the presupposition that it is only a particular form of the general phenomenon of "religion." In the New Testament this faith presents itself as a gift of the Holy Spirit, a fruit of election, a special revelation, an insight which no human heart has conceived. It is no small matter to deny from the start this basic religious conviction in the method we choose to employ. But the big question is how to give expression to this conviction in the method (*met-hodos* = "access") we decide to use. How can access be gained into something which presents itself as a leap into a strange reality? But, conversely, how can we abandon such an attempt if at the same time this Christian faith somehow and somewhere "lands" in our reality and becomes part of it, though perhaps a very strange part? The problem we are faced with is that of the legitimacy and contents of the so-called "Prolegomena" to Dogmatics.

This problem has always played a large role in theology. As early as the 2nd century, the Apologists searched for experiences and convictions they had in common with their opponents. Since the Middle Ages, Roman Catholic theology has held to the doctrine of the *praeambula fidei* (portals of the faith), especially the proofs for God's existence. See Aquinas, *ST* I, q. 2, art. 2, and II, q. 1, art. 2. The Reformers saw little or no value in this search. But Protestant Scholasticism soon continued the medieval tradition by giving dogmatics an infrastructure of natural theology. In the 17th century, under the influence of Descartes, this infrastructure came to be viewed as a help to prove the truth of the Christian faith. In the 18th century the Prolegomena became for many the real contents of theology. Kant's *Critique of Pure Reason* (1781), however, demonstrated the inability of reason in this area.

But that was not the end of the problem of the Prolegomena. The formulation of the problem was changed, however. The increasing secularization of life in Europe led to a deeply felt need, more than ever since the Apologists, for an access to the Christian faith from within experiences and insights common to all people. To Schleiermacher, *CF* pars. 1–14, goes the honor of having grandly inaugurated the modern tradition of Prolegomena by anchoring the Christian faith in "the feeling of absolute dependence," regarding it as its highest developed form. Nineteenth-century theology continued and elaborated this tradition; the essence and truth of the Christian faith were now built on the essence and truth of the general phenomenon of religion.

Schleiermacher was or did become aware, however, that there was something problematic about his Prolegomena. He revised them in the second edition, and with that, in his *Zweites Sendschreiben* (Second Open Letter; to Dr. Lücke, 1829), he clarified his changed viewpoint together with some of the reasons for the change. He says there that there is a chasm between his "Introduction," which contains the Prolegomena, and his Dogmatics, and that no one should think that "I want to use a common religious consciousness to account for Christian piety." This substructure, while being able to give us the concept of "redemption," can never give the redeemer himself. Hence it follows that "Für die christliche Glaubenslehre ist die Darstellung zugleich die Begründung" (for the Christian doctrine of faith the exposition is at the same time the foundation). Hence the remarkable line of thought in the second edition of *CF,* par. 11, 5, that all he was after was to arrive at a phenomenological description of the unique character of the Christian faith, and in no way did he pretend to furnish a proof for its truth. "Everything we say in this place is relative to dogmatics, and dogmatics is only for Christians; and so this account is only for those who live within the pale of Christianity." Thus there lies a gap between the general religious consciousness and the Christian faith. And calling the latter the highest form of the former is not making a general statement but a statement of faith.

In the 20th century this methodological uncertainty has become dynamite under the Prolegomena. The best example is Barth's *CD,* esp. I,1 and I,2: "The Doctrine of the Word of God: Prolegomena to Church Dogmatics." Schleiermacher's concessive statement, "The exposition of Christian doctrine is its proof as well," now becomes the starting point. "Prolegomena to dogmatics are possible only as a part of dogmatics itself. The syllable pro- in the word prolegomena is to be understood figuratively. What is in question is not the things that must be said previously, but the things that must be said first" (*CD* I,1, p. 45). And what is to be said first is that God makes his Word happen without root or point of contact in human possibilities.

Barth thus completely rejects the search for an access from the surrounding territory. This honesty made a great impression, because it freed dogmatics from forced attempts to suggest a way and camouflage a chasm. It was not surprising that this radicalism was followed by others. Examples are the systematic theologies of Brunner, Vogel, and Weber. But certainly not everyone followed. Especially the opposite "method of correlation," employed by Tillich in his *ST*, had a great influence. Tillich wanted to correlate human consciousness and Christian faith as question and answer to prevent the Christian faith from operating as it were in a vacuum, unrelated to human thinking and searching. Many saw this danger in Barth. Of his own method Tillich says: "In using the method of correlation, systematic theology proceeds in the following way: it makes an analysis of the human situation out of which the existential questions arise, and it demonstrates that the symbols used in the Christian message are the answers to these questions" (*ST* I, p. 662). But this brief quotation is sufficient to show that this method, too, evoked opposition. Do only questions arise out of the human situation and no answers? And are these questions of such a nature that the Christian faith is the fitting answer? Or do the questions presuppose the answers?

The present situation in Prolegomena shows great confusion. Most theologians are of the opinion (contra Barth) that something should be said *before* to bring out the relevance and importance of the basic concepts of the Christian faith, but they differ widely about what is to be said before. Protestant theology thinks of such questions as the structure and needs of man's existence, his being part of history *(Geschichtlichkeit)*, and his orientation to a utopian future.

This question has always been of special concern to Roman Catholic theology. It emphasizes especially man's innate urge to transcend himself: man is made for more than he himself has or can achieve by his own powers, and that "more" he finds in revelation. K. Rahner is regarded as the champion of this method (see his *Grundkurs des Glaubens,* 1970).

Both the similarity to and the differences from the 19th century are striking. Now, too, there is the urge for a solid anchoring of the Christian faith in man's natural existence. This concern includes more than religion as such (which due to secularization has lost much of its anthropological relevance); it now includes the whole search for something for man to hold on to, for meaning, for a mandate and a perspective for life. This greater comprehensiveness is to be welcomed as an enrichment of our thinking about Prolegomena. But this broadened perspective cannot hide the fact that the chasm, which Schleiermacher came up against and which led Barth to give up traditional Prolegomena, remains. More on this theme in par. 10.

We opt for the legitimacy of Prolegomena. The discussion about it has been unnecessarily burdened by the idea that if something is said "before," the Christian faith has to relate harmoniously with it. Relationships in our world can be of many different kinds: synthetic, antithetic, dialectic, complementary. The conviction that the Christian faith sustains a special relationship to particular areas of our experiential reality does not necessarily require that we now determine the nature of that relationship. Of the reality of that relationship we are convinced; more than that, we are convinced that the Christian faith is related to the totality of our experiential reality. This conviction is implicit in the Christian faith itself, proceeding as it does on the premise that the Word that has happened to us is also the ground of all created reality. "He came to that which was his own" (John 1:11). The firstborn from the dead is also the firstborn of all creation (Col. 1:15ff.) and the one in whom as the Head all things will be brought together (Eph. 1:10). Therefore divine salvation and earthly reality are complementary concepts; it is only in relation to each other that they can become visible. God's healing and salvation-bringing work is directed to us and the world in which we live. From this it follows that in principle there is nothing that does not touch on the contents of the Christian faith and that there is no area from which no road leads to it. All of existence could thus properly be regarded as the domain of Prolegomena. Practically such is of course impossible. No one is able to know and to take everything into his purview. Everyone has his limitations. For that reason there is such a wide divergence among theologians in their Prolegomena, though that does not allow one to say that the approach of the one is right and not that of the other.

These insights, however, make the writing of Prolegomena very difficult. One could ask, moreover, what is gained by it. Should not the manner in which God's saving work touches and affects our reality much rather become clear from the description of the saving work itself? There seems to be much in favor of the practice of the Reformation theologians, who did not bother with preliminaries but went straight to the point.

This wise soberness can no longer be followed, we believe, because of the different times in which we live. Between us and the Reformation lies the Enlightenment and everything that followed. As a result, human self-awareness has become infinitely greater while God has become more of a question mark. For modern man, God's salvation and the reality he knows have become two separate things; the world has become increasingly more prominent and salvation increasingly more vague. The Christian believer, too, cannot get away from that climate. A contemporary book about the Christian faith can ignore this climate only at the cost of some or much of its effectiveness. At certain periods in the past, omitting the preliminaries was no doubt the proper thing to do, and the writer did his readers a favor with such a direct approach. Today, however, a similar directness might fall cold on the reader and give the impression that the writer does not really care for him. It could foster the idea that when we speak about the faith, we deal with a world which exists all by itself, alongside of the ordinary, real world. We therefore opt for Prolegomena.

But the moment we have made this decision, the objections are there again. To begin with, there is the question which aspect of reality we shall make the base from which to understand the revelation the Christian faith speaks about. Will not this choice itself already prove an unquestionable decision, one based on unargued prior philosophical, ethical, or theological presuppositions? Right from the start, beginning with the Prolegomena, these presuppositions would thus have a determinative influence on the whole of our dogmatics. Or the other way around, is not the choice and description of the area from which to tackle the faith already dependent on how the faith will be described? It is also very well possible that both perils are acute at the same time. In any case, ending in a vicious circle is far from imaginary. Stated differently, purporting to give an objective analysis of a segment of reality, we may be looking at it from a perspective that corresponds with our understanding of the Christian faith, with the sketch of the reality from which we will look at the faith already hiding a religious decision.

Can we escape this danger? Not really, because no one can step outside himself and adopt a totally objective standpoint, especially not when such fundamental questions are at stake. What can be done is to be aware of the pit falls so that the dangers are minimized. One who is conscious of the dangers will be on guard against devising his Prolegomena purely on the basis of a philosophy that happens to be in vogue at the time, or with the use of trends that happen to be fashionable in literature, natural science, or the social sciences. Such would be proper enough, and perhaps even necessary, in a sermon or articles of a pastoral, apostolary, or apologetic nature; but a book on Christian doctrine has its own requirements.

Considering how easy it is to get on to the wrong track, in our Prolegomena we use as our starting point the area of reality in which the Christian faith was initially "developed" or "entered" (which of these terms is correct can only later become clear), namely the area of religion. Thus we have a combination of a phenomenal and a historical approach. And at the same time we go back to an age-old tradition in the Prolegomena. This may seem less than a felicitous choice in an age which is often emphatically presented as post-Christian (*religionslos*). But even in such an age honesty compels us to recognize that the origin of Christianity lies in the world of religion. We could not very well ignore or deny this anyway, because our world continues to regard the Christian faith as a form of "religious life." In view of the secularization of other aspects of reality, this outlook is correct to this extent, that those other areas are suitable for the construction of our Prolegomena only if we add a transcendental dimension to them. Experience teaches that that is considered questionable and dishonest by our modern world. It is, as a matter of fact, a question whether we run the risk of a loss of intelligibility if we make religion the content of our Prolegomena. Furthermore, in our culture the search for religion continues, and is even increasing in intensity. Modern man retains a vague awareness that it is precisely religion that deals with the ultimate and most comprehensive questions. We will have little difficulty to relate these question to many others occupying the mind of contemporary man, such as the meaning of life and of existence, freedom, death, man's place in the cosmos, the direction of evolution, etc. From the whole of reality we shall take the aspect of religion and use it as the basis from which to acquire an understanding of the relevance of the Christian faith for that total reality.

At the present time, theology in the Western world shows a strong tendency to construct Prolegomena with the use of contemporary philosophical thought, even though the results are rather ephemeral. Kant, Hegel, Heidegger, Jaspers, Whitehead, Wittgenstein, Merleau-Ponty, Teilhard de Chardin, Bloch, Levinas, Ricoeur, and others have been used to develop some type of theology. As such there is nothing against this ("all things are yours"!), provided one realizes that these thinkers are often interpreted in a way that they themselves reject (Teilhard de Chardin, Levinas, and Ricoeur are "believing" exceptions). Then, however, it becomes a question whether there is much in favor of "baptizing" them against their will and so have them build "vestibules of the faith."

It would be different if a theologian of great intellectual ability and clear vision were able to offer Prolegomena which would be an analysis of existence *(Daseinsanalyse)* in which many of his contemporaries could recognize themselves and which would at the same time give them a new outlook on the Christian faith as contradiction *and* fulfillment of their understanding of life. Pascal's *Pensées* are an excellent example of this. Steps in that direction can also be found in Kierkegaard, J. H. Gunning, and, more systematically, H. Thielicke, *The Evangelical Faith,* I (E.T. 1974).

2. RELIGION

THE FIELD OF HUMAN RELIGION is so vast and varied that after a long period of passionate searching for "the essence of religion" (eighteenth and nineteenth centuries) many now have given up hope of finding a comprehensive definition. Even so, every explorer has a more or less clear picture of what he is after. And despite the variation, the pictures are more similar than dissimilar. The same is true of the definitions that are given. This encourages us to come with our own definition. In the awareness of its inadequacy, and thus being open for a better one, we describe religion as: *the relationship to the Absolute.*

This description has the advantage that it states both what is unique about religion and what its function is in human life. Human life is, after all, living in relationships. We are human in and through our relationships to the world around us, to our fellow human beings, our job, societal structures, culture, science, nature. Religion as relationship to the Absolute is our awareness that we stand in yet another altogether different relationship, to something which is not part of our phenomenal world, though it cannot be known apart from it either, a reality which is the ground of our existence.

Does such a ground needing no further ground exist? Is there amid all the limitations, finitude, and relativities of the phenomenal world a power which is absolute, self-contained, not dependent on something else, and which upholds this world of relativities? Here we can say no more than that the search for this absolute seems to indicate that it belongs to being human to want to think and to need it, and that with it there is the certainty that this absolute can be found and that people can enter into relationship with it.

We mention two things here, *need* and *certainty.* We can also say that religion is a question and an answer at the same time. This inner need and questioning attitude may well be the most enigmatic and fascinating aspect of what we call man. Repeatedly it can be seen that his relationships with the world as it presents itself to him and which he needs do not seem to be enough for him. He cannot help reaching beyond this world and thereby beyond himself. The answers the world gives to his questions and the satisfaction it offers him leave him unfulfilled. He keeps on asking questions, beyond all the answers that have been given. His nature is apparently such that he cannot be content with the world that is and its relations and relativities. There is within him a permanent restlessness, a thirst, a void, clamoring for filling and fulfillment.

The reverse side of religion is its certainty, its being-an-answer. Religious man regularly experiences that he receives a final answer, that the Absolute enters into a relationship with him, and that in this way he is initiated into a depth of knowledge and life in which his humanity finds the fulfillment for which it is made.

Intentionally we use two words here, *knowledge* and *life.* For man's fundamental discontent is related to both. His thirst for knowledge is too great to be quenched by the knowledge that can be gained from this world of relativities. He keeps asking all the way to the absolute ground. And his yearning for fulfillment is too great to be satisfied by the satisfactions and happiness which his limited, faltering, earthly, and care-filled existence can offer him. He keeps pressing for a knowledge of the Absolute and for complete self-fulfillment. For him the two quests are apparently one. He hankers after truth and happiness, revelation and salvation. And in his religion, through his relationship with the Absolute he hopes to find both of these together: the revelation of the divine is at the same time in some way revelation of the way that leads to salvation and bliss.

Religion is thus a relationship going beyond phenomenal relationships, while complementarily most intimately connected with these. The latter fact explains the bewildering variety there is in religion. All these religions, being both question and answer, belong complementarily to widely varying human situations, in each of which the questions concerning knowledge and salvation are put differently. Religion is thus embedded in a specific cultural-anthropological pattern, while breaking through it in one way or another at the same time. Not in respect to its essence, but certainly in respect to its manifestations, religion is conditioned in many ways: geographical, psychical, social, cultural, historical.

Hence the great variety of questions, particularly where it concerns salvation. In one religion the human deficiency is experienced especially in man's sense of smallness and powerlessness in a great and threatening world. In another religion it is the mystery of pain and suffering, or of mortality and death, or of man's constant failures and guilt.

And even greater is the variety of answers. Now man finds rest in the tribal bond, in the belief in an immortal soul, in knowing himself part of the world of his ancestors which supports and surrounds him; then again in the eternal cycle of nature, the cosmic order in the solar and stellar world, the correlation of act and fate, or the polarity of light and darkness. Still others look to the life of the nation or the idea of a universal humanity, to man's spirit as a divine spark, or to losing oneself in the world-soul. In Judaism and Christianity redemptive history is the means whereby man enters into fellowship with God.

This great variety as to content notwithstanding, structurally the religions exhibit a great uniformity. Nearly all have three elements: the element of myth, teaching, or proclamation; a sacred rite or cult; and rules for moral conduct. The first concerns the manner in which the Absolute opens up, the second man's immediate response, and the third the consequences of such knowledge and salvation for his everyday life. Many are inclined to add yet a fourth element, that of inner experience, the mystical component of religion. This, however, presupposes a measure of individuality and a corresponding contact with the deity which was and is by no means found in all religions.

Returning to the variety in religion and its causes, we have now come up against the problematic inherent in religion. For we have seen that the religious answers that are given differ greatly, varying with the kind of world the people, tribes, nations, or cultures giving the answer live in. The Absolute cannot be known or experienced apart from the world one lives in. By its very nature it is that which infinitely transcends the phenomenal and the relative, but which at the same time, due to the fact that we are bound to the phenomenal world, can be known only when and insofar as it appears in these relative phenomena.

And that is where the differences begin. For the one the cycle of nature is the window to the Absolute, while for the other this is a purely phenomenal and secular event. The same holds for history, or the world soul, or the cosmic harmony. For some these are only secular matters, for others they are sacral happenings. Behind these differences lies a much more serious problem: is it not a contradiction to look for the Absolute in the relative? But where else can man, bound as he is to the phenomenal world, find the Absolute? But does this not mean that he looks for something which by definition cannot be found, making religion a noble form of self-delusion? For the Absolute is simply nowhere. Trying to find it in a secular fact or happening, one is in great danger of overemphasizing and sacralizing the secular and of misunderstanding its secularity, and simultaneously of relativizing and secularizing the Absolute.

At this critical juncture there emerges in the field of religion the phenomenon of atheism. It is commonly presented as the enemy that totally denies religion. But then one fails to recognize that religion and atheism are dialectically related as opposite answers to the problematic inherent in religion. This is clearly seen in the atheistic religion of Buddhism. This polarity is equally evident in Graeco-Roman and Enlightenment atheism. The fact of the matter is that atheism shares in the religious questions but not the religious answers. It asks for the Absolute, but observes that it is nowhere. It is characterized by a passionate desire to do complete justice to the bare facts and the relativity of the profane world. Often it also exhibits a deep piety which seems to grasp how absolute the Absolute would really have to be, one which does not want to offend the deity by believing in its existence after the manner of religion. This religious root of atheism explains why so often it issued in new forms of religion, forms in which the totality of the profane and relative phenomenal world was mystically experienced as an absolute process or as a birth from an absolute abyss. Generally speaking, sacralizing and secularizing tendencies in history continually alternate as the answers to the universal and ineradicable question articulated by religion.

The assertion in these last words, *universal* and *ineradicable,* requires elucidation. This thesis has been attacked through the ages, especially since the Enlightenment. To the extent that appeal was made to the phenomenon of atheism, this attack is unconvincing, considering the polar relationship between religion and atheism. With more reason one might point to the widespread religious indifference in the Western world and the prevalence of agnosticism and skepticism, which seem to have put the whole problem aside. Likely these are things that happened and happen in all cultures. Religion presupposes a measure of conscious depth in one's experience of reality and existence which many people simply do not have. Furthermore, in many people the awareness of the aesthetic, historical, and social dimensions of life is hardly or not at all developed, yet it does not lead us to deny the universality and ineradicability of such forms of awareness.

An effective denial needs better proof than static facts. A denial can be successful only if the source of religion can be traced back to another, more essential element of man's nature. One would thus have to demonstrate that the religious question is at bottom a nonreligious question, and that for that reason the religious answer does not fit the question, with the result that the answer is exposed as irrelevant. Many have sought to do just that, attempting in this way to reduce religion to nonreligious factors. The source of religion has been said to be deceptive priestcraft, fear of the unknown, a primitive scientific instinct, the need for security, neurotic disturbances, support of the established order, compensation for human weaknesses, finding support for a moral code, etc. So religion was reduced to psychic, social, intellectual, or moral factors. The best-known and most widely accepted reduction is the Marxist, which views religion as the reflection of economic conditions: the suppressed social classes try with this opium (especially its promise of a blissful hereafter) to forget their chains.

All these theories have their strong points. Since by its very nature religion affects the whole person, it is also nourished and colored by the whole person. One can thus point to a great many connections. That, however, is something else than reducing it to any one of these connections. So far no attempt at such a reduction has succeeded. Marxism is confident that it can give this practical proof, expecting that with the liberation of the suppressed classes their need for religion will eventually disappear. But this proof has not yet been given, and the confidence that it can be done in the near future is diminishing.

If our definition touches the heart of the matter, religion as relationship to the Absolute cannot be reduced to another relationship or another aspect of man. Even if it could be shown that it corresponds to other human needs, the fact remains that positing the Absolute and a relationship to it amounts to a mental jump within the human consciousness, one which as such is not required by the segment of reality from which it is made. Unless one assumes that in this aspect of reality there is already a latent tendency toward the Absolute. But post-Enlightenment man no longer perceives that tendency.

This irreducibility does not necessarily imply the universality and ineradicability of religion. (Mental illness may be irreducible too.) But assuming that the jump to a relationship with the absolute is characteristic of human consciousness, in practice they belong inseparably together. This obvious assumption is strengthened by the fact that religion is a universal phenomenon, which leads to the conclusion that it cannot be eradicated. Scientifically we can make progress only if we zero in on what is unique in this phenomenon. "Religion begins with itself" (R. Otto). A human being cannot escape the religious problematic (note: I do not say "religion"). In this problematic he reaches out for and past his final boundaries, and only in that reaching out is he fully human. Without this urge for the infinite he remains a two-dimensional being.

But this urge stands out more clearly as question than as answer. The answers are too diverse and too uncertain to carry the pretension of expressing universally valid truth. So we hit upon the ultimate problem, that of the truth of religion. If religion is an irreducible activity of the human spirit, then it contains anthropological truth. It proves then—something at least hinted at by other human activities—that man is a being who cannot be satisfied with the world he is situated in. "Man infinitely surpasses himself" (Pascal). Does this innate dissatisfaction prove the existence of "another world" for which man is intended? The phenomenon of religion does not allow this conclusion. For it is always bound to look for the Absolute in the relative and then gets entangled in a problematic which rightly invites the opposition of atheism. It appears that in his religion man reaches beyond himself and his world and then inevitably falls back on himself and this world. With that, something most remarkable and mysterious is said about man. Nothing less; but nothing more, either.

On the subject of viewing religion as an existential aspect of human existence, the following important and influential thinkers are to be mentioned. The first is Schleiermacher with his *On Religion. Speeches to its Cultured Despisers* (1799; E.T. 1958). His second discourse is especially significant. He argues against reducing religion to the intellectual or the moral. According to him religion is "a separate province in the soul," and characteristic of it is its "apprehension and taste for the infinite," as "feeling" and as "perception of the universe." Ignoring the romantic and even pantheistic garb in which he often expressed his thoughts, we can view Schleiermacher's conception of religion as man's being grasped by the one creative, foundational power which can be "felt" or "perceived" amid the many relative phenomena, that is, forces itself upon man as a revelation.

The 19th century has thought and written much about religion. Unfortunately, evolutionistic theories (which from the perspective of Christianity as the "highest" religion sought to determine what may and what may not rightly be called religion) and the inclination to anchor religion in other aspects of reality often obscured an honest and open-minded consideration. Preferably, with the aid of faculty psychology, one tried to locate this basis of religion in man's reason, his feelings, or his moral awareness. Under the influence of Kant religion was linked especially to man's awareness of right and wrong. In all these cases religion itself was not permitted to express itself fully and radically. Nor was that done by others who followed and who desired to base religion on feeling. Schleiermacher, however, was an exception. He understood the confusing *Gefühl* as, in his own words, "an immediate existential relationship."

A hundred years after their appearance Schleiermacher's *Discourses* were reissued by R. Otto, a young historian of religion who in 1917, with his great work *The Idea of the Holy,* in his own way carried on Schleiermacher's tradition. As Otto described it, the uniqueness of religion is man's being alternately attracted to and repelled by "das Ganz Andere," "das Numinose," "das Heilige" (the wholly other, the numinous, the holy). This description enabled him to account for the many bizarre and repulsive forms and aspects of religion, something for which the 19th century as a rule lacked the apparatus. Otto's view has till now prevailed.

The third who after Schleiermacher and Otto deserves mention is N. Söderblom. He, too, was interested in articulating religion as an entirely unique phenomenon. Like Otto (though his views are less systematically worked out), he took the category of "holiness" as typical for religion. His major work is *Das Werden des Gottesglaubens* (Swedish 1914; German 1916). A generation later G. van der Leeuw built further on the foundation laid by Söderblom and Otto. See his *Phaenomenologie der Religion* (1st ed. 1933; E.T. *Religion in Essence and Manifestation,* 1963), *passim,* and his brief but meaningful introduction to *De godsdiensten der wereld* (2nd ed., 1948).

After Van der Leeuw, the attention of historians of religion shifted strongly to concrete religious expressions and their coherence with the totality of culture. Among present-day philosophical theologians who have concerned themselves with the phenomenon of religion, particularly Tillich is to be mentioned. See his *ST* III, pp. 86–106, 162–244, and his brief study *Christianity and the Encounter of the World Religions* (1963). Not all his descriptions are equally useful. "Self-transcendence of life" fails to indicate direction; "experience of the unconditional" is much more precise. The latter is also true of the description in his above-mentioned brief study: "Religion is the state of being grasped by an ultimate concern. . . . This concern is unconditionally serious. . . . The predominant religious name for the content of such concern is God" (p. 4). In his theology Tillich gives much attention to the dialectic of the relationship between the absolute and the relative in religion, what he calls the universal and the concrete. On religion as expression of the "offene Lebensproblematik," see also G. Ebeling, *Dogmatik,* I (1979), pars. 5 and 6).

Atheism in its polar relationship to religion is fed mainly by three sources: the rule of fixed natural law, the suffering in the world, and human autonomy, each of which in its own way (seems to) argue against the existence of an absolute which gives meaning and blessings to the world. It is no accident that both OT and NT lend support to this atheistic critique of religion (see Isa. 44:9–18 and Rom. 1:18–25). For a thorough treatment of atheism, see Barth, *CD* I,2, 320–325; for the historical facets, H.-J. Kraus, *Systematische Theologie* (1983), pp. 302–317; and for the discussion with the "God is dead" thinkers, H. Thielicke, *The Evangelical Faith,* I (E.T. 1974), from par. 13.

3. FAITH

THE CHRISTIAN FAITH is a phenomenon in the wide field of religion. Considering the enormous variety of phenomena in this field, this localization is not all that helpful. Happily we do not have to leave it at that. Both the historical and the phenomenal approach urge us to be more specific as to the area of reality which constitutes the context within which the Christian faith has occurred. Within the wider field of religion we call this the area of faith. In view of its specific nature it is possible, even preferable, to approach this context historically.

It so happens that in the history of religion we are able to point with considerable precision to a period, a geographical area, and a group of people that were involved in one of the greatest, if not the greatest, religious leap that has ever occurred in religious history. Its matrix was the Sumerian-Akkadian culture in Babylon in the first half of the second millennium before Christ, likely about 1700 B.C. We know that at that time groups of people and tribes left Mesopotamia for the regions west of the Syrian desert to start a new life in Palestine and other countries (some trekked as far as Egypt), living there as semi-nomads among the native population of the cities and working with varying degrees of success for their future. We know about this from archeological excavations, but we possess a close-up of these people and their experiences only in the ancestral traditions preserved by the people of Israel as these are compiled in the book of Genesis. That compilation, which involved some stylization, was done by later narrators. But on the whole the narrative presents a reliable picture of the history, as is evident from the fact that the narrators mention names of deities, cultic practices, family relationships, and laws which were unknown or taboo in their time but are now known to us as the result of the excavations in second-millennium Babylon and Phoenicia.

A reconstruction of the historical nucleus yields the following result. For economic reasons a Babylonian shepherd prince (perhaps there were more, either close together in time or separated by large intervals—it is not important for our purpose) left the famous city of Haran in Mesopotamia, at that time a center of the moon-god cult, together with his family, tribe, or a group of like-minded people. This transmigration meant that he could no longer count on the protection of the city god or of the other gods that represented and protected Babylonian life. Nor could he, of course, count on the gods of the unknown land to which he went, for those gods were the deities of the indigenous city population there. Even so, this man with the Babylonian name Abraham dared to undertake the migration, in a strange new confidence that he would be led and protected by a higher, as yet nameless God who called him, a God who ruled over the old country he had left and the new country to which he was going as well as over the dangerous desert lying in between, a God who was not confined to a particular territory but who because of his transcendence was mobile and able to protect him as he trekked to new worlds. This trust was not disappointed. Therefore it could afterwards be nourished and enriched by continually new experiences. This had a contagious effect on his family and following generations. They began to speak of "the God of our father," later "the God of our fathers," and they, his semi-nomadic descendants, felt secure in the confidence that this God guaranteed the fulfillment of their two greatest needs: a numerous offspring and a country of their own for permanent settlement.

Some centuries later the relationship with this God received a new impulse when Moses, in the name of this God, led Abraham's oppressed descendants in the Nile delta out of Egyptian slavery. Inspired by his religious experiences during his wanderings in exile in the Sinai desert, he gave a new and mysterious name to this deity: Yahweh. In this name he proclaimed the so-called "ten commandments" (a brief pre-form of the present decalogue) and made it the basis of the relationship between these tribes and their God. That concluded the pre-history of Israel's faith. The history that followed, in Canaan, was a tremendous struggle between this faith and the religious beliefs and practices that were current there as well as elsewhere in the Middle East.

The question how this religion differed from the other religions of that time is best answered by recalling what we said in paragraph 2 about the problematic inherent in religion. Religion is a relationship with the Transcendent and the Absolute, but man can have such a relationship only through the immanent and the relative. As far as we know, from the genesis of man and his religion to the days of Abraham, no one, or at most very few, felt this as a problem. The world was experienced as a cosmic natural process which was the expression of the divine power. The Absolute expresses itself in the relative. All of reality is "der Gottheit lebendiges Kleid" (the living garment of the divine). The implication is that the deity is similar to reality: infinitely multiform (hence polytheism), majestic, opaque, contradictory, freakish, having many faces and therefore faceless. With the help of sacrifices and incantations man must secure for himself the favors of the divine powers.

Abraham forsook that path. In his migration he listened to and put his trust in the call of a transcendent deity whose power and sphere of influence are not limited by that of other gods. Many religions, to be sure, had a "highest god," but he was then as passive as he was high. For effective help in concrete needs one had to go to the lower gods. The remarkable thing about Abraham's religion is that here transcendence and nearness with respect to the concrete problems of life go hand in hand. The transcendence of this God makes it impossible to understand that nearness as a general presence and as something inherent in the reality of nature itself. But this transcendence is not experienced as passivity either. This deity is living and active, but as such he must make himself known in the relativity of the phenomenal world; not, however, as revelation of a static Existence which of necessity permeates the entire world, but in a liberating and guiding acting in which he distinguishes himself from this world. This new relationship between a transcendent God and his human world thus implies a radical desacralization of the world. God is above the world and now here, now there enters into a judging or saving relationship with it, an entrance depending on his divine will, a will not susceptible to influence by magical means. Man may call on God, implore his help, wait upon his intervention. But in a profane world it is not possible to force him to be present by naturalistic, magical, or mystical means. With Abraham begins the awareness of a break between the deity and the experiential world. Religion loses its self-evidence. God is now far away and hidden. But when he comes and helps, he is infinitely closer than any god of naturalism could be. Then he has a face, then he has an unambiguous purpose, then he is present as the great covenant partner, and it takes the most daring anthropomorphisms to describe his saving nearness.

Thus we cannot say that the problematic inherent in religion has been overcome here (for that it is too directly interwoven with our whole human existence). We can say that it has received a totally different structure. That is not primarily an intellectual conclusion, for it began as an existential experience. The narrators of Genesis leave no opportunity unused to make clear how "difficult" this faith was for Abraham and his followers. For long periods they could go through life without receiving any sign of the saving nearness of their God. Their life could thus be called "a-theistic," were it not for the fact that this "emptiness" which they experienced as the hiddenness of God must have been very trying for them, so much so that it could assume the form of a "contending with God"; they were able to bear it only because they remembered former saving encounters on which they could base expectations of help for the future. The biblical narrative views Abraham's whole life from this perspective. In a groping sort of way he goes from promise to fulfillment and thence again to new promises, living a life of belief that exists on the brink of unbelief. This outlook remained characteristic for Israel's faith, as is seen in the Psalms.

Another characteristic of the nature of this relationship with God is the prohibition of images. In the image of the deity, which he could carry along from place to place if he so desired, ancient religious man had at his disposal the helping presence of the deity. God strictly forbade this to Israel. He refuses to be manipulated by man. Related to this is the important place assigned to speech in the divine-human relationship. Speech is the most personal and most direct form of mutual contact. Hence the *word* was central in Israel. That word comes sovereignly from God, or it does not come at all; it cannot be manipulated or conjured up, but demands total trust and obedience. Especially the first three of the so-called ten commandments articulate that fundamental and strict relationship.

It is not hard to see why from the start and increasingly more so with the passage of time, the future became the focal point of this relationship to the deity. The hidden and incidental presence of Yahweh marks this presence as provisional and contains the promise of a time when Yahweh will be permanently revealed and all his promises fulfilled. God accompanies his people on the way, and this way must have a goal.

The term "religion" is no longer adequate to express the human correlate of this mode of Yahweh's association with his people. The term is much too general for that. The customary designation for this correlate is *faith.* It contains the notion of distance between the deity and man, it is not as closely linked to experience as "religion," it suggests a reaching beyond experience, even a holding on against experience; it speaks of a trust which can at times become totally blind; and it has the undertone of the "not yet," of living by a promise. The word *faith* is used very often in the New Testament; it is derived from the Old Testament where it is still sparsely used, though in some passages it becomes a very important word.

On the origin of faith-religion see H. Berkhof, "Openbaring als gebeuren," in the collection *Geloven in God* (1970), pp. 101–132, and the literature mentioned there. The root *'m-n* denotes "to be firm"; the niphal *ne'^{e}man* means "to be constant," "prove oneself faithful"; and the hiphil *he'^{e}mîn,* "to consider someone faithful." That is what man does with respect to Yahweh and his promises. He must often do that directly contrary to his own experiences and calculations.

This is beautifully illustrated in Isaiah 7 where the prophet Isaiah calls on King Ahaz to trust, in the midst of war, Yahweh's word that the city of Jerusalem will remain unharmed. With a play on words he exhorts the nervous and discouraged king: "*'im lō' ta'^{a}mînû kî lō' tē'āmēnû,*" literally translated: "If you do not hold on, you will not remain firm," or: "if you do not stand by me, you will not stand at all" *(Jerusalem Bible)*. Israel's existence depends on her readiness to live by trust in Yahweh's promises.

The same is said in another key passage, Gen. 15:1–6, where God promises doubting, childless Abraham that he will give him a son and innumerable descendants, and where it is then said of Abraham: "And he believed the Lord *(w^{e}he'^{e}min bayhwâ)*, and he reckoned it to him as righteousness." That is, God regarded Abraham's faith and trust as the proper and only right response to his promises.

For the OT concept of faith, see the art. *pisteuō B* (Weiser) in *TDNT* VI; Botterweck–Ringgren, *Theological Dictionary of the OT, s.v. '-m-n* (Jepsen); Jenni–Westermann, *Theologisches Handwörterbuch zum AT, s.v. 'mn* (Wildberger); and T. C. Vriezen, *Geloven en vertrouwen* (1957).

This faith-religion was bound to clash with the religion that was current everywhere else. Not that this conflict immediately assumed the form of monotheism versus polytheism. The existence of other gods was not denied. Heaven and earth, sun and moon, vegetation and fertility, society and state are undeniably powerful realities. But they are not able to make and keep promises, and they cannot enter into a covenant relationship with helpless man. That is why those who put their trust in these powers are let down in their faith. For that reason, in Canaan Yahwism could not make peace with the agricultural religion of the indigenous inhabitants who worshipped Baal, the god of the fructifying heavens. The clash between these two opposing forms of religion was very strong and lasted for centuries; only the Babylonian captivity put a kind of end to it. Baalism could hold out so long because for the Israelite, too, the Baal cult had such a great appeal, appearing so much easier, more natural, and more meaningful than the Yahwistic faith. Baal's presence was visible and his blessings were more or less predictable; moreover, one could use magical means to force these blessings in case they were long in coming. The faith in Yahweh made a poor showing compared with this fertility religion. Many found themselves unable to resist the powerful lure of Baalism, while many others began to worship Yahweh as a higher kind of Baal, as the real and better fertility god of Israel. That Yahwism ultimately won the day was owing to small, dedicated groups and to prophetic individuals whose faith and the preaching, promises, and admonition based on it were apparently again and again confirmed by the course of events.

Yet this victory left much to be desired. After the exile, legalism became Israel's predominant religious outlook. All the emphasis was put on keeping a growing list of strict legal precepts of do's and don't's. This development was at variance with the original faith perspective of Yahwism. With Baalism it had in common that for Israel it was again a means to get a hold on her sovereign God. Reading the pre-exilic and post-exilic prophets, we get a negative picture of Israel's religion. For the majority the faith-religion of Abraham and Moses was too much. It demanded an abandonment of certainties (or pseudo-certainties) and a taking of risks (or a trust in unverifiable promises), things in which, according to the witness of the Old Testament, at critical moments even great men like Abraham, Moses, and David failed. That is why the Old Testament record speaks frequently and very radically about man's guilt, which constantly breaks the fellowship with God. Hence the course of the Old Testament makes such a strange impression on the reader: there is no progress, and it is anti-climactic, ending with the same problems with which it began.

Contradictory as it may seem in view of these observations, this faith-religion has become the structure and infrastructure of a number of later forms of religion and as such has attained worldwide significance. For from it have sprung three world religions: Judaism, Christianity, and Islam. The relationship of these three to the mother differs considerably, with none of them clearly resembling her. But all three are shaped by the Old Testament infrastructure. All three start from the assumption of a sovereign relationship of a transcendent God to a desacralized world. In contrast to primitive naturalism and a variety of modern ideologies which absolutize certain aspects of reality, these three religions have taken a new and different direction. How they nevertheless happened to go in three different directions will be discussed in the following paragraph.

Here we are interested in the fact that within the wide field of religion we see the Christian faith situated in the field of faith. That leads us to raise the question about the relation of religion and faith. Earlier we used the term "religious jump" to indicate both the continuity and the discontinuity. Faith is not just a variant or a "higher rung" of the multiform and richly diversified phenomenon of religion. One who says that does not do justice to the structure of faith and its awareness of an uncompromising opposition to all sorts of religious forms. But one who is keenly aware of that can by way of reaction go so far as to regard faith and religion as opposites. Then we must not forget, however, that these are opposites within one field because they give contrasting answers to a religious problematic they have in common.

When we have a clear eye for the dialectical relationship between faith-religion and other forms of religion, the question as to the truth presents itself. We have to choose in what direction we wish to go. But the phenomenological approach we follow in this Introduction offers no insights we can use to solve the truth question. It rather suggests that such a "solution" in the sense of a theoretical or empirical verification cannot be given here. In the final analysis only a devotee of a religion is qualified to speak about it. Objective information alone is not sufficient to choose this or that religion; and it is an existential delusion to think that it can be done. It thus appears that there is a gap between examining and choosing a religion. Religious truth is existential truth; such truth is a matter of choice. That choice is subjective in this sense, that there is no objective agency outside the subject that can make the choice for him. At the same time the choice is not subjective in this sense, that it is not so much a choice which the subject makes and something he experiences as being done to him, but rather a being overwhelmed by truth that discloses itself. In paragraphs 2 and 3 we tried to make clear that the Christian faith implies such presuppositions of "choice" and of "being chosen," first (this "first" is meant logically and anthropologically) that of religion, next that of faith. They are both subsumed in the first and most basic choice by which the Christian faith itself is formed, the choice that will occupy us in the following paragraph.

Unfortunately, students of the phenomenology of religion have not always clearly recognized and articulated these phenomenological distinctions and connections. The distinction between "religion" and "faith" is often overlooked and the terms used interchangeably. Then it is not surprising that Judaism, Christianity, and Islam are usually not treated as a separate group, but on the basis of one or more characteristics are lumped together with other religions and discussed under one heading, e.g. monotheism, ethical monotheism, a personal God concept, redemptive religions, historical religions, religions derived from the particular founder. See *RGG* V, *s.v. Religion II: Typen der Religion.* Such a delineation, which could even include entirely different religions such as those of Zarathustra and Buddha, obscured the uniqueness of the three mentioned above. Yet historically this uniqueness can easily be shown, namely from the OT, which is the source of all three. The OT makes it clear that this uniqueness is not so much a matter of certain ideas as a new way of experiencing the triangular relationship of God, man, and the world, with other characteristics bearing on belief and practice following from that by way of consequence. In my judgment K. A. H. Hidding offers a more satisfying phenomenological order in many of his writings; see especially *God en goden* (1960) and *De evolutie van het godsdienstig bewustzijn* (1965). He distinguishes between religions of the image, which orient themselves to nature; religions of the word, which orient themselves to the spirit and the law (Judaism and Islam), and Christianity, which orients itself to the/a person and to love.

In our time, in which the religions are becoming intermixed geographically, there is a clear preference for minimizing the differences and instead focusing on the at first sight remarkable similarities. But a closer look shows that making a choice is unavoidable.

In direct contrast to the levelling tendency is the school of Barth, which both phenomenologically and theologically sees an absolute contrast between religion (understood as self-projection and maintaining the existing order) and faith (as the revelation of the Name in OT and NT, which subjects all religions to critique). Barth himself coined the famous characterization "Religion as Unbelief" (*CD* I,2, par. 17). But he does not see it as a mutually exclusive contrast, but rather as a dialectical opposition. In revelation he sees "the abolition of religion," which also involves being taken up in a new relationship in virtue of the justification and sanctification of religion. For that reason he can call Christianity "the true religion." This dialectic is dropped by his followers; see Beker-Hasselaar, *WK,* ch. 1, and H.-J. Kraus, *Systematische Theologie,* par. 34. But "faith" means going in an opposite direction in the field of "religion." Ebeling, *Dogmatik,* I, pars. 5 and 6 (who, however, equates the dialectic between religion and faith with that between law and gospel), is good on this. "For the gospel can make itself heard in no other way than in its tension to religion" (p. 139). See also par. 8.

4. CHRISTIAN FAITH

NOWHERE IN THE WORLD is Israel's faith, as we have described it, any more the sole determining factor for the religious beliefs people hold. Till the present day this faith, like a leaven, does, however, work as an inspirational and critical ferment in other forms of religion. Here we take up again the earlier-used word *infrastructure.* This book aims to set forth the Christian faith. Here we have to ask what the determining structures of this faith are and how these rest on the Old Testament faith as their infrastructure.

The best way to begin is by stating in what elements and in what way the Israelite infrastructure remains determinatively present in the Christian faith. That is especially in the ideas of transcendence, divine freedom, God's personal coming to man in the word, sinful man's resistance to this coming of God, and the confidence of a radical solution in the future.

That all this has now become infrastructure is not so much the result of new ideas as of belief in new facts. The Christian faith consists primarily in the conviction that the radical solution which will become manifest in the future is now already present in principle and has been realized in the ministry, suffering, death, and resurrection of Jesus of Nazareth. This event adds the following seven elements to the existing faith:

1. The very personal coming of God to man in the Old Testament, to the point of being anthropomorphic, is here immeasurably intensified, and thereby completed as well: he comes to men in a man, in one who as "the Son" stands in a unique relationship to him as "the Father."

2. This unique and all-surpassing coming evokes an unequalled and unsurpassable act of guilt: the condemnation of "the Son" as a blasphemer. Apparently men are not able to endure God's nearness to them.

3. God raised Jesus from the death to which men had condemned him. He rises as a renewed man—*the* man—in whom God, as with "a firstfruits," makes a new beginning for the salvation of mankind.

4. In the light of the resurrection the crucifixion is shown to be not only a human crime but especially a substitutionary suffering in which the Son, according to the will of the Father, identifies himself with his enemies and so brings about reconciliation between God and the guilty human race.

5. From the risen Jesus proceeds the "Spirit." He alone is the guarantee that human beings, who in themselves are unable to remain faithful to a relationship with God, can remain in such a relationship. He causes people to believe that in Jesus God's grace has definitively appeared, and so enables them to achieve a measure of new obedience.

6. Now that the gracious coming of God has become definite in Jesus, the Spirit goes beyond the confines of Israel. God's salvation becomes universal. The good news is proclaimed everywhere to religious and atheistic people. The church emerges and spreads as a worldwide community of people who believe that in Jesus God has come near to us.

7. In the Christian faith, just as in the Old Testament, the fullness of salvation lies in the future. But that future is now viewed as the return of Jesus to establish his Kingdom, as the unfolding and disclosure of the powers already operative in our history in his resurrection and in the work of his Spirit.

The relationship to the infrastructure of Israel's faith comes out in the place which the Old Testament has in the Christian faith. From now on it is read as preparation for the fulfillment in Christ, though the awareness remains that what the Old Testament ultimately looks forward to has not yet been fulfilled. In comparison with the New Testament there remains a "plus" in the Old Testament. It is also true that the Old Testament furnishes most of the concepts and terms that are employed in the New Testament. On the other hand, the "plus" in the New Testament receives at least as much emphasis, a "plus" consisting in the fact that Jesus, on behalf of God, in his work and his destiny has removed the estrangement between God and man as this became visible in the Old Testament and could not be decisively overcome there. As a rule, therefore, the New Testament connects the redemption which the Old Testament expects from the future primarily with the coming of Jesus.

This relation to the Old Testament infrastructure is also exhibited by the conception of faith that is found in the New Testament. This conception is both closely related to and different from that in the Old Testament. In the New Testament, too, faith is the human correlate of the words and deeds through which God associates with man, namely as a posture of "firmly believing" and thus of "trusting in." In the New Testament that faith is related primarily to a person to whom man may entrust himself, because in him salvation in the sense of reconciliation and of adoption as children of God has already become a reality.

This is really no more than a difference of degree. For the salvation that has been accomplished also points to the future for its full realization. This makes it understandable that the NT, beside the Pauline conception of faith as trust in the salvation that has happened, contains that of the Epistle to the Hebrews, a book which is primarily future-oriented and in which faith is structured much more along OT lines. Thus in Hebrews the Christian community is assumed to have the same future-oriented religious posture as the OT heroes of faith (Heb. 11). Therefore we have to reject the contrast made by M. Buber in his *Two Types of Faith* (E.T. 1951). He sees in the OT an existential faith in the sense of a trusting in the covenant relationship between Yahweh and Israel, and in the NT, since Paul, an intellectual faith in the sense of accepting a doctrine regarding facts. But in the OT as well transmitted facts are constitutive for faith, and in the NT faith is also a relation of trust and obedience. See contra Buber, T. C. Vriezen, *Geloven en vertrouwen,* and E. Brunner, *Dg* III (E.T. 1962), pp. 159–162. The difference between OT and NT is not primarily in the concept of faith itself, but in the different nature of God's presence in human existence to which it directs itself.

As we thus explore the manner in which the Christian faith assimilates and transcends the Old Testament faith, the truth question asserts itself again, as in paragraphs 2 and 3. Can one, on the basis of a description of these phenomena in the areas of religion and culture, demonstrate the truth of the transition from the one form of faith to the other? Twice already we have seen that the nature of the access we seek here gave no answer to the question as to the truth. Now that we ask the question for the third time, we want to ask the less pretentious question whether the transition from the Old Testament faith to the Christian faith was the result of an inner necessity. Though not the religious person in general, in that case at least the person who has faith could be convinced of the truth of the Christian faith. The fact, however, that the transition beyond the faith of the Old Testament has been in three entirely different directions makes it likely that we expect too much. The question would then have to be phrased like this: can it be shown that the transition to the Christian faith rests on an inner necessity, one which is quite different from or at least manifestly superior to the pressures which led a later Judaism and Islam to go beyond the Old Testament?

Many still make the mistake of identifying Judaism with the faith of the OT. This mode of faith began with the groups who returned from the Babylonian captivity in the 5th and 4th centuries before Christ, but did not get its specific structure until after the fall of Jerusalem (A.D. 70) in the exegetical methods applied to the OT by Jewish scribes, an exegesis and application that is embodied in the Talmud which received its definite shape about A.D. 500. The Talmud may be regarded as a parallel of the NT, since both integrate the OT in a new faith perspective. That implies also that the two employ entirely different hermeneutics for their reading of the OT. For the many variants of Judaism, the orthodox, the conservative, the mystical, and the more liberal forms, the realization of the covenant remains co-dependent on the obedience of the human covenant partner. The crisis in which the covenant, according to the OT, finds itself, and which according to the Christian faith has been overcome by God himself, is of a permanent nature in Judaism. This permanence is bearable, however, because according to Judaism man is not powerless; sin is limited to the deed, and every subsequent act of *t^{e}šûbâ,* or "turning," can make up for it. The Jew is therefore obligated to respond to God's covenant faithfulness with his keeping of the law or his striving after obedience, and so to promote the realization of God's Kingdom. Thus in the guilt of his OT ancestors he does see a continually repeated failing, but not a disclosure of what man is really like. Whereas the Christian reads the OT especially as a book providing him with the guidelines for meeting his ethical responsibilities as God's covenant partner. The law of Moses as the road to obedience (*halakah*) is central. He regards the Christian faith with its trust in a definite and substitutionary atonement which presumably has already happened in history as an illusion or at least as a premature claim of victory. For a deeper analysis of these differences we refer to L. Baeck, *The Essence of Judaism* (E.T. 1961); K. H. Miskotte, *Het wezen der Joodsche religie* (1933); and H.-J. Schoeps, *Jüdischer Glaube in dieser Zeit* (1934) and *The Jewish-Christian Argument* (E.T. 1963). Cf. also the end of par. 31.

Islam, particularly as a post-Christian religion, presents us with special problems. It arose at a time when Christianity and Judaism were already firmly established. From the Koran it is difficult to say how much Mohammed knew and understood of Christianity. It is certain that at first he had a strong attachment to Judaism. His prophetic consciousness and the contents of his prophecies in the early stages of his career strongly remind us of some of the OT prophets. He proclaims the one God as creator, his gracious upholding of the universe, and his judgment of all humanity at the end of time. As a prophet he thinks of himself as standing in the line of the OT prophets and the NT apostles; he has the same message, except that he has been sent to a people that has not yet heard this message. This changes after his emigration to Medina (622). The result of closer contact with the Jews is that they refuse to acknowledge him as a prophet. Over against them, he appeals to Abraham, whose mode of faith he thinks he continues. The Medina period was also the transition from suffering to fighting and from prophecy to theocracy. The difference from Judaism now becomes marked by the emphasis on the universality of Islam and by other prescriptions, including the change in the direction one faces in prayer from Jerusalem to Kaaba, an ancient naturalistic shrine in Mecca which is now said to have been established by Abraham. All these changes combined set Islam apart from Judaism and consolidated it as a faith with a structure of its own. Here, too, the covenant relationship between a transcendent God and man is central. And as in Judaism, this covenant is not established by a unilateral gracious act of God; it is especially an assignment to man to make sure that by fulfilling the law he will be able to stand in the coming judgment. This keeping of the law, however, is here thought of in terms of outward conduct even more than in Judaism. In that way Islam leaves room for the counterbalance of a strong collective consciousness of belonging to the chosen community, provided one observes the few easy-to-live-up-to commandments. So Islam seems to combine the Jewish element of keeping the law with the Christian element of covenantal security. Moreover, the nature and universality of this combination make it very adaptable to existing naturalistic and nationalistic patterns of religion and life. Through this all Islam presents itself as the final and thus highest world religion, which in contrast to the West offers a conscious identity to millions, especially in the developing countries. For an insight into Islam and its differences with the Christian faith, see the classic book of K. Cragg, *The Call of the Minaret* (1956), and further W. A. Bijlefeld, *De Islam as na-christelijke religie* (1959); J. Jomier, *Bible et Coran* (1959); and J. Bouman, *Das Wort vom Kreuz und das Bekenntnis zu Allah* (1980).

The way in which the Old Testament pictures the covenant and its crisis calls for a sequel. But if it is to be a genuine sequel, it has to add a new element by which the crisis either is overcome or made bearable. Such is in fact done in all three of the religions. The three "solutions" can be looked at from various angles. One can say that the love of God as an inspiring power is nowhere seen as clearly as in Christianity; or that the moral responsibility of man is nowhere taken as seriously as in Judaism; or that no religion is as rational and as adapted to human capabilities as Islam. One can also, with Lessing in his "Nathan the Wise," apply the moral level of the followers (e.g. the measure of love they show to the followers of the other two religions) as the norm for truth. Lessing's play, however, intends to say that truth cannot be determined in this way. And the same holds for the other means of comparison. They all proceed from a presupposed norm which is uniquely rooted in *one* particular faith; they are thus based on circular reasoning.

Meanwhile, the real decision as to the truth is made in an entirely different area. The Jew believes that there are no new revelations from God after the Mosaic laws and the prophets and before the coming of the Messiah, and that such revelations are not necessary. The Christian believes that a very radical and liberating revelation has happened after that. The Muslim believes that the series of revelations was concluded with a final and highest one which comprehends and sums up for all time the truths of all earlier revelations. Whether certain events in history are revelations from God or not—that is the real question deciding the truth. This question cannot be answered with rational arguments. Rationality and factuality are two quite different categories. Nonetheless, people have always tried to combine them in religion. Every religion has its apologetic literature in which an attempt is made to demonstrate the rationality of one's own faith. The undertaking is not entirely meaningless. It is clear, however, that the arguments are really convincing only for the person who is convinced to begin with.

In the Christian faith the thought of a methodological solvability of the truth question is cut off at the root by the confession of the Holy Spirit. For this confession implies that by himself man cannot discover the truth about God because only God can make God known to us. Methodologically this means that while we are able to point out the area of reality within which this mode of believing appears (as we have now done), we cannot point to an access, a *met-hodos,* which with an inner necessity leads from the wider circle to that specific area. Methodologically, but now viewed positively, it implies, too, that the truth of the Christian faith cannot be articulated beforehand ("*prolegein*" in the Prolegomena) but only reveal itself to the hearer or reader in the proclamation and the exposition of the contents of the faith, because he becomes aware that this is the *true* knowledge of God and this is man's true salvation. But the deepest ground for this awareness of the truth remains hidden to him, let alone that he would be able to make it clear to an outsider.

At this point it may be illuminating to compare our access with the one Schleiermacher made for himself in the opening paragraphs of his *CF.* After some introductory remarks about the church, Schleiermacher turns first for basic assumptions to what he calls "Ethics" and what we now call "philosophical anthropology." He takes his starting point in the human self-consciousness (3) of which religion as "the awareness of absolute dependence" is the "highest grade"

(5). To get the necessary differentiation Schleiermacher needs basic assumptions from what he calls the philosophy of religion and what we would rather call the phenomenology of religion. With the help of these he examines the religions as concerns differences in their degree of development and as concerns differences in essence. From the evolutionary point of view the monotheistic religions are the highest, particularly because in these religions man's religious awareness has become entirely independent of his "sense" awareness, of his awareness of "being-in-the-world." There are three monotheistic religions. Judaism still contains an admixture of nationalism, though for that matter "being almost in process of extinction!" (8,4). Islam remains characterized by a strong attachment to the world of the senses. "Christianity, because it remains free from both these weaknesses, stands higher than either of those other two forms, and takes its place as the purest form of Monotheism which has appeared in history." Changing over from Christianity to Judaism or Islam can only be a kind of illness (8,4).

Yet Schleiermacher is not satisfied with this purely "empirical" mode of reasoning. He buttresses it with a more phenomenological approach in which he contrasts Christianity and Judaism as teleological religions (in which everything serves the purpose of the coming of the Kingdom of God) with Islam as an "aesthetic" religion, that is, as a religion of contemplation, surrender, and acquiescence. Because the moral is higher than the natural, the religions in which morality plays a dominant role are higher than the naturalistic, and among these ethical religions Judaism, because of its system of rewards and punishments, ranks lower than Christianity (9). Thus along two lines, that of the level of development and that of an analysis of the essence of each religion, Schleiermacher gives conclusive proof for the truth of the Christian faith. At least that is how it looks. When he is set to reap the harvest (in 11), he suddenly pulls back. See what we wrote about that on p. 2. Much to our surprise, Schleiermacher assures us in par. 11,5 that it was not at all his intention to give that kind of proof, but that he was interested only in bringing out the decisive difference between Christianity and the other religions. For the phenomenology of religion "could not establish any necessity, either to recognize a particular fact as redemptive, or to give the central place actually in one's own consciousness to any particular moment." In the first half of this sentence Schleiermacher says that there lies a gap between factuality and having insight into it, and in the second part that there is a gap between contemplative objectivity and existential choice. After having walked to the end of the long road of the Prolegomena, Schleiermacher admits that on the way to the Christian faith he has come upon a chasm and that taking a leap is the only way to get across. Therefore par. 11 ends with the words: "We entirely renounce all attempts to prove the truth of or necessity of Christianity; and we presuppose, on the contrary, that every Christian, before he enters at all upon inquiries of this kind, has already the inward certainty that his religion cannot take any other form than this."

The reader will notice the similarity, both in method and result. First Schleiermacher surveys the whole area of religion, then he finds three religions which together form a separate category, he contrasts them with each other, he describes what is peculiar to the Christian faith, and he concludes that all that does not answer the truth question because a phenomenological description is inherently incapable of that. The differences between our way of tackling the subject and that of Schleiermacher are the following: (1) Due to the study of the history of religion in the century and a half after Schleiermacher, we cannot place the religions in such a harmonious hierarchy from lower to higher. We do not deny that there is some truth in an evolutionary development, but this does not exclude, rather includes, breaks, religious leaps, and antitheses; and our vision of the evolution is decisively dependent on the choice which we ourselves make at a number of crossroads and intersections. (2) Related to that it must be said that Schleiermacher had to do injustice to the peculiarities of many religions by the place he assigned to them on the hierarchical ladder. Such is the case with polytheism, and even more so with Islam when, on the basis of only a few features, it is regarded as belonging to the "aesthetic" type. (3) For Schleiermacher the world of religions is primarily a world of ideas. The highest religions distinguish themselves by having the purest idea of God, namely the monotheistic. In Israel, however, monotheism was the correlative and consequence of the special relationship in which they stood *to* one particular God and the experiences they had *with* him. The religions are not ideas that reflect the nature of our awareness of absolute dependence, but encounters with a supernatural reality in the midst of the reality of this world. Schleiermacher's earlier definition of "perception of the universal" (*Anschauung des Universums*) does more justice to that. (4) We noticed that Schleiermacher at the end, in par. 11 (in an addition to the second printing!), sees the ineffectiveness of his apologetic prolegomena. But that insight comes too late. It should have led him to a revision of his evolutionistic and typological considerations—and that did not happen.

In broad outline we follow Schleiermacher. But we shall not try to come with a neat hierarchical system with built-in proofs that go beyond the limits of the phenomenal. In all honesty we have to admit that phenomenal reality does not offer criteria for answering the truth question. That admission allows us the freedom to let the phenomena speak for themselves. We shall then observe that, while not proving anything, they do repeatedly place us before forks in the road and opposite directions which compel us to make very personal and decisive choices. This is the only insight the prolegomena to a study of the Christian faith can offer us. There is, however, every reason to express this insight beforehand. This is certainly so if this insight is based on a clear determination of the place which the Christian faith occupies in the whole of experiential reality. For that is the real reason for prolegomena: not to prove truth but simply to indicate the position of the Christian faith. The surrounding areas cannot further elucidate the right of the gospel to that particular position. For that the subject will have to speak for itself.

5. STUDY OF THE CHRISTIAN FAITH: MOTIVES AND ESSENCE

THE CHRISTIAN FAITH begins past a number of forks and some clefts. Moving about in this new territory one senses the need for reflection on the new situation. This need is inherent in being human. With the believer this urge for elucidation can go in either of two directions.

Looking back, he can think about and desire to give an account of his relationship to what lies *before* the crossroads and clefts. In that case he seeks to enter into dialogue with those who have not made that choice with him. This account and elucidation can assume different forms and be carried on under different names: philosophy of religion, apologetics, polemics, eristics; earlier we saw that the prolegomena to the study of the faith aim at something similar. But the believer may also be interested in satisfying a more basic need, namely to obtain greater clarity about his own situation and what is unique about it. Then the question is not, Why do I believe? but, What do I believe? Then one does not think toward the faith but one proceeds from the faith itself. This is done in what we call here the "study of the faith." Presupposed thus from beginning to end is that anyone seeking this clarification is already a believer and wants to be questioned about his faith. It is important to establish this clearly at the outset, because many look to the study of the faith to provide the basis or even the proof for the faith. We have argued that such cannot be done. The question whether that proposition is true, and if not, what then can be said in this area, belongs to the above-mentioned "backward-looking reflection." One who sets himself to engage in the study of the faith has to abide by its rules and take his starting-point in the faith itself. It might even happen that in this way he will find an answer to his quest for a foundation for his faith. At any rate, the Christian faith entails its own certainty; and if it is studied properly, that fact will become clearly evident. In the study of the faith one thinks about his relationship to God in Jesus Christ. The need for such thinking about the faith has always been strongly felt in the Christian church. This may seem strange, for a relationship by no means always compels one to reflect on it. Does one constantly need intellectual elucidation of one's marriage relationship, one's friendships, one's citizenship? Normally that need arises only when something is amiss with these relationships. Is this different with the faith?

In the history of the church we find several motives that have led to reflection on the faith. The very earliest articulations, consisting of longer or shorter creedal statements, had their origin in the missionary situation and the catechetical needs of the church; the core of the faith-relationship needed to be articulated so that outsiders would know what it was about. Soon afterward another motive was added: the church needed help so that it could cope with the confusion being caused by contradictory presentations of the gospel. In addition, through the ages, regular church life, and especially preaching, has had a need for a brief and more systematic summary of the contents of the faith, within which could be placed the results of individual interpretations of the Bible. Most recently yet another motive has strongly come to the fore: since secularism radically took over the dominance Christianity used to have in Europe, including the church, many have become deeply alienated from the language of the Bible and of the church. This gap, which is very much a gap between the generations, at least in part must be bridged. To the study of the faith falls then the task to come with the language and the concepts that are needed for a translation of the faith that bridges the gap. It thus becomes primarily a handmaid of the hermeneutical process of the *traditio,* the transmission of the faith to those who have not understood it in the traditional forms. Study of the faith must be carried on with an awareness of the mentality and the situation of the people whom it can help. Thus the church not only needs study of the faith in this sense for the translation of the faith to others, but also to gain a clearer and deeper understanding of what she believes herself, and so to be strengthened in her struggle to live by that faith. Summarizing, we can thus say that reflection on the faith, apart from arising out of the general human need for clarification, arises from the needs of exegesis, catechesis, polemics, hermeneutics, and the confrontation between the world and the church which is constantly subject to its attacks. Behind that we perceive the deepest and most comprehensive motive, what we may call the "non-self-evidence" of the Christian faith. This faith, as we saw, arises by no means, as with an inner necessity, out of the given reality. It is rather loosely attached to it. It is, as Luther said, "a restless thing." That tense situation heightens the need for reflection, as a defense against the suction of doubt.

Corresponding to these above-mentioned motives, history exhibits a great variety of designs in the area of the faith. Some were born especially out of the need to provide catechetical instruction, such as that of Gregory of Nyssa, *Oratio catechetica* (383), and of Calvin, *Institutio christianae religionis* (1st ed. 1536). Others were especially intended to refute erring opponents, such as Irenaeus, *Adversus haereses* (ca. 185), and M. Chemnitz, *Examen Concilii Tridentini* (1573). In the Middle Ages the exegesis of the Bible and of the fathers was the basis of the study of the faith. Barth wrote his *Church Dogmatics* (1932ff.) for the sake of the church's proclamation. Even more emphatically, Noordmans offered his *Herschepping* (1934) as an articulation of the "rule" for the speaking of the church. The need to formulate the faith in conscious confrontation with the intellectual climate of one's own time is especially something from after the Enlightenment. Schleiermacher's *Christian Faith* (1822) may be regarded as the first and outstanding specimen. But this motive is strong already in Origen's *De principiis* (ca. 220). It was very strong in the 13th century when theology was confronted with the rising Averroistic Aristotelianism. Thomas Aquinas' *Summa Theologica* (1274) is a grand attempt to express the gospel in the (for that time) modern categories of Aristotle. In our time the most significant alternative motivations and methods of dogmatics are those of Barth in his *CD* and those of Tillich in his *ST.* Barth in his Dogmatics inquires after the Word of God as the norm for preaching. Tillich calls that approach "kerygmatic theology," and to it he wishes to add his "apologetic" or "answering theology." His primary concern, however, is not to give answers to needs of the hour. The 'situation' to which theology must respond is the totality of man's creative self-interpretation in a special period" (*ST* I, pp. 3–8). In contrast Barth holds that it is only from the Word of God that we can learn what our real needs are.

From the foregoing it should not be concluded, however, that dogmatics should be constantly aware of the service it has to render to the believer, the church, and the world. That would not even be desirable. Here it is necessary to distinguish between motive and purpose. The call for good instruction, for example, may compel to reflection on the faith. But it would be wrong if in this reflection the question is continually asked whether the results are really suitable for the instruction. That is exactly what would not be good for the instruction. For instruction does not seek to serve itself, but the truth of the faith. Theology serves the church best if it does not try to be always one step ahead of every need that may arise, but aims to articulate the truth for the sake of the truth itself. Precisely because it is concerned with life, it is obligated to proceed in a kind of "aimlessness." It serves all needs not primarily by trying to meet these needs, but by serving the truth. It is not correct, however, to speak here in terms of absolute contrasts. That is why we speak of "a kind of" aimlessness. An analogy would be the preacher who concentrates on his text, yet without ever forgetting the hearers he is addressing. That can lead to tensions. Conformistically the study of the faith can become a slave to needs, or, narcissistically and by losing itself in abstractions, it can become unfruitful. But these are extremes which almost never, if ever, occur in their pure form. If the student of the faith is a living human who himself, in his own soul, senses the tension of the faith and is deeply aware of what is involved in translating it to others (which is a prime requirement for any student), the danger of abstraction is small. In fact, such a student should try to consciously put the aimlessness of his labor first, in the knowledge that this detachment is the guarantee of a fruitful pursuit.

For all times to follow, Anselm of Canterbury has hit upon the formula that captures this aimlessness of dogmatics with his statements, *fides quaerens intellectum* and *credo ut intelligam.* This fruitful aimlessness can regularly be observed in the history of theology, also in those thinkers whose work was prompted by very specific needs. Fine examples are the earlier-mentioned *Summa* of Aquinas and Barth's *Church Dogmatics.* In the early church the sense of need was the predominant motive. In Protestant Scholasticism (17th century) such investigation of the faith was mainly done for its own sake. Which is not to say that in both periods no other motives played a role. In the 19th and 20th centuries, subject specialization in the universities meant that the study of the faith, too, became very much an independent subject of study. But in both centuries it has met with strong reactions. See H. Berkhof, *Introduction to the Study of Dogmatics* (E.T. 1985), 2.6.

The essence of the study of the faith is best grasped if we regard it as an element in the sanctification of the church. In the faith-relationship God seizes us for himself with his love. We may respond to that by loving him with our whole being and therefore with all our mind. The study of the faith is not the only form, but certainly one of the forms of our loving God with the mind. Only in the context of sanctification do its nature and contours come out. To love is an aimless something, because it finds its purpose in itself. If this love is an element in the sanctification of existence, it is part of the struggle the believer and the people of God are engaged in against the forces within and without that draw them away from the faith.

This context of sanctification makes us aware, however, of still another aspect. Sanctification happens in what systematic theology calls "works" or "good works." Everywhere, however, the New Testament shows us the ambivalence of these works. Imperceptibly the aimless work of gratitude can become an achievement in which man seeks himself and lives for himself. This danger is particularly great in the exercise of the study of the faith. Because of the intellectual nature of this activity, the threat of intellectual pride is ever present. Someone has said that the lowest reaches of hell are reserved for theologians who are more interested in their own thoughts about God than in God himself. The church has always had a keen nose for this danger of theological self-justification, more than most theologians themselves. True theologizing is only in part dependent on the intellectual capacities of the student of theology. It has just as much to do with the encounter between God and the person practicing theology, that is, with the right relationship.

By putting it this way, we hit upon what is often regarded as the basic problem of dogmatics, the contrast between relationship and objectification. "Faith" is a relationship, "study" or exposition is an objectifying activity, and consequently study of the faith looks very much like a contradiction in terms. A love relationship can be experienced; it can also be studied; but can one ever do both at the same time? Especially due to the influence of post-war existentialistic thinking which assumed a contrast between existence and objectification, this has become a much-discussed problem. This was correct insofar as one had in mind with it the fatal reversal referred to above, being more interested in one's own thoughts about God than in God himself. But the philosophical setting and underpinning that were given to the problem do not agree with reality. Relationship and objectification do not necessarily exclude each other. Love, in fact, may compel to objectification. The term "objectification" can mean two quite different things: both the reverent contemplation of an object of affection and the irreverent attempt to overpower it, while disregarding its unique nature. These two may not be identified. In theology the second is a constantly present threat, and the first is the only thing that may legitimately be done. It does mean that all right thinking about God arises out of the encounter *with* God and is aimed *at* the encounter with God. When we are engaged in this thinking, we are involved in it, more than in other intellectual activities, with our total existence. Whether this thinking becomes true and meaningful thinking depends on the relationship which from the other side is established by the Holy Spirit. That, however, such thinking is possible is evident from many pages in classical and modern theology.

A classical definition of theology says correctly: "Theology teaches God, is taught by God, and leads to God." For a further investigation of the problematic of relationship and objectification, see H. Gollwitzer, *The Existence of God as Confessed by Faith* (E.T. 1965), esp. II,4; T. F. Torrance, *Theological Science* (1969), esp. pp. 295–303; H. Berkhof, *Introduction to Dogmatics,* 2.5.

The study of the faith has a modest but indispensable function. It can be compared to a map of a geographical area. Such a map is based on acquaintance with the landscape and is intended to familiarize the user with the totality and the coherence of the area. Detached from that coherence the map becomes an abstraction or a substitute. The drawer of the map knows that he does it for the user and with a view to his needs. But while drawing, his only concern is to draft as good a map as possible.

Another clarifying illustration of the function of the study of the faith is given by Brunner: "As the analytical chemist analyzes in his retorts edibles which are offered for sale in the marketplace, and thus is able to distinguish that which has real food value from all mere substitutes, yet in so doing diverts the material intended for human nourishment from its actual purpose, and indeed even destroys it, and yet the result of all his methods of separation and examination serves the nourishment of the people as a whole, so that which the theologian clarifies, separates and re-unites, his dogmatic concepts and his systematic processes, are not the 'food' that the believer needs, and not that which has to be preached, and yet it is serviceable to the preacher and the pastor" (*Dg* I, pp. 64f.).

Having considered the motives and character of this reflective labor, there remains the question of the designation we are to give to this work. The commonly used name for this discipline is *dogmatics* (in the English-speaking world: *systematic theology*). Though in this book we shall not entirely avoid this designation, we do not regard it as an adequate description, certainly not for our time. The term "dogma" reminds us of the classical doctrinal pronouncements of the church, especially those from the fourth to the sixth century about the Trinity, the relation of God and Christ, and of the divine and the human nature in Christ. The term "dogmatics" tends to suggest that this theological discipline is primarily or solely concerned with those doctrinal pronouncements and takes its starting-point in their authority.

This is somewhat true of Eastern Orthodox dogmatics, much less of Roman Catholic theology, and not at all of Protestant dogmatics. Hence most Protestant dogmaticians understand the term "dogma" differently; but the reader often finds it hard to see that. The terms "dogmatism" and "dogmatic," which have acquired a much wider meaning, still suggest authoritative assertions that are laid on people's shoulders like a yoke, assertions that are contrary to reality. For these reasons we drop this term (it is only three centuries old anyway).

We prefer the name *study of the faith.* However, it, too, has its drawbacks. As "dogmatics" had objectivistic overtones, so study of the faith could smack of subjectivism. It may seem that the writer of the study articulates only his personal viewpoint, without any pretension of a more universal validity. This misunderstanding disappears, however, when we recall the meaning which the term "faith" has in the world of religions. Faith is a relationship between God and man. One who describes a relationship does not describe something subjective, nor something objective, but a coming together of two subjects in an encounter which for both of them possesses a trans-subjective, and thus objective reality. One who reflects on the Christian faith is not reflecting on a human disposition as such. Faith is an act by which man points away from himself. It is always "believing in." When we deal with faith as a subjective attitude (the *fides qua creditur*) we deal at the same time with the faith that is believed, the contents of faith (the *fides quae creditur*). In our opinion the danger of subjectively misunderstanding the term "study of the faith" is much less than the danger of objectivistically misunderstanding the term "dogmatics."

The word *dogma,* plural *dogmata,* has had a far from uniform use in Hellenistic and Christian Greek, embracing in its range such diverse meanings as "government edict" and "private opinion." This semantic range has often been conveniently used to explain and defend the term "dogmatics." For the historical problematics see *TDNT* II, *s.v. dogma* (Kittel), *RGG* II, *s.v. Dogma II* (Gloege), Brunner, *Dg* I, pp. 103–107, and many handbooks on dogmatics. On the changed and diverse modern meanings of the word see Gloege, *RGG* II, *s.v. Dogma II.* Well known is Barth's reinterpretation in *CD* I,1, pp. 304–309. "Dogma is the agreement of Church proclamation with the revelation attested in Holy Scripture" (p. 304) and is therefore "an eschatological concept" (p. 309).

For centuries the term "dogma" has especially signified an infallible ecclesiastical pronouncement about divine revelation. Since the Reformation, in the Protestant churches, this use could no longer be maintained. For two reasons: (a) all ecclesiastical pronouncements have to be tested by the infallible Word of God in Holy Scripture; (b) faith is no longer "accepting whatever the church says must be believed," but a personal relation of acceptance and trust in God's promises in Christ. That is in principle the end of objectivism.

The Reformation did not express its faith in dogmas but in creedal statements, fallible human summaries of the Word of God. It appears as if lately, also in the Roman Catholic Church, dogma has lost its credibility as a means to proclaim truth; intentionally the Second Vatican Council refrained from proclaiming dogmas.

It is remarkable therefore that the word *dogmatics* arose in a Protestant climate. It was first used by L. F. Reinhart in his *Synopsis theologiae dogmaticae* (1659). Before that *theologia* was used, with additional specifying terms such as *Summa, Sententiae, Institutio(-nes), Loci, Syntagma, Systema.* The name "dogmatics" found general acceptance, likely because the increasing specialization in theology required a new name. But a century later another name was introduced: study of the faith (Dutch *Geloofsleer*). S. J. Baumgarten, a conservative follower of Christian Wolff, named his dogmatics, posthumously issued by Semler in three volumes (1759f.), *Evangelische Glaubenslehre.* But only through Schleiermacher's *Christian Faith* (1822) did it become a widely used name. At the same time, however, there remained considerable opposition to the name, because in Schleiermacher it was clearly linked with a method which in the eyes of many was plainly subjectivistic. Think of the famous par. 15: "Christian doctrines are accounts of the Christian religious affections set forth in speech." (One should bear in mind, however, that for Schleiermacher the subject is not the believing individual but the church—see already par. 2—and that Schleiermacher also wants to use the description of the Christian states of mind to base on it theological and cosmological statements, according to par. 30.) As a consequence many orthodox theologians rejected the term "study of the faith," for the most part preferring the term "dogmatics." This contrast is not yet a matter of the past; wrongly in my opinion, as argued above. See also H. Berkhof, *Introduction to Dogmatics,* 2.1–4.

We may not conclude this paragraph without asking for something like a definition of the concept of the study of the faith. The objection could be made that a definition should come first. But in that case the writer is too quick with forcing his own viewpoint upon his readers. A definition should arise out of a preceding broader orientation. Then, at least, we have some conjecture as to the choice we make with our definition (= limitation). Moreover, beginning with a definition might suggest that a precise definition is of decisive significance. Every definition has, however, something artificial about it. No one should become the slave of his own definition. With this reservation we describe the study of the Christian faith as: *a systematic examination of the contents of the relationship which God in Christ has entered into with us.*

To that we add the following remarks: (1) This examination is not directed to human states of mind, nor directly to God himself, but to an encounter between God and man in which faith professes God as the one taking the initiative. (2) This examination is directed to the contents of that relationship (of course never detached from the relationship as such), without our being able in the definition to run ahead to a description of those contents; the description will have to become clear as step by step the reflection proceeds. (3) Our concern is the intellectual penetration of the relationship. That is not the first, let alone the only thing the believer does with that relationship. First comes his entrance into it by faith, and his practice of it in prayer and praise, in experience and deed. Therein his intellect always plays an active part too, even though there is no deliberate examination here. (4) It concerns a systematic examination, which differs from that which is done, for example, in the study of the Bible, meditation, sermon preparation, or discussion with an eye to contemporary problems. A systematic exploration is done for its own sake; it is a probing of God's association with us, with the intent of getting a better and deeper understanding of it, and (especially) to be able to understand the various elements and aspects in their interrelation as a unified whole. To what extent the latter is possible—in other words, what the limits of this pursuit are—is one of the subjects that will come up in the next paragraph.

6. STUDY OF THE CHRISTIAN FAITH: REACH AND LIMITS

WHAT VALIDITY can be ascribed to the results of this "systematic examination of the contents of the relationship into which God in Christ has entered with us"? Here again we face the question concerning the *truth,* without being able to solve it. What we can and must do is have another look at the place and significance of the study of the faith, trying to further elucidate it in the light of this question which lies behind all such theological study.

The truth contents of the Christian study-of-the-faith are entirely dependent on the truth which we ascribe to the Christian faith-relationship. At the same time it must be said that the truth of a study of the faith remains as such far behind that of the faith itself. For every study of the faith is an intellectually clarifying reaction of an individual believer to the faith-relationship, a reaction determined by particular needs, by his tradition, and by individual preferences. A study of the faith may thus include all kinds of things that cannot be derived from the faith itself, and it will always leave out much that does belong to a total experience (which no one has) of the faith-relationship. It is thus impossible that the faith could ever be identified with any theological model. The danger of such an identification is by no means imaginary. Yet all churches correctly maintain the principial difference; even the proclamation by the Roman Catholic Church (1879), making Thomas Aquinas the *Doctor Ecclesiae,* was never intended to do away with this difference.

Trying to express the above in positive terms, we may say that the study of the faith shares in the truth of the Christian faith which it assumes and aims to articulate. One can, however, ask what that means. Can the study of the faith pretend to enunciate truth? Is it not a contradiction in terms to speak of the *truth* of *faith?* Does truth not always pretend to possess universal validity and verifiability? And according to that criterion, can study of the faith be anything more than a subjective pursuit (even though a large community should stand behind it)? Against that it must be remarked that faith is more than a subjective relationship of trust. Trust is based on knowing of the dependability of the person or object that is trusted; it therefore includes and presupposes knowledge. It belongs to the essence of the faith that it pretends to have to do with truth, and even with the all-inclusive and universally valid truth. Thus the study of the faith cannot relinquish the claim that it tries to articulate the truth. But what does that mean, if its truth is not acknowledged outside a particular group, or even firmly rejected?

The questions arising here can be summarized in the question: is study of the faith a *science?* Scientific activity always presupposes an a priori given reality which it seeks to penetrate and elucidate with the use of analytical and combinative concepts that bring order, coherence, and insight into that reality. The same is true in the study of the faith. And for that discipline it may be useful if it presents itself as a science, since scientific activity as such is a modest enterprise, being a task with which man is never finished. This awareness keeps the study of the faith from ascribing to itself the absoluteness which belongs only to its object. There is, however, a great difference from what is usually understood by science. Science is based on a mode of experience, investigation, and verification which in principle is common to everyone. But the study of the faith is based on a conviction that lacks this commonness and of which it is said that it is brought about by a special working of the Holy Spirit. Must we not say that because of this appeal to the Spirit the study of the faith is not really a scientific pursuit? But then the question comes up: when is something scientific and when is it not? After all, the deeper the scientific probing and the more is included in the truth one seeks, the stronger will be the subjective element in the scientific pursuit and the smaller its comprehensibility and verifiability. Reflection on the ultimate truth will always be in the nature of a choice. To exclude this area of reflection from the scientific pursuit implies that one condemns science to limit its investigations to surface phenomena and to ignore all questions about ultimate presuppositions, connections, and perspectives, which must lead to the conclusion that the knowable is not really important and that the important is unknowable. Looked at from this angle, the question whether the study of the faith should be called a science is of decisive significance for science itself and its scope and aims.

From the perspective of what is meant by science, the question as to its scientific character not only concerns the study of the faith, but also all kinds of other forms of systematic thinking, especially of course philosophy and ethics. Is Hegel's intellectual labor science? Or that of Marx, of Jaspers, of Bloch, of Teilhard de Chardin? Or in the Netherlands that of W. Banning, J. H. Vanden Berg, or H. Fortmann? This is more than a matter of definition. The whole relation of science and society and the service which the university is to render to society is at stake.

The study of the faith can hardly think of itself as anything else than a form of the human activity called "science." For faith implies the conviction that it directs itself to reality, namely the highest reality. It also wishes to concern itself with this reality using the conceptual approach that is characteristic of science. At the same time faith knows that its claim to truth and that the claim of the study of the faith that it is scientific in character find no recognition outside the community of believers. This is the direct consequence of the non-self-evident place the Christian faith has in the whole of reality, because the encounter with God is unpredictable and on account of sin even improbable. But the study of the faith cannot let go of the claim that it is scientific in character. Moreover, she will be conscious of the fact that by this insistence she makes her own contribution against an empiricistic narrowing of the concept of science. Beyond that she will simply have to wait and see whether with this claim she finds acceptance in her cultural environment. Whether she gets this recognition or not will have no influence on how she understands herself and her task.

On theology as a science see Barth, *CD* I,1, pp. 3-11; Brunner, *Dg* I, pp. 60-66; Trillhaas, *Dg* pp. 48-57; very good is Weber, *Gl* pp. 56-64; further also G. J. Heering, *Geloof en openbaring* (3rd ed. 1950), II, II, par. 2, and Ott, *AG* art. 7. An extensive survey of the problematics in Germany since the Enlightenment is found in G. Sauter, ed., *Theologie als Wissenschaft* (1971), especially the thorough survey article by Sauter himself.

This is not the first time that the scientific character of dogmatics has been discussed. Barth gauged it only in terms of its "Sachgemassheit." H. Scholz (contra Barth) spoke of "controleerbaarheid" (possibility of being checked), while today the term "verifiability" is frequently used. But these terms, derived from the physical sciences, are not suitable in the humanities, certainly not in theology (see above, large type, and my *Introduction to Dogmatics,* 6.7). Defenders of the scientific character of dogmatics speak of "inzichtelijkheid" (comprehensibility), "plausibiliteit" (plausibility), "Sinnzusammenhang aller Wirklichkeitserfahrung" (coherence of meaning of all experiences of reality—Pannenberg), "navraag kunnen lijden" (ability to stand inquiry—Kuitert), "Grundvertrauen als rationale Verantwortbarkeit" (basic confidence as rational accountability—Küng), "Lebensbezug als Kriterium" (relatedness of life as criterion—Ebeling). Pannenberg in particular has grappled with this problem. See his *Wissenschaftstheorie und Theologie* (1973) and the discussion with G. Sauter in W. Pannenberg et al., *Grundlagen der Theologie—ein Diskurs* (1974).

In the Netherlands the question concerning the scientific character of dogmatics has again become very relevant in connection with the restructuring of the university. See H. Berkhof, *Introduction to Dogmatics,* 4.1, and "God voorwerp van wetenschap?" II, in *Bruggen en bruggehoofden* (1981), pp. 208-216.

We noted already that the pretension of being "science" points to the limitations inherent in the study of the faith. It is necessary that we try to get a deeper and more concrete understanding of this limitation, lest—as has often happened—we should be tempted to overestimate the importance of this discipline. All disciplines have their limitations, depending on the object and the methodology, and also on the investigating subject. In the study of the faith this limitation is of a unique and weighty character, due to the very special relationship between subject and object here. This special limitation consists in the following:

1. The limitation lies herein that we are *creatures.* Our object is the God who has created us. We cannot comprehend him. On the contrary, he comprehends us. The object of theology is the relationship to him who is pre-eminently Subject. Scientifically this makes for an almost unbearable situation, one which becomes bearable only because, according to the Christian faith, the Subject so completely enters into our reality that, while remaining Subject, he makes himself therein object for us as well.

2. The limitation lies herein that we are *sinners.* In ourselves we are not willing to direct our life, and therefore not our thinking, according to the revelation and the will of this God. Instead of being transformed after his image, consciously or unconsciously we always try to picture him after our own image, as a reflection of our own ideas and ideals. It is the Holy Spirit himself who constantly has to overcome our resistance against fully walking with this God, also in our theological thinking.

3. The limitation consists therein that we are *on the way.* God goes a way with us through his history toward the fullness of salvation. Now we do not yet know as we ourselves are known. In new situations God shows himself in constantly new ways to mankind. Revelation is not yet completed, and therefore our knowledge is fragmentary. Every exposition of the faith is thus a dated snapshot. If taken correctly, the picture is indeed a snapshot of an eternal reality. But that eternity is not only the firma-

ment above us but also the distant horizon before us. Consequently, dogmatics should never take on an air of definitiveness. For the faith itself is not definitive; it is meant to become sight.

A good discussion of this limitation of theology is Althaus, *CW* I, pp. 288ff. There is the classical contrast between the coming *theologia visionis* and the present *theologia viae* or *viatorum* —though one does not always receive the impression that the expositors really reckon with this eschatological boundary.

Several biblical elements and passages also serve the purpose of reminding us of this limitation. According to the OT anyone who sees God must die. According to the NT we see him indirectly, in Christ, by faith—but faith and sight are essentially opposites. Not even Moses was permitted to see God's glory; he may hear the "name" and see God's "back," thus "a posteriori," indirectly (Ex. 33:18–23). The OT warns strongly against the manipulation of God by sinful man (2nd and 3rd commandments of the decalogue; warnings against false prophecy; and Ex. 3:13–15 where "I am who I am" also implies that the name must be protected against magical manipulation). In the NT we think especially of 1 Cor. 13:9–13: now we know "in part" (fragmentary), now we see in a mirror ("in an enigma"), to which the solution still has to come.

At this point it is necessary to consider more closely that the study of the faith is a *systematic* reflection. Thus far we have used this term in a limited and plain sense: it is a reflection which makes use of concepts by which divisions and combinations are made in the subject matter so that it becomes structured, ordered, and rationally transparent. The question must, however, be asked what the purpose of this ordering activity is. In the past it used to be said that this purpose was the construction of a system, a large, organic, conceptual unity, as a mirror of the unity of the divine thoughts as they are revealed to us. Nowadays one seldom hears this answer. We know too much of the limitations of our theological thinking. We regard the grasp for the system as a grasp in a vacuum, or at least as grasping for something which is beyond our ability.

From what we noted about the limitations it follows that we agree with that. But with that not everything has been said. For now the question is: what do we aim at, if it is not a system? What alternative is there? We can discuss all kinds of subjects without relating them. But scientifically this means that we do only half the work. The human spirit wants to go on and find analogies and connections. Systematic reflection has no boundary. This is particularly so in theology, because we believe in the unity of God and thus in the unity of his thoughts and works. The ultimate and highest ambition of dogmatics is to make its entire thematics transparent all the way to this unity. What is true everywhere is true especially here: systematic reflection tends toward the system.

But the system is unattainable for us. This unity is God's privilege and it is not at our disposal. And what God works is history, history concentrated in a person. The facticity of history and the subjectivity and uniqueness of the person that history is about limit our systematizing ability. Like Moses we can see only the back of God. As we noted earlier, there are definite limits to our ability to know, and that implies that the system lies beyond our reach.

This does not mean that the term "system" is meaningless for us. It indicates the limit and the horizon of our thinking. It is an eschatological concept for which we reach from afar. It is the polestar by which we sail and chart our course. The search for the coherence and unity in what God reveals to us is a task without end. Only the one who has a clear perception of this task is keenly aware of the inherent limitations of his systematizing ability. The less one is interested in a system, the fewer limitations one will find, and the more one will be satisfied with a disparate and diffuse presentation that does not serve the cause one has in mind.

On the systematic character of dogmatics see Heering, *Geloof en openbaring,* II,II, par. 3; Barth, *CD* I,2, pp. 861–870; Althaus, *CW* p. 299; Tillich, *ST* I, pp. 58f.; esp. Weber, *Gl* I, pp. 66–70. The systematic contents of a study of the faith (not to be confused with the systematic *form*) vary considerably. There was little in the first edition of Melanchthon's *Loci Communes* (1521), which was a reaction to the medieval systems. Highly systematic contents are found in the works of great dogmaticians like Aquinas, Schleiermacher, Barth, and Tillich—with the danger, which they themselves are aware of but did not always avoid, that the step-by-step-discovered unity and convergence becomes a principle from which the next step can logically be deduced.

Every systematic theologian will more or less consciously make a certain theme central, e.g. the sovereignty of God, incarnation, reconciliation, justification, the new life, or the future. In such a dominant theme he tries to express the unity or approximate it. The reader usually discovers without much difficulty that in this way such a concept is being overburdened and that consequently other equally necessary concepts do not receive the required emphasis. On the impossibility of a closed system see also par. 18, the larger type.

We end by inquiring after the *division* of the study of the faith. It can be structured from at least three points of view. Because it concerns the relationship between God and man, our starting-point can be God or man or the relationship. If we start with God, the usual order is a trinitarian design in which successively the Father, the Son, and the Spirit are the center. If we start with man, we can view him in his different relations to God: as a creature, as a sinner, as redeemed, and as sanctified. If the relationship is made central and one bears in mind that this relationship has a history, the result is a design which is either redemptive-historical (*heilsgeschichtlich*) or Christocentric. Owing to the scope of the material, a theologian hardly ever sticks consistently to his design. Most works on dogmatics exhibit a combination of methods. While detracting from the methodological strictness, this makes it easier to be comprehensive and thus makes for greater flexibility. So this combination does greater justice to the object of dogmatics, "the manifold wisdom of God." This order is crystallized in a centuries-old dogmatic division (which, moreover, is found in many confessions and catechetical instruction books) which, though with individual variations, was and is in the main adhered to by a great many theologians. We wish to do the same—both in the adherence and in the variation.

This order begins with God, his being and revelation, and next takes up man, as creature and as sinner. Then it follows a more redemptive-historical and Christocentric approach (Israel; the person and work of Christ). In the then-following pneumatological division, man and his renewal are central, which is for the most part also the case in the concluding eschatological section. The whole is usually preceded by a discussion of the source and norms for our knowledge of God. In general we shall adhere to this tradition. Where we strikingly depart from it we will give the reasons for it.

In earlier centuries dogmatics often included what is now called theological ethics, the doctrine concerning the Christian life. The separation of ethics from theology began in the first half of the 17th century (Amesius, Calixtus). For neither of the two branches was this severance without danger. Faith and works belong together as the two sides of a coin. Isolating them from each other can easily lead to an intellectualistic misunderstanding of the Christian faith and a moralistic view of the Christian life. For that reason systematic theologians have never really acquiesced in the split and continued to combine dogmatics and ethics. A good illustration from the previous century is M. Kähler's *Die Wissenschaft der christlichen Lehre* (1883); well known from our century is Barth's *CD* of which II,2 contains important sections on ethics, III,4 discusses the entire ethics of creation, and IV,4 (of which Barth was able to finish only a small part) was to give the ethics of reconciliation. Yet these remained exceptions. In our pluralistic society in which ethics is confronted with ever more varied and dynamic situations, it is becoming such a specialized undertaking that the combination with dogmatics can perhaps only be made by an occasional highly talented student.

A trinitarian division of dogmatics is found in Calvin's *Institutes* in its final form (1559). Anthropological in design are Melanchthon's *Loci communes* in its original form (1521), Schleiermacher's *Christian Faith* (which starts from the "pious self-consciousness"), and Kähler's book referred to above (which starts from "faith in justification"). Barth's *CD* has a trinitarian design. Classical examples of salvation-history theologies are Cocceius' *Summa doctrinae de foedere et testamento Dei* (1648) and J. C. K. von Hofmann's *Der Schriftbeweis* (1855). The foundation for the classical combination was laid by P. Lombard in his *Sententiarum libri* IV (1157) with the division: Trinity, creatures, salvation, sacraments, and last things. On the division see also my *Introduction to Dogmatics*, 7.1.

In the design for *CD* IV,1–3, Barth has made a drastic correction on the traditional scheme. Three times and from three different angles he discusses the large dogmatic core (from the doctrine of sin to that of the church and of sanctification): (1) the saving condescension of God; (2) the exaltation of man implied in it; (3) the calling and task of man which is likewise implied in it. The cross-connections to which this leads often yield surprising discoveries and vistas. The reverse is that every theme is dealt with three times, resulting in breaking natural connections. It is still too early to consider the pros and cons of this new design. Mindful of the *in dubiis abstine* we stay with the classical order.

Revelation

7. INTERNAL PROLEGOMENA

AT THE END OF PARAGRAPH 6, speaking about the classical dogmatic order, we remarked in passing, "The whole is usually preceded by a discussion of the source and norms for our knowledge of God." We are thus at the point where we have to ask whether we, too, want such a preceding discussion, and if so, what its nature will have to be. The need for such a discussion did not become apparent from the considerations in paragraph 6 on the division. It rather became clear that when we are engaged in the study of the faith we enter a closed circle, and that principially it does not matter in which direction we move as we try to find the coherence and the connections. From the fathers we have the wise statement, "the access to it does not matter" (*methodus est arbitraria*). Without embarrassment—for it derives from the subject itself—we find ourselves in a circular argument. In token of that we might do well to jump without further ado into the subject and thus, if we follow the classical order, begin with a chapter about God.

Yet for centuries this has been more the exception than the rule in dogmatics. This is partly due to the liking which many have for Prolegomena; there is an eagerness to determine beforehand the position of the Christian faith within the whole of reality. But beside that or instead of it, many theologians, also when they have already entered the circle, want to present a methodological account of what they do before they plunge completely into the subject. Rather confusingly, such an account-within-the-circle also goes by the name of Prolegomena. To guard against this confusion we have named this second "start," which in contrast to the first is made *after* the jump across the gap, *internal* Prolegomena. Barth calls them "the things that must be said first" in contrast to the external Prolegomena, which he calls "the things that must be said beforehand" (and which he rejects).

The question is whether, inside the circle, the subject itself compels us to say certain things of a more methodological and formal nature *first,* before we can begin to explain the contents of the faith. If we say "compels," the answer, on the basis of all that we have seen so far, must be negative. Hence many theologians, including some of renown, have felt no need for internal Prolegomena. But for the majority of theologians, past and present, the need did and does exist. This need not surprise us. Even if the subject itself does not force us, the times and the circumstances within which and from which we theologize may yet compel us. Surveying the circle, the theologian may become so impressed with regularly recurring starting-points and structures that he considers it best to deal with them separately in a more formal and detached manner first, so that later in each chapter he does not have to come back to them. He will especially sense this need if he assumes that many of his readers will come up against these starting-points and structures and will regard them as obstacles which they find hard to overcome. The concern is then not to provide an introduction to the subject, as in the external Prolegomena, but an open and honest placing of all the cards on the table, so that the reader knows from the start what the rules are in the circle he now enters. Stated briefly, in the internal Prolegomena the epistemology which is implicitly given in the relationship between God and man is abstracted from it and considered first.

The objections against this, it must be said, are not small. God's relationship with man is a very intimate one and full of deep personal concern. One who is engaged in internal Prolegomena starts out with an alienating reflection, one fraught with possible dire consequences. Can the relationship take such a formalization? Is one then still busy with the subject itself? Is there not a very great danger of lapsing back into apologetic external Prolegomena? And if one manages to avoid that, how can one take up internal Prolegomena without constantly anticipating the material discussion of the subject proper?

These objections seem weighty enough to abandon the whole undertaking. The reason that we go ahead anyway is that the estrangement between the Christian faith and the secularized cultural mentality in the Western world and in our time is so great and so strongly felt that we should take the risks, if at the outset we can do something to shed some light on this situation of estrangement. Precisely where modern autonomous thought likes to reject the Christian faith on methodological and formal grounds, theology should be willing to walk the second and the third mile with modern man; not in order to agree with him, but to be able to firmly contradict him precisely in the area in which he himself wants to oppose Christianity. Therefore we begin our study of the faith here with epistemology, with the formal structure of the relationship which God in Christ has established with us. Thereby we shall not hesitate regularly to look or point ahead, to protect the structural from dry abstraction and the formal from formalism.

But where then must we look for that formal structure? In the main, three answers have been given to this question.

Roman Catholic theology used to present mainly a doctrine of the *church* as internal Prolegomena. For the relationship of God with man is effected in and through the church as the guardian of salvation and revelation. This mode of Prolegomena arose at the time of the Counter-Reformation and flourished at least till the First World War. In accordance with the times in which it arose, it was rationalistic-apologetic in character. In these Prolegomena the four marks of the church were dealt with (unity, holiness, catholicity, and apostolicity), and it was demonstrated that these are found only in the Roman Catholic Church.

Over against this, Reformation theology developed as its internal Prolegomena a doctrine concerning the authority of the Bible, following the same rationalistic-apologetic pattern. It was demonstrated that the Bible has four characteristics which guarantee its infallibility: divine authority, necessity, perspicuity, and perfection or sufficiency.

Nowadays both modes are usually replaced by a third: the discussion of the concept of *revelation* as the internal Prolegomena. This is not something absolutely new after both previous traditions. These traditions also had in mind to design a doctrine of revelation, of which respectively the church and the Bible were the main and infallible bearer. The accent, however, has shifted. Roman Catholic theologians became dissatisfied with developing the doctrine of the church mainly in the Prolegomena and with a rationalistic-apologetic bent. And after the rise of the historical criticism of the Bible, Protestant theologians could no longer start from its demonstrable infallibility. So both sides went back, beyond church and the Bible, to a more comprehensive concept to which both refer and from which they derive their divine authority.

Revelation as the theme of the internal Prolegomena answers, it seems to us, the needs we mentioned above. This concept contains precisely that presupposition of all speaking about God which modern man regards as strange and debatable. Consciously or unconsciously he lives in a world which is everywhere governed by the same laws and which is intelligible by itself. The offense for his thinking is that there is a God who should enter this world from the outside and interfere in its affairs. And precisely this conviction forms the basis of all Christian speaking about God's dealings with man.

Implied, however, in what we say here is that this form of internal Prolegomena is not the end but the beginning of the difficulties. In the Bible this concept is so much a matter of course that it does not play a central role. And for centuries such was also the case in the study of the faith. The fact that it has now become such a central concept is because it has lost its self-evidence. Anyone who now posits it as the summary of the Christian epistemology thereby takes on his shoulders all the opposition of modern immanentistic and empiricistic thinking. In his Prolegomena he may not ignore all these questions nor can he quickly resolve them.

He has to consider the following facts: In the Bible revelation is a marginal concept; nowhere does it speak of God as totally unknown; and if there is something like revelation, it happens in secret, always hidden in the forms in which the life of man and the world take place; the real revelation will happen only in the great future. Most other religions, too, pretend to live by revelation. Thirdly, to modern ears the term "revelation" has intellectualistic and supernaturalistic (sometimes also mystical) overtones.

The subject matter of the Bible is the contents of the words and deeds, which the witnesses believe and experience as being from God. In their situation there was little need for reflection on the concept "revelation." But that is no reason not to engage in such reflection in another situation. There is not much conscious reflection on the church in the New Testament either, and the Bible is never the subject of such conscious study. What is important is that we are aware of the dangers and limits of every choice. Otherwise the internal prolegomenon isolates itself from salvation or even crowds it out. Relative to the concept of revelation, this means that the epistemological question may never become more important than the ontological question and the salvation question. We do not know of revelation except through what we experience as being revealed and liberating. The broadening of our knowledge is only a part of the intended renewal of our life.

In my *Introduction to Dogmatics,* 6.1–6, I have pointed out that all concepts that were and are being used as prolegomena must constantly refer to each other, in order not to derail.

For centuries there was little or no need for prolegomena. Aquinas, before he begins his dogmatics (*ST* I) with the doctrine of God, submits one introductory question under the heading: "The Nature and Domain of Sacred Doctrine," where he briefly discusses a number of preliminary questions. Calvin (*Inst* I, 1559) precedes his treatment of the doctrine of God with twelve chapters on the knowledge of God (on the natural knowledge of God, Scripture, and other religions), which makes an almost modern impression, but it lacks the methodological deliberateness found in later discussions. One sees the difference when it is compared with the iron-clad treatment of Scripture as internal Prolegomena which Polanus developed in his *Syntagma theologiae christianae* (1609). That treatise arose in part from the need to refute the predominance of the church-principle in Roman Catholic theologians like Bellarmine and Stapleton. A parallel, though less rigid treatment of the Scripture-prolegomena began at the same time among the Lutherans (Wigand, Heerbrand, and especially J. Gerhard with his *Loci theologici,* 1610ff.).

In Roman Catholic theology the reaction against the imprisonment of ecclesiology in the Prolegomena began with J. A. Möhler, and it is especially strong in and since M. J. Scheeben. Schleiermacher strongly opposed the

Scripture-prolegomena of Protestantism. In the orthodox camp they were maintained for a long time. But already Bavinck, following Calvin's lead, put them in the wider famework of revelation-prolegomena (*GD* I, pars. 9–14).

Though with considerable variation, nowadays it is common practice to begin with revelation. See the dogmatics of Althaus, Brunner, and Weber. Trillhaas, *Dg*, p. 44, and Weber, *Gl*, I, 187f., express doubt about the correctness of this practice. The best-known example is Barth, who discusses revelation as internal Prolegomena in both volumes, *CD* I,1 and 2, as "The Doctrine of the Word of God." In that discussion he anticipates very much his dogmatics proper by his extensive discussion of the Trinity and to a lesser extent of Christology and pneumatology. It is remarkable that Barth wants to base the necessity of these internal Prolegomena only on the presence of heretical opposition within the church (I,1, pp. 33–38). The Lutheran Prenter does the same (*Creation and Redemption*, E.T. 1967, pars. 2ff.). It appears to me that this motivation is unnecessarily limited and that the actual treatment, especially in Barth, goes far beyond this motivation.

Biblical theologians have repeatedly pointed out that "revelation" is a marginal and/or eschatological concept. For the OT see C. Westermann, *Theologie des AT in Grundzügen* (1978), pp. 19-21; for the NT see H. Schulte, *Der Begriff der Offenbarung im NT*, and A. Richardson, *An Introduction to the Theology of the NT* (1958), ch. II.

These insights led to two strong attacks on the present centrality of the concepts of revelation: F. G. Downing, *Has Christianity a Revelation?* (1964), and James Barr, *Old and New in Interpretation* (1966), pp. 82–94. See further par. 18, small type.

More comprehensive examinations of the concept of revelation in the study of the faith, and thus separate from the prolegomena, are H. Thielicke, *The Evangelical Faith*, II (E.T. 1977), esp. pars. 1-8, and G. Ebeling, *Dogmatik des christlichen Glaubens*, I (1979), par. 10.

8. REVELATION: PHENOMENOLOGICAL AND THEOLOGICAL

COMMENCING THE STUDY of the Christian faith with the revelation concept is not always greeted with approval. It seems to carry the implied suggestion that only the Christian faith rests on revelation; all other religions are illusions and misconceptions. Are not all religions based on revelation? Implied in that questioning remark is often the suggestion that all religions are consequently equally true or equally untrue. These various suggestions require further critical scrutiny.

The thesis *all religions are based on revelation* is derived from the phenomenology of religion, where it is meant to note a fact which can be more accurately described in this way: "all religions live by the conviction that the absolute is known through revelation." Not only is this thesis correct, but it almost sounds like a tautology. If religion (as we saw in paragraph 2) is a relationship with a world which far transcends us and which appears in the phenomenal world, then human religiousness is always dependent on such an appearance, disclosure, manifestation, epiphany, revelation, or whatever one wishes to call it. The question whether a real revelation of the true God corresponds to this idea of revelation as held by the religions is one that can neither be asked nor answered by the phenomenology of religion. "Vor der Offenbarung macht die Phänomenologie halt" (Phenomenology comes to a stop when it meets revelation; Van der Leeuw).

J. Huxley's *Religion without Revelation* is an abstraction. Of how little use the phenomenological approach is, is shown by T. P. van Baaren, *Voorstellingen van openbaring phaenomenologisch beschouwd* (1951). Even where he limits "revelation" to "intentional" revelation, he finds ten different types (p. 113). Some of these he regards as "higher" or "in a meaningful sense," but without making a convincing case for this approach and distinction. See also *RGG* IV, *s.v. Offenbarung I.* In our time Tillich, as a lone exception, tries to combine the phenomenological and the theological viewpoint; see *ST* I, pp. 106–108.

Yet as human beings we want to know more than phenomenology can tell us. The question we raise is: can the idea of revelation common to all religions be subsumed under one denominator in such a way that it offers universally valid criteria for truth? In other words, can we objectively determine the verity of all these pretensions to revelation?

These pretensions occur in a near-limitless variety, ranging from the fetishism of the primitive tribal religions to, for example, the a-cosmic mysticism of Buddhism. Within that range are found, for example, ancient man who receives instructions on how to get rich from a divine oracle, the *daimonion* of Socrates, the fascist for whom the divine resides in the race, the prophet Jeremiah for whom revelation went directly counter to the national mood, the Quaker who is guided by the inner light. This is not just a matter of a diversity of phenomena which become the vehicle for revelation, but a diversity and even a contrast of experiences of the divine. Does this variety itself yield a criterion for truth? In the nineteenth century this question was often and easily answered in the affirmative, also by students of the phenomenology of religion. One spoke of "lower" and "higher" forms of revelation. Such value judgments require a truth criterion about which usually little or nothing was said. Tacitly this criterion was assumed to be: whatever is thinkable and acceptable as revelation in accordance with the life-style of a secularized European-American culture. This criterion has no deeper basis and cannot be further verified; moreover, it is quite elusive because modern man, precisely because of his cultural pattern, has very few experiences of revelation. In fact, here we again hit upon the epistemological crux which we referred to in paragraph 2 and which we formulate here as follows: one who places himself above the pretensions to revelation with an objective criterion stands as such outside the experience of revelation; and one who has such an experience finds in it the criterion for which the neutral observer searches in vain.

Anyone deeply aware of the full weight of this crux knows that he has come to a fork in the road. He must either drop the whole subject of "revelation" as to its truth content and limit himself to the phenomenology, or make his own experience of revelation the starting-point of his reflection. Scientifically both ways are proper. Phenomenology chooses the first road, dogmatics the second. While able to help each other, they follow entirely different paths, which also implies that they do not stand in each other's way.

That last point has not always been accepted and has been contested. It is thought then that the Christian faith, owing to the fact that it finds the relationship with God in Israel, in Jesus Christ, and in the Spirit who proceeds from him, rejects as illusionary every other claim to a divine revelation. But that conclusion is neither logically compelling nor materially correct. The Bible contains statements to the effect that there is revelation from God also outside of Israel and Christ. It is a fact, however, that within the church frequent attempts have been made to minimize these statements. That is understandable because it seems difficult or even impossible to combine the uniqueness of the Christian revelation of God with much that passes for revelation in the world of religions. The belief that Jesus Christ is *the* way, the truth, and the life, and that no one comes to the Father except through him, seems to lead to the conclusion that there is no real revelation apart from him. But at the same time, that same belief pushes us in a seemingly opposite direction: If in Jesus Christ the Father is revealed who is the creator of heaven and earth, then in Christ also the ultimate mystery of created reality must be manifest. Then it must be so that in the Word-made-flesh there is revealed *that* Word by which all things were made (John 1:1–14) and that all things were created by and for Christ (Col. 1:16). But then it is impossible that this reality, which inalienably remains God's creation, should not in all kinds of ways, no matter how fragmentary, incidental, or broken, bear witness to the purpose of its creator. Then it is also certain that man was created for a relationship with God and that his thirst for the Absolute corresponds to a reality. Then it must also be a fact that this man in this created reality must regularly detect signs, rays, and disclosures of God's nature and purposes. Precisely because we believe that Jesus Christ is the central revelation of the creator of the world, we cannot believe that outside of him and the history of which he is the center there would be no inkling at all of this central creative will. He is the key to the understanding of the world, and this world is the door to which that key fits.

But that is something that can only be believed and thus more or less perceived by the person who believes in Christ. One who does not believe in him sees the same reality, but of necessity will have to understand its revelational caliber from a different perspective and thus (as Christians see it) must misunderstand it. But *mis*understanding is not the same as *not* understanding it. Expressed positively we have to say: *the divine revelation in Christ is indeed normative, but not exclusive.* The indiscriminate use of both these adjectives has caused much confusion. That Christ is *the* truth does not mean that there are no truths to be found anywhere outside of him, but it does mean that all such truths are fragmentary and broken unless they have become integrated in him as the center. Therefore he who in Christ has found the Father will with a receptive mind look around in this world to discover in it traces of the character and work of the Father. These would not be real traces if men could not also perceive them outside of God's revelation to Israel and in Christ. But at the same time, apart from this revelation they cannot be understood in their true context and significance. So the Christian belief in revelation stands necessarily in a dialectical relation to the beliefs in revelation as these are found in the world around.

This dialectical character is clear in the biblical data. There is no doubt that the people who do not know the God of Israel (in the OT) live in the darkness of being alienated from God. At the same time the OT is aware of a knowledge of God outside the pale of Israel: Melchizedek, Balaam, Job. In the NT it is stated more than once as something which is quite natural that God reveals himself also outside of Israel and Christ. But in the same breath it is then added that this does not liberate man from his alienation from God. In John 1 we read that the eternal Word is the light of the world, but that this world in its darkness has not "grasped," "understood," or "overcome" (Gk. *katelaben;* 1:4f.) this light. A little further, in parallel fashion, it is said about the incarnate Word that he came to that which was his own but that his own did not receive him (vv. 10f.). According to Acts 14:16f., through the blessings he gave everywhere God did not leave himself without witness to the world, while at the same time he let all nations go their own way. In his Areopagus address the apostle Paul expresses the same thought when on the one hand he says that God gave sufficient blessings to his creatures to make it possible for them to seek him and to find him, and on the other hand that they remained in "the times of ignorance" and perverted the worship of God into idolatry (Acts 17:27, 29f.). This thought is given clearest expression in Rom. 1:18–22: God's eternal power and divine nature are clearly revealed to men, but they suppress the truth by worshipping and serving created things rather than the creator. Especially this last passage shows that one cannot simply say that God did indeed reveal himself, but that somehow it did not get through to man. On the contrary, man becomes guilty because something essential does reach him, something which he, however, cannot endure and therefore must incorporate into his self-chosen conception of life.

Only a few biblical passages touch on this matter, but whatever the tradition from which they derive (John, Luke, Paul), all speak a dialectical language which has seldom been maintained in the history of the church. Either one saw only demonic darkness outside the Christian faith (so especially orthodox Protestantism) or the relation was interpreted as a harmonious preparation leading to Christ (especially in Roman Catholicism, Anglicanism, and liberal Protestantism). A much more dialectical view is found in the *Apologia* of Justin Martyr (ca. A.D. 150), who on the one hand sees the religions as the product of demonic illusion, and on the other sees the "logos spermatikos" operative in Heraclitus, Socrates, and Plato (I.46; II.8, 10, and 13). Justin makes one think of the Reformer Zwingli who, particularly in his posthumously published *Brevis et clara expositio* (1536), expressed the conviction, much to the indignation of Luther, that in eternal life he also expected to meet people like Socrates, Aristides, the Catos, the Scipios, Seneca, and many other Greeks and Romans. With more reserve but with great acumen Calvin (*Inst* I) has expressed the dialectic between divine revelation and alienation from God in the careful sequence of chapters 3 to 6. For this dialectic see also H. Kraemer, *Godsdienst, godsdiensten en het christelijk geloof* (1958), esp. V, and H. Thielicke, *The Evangelical Faith,* II, par. 6.

When the so-called "German Christians" in their political blindness lost sight of the normative place of Christ and began to see in the Germany of Hitler a new divine revelation, the "Confessing Church" had to take firm measures (1934), which it did in the first statement of the Barmen Declaration: "Jesus Christ, as the Bible declares him to us, is the one Word of God which we have to hear and which we have to trust and obey in life and in death. We reject as false teaching the view that the church could and would have to acknowledge as a source of its proclamation, outside and beside this one Word of God, still other events and powers, circumstances and truths as divine revelation."

A few years later Barth provided the theological basis for this declaration in *CD* I,2 in his much-discussed par. 17: "The Revelation of God as the Abolition of Religion," Outside the prophetic-apostolic witness to Christ he sees only human religion, and he sees it as "unbelief" (par. 17,2), as "the one concern of godless man" (p. 300) in which he contradicts the revelation both by his idolatry and by his self-justification. Does religious man then have a certain knowledge or suspicion of revelation? The main impression, according to Barth, is that religion is not a response to a transcendent event but a projection of autonomous men (there is an exception on p. 305). Only much later did Barth clearly express the thought that the revelation in Christ not only throws a negative light on the world but also presupposes a worldwide engagement of God with the world; see *CD* IV,1, pp. 483f. and the doctrine of "the lights of creation" in IV,3, pp. 135–165.

The changed cultural climate and the broadened perspective after the Second World War have led to a shift of accent in the direction of a more positive evaluation of the dialectical relation between the Christian faith and other religions. The awareness of the oneness of mankind is so great that many find it hard to conceive of a breach between biblical revelation and human religions. It is correctly pointed out that biblical revelation derives its religious vocabulary, including the name "God," from its "pagan" environment. A typical illustration of the dominant mode of thought is the presentation of this subject in the (Dutch) Roman Catholic *New Catechism* (E.T. 1969). Under the heading "The Way of the

Nations" it briefly discusses the most important religions and ideologies (pp. 25–32), concluding this survey with a paragraph about "The Spirit of God in the Whole World" (p. 33). At first sight it may appear that what we have here is a broad appreciation of religious truth as this is known by revelation. A closer look makes it clear that the norm for this appreciation is entirely the faith in Christ as the final revelational truth. "The gleam of truth in another way of life can help Christians to gain a deeper and more vital conviction of Jesus' truth" (p. 33). H. Küng in *On Being a Christian* (E.T. 1976), A, III, and M. M. Thomas in *Man and the Universe of Faiths* (1975), esp. pp. 146–157, relate Christ as "critical catalyst" to the religions. Cf. also Choan-Seng Song, *Third-Eye Theology* (1979). Using the concepts of the process philosophy of A. N. Whitehead, J. B. Cobb does something similar in *Christ in a Pluralistic Age* (1975), where he presents Christ as the cosmic principle of "creative transformation."

This "dialectical relation" of which we made mention also turns out to be dialectical in this sense, that an examination of the one pole inevitably points to the other. One who understands the religions as rebellion against God must assume that there is some consciousness of this God; otherwise there could be no rebellion. Conversely, one who takes the view that religions are expressions of revelation, as soon as he wants to do more than speak in generalities, will have to distinguish between what he regards as true and not true, as pure and impure; and then it will have to come into the open where he finds his criterion for truth.

Meanwhile we should not forget that between Christ and the Christian churches there exists a dialectical relation which, though not identical to, is analogous to that between him and the religions. But this relation will be discussed in another context.

9. THE EARTHLY CHARACTER OF REVELATION

CHRISTIAN THEOLOGY is based on the conviction that in the coming, humiliation, and exaltation of Jesus of Nazareth we have to do with the revelation of the very heart of God, and that therefore this event must be the starting-point and guide for our thinking about revelation in general. This conviction is not at all unreasonable, but it has in common with many deep-seated human convictions that it cannot be rationally proven beforehand. That holds all the more here because it concerns an encounter which as such is not predictable and which cannot be made rationally transparent. If we can speak of proof at all, then faith itself implies it and consequently it is only in retrospect that it can be seen as proof. But one does not have the option of refusing to make a choice on the ground that it is inherently undemonstrable. Such a refusal would entail the end of one's thinking. For then one remains stuck in a hodgepodge of unorganized and contradictory statements about revelation. Only when the leap across the gap has been made can our thinking proceed again. The first thing we then have to do is survey that new territory and trace and formulate the presuppositions that underlie the

Christian faith in revelation. We thus give an "account"; that is less than making a compelling demonstration, but much more than making authoritative assertions. In the following paragraphs we shall juxtapose a series of elements. Hopefully their inner coherence will become clear as we proceed. This series is by no means exhaustive. In the doctrine concerning the Christian faith no one analysis or presentation can carry such a pretense. We shall mention those elements which are seen to be the most significant.

We begin with the earthly character of revelation. Revelation is not a heavenly event. It happens on earth and in modes that are given with this earthly life. For man in his present mode of existence, for reasons we cannot fathom, depends on the phenomenal reality within and around himself for the inspiration and nourishment of his spirit. Man is thus not constituted for a direct encounter with God, only one that is mediated. We cannot even imagine what a direct encounter would have to be. Even if God, for example, would reveal himself in a mysterious voice, a blinding flash, or an experience of rapturous ecstasy, these would still be phenomena that are part of our earthly reality. They are thus thinkable apart from an encounter with God, and in themselves do not prove anything. Simultaneously they mediate and veil revelation. Some have related this problematic to man's sinful alienation from God. But it is just as much and in the first place related to our creaturely finitude. The Bible presents many earthly forms of revelation: trees, natural catastrophes, thunder and lightning, a burning bush, a voice in the night, a vision, and many others. It has been pointed out that these means of revelation became increasingly more spiritual in character with the passing of time, so that eventually they consisted mainly of audible words and inner experiences. If this is so, it still would not mean anything for our subject, for then, too, we have to do with earthly phenomena. This is no less true of the central revelation in Jesus, for he was a man and a Jew, and he appeared as a Jewish rabbi.

This problematic of the earthly character of revelation is not specifically Christian. It presents itself wherever there is an experience of revelation. It is simply a fact that the earthliness of the revelation in Israel and in Christ shares in the general religious problematic inherent in earthliness. Therefore it also shares in the defenselessness and the contradictability of everything that offers itself as revelation. It is always "a sign that is spoken against" (Luke 2:34). Therefore faith cannot regard atheism and agnosticism as abnormal attitudes. The earthliness of revelation evokes such attitudes. In a salutary way they accompany the faith because they remind it of its non-self-evident ground.

All this now makes it a pressing question: how can the supernatural be perceived in natural phenomena? Not, as we have seen, by the supernatural forcing the natural away or absorbing it or infringing on it. Nor, as it has sometimes been presented, that a normal earthly event was "afterward" by certain witnesses "shown to be" revelation from God. The first is an objectivistic, the second a subjectivistic misconception of what happens. The real event is an encounter in which the natural becomes the transparency of a divine word or act. The person perceiving that is thus by means of the natural brought to a direct encounter with God. Outsiders can neither confirm nor deny this. Yet it is always connected with earthly experiences.

"Gott ist mitten in unserem Leben jenseitig" (In the midst of our life God is opposite—Bonhoeffer). "God without ground among us" (Miskotte). In the Bible the earthly character of revelation is always presupposed but seldom specifically stated. Where that is done it takes the form of a profession of the principial indirectness of all revelation. "No one has ever seen God" (John 1:18). Whoever sees God shall surely die (Ex. 19:21; Judg. 13:22). "For now we see in a mirror dimly" (1 Cor. 13:12). The deepest reflection on this theme is Ex. 33:18–23 where Moses desires to see the face of God, that is, where he asks for a direct revelation and encounter; he is refused, but he does hear the name of God proclaimed and he sees the back of God—afterward, after he has passed by. The direct vision of God is indeed a biblical theme, but then a promise to be fulfilled at the end of time. In the study of the faith the earthly character of revelation is variously appreciated. Many, especially from times with a greater sensitivity for the supernatural, saw the natural as a necessary and willing instrument for the revelation of the supernatural. Calvin was among those who realized the problems here. He saw in revelation a divine accommodation (see, e.g., *Inst* I,x,2; I,xi; I,xiii,1, and *passim*). Particularly the prohibition of images led him to it. When God reveals himself in visible and material forms, this is not because he is like that, but for our sake. God uses pedagogical means as a mother does when she speaks to her child. " . . . as nurses commonly do with infants, God is wont in a measure to 'lisp' in speaking to us" (I,xiii,1). In his earlier thinking Barth has made use of the more extensive concept of paradox: as a result of the gap between God and man there is a contrast between the contents and the form of revelation. In *CD* I,1 he makes many worthwhile remarks about the "Welthaftigkeit" (earthly character) of revelation (pp. 189–198). There he writes about the word of God: "Its form . . . does not correspond to the matter but it contradicts it" (p. 189). On Calvin versus Barth, see Schilder, *Zur Bergriffsgeschichte des "Paradoxon,"* 1933, esp. ch. IV. In his *De mensvormigheid Gods* H. M. Kuitert takes issue with both; according to him God's essence lies precisely in what we call accommodation, in his becoming our covenant partner in the encounter. The basic question behind the differences is whether the earthly form of the revelation is to be regarded as hampering (if at all, or to what extent) the revelational event. In our view this earthliness is not a result of sin, but it is not an adequate instrument either; it belongs to the provisional form of the first creation, of the "physical," material mode of existence (cf. 1 Cor. 15:44–49). God certainly reveals himself, his essence. His accommodation is not an "as-if." But his revelation takes place within the limits of this provisional existence and is thus determined and limited by that context.

10. REVELATION AND EXPERIENCE

IF REVELATION is always linked with earthly experiences, while yet, in virtue of its nature, it transcends it, the relationship of revelation and experience is an issue that is bound to come to the forefront time and again. Such is especially the case in our time, in which our experience of reality is so secularized that many can hardly conceive of experience as providing access to revelation. The fact that experience is a vague term that regularly causes confusion makes the investigation even more difficult. In the study of faith it legitimately comes up for discussion in three ways: 1. as experience that precedes the revelational encounter and leads up to it; 2. as another term for the faith encounter itself; 3. as designation of personal experiences and experiences with the world that are evoked by the faith encounter. In the context of the Prolegomena we are concerned only with the first meaning. In its second meaning it is used only in passing in this book, because we have more specific words (repentance, faith, hope, etc.) for it. In its third meaning it regularly comes up in the last two chapters, and more deliberately in par. 45 and par. 50.

"The word 'experience' is one of the most deceitful in philosophy" (Whitehead).

It is often contended that the Christian faith as "conviction of things not seen" (Heb. 11:1) and as something that is accepted on authority from the outside, as such excludes experience. Indeed, in the Bible it is contrasted with our daily experiences, which are often called "seeing." By contrast faith is usually presented as "hearing" (namely, of the Word of God). This is a way of saying that this experience is of a different kind. But hearing, too, is definitely an experience. A person who in faith is willing to listen to a higher authority thereby surrenders to a new experience (meaning 2 above).

As regards meaning 1, one can think of at least three periods in the history of theology when the relationship experience-revelation received a great deal of attention. The first period was that of the Apologists in the first centuries of church history. At that time the fledgling and frequently persecuted Christian church defended itself against its enemies and despisers by appealing to universal experiences and insights, which they then placed in a new framework. The second period was that of Medieval Scholasticism, which in the course of a few centuries, from Anselm to Occam, discovered that the harmony of reason and revelation they searched for became more and more unreachable. The third period began with the Enlightenment and continues till the present time in secularized Western culture. The Enlightenment sought harmony by way of the *ratio,* Reason. Schleiermacher and many after him tried to build a bridge using religious experience as the core of human existence. When this approach began to lose its appeal after ca. 1870, the preferred access, in the wake of Ritschl's example, shifted to man's moral experience, the human conscience, or the awareness of values, which enables one to discover one's responsibility and failures

Because all these approaches threatened to reduce God to a reflected image of a human's higher ego, many after the First World War, especially under the influence of Barth, rejected all "points of contact." The main concern now was to start radically from the side of revelation, in the conviction that if one does not begin with God, one does not end with God either. (Not all felt this way. There were at least two other great theologians, Bultmann and Tillich, who radically rejected this alternative.) Many banished the concept of experience from dogmatics.

In the sixties the scene shifted again. To many the concepts used by Barth were no longer meaningful. They looked for new connections between revelation and experience. Their attempts were in part enforced and in part made unnecessary by the rapid emergence of theological designs coming from the nonacademic world of oppressed groups: blacks, the exploited, women. Since then almost everywhere in the world the relationship between revelation and experience (usually called "contextualization" in the Third World) has become a central theme.

Barth's followers are the most strongly opposed to a theological role for experience. See Beker-Hasselaar, *WK,* passim. At the same time, other historical investigations (C. Gestrich, F. W. Marquardt, J. Wissink, et al.) show how much Barth's thinking has been influenced by experience, and how his final rejection of experience as a theologically useful concept was precisely due to (negative) experiences. N.B.: The segment in *CD* I,1, par. 6.3, "The Word of God and Experience," is not about experience in the first but in the second sense.

The positions on this point taken by those not following Barth are innumerable. This is not surprising, for as humans we have a host of experiences. Yet two distinct kinds of experience occupy believers and theologians in their studies today. In the first world these are especially *experiences of meaning* (and meaninglessness), and in the Third World and in feminist theology, experiences of *oppression and liberation.*

The experiences that are being analyzed in the first world are experiences that, provided they are examined in great depth, theologians believe point toward revelation. The classic precursors in this respect were Bultmann and Tillich, both of whom took their starting point in human existence, understood in the sense of Heidegger (ek-sistence as "to step out" from the world of objective data). According to Bultmann a person cannot "exist" without having his support in God, after the example of the crucified Jesus. According to Tillich all of the "existing" of man out of the ambiguity of his position is a quest to which only the revelation in "the Christ" is the reconciling answer.

Roman Catholic theologians in particular, using as a base their belief in the interrelation between nature and grace, have developed this theme, usually from the vantage point of self-transcendence as a central anthropological dimension: man searches for the meaning of his existence in what supportingly and savingly transcends his present existence. Grandmaster of this method is K. Rahner; see his summarizing *Grundkurs des Glaubens* (1976). Others thinking along these lines are B. Lonergan, *Method in Theology* (1972); D. Tracy, *Blessed Rage for Order* (1975); E. Schillebeeckx, *Gerechtigheid en liefde* (1977), Vols. I and IV; and G. O'Collins, *Fundamental Theology* (1981). Most of these theologians combined the experience of self-transcendence with other experiences: emancipation, border situations, contrast experiences, hope, and also the scientific world picture of Whitehead's process philosophy with its emphasis on God as involved in temporality, growing along with the world process. Among Protestant theologians, particularly the influence of Tillich is evident, now often combined with process theology. For process theology see especially J. Cobb, *God and the World* (1969) and *Process Theology* (1976). Self-transcendence and process theology combined are found in L. Gilkey, *Naming the Whirlwind* (1969) and *Reaping the Whirlwind* (1976). Self-transcendence toward what is above and lies in the future is dominant in the young Pannenberg as experience of "Weltoffenheit" (world openness) in *Was ist der Mensch?* (1962), broadened and deepened in his *Anthropologie in theologischer Perspektive* (1983) through the tension of identity and communion as pointing to the image of God. H. M. Kuitert, in *Wat heet geloven?* (1977), goes his own way by starting from the venture of culture that requires a meaning guaranteed lastingly only in the universal love of God in Christ. These and virtually all other designs based on experience touch directly on the questions concerning the plausibility and rationality of the faith; see par. 6, p. 34.

In the Third World the field of experiences that occupies and shapes theology is quite different. Important there are the opposite experiences of poverty, exploitation, and discrimination, and the ardent longing for deliverance from it. (Feminist theology in the first world provides a parallel.) In the lead here is liberation theology in Latin America. See especially G. Gutiérrez, *A Theology of Liberation* (E.T. 1973), and his Protestant counterpart J. M. Bonino, *Theologie van verdrukten* (1974, Dutch translation). Liberation theology views these experiences as the real (and only?) entrance to the salvation event, which is focussed in the exodus out of Egypt and the resurrection of Jesus Christ. Besides this there are, especially in Africa and Asia, forms of experience theology that start from the cultural and religious traditions in these countries (tribal religions, Hinduism, Buddhism) and can be summed up by the name *contextual theology.* For examples, see H.-W. Gensichen, et al., eds., *Theologische Stimmen aus Asien, Afrika und Lateinamerika,* 3 vols. (1965–1968), and D. J. Elwood, ed., *What Asian Christians are Thinking* (1976).

The experience theologies from the first and the Third World oppose each other on several points. The first group feels that the field of experiences in the second group is too limited and that it establishes a link between these experiences and revelation that is too exclusive and direct. The second group is of the opinion that the field of experiences of the first group is a costly academic abstraction, which only confirms the oppression. An attempt to combine the two in a new *theologia crucis* is D. J. Hall, *Lighten Our Darkness* (1976).

The group of theologians who work with experience can also be divided in a different way. On the extreme "right" is a group that strictly separates revelation and experience, and sometimes comes close to Barth. This group includes J. Moltmann, *Theology of Hope* (E.T. 1967), who hooks in on Bloch's idea of hope, and H. Küng, *Does God Exist?* (E.T. 1980), who views revelation as answering our need for meaning and rationality. Some of these, using Barth's concept of analogy, try both to connect and to separate revelation and experience. See T. F. Torrance, *God and Rationality* (1971), esp. ch. V; C. Link, *Die Welt als Gleichnis* (1972), and especially E. Jüngel, *God as the Mystery of the World* (E.T. 1983), who understands the gospel as "Ereignis der Entsprechung" (event of correspondence) relative to our reality. Starting from a Thomistic doctrine of analogy (see also par. 14 end), this could lead to new convergences; for a Roman Catholic approach see D.

Tracy, *The Analogical Imagination* (1981), esp. pars. 5, 9, 10. On the extreme "left" are especially designs from feminist theology, in which revelation seems almost to coincide with the experience of being a woman. For a more moderate example, see Rosemary R. Ruether, *Sexism and Godtalk* (1983). On experience as a component in theology, see also H. Berkhof, *Introduction to Dogmatics,* 3.4, 5.2, 5.4, 6.4, 6.7.

In view of the endless variety, the relationship between experience and revelation can be set forth and illuminated in a number of ways. Dogmatics cannot possibly map these out. Its concern is the possibility and the nature of this relationship in general. Actually, even that is saying too much. It ought to determine the possibility, the structure, and the boundaries of this relationship. As we see it, the following three perspectives are significant in that case.

a. Revelation is directed to people in the world of their concrete experiences.

That is where the encounter begins; there they are met, in order from there to move far beyond the boundaries of their world. Humans bring with them their experiences, which help color and determine the encounter with God. The freedom of the Spirit, who blows where he wills, entails that all experiences, ranging from the very intimate to the very universal and from the extremely negative to the extremely positive, can become entrance gates to salvation. The study of the faith must reverently and thankfully recognize this fact. It may not canonize one or a few experiences. What it may do, if need be, is refer to certain experiences of a general or contemporary validity that can illustrate the encounter with revelation. What dogmatics in virtue of its nature will do only in general and with reserve, can and should be done much more emphatically in preaching, teaching, and discussion.

Twentieth-century research into the form, the passing on, and the redaction of many biblical witnesses has opened our eyes to the great many variations brought about by the variety in experiential and linguistic background of the writers or the readers, or of both. The same message is expressed in various ways, depending on whether the addressees were nomads, farmers, exiles, city people, citizens of a free country or living in occupied territory, oppressed, philosophically trained, etc. The small differences between the three synoptic Gospels, for the most part due to the nature and situation of the addressees, are striking. We should not try to harmonize those differences, but look on them as a challenge to make proper use of human experiences in the proclamation of the gospel in our time.

b. This approach always both determines and delimits at the same time.

Everyone who articulates the gospel consciously or unconsciously proceeds in this articulation from his or her world of experiences. Without it, this articulation would remain hanging in mid-air. The theologian must become conscious of this fact (to the extent that a human can objectify himself). If that is done, the utmost use can be made of this relationship. One can then at the same time become keenly aware of the limitations this relationship entails. These limitations challenge us always to seek to go beyond them and to look for further revelational experiences. Otherwise revelation threatens to change from being an encounter to becoming a self-affirmation.

It is clear that these limitations have an adverse effect if one does not become aware of them. The adverse effect is even worse if deliberately only one field of experience (e.g., that of oppression and liberation) would be proclaimed as the legitimate correlate or "Vorverständnis" of the revelation. The most damaging approach is that of the theologian who does not take certain experiences as his theme, but certain philosophical or sociological theories *about* experiences. In that case the intelligibility of the faith systems constructed with the use of such theories will remain limited to a small group, and these systems are destined to disappear with the rapid changes in culture and cultural expressions.

c. Experience itself can never bridge the gap between the person and revelation.

Every genuine encounter in which another meets us is unpredictable and unmanipulable; and only as such does it widen our horizon. From the vantage point of our limitations and alienation from God, the encounter with God is astonishing, threatening, and liberating. Therefore the experiences we ourselves bring along can have only a preparatory input. Most of the time the significance of that input will only afterward be realized. We are dependent on the miracle that comes from the other side, forcing us to make the jump that antedates all our experiences.

With these considerations we run ahead of the full scope of the concept "covenant," which will play an important role later in the book. In a covenant two parties get together. Viewed from our perspective, in the covenant between God and man everything depends on the divine initiative and perseverance. At the same time, in the Bible God is presented as dependent on us. Many passages in the Bible speak of the searching, asking, pleading, and knocking of God and of Christ. Later we shall talk about how this searching of God and our own searching are related to each other.

We noted that there was a great deal of difference in the linguistic contexts in which the biblical witnesses brought their message. Closer scrutiny shows that the meaning of the words and concepts they used changed under the impact of the divine encounter and received a new content. Every theology that proceeds from experience will prove its encounter-genuineness by its willingness to submit to continual correction and change. It is remarkable how often converts, especially from cultures without a Christian tradition, afterward make two apparently contradictory statements: "Long before my conversion God was working in me," and "Only through Christ was I changed from darkness into light." On the relationship between preparation and surprise see the beautiful section in Augustine, *Confessions* VII.9.

On the theme of this entire section, see also H. Berkhof, *Introduction to Dogmatics,* 3.4, 5.2, 5.4, 6.6. All three of the perspectives set forth here are found together in the address of Paul on the Areopagus (Acts 17:16–34).

11. REVELATION AND HIDDENNESS

THIS SUBJECT is closely related to that of the earthliness of revelation (par. 9), but it covers another and broader problematic. For the concept of revelation cannot be defined unless it be related to its opposite and correlate, the concept of "hiddenness." Both concepts accompany each other in a dialectical relationship, or rather, in three different dialectical relationships.

a. Revelation presupposes hiddenness.

Only what is hidden needs to be revealed. From the fact of revelation we learn that apart from this event God is for us the hidden one. So revelation confirms what we could surmise beforehand or after a long search sadly had to discover: that God is hidden from us. A mysterious, indirect light may shine through the earthly reality, but the face of God does not become visible in it. Reality is poly-interpretable and not transparent all the way to God. The revelational encounter tells us that this is not just our short sighted imagination. It confirms our doubt at the moment that it abolishes it. Because God makes himself known, we know once and for all that God can only be known by God.

In the OT this truth is especially attested in the book of Job: With their talk about God, people darken God's "counsel by words without knowledge" (38:2); when God reveals himself it becomes apparent how much he was previously hidden from Job and his friends. In the NT Paul touches on this problematic in 1 Cor. 2:6–16: "God has revealed [it] to us through the Spirit. . . . No one comprehends the thoughts of God except the Spirit of God."

An impressive study of this aspect is given by Barth in *CD* II,1, par. 27,1, pp. 179–204, under the heading "The Hiddenness of God." But unlike Barth we do not regard man's surmise of God's hiddenness (Plato, Plotinus) as purely a contrast to the hiddenness that is revealed, but also (objectively) a reflection and (subjectively) a surmise of it.

b. Revelation reveals hiddenness.

When God in his revelation emerges from his hiddenness, he does not by that act cease to be the hidden God; rather, that hiddenness is now fully disclosed. What we could before at best only surmise, now becomes a clear certainty: how immensely exalted and hidden God is, how unspeakably and surprisingly marvelous his gracious condescension, how unimaginably glorious the future he discloses to us in it. Revelation initiates us into a great mystery. This does not make the initiate feel proud; rather, each step makes him smaller and humbler. God would not be God if it were otherwise. The more we come to know him, the less we are able to comprehend him with our intellect.

We hear these notes especially in the OT. The revelation at Sinai is a revelation of God's majestic hiddenness. The Psalms sing about it (see e.g. 77 and 139). In this connection, too, Job is to be mentioned; for when God reveals himself to Job (chs. 38–42), pointing to the incomprehensibility of his creation, he reveals himself precisely as the incomprehensible God. The most striking utterance in this respect is Isa. 45:15, where the prophet, thinking of how marvelously God acted in rescuing his people, exclaims: "Truly, thou art a God who hidest thyself, O God of Israel, the Savior." Saying it with Luther, the *Deus revelatus* is precisely the *Deus absconditus,* the opposite of a *Deus publicatus.*

Of the dogmatic literature on this aspect we must especially refer to the earlier-mentioned (sub *a* above) discussion by Barth. We also refer to G. J. Heering, *Geloof en openbaring,* II, II, "Revelation," and esp. par. 5, "Revelation and Hiddenness."

c. Revelation assumes the form of hiddenness.

With this we touch on what we have said about the earthly character of revelation. We saw that this is entirely due to the creation itself and is not a consequence of man's guilt. By this guilt, however, it is as it were intensified. The earthliness now becomes hiddenness, making for a double hiddenness of God. He can be present in his world only as a stranger, the suffering servant, the crucified one. The concept of *paradox* is suitable here: God is present contrary to *(para)* the appearance *(doxa)* of the opposite. This appearance is forced upon him because man by his thinking and striving contradicts the thoughts God reveals about him. Such is the case in the history of salvation, the center of which is the stumbling block and the foolishness of the cross. Such is also true for the personal association of the individual with God, in which he constantly experiences that God must hide his face from man, because in this association man tries to force his will upon God. That is true also of the judgments God sends upon his people and the world in which in a hidden manner he is present as the one who has no other choice but to let us walk in our self-chosen way and so to show us how things stand between him and us.

These are three aspects of a hiddenness forced upon God but actively accepted by him, and which he turns into revelation. All these aspects are found particularly in the OT. The first is found especially in the later writings with their emphasis on the suffering of the righteous, of the faithful remnant, of the suffering servant—all as forms of the hidden presence of God. See especially G. von Rad, *OT Theology,* II (E.T. 1965). The second aspect occurs especially in the Psalms. Kuitert has written incisively about this aspect in *De mensvormigheid Gods,* pp. 245–267: "The Hiddenness of God." For him this concealment of God is exclusively a form of his covenantal association with man. We reject, however, this "exclusively," which is based on Kuitert's belief in the identity of God's essence and revelation (see p. 265). The third aspect is found very much in the Deuteronomic and prophetic literature: owing to the disobedience of his people, God is forced to be present as the chastising, abandoning, and hidden one. In the NT, on account of the joy of God's gracious presence in Christ, these second and third aspects recede (though they do not disappear). But the first asserts itself all the more. All appearance to the contrary, God is present in the suffering and crucified Christ. Particularly Paul has reflected deeply on that. See especially 1 Cor. 1:18–2:5 where he contrasts human self-justification and wisdom with the stumbling block and the foolishness of the cross. In the history of the church, Luther, far ahead of all other Christian thinkers, has reflected on hiddenness as a form of revelation. Only to a very limited extent has the church been able to appropriate his penetrating thoughts. At stake here are his doctrine of the *theologia crucis* and the *Deus absconditus.* These ideas are not limited to a particular period or writing, but permeate all of Luther's thinking. A forceful expression of these notions is found in one of his earliest Reformatory writings, The Heidelberg Disputation (1518), in which, on the basis of his Pauline studies, he submitted 28 *theologica paradoxa* to his fellow Augustinian monks, of which we cite the famous 19th and 20th conclusions: "He is not worth calling a theologian who seeks to interpret 'the invisible things of God' on the basis of the things which have been created (Rom. 1:20); but he is worth calling a theologian who understands the visible and hinder parts of God to mean the passion and the cross." The clarifying comment is added: "The visible and hinder parts of God are set over against those which are invisible. These invisible parts mean the humanity of God, his weakness, his foolishness." God is thus paradoxically visible in what is his opposite. Though as the exalted one he is (often) the hidden God, he is that especially as the humiliated and suffering one, in his presence in the crucified. Hence Luther's favorite expressions: "The hidden God (revealed) under the opposite form, in suffering," etc. Here are two other characteristic quotes: "God is the One who is hidden. This is his peculiar property"; see J. T. Bakker, *Coram Deo* (Dutch 1956), p. 159: "God hides his own things in order to reveal them. . . . By his concealment he does nothing else than remove that which obstructs revelation, namely, pride"; see W. von Loewenich, *Luther's theologia crucis* (E.T. 1976), p. 30.

These thoughts were further worked out by Kohlbrugge and by Barth in his younger years. In some passages in his *Letters and Papers from Prison* (E.T. 1953) Dietrich Bonhoeffer comes with his own modern version of the hidden form of revelation. Often cited are these words from his letter of July 16, 1944: "God lets himself be pushed out of the world on to the cross. He is weak and powerless in the world, and that is precisely the way, the only way, in which he is with us and helps us." The Death-of-God theology, with an appeal to Bonhoeffer, also wrote often about the hiddenness of God. There, however, these ideas are no longer related to man's rebellion, but to his having come of age for the sake of which God is readily willing to step back (in Bonhoeffer being of age and rebellion still hang together). However, in Gen. 3:4f. man's having become like God in competition with God is precisely rejected as a demonic seduction. On the hiddenness of God see also G. Ebeling, *Dogmatik,* I, 254ff.

The many remarks made so far about the hiddenness of revelation can give the uneasy feeling that the hiddenness threatens to negate the revelation, and that under these circumstances one can no longer honestly speak of revelation. That this, nevertheless, can and must be done is only due to the fact that the revealing God himself through his Spirit opens man's eyes for his hidden presence. We shall deal with that under the next heading. Here it must be noted that we can speak meaningfully about the illumination of the Spirit only if we are deeply aware of the hiddenness of revelation, and thus of the necessity of God himself opening our eyes to it. Otherwise we are again inclined to base our revelational insight on our own powers and so by way of this wrong basis to construct a less hidden revelation which intellectually or in some other way would be at our disposal. Only if we know of the unveiling by the Spirit can we bear this hiddenness of God in this provisional world which, moreover, is estranged from him.

In conclusion we point to the story of Yahweh's revelation to Moses (Ex. 3) in which the hiddenness of God in his revelation is so strongly emphasized. The burning bush speaks of the earthliness of revelation. But the hiddenness deepens when God refuses to mention his name and wants to be known only as *'ehyeh* or as *'ehyeh '^{a}šer 'ehyeh* (v. 14). With that he withdraws himself from the possibility of human magical manipulation. That is, however, something else than a basis for agnosticism. For this "non-name" which cannot be manipulated is at the same time a testimony to God's faithfulness and a pointer to the future, in which he who responds to it in faith and trust will see this faithfulness again and again confirmed in the deeds of God. So revelation occurs in a sphere of hiddenness which provides a screen between God and man, but which precisely in this way serves as the protective layer within which God can become a real covenant partner for his small and guilty creatures. The same meaning is found in the story referred to earlier in which God refuses to show his face to Moses and lets him see only his back (Ex. 33:18–23).

12. THE DUALITY OF REVELATION: WORD AND SPIRIT

REVELATION IS AN EVENT of encounter. It always involves two parties, and the approach must come from two sides. Revelation has in common with all other forms of encounter that it is a getting together, and therefore it can never be described only as a divine (objectivistic) or a human (subjectivistic) happening. It differs from what we usually call an encounter in that in this case the initiative is entirely from one side. It is God, and God alone, who by entering in a hidden form into our reality makes the encounter possible. We write "makes possible" and not "effects." For God cannot effect this encounter unless his partner, man, from his side responds to the revelation. In fact, revelation is not even revelation if it is not perceived and acknowledged as such from the other side. Viewed in that light, structurally the revelational event hardly differs from our encounters, even though in this case the initiative to it is strictly unilateral.

There is, however, another and much more radical difference: as a result of the earthly distance and man's guilty estrangement from God, revelation now takes place indirectly and in a hidden manner, while man, owing to the way in which his cognitive faculties function in this situation, is by himself either unwilling or unable, or in any case fails to recognize the revelation. To God's coming down into our world must therefore correspond a creative leap of our cognition beyond its own limitations. Both a heightening and a liberation of our cognitive faculty are needed; and that is beyond our ability. Beside the revelation we need the illumination of our mind to be able to perceive the supernatural in the natural and the divine majesty in the humiliation. No revelation will be effected unless God works in us with this double revelational activity. He must make himself present in our reality *and* he must open our eyes to make us see his presence.

For this double activity dogmatics uses the concepts *Word* and *Spirit.* Separately as well as together, both play a large role in the Bible. There Word is often used as the denominator for the whole of the revelational event. Yet revelation is by no means always in the form of words; it happens also in events, visions, cultic rites, and (in Christ) in a person. By labeling all this as "word," the communicative nature of revelation receives all the emphasis; it happens as an appeal to our existence, and it wants to be heard, understood, and obeyed. But if the latter does indeed take place, the word event, the speaking of the word, has apparently been augmented by another event, the hearing of the word. To bring that about is the work of the Spirit, that is, of God who not only comes to us from the outside, but who is also the one who transforms our life and our existence, giving us ears and enabling us to let him come to us as the speaking and revealing God.

This duality and "biunity" of Word and Spirit is thus the description of the encounter event that takes place in the act of revelation. We may in fact say—despite the difference mentioned earlier—that when two people genuinely meet each other, this is an analogy from the "outside" and "inside" which can in some way serve as an illustration of the Word-Spirit relation. Believers have always lived out of this dual reality. Theology, however, has often had great difficulty in finding somewhat adequate concepts for it. Only very seldom has the European mind been able to verbalize this specific category of encounter. Either the thinking proceeded objectivistically from God or subjectivistically from man. But the language and concepts of the Bible are oblivious of this alternative. Especially on two points has theology had difficulty with the dialectic of Word and Spirit:

The first problem is that of the *mutual relation of Word and Spirit.* Does this duality mean that there are two cognitive sources of revelation? But if the Spirit is a separate source beside the Word, does this mean that man, with an appeal to illumination by the Spirit, can rise above the objective Word revelation? On this way lurks a subjectivism which makes of the Spirit a pseudonym for our personal notions. Must we then, conversely, regard the Spirit as the convincing power residing in the Word itself, which would make him as it were the inside of the Word? But the Word by no means always has this convincing power; it can also leave its hearers cold or even provoke to resistance. The incarnate Word certainly did not automatically convince people but evoked the most diverse reactions. There is no such thing as word-magic. Word and Spirit are thus not interchangeable. Yet they are one. For what we call Word here is already the work of the Spirit who inspires people. Also, when we limit ourselves to the working of the Spirit in the believer, Word and Spirit are complementary, namely in the sense that the Spirit incites our spirit to listen to what he says to us in the Word. It is not spiritual or mystical characteristics in the believing subject by which the Spirit is recognizable, but therein that a man discovers the revelation outside himself, in the hiddenness. At the same time, however, it must be said that by the Spirit we make this discovery within the structures and limitations of our spirit; and that thus our subjectivity is put to work in understanding the Word. All understanding is subjective; but it is always the subjective understanding of a trans-subjectively experienced reality. Through the "bi-unity" of Word and Spirit man becomes involved in a process of encounter and understanding in which his subjectivity is fully engaged and at the same time divested of its biases and projections, making it increasingly more open to the saving event it has encountered. This formulation makes it easy to see the analogy with what happens among people in a growing relationship of love or friendship. This ongoing interplay of Word and Spirit brings about the encounter and continually purifies and deepens it.

The relation of Word and Spirit is not a theme that is prominent in the OT. There the working of the Spirit is restricted to the small circle of bearers of revelation to whom the Word "comes" or "happens." It is not until we come to the NT that we see how the revelational event happens in this dual working, proceeding from the incarnate Word and the pentecostal Spirit. Though the affirmative response to the revelation remains the work of man, in this response he is entirely dependent on God. "Flesh and blood," that is, man's own insight, does not reveal to him who Christ is (Matt. 16:17). " ... we have received ... the Spirit which is from God, that we might understand the gifts bestowed on us by God" (1 Cor. 2:12). We touch here on the concept of "election"; see par. 50 G.

The Spirit as man's renewer does more than put him into contact with the revelational event. Later, in a different context, we will deal with this "more." Wherever his revelational function is mentioned, this is strictly of a referential nature. He opens the eyes, not for his own presence in us, but for that of Christ outside us. "When the Spirit of truth comes, ... he will not speak on his own authority, but whatever he hears he will speak. ... He will glorify me, for he will take what is mine and declare it to you" (John 16:13, 14). According to Acts 2, the setting of the coming of the Spirit was a sermon on the resurrection of Jesus. But as such the working of the Spirit is an event having its own origin and order. Acts 16:14 provides a good illustration of its relation to the objective revelational event; there it is said of Lydia, as she was listening to Paul's preaching, that the "Lord opened her heart to give heed to what was said by Paul." In the epistles (and later in the early church) this referring activity of the Spirit is for that reason often described as "giving light," illumination (*phōtizein, phōtismos*): "For it is the God who said, 'Let light shine out of darkness,' who has shone in our hearts to give the light of the knowledge of the glory of God in the face of Christ" (2 Cor. 4:6). On the question why the Spirit does not do this with everyone and the role of man in relation to the Spirit, see par. 50 sub c.

For centuries, in the history of the church, there was only scant attention to this specific function of the Spirit in the revelational event. Western theology has indeed always had an eye for the subjective role of man in his relationship to God, but then on the point of the fruits of the faith (sanctification, good works, merits). Theologians did not really become aware of the unique role of the human subject in the matter of revelation and faith until after the Middle Ages, at the dawn of the new era. From Luther to Schleiermacher and from Descartes to Kant, man's own role takes on an increasing prominence. In theology this meant an increasing investigation of the role of the Spirit as a medium of revelation beside the Word. The Spiritualists and Quakers went so far that they appeared to ascribe to the Spirit, and thus to the subjective pole, an independent content over against the objective event of revelation; they overemphasized the subjective pole. Luther and Calvin strongly rejected this development, strictly maintaining the referring function of the Spirit. But their followers became divided about the "how" of this referral. The Lutherans spoke of a working of the Spirit *per verbum;* the Reformed of a working *cum verbo.* The former threatened to lead to an automatic working of the Word, the latter to the separation of the Spirit from the Word and an autonomous operation of the Spirit. The Canons of Dort (1619) with their *cum verbo* moved dangerously far in this direction (see I,12 and III/IV,13). Laboriously theology has tried to find a way between objectivism and subjectivism. See H. Berkhof, *The Doctrine of the Holy Spirit* (E.T. 1976), pp. 36–38, and G. J. Hoenderdaal, *Geloven in de Heilige Geest* (1968), esp. ch. 6. How relevant these problems have remained, also for today, is evident from two Dutch theologians. As is shown by the sequence in the title, G. J. Heering, *Geloof en openbaring* (1st ed. 1935, 3rd ed. 1950), seeks to assign to the Spirit, and through him to the human subject, its own place and function over against revelation, yet he seeks to closely connect both (whereby, however, the referring function of the Spirit does not always become clear; see esp. II, II, par. 7). J. G. Woelderink, among others in *De gevaren der doperse geestesstroming* (1941), ch. 5, and *Van de Heilige Geest en van zijn werk* (n.d.), ch. 6, was so afraid of a passive waiting for a revelation from the Spirit (among so-called experiential Christians) that he veered dangerously close to the Lutheran *per verbum.*

The second problem, already touched on above and in principle answered, is that of the *relation between the Spirit and our spirit.* One can speak about the necessary and dominant role of God's Spirit in the perception of revelation in a manner which might give the impression that no room is left for any activity of the human spirit. This would be a fundamentally erroneous presentation, since it threatens to deny the very aim of the work of the Spirit: to bring about a real encounter between God and man. As a reaction, to save the human subject, mention has been made of a cooperation and interaction between the Spirit and the spirit, with an appeal to the words of Paul: "it is the Spirit himself bearing witness with our spirit that we are children of God" (Rom. 8:16). Words like "cooperation" and "interaction" can be used, provided they are given the proper meaning. Paul means to say that the Spirit witnesses so strongly to our spirit that it cannot but agree with him and adopts this witness as its own. In this cooperation the Spirit is thus primary and dominant. His intention, however, is not to displace our spirit, but to awaken it to a new life of its own that continuously interacts with the Spirit. It is not the Spirit who believes in us. We believe, illumined by the Spirit. In the encounter we are not treated as objects, but respected as subjects and lifted to the highest subjectivity, the level on which we are truly subjects.

The problems uncovered here have for centuries, until today, engaged western European theology and the theology influenced by it. The Western spirit is highly active, aware of its own subjectivity. It views the world around as its object and as such it has the urge to dominate it. It is inclined to apply its subject-object scheme also to the relation with God. Then either God must be subject and man purely the object of his love or wrath, or man is subject, in which case the decision about his encounter with God and his salvation rests ultimately in his own hands. The contrast was hardly ever put so sharply; it would have made it too clear that both sides were doing injustice to fundamental biblical and religious categories. But the conflicts have always been fierce: between Augustine and Pelagius, Luther and Erasmus, Calvin and Bolsec, Remonstrants and Counter-Remonstrants, Molinists and Thomists. It becomes increasingly clear that we are here the victims of a wrong alternative. But our Western mind has difficulty finding somewhat adequate concepts. A happy formulation is offered by the Canons of Dort which profess: "Whereupon the will thus renewed is not only actuated and influenced by God, but in consequence of this influence becomes itself active. Wherefore also man himself is rightly said to believe and repent by virtue of that grace received" (III/IV,12). What is said here of the renewal of the will also applies to the renewal of the mind. In the Netherlands, in the previous century, especially the older ethical theology (Chantepie de la Saussaye, Sr., Gunning) tried to do justice to man as subject beside and under God. An extensive treatment of the reciprocal relation of God's activity and ours is given in the (in a sense classical) work *Grace and Personality* (1917) of the English Reformed theologian J. Oman. On this theme see further Berkhof, *The Doctrine of the Holy Spirit,* pp. 96ff., and Hoenderdaal, *Geloven in de Heilige Geest,* ch. 4.

13. REVELATION AS HISTORY

THE EXPRESSION "REVELATIONAL EVENT" which we have repeatedly used suggests that revelation comes to us on the plane of history, in consecutive and connected historical events. This is indeed so, provided we do not limit the expression to that. For God is as much the God of nature as he is of history. From our vantage point he is hidden in both and traces of his presence can be expected in both. As concerns God, both can become the stage of his revealing presence. The separation of the two is really only a product of the European mind; the Bible knows at most only a distinction, and does not have separate words for what we call "nature" and what we designate "history."

Yet we may emphatically speak of God's revelation in history. The Old Testament does mention divine revelations in natural events (Abraham's sacred trees, Moses' burning bush, the east wind which made a path through the Red Sea, the natural phenomena at Mount Sinai, thunder and lightning, etc.). Even so, these things were more in the nature of phenomena accompanying God's association with his people in history, to which history they also constantly pointed. Hence with increasing emphasis the revelation in history became the guide and touchstone for discerning the revelation in nature. In the Old Testament we observe a loosening of the revelation in history from its matrix, the natural revelation from which primitive religions lived. The difference between the two worlds was not that for the one revelation was exclusively an event in nature whereas for the other it occurred exclusively in history, but that with the one history was regarded as part of natural revelation and that the other saw natural revelation as an element in the historical revelational process.

How are we to imagine or conceive of divine revelation in history? There are three "models" which we must exclude as being in conflict with the nature of the biblical revelational event. *Revelation does not coincide with history.* History is first of all the sphere of man's activity, and thus of man's alienation from God and rebellion against him. In itself, therefore, history has no revelational powers. Its period of growth and decay, its catastrophes and surprises may suggest that there are "lessons" to be learned from history, yet there is so much that conflicts with it that history as such is to be regarded as the sphere in which God is hidden. In this area, beside and over against humans, God also makes himself a "factor," an "actor," who makes his own path through history.

Furthermore, *revelation is not an organic-evolutionary historical process, clearly distinguishable from the rest of history.* For that the lines between this "process" and that of "profane" history are much too blurred and fluid. "Sacred history," a favorite term with those who hold this conception, is totally embedded in ordinary history. Moreover, this process is far from organic-evolutionary. It is full of twists, gaps, and repetitions, and most of the time it gives more the impression of decline than of incline. We see nothing here of an organically unfolding principle. It looks much more like a battle, a continuous struggle on the part of God to bring his unwilling creature into line and to keep him in his way. But this struggle takes place in the arena of history.

This led others to an opposite viewpoint, which, however, likewise is untenable: *revelation does not consist in a series of purely momentary and vertical incursions into history.* The salient points (what are these, anyway?) may not be part of an organic whole, much less are they detached from each other. What follows presupposes what preceded and sheds new light on it. There is progress in it, a progress which is the direct result of the nature of God and man and their interaction. This progress has nothing of a biological unfolding; it rather resembles the movement in the plays of classical writers: the themes are developed to a climactic crisis, from which a new beginning is then made. But there is a clearly irreversible coherence in which Moses cannot be understood without the promises to the patriarchs, the prophets without the law, Jesus without the Old Testament, and the Spirit without Christ.

It is difficult to describe, even approximately, how revelation assumes shape in history. We choose the description: *revelation consists of a cumulative process of events and their interpretation.* God establishes his own history, which on the one hand follows the regular laws of history, while on the other hand it establishes, within that history, its own tradition, by means of interruptions, turns, catastrophes, and liberating events. This history links up with existing religious traditions. God "began small" as the tribal god of semi-nomads. He induced people to put their trust in him, and he rewarded that trust beyond expectation by deeds of protection and deliverance. These acts stimulated further trust, which was likewise confirmed. So God's revelational deeds cut a trail through history. Events led to insights, and insights shed a particular light on events. So a special history is formed which is passed on through interpretations and applications. The story induces visions and expectations which then form the basis for understanding other events as revelational. At the same time a reverse process begins to take place: later events throw new light on earlier events; they become better and more correctly understood. The facts are accompanied by the words of visionaries who prophesy of the facts beforehand or interpret them afterward. Such a cumulative process happened in Israel. Its major segments were: the migration of the patriarchs, the deliverance from Egyptian bondage, the settlement in Canaan, the kingship of David and Solomon, the messages of judgment and deliverance of the great prophets, the Babylonian captivity and the return from it, the slow and difficult rebuilding of the nation around the second temple. The revelational elements which become visible in this history then reach a decisive climax in Jesus' proclamation, in his sufferings and death, and in his resurrection. These events are interpreted in the light of all of Old Testament history with its blessings and deliverances and its curses and calamities. And, conversely, in the light of Christ the whole Old Testament is now reinterpreted as the history leading up to him.

It is not possible to capture this cumulative process, issuing in cross and resurrection and then continuing from that point, in a harmonic evolutionary model. In this story of repeated conflicts, defeats, and deliverances, a constantly sharper picture of the fact of God and of his thoughts concerning his people and mankind becomes visible. This "constantly sharper" means that this is a process in which there is progress and development. We should see clearly what this progress means and what it does not mean. It does not mean, for example, that Ezekiel's contemporaries knew God much better than Abraham. Wherever God makes himself known in what is happening, he makes himself known, he discloses his heart. But such happenings create ever-new encounter situations, making more of the implicit aspects of God's self-revelation explicit. We see the same happen in human love relationships. Another illustration would be that of the full sun, which can shine through the window of a small attic and also through a big window that gives a panoramic view of a wide landscape. These analogies must, however, be augmented with the insight that revelation as history, owing to its disclosing function, regularly forces the relationship between God and man into a crisis situation, while God then confirms his saving will by the way in which by his grace he overcomes the crisis.

An inevitable question is whether this cumulative process, often called "history of salvation," continues after the decisive crisis and freedom that have come with Christ. This is certainly the case. Now it is Christ's church which dares to live out of his salvation and under his lordship and which in constantly changing situations constantly gains new experiences with her Lord, in which his deeds of judgment and of grace are again understood in new ways. The difference from the time before Christ is that the crisis and the liberation for which this cumulative process are headed now are the crisis and liberation of all of human history. We are now in the "between the times" phase in which what has happened in Christ is worked out worldwide. What has happened in him is and remains the basis, the limit, and the norm for all revelational events after him. Faith, believing in him as the central revelation, can only accept as revelation whatever can be discerned as a disclosure of God's heart in human history. To this problem also applies what was said earlier in a different context. Though not exclusive, Christ is normative.

For biblical-theological arguments see H. Berkhof, "Openbaring als gebeuren," in *Geloven in God.* For the systematic argumentation about the historical dimension of revelation see the Faith and Order report of the Bristol Conference, *God in Nature and History* (Faith and Order Papers, no. 50, 1967). With the first model we rejected we had in mind Hegel; with the second the salvation-history theology of J. C. K. von Hofmann in the 19th century; with the third the thinking of Barth in his earlier years, and especially of Bultmann for whom revelation as an "Existenzergreifung" (apprehension of existence) time and again happens vertically, outside the horizontal plane of history.

Attempts to connect revelation and history in a manner that does justice both to the biblical perspective and to literary-historical and the tradition-historical insights are found (following von Rad's example) in O. Cullmann, *Salvation in History* (E.T. 1970), however insufficiently worked out dogmatically, and in W. Pannenberg, especially in his contributions to the symposiums *Offenbarung als Geschichte* (1961) and *Theologie als Geschichte* (1967), with their fruitful starts toward a concept of revelation. These, however, are intersected by his advocacy of the demonstrability of revelation, his denial of God's self-revelation, and his subordination of word-revelation to deed-revelation. J. Barr, in *Old and New in Interpretation* (1966), ch. 3, in discussion with Pannenberg, has refined and corrected the concept of history from the viewpoint of biblical studies. In the absence of a better term, I derive from him the term "cumulative process," which suggests a looser connection but not (p. 92) a quantitative increase of revelation. But I differ from Barr in that for me this does not imply a rejection of the "revelational model." See the large type on pp. 68–71.

The modern study of the Bible has taught us to take much of what is presented in the Bible as history as (later) interpretation. Yet that has not altered the principial relationship of revelation and history. For the interpretations have to do with historical explosions, turns, and accelerations in which revelation was detected (exodus and conquest, Davidic monarchy, exile as punishment, return from captivity as salvation, ministry and resurrection of Jesus, the work of the Spirit). The interpretations of these events verbalize what eyewitnesses or later generations experienced as salvation in these saving events; and that was subject to change, depending on the situation and on adjusting or complementing what had been said by others.

A consequence of the cumulative model is the suggestion that the Intertestamentary Period is also theologically important, at least as a link. For that matter, the NT cannot be understood without taking into account the meaning that key words, such as law, Kingdom of God, Messiah, Son of man, wisdom, etc., acquired in that period. It was a period in which revelation through history was viewed as belonging to the past, and from different sides there was a search for the correct interpretation to make that history relevant for the present. The probing of the revelational content of that period must be done from the perspective of what preceded it (OT) and what followed it (NT).

The cumulative model also entails the suggestion that revelation continues after Christ. If that is so, can he then still be called the definitive revelation? See on that the final lines of the large type above. The concepts "definitive" and "progress" are not mutually exclusive. In addition, Christ is provisional (see par. 18), and through the Spirit his provisional definitiveness must be made clear in ever new interpretations (John 16:5–15).

The cumulative model is especially contested by followers of Barth, who have an aversion toward connecting the vertical "Geschichte" (i.e., revelation) with the horizontal "Historie." In the Netherlands, the so-called Amsterdam school puts all the emphasis on the proclamation embedded in the historical stories of the Bible, and regards the historical content as irrelevant. (The historicity of Jesus and his life and mission, too?) Revelation is then only the becoming-word of the Word (which must make history in our present). This view fails to see that proclamation (*kerygma*) always points to a preceding or following event. See K. A. Deurloo, *Waar gebeurd. Over het onhistorisch karakter van bijbelse verhalen* (1981), esp. ch. 8.

For the difference on this point between the Amsterdam school and the current study of the Bible, see "Een geschil over de uitleg van het OT," in *Kerk en Theologie* (April 1976), esp. pp. 95–98; and the discussion between K. A. Deurloo and A. S. van der Woude in *Kerk en Theologie* (October 1979), pp. 265–284. Cf. also H. W. de Knijff, *Sleutel en slot* (1980), ch. 11. But history as a medium of revelation does have a central place in others who think along the lines of Barth. Such is the case with A. E. Loen, *De geschiedenis* (1973), esp. IIb, whose orientation is more philosophical; and H.-J. Kraus, *Systematische Theologie im Kontext biblischer Geschichte und Eschatologie* (1983), pars. 12, 26, and passim, whose orientation is more biblical-theological.

14. THE SYMBOLIC LANGUAGE OF REVELATION

REVELATION OCCURS in an interaction of experiences and insights which are continually retold in such a way that the hearer can understand their liberating power for his life. The important role of language in this process is clear. If the revelation is going to be revelation for man, it has to be expressed in such a language that it can be understood as revelation. But is this possible? We have spoken about the "earthly" character of revelation. This is as it were heightened by the language in which it is expressed. For this language is earthly language, also therein that, like everything human, it is tied to this earthly experiential world. We have words for these earthly experiences and only for these. If in such experiences man discovers the new dimension of revelation, he has to borrow words for it from his "ordinary" world. With these borrowed words he aims to facilitate the transfer, but he can just as well use them to obstruct it.

We must make a distinction here. Like poetry and similar linguistic subjects, revelation employs what is called figurative language. We can speak about God as a rock, a shield, a light, and so on. We mean to compare him with these things only in a certain context. Also, when we speak about God's throne, his dwelling, his eyes, his right hand, and so on, the linguistic question does not yet need to worry us. We are still in the area of the transitive use of language. Our difficulties begin when we try to express which reality in God answers to these symbols. The real linguistic difficulties arise when we try to express in human language what the essence of God is, his heart, his character. For that the Bible uses words like "lord," "judge," "creator," "king," "father"; and to indicate God's relationship to us it employs words like "wrath," "love," "repentance," "mercy." These are all words derived from man's personal and social relationships. What right do we have to apply these to God? Through the centuries theology has wrestled with that question. Lately this grappling has become intensified. Depth psychology has made us discover the phenomenon of "projection." It could be that with words like "father," "judge," "wrath," and "love" we are projecting onto a blank screen an enlarged image of our earliest childhood experiences and desires. Another problem that has lately come up is whether these words are still sufficiently meaningful for us. To modern city man the image of God as a "shepherd" does not mean much; to one living in a communist country a "king" is the exponent of a bygone feudal society; for people in an industrialized world the "father" function has shrunk so much that many of the biblical connotations of this word have become strange to them.

There has always been the inclination to escape the linguistic problems by choosing other words. Thus theology has always had the tendency to designate God by means of word formations with *omni* (all): omnipotence, omniscience, omnipresence. But this does not in the least solve the problem. We still start from known earthly realities: power, knowledge, presence, which are then infinitely extended. The implied but unproven premise is that the world of revelation is the infinite extension of our world. One who shies away from that can take the opposite course and add the prefix "in" (un) to earthly words: infinite, unchangeable, and so on. But such designations, too, remain tied to earthly experiences of finiteness and transitoriness; by prefixing a minus sign their content is negated, without, however, filling them with a new content.

An often-followed course to get rid of the problem of figurative language is the substitution of impersonal, abstract concepts for personal and concrete expressions: the spirit, the ontic, the universal, the ground, the absolute, etc. But that does not help either. One may think he has exchanged the "lower" figurative language for the "higher" language of the abstract concept. The concept, however, is always a faded image. In our speaking about God, the concept suffers from the same problematic as the image. We are always engaged in speaking about God in terms derived from the reality of this world. The problem has only been shifted, because the terms are now derived from impersonal realities. The underlying assumption is that one comes closer to God and expresses him more adequately with the use of impersonal instead of personal categories. That assumption needs verification. And the Bible cannot be used for that. Biblical language exhibits a sustained preference for personal and social imagery.

There is no way to escape the symbolic character of the language of revelation. This fact as such does not need to perplex us. After what we noted about revelation itself, we could not expect anything else. For this occurs hidden in the structures of our earthly reality. It does not eliminate this reality. Nor does it occur outside or beyond it. God expresses himself in, with, and through earthly realities. Everywhere revelation and earthly reality go together. This makes that reality sym-bolic, that is, coincide with another reality. And the adequate language for a symbolic event is symbolic language.

Then, however, the question remains whether the language of the personal and the social symbol used by the biblical interpreters of the revelational event is the most adequate, or needs to be replaced by other expressions. This, however, is a question which cannot be answered from the outside. The functional adequacy of a language is judged only by those who through the medium of this language understand what this language tries to say. Such persons can afterward assess the language in terms of that intention and then proceed from that intention to devise other more adequate symbols. But since we have access to the intention only via the medium of the language we move principially in a closed circle. We have come across this circle more often. When we jump out of it, it means the end of our thinking about the faith. We thus stay inside it, and need to be continuously aware of that.

The casual manner in which the biblical witnesses apply the language of human existence and interpersonal relationships symbolically to revelation is due to the fact that in this revelation they encounter a God who enters into a personal relationship with them in which he behaves very humanly. Their anthropomorphic language corresponds to the nature of the encounter they describe. Their figurative language, whether "primitive" or not, may not be absolutely adequate, but it is certainly analogically adequate to describe the event in which they are involved and the person whom they meet in it.

From the witnesses in both OT and NT we cannot expect a conscious reflection on their own use of language. This is not done until there arises a scientific detachment or an existential estrangement. Yet we do come across a number of significant statements that disclose the basis for this lingual symbolism: "God created man in his own image" (Gen. 1:27). "He who planted the ear, does he not hear?" (Ps. 94:9). "For this reason I bow my knees before the Father (*pros ton patera*) from whom every family (*patria*) in heaven and on earth is named" (Eph. 3:14, 15). "This is a great mystery [the "biunity" of man and wife], and I take it to mean Christ and the church" (Eph. 3:32). These words denote the awareness that through God's creative and saving fellowship with man, our earthly, human realities are made the "image" and "mystery" of his essence and work. The fact that we can meet God is evidence that from the side of God there is an analogy. That is because he projects himself in us. Therefore we can speak meaningfully about him by means of projections. "Den Menschen bildend theomorphisierte Gott; notwendig anthropomorphisiert darum der Mensch" (F.H. Jacobi; "making man, God theomorphized; of necessity, therefore, man anthropomorphizes"). Outside the reality of the encounter, this image-language is bound to be one-sidedly and anthropologically explained as a "projection" in the modern sense of the term—as is done since Feuerbach.

It may seem that the anthropomorphic symbolic language recedes in the NT. Insofar as this is so, it has nothing to do with a "more sublime concept of God." On the contrary, the human God of the OT covenantal relationship has now come directly to us in a man. Now we have the *nous* of God in our midst in the *nous* of Christ (1 Cor. 2:16). We have no other "knowledge of the glory of God" except "in the face of Christ" (2 Cor. 4:6). The language of the symbol does not evaporate in the NT, but is now concentrated in the life of one man and in his work and destiny.

Yet the biblical writers are clearly conscious of the permanent distance between God and man without which the encounter with him would not be what it is. Precisely the OT which finds it so easy to speak anthropomorphically does not forget for one moment that this is analogical speaking. Man is not God —he is not even the image of God (so Christ is called in the NT); he is created "after" his image and likeness (literally: "in his image," after his "likeness," *bᵉṣalmēnû kiḏmûṯēnû*, Gen. 1:26). With such prefixes the distance is carefully preserved. Ezekiel too, when in a vision he sees the human God of the covenant, speaks of "a likeness as it were of a human form" (Ezek. 1:26). In the OT the language of image combines marvelously with the prohibition of images. The latter does not nullify the import of the first, but keeps alive the awareness that we have here (adequate) image language. It points to what goes beyond the image. We cannot through objectification and manipulation capture God in the image. That would infringe on the sovereignty of God in the encounter and the word event. ". . . you heard the sound of words, but saw no form; there was only a voice" (Deut. 4:12). Therefore we read: "To whom then will you compare me, that I should be like him? says the Holy One" (Isa. 40:25). This tension between the use and the prohibition of images poses dogmatic questions which we shall now take up.

The expression "analogically adequate" implies that there are limits to this adequacy. The symbol remains pointing—beyond itself. Does this not mean that thus it loses its adequacy, or at least that it becomes unclear? What does this adequacy consist of and how far does it go? In answering this question we need to realize that the belief in the analogical character of the language of revelation results from the belief that God in his revelational association with us in the present world (thus *before* the full revelation in the eschaton) creates a relation of analogy. This consists herein that he forms us in his image, that he deals with us accordingly, and that he then inspires his witnesses to return as it were to him some of the elements of our world as being made in his image. The belief that this is the structure of the encounter and association is the ground of our confidence in the comparative adequacy of the symbol language in which we express this association and its consequences. Thus we may speak of words like "Father," "Lord," "justice," "mercy," and the like: God's essence and his deeds are something like that. As God he is not less but infinitely more "Father" than those who on earth go by that name. He is thus always more than is expressed in these terms, but not essentially different. From this it follows that God's revelational association with us is itself the ground, the norm, and the limit of the symbol language. Which of the characteristics of an earthly father we may analogically ascribe to God, we can find out from a comparison with other symbolical terms that surround this symbol. Therefore we may not characterize revelation or the God of revelation with just one single term. Detached from other terms and what they intend to express, every symbolical term loses its revelance and transparency.

But when the symbolical terms function in the context to which they belong, they are so relevant and transparent that we may no longer say that they are used in a "figurative" sense. For then they share in the true analogy as it is grounded in the creation and actualized in the revelational encounter. When certain concepts are ascribed to God, they are thus not used figuratively but in their first and most original sense. God is not "as it were" a Father; he is the Father from whom all fatherhood on earth is derived. The same applies to words like "Lord," "community," "love," etc. Because of this the symbol language of revelation can also serve a critical function with respect to our earthly reality. We see this clearly in the parabolic language of Jesus, in which God who is presented as a father, the owner of a house, a farmer, an employer, etc., at the decisive moment reacts surprisingly differently than his earthly analogues are wont to do. That he is different does not mean that God is not really a father, etc., but that we are estranged from its essential meaning.

God created man after his image and therefore he deals with him in personal-social categories. This relation is irreversible. Therefore one cannot say that all images derived from man and human associations would be applicable to God in a more than figurative sense. The OT contains rich imagery about God, but two series of images that played a large role in the religious world of that time are in the OT nowhere analogically applied to God: that of the animal world and that of sexuality. (Yahweh may not be portrayed as a young bull.) Both are not sufficiently personalizing for that. That perspective and norm is also valid for us. But in a constantly changing world we are not biblicistically bound to the biblical imagery.

For centuries the Christian church has had great difficulty with the symbol language of the Bible. Identifying the God of the Bible more or less with the deity concepts of Plato and Aristotle (who through a process of extrapolation thought of God as absolutely beyond this world), she regarded the anthropomorphic manner of speaking as of a lower order, figurative, which needed explanation and excuses. On that see H. M. Kuitert, *De mensvormigheid Gods,* esp. III-V.

Tillich is the theologian who in this century thinks most clearly along this line. Because according to him there is only one adequate description of God, namely "being itself" (the Scholastic *ipsum esse*), he has great difficulty giving due weight to the truth content of the symbols used by Christianity. Their truth is very indirect. The symbol utilizes "a segment of reality." So "the realm of reality from which it is taken is, so to speak, elevated into the realm of the holy" (*ST* I, p. 241). But the holy is not this segment, but its infinite ground. That means that the truth content of the symbols has lost its basis. See p. 242: "Theology should not weaken the concrete symbols, but it must analyze them and interpret them in abstract ontological terms." In our opinion, this sentence contradicts itself. One who does not understand the biblical symbolic language analogically, but as the expression of an abstract ontology (being itself) does not interpret it but abolishes it.

Whereas Tillich puts all the emphasis on the inadequacy of symbolic language, Kuitert stresses its adequacy. (See par. 9.) One of his theses is: "That in Holy Scripture God resembles biblical-Israelite man is to be understood as Israel's adequate expression of the being of God as that of being a Covenant-partner in his words and deeds to Israel." Here hardly anything is left of a secret of God behind the relationship. See also par. 20, end.

Two great theologians have in this connection attempted a strict and consistent examination of the analogy concept. The first one is Aquinas. See especially *ST* I, q. 13: "De nominibus Dei." He rejects the idea that our language would inadequately and ambiguously *(aequivoce)* express the things of God, but likewise that it would be purely adequate *(univoce)*; he opts for analogical *(analogice)*, whereby, due to the infinite difference between God and man, the dissimilarity is to be regarded as greater than the similarity. Furthermore, it needs to be kept in mind that the analogy finds its source and norm in God. He is the *analogans,* our language and concepts are the *analogatum.* But in the epistemological order we have to start from the latter: "We conclude, therefore, that from the point of view of what the word means it is used primarily of God and derivatively of creatures, for what the word means—the perfection it signifies—flows from God to the creature. But from the point of view of our use of the word we apply it first to creatures because we know them first" (I, q. 13, art. 6).

Aquinas' confidence in the adequacy of symbolic language is based on the analogical relation in which man, by virtue of his creation in the image of God, stands to God.

The second great analogy thinker is Barth. See *CD* II,1, par. 27,2, esp. pp. 224–243. Different from Aquinas, less philosophical, more concrete, biblical, historical, he strongly emphasizes that God in his gracious association with man creates the analogy. We cannot operate with it as with a fixed *analogia entis,* but have to receive it from God in his self-revelation as an *analogia revelationis* or *fidei:* "Our words are not our property, but His. And disposing of them as His property, He places them at our disposal when He allows and commands us to make use of them in this relationship too" (p. 229). Barth rejects the analogy as if it would be "something existing and capable of proof" (p. 231). "When we make this repudiation, when we understand that the analogy has its basis in the being of God as He may be comprehended by creation and is therefore a mode . . . of His revelation, and the work of His grace, the peculiar overweighting of the concept, and the danger which its use incontestably involves, is eliminated" (p. 231). It is thus not true that Barth denies that analogy has its ground in creation, but this ground recedes entirely behind its actual happening in revelation. As a result, Barth sometimes seems to move on the brink of nominalism and to give the impression that, from our perspective and the terms we use, the connection between the word and the subject it stands for is arbitrary. He also wants to limit the use of analogy to "the selection made by God Himself" in revelation. This tension in his view of analogy stems from his view of the relation between creation and redemptive event; since *CD* III,1 he has, however, drawn them more closely and clearly together, so that with III,2 he has begun to speak of an *analogia relationis.*

For other Protestant considerations on the analogy, see G. J. Heering, *De Christelijke Godsidee* (1945), esp. III; H. Gollwitzer, *The Existence of God as Confessed by Faith* (E.T. 1965), pp. 142–201; G. D. Kaufman, *Systematic Theology* (1968), par. 8; and in particular the incisive critique *on* and deepening of Barth's analogy doctrine in E. Jüngel, *Gott als Geheimnis der Welt* (1977), pars. 17 and 18, from the perspective of the insight that God's love in becoming man creates an analogy: "It means that the Gospel is to be understood as event of what we are meant to be" (p. 390).

Aquinas as well as Barth emphasizes that the language of symbol, applied to God's being and acts, is not used figuratively, but is instead again given its most essential meaning. Aquinas says: "So far as the perfections signified are concerned the words are used literally of God, and in fact more appropriately than they are used of creatures, for these perfections belong primarily to God" (*ST* I, q. 13, art. 3). And Barth continues the sentence we quoted from p. 229: "The use to which they are put is not, then, an improper and merely pictorial one, but their proper use. . . . When we apply them to God they are not alienated from their original object and therefore from their truth, but, on the contrary, restored to it." In what follows, Barth elaborates this thought more fully than Aquinas. But Aquinas considers more intensely that symbolic language hangs together with the provisional character of the present existence and the revelation given for it. Repeatedly he points out that the analogy is valid only *in hac vita, secundum hanc vitam,* because here we do not yet know God *per essentiam.* For the convergence of Aquinas and Barth see J. Wissink (R.C.), *De inzet der theologie* (1983), V, 2.2. An incisive analysis of the analytical-conceptual problems in this area is offered by V. Brümmer in "Over God gesproken," *Kerk en theologie* (July 1982).

15. SELF-REVELATION OR REVELATION OF TRUTHS

ON THIS SUBJECT we can be much briefer because theologically it does not present such great problems. But it is necessary to touch on it, because in the history of the church wrong formulations of the problems in this area have had a bad influence up to the present. With "revelation" many thought and think of a *plural,* a series of "truths," a number of propositions on a variety of "super natural subjects" such as: God, creation, angels, providence, sin, the incarnation, the Trinity, the last things, etc. This plural concept of revelation focusses on impersonal ideas; but encounter and trust are directed to a personal *singular.*

Implied, too, is that if the Christian faith is regarded primarily as a trust-encounter with the living God, there is no longer room for the plural concept of revelation. Instead of speaking about "revealed truths," one begins to speak about the Truth as a person or as a singular event. This does not appeal first of all to the understanding intellect, but to the loving heart, to the self-surrender of the person, to the human existence risking itself and winning.

Since this sharp distinction has come into vogue, a wholesome change and purification have taken place in the way of speaking about revelation. The intellectualizing plural has made way for the personalizing singular. One no longer speaks of revealed truths, but of the God who reveals himself, and preferably of God's "self-revelation." It is questionable, however, whether we may think in terms of opposites here. Where it concerns saying what revelation is like, singular and plural do not exclude each other. The same is, for that matter, the case in our earthly reality, where organisms, processes, institutes, and events can often be described only in a combination of singular and plural.

The same applies to revelation when we think of the revealing God who is indeed singular, but who in his infinite fullness cannot possibly be described in a singular human word. It also applies to man who in a creaturely-analogical manner comprises in his unity a plurality and fullness of aspects and situations. It applies therefore also to the encounter between the two, particularly where this occurs in history with its constantly changing situations, constellations, and challenges. In revelation the "eternally rich God" enters the plurality of our human existence with its physical and psychical, its spatial and historical aspects. Yet in all this it remains one encounter. Therefore the Christian concept of revelation will always have to be described in a tension between singular and plural.

Dogmatics, therefore, does not have to be in the least ashamed of having a great many themes. On the contrary, it should always realize that it has not yet discussed enough. There is a truth of creation, but also of sin, of reconciliation, of the last things, and of many more subjects. It is thus entirely to the point, in many cases, to use the plural "truths." As long as it is realized that this plural can be compared with the many segments into which the one circle can be divided, which all radiate from one central point and point back to it. Taken out of context, these truths turn into aspects of a world view and theory, differing from other such conceptions and constructions only in the supernatural authority they are invested with and the *sacrificium intellectus* they demand. But one who shrinks the circle, limiting it to the center, being only concerned with the existential encounter, evaporates the encounter, since it occurs and evolves in the concreteness and plurality of insights and perspectives.

This convergence of the one and the many is not easily expressed in a usable formula. As a rule, we who are the recipients of revelation will do well not to begin with the singular but with the plural, not in the center but at the periphery. From there we should then try to find the revelational content of the various themes. Thus, for example, in the theme of "creation" our concern is not information about the created world and not even primarily the creative act, but the manner in which God as creator comes to us his creatures. Or, using another illustration, in the theme "the earthly work of Jesus," our concern is not all kinds of historical details, but how in the words and deeds of Jesus the encounter between God and man is disclosed. Fortunately, in many systematic theologies of the present time such a combination of Truth and truths has been fruitfully brought about.

Especially in the Roman Catholic Church and in Roman Catholic theology this speaking in the plural has been dominant for centuries, with all the resulting consequences. Until very recently one spoke there smoothly of *veritates, mysteria, doctrinae, dogmata revelata,* and the like. Central in this connection are the pronouncements of Vatican I, in the *Constitutio dogmatica de fide catholica,* esp. ch. 2: "De revelatione," and ch. 4: "De fide et ratione" (D 3004–3007, 3015f.). Interesting in it is the description that it pleased God "to reveal to the human race both himself and the eternal counsel of his will" (D 3004); next to the plural we have here the singular of the self-revelation.

The singular has begun to play a much larger role in the pronouncements of Vatican II, especially in the *Constitutio dogmatica de divina revelatione,* of which ch. I, "De ipsa revelatione," begins with the words: "In his wisdom and goodness it pleased God to reveal himself. . ." and then continues with a description which admirably links the singular and the plural together. In the following chapters, too, revelation is not viewed as a series of dogmatic propositions but as mediation of a new relation of friendship with God. It is unfortunate that the final chapter, ch. 6, "De veritatibus revelatis," reverts to the language of the First Vatican

Council. Of no less importance is the famed statement in the *Decretum de oecumenismo:* "In the comparison of each other's teachings, they [that is, the Roman Catholic theologians] must keep in mind that there is a progressive order or 'hierarchy' in the truth of catholic doctrine, because they differ in their relation to the basis of the Christian faith" (par. 11). The encounter with God is the basis determining the weight of the different truths. From the viewpoint of the earlier *veritates*-concept this is a revolutionary thought.

Protestant theology, born of Luther's question: "How do I find a gracious God?" began with the singular and has never completely denied this origin, not even in the two centuries of Protestant Scholasticism when *veritates*-thinking had a heyday again. The Lutheran *was Christum treibet,* as well as the focusing on the covenant in Reformed federal theology, had to lead to the formation of a concentric hierarchy of primary and secondary truths around the center, Christ as the Savior of sinners. See S par. 13; R I, ch. III; H III. When this led to an ecumenical, irenical attitude with Calixtus, the so-called syncretistic controversy about the *articuli fundamentales* broke out (first half of 17th century). After Kant's separation of pure and practical reason, and implied in it the separation of knowledge and faith, in Schleiermacher and succeeding theology the plural in the concept of revelation was pushed back as far as possible, especially in liberal theology. This tendency was given further impetus by Ritschl, and in our century in the existentialism of Bultmann. This meant a steady reduction in the contents of revelation. Every plural became suspect, being regarded as the consequence of contemplative, objectifying thinking, instead of articulating an existential attitude. Faith was thus abstracted from reality, emptied of its contents, and reduced to a human attitude. Farthest in this direction went F. Buri in his *Dogmatik als Selbstverständnis des Glaubens* (I, 1956; II, 1962) and *Der Pantokrator* (1969). Much more thought-out and restrained is G. Ebeling in *Dogmatik,* I, par. 10. But "what comes to light in revelation is man," who is revealed to himself in judgment and acquittal (p. 253). He precedes his discussion of the concept of revelation with that on prayer (par. 9), which presupposes the nonobjectifiability of God, but precisely from that vantage point attributes to God very specific characteristics. Diametrically opposed to this is the fundamentalistic dogmatics of C. F. H. Henry, *God, Revelation and Authority* (1976ff.), which is based on the propositional character of the revealed truths (plural).

16. GENERAL AND SPECIAL REVELATION

IN A THEOLOGICAL DISCUSSION of the theme of revelation, the distinction now under consideration is usually elaborated in great detail. This will not be so in our discussion. We already discussed the core of this subject in paragraph 8. The contrast "general" and "special" is not really suitable to clearly express the problems that arise here. In fact, the terminology itself is unclear. One may think of general revelation, as is usually done, both as a revelation which does not depend on a special act of God but which is given with his relation to his creation, and as a revelation which people can everywhere and always experience. In contrast, special revelation refers both to the revelation which is regarded as based on a special act of God and to the revelation which comes only to particular individuals or groups; in this connection one thinks of the revelation to Israel, in Christ, in the Bible, and through the church. The terms "general" and "special" are intended to distinguish these revelations from other divine revelations. This seems to suggest, however, that the special is to be regarded as a specification of the general. That is not at all what is meant here; the intention is rather to contrast the special, as that which is richer and fuller, with the general, as that which is dimmer and poorer. The couplet of terms is therefore not really suitable to express what is meant.

Beside the linguistic arguments there are four theological considerations that confirm this conclusion:

a. The term "revelation" is too strong to indicate the manner in which God is knowable in his works of creation. Earlier we used the picture of an indirect light that shines through our experiential reality. It directs men to a humanly unknowable mystery. At the same time this light is so indirect and diffuse that one can have the most diverse ideas as to its source and can even deny the existence of a separate source.

b. If revelation is an encounter event, each revelation is a very "special" event in which an individual or group experiences the presence of God as a communicating event; "general revelation" is then a contradiction in terms.

c. There is no good reason to think of God's revelational encounters with man as limited to the history of Israel and of Christ in the Old and New Testament. We believe that in that revelation is expressed the last truth about God, enabling us to look as deeply as possible into his heart. It is therefore the gauge with which we measure everything else that presents itself as revelation. This implies, as noted earlier, that the revelation in Christ is normative, but not exclusive. The confusion of both these concepts has so far been one of the burdens of the general-special problematic.

d. The contrast general-special, suggesting a kind of break between biblical revelation and what passes for revelation outside of it, is also insufficiently able to show the common background of both, or, stated differently, how the revelational event is rooted in the world of its time. The terminology is too imprecise to indicate the historical connection and growth and the dialectical relation between God's concern with the nations and his concern with Israel.

We live by the revelation of God to Israel and in Christ. This is for us the revelation, the self-disclosure of God. What we know about other revelations can only confirm our conviction that here the deepest word has been spoken. But we cannot characterize those other revelations with a term like "general." Standing in the fullness of Christ, we might perhaps use words like "partial," "groping," "dim," "unfulfilled," etc.

But all these terms, too, have their drawbacks, and they say very little. Moreover, we apply these qualifications to phenomena of which we have no inner experience ourselves. Is it then still necessary to apply dogmatic categories here?

In the NT, Rom. 1:18ff. has always been the starting-point for the consideration of what is called general revelation. How little this section of Paul refers to what is meant by that term is evident from the following: (1) What Paul says is meant to prove the statement in v. 18 that "the wrath of God is revealed from heaven against all ungodliness and wickedness of men." (2) In contrast to his usual terms for revelation, Paul uses neutral terms here to designate "what can be known about God" *(to gnōston tou theou)*. (3) The effect of this "revelation" is negative; it lures men to idolatry and serves only to make them "without excuse"; thus revelation in the sense of an encounter does not take place.

These three limiting aspects have often been overlooked. This is especially so in Roman Catholic theology, which appeals to this passage in support of its distinction between what it commonly calls natural and supernatural revelation. Vatican I canonized the doctrine of natural revelation when it stated, with an appeal to Rom. 1:20, that God "can be known with certainty from the things that were created through the natural light of human reason" (D 3004), though supernatural revelation is necessary in order that the natural can be known "with no admixture of error" (D 3005).

The terminology "natural-supernatural" was also taken over by Protestant theology; beside it the terms "general-special" came up. With the Reformers this duality played only a subordinate role, preoccupied as they were with the special revelation of God's grace in Christ. Calvin is in this respect an exception, in that he devotes a careful and penetrating discussion to this problematic in the opening chapters of the *Institutes*. In I,iii–I,v he gives a broad exposition of the "sense of divinity," the "seed of religion," which is found in all humanity. But as strongly as Calvin avers general revelation, so strongly he denies that this revelation leads to a revealing encounter. We need the spectacles of Scripture to perceive general revelation (I,vi). With less precision, art. 2 of the Belgic Confession expresses the relation of the two revelations in the spirit of Calvin.

This dialectic of Calvin and of the Lutheran confessions soon faded among the proponents of Protestant Scholasticism (Lutheran and Reformed). General revelation now became the basis for a comprehensive natural knowledge of God *(theologia naturalis)* which increasingly came to function as the substructure and infrastructure of special revelation. The marginal role became a fundamental one. See S pars. 2–5; R II, par. 16; H 1; and on the development in the Netherlands from 1650–1750, P. Swagerman, *Ratio en revelatio* (1967).

Since the Enlightenment and in the 19th century, the Christian faith became for many a special, be it the highest, form of the common religious awareness. The 20th century, which observed the fruits of this type of thinking in the so-called "German Christians," also witnessed a sharp reaction against natural theology in the Barmen Declaration (1934). General revelation was also drawn into this crisis of natural theology, especially through Barth with his strict Christocentric concept of revelation, the reverse of which was the total rejection of all other forms of revelation (*CD* II,I). See also Beker-Hasselaar, *WK* I, ch. 1, and more nuanced Kraus, *Systematischer Theologie,* par. 114.

Going back to Calvin, G. C. Berkouwer, *General Revelation* (E.T. 1955), tried to keep general revelation and the natural knowledge of God strictly apart. He also presents an extensive overview of the controversy between Barth and Brunner and of other recent discussions on this subject.

Even after all these discussions, contemporary Roman Catholic theology maintains the duality of natural and supernatural revelation. But the role of the first has become less important, and to the extent that it is recognized is often anchored in (a cosmic) Christology: as the mediator of creation Christ is also the source of natural revelation. This theology is more optimistic about the effect of this revelation than were Calvin and others. Often only the positive statements in Rom. 1:18–22 are referred to. Subdued formulations come from Vatican II in the constitution *De revelatione,* pars. 3 and 6. This is also true of the *New Catechism,* which gives, for instance, this typical sentence: "Humanity's groping quest for God is animated by God's quest for man" (p. 33). Lutheran theology, with its opposition of wrath and love in God, and of law and gospel, has a tradition of perceiving of general revelation as revelation of law and of wrath (cf. Rom. 1:18), and even of constructing a broad and ambivalent view of culture on the basis of it. See R. Prenter, *Creation and Redemption,* par. 16, and G. Ebeling, *Dogmatik,* I, 252.

The view which I have defended here contains many points of contact with that of H. Kraemer in *Religion and the Christian Faith* (1956), ch. XX. He calls "general revelation" a "misleading term." His conclusion is: "As to the whole question of terminology, we have little hope that these time-honored terms 'General and Special Revelation' will be abolished. It is very difficult to find satisfying, generally acceptable new terms. The most feasible way is a persevering struggle for their purification" (p. 355).

17. FIXATION AND TRANSMISSION (SCRIPTURE AND TRADITION)

FROM THE PRECEDING it is clear that in our opinion revelation occurs in what we called a cumulative process of events and the interpretations put on them. If it is true that in history persons emerge and events happen in which God discloses himself and his eternal purposes with us, then such revelations are also valid for the times to come. This validity, which came to the first witnesses in the cultural forms and thought modes of their situation, needs to be passed on to succeeding generations in their situation. But that will have to be a genuine interpretation and transmission of the past events, not a transformation and adaptation to the new situation in which the uniqueness, the revelational dimension of the earlier happenings, is swallowed up by and lost in the ongoing stream of history. This evokes a double need in the following generations that want to live from the earlier revelational events: on the one hand, to fixate these events in a way which protects them against fading and misrepresentation; and on the other hand, to throw fresh light on and to articulate, perhaps also in the light of later revelational events, for the times to come these fixated events. Only so does each new present get an encounter with the eternity dimension of an earlier revelational event. Through the centuries this double need has expressed itself in the dual activity of fixation and interpretation. That has led to the duality which is usually discussed under the terms "Scripture" and "tradition." We will first consider each separately and then in their connection.

a. Scripture as the fruit of fixation

The revelation to Israel and in Christ can only be permanently passed on and penetrate if it is fixed in written documents. For that is the only responsible way in which history can be passed on to later generations. If God had revealed himself in different ways, such a fixation would perhaps have been unnecessary or even impossible. If God had revealed himself in the events of nature or in the quiet depth of each human heart, the documentary form would have been alien to this revelation. Hence where naturalistic, spiritualistic, or mystical conceptions of revelation are held, one usually speaks disparagingly of "book religions" (Judaism, Christendom, and Islam). But where a book or books have a central place, the important thing is not the book as such, but the fact that the revelation was experienced in history. Where such is a case, written fixation eventually becomes an inner necessity.

Eventually—for it is only natural that there is first a period of oral tradition. But that can only be temporary. The written fixation commonly happens when the distance between the events and the present can no longer be bridged by ear- and eyewitnesses, and when the twofold danger of oral tradition, namely abridgment and trimming, and elaboration and embellishment, becomes too great. As far as that is concerned, one can conceive of various connections between revelation and fixation. Sometimes they almost coincided; examples are the scribe Baruch who wrote down Jeremiah's prophecies and Paul writing his letters. Sometimes there was a large span between revelation and fixation, especially in those centuries when only a few were literate and many were skilled in oral transmission. We must assume such a large span with the patriarchal narratives and those about the exodus and entrance into Palestine. The greater the distance, the more the fixation will already comprise interpretive transmission. In that case Scripture is based on a segment of tradition, being its crystallization. The significance of this insight is especially felt in the four different versions of the life of Jesus. They originated in the period following the death of the eyewitnesses, in different localities, and against the background of the various situations in the early Christian church. That is reflected in the manner in which each of the evangelists narrates what has been handed down. In the narrating process he actualizes it for the people for whom he writes. This results in differences and occasionally even in contradictions in the fixation. These four versions show us how the historical is to be passed on. The variations in them tell us that there exists not just *one* normative narrative (in view of the continuance of history such would be impossible); this difference is an invitation and guide to us to interpretively pass on in our situation and in our own way the fixed tradition.

It is interesting to trace in the Bible the role of the verb "to write" and (in the NT) of its noun "writing." The great recipient of revelation, Moses, is in the Pentateuch also described as a great writer. In Joshua and several of the prophets, writing also plays a role at significant moments. When the central revelation in the decalogue is at stake, God himself is described as writing (Ex. 24:12). For the NT we think of Luke 1:1–4; John 20:30f., and Rev. 1:3, 11, and *passim* to 22:18f.

Above we have tried to draw systematic conclusions from the results of the tradition- and redaction-history approach. As a result of the historical-critical study of the Bible we possess a global insight into the tradition process that has led to the formation of the Bible. Where it concerns the details much remains unsolved and is perhaps even unsolvable. Perhaps oral and written tradition not only followed each other but also developed alongside of each other, be it in different social strata. Possibly the earliest form of the decalogue was one of the earliest fixed documents. The sanctuaries of the first centuries after the entry into Palestine must have had a large role in the process of committing the traditions to writing, and later the chronicle writers at the Jerusalem court and the priests in the temple. When the tradition was threatened by the Babylonian captivity, there arose a strong and lasting interest in the fixation of the past, and that fixation was done in such a way as to elucidate the relevance of that past for the present. The gospel literature was produced between 60 and 100 after Christ, when the eyewitnesses had died and the danger existed that for the Gentile-Christian churches Christ would evaporate into an idea.

Thus far we have limited ourselves to the separate documents which in the course of the centuries of the fixation process were singled out for acceptance. Eventually these documents were collected into larger units. And finally this process came to an end because a consensus was reached concerning the scope and the limits of the body of documents that could be regarded as the written fixation of the event of revelation. We call this the *formation of the canon.* This could only begin and be completed in times when the revelational event was thought to be essentially finished. The norm for determining whether a document was canonical or not was the chronological and personal proximity of the writer (real or presumed) to the revelational event to which his writing seeks to bear witness. To a large degree, therefore, the formation of the canon rests on historical considerations; rightly so, because of the historical nature of revelation. Consequently, the final determination of the canon was not so much an ecclesiastical decision as the result of much discussion and thinking and of a long period of weighing the pros and cons of historical arguments by theologians. To the present day this has not led to total consensus concerning the extent of the canon. The so-called "apocrypha" (the canonicity of which remains a point of discussion till today) are accepted only in the Eastern Orthodox and the Roman Catholic Church, somewhat by the Lutherans, and not at all by the other Protestant churches. This lack of clarity is occasioned by the historical character of revelation; the flow of history, after all, knows no boundaries. And if, moreover, principially no sharp distinction can be made between fixation and interpretation, it is clear that the limits of the canon will naturally be vague and fluid. Therefore the churches show little or no inclination to revise the existing limits of the canon, even though due to historical-critical investigation we may have quite different ideas about the "authenticity" of some of the documents than those who long ago included them in the canon. However, what we today can no longer accept as authoritative fixation, we can often appreciate as an example of interpretive transmission. The canon which we now have contains very varied and often contradictory reactions to the revelational process. So this canon reminds us that the revelation is not a system or an ideology, but an encounter of the living God with living people in history. The unity of the Bible does not lie in itself but in the oneness of the God who remains the same in the continually changing encounters. The canon marks the area within which we can find these encounters. When we have thus met the living God, we can also go the opposite way; that is, from within what all the writers point to, we can now evaluate whether and to what extent their pointing is in agreement with that to which they point.

The Greek word *kanōn* means "list," "catalog," or "table," as well as "rule" or "measuring instrument." Both meanings are to be applied here. The formation of the canon of the OT began during the time of the Persians (5th and 4th centuries B.C.). Israel, now no longer an independent nation, had to find her national identity in the clarity as to the revelational sources of her faith. The Pentateuchal books likely became a collection either during the time of Ezra (see Neh. 8:2) or after him, but at least before ca. 300 B.C. when the Samaritans separated themselves and adopted the Pentateuch as their only sacred book. From the Wisdom of Jesus the Son of Sirach (39:1; 44f.) we gather that around 200 B.C., in addition to the law, the prophets were collected and given canonical status. The prologue which the grandson of Jesus Sirach, ca. 130 B.C., added to the work of his grandfather shows that at that time there did not yet exist a definite list of sacred books. Beside the law and the prophets there was a third category, the "writings," the core of which was formed by the Psalms, and to which the grandson also reckoned what was written by his grandfather. The growth of this category continued yet for some time. In the Septuagint, in addition to the Wisdom of Jesus Sirach, such books as Wisdom of Solomon, Tobit, Judith, Daniel, Bel and the Dragon, the books of the Maccabees, and others were included. In Jesus' day there was no unanimity yet about the limits of the canon. The Song of Solomon, Ecclesiastes, and Esther were disputed. The NT does not quote from them. The Sadducees recognized only the law (Pentateuch) as canonical. This situation of uncertainty came to an end when, after the fall of Jerusalem, the high council of rabbis, which settled in Jamnia, assumed the spiritual leadership of the defeated and dazed Jewish people. During the nineties of the 1st century they drew up a list of canonical books that was considerably shorter than the series that had been translated as sacred by the Septuagint. It is possible that with this the rabbis turned themselves, on the one hand, against the Hellenistic spirit (which is evident in several of the later writings) and, on the other hand, against fanatic nationalistic expectations of the future that were nourished by the apocalyptic genre. They rejected the idea of a continuing revelation; Malachi was taken to be the last prophet. Daniel was included, but they did not know that this was a pseudepigraphal work. The Septuagint, which had become the missionary Bible of the Christians, was rejected; its free renderings made it too easy for the Christians to interpret the OT as prediction of Christ. The Jews now made their own new translations. The first one, made about 130, was from Aquila; it was a woodenly literal rendering. The influence of Jamnia is seen in Flavius Josephus, who knows a strictly limited canon of twenty-two inspired books (*Contra Apionem* I.8), and in 4 Esdras, which speaks of twenty-four canonical books (14:18–48).

The Christian church did not follow the decision of Jamnia. It retained the larger canon of the Septuagint, though, like the Jews, it was aware that not all books were on the same level. But in the second half of the 4th century, Jerome attacked this broader canon as being in conflict with the one of the synagogue which he regarded as the original and genuine canon. The success of his rejection of the so-called apocryphal books had to wait until many centuries later, until the time of the Reformers who, also on the point of the canon, wanted to go back to the sources. Calvin was in that respect more radical than Luther. Trent, on the contrary, maintained the canon of the Septuagint.

Since then the extent of the OT canon has been one of the points of difference between the Roman Catholic and the Protestant churches. One should not underestimate this difference, for it also concerns the greater influence of Hellenistic thinking on the Roman Catholic Church and its theology. But one should not exaggerate the difference either: The Lutherans kept the apocrypha in honor. The Synod of Dort ordered that they also be translated (but not supplied with annotations), with a "warning to the readers" to compare their content with that of the canonical books. And the Roman Catholic *New Catechism* says: "The question is not so important as it may appear. The fact that these books, which are, incidentally, often very beautiful, are part of Scripture does not mean that they are as important as the rest. And they add no new message" (p. 47).

From the preceding the question is bound to arise as to what may properly be regarded as the extent of the OT canon. Putting it concretely, the question is whether Jerome and the Reformers did the right thing when they switched from the Septuagint canon to the one of Jamnia. The question becomes urgent if the decision of Jamnia was a defensive reaction to developments in Judaism and to the appeal of the Christian church to the Septuagint canon of the OT. We might maintain the canon of Jamnia on the objective ground that we, too, would hold that the era of revelation finished with Malachi. But in that case there are other books, too, which we cannot retain, such as Daniel (2nd century). That conflicts, however, with the concept of revelation as we have developed it in the preceding. For the ministry of Jesus cannot be thought of apart from the interpretations of revelation that arose in the so-called interim period between OT and NT. In this connection we think especially of apocalyptic literature and thought. This development was possible because, as we saw, the canon was not yet regarded as closed. Hence in the NT an apocryphal writing is more than once authoritatively quoted as "the Scripture" (Luke 11:48; John 7:38; 1 Cor. 2:9; Jas. 4:5; Jude 14ff.). The manner in which the interpretations of the interim period are connected with the revelation in the NT has made them a part of the history of revelation. In the NT these interpretations are sometimes accepted, sometimes rejected, and sometimes altered. The revelation in Christ is the criterion by which we measure the value of these interpretations. But the same applies to all the books of the OT and NT. Our conclusion, therefore, is that as such there is no reason why the Protestant churches should not return to the earlier, wider canon. We cannot put it stronger, however, because the accepted Septuagint canon lacks, on the one hand, precisely apocalyptic writings such as Enoch which have prepared the climate of the *Naherwartung* (imminent expectation) of John the Baptist and, on the other hand, contains much apocryphal material that reflects a certain Hellenization of Yahwism and which in this form has hardly or not at all influenced the NT.

For us the ideal canon is thus not identical with either of the existing two. The present canon would have to be augmented with those writings that form the interpretative bridge between the revelational event in the OT and that in the NT. But who is authorized to make this decision?

The formation of the NT canon shows similarity to and difference from that of the OT. For the NT, the historical books were written after the epistles, and due to the brief historical time span the eyewitness criterion played a major role. The Pauline epistles were combined in the course of the 1st century so that they could be read in the churches. We know that in the middle of the 2nd century our four gospels formed a collection (think also of Tatian's *Diatesseron,* his harmony of the four gospels made about 170). Meanwhile, following the Pauline collection, epistles from other apostles and their pupils, with some other early Christian writings, had also been brought together for reading in the churches. After the collecting process came the task of delimitation. The church felt urged to do this when her antagonist Marcion, in the 2nd century, issued a sharply abridged canon which included only a "purified" Luke and Paul; while on the other hand, through Gnosticism, she was faced with an expansion of sacred writings, and in the Montanist movement with the belief in a continuing revelation. The church had to learn to find her own way in between this increase and decrease. Her aim was to acknowledge as canonical the writings of the eyewitness-apostles and those of their immediate followers. Agreement existed about the four gospels and the Pauline epistles (the so-called pastorals included). For a long time afterward there remained uncertainty about other letters and writings, such as Jude, 2 Peter, Hebrews, Revelation, Barnabas, 1 Clement, and the Shepherd of Hermas. Were these apostolic in origin or not? Basic historical and secondary dogmatic arguments carried weight for and against the canonicity of each of these books. The result that lies before us in the twenty-seven books of the NT comes from the enumeration of Athanasius in his 39th Paschal letter (367), which later for the Western church was adopted by Augustine and ratified by some synods. Only a few Oriental churches have retained a different canon. In another century Luther questioned the canonicity of some books on dogmatic grounds. But at that late date this did not lead to changes in the extent of the canon.

Despite the existing consensus, the NT canon is as much surrounded with questions as the OT canon. Those who determined it started from the question concerning the apostolic origin of the various writings. From that perspective they rightly excluded some books. But they also included a number which they wrongly thought were apostolic, such as Hebrews and 2 Peter. Should these now be removed? That depends on whether we must use the same criterion they did. That question will be discussed later. Another question arising here is this: if another apostolic writing, e.g. a letter of Paul, were discovered, would it yet have to be included in the canon? So far the question has remained theoretical, but that can change any time. Following the standards of the early church, such a letter would indeed have to be put in the canon. And that will have to be done, too, according to our criteria if we follow the early church and ascribe canonicity in the first place to the generation of eyewitnesses and their immediate successors.

For the historical side of the question of the canon we refer to the Introductions to the OT and NT, and to H. F. von Campenhausen, *The Formation of the Christian Bible* (E.T. 1972).

The fact of the canon is thus an inevitable result of the necessity of having a permanent record of the history of revelation which reached its climax in Christ. Canon presupposes a situation in which this history has reached its climax and now continues in a history of interpretive transmission. The canon is not only necessary due to the need for a fixed record, but as much for the sake of ongoing translation. The latter, which happens primarily in preaching, always presupposes a narrative or a text which is to be interpretively passed on and which is the source and norm of every transmission. Without this permanent "foil" of the canon, every articulation sooner or later degenerates into an adaptation to the spirit of the age or into an ecclesiastical monologue. From this perspective it is significant that the church gave canonical status to books (for example, the letters of Paul) which at that time she hardly understood, and rejected books (for example, 1 Clement, Barnabas, Hermas) which were much more a reflection of her faith. This underlines once again that the church was not the "creator" of the principal content of the canon and that she hardly "determined" what this content was. Actually she did no more than "recognize" it.

As lucid as the fact of the canon thus is, so impossible is it to make its existing extent perspicuous. An older Protestant theology sought refuge in the idea of a special divine providence which supposedly led the church to an infallible fixing of the limits of the canon. That idea is untenable. The determination of the precise extent was the result of debatable and sometimes even erroneous considerations. It was a fallible human response to the revelation, basically of the same order as dogmas and creeds.

For the study of the faith two questions arise here that need an answer.

The first question is: *Which conditions must be met in order to admit a New Testament manuscript to canonical status?* The early church operated primarily with the condition of apostolicity, a condition also met by the immediate disciples of the apostles (hence the recognition of the gospels). Theologically, too, this was a proper norm to use. The apostles were the witnesses of the first hour, called specially by the historical Jesus or the exalted Christ to represent and to proclaim him. With this formulation we also say that their authority does not lie only in the fact of their historical nearness. There were many eyewitnesses who were not called. And the greatest witness to be called, Paul, can hardly be called an eyewitness. The canonical witness needed, beside historical proximity, insight into the revelational caliber of the historical. In the extant documents of the apostles and of some of their first disciples the church perceived this twofold dimension. For that reason she has never used only the eyewitness concept, but also the concept of inspiration—of which being an eyewitness was an aspect. Attempts to make the origin and content of inspiration further conspicuous have never been successful. The "how" we cannot fathom. The "that" we must acknowledge on the ground of the permanent authority these witnesses have over us. We will come back to that later.

The difficult question is: where did this combination of historical nearness and inspired interpretation exist and where did it end? One knew it was present in Paul, and one knew, too, that it was no longer present in the writers of the third generation. But how was this with the second generation? For a long time there was no agreement about this. The church managed by using only the historical norm of supposed apostolicity. Because writings such as 2 Peter were mistakenly ascribed to an apostle, later and better-informed generations face anew the question whether or why certain documents should be in the canon. If apostolicity is lacking, canonicity can be based only on a possible elementary inspiration. That inspiration would be perceptible only in the light of the other parts of the canon that are unmistakably experienced as inspired. But is it possible to point out those parts? With this our first question passes over into the second.

The second question is: *Can we find a "canon within the canon" in the New Testament?* That is, are there parts, writings, or writers that give such a normative interpretation of the heart of the gospel that they can be used as a norm for the other articulations? Here we could think of the common tradition of the gospels and of the central epistles of Paul

(Romans, Corinthians, Galatians) and the understanding of the Christ-event which they offer. We are inclined to accept the canonicity of other writings to the extent that they agree with the vision of Paul. But what does "agreement" mean here? Other situations and generations may require different terms and emphases, and these differences may be so great that only a careful reading brings out the agreement. Other writers may develop lines of thought which are hard to imagine in Paul and which do not seem to fit his thinking, while precisely for that reason they may be an indispensable reminder of the inexhaustibleness of the revelation, which can never be adequately articulated, not even by the most inspired witness. Standing on the foundation of the gospels and Paul, believers may in certain situations find much help in other interpretations in the New Testament, while still other interpretations do not communicate to them. Certain writings will always be regarded as secondary in importance. But church history teaches that our accidentally fairly large canon has been a big help to the church and individual believers to find a new understanding and a new interpretation of the gospel in new situations. Conversely, the tendency to limit the canon to Paul or reduce it to what was considered consistent with his outlook (Marcion, Luther) stemmed from too narrow a view of the gospel, and contained the threat of changing the gospel into a concept, a dogma, or an ideology. Therefore we do well to distinguish in the canon between center and periphery, and between peaks and plains, without prematurely rejecting the second for the sake of the first. No one can inwardly appropriate the whole. But in that awareness, every believer should be open for new insights into passages and lines of thought which thus far had remained strange to him or her.

The problem of the canon has again become acute after the Second World War. After a period when the main emphasis fell on the message of the various books of the Bible, it is now the differences that are preferably accentuated. Especially the school of Bultmann is inclined to go so far as to speak of irreconcilably contradictory interpretations in the NT. This one-sided interest in the differences easily leads to overlooking the basic agreement among the various witnesses. But the great differences in the presentation of the gospel in the NT are clear enough: between the synoptic gospels and John, between Paul and James (Rom. 3:28 over against Jas. 2:24!), between the proto-Pauline writings and the Epistle to the Ephesians (with its emphasis that we have already been raised with Christ and on the cosmic scope of redemption), between Paul and the pastoral epistles (which breathe the atmosphere of the second generation, with their interest in the confession, the church, office, and church polity), between the here-and-now eschatology of the Johannine writings and the apocalyptic of Revelation, between Paul's concept of faith (the correlate of justification) and that of Hebrews (the correlate of the promises for the future), etc.

E. Käsemann, in several essays in *Exegetische Versuche und Besinnungen* (I,

1960; II, 1964; E.T. *Essays on NT Themes),* saw such irreconcilable contradictions here that he looked for a "canon within the canon," which he found in Paul's *theologia crucis* as expressing the "biunity" of "the lordship of the Crucified" and the "justification of the ungodly." On this basis he rejected other expressions in the NT, either as fanaticism (Ephesians) or as institutionalism (pastoral epistles). This standpoint, an intensified continuation of that of Luther, was disputed by H. Küng, who labeled it sectarian and subjectivistic, and argued that the other voices in the canon cannot be regarded as anti-Pauline but belong together with that of Paul as periphery and center. See especially his *Kirche im Konzil* (1963), D I. For significant publications and a survey of the present discussion, see the symposium *Das NT als Kanon* by E. Käsemann and others (1970), where Käsemann once again formulates his standpoint (pp. 336–410) and sees the canon as the theater of the struggle between truth and its deviations; see the concluding sentence: "It is the documentation of that history in which the gospel of the unknown God for the first time thrusts into the world of the gods" (p. 410).

In principle we agree with Küng. God's revelation transcends all human comprehension. No man can adequately articulate it, not even a witness of the stature of Paul. It cannot be captured and formulated in a "central idea." It is, moreover, historical and wants to move with the times. To say what Paul had in mind, in a different situation and against other temptations, James has to express himself quite differently, even in terms contradicting Paul's. It has been a blessing that the church, consciously or unconsciously, chose a canon with such great variations (against Marcion). Interpretations in the NT which we today find hard or impossible to recognize as legitimate may later prove to contain the liberating answer to questions and temptations which we cannot now imagine. Only he who realizes that has the right to point to the defects and deviations in the canon. He will do so with great modesty and will not be led by just one witness but will take as his standard the entire choir of interpretive voices. For that reason the search for a "canon within the canon" is not really to the point.

In the above discussion we left out the OT. In principle the case is the same there. But on the one hand, due to the much greater time span, the variations are far greater (Genesis compared with Daniel, Leviticus compared with Amos, Isaiah compared with Ecclesiastes, etc.). On the other hand, after the Babylonian exile, the editors of the canon which has been transmitted to us have consciously edited the books in a prophetic-deuteronomic spirit. Particularly the Song of Solomon, Ecclesiastes, and Esther have again and again been doubted as to their right to be in the canon. But at other times precisely these books have functioned as the bridge between revelation and human experience. Of greater difficulty, in my opinion, is the question how the transparency of God's direction of history as the Chronicle-books see it can be harmonized with its obscurity according to the book of Job. As regards the OT, we will sometimes in the light of the NT have to choose for some and against other lines in the proclamation.

Nowhere in this great process of tradition are we provided with easily and readily usable norms. One could ask of what value the canon then is. The answer must be that the canon is the horizon within which the church has found the revelation in its original form, its depth, and its breadth, and through the centuries has constantly encountered it there. See the Faith and Order publication *The Bible, Its Authority and Its Interpretation* (1980), esp. ch. 4, III.

This brings us to the much-discussed question of the *authority of Scripture.* It is doubtful whether the term "authority" is quite relevant in reference to the encounter with God in Christ. Paul describes what happens in this encounter in the words: "it is the Spirit himself bearing witness with our spirit that we are children of God" (Rom. 8:16). And the life based on this he describes as a life of freedom and confidence. Can one justly apply to this life the term "authority" with its correlates of obedience and subjection?

"Authority" is, however, a term which properly belongs to an encounter situation. The exercise of power and blind obedience are foreign to a situation in which one encounters the authority of the other. It does, however, presuppose a higher and a lower. And precisely that is essential for the encounter with God. The witness of our spirit follows upon and joins the witness of the Spirit. Therefore there is every reason here to maintain the concept of "authority."

This does not yet imply, however, that the combination "authority of Scripture" is to the point and clarifying. After all, the Bible cannot be identified with revelation. It is the human reaction to it. Here we meet revelation indirectly, in the mirror of the human witness. And when this witness is itself the product of a history of interpretation, we have to speak of a double indirectness. In general this indirectness is presupposed and respected in the language of the church. One who has a Bible in his pocket will not say that he has the Word of God in his pocket.

But in our century more than ever we are impressed by that indirectness. To a great many people that has made the Bible a purely human book, without special authority. But all these biblical testimonies have in common that they react and respond to faith encounters with the same God (Old Testament). The reports on that cover centuries. Earlier we remarked that God began small. In the course of revelational history he adapted himself to humans, in order to make them more and more suited to his purposes. In those encounters this leads to renewals and reversals, as well as to contradictions and corrections. These changes also have to do with the quite different situations in which the witnesses and addresses found themselves. Therefore the Bible is not a totally uniform authoritative book. It is not a photo but a film; not a law but a way. The authority is not found in a particular snapshot on that way, but in the way itself. We cannot randomly appeal to texts outside their contexts, but must see their place on the way. That can be done only as we join in that way and pursue it in our situation. Thus Scripture receives its intended authority.

But then it is also true that the relationship of revelation and Scripture is precisely in its indirectness very intimate and positive. Nowhere else but in the Bible does the word of the primary witnesses to revelation come to us. Their authority, that is, the authority of revelation that came to them, comes to us in the words of Scripture. In the name of God we let ourselves be addressed by those words. Therefore one can say that the authority of Scripture is essential for the Christian faith.

But if the relationship of the Bible and revelation is indirect, then the authority of Scripture is also of an indirect character. Concretely this means: first, with an authoritative voice Scripture refers us to the revelation; next, on the authority of what we have understood of the revelation we evaluate the testimonies of the Bible, and so there arises an interaction between them. The concept of the "authority of Scripture" is part of this process and is qualified by it. One who tries to use it apart from that context fails to recognize the indirect relationship between revelation and Scripture and cannot, or only with difficulty, do justice to the humanness, the historicity, and the variety in the biblical testimonies.

A discussion of the authority of Scripture as brief as ours is uncommon in the tradition of Protestant dogmatics. As a matter of fact, from the perspective of the viewpoint which we have presented here there would be much in favor of complementing the term "the authority of Scripture" with that of "the confidence in Scripture." The description above is not much different from the way Luther both acknowledged and delimited the authority of Scripture with his "was Christum treibet" (see his *Vorreden zur Heiligen Schrift,* 1522). In Calvin Scripture has more distinctly its own character and authority, but he does not present a detailed theory about it. On the one hand, Scripture is for him the instrument through which God speaks directly: "Thus, the highest proof of Scripture derives in general from the fact that God in person speaks in it" (*Inst* I,vii,4); on the other hand, through its human mode of speaking it shows God's accommodation to the limited comprehension of his creatures (he gives many examples of this in the commentaries). In the conflict with the Counter-Reformation to the one side and with Spiritualism to the other, this casual speaking had to give way to a deliberate doctrine of the authority of Scripture. As such this was normal. But the real motive was the need for a demonstrably certain foundation of the Protestant faith similar to that which the Counter-Reformation had made for itself in its doctrine of the church (cf. par. 7). Thus arose the inspiration doctrine of Protestant Scholasticism which eventually left no room for the individual authors of the Bible other than that of being stenographers of the dictation of the Spirit; an inspiration which also pertained to chronological, geographical, and physical data and which left no room for deviation and contradiction among the writers. See S pars. 6ff.; R par. 6; H II. The climax of this development was the Swiss *Formula consensus* (1675), which declared the Massoretic Text fully inspired, including its consonants and vowel points. For if anything remains doubtful on this point, in principle the authority of all of Scripture collapses.

The *Formula consensus,* far from preventing this with its rationalistic argumentation, has actually set the stage for that development. Already in the 17th century errors and contradictions were discovered in the biblical text and narratives. The Enlightenment concluded from this that there is no infallible authority of Scripture. In the orthodox camp this conclusion was countered with a somewhat moderate and modified "apologetic theory of inspiration." For the Netherlands we refer to the so-called "organic" theory of inspiration as developed by Kuyper and Bavinck. These rearguard skirmishes continue till the present, though with decreasing frequency.

All this does not mean, as we noted earlier, that concepts such as inspiration and the authority of Scripture have become meaningless. What has happened is that they have been removed from the sphere of things that are rationally and empirically verifiable. The so-called "higher criticism" of the Bible was a salutary judgment on the attempt to make God's authority humanly transparent and accessible. The confession of the inspiration of the Bible and the authority that is based on it expresses the experience of faith that the words of Scripture give genuine guidance, that they mediate an encounter with God. This irreducible experience is based on certain words and passages in the Bible, and it evokes the expectation that eventually it will be enriched and deepened by further words from Scripture. The term "inspiration" expresses this union of experience and expectation. Unfortunately, it is so closely linked to the inspiration theory of the seventeenth century that its usefulness has become dubious. To many it suggests something that leaves no room for humanness, fallibility, and incorrectness. Faith, however, perceives in all these fallible human words the echo of the voice of God. It knows that it is placed in the presence of the living God through, and in spite of, these human reactions with all their limitations. This knowledge cannot be made transparent. This cannot be done because the manner in which God in his revelation conceals himself in our human reality and at the same time is distinct from it goes beyond our imagination and conceptual ability. Therefore we have no reason to expect that we will be able to capture the indirect presence of the Word of God in the words of the biblical witnesses in an exact and comprehensive formula. The concrete implications of the belief that the Bible mediates the Word of God will have to become clear throughout this book.

In *CD* I,2, par. 19, Barth made a new start in the doctrine of Scripture: "Scripture is holy and the Word of God, because by the Holy Spirit it became and will become to the Church a witness to divine revelation" (p. 457). The words "through the Holy Spirit" and "witness" turned the identification of the Word of God and the Bible into an "indirect identity" (p. 492), which does not exclude human failings but makes use of them (pp. 507ff.). Due to the much greater attention to the human side of Scripture, this conception, long and fiercely opposed by the orthodox, now has turned out to be insufficient. Initiatives toward a reformulation of the authority of Scripture are offered by the reports of Faith and Order, in *The*

Bible; J. Barr, *The Bible in the Modern World* (1973); D. H. Kelsey, *The Uses of Scripture in Recent Theology* (1975), esp. chs. 8–10; P. Stuhlmacher, *Vom Verstehen des NT* (1979), par. 14; and in the Netherlands H. M. Vroom, *De Schrift alleen?* (1978), esp. IV; the study of the synod of the Reformed Churches in the Netherlands on the nature of the authority of Scripture, *God with Us* (E.T. 1981); and J. Verburg, *Canon of Credo* (1983), V and VI. In contrast, Beker-Hasselaar, *WK* I, with its extensive doctrine of Scripture (pp. 83–173), stays with Barth, without discussing questions that have been raised later. Such in contrast to H.-J. Kraus, *Systematische Theologie,* who seeks to carry forward academically Barth's insights (see pars. 14–19).

More and more the doctrine of Scripture is connected with that of tradition and the church. The result is that the boundary with the interpretive transmission becomes blurred. That would be alright if the origin of Scripture was perceived as an aspect of the way the Spirit goes through history in his coming to man. But in modern hermeneutics the danger is real that the character of Scripture as the element of "fixation" no longer functions, and that Scripture is used to justify one's own ideas. "Scriptural criticism" should first of all be Scripture's criticism of us!

This is the place to say something about the concept of hermeneutics as it bears on the study of the faith, and especially to give an account of the varied manner in which the Bible is being used in this book. For centuries it was customary in dogmatics to find a set of proof texts *(dicta probantia)* for each subject, without much regard for the context, function, and quality of the texts themselves. In our century this is no longer possible. Hermeneutics has given us a more critical disposition. The appeal to the Bible has become much more discriminate and selective, and therefore often much more indirect and general than used to be the case. "Hermeneutics" is the theory of interpretation, the whole of the rules to be observed in the interpretation of a book or passage. Modern hermeneutics teaches us to make a threefold distinction in the Bible: (a) between what is said and what is intended with it; (b) between the different authors, books, and witnesses; and (c) between then and now. Once we are aware of this distinction, an indiscriminate appeal to a text is no longer possible; instead we have to restate what the authors intended to say, in its agreement with as well as deviation from other biblical writers, in such a way that we today can hear it as the Word of God. Theological hermeneutics thus serves to facilitate the double process of making the connection with the past and of interpretively passing this on to the present. In this study of the faith we shall keep this threefold distinction in mind, and it will determine whether or not and the manner in which appeal is made to the authority of Scripture.

This manner can be clarified by distinguishing four levels in the Scriptural witness.

1. The direct witness concerning God and the words and acts in which he savingly reveals himself. Examples: the story of the exodus, the revelations to the prophets, the praise of God in the Psalms, the story of Jesus and his resurrection, brief kerygmatic nuclei in the epistles.

2. The insights which are directly based on this witness and follow from it. Examples: the confession of creation, of sin, of justification by faith, of eternal life.

3. Representations in which these insights are figuratively or in other ways expressed and elaborated without a definite connection with these insights. Examples: the various traditions of creation, the views about the eschaton, the ideas about heaven, angels, and the devil.

4. The representations which, though related to these three levels, are not derived from them but rather originate from other (social and religious) traditions. Examples: the three levels of the cosmos, the sacrificial cult, the dietary laws, the position of woman, psychological, medical, and other views.

In the actual texts these four levels are combined. The first is nearly always interwoven with all kinds of presentations (e.g. the exodus narrative), the fourth is almost never without a relation to the kerygma (e.g. the sacrificial laws). For the sake of the interpretive transmission we make distinctions which were mainly foreign to the writers of the Bible. Mainly, not always; see e.g. Amos 5:25f.; Matt. 19:7ff.; 1 Cor. 7:25. We have to put them into a much more systematic form so as to be able to do justice both to the historical form of the revelation and to its relevance for the present.

The danger exists that we make such distinctions indiscriminately, with the conscious or unconscious intention to cast what is said to us from the other side into our own mold. But the aim of hermeneutics is precisely that we learn to make such distinctions properly and responsibly. We will thus have to be critical with respect to our own feelings and desires. On the other hand, genuine insights of our culture, which were unknown to the writers of the Bible, may be taken into account (e.g. when we think about the connection Gen. 3 and Rom. 5 make between sin and death). But it is especially Scripture itself that will have to give the criterion for discerning the four levels. This totality of Scripture is indeed a combination of all the parts, but from that totality new light is shed on the parts, showing which are more or less central and which are more or less peripheral. This double movement from the parts to the whole and vice versa we call the "hermeneutic circle."

Two examples: If we reckon the resurrection of Jesus to the first level but the virgin birth to the third, the decisive consideration is that the first is mentioned everywhere in the NT and the second only in the introduction of Matthew and Luke. If we reckon what is said about the devil to the third level and not to the second, this is because the figure of a satan seldom occurs, and where it does, in very different ways (e.g. in Job and in the synoptic gospels). Thus hermeneutics does not in the least aim at a cheap reduction. It seeks to place the biblical data in their proper context and perspective, and so to sharpen our eyes for the limits and the freedom with which we are to pursue the translative task. A kind of consensus on this is found in the Faith and Order report *The Significance of the Hermeneutical Problem for the Ecumenical Movement* (Bristol Conference, 1967); see also the above-mentioned report *The Authority of the Bible*, III.

b. Tradition as the process of transmission

As a rule Protestant dogmatics has no separate chapter on tradition. This is not the case with Scripture; its perspicuity, infallibility, and sufficiency are thoroughly discussed. That seemingly leaves tradition no other role than that of a continuous reference to the authority of Scripture. There certainly is no room for the idea that it could itself be an element in the revelational event.

This disregard of the concept of tradition in the study of the faith cannot be maintained, however. Revelation means that God enters the field of history to bring about an encounter with man which transcends human history, and which therefore goes far beyond the temporal and spatial bounds of the original field of revelation. The encounters which took place at that time were meant and suited for leading to further encounters in other times and places. Hence the revelation of Christ in the New Testament, in spite of, or rather because of its definitive nature, is not the end but calls forth as its sequel the coming and the work of the Spirit. The Spirit proceeds from Christ to continue and interpret his saving work worldwide. This coming of the Spirit is a new redemptive act, of the same importance as the coming of Christ of which he is the complement and counterpart. The events would remain hanging in mid-air without the interpretive transmission. It is one continuous revelational event. Fixation without interpretive transmission petrifies the faith; interpretive transmission without fixation makes it evaporate. The relation of fixation and interpretive transmission is a particularization of the relation of Word and Spirit.

The oneness of Scripture and tradition is underlined and at the same time complicated by the fact that they cannot be neatly separated as fixation and interpretive translation. The Old Testament records in written form God's redemptive ways with Israel. But in its various historical traditions it also presents a variety of reinterpretations of these traditions (Yahwist, Deuteronomist, etc.). The New Testament is the written record of the Christ-event. At the same time it offers, in the four gospels and in the divergent interpretations of Paul, John, James, Peter, and in the narrative of the history of the early church in Acts, *et al.*, a wide scale of elucidations, reinterpretations, and applications. Scripture as the product of fixation is simultaneously an anthology of interpretive models which for the most part arose close to the source. These are not handed to us for simply repeating them in the coming centuries; they are there especially as an invitation and a command to continue the interpretive translation in the same spirit and along the same lines for the benefit of later times and situations.

If the concern of revelation is the continuing encounter between God and man, then tradition is theologically of the same importance as Scripture. Thereby one has to keep in mind that it is a two-sided act. *Tra-ditio* means a "handing-over." This is accomplished only when, on the one hand, the matter to be handed over remains preserved intact and, on the other hand, actually enters into the lives of those for whom it is meant. The tradition of the redemptive work of God must on the one hand carefully guard this redemption so that nothing of it gets lost; for that a continuous return to Scripture as the fixation of the revelation of redemption is necessary.On the other hand, the tradition should be equally energetic in verbalizing this salvation in such a way that it becomes intelligible in other times and places by people who do not understand the language in which the event was originally expressed or the people and cultures who long ago expressed it. Unfortunately, in the term "tradition" one usually hears only the first activity, the need to preserve, but not the requirement of passing it on, the reiteration but not the reinterpretation. This dangerous one-sidedness has caused many tensions, obstructions, and crises in the process of tradition.

This is true of all churches, and it is so obvious now that not much needs to be said about it. As concerns the Protestant churches, there is the additional factor that they try to live by the illusion that they are purely "biblical," "Scriptural." The role of tradition is valued mainly negatively and therefore ignored as much as possible. Historically this is explainable, but therefore no less harmful. The Reformation churches, too, live fully in and from the process of tradition. Otherwise the translation and the reading of the Bible would there be experienced as sufficient for creating and sustaining faith. In reality preaching has the central place in these churches. In preaching, Scripture is interpreted and applied. The sermon is therefore the central act in the interpretive process, as based *on* and distinguished *from* the Scriptural fixation. Also in their catechetical instruction, youth work, theological studies, devotional literature, and so on, the churches of the Reformation are fully engaged in the process of tradition. But this almost total lack of reflection on the theological significance of this process has unfortunate results. Different traditions operate within the churches; particularly the so-called viewpoints could stand more objective and critical evaluation, both as to their positive value and as to their limited perception. Every tradition is eager to be known as "biblical Christianity," while unawares tradition plays the decisive role. It is insufficiently realized that the latter may and even should be the case, but can be done responsibly only if the basis, the purpose, and the limits of the process of tradition are understood.

Scripture is always transmitted and interpreted. It lives in a community which lives from it and which passes it on. If it were not so, it would not be operative in history. The interpretive process which it evokes and in which it is embedded proves that its importance far exceeds its historical limitations. The duality of Scripture and tradition expresses the fact that eternity has entered our history. Therefore the interpretive process is not accidental and arbitrary. One who believes that it is God himself who goes with us through history, revealing himself to us and meeting us, believes on that basis that the same Spirit who speaks through the inscripturated testimonies is the ultimate bearer and director of the process of interpretation.

The assertion being made here becomes more concrete to us if we inquire about the theological necessity of the transmission. Why not hand out Bibles and await the results? The Bible is, however, a library full of heights, depths, and plains, with central and marginal sections. To gain entrance and to find its central perspective the reader needs help. The community of believers must offer an introduction, a guide, a summary. This is a daring undertaking which nevertheless, in reliance on the guidance of the Spirit, must be undertaken, and which through the centuries has been undertaken. For evidence we can point to the liturgical creeds of the early church, the confessions of the Reformation, the catechisms, and all kinds of other ecclesiastical statements. Tradition has the never-ending task of preparing explanatory summaries and abridgments of Scripture.

An equally important function of tradition is to show the relevance of the biblical message for each new era and situation. Each human being, every era, and every situation is unique and nonrepeatable. Because eternity confronts specific people, times, and circumstances in the Scriptural testimonies, a re-formulation is continually necessary. And because eternity is operative in that witness, it can be done too. What is recorded in Scripture contains in principle the word and the answer for all people and all times. But that is something which the interpretive translation in the tradition process must make clear. For the sake of further encounters, fresh light, other emphases, elaborations, and abridgments will always be necessary. These we receive in the preaching, in the religious instruction, through pastoral contacts, Christian literature, theological reflection, and the like. (This book, too, is meant to be a small element in the tradition process!)

We do not suggest with this that Scripture itself exhibits a harmony and synthesis which (unfortunately) has to be distorted by tradition. As we noted, Scripture itself is a collection of variously accentuated traditions. Every new situation helps to clarify and heighten revelational elements which may or may not be found with equal emphasis in Scripture. Tradition discloses the inherent potential of the gospel to know all situations and answer all needs; it shows how much all of human life is understood, judged, forgiven, and sanctified by that gospel.

Note, for example, in the OT the different slants given by the Yahwist, the Deuteronomic historians, the Priestly writers, and the Chroniclers as they narrate the great deeds of God to their contemporaries. Or the differences in terminology in the NT when it speaks to Judaists (Rom., Gal.), Hellenists (Col., Eph., Heb.), or Gnostics (John); or to first-generation Christians (Paul), or to following generations (deutero-Pauline epistles, general epistles). Church history continues this and offers an overwhelming panorama of interpretations. This time the emphasis is on the person of Christ (Eastern church), another time on his work (Western church); now on him as an example, then again on his cosmic significance or on his way with the individual soul. Mysticism and activism, extroversion and introversion, traditionalism and future-orientedness, self-justification and fatalism, romanticism and realism, skepticism and speculation continually alternate and follow each other (accelerating, so it seems, all the time) as the dominant factor in the mood of cultures and periods. In the alternation many traditional Christian words lose their color and new words come on the scene. This is not a catastrophe but a necessity and a calling. The history of the church is the history of her transmission activity.

It would be wrong, however, to think of this tradition as a quiet and smooth happening, as if, for instance, it were like a softly flowing stream or a growing organism. All of church history argues against that. Precisely because interpretation often means a change of emphasis, revelation is in danger of being distorted and deformed, so that it conforms to the ideas and ideals of the time instead of giving the reforming answer. Then revelation is obstructed instead of speeded on its way. In many forms, individual and collective, Christianity has constantly succumbed to this danger. It would be strange if it were not so; for as to its contents revelation contradicts our aspirations, also our religious aspirations. Man will seize every opportunity to turn it into a harmless reflection and confirmation of his own aspirations. Many traditions are false traditions in which the Spirit is contradicted and suppressed. One who sees that may even be inclined to ask whether the Christ-event has ever really gained a foothold in this world, and whether Christianity is not a sustained and successful attempt to immunize mankind against it. But the fact that precisely this question has been asked, and that it has regularly led to protest and renewal, may be an indication that more than a negative answer is needed. As surely as the crucified Christ is also the risen Christ, so surely may we believe that in the ways of the Spirit the cross is not the final word, but that the pure interpretation and the true understanding will prevail over contradiction and obscurity. By implication this means too, however, that we are not to think of tradition as a harmonious development; it also evidences confusion and detours, contradiction and conflict.

The conception of the process of tradition as a harmonious and organic development has been dominant in some quarters of Roman Catholic theology since the days of Romanticism. The foundation was laid by J. A. Möhler and continued by M. J. Scheeben, J. H. Newman, K. Adam, and many others. This conception still finds support, but has since Vatican II been displaced by a more dialectical conception with greater nuance.

The term "tradition" *(traditio, tradere)* itself is ambiguous. It means "transmit" but also "betray." This linguistic similarity may seem accidental. But in both cases there is someone or something who is removed from his (her) own setting and put in a foreign context. Transmission and betrayal are right beside each other and easily become the same. Compare the Italian expression: *tradut-tore traditore.*

In the OT the tradition process is far from gradual. For centuries the transmission of prophetic Yahwism was threatened by a Baalistic naturalism and after that by a moralizing legalism (overemphasis of the law aspect of Yahwism). The clash between "true" and "false" prophets was a clash between two opposing traditions. In the NT it is noteworthy that the verb *paradidonai* is mostly used positively, but the noun *paradosis* more often negatively, as the false tradition of men which contradicts the word of God (Mark 7:1–13; Gal. 1:14; Col. 2:8). The NT also exhibits from the start a clash of traditions: Judaism over against Paul, Gnosticism over against John.

It would not be difficult to describe church history as a history of conflicting and antagonistic interpretations. And it would be quite well possible to view the whole as a history in which the divinely upsetting power of revelation is suppressed and rendered innocuous by misinterpretation and conformism. For the most part it can be described as the history of the successive and simultaneous Hellenization, moralization, Germanization, nationalization, scholasticization, and liberalization of the gospel. Think of what men like Kierkegaard and Franz Overbeck said about church history! The true history of the church has mostly been the history of lone individuals, martyrs, and minorities.

Our investigation of these problems leads us to the final and most difficult question of all: What criterion do we use? How can we recognize the true tradition? How do we determine where the path of true interpretation is? Or, to be more exact, where the paths are? For due to the great differences in people, periods, and cultures, the revelation can be transmitted only in a multiplicity of traditions. This multiplicity can be so varied that what is here or now the right interpretation may somewhere else or at a later time be insufficient, beside the point, or even deceptive.

Which institution, agency, or person can authoritatively show us the paths which come from and go in the right direction? The Eastern church answers: the official pronouncements of the original and undivided church, concretely, the doctrinal pronouncements of the seven councils from Nicea (325) to Nicea (787). This answer cannot help us to meet the changing challenges and conflicts of the many following centuries; it leads to traditionalism and petrification. The answer of the Roman Catholic Church is that the true tradition is determined by the official teaching authority of the bishops, and in particular the infallible teaching office of the Pope. But the consideration that this teaching office has rejected what are, in our opinion, biblically prophetic interpretations (the Reformation, for example) while sanctioning strange growths (for example, the Mariological dogmas) makes it impossible to acknowledge this authority as the rightful arbiter. A third answer, in a variety of forms, is given by "spiritualistic" groups and movements; they regard the inner light of the Spirit-led individual as decisive. But this authority is so individualistic and subjective and offers so little resistance against a blurring of Spirit and spirit that it cannot possibly serve as a counter-authority against subjectively arbitrary traditions.

The Reformational answer is that only revelation as it is recorded in Scripture can be the counter-authority which can act as the arbiter of the divergent traditions. In principle we consider this the only possible answer, considering what we have said about the complementary relationship between Scripture and tradition; a proper interaction between them is possible only if the traditions continually become legitimate by falling back upon and evaluating themselves in the light of Scripture. For us this answer has, however, lost the self-evidence which it has in most Reformational books on dogmatics. For we know that Scripture, in addition to the central revelational cores, contains a variety of divergent interpretations. Upon which of these are we to fall back? Everyone makes a choice on the basis of his own standpoint in the tradition process. Every heretic has his own text.

It is indeed true that Scripture cannot be directly and easily used as the arbiter in the conflict of the traditions. Often in fact the judge seems himself to sit in the dock. This counter-authority, Scripture, does not therefore relieve us from having to make our own choice as to where we wish to stand in the tradition process. Yet the history of the church is full of indications that Scripture has again and again acted as a guiding, correcting, and liberating counter-authority. There is a subtle but profound difference between usurping Scripture for our own views and desires and the willingness to be guided by what it really says. The traditions are more adequate in the measure in which, while taking into account the situation of the addressee, they confront him especially with the authority of a revelation which liberatingly contradicts him. The hallmark of the true and legitimate falling back upon Scripture is that the tradition orienting itself to it echoes the cross which is the heart of the gospel.

But this hallmark of which every transmitter should be sure in his own conscience is not an easy "Scriptural criterion," readily intelligible to all. It cannot with a magical formula put an end to all the confusion. Every new step we take with the revelation in history is a step into an area where we have not been before. There are times that the doubt-ridden transmitter can do no more than remain standing in the certainty that he (does not repeat but) continues the true intent of traditions of Scripture. In this he is supported by the ways of the Spirit in the preceding centuries of tradition. Likewise the whole church of Christ is in these cross-currents of tradition upheld by the confidence that the Spirit regularly makes the necessary corrections as well as the final decision, because he knows and points the way.

The discussion of the relation between Scripture and tradition presented here coincides only partially with what is usually meant by it in dogmatics. For the term "tradition" has two meanings: (1) the *traditum* or *tradendum*, that which is or must be transmitted; (2) *tradere*, the act of transmitting. Sometimes they are distinguished as *traditio passiva* and *activa*. We presuppose that the *tradendum* is found entirely in the (very broad) canon and therefore has no content of its own beside that of Scripture. For that reason we concentrated on the problematic of the act of transmission. In Roman Catholic circles and its theology one speaks, however, of a *tradendum* beside that which is contained in Scripture. This gives an entirely different meaning to the juxtaposition of "Scripture and tradition." Then the question becomes: Are there aspects of the faith that are not found in Scripture but outside it? If so, what are these? Roman Catholic theology speaks of two sources of revelation; Protestant theology puts the *sola Scriptura* over against it. Though this formulation of the problem is not ours, we have to say something about it in this connection, the more so because it has played a large role, and to some extent still does, in ecclesiastical controversies.

In the NT, when *paradidonai* and *paradosis* are used in a positive sense, they refer to the event of Jesus Christ, as the content of the kerygma as it is transmitted by the apostles (Luke 1:2; Acts 16:4; Rom. 6:17; 1 Cor. 11:2, 23; 15:3, and other passages). This *traditum* is fixed and entirely Christocentric. Yet the formulation is far from uniform. Early summaries of it are found e.g. in Rom. 1:3f.; 1 Cor. 8:6; 12:3; 15:3ff.; Phil. 2:11; 1 John 4:15. In the immediately beginning process of transmission this nucleus is expressed and elaborated, applied and accentuated, in a great variety of concepts and terms. Likely the "prophets" of the early church played a large role in this (Acts 11:27; 13:1f.; 1 Cor. 12:28, etc.) as the organs of the Spirit, actualizing God's salvation and commandments for specific situations. But alongside them there also arose the false prophets, and thus the acute need to discern the spirits.

This problem reached a climax in the 2nd century in the conflict with Gnosticism which presented itself as the true interpretive translation and which, to support its claims, appealed to further writings and oral traditions. Its main antagonists were Irenaeus *(AH)* and Tertullian *(De praescriptione haereticorum)*, who examined the relationship between Scripture and tradition (church). The same Spirit is at work in both. The church lives from Scripture and she alone understands Scripture. To understand Scripture one has to go by the *regula fidei*, the summary guidelines made by the church for the understanding of Scripture. All the emphasis falls on the interaction between Scripture and ecclesiastical interpretation, and on what we have called the summarizing and abridging function of tradition. A further consequence of the intense struggle with Gnosticism was that the preservation element in the tradition concept, in other words the backward look, displaced the interpretive duty. For centuries the discussion about tradition was dominated by the definition of Vincent of Lerins (in his *Commonitorium*, A.D. 434, 2:5): "that which has been believed everywhere, always, and by all." (With this formula he wished to put an end to the "novelties" of Augustine!)

This led the doctrine of tradition into a blind alley from which it found a dubious way out in the late medieval period. The doctrine and practice of the church contained too many elements which were not directly derivable from the Bible (five of the seven sacraments, infant baptism, the filioque, etc.). To justify these elements one sought refuge in the idea of a separate oral tradition from the days of the apostles. This belief was Gnostic in origin and had been rejected by the church fathers (with the exception of Origen and Basil). Now it was necessary to create a separate area for tradition, in a culture which had not yet learned to think historically. Thus arose the Roman Catholic doctrine of the "two sources." The Council of Trent declared that beside the books of the Bible it accepts and venerates "with the same sense of loyalty and reverence" the truth insofar as it is contained "in the unwritten traditions that the apostles received from Christ himself or that were handed on, as it were from hand to hand, from the apostles under the inspiration of the Holy Spirit, and so have come down to us" (D 1501). Two sources of revelation are thus put beside each other. The content of the second source is not further indicated. Every further indication would historically have been unverifiable. This specification of the content will thus have to come from elsewhere. Vatican I declared that only the Pope can infallibly determine the apostolic tradition (D 3074). "I myself am the tradition," as the Pope of that time, Pius IX, put it.

Meanwhile in Roman Catholic theology since Möhler another concept of tradition began to break through. The two-sources theory suggested too much that revelation is an intellectual communication of various truths. In contrast it was increasingly asserted that revelation is communion with God and the bestowal of divine life. Tradition was here regarded as a flow of life, an organic process of development of which Scripture is one element, be it a very fundamental one. The result of this opposite line of thought was, however, not all that much different from the traditional approach. In both cases revelation is more than its Scriptural deposit and the ecclesiastical teaching office decides what belongs to revelation. The idea of oral apostolic traditions was, however, increasingly abandoned. The revival of Roman Catholic biblical studies in the 20th century led more and more people to become critical of so-called revelational truths for which no basis can be found in the Bible. Many are inclined to regard Scripture as the material principle and tradition in the church as the formal principle of revelation. (Because Trent gives no specific content to the oral tradition one can also interpret its pronouncement in this way.) The conceptions come close to those of Irenaeus and Tertullian. But the two-sources theory has never been denied and comes through in several recent papal pronouncements.

In the Constitution *De divina revelatione*, Vatican II has freshly formulated the relationship of Scripture and tradition. Dominant here is the conception of revelation as the self-giving of God. A speaking of two sources does not fit here. *Traditio* is used in the singular and understood as *divinae revelationis transmissio* (cap. II). This *transmissio* is understood as an organic growth process which leads to a continually deeper understanding of Scripture (II 8). But at the insistence of the Pope this was followed by a quote from Trent (D 1501; see above), preceded by the sentence: "Consequently, it is not from Sacred Scripture alone that the church derives her certainty about the whole content of revelation" (II 9). This addition opens up the possibility of again interpreting everything that has been said so far in the sense it has in the traditional two-sources doctrine. The official Roman Catholic standpoint thus remains unclear on this subject. But not in the least unclear and of decisive importance is what follows (II 10): "The office of authentically interpreting the word of God, whether written or handed down, has been entrusted to the living teaching office of the church alone."

Holding to the doctrine of the perspicuity of sacred Scripture, the whole

Reformation vehemently opposed the idea that Scripture would have to be supplemented by tradition, or that the church would have to interpret a Scripture which in itself is insufficiently clear. See e.g. Belgic Confession, art. VII: "Neither may we consider any writings of men, however holy these men may have been, of equal value with those divine Scriptures, nor ought we to consider custom, or the great multitude, or antiquity, or succession of times and persons, or councils, decrees or statutes, as of equal value with the truth of God, since the truth is above all." This enabled the Reformation to come with a new and legitimate reinterpretation. Yet even the Reformation did not think historically, so that the interest was one-sidedly and biblicistically oriented backward.

Modern historical thinking since the 19th century and the rise of the tradition-historical method in the field of biblical studies have led to a great variety in the formulations of the problem Scripture-tradition in modern Protestant theology. This variety became more pronounced through contact with the Eastern church in the World Council of Churches. The newer conceptions are more or less officially expressed in the report of the second section (on "Scripture, Tradition and Traditions") of the Fourth World Conference of Faith and Order in Montreal (1963). There it was declared: "By the Tradition is meant the Gospel itself, transmitted from generation to generation in and by the Church, Christ himself present in the life of the Church. By tradition is meant the traditionary process" (par. 39). And: "We can say that we exist as Christians by the Tradition of the Gospel (the *paradosis* of the kerygma) testified in Scripture, transmitted in and by the Church through the power of the Holy Spirit" (par. 45). "But this Tradition which is the work of the Holy Spirit is embodied in traditions" (par. 46). As regards the final norm to judge the legitimacy of the traditions, the Protestants and the Orthodox were unable to reach agreement in Montreal. The Protestants looked for the ultimate norm partly in "Scripture as a whole" and partly in "the centre of Holy Scripture" (par. 53).

It is clear that theologically the standpoints come close together, but the hard core of the difference does not disappear. See E. Flesseman-van Leer, "Plaatsbepaling in de hedendaagse discussie over de traditie," in *Nederlands Theologisch Tijdschrift,* Feb. 1967; and on the historical perspective: J. N. Bakhuizen van den Brink, *Ecclesia,* II (1966), arts. 1–7. Nevertheless, one stays with a traditional backward-oriented concept of tradition. The challenge of a continual interpretation and the question as to the norms for judging its validity do not yet receive the needed attention, let alone that there is a readiness to accept a plurality of traditions (though Montreal does touch on this question, pars. 50 and 56). Especially the battle around the Roman Catholic two-sources doctrine, a doctrine still not rejected by the Roman Catholic Church, has sapped the energy of the Western churches and theologies from what is, in our opinion, a broader, better, and more productive way of posing the problem.

Meanwhile, this problematic presents itself to us in the 20th century with greater force than ever before. The 19th century was a time of intense confrontation with the modern spirit of the time. After the First World War one discovered that as a result of this interest the uniqueness and the peculiarity of the *tradendum* was in danger of getting lost. This led to a renewed interest in what is called "biblical theology." In our day, after the Second World War, when the forces of secularism assert themselves with renewed force, we note a shift again from the content and norms for an interpretive articulation to the concepts and accents of a modern interpretive transmission. Such a pendulum movement is a natural consequence of the two-sidedness of the tradition concept. Paul writes: "Do not quench the Spirit, do not despise prophesying, but test everything; hold fast what is good" (1 Thess. 5:19f.). This twofold challenge puts the Christian church in a situation of tension from which she may not withdraw. There are all kinds of ways in which she can withdraw from it, and very often she has succumbed—biblicistically, traditionalistically, spiritualistically, etc.—but this has always been at the expense of her calling.

18. THE PROVISIONAL CHARACTER OF REVELATION

WE HAVE COME to the conclusion of our discussion of the concept of revelation. Our aim here was to provide an introduction setting the stage for the whole of the material. But already at the beginning we mentioned the difficulties concomitant with this concept. These difficulties became clearer with each successive delineation of the subject. Think of the discussion of the earthliness, the hiddenness, the symbolic character, the role of the Spirit, and the function of history and tradition. This made it evident that we cannot simply and self-evidently use the term "revelation" to capture the encounter with God as this is experienced in the Christian faith. If we use the term, we immediately need adjectives to make it more specific and delimit it by speaking of revelation as "hidden," "indirect," and the like. These appositions almost obliterate the concept of revelation. Not altogether. Faith discerns just enough in the hiddenness and indirectness to keep speaking of revelation. But that is just enough, too, to long for and expect much more. The fellowship with this God who reveals himself indirectly and in secret inspires in us the confidence and the certainty that he is on the way with us to a much more direct and fuller encounter, in which the sun of his presence will break through the thick fogs of the present and we shall see him "face to face."

Therefore we may and must call the hidden and indirect revelational fellowship, as we now know it, "provisional." With this term we say not only that this form of fellowship is temporary, provisional, imperfect, but also that it prepares for what is higher and that in this contact God anticipates what he has laid up for us in his future: that which at last can fully and really be called revelation.

There is thus no way to avoid labeling "provisional" what we know as revelation. At the same time we are aware that so we call up a series of new questions to which we are unable to give the final answers.

To begin with, we would like to know why it is that in the only form of human existence we know we come in touch with God only in such a hidden and indirect manner. We know that one reason is our sin, due to which we as God's children are estranged from the house of the Father. But we saw also that it is very closely bound up with the earthliness and the historicity of our human existence. Then, too, apart from sin God cannot in this life realize the destiny for which he has created us. He cannot because for some reason, unfathomable to us, he does not want to. Apparently he has decided to go through a process with his creatures. Because of what we by faith come to know as revelation, we know of this process, we know that he himself is present in it, and from a distance we know, too, of the destiny of this process.

Can we perhaps say more about the goal of this process when we view it from the perspective of revelation? In biblical terminology we are accustomed to speak of "seeing God" "face to face." The mists clear up, the scales fall from our eyes, and we look into the heart of God and thereby into the heart of all reality. Then our thirst for full knowledge will be forever and fully satisfied. But these are all limiting concepts which we posit from the world of our present imperfect knowledge. As limiting concepts they admit of no further clarity.

Meanwhile, as human beings we can hardly imagine that perfect knowledge would not also have its own limits. Is direct contact with God ever conceivable for the creature? Would that not be the end of our creaturely existence? Must we not assume that throughout all eternity our fellowship with God will be a mediated and indirect one? Will we ever know God otherwise than by orienting ourselves to a man, to Jesus Christ who became a man? We could even ask whether we will ever cease to be historical beings. Perhaps we must, however, also conceive of the full revelation as a progressive discovery, forever penetrating deeper. These considerations make us less certain as to what is to be regarded as provisional and what as permanent in the present revelational fellowship, and whether we are to conceive of the difference between the provisional and the perfect as fundamental or gradual—and, incidentally, the difference between these might be one of degree. Thinking along these lines we have, however, moved into the area of eschatology (see par. 59). That was unavoidable because it turned out that revelation is to be seen as aneschatological concept. But then we must understand "provisional" as an ontological declaration about our entire created reality. See par. 25, point 7. But we conclude the train of thought by returning to the provisional character of the revelation which we have used as internal Prolegomena and made the basis for this study of the faith. From that we need to draw one more conclusion, for this study of the faith and for systematic theology in general, one we made earlier, in paragraph 6, in a different context and from a different perspective: if revelation is provisional, man's faith response is even more so, and then conceptual reflection on it is entirely provisional. For that reason a closed system is dogmatically an impossibility. That would contradict the very material which is to be systematized. The systematic is indeed an aspect of the reflection. But in its fragmentariness and incompleteness it will have to reflect the provisional character of the revelation to which it directs itself. The more the reflecting subject (a church, a group, an individual) dominates the object of the reflection, the more it will be a closed dogmatic system. It might even create the illusion of being able to anticipate the eschatological truth. But the system collapses as history and reflection continue and its unintentional provisional nature becomes evident. The more a dogmatician is convinced of the provisional nature of his designs and tries to stay open to new insights, the greater the likelihood of a measure of permanency in his work.

It has been noted more often that the OT does not have a central term for "reveal." The idea itself is of course present. It is described in various ways (with forms of the verbs *gālâ, rā'â, yāda', yārâ, dāḇar, 'āmar,* and others). The OT witnesses lived with a great variety of divine encounters without feeling the need for a central and comprehensive concept. We recall Ex. 33:18–23 where Moses is unable to bear the full glory of God's revelation. And in the NT this is really no different. There, however, the expectation of a future revelation is particularly strong, while the revelation in the present is sometimes intentionally disparaged: "We do not yet 'see'" (Rom. 8:24; Heb. 2:8; 11:1, and *passim*), or "For now we see in a mirror dimly" (1 Cor. 13:12), or "It does not yet appear what we shall be" (1 John 3:2). While the terms for revelation and reveal (*apokalypsis, apokalyptein, epiphaneia, phaneroun, phanerōsis*) do indeed often refer to the revelation in history, they refer mainly to the eschatological revelation; see e.g. Luke 17:30; Rom. 8:18f.; 1 Cor. 1:7; Col. 3:4; 2 Thess. 1:7; 2:8; 1 Tim. 6:14; Tit. 2:13; 1 Pet. 1:5, 7, 13; 4:13; 5:4. This use of the terms is related to the fact that the central revelation for the present, that in Jesus Christ, happened in a condemned and crucified man, whose resurrection as the anticipation of the full revelation became known only to a few, indirectly, through appearances. One may rightly speak of revelation here, but then in the sense of "firstfruits" and "deposit" of what only later will really be revelation. See the literature mentioned at the end of par. 7.

In the history of the church the awareness that revelation is provisional has often been pushed to the periphery, yet it has never disappeared. It is very much present in Irenaeus in this sense, that he distinguishes three levels of revelation: in the OT, through Christ, and in the eschaton (*AH* IV.20). The revelation in Christ is also provisional and points forward: "Thus does the Word of God always preserve the outlines, as it were, of things to come" (*AH* IV.20.11). His vision of a progressive disclosure leads him so far as to assume that even in the eschaton there will be a progressive knowing of God: "We are able by the grace of God to explain some of them [the things of the Scriptures] while we must leave others in the hands of God, and that not only in the present world, but also in that which is to come, so that God should forever teach, and man should forever learn the things taught him by God" (*AH* II.28.3).

Since the Middle Ages the distinction between the *theologia viae, viatorum,* or *revelationis,* and the *theologia gloriae, patriae,* or *visionis* has been in use. Thomas always kept it clearly in mind, because only in the state of glory will man so much be lifted above his creaturely limitations that he will be able to see God in his essence *(visio Dei per essentiam)*. Our present knowledge of revelation is limited especially by our earthliness; being physical, mortal, and dependent on our senses, even by the light of his grace we can know God only in his acts *(effectus)*, not in his essence. See *ST* I, q. 12; cf. *Summa contra Gentiles* III, chs. 38–63.

Appealing to the Greek church fathers, Eastern theology rejected the doctrine of an eschatological vision of God *per essentiam*. Supported by a series of Eastern synods, Thomas' contemporary Gregory Palamas taught that man can never know God in his essence, but only in the "energies" emanating from him, in Christ's human nature, in the nature of grace. See V. Lossky, *Vision de Dieu* (1962).

Reformation theology rejected Thomas' doctrine on entirely different grounds. It did not regard the earthly created reality but sin as the great and only obstacle standing in the way of full communion with God; grace does not lift nature to a higher level, but restores fallen nature. See G. C. Berkouwer, *The Return of Christ* (E.T. 1972), pp. 374–381. In our opinion Reformation theology, against Roman Catholic theology, rightly put the hamartiological aspect first, but it erred by rejecting for that reason the ontological aspect.

Lately, however, lines of thought are being developed in Protestant theology which more than ever before emphasize the provisional nature of revelation. Unlike Thomas', the Protestant motive for that is a historicistic or futuristic view of existence. See *Revelation as History* by Pannenberg and others in which, among others, Pannenberg defends the following theses (pp. 123ff.): "1. According to the biblical witnesses, the self-revelation of God has not come about directly, in the form of a theophany, but indirectly through divine acts in history. 2. The revelation does not happen at the beginning but at the end of the revelational history." What he says in 2 must be true because it is only at the end that all the revelational elements in the historical process are disclosed.

Moltmann likewise reaches the conclusion that one cannot yet speak of a self-revelation of God within the frame of our history. Revelation does not have the form of "epiphany" but of "promise"; it points forward to an eschatological self-disclosure of God. See *Theology of Hope* (E.T. 1967), esp. I, par. 2; and the article "Gottesoffenbarung und Wahrheitsfrage," in *Perspektiven der Theologie* (1968), pp. 13–35. On similar grounds G. Sauter in *Zukunft und Verheissung* (1965) also argues for "the 'not-yet' of revelation," which "expresses God's acts in his revelation, which is promise and not disclosure (apocalypse)" (p. 367). These ideas could lead to an emptying of revelation. However, the heavy emphasis on Jesus' resurrection as a promise-event in these theologians prevents them from doing this.

God

19. REVELATION AND ESSENCE

HAVING DEALT WITH THE REVELATION OF GOD, we must now venture to speak about God himself. This transition from the one theme to the other may seem an enormous step, even a jump. Thus far we spoke about an event coming from God. Now we move from the event to the subject, from the river to the source. In this really such a big step, however? We may say just as well that we do not take a step at all. For speaking about revelation, did we not all the time speak about God himself? Either revelation is revelation of God or it is no revelation at all.

By formulating the relationship between God and his revelation in these seemingly contradictory ways we are already at the heart of the subject. On the one hand, we cannot relate the revelation and the essence of God closely enough to each other. *Revelation is by definition revelation of the essence*, self-revelation. Therefore the essence of God is known from his revelation. The many nuances and limitations which we added to the concept of revelation in the previous paragraphs do not detract from this thesis. They remind us of the indirectness and the brokenness of revelation. But they do not deny that in its indirect and provisional character we perceive not just a something, an aspect, a segment of the divine mystery, but God himself, his heart, his deepest essence. We see in a mirror and thus do not see God face to face. But what we see in that mirror is God himself in the face of Jesus Christ.

God's revelation is revelation of his essence. That is true of the content of revelation: God's acts and virtues, his words and attributes which we encounter in the revelational event, disclose to us the character of God. These attributes of God will be the subject of the following paragraphs. But if revelation is revelation of his essence, then that statement cannot only have reference to the content of revelation but must also apply to the fact of revelation. Then it also belongs to the essence of God that he wants to reveal himself and enter into fellowship with his creatures. As such revelation is communication. Even apart from any concrete content, it reveals to us a communicating God. This God, so to speak, fully lives, finds self-fulfillment in his revelational act.

We began the line of thought formulated above with "on the one hand." For more needs to be said, without detracting from what has been said so far. On the one hand, revelation is revelation of the essence; on the other hand, God is more than his revelation. *God's essence transcends his revelation.* This is true in more than one respect. God's revelation is directed to human creatures and its nature is determined and limited by this address. No creature is capable of making the infinite and inexhaustible richness of the essence of God his own. Yet he does reveal his essence to us. We look into his heart. We do not meet something of God, but God himself. But at the same time that self contains worlds of inaccessible divine secrets. We can, however, be sure that there is nothing in these infinite worlds that conflicts with what we can know of God. To use an illustration taken from geometry: in revelation we do not have a random slice from the circle of God's essence, but a section, a piece that reaches to the very center. However small the slice, it leads to the heart.

However, when we say "God's essence is more than his revelation," we do not think so much of what we may call the "quantitative" problematic. The thesis also aims at something more essential, namely that *God is the subject* from which the act of revelation proceeds.

The subject precedes the act and makes it possible. If revelation is revelation of the essence, then logically the essence precedes and comes first. Far from being exhausted by its relationship to us, the subject can only effect it because it transcends this relationship. That God is not absorbed in his revelation and is not identical with it is precisely the presupposition that makes the revelational event possible. The horizon of revelation is not the horizon of God himself, as certainly as it is true that it is God who appears within this horizon. As subject God transcends the act of his self-revelation.

The above implies that God appears in revelation in a dual way. He is, on the one hand, the one to whom all revelation points as the source and the lord of this event. He is, on the other hand, the one who in all revelation emerges from his majesty to give himself to what lies outside him. God is free and sovereign and does not need us. But at the same time he is no less the God who has decided not to be alone, all by himself. And that decision is in full accord with his essence. The God who is free uses his freedom to establish communion. The sovereign one gives himself away. He does not want to be the only one who exists. But this does not mean the end of his freedom and sovereignty. The fact that God is himself is not sacrificed or eliminated in the revelational partnership, but precisely realized through it.

For the time being we shall indicate this two-sidedness with the rather formal terms *transcendence* and *condescendence,* since in this paragraph we deal with the question concerning the formal relationship of the fact-of-revelation to the fact-of-the-essence. In the following paragraphs this formal relationship will be given content, and then the concepts of transcendence and condescendence, "surpassing" and "stooping down," can be replaced by more specific concepts.

In the Bible this two-sidedness occurs regularly, but rarely if ever as an intellectual problem, and almost always in such a way that the distinction between the two aspects remains entirely in the shadow of the unity which both have in the one essence and the one act of God. The duality comes out in the well-known words from Isa. 57:15: "For thus says the high and lofty One who inhabits eternity, whose name is holy: 'I dwell in the high and holy place, and also with him who is of a contrite and humble spirit, to revive the spirit of the humble, and to revive the heart of the contrite.' " We detect the tension of this "biunity," too, in the Isaianic description of God as "the holy One of Israel." And even more in the interpretation of the divine name Yahweh in Ex. 3:13–15 (cf. also pp. 37f). On the one hand it is clear that God refuses to entertain the question: "What is his name?" (v. 13); he answers, "I am who I am," an evasive tautology of one who himself wants to remain subject and lord and refuses to be manipulated. On the other hand, this name also contains a promise: "I shall be with you," and you will experience my saving presence—making the name virtually identical with the name "the God of your fathers" (v. 15, cf. also v. 12). The ring of duality here is also the undertone of the designation "the Name" which is often used of God. In the East the name is a revelation of the essence. Essence and revelation are comprehended in the name. There is one concept which seems one-sidedly to express God's sovereignty, apart from his reaching out to us. That is the Hebrew *kāḇôḏ* and the Greek *doxa,* both translated by "glory" and sometimes as "honor." These terms express particularly God's transcendence. But that transcendence is never viewed apart from his condescendence. His *kāḇôḏ* is concretized in his Name, revealed in his temple, and realized in the salvation he gives to his people (see e.g. Ps. 29). And the *doxa* of which the angels sang on the first Christmas night means for us "peace on earth" (Luke 2:14); it is the *doxa* which we come to know "in the face of Christ" (2 Cor. 4:6), and which, very paradoxically, in the Gospel of John is connected with Jesus' death on the cross (verb *doxazein,* 12:23–33; 13:31f.).

The theological insight into this unity of transcendence and condescendence has by and large become a lost theme in the history of the church, especially due to the great influence of Greek philosophy on Christian theology almost from its beginning. Greek philosophy was a reflection on the ultimate grounds of our reality. By his thought the philosopher reached as it were higher and higher till he came upon the concept of deity. The consequence of this intellectual approach was that God had to be far away from us and as high as possible; he had to be one-sidedly conceived of as the transcendent one, as the final (non-active) object of our thought, and so as the ground, horizon, and eschaton of our thought. In Plato this is not yet consistently and clearly developed; he has, however, exerted great influence through his (incidental) description of the godhead as the highest idea, that of the good, which is "beyond being" (*epekeina tēs ousias, Republic* VI.509b). For Aristotle God is perfect being, thinking which thinks itself, the "unmoved prime mover" *(prōton kinoun akinēton)*. In Stoicism the godhead is the cosmic harmony, the logos, the designation of the natural order. Most transcendent of all is the god-concept of neo-Platonism which preferably called God "the first" *(to prōton)* or "the one" *(to hen)*.

The bridge from these traditions to Christian theology was the Hellenistic Jewish thinker Philo of Alexandria (B.C. 25–A.D. 42), who tried to show to his educated contemporaries that the pure transcendental and monotheistic conception of god they sought could be found in the OT; accordingly, following the Septuagint, he construed the divine name in Ex. 3:14 as "the one who is" *(ho ōn)*. The church fathers followed him in this. Already Aristides in his *Apology* (ca. 140) presents the Christian faith as the true philosophy and describes God in the form of negatives: "imperishable, unchangeable and invisible" (4). The Patristic development of the concept of God followed the same pattern; for the church fathers God is especially (using a favorite definition of Athanasius) "incomprehensible being" *(akatalēptōs ousia)*. The medieval doctrine of God received a fresh and strong impulse from about five hundred writings of an unknown author, who was later thought to be Dionysius the Areopagite (see Acts 17:34), and who for that reason was accorded nearly apostolic authority. The intimate connection with the neo-Platonic *theologia negativa* derives from him: God lives in an inaccessible light to which man can approach only by the constant negation of all earthly analogies.

Aristotle became the other dominant influence on the (Western) medieval doctrine of God, especially through Thomas Aquinas. Following Aristotle, he regards God as *primum movens omnino non motum*. He is the ground of all, true being, *ipsum esse*, and the goal toward which everything tends: the *summum bonum*. See *ST* q. 2–13. According to Thomas the most appropriate name for God is *Qui est*, the name God uses himself in Ex. 3:14 (*ST* q. 13, art. 11).

This one-sided emphasis on the side of God that is turned away from us, his transcendence, has until recently governed the doctrine of God both in Roman Catholic and Protestant theology. For Roman Catholic theology see the definition of God in Vatican I: ". . . mighty, eternal, immense, incomprehensible, infinite in his intellect and will and in all perfection. As He is one unique and spiritual substance, entirely simple and unchangeable, we must proclaim Him distinct from the world in existence and essence, blissful in Himself and from Himself, ineffably exalted above all things that exist or can be conceived besides Him" (D 3001).

Compare this with the introduction of the Belgic Confession: "We all believe with the heart and confess with the mouth that there is one only simple and spiritual Being, which we call God; and that He is eternal, incomprehensible, invisible, immutable, infinite, almighty, perfectly wise, just, good, and the overflowing fountain of all good." Protestant orthodox scholastic theology from the 16th to the 18th century, both Lutheran and Reformed, moves entirely along these lines. God is preferably called *essentia spiritualis (infinita)* as well as *spiritus independens, actus purissimus, spiritus simplicissimus, ens spirituale a se subsistens,* and the like. See S par. 17; R par. 17; H IV.

It would have been strange indeed if the Christian church through the centuries would not have been able to say more about God. Fortunately, there is another, entirely different vocabulary, the one used in sermons, liturgies, hymns, and meditations, which not only speak of God's transcendence but are also filled with praise for God's condescendence. Dogmatics, however, saw this latter aspect as limited to the area of revelation and not as belonging to the essence of God. This is the reason that the doctrine of God was such an abstract and sterile part of the study of the faith.

In our age we have come to see how untenable this separation of essence and revelation is. By way of reaction, that has led to the rejection of the traditional doctrine of God as a heterogeneous element, as the product of Greek thinking that does not know revelation. We may not forget, however, that dogmatics can never do without philosophical means of articulation and that it needs to express the faith in a language that is intelligible to the educated man and woman of its own time. By adopting the terminology of Greek thinking about God, the church sought to express in contemporary terms the message of God's transcendence as she had heard it in revelation, and tried to proclaim to the searchers in the Hellenic world that the God of Israel was what they were searching for. If it now turns out that in this partnership Hellenism proved to be stronger than Israel, then this should especially serve as a constant warning to us in our labor of articulating the faith.

This development of the doctrine of God under the influence of Greek thinking was not altogether wrong because of the reliability and superior power of God. But it was terribly one-sided due to the fact that one tried to derive God's essence from abstract thought instead of reading it exclusively from his revelation to Israel and in Christ. Thus there was imprinted upon the minds of many the image of a distant and cold deity. For a balanced evaluation see Althaus, *CW* II, pp. 10–13, and especially Pannenberg, "The Appropriation of the Philosophical Concept of God as a Dogmatic Problem of Early Christian Theology," in *Basic Questions in Theology,* II (E.T. 1971), pp. 119–183.

The attempt has been made to lessen the one-sidedness by speaking of God's *immanence* beside his transcendence: God not only stands over the world, he also lives within it. This follows both from his so-called "general revelation" (par. 16) and from his omnipresence (see par. 20). But this static concept is even more philosophically burdened than "transcendence." The emphasis on it often led in the direction of pantheism. "Condescendence" is a better word for God's sustaining and providing activity in our midst (see par. 28).

It would be very strange if in all these centuries there had been no theologians who had formulated a doctrine of God from the perspective of God's condescension in his revelation. Yet in a real sense this can be said only of Augustine and of Reformed theology till the middle of the 16th century.

Augustine saw increasingly that God's essence is to be learned from his revelation in Christ. For him God is not only and in the first place the high and exalted one, but the one who in love stoops down to man. Over against the *superbia* of the natural man he goes so far as to put all the emphasis on the *humilitas Christi* which is the *humilitas* of God himself: "Then there is also this reason: that the pride of man which more than anything else hinders him from cleaving to God might be refuted and cured by such great humility on the part of God" (*De trinitate* XIII.17.22). Well-known is his exclamation in *Sermo* 142.6 (a sermon on John 14:6): "How humble God is and yet how proud man is!" See A. D. R. Polman, *De leer van God bij Augustinus* (1965).

Much of this is found back in Calvin, Augustine's great disciple, though with less warmth, tempered by a strong awareness of God's transcendence which Calvin preferably calls the *gloria Dei.* He has a remarkable balance between transcendence and condescendence: God's glory expresses itself in his mercy and his mercy on us serves his own glory. Note the beginning of the Catechism of Geneva: "He has created us and placed us in this world in order that he might be glorified in us. And it is certainly proper that our life, of which he is the beginning, be directed to his glory" (2). And this happens, according to 7, if we "put all our trust in him." This is further explained in 14: "The foundation and beginning of faith in God is to know him in Christ." There is, however, no one in all of theological history who rejected the traditional doctrine of God as radically as Luther, for deeply personal reasons. The high and majestic God of Scholasticism had become a terror to him. For "he who beholds his majesty is overwhelmed by his glory." He calls God the *Deus absolutus* (separate from us and from his revelation), the *Deus nudus* (not veiled) or *vagus* (indeterminate). We would have perished in his wrath if he had not stooped down to us in his revelation in the manger and at the cross, *absconditus sub contrario.* This hiddenness reveals precisely his true loving essence. "God is the one who is hidden; this is his special characteristic." Luther emphasizes this so much that at times it appears as if God and his condescendence are one. But then suddenly (in an entirely different sense) there looms again, behind the revelation of God's love, a *Deus absconditus,* an awesomely transcendent God who is exalted far beyond his own revelation. There is in Luther an awesome tension, even a conflict between transcendence and condescendence; he calls the tortured souls to flee from the first to the second. This tension is absent in Calvin because for him the two sides of God are not contradictory but complementary. Lutheran orthodoxy has not been able to work with Luther's doctrine of God either. Not until the classical work of T. Harnack, *Luthers Theologie* (1862), did interest in it revive. See further J. T. Bakker, *Coram Deo* (Dutch 1956). For Luther's doctrine of God especially, but also for the whole history of the doctrine of God from the Patristic age to Ritschl (it has its importance, too, for the following paragraphs), we refer specifically to G. Aulén, *Het christelijk Godsbeeld* (Swedish 1927; Dutch 1929).

Owing to its philosophical orientation to German Idealism and because of its starting-point in the religious subject, 19th century theology meant a clear break with the metaphysical doctrine of God of the previous centuries. In general, however, this break did not lead to a new theological combination of God's self-revelation and essence. There were indeed fruitful new beginnings, especially in the so-called *Vermittlungstheologie* (mediating theology), which under the inspiration of both the Bible and Idealism rejected the traditional transcendentalism and supernaturalism. But elsewhere the doctrine of God, to the right as well as to the left, continued to be controlled by general and abstract categories. Only the 20th century witnessed a profound change, mainly through Barth's exposition of the doctrine of God in *CD* II,1,vi: "The Reality of God" (pars. 28–31). Barth derives the essence of God strictly from his revelation in Christ. In this revelation he makes himself known as the loving God. But this love is not a necessity, nor an arbitrary whim. It is the free choice of God's essence, the manner in which God realizes his freedom. Hence the heading of par. 28, which aims to give a "definition" of God: "The Being of God as the One Who Loves in Freedom." Freedom constitutes as it were the background, and love the foreground. Transcendence is not abstracted from condescension here, as was traditionally done, nor opposed to it, as in Luther. Transcendence realizes itself in condescension. Revelation is fully disclosure and actualization of the essence. Therefore Barth begins his doctrine of God with the par.: "The Being of God in Act," where we read, among other things: To its very depths God's Godhead consists in the fact that it is an event—not any event, not events in general, but the event of His action, in which we have a share in God's revelation" (p. 263).

This fresh formulation of Barth in the doctrine of God has exerted a greater influence than any other part of his theology. See esp. Weber, *Gl* I, pp. 439–450. Even many who in no way follow him know that on this point they cannot disregard Barth, and return to the God of the philosophers who is construed apart from Christ. That nonetheless the philosophical concept of God keeps influencing theological thinking is shown in Tillich, who again takes up the Scholastic definition of God as *ipsum esse*. "God is not a being, but the ground of all being." He is the Being that upholds all beings, Being itself. At the same time, as a Christian and as a theologian influenced by Luther, Tillich wants to connect the revelational aspects (righteousness, love, holiness, I-thou relation, and others) with this transcendental deity concept. He is, however, able to do this only through a process of radical abstraction. See *ST* I, esp. "The Reality of God."

The contrasting thought patterns of Barth and Tillich symbolize the alternative that confronts each thinker on the doctrine of God; to make either a biblical condescension or a philosophical transcendence the dominant motif. Compare, by way of illustration, the following two brief studies: Barth's *The Humanity of God* (E.T. 1960) and Tillich's *Biblical Religion and the Search for Ultimate Reality* (1955). In our opinion the first alternative is able to do justice to the transcendence aspect, but the second is not able to do justice to that of condescension. With that we do not deny that the first alternative, on further examination, also causes serious problems which will be discussed later.

20. ESSENCE AND ATTRIBUTES

WE CONCLUDED the main text of paragraph 19 by saying that the formal concepts of "transcendence" and "condescendence" presented there would be replaced by other more substantial concepts. If that could not be done, we would still not really know God. For to know him means to know him in his disposition toward us. Thus inquiring after the essence of God means that we inquire after his "character." With the answer to this question we stand or fall as believers. Through the centuries the study of the faith has attempted to give this answer in the doctrine of the "attributes" of God.

That term is not a happy choice. The terms properties, predicates, virtues, or perfections have also been used. But none of these is fully satisfactory either. We shall stay with the generally accepted terminology. Immediately this raises the question whether in the case of God we can speak of something like attributes. After all, attributes determine and delimit. Is God not all-comprehensive, without special characteristics that would only delimit his essence? But one who asks that operates with a specifically determined or rather *in*determinate concept of God. The God whom we meet in revelation is definitely not everything. He is, for example, not created, nor is he sinful. For that reason already he has certain attributes and does not have others. In paragraph 19 we used two terms to designate him. Two is not the same as infinite. But at the same time it must be said that each of these terms stands for an infinite abundance of virtues and attributes.

Of course these attributes do not have an independent existence beside the *one* being. Together they constitute and describe that being. Formally speaking, the relation of essence and attributes is similar to what we find in man who is created in the image of God. God who is one and simple is at the same time the infinitely rich and differentiated God. We certainly do not come close to the simplicity of his being by using a meager singular appellative for God; we can only approximate that essence by collecting and accumulating an abundance of adjectives. The church and the believing individual do this especially in their hymns of praise. In song and liturgy the glorious attributes of God are continually extolled. Beside that stammering of love and ecstasy, the doctrine of the attributes in traditional dogmatics makes a cold impression indeed. This is partly due to the fact, mentioned earlier, that dogmatics has wrongly oriented itself to an abstract and one-sidedly transcendent concept of God. But partly it cannot be helped, because in our intellectual quest we need to concern ourselves with questions which we may forget in our praise and adoration of God.

We can then begin with the question how numerous the attributes of God are. In passing already we gave the answer: though God is not everything, in his essence and virtues he is immeasurably rich. There is no limit to his attributes. This does not mean that it is pointless to start enumerating and studying them. After all, we know God in the "sector" of his revelation, and there he appears to us with distinctive qualities. We can and will have to speak about that, all the while knowing that the limited number of attributes we meet there denote the true essence of God, thereby assuring us that the attributes of God we have no knowledge of do not contradict that essence but confirm it.

Further questions arise when we try to get an idea of the relation of God's being to his attributes. Here, too, we think analogically of the way they are related in man. We may thus not conceive of the attributes as if they would make a composite of the simple being of God. Nor may we conceive of the attributes as a separate world of energies and substances next to the being of God, much like appendices from which he himself can be separated. Conversely, we may not do away with the plural to save the singular. We can thus not say, however profound it may sound, that in the final analysis all the attributes of God denote the same thing, namely the simple being of God; that would reduce the richness of the plural to mere appearance. Nor will it do to say that the plurality of attributes exists only in our subjective comprehension, so that it would not be the expression of God's essence but only of our limited view on it. What we may say is that what we call attributes denotes the manner in which we meet God, as singular-plural, in his revelational history. But that is then no projection or arbitrariness because we may believe that he is as he appears in it (par. 19).

Consequently, we have to say that the attributes of God are his being itself as it is facing us. His attributes are one with each other and one with his being. God is his attributes. This does not mean that the differences in the attributes are abolished. In each attribute we confess the fullness of God's being from a different perspective. These perspectives are derived from our experience of revelation (holiness, love, justice) and from our common experience (time, space, knowledge, change, etc.). While adding a subjective element, it does not render these statements in human words subjectivistically false; instead it makes them analogically true. In this connection one should bear in mind what was said in paragraph 14 about the symbolic language of revelation.

In passing we noted that the attributes we can ascribe to God add substance to his transcendence as well as to his condescendence. Due to the one-sided emphasis on God's transcendence in the traditional doctrine of God, in the history of theology especially the attributes that denote God's supernatural exaltation have been studied and developed, such as his infinity, incomprehensibility, immutability, omnipresence, omniscience, omnipotence, simplicity, eternity, spirituality, holiness. The attributes of God's condescendence remained much more obscure, the most significant of which were wisdom, goodness, love, and righteousness. God's essence was not derived from his condescension to Israel and in Christ. In that way there was constructed the image of a God who is far away, aloof, and cold.

Our repudiation of this image of God, and making God's condescendence our starting-point, does not imply that God would not have all the attributes we have just mentioned. But the importance they obtain in a reevaluation depends on the manner and extent to which they function in the revelational encounter and are derivable from it.

To give some examples:

We profess the *omnipresence* of God. This profession rests on the belief that God, who often seems far away, has the unlimited ability to be present with his judgment and grace, his help and his guidance, even when man does not in the least expect it. One who begins to see that dares to believe that such a God will never and nowhere lose sight of his creation, and may therefore be said to be everywhere present.

We profess the *omniscience* of God. As with the omnipresence of God, the poet of Psalm 139 sings about it, not to frighten small children with it, but to comfort God's lonesome and tormented children. The fact that the merciful God wants to know us completely, in even the deepest recesses of our existence, means that he accepts us and that he loves us. It is obvious that from a God who deals with us like that nothing in creation can be hidden. Therefore we may say that he is all-knowing.

With a term which is not very clear we profess the *simplicity* of God: there is *one* name, *one* salvation, *one* comfort, *one* faith. They come from a God who is unequivocally and consistently one, in whom there is no contradiction, no duplicity or change. He is the simple (not composed of parts) and only God who deserves all our trust.

We profess the *eternity* of God. By that we do not mean that God would not be in time, that he would be far outside it, in a timeless eternity. On the contrary, it is precisely in time that we come to know him as the one who goes with us through time. In that respect we come to know him as the one in whose hands are our times, who makes our time possible, and who guides and directs it from what transcends and surrounds our time: eternity.

So we could go on for a long time. But these examples are sufficient to make us aware that many of the attributes which are usually regarded as uniquely divine are definitely not the ones that impress themselves upon us first in the revelational encounters. They are rather the presuppositions or consequences of such experiences. For that reason we prefer, in the following pages, to deal with those attributes which according to his revelation are his primary and fundamental attributes. These are definitely not only attributes of his condescendence, though they are all derived from it. But from this condescendence we learn the one God and the whole God, and thus the transcendence on which condescendence rests. To make this clear we will, in the headings of the following paragraphs, always combine a noun with an adjective, the one denoting the aspect of transcendence and the other the aspect of condescendence. These headings make it obvious that the respective paragraphs will involve the discussion of several classical attributes of God, such as holiness, love, omnipotence, and immutability. But they are not developed from the perspective of an abstract concept of deity, but read off from an experience of God in history. Thereby it will become clear that these attributes never exist apart from their apparent or real opposite, something that could not become visible in the traditional doctrine of the attributes. Only in this context do they stand out as attributes of a wholly unique God who consistently wants to be a God of people.

Like the theme discussed in par. 19, the doctrine of the attributes has had a tedious history due to the attempt to harmonize the Greek and the biblical concept of God. The tremendous distance between the two concepts becomes apparent when one compares, for example, the story of Moses who wants to see the glory of God and then hears the Name proclaimed: "I will be gracious to whom I will be gracious, and will show mercy on whom I will show mercy" (Ex. 33:18f.) with Philo's statement that God is without attributes (*apoios gar ho theos; Legum allegoriae* I.13.36). Following his approach, the church fathers attempted to reconcile these two visions. In this attempt they usually assumed, wittingly or unwittingly, that the deeper and ultimate truth had been set forth by the Greek philosophers, for which reason they could only minimizingly and apologetically speak about the attributes of God as something unessential. Justin contends that God has no name and that the names we give him are predicates of his benefits and works (*ek tōn eupoiiōn kai tōn ergōn prosrēseis, Apologia* II.6). This is how the problem was formulated for centuries. We could, however, expect, on the basis of par. 19, that Augustine would be more positive on the attributes. For him they coincide with God's essence. "For whatever seems to be said there according to qualities is to be understood according to substance or essence" (*De trin.* XV.5.8). "But for God to be is the same as to be strong, or to be just, or to be wise, and to be whatever else you may say of that simple multiplicity, or that multiple simplicity, whereby his substance is signified" (*De trin.* VI.4.6). Since then Western theology has desired to maintain, in spite of the problems, that "the virtues are the essence itself." That was not the case in the Eastern church. There the attributes were viewed as "energies" which emanate from the being of God but which are not that being itself (see par. 18). This doctrine was especially set forth by Gregory Palamas (1296–1358) and elevated to official church doctrine at the Synod of Constantinople of 1351.

The Western church was of a mind to follow Augustine but found it impossible to break with the attribute-less God of the philosophers. That is why Thomas is not always clear. See *ST* I, q. 3, art. 3 and I, q. 13 (esp. art. 12). One characteristic quotation: "Now God is both simple, like the form, and subsistent, like the concrete thing, and so we sometimes refer to him by abstract nouns to indicate his simplicity and sometimes by concrete nouns to indicate his subsistence and completeness; though neither way of speaking measures up to his way of being, for in this life we do not know him as he is in himself" (*ST* I, q. 13, art. 1, ad 2).

Theology continued in this ambivalent direction, including Protestant Scholasticism. See S par. 18; R par. 18; H V. The universal uncertainty (on the one hand the attributes exist objectively in God, on the other hand they are projections of the knowing subject) is particularly clearly expressed in the *Leidse synopse* (*Synopsis purioris theologiae*, 1625), Disp. VI 21: "Although this essence is indeed perfectly adequate to God, so that there are not various parts in God, but whatever qualities he has belong to that essence; yet we assign various properties or attributes to him . . . as though they could be distinguished from each other and that essence; nevertheless they are not really separate attributes but the kind of distinctions made by rational creatures."

We should bear in mind that at that time one thought in terms of the objective-subjective theme, while lacking concepts and terms to describe what happens in a personal inter-subjective encounter. And that is precisely what the back-and-forth movement of objectivizing and subjectivizing concepts was intended to articulate. See on this entire problem Bavinck, *GD* II, par. 27, no. 185, and Barth, *CD* II,1, pp. 327–330. Only Nominalism (Occam, Biel) chose radically for the direction of Justin: the attributes are only *nomina* referring to the various works of God, grounded not in God's objective reality *(ratio ratiocinata)* but only in the subjective human conception *(ratio ratiocinantis)*. Eckhart also, on the basis of the unity of God, rejected every differentiation within his being: "omnis distinctio est a Deo aliena." In 1329 this thesis was condemned by the Pope (D 973f.). Usually this view is also attributed to Schleiermacher because of *CF* par. 50: "All the attributes which we ascribe to God are to be taken as denoting not something special in God, but only something special in the manner in which the feeling of absolute dependence is to be related to Him." Likely, however, within the whole of Schleiermacher's conception of the relationship of God and man, this is to be understood more as relational than as subjective, and thus more in line with the classical conception. See G. Ebeling, "Schleiermachers Lehre von den göttlichen Eigenschaften" (1968, in *Wort und Glaube*, II, 1969, pp. 305–342). Meanwhile, in her life and liturgy the Christian church has never doubted that God really has attributes, even though she did not see clearly how this belief could be squared with the oneness and simplicity of God which she regularly put first at the authority of Plato and the church fathers.

As soon as, in a sense, attributes were ascribed to God, the question about their division came up. In view of the duality of transcendence and condescendence in the God who reveals himself, a bipartite division of the attributes would seem most natural. But the biblical concept of God on which this is based was so much overshadowed by the philosophical Greek concept that this bipartition could be accepted only with the help of the philosophical doctrine of the "three ways," developed by Pseudo-Dionysius the Areopagite (ca. 500) in *De divinis nominibus* VII.3, according to which we know God either in the abstraction of all things, or in being superior to all things, or in his being the cause of all things, better known in the Latin as *via negationis, via eminentiae,* or *via causalitatis.* In other words, one ascribes to God the opposite of a human characteristic (e.g. infinity), or what is its highest degree (e.g. omnipresence), or—but this is implied in the previous two—one argues back to him as to the final cause of our earthly reality. In Pseudo-Dionysius this type of reasoning serves a neo-Platonic, extremely transcendent concept of God, which continued its influence in succeeding centuries. The result was that on the one hand a twofold division was introduced into the divine attributes, and on the other hand the attributes of transcendence almost completely overshadowed those of God's condescendence. The division into two was variously designated: *attributa negativa et positiva, interna et externa, quiescentia et operativa* (Luther); *incommunicabilia et communicabilia* (Reformed). Not only these names, but also the twofold division itself is open to criticism. See Bavinck, *GD* II, par. 27, no. 187, and Barth, *CD* II,1, pp. 335–345. Only when these two series of statements are constantly related to each other do they not detract from the unity of God and can they be used to indicate both the distinction and the connection between transcendence and condescendence. Our objection, therefore, is not against the twofold division and the terminology as such, but against the fact that the attributes are not given their substance from the revelation to Israel and in Christ but from an abstract Greek philosophical concept of the unity and the exaltedness of God and that, as a result, the treatment of the second series of attributes was far less adequate than that of the first series. So over the centuries the books on dogmatics have presented a cold and abstract doctrine of God, one that did not correspond to the Christology and the soteriology they contained.

The Reformation meant a radical but brief interruption. See par. 19. The Reformers wanted to design a doctrine of the attributes that was based completely on revelation. But shortly after the middle of the 16th century, Protestant theology returned at this point to the Scholastic tradition. Even Schleiermacher, whose doctrine of God was oriented to the concept of German Idealism, was not able to bring about a renewal, since this concept was more like the Greek than the biblical one. One can only be amazed at the persistence of this conception of a distant and passive God. After all, of what use to man is such an *essentia spiritualis infinita?* But it does have the great advantage that it leaves us undisturbed! Perhaps here we have one of the roots of its tenacity.

The Lutheran H. Cremer, with his study *Die christliche Lehre von der Eigenschaften Gottes* (1897), was the precursor of the biblical transformation of the doctrine of the attributes. He aimed to derive this doctrine entirely from revelation, more specifically, from the contrast of sin and grace. "The will which is active in all the attributes is the will which opposes sin so that his love may be served, and the main characteristic of all the attributes is the self-manifestation of God in the unity of judgment and grace in the service of redemption" (p. 109). Elsewhere in the same period one comes across new and better approaches. See e.g. T. Haering, *The Christian Faith* (E.T. 1915), Vol. II, pp. 488–513.

But the real transformation came only with Barth, *CD* II,1 (1940), par. 29: "The Perfections of God." While going along with the traditional twofold division, he avoids its drawbacks by giving a christological foundation and content to each of the attributes, and by always combining an attribute of condescendence (love) with one of transcendence (freedom) (see *CD* II,1, pars. 30–31). We shall follow this method, with the understanding that we are less inclined to defend an objective over against a subjective interpretation of the attributes because we are more inclined to connect the statements with their *Sitz im Leben* in the revelational events. An implication is that we, in distinction from Barth, do not feel the need for a special treatment and reinterpretation of attributes such as wisdom, omnipresence, and eternity, which, as we see it, have loomed so large in dogmatics more because of their Greek than their biblical roots.

Many handbooks on dogmatics that have appeared after Barth start from these viewpoints as explicated by Barth. See Brunner, *Dg* I, pp. 241–247; *MS* V, IV; Trillhaas, *Dg* pp. 119–132; Weber, *Gl* I, pp. 450–508, and (to a lesser extent) Althaus, *CW* II, pars. 25–27. But later the tendency arose to glean God's characteristics even more from the relationships of his condescension: from the covenant with Israel, as in H. M. Kuitert, *De mensvormigheid Gods* (1962); from the nature and content of prayer, as in G. Ebeling, *Dogmatik,* I (1979), par. 9 G; or even more radically, as in "process theology," from the processes in nature and life, in which God is the player who changes right along with the world; see, e.g., C. Hartshorne, *The Divine Relativity* (2nd ed. 1964), ch. III, and J. B. Cobb, *A Christian Natural Theology* (1966). This may not leave enough room for the confession "deus semper maior." The consequences would be fatal, for only as the Wholly Other can the Condescendent One be salvation to us. His simplicity consists in this two-sidedness. A penetrating dialogue with the doctrine of God of process theology is carried on by W. Welker in *Universalität Gottes und Relativität der Welt* (1981).

21. HOLY LOVE

WE HAVE DEALT LONG ENOUGH in general and abstract terms with transcendence and condescendence, with revelation, being, and attributes. The usefulness of this discussion will depend on the concrete meaning we are able to give to these concepts. Perhaps nowhere in the world is a formal-material separation really possible, but certainly not where it concerns God's revelation. More than once, therefore, we found it necessary in the two preceding paragraphs to anticipate what we were going to say on this subject. But only now do we actually address ourselves to it. In this paragraph we may and must dare to speak not just about God's being but about his "character," and with that about what is the heart of the Christian faith. We do that by stating first of all that the high and holy God in his coming to us manifests himself as Love.

In paragraph 19 we inferred from the fact of revelation that God must be a communicative God. That, however, he could be in different ways. In view of our relation to him, communication could be in the form of a revelation of denunciations, even of wrath, perhaps even of hatred. In any case, one could conceive of the communication (as many in fact do) as a revelation of commandments, information about rules of conduct. In his communication God can manifest himself as an angry, an instructing, a commanding, or an inspiring God. But the amazing discovery faith puts us in touch with is that in his condescension God is above all the one who gives, the one who gives himself, the one whose aim it is to make man happy by making him share in the richness of his own being.

In these last words we attempt to describe what is usually called the love of God. They denote what is most amazing, incomprehensible, and marvelous in all our human existence, namely that we are supported and surrounded by a final reality which we may call Love. With this confidence our Christian faith and our Christian existence stand or fall. Here we stand at the center of everything, and thus also of our study of the faith. Everything yet to follow will be an elaboration of this wonderful reality.

In this paragraph we shall thus not try to survey the immense field that opens up when we come to know God as love. We are not concerned here with the wider circle but with its focal point. The Bible uses not only the word *love* but many other words as well, of which grace and mercy are the most important. We do not use those here because they refer especially to the concrete content of the relationship God enters into with us. Relative to our sin it is called grace; and relative to our need it is called mercy. But this paragraph is about the permanent attribute of God which comes to expression in this relationship and which is also a reality apart from need or guilt. For that attribute we have no better word than "love."

But the use of this word has its dangers, too. Like all revelational words, it is derived from the language of human experience. In that language "love" is a word covering a wide range of emotions and relationships, from the crassest form of greed to the most sublime form of self-sacrifice. Therefore current usage of the word cannot tell us what it means that God is love; only the revelation wherein God manifests himself as the one who loves can do that. Love as such is not divine in character; rather, God's basic character is that he is love, a most unique love, with which he gave himself to man in his covenant with Israel and in the life of Jesus Christ.

It is thus not possible to find the love of God by an infinite extension of what the word *love* means to us. But it is not accidental either that precisely this earthly word is needed to express what lives eternally in the depths of God's heart. In paragraph 14 we established that such words, applied to God, are "analogically adequate." They signal in what direction the reality we seek becomes visible. In the Bible the love of God is sometimes compared with that of a father or mother, then again with that of a husband or a friend. But at the same time it is made clear that God's love is only comparable to it and goes far beyond what we mean by these forms of love.

Deriving the nature of God's love from the story of his struggle with the people of Israel and from the Son who was prepared to die for a sinful world, one becomes impressed with the strangeness and incomparableness of this love. We characterized it as self-giving love. But that is still too pale when we realize what we have here. It is a love that stops for nothing, that is resolutely devoted to the other, however far away and hostile that other may be; it is a love which is unmotivated and for which no sacrifice is too great to enrich people who did not ask for it or even oppose it. For this strange and amazing attitude we have no better word than love. But what we normally think of with this word falls far short of what is actually found in God's heart.

"God as Holy Love—The dogmatic exposition of this doctrine of faith is rendered difficult by the very circumstance which constitutes its merit, namely that it is as inexhaustible as it is simple. . . . it makes it difficult in any single section like the one before us, to say what is most necessary, without unnecessary repetition in other places" (Haering, *The Christian Faith,* Vol. I, pp. 337f.). This observation holds for many handbooks. For rather good treatments see Barth, *CD* II,1, par. 30, esp. 1; Althaus, *CW* II, pars. 25–27; Brunner, *Dg* I, chs. 14–15; Weber, *Gl* I, pp. 466–483.

The Bible witnesses to God's holy love in many passages. It is found especially 1 John 4:7–19. There we find the well-known *ho theos agapē estin* and passion of Jesus. Sometimes it is held that in the OT the love of God appears only dimly and that only in the NT does it shine forth in its true brightness. But that is a faulty formulation of the difference between OT and NT. In the OT we see especially the covenant love of God for his chosen people; in the NT, in and through Christ, this love receives a more radical, universal, and individual expression. In the OT the love of God is movingly proclaimed especially in the psalms and many of the prophets. Note Psalm 25 or 103, Hosea, esp. 1–3, Deutero-Isaiah, and Deuteronomy with its conscious theological use of *'āhaḇ* and *'^{a}hāḇâ.* In the NT this theological use is found most frequently in John; see especially 1 John 4:7–19. There we find the well-known *ho theos agapē estin* (v. 8), which, to be sure, is not to be taken as a definition (God "is" also "spirit" and "light"), but according to the context is certainly meant to express the ultimate truth about God. Note how much John is aware that he derives this love from God's saving work in history (see the two verses that follow; cf. John 3:16). Paul, too, frequently reflects on the love of God. The "hymn of love," 1 Cor. 13, must in the first place be understood as a description of God's disposition toward us as this became manifest in Christ. See further, *inter alia,* Rom. 5:5ff.; 8:31–39. Cf. also *TDNT* I, *s.v. agapaō* (more because of the passages than the discussion itself). One should note, however, that in the Bible the love of God is by no means expressed only by *'^{a}hāḇâ* or *agapē.* In the OT, e.g., it is also expressed in words like *b^{e}rîṯ, mišpāṭ, ḥeseḏ, ḥēn, ṣ^{e}ḏāqâ,* etc.

As regards the symbolism and analogy, already in the OT God's love is repeatedly compared with the love of a father (e.g., in Deut. 32:6; Ps. 103:13; Isa. 66:13). Following Jesus and on his authority, the NT refers to God primarily as "Father"; also to Israelite ears the name *abba* had the ring of an unusual intimacy. At the same time the comparison in Matt. 7:9–11 and the parable of the prodigal son (Luke 15) prove how far the fatherhood of God exceeds that of an earthly father. Israel's being called a foundling (Ezek. 16:5) and Paul's calling believers God's children by adoption (Rom. 8:15, 23; Gal. 4:5) also emphasize the distinct quality of the fatherhood of God. The self-sacrificial love of Jesus can be compared with that of a friend (John 15:13), but as love for those who are enemies it far exceeds that analogy (Rom. 5:7f.). The prophets like to compare God's love with that of a man for his wife, but because of the continual unfaithfulness of this wife, Israel, God's love also transcends this analogy (Jer. 3; Ezek. 16 and 23; esp. Hos. 1–3). In his love God is also likened to a mother. See, e.g., Isa. 66:13 and Jas. 1:18. But God's love also transcends this love; see Isa. 49:15. The emphasis on the mother image by feminist theology is useful in removing despotic traits from the father image. But if this emphasis leads to a misconception of the transcendent authority of God's love, it is subject to the danger that was pointed out in the last few sentences of par. 20.

In church history we face the remarkable fact that the love of God, which is, of course, the subject of endless discussion, reflection, and song, is hardly the central and overwhelming subject in the church's confession and instruction. The best in this respect are the Eastern churches who owe their Johannine reputation especially to the central place they give to *agapē*. That this is not the case in the Western churches is likely due to more than one factor. We in the West are more inclined than the East to relate God directly to everyday reality in which often little is seen of his love. Not only does the absurd trouble us, but the question of guilt receives much more attention in the West. Add to that the Scholastic elaboration of the Greek concept of God, and it will be clear that there was much to mute the doxology to God's love. In the Protestant churches, moreover, the question concerning the relation of God's love to his just anger and punishing justice played a large role. Later the combination with modern philosophy had an unfavorable effect on the (personalizing) understanding of God as the one who loves. See the abstract treatment of this theme in Schleiermacher at the end of *CF* pars. 165–167 (par. 165 reads: "The divine causality presents itself to us in the government of the world as love and as wisdom"). For Ritschl the love of God is only the means to bring about the moral world order, the Kingdom of God. "Love is the constant purpose to further another spiritual being of like nature with oneself in the attainment of his authentic destiny *(Bestimmung)*, and in such a way that the one who loves in so doing pursues his own proper end *(Selbstzweck)*" *(Unterricht in der christlichen Religion,* 1875, par. 12d). In Tillich as well, who defines God as Being itself, the concept of the love of God has only a minor and symbolic role: "If we say that God *is* love, we apply the experience of separation and reunion to the divine life" (*ST* p. 280). Each of these is a good example of how, respectively, the philosophies of German Idealism, Kant, and Heidegger are obstacles that prevent the heart of the gospel from coming through loud and clear. Unfortunately, they are more the rule than the exception. Of course there are others too, such as T. Haering mentioned above. From the previous century should be mentioned especially F. D. Maurice, who on the basis of Christ's oneness with God wanted to see the latter exclusively as "an abyss of love," even going so far as to see self-sacrifice as God's essence. As to its consequences, Maurice reminds us strikingly of Barth. See on this spiritual affinity E. Flesseman-van Leer, *De overmacht van de liefde: Inleiding in de theologie van F. D. Maurice* (1968).

It was Barth, *CD* II,1, who finally gave the confession of God's love the central place it should have in dogmatics, through his definition of God as the one who loves in freedom and by the consistency with which he made this insight the methodological basis of his thinking. Since then other theologians have done the same. But there are others, too, who do not follow him in this (Prenter, Trillhaas, Ebeling). We seem to find it very difficult to believe and accept with heart and mind the wonder of God's love.

The love of God is infinitely more than what we call love in earthly relationships. It is as much more and different as God is more and different than man. He is the subject who determines the content of this love. The concept of love does not determine what God is, but God determines what love is. He is the subject and love the predicate. These two are not interchangeable. To express the uniqueness and divine character of this love we add a further qualification and speak of God as *holy* love. In this way we express the unity of his transcendence and condescendence. This was already presupposed in the preceding discussion, but it needs a separate discussion, too, in which we speak of holiness as the attribute of God which further defines his love. Now, too, our concern is not so much the manner in which this attribute manifests itself in God's relationship to us; we shall thus, for example, speak only about "righteousness" and "wrath" insofar as they shed light on the essence of God himself which is the basis of these relations. We thus ask strictly: what does it mean that God's love is holy love, that is, that it comes from a God who in this love acts as the one who is completely sovereign and free? A simple answer is not possible. We present various aspects of it in the following points:

1. The love of God is the coming and bending down to us of the infinitely high God. In a manner and measure that is without earthly analogies it is, therefore, a love from the higher to the lower, and so a love which indeed bridges the gap, yet in that bridging not only presupposes the gap but also confirms it. Already for that reason alone man can experience it only as an undeserved and unexpected favor. Here we hit upon one of the limits of our analogical symbols. Comparing God's love with that of a father or mother, or that of a husband or friend (these are the four analogies that occur in the Bible), it is precisely this element of a basic difference that we cannot express in these comparisons.

2. In this love God acts freely. He is and gives himself fully in it. We cannot say that God needs us as objects and partners of his love, for example, to relieve his loneliness, to have someone to share his love with, or to be enriched himself by a partner. As soon as we would ascribe such motives to God, his sovereign and gracious turning toward us, as we witness it in his revelation, would lose its luster and power. But we cannot say the reverse either. For then in the depth of his heart God would not be related to his creatures; then our situation would not touch him *essentially.* All we can do is note with amazement that his freedom coincides with his love, his ability with his willing. Apparently he wants to be able to do nothing else than be our covenant partner.

3. That in his love God gives himself to us implies that he does not deny himself in his turning toward us. He remains himself. If this were not so we would not experience the love of God himself, but that of a God who had changed himself into this love. In order to really love us and give himself to us in his love it is necessary that God does not abandon himself but fully maintains himself, precisely in his being God, his transcendence, his holiness. Only by fully maintaining himself can he fully give himself. The reverse is likewise true: by giving himself he fully maintains himself.

4. In the Bible it is as the one who loves that God is called a jealous God. The holiness of his love means that in his love he really and fully wants us for himself, that he wants to be fully with us in the oneness and exclusiveness of his divine being and wants to be accepted by us. This meets with our resistance because we want to belong to other powers as well, and especially to ourselves. God's holy love cannot acquiesce in that. It cannot tolerate opposition. It crosses our path to break our resistance. In his jealous love God demands our total surrender to fellowship with him.

5. This jealousy is the negative side of the purpose which in his love he has with us. He not only wants to be present in our life, but being present he wants to change and renew that life. He wants us to look like him and to imitate his holiness and his love. We imitate his love if we choose just as unmotivatedly for others, even our enemies, as God has chosen for us. And we are representatives of his holiness if we give full play to God's otherness in our lives and acknowledge his priority. But holiness and love are inseparably one. God's otherness is the otherness of his fatherhood, of his name, of the revelation of his love which through us wants to make its way in the world. Therefore we pray in word and deed:

> Our Father who art in heaven,
> Hallowed be thy name.

"God's loving is a divine being and action distinct from every other loving in the fact that it is holy. As holy, it is characterized by the fact that God, as He seeks and creates fellowship, is always the Lord. He therefore distinguishes and maintains His own will as against every other will" (Barth, *CD* II,1, p. 359).

It is especially because of the widely read book of R. Otto, *The Idea of the Holy* (E.T. 1928), that the concept of holiness is not in the first place regarded as a moral quality, but as expressing the fact that God is wholly other, the numinous, the majestic *mysterium tremendum* which is at the same time *fascinans.* In the OT, too, the words *qōḏeš* and *qaḏōš* denote first of all God's unapproachable majesty. In older texts this majesty is still closely bound up with taboo ideas as we know them from primitive and ancient religions (see Lev. 10:1–5; 1 Sam. 6:19f.). The classical passage on the holiness of God in Isaiah 6, the vision of the calling of Isaiah, is completely free from such ideas. This prophet's favorite name for God is "the Holy One of Israel." The addition "of Israel" reminds us that it is precisely in his turning toward us, in his nearness, that this awesome exaltedness of God is experienced (see e.g. Ex. 15:11; Ezek. 20:41). Especially in Deutero-Isaiah it is clear that as the Holy One of Israel he is the redeemer *(go'ēl)* (41:14; 43:3, 14; 47:4). Reversing the emphasis, Ezekiel says the same: "Thus says the Lord God: It is not for your sake, O house of Israel, that I am about to act, but for the sake of my holy name, which you have profaned among the nations to which you came" (36:22; see all of 22–32). The deepest expression of the unity of holiness and love is given by Hosea: "for I am God and not man, the Holy One in your midst, and I will not come to destroy" (11:9). In the cultic tradition the awareness was very strong that it is characteristic of holiness that it wants to take possession of men and to sanctify them (see 5 above). This is especially evident from the so-called law of holiness, Lev. 17–26, esp. Lev. 19, where Israel is called to a new way of life because of God's otherness, God's holiness. For the concept of holiness in the OT see especially the biblical theologies of Eichrodt and Vriezen.

Terminologically the holiness of God is not prominent in the NT. Jesus is sometimes called "the Holy One of God" and the Spirit throughout is called the Holy Spirit. In this closest nearness to men, God's holiness manifests itself. Because of the work of the Holy Spirit all the emphasis falls now on man's participation in the holy love of God through his imitation of Christ and sanctification of God's name. As participants in this reality believers themselves are now called "holy." But one can sense that the numinous holiness of God in the OT remains the background, and in passages such as Heb. 12:29; 1 Pet. 1:15f., and Rev. 4:8 it is clearly expressed. For the concept of holiness in the NT see *TDNT* I, *s.v. hagios.* See further par. 47.

In the theology of recent decades, the subject of the love of God as a holy and thus entirely unique kind of love has been repeatedly discussed in the form of the theme of the relation of *erōs* and *agapē.* The Greek *erōs,* which ranges in meaning from sensuous desire to mystical ecstasy, expresses man's desire for another human being or object by means of which he hopes to find satisfaction or the enrichment of his own self. The Septuagint was unable to use this word for the OT concept of love, and therefore adopted as the equivalent of *'ahăḇâ* (because of the similarity in sound) the less common and weaker term *agapē* (*agapan:* to "like" someone or something), and so this became a key word in the NT. Building on this fact, A. Nygren constructed his great work *Agape and Eros* (E.T. I [1932], II [1938–39]). Systematically and historically he contrasts the eros which is egocentric and enriches itself from the value of its object, and the agape which selflessly gives itself away to what has no value. Several theologians and philosophers have followed him in this contrast. Nygren's starting-point is no doubt correct. As holy love, the love of God which gives itself away is *sui generis.* But he misses the mark when he posits an absolute contrast between this love and the human eros which is regarded as sinful. It must mean something that in the Bible the love of God is regularly expressed in symbols which are derived from the human eros: marriage, parenthood, friendship. It seems to me that this indicates that the love of God is not only viewed as unmotivated, giving itself away, but also and precisely as realizing itself. In his giving away of himself God realizes himself. Nygren noticed correctly a great difference, but incorrectly a gap. Agape and eros are reconciled in God. Therefore in man a purified eros must be reconcilable with agape. (See *RGG* II, *s.v. Eros und Agape;* to the literature there has to be added Barth, *CD* IV,2, pp. 734–751.) In my judgment a proper correction on Nygren (and Barth) is E. Jüngel, *Gott als Geheimnis der Welt,* pp. 436ff. and 461ff. (See further *RGG, s.v. Eros und Agape.*)

It might seem that we have now rounded off our subject. For we have presented God's holy love as a vital unity in God which is to be seen from two perspectives, from his condescendence and from his transcendence.

But reality makes such a rounding off impossible. On the contrary, at this point we are faced with the most difficult question. Everything would run smoothly if the holy will of God's love would manifest itself so forcefully or would everywhere be so gratefully accepted by man that a serious and permanent resistance against this will would be out of the question. But the opposite is the case. No matter how well man is suited for this love, in the presence of this unique, unasked for, and jealous love man turns out to be an enemy and a rebel. In the encounter God wants to give himself to man as holy love. But if man refuses this encounter, then God, if he still wants to encounter man, will have to manifest himself in another way and will have to deal in a different way with man, in a manner that will make man realize his situation and force him to turn around. But how else is God to relate himself to us? If there is change in the way in which he continues to give his love, regardless of our refusal, it does not become manifest that it is God's love which we reject. And if God rejects us forever because of our refusal, his attitude is determined by ours and his love fails to reach its goal. Either God abandons himself, or he abandons us, or he does both. The conflict with man who is hostile to him seems inevitably to lead to a conflict in God. And this is indeed the strong impression which we get from the historical and prophetic witnesses in the Old Testament. There we find a continuous alternation between God's grace and his justice, between his wrath and his love. This is a movement that does not seem to be able to come to a stop. The collision with rebellious man seems to cause a split in the being of God, a holy justice on the one hand and an indulgent grace on the other. In the New Testament this polarization is much less strong. Yet there, too, it is everywhere noticeable. God is a consuming fire for those who resist his purposes. For the sake of his holiness there is somewhere a limit to his love. It is understandable that as a result of this supposed or real contrast in God as concerns his relation to sinful man, the testimony to God's love has often sounded much less clearly in the life, confession, and thinking of the church and believers than might have been expected with so central a theme. Many find it difficult to get away from the idea that God is undependable and arbitrary, and this keeps them from fully surrendering themselves to the joyful message of God's love.

That is then due to a great misunderstanding. The gospel leaves no doubt whatsoever that we may surrender ourselves in complete confidence to the gracious love of God. Only when we refuse to do that do we become the guilty victims of a duality in God. We are then confronted with his justice in which he claims the refusing person for himself, and with his wrath by which he accompanies our estrangement. But these are and remain the expressions of his holy love. God meets us here as injured love, by which he tries to make us aware of our estangement in order to induce us to surrender to his love. The exemplary history of God's association with man in the Old and New Testament is one continuous announcement of that fact. This story culminates in the death and resurrection of Jesus Christ where holiness and mercy come together: the one righteous Man bears vicariously the estrangement of all, and thus bridges the gap. But then, too, grace is not turned into a principle or ideology. It does not come automatically. In the encounter God respects his partner; whoever rejects his grace chooses to remain under his wrath.

But neither are believers free from this dialectic. For they, too, try repeatedly to free themselves from the dominion of his grace. Mirrored and refracted in our guilty existence, the oneness of God's holy love can never become clearly and permanently visible. But to believe means always that in spite of what we experience, there is this oneness in the great Partner. His unconditional and limitless love are also operative in his hiddenness, his judgment, and his wrath.

The final question to come up then is this: will this oneness of God as it relates to man not eventually triumph over every dialectic and division? Can God acquiesce in the fact that his rebelling partners force him to perpetuate his attitude of wrath forever? This question can be discussed only at the end, in paragraph 58. Here it is sufficient for us to know that, however much the light of God's being is refracted and obscured in the prism of the revelational encounter, this refraction nevertheless bears witness that God is the one light of holy love.

One should consider here, side by side, two biblical statements: "With the loyal thou dost show thyself loyal . . . and with the crooked thou dost show thyself perverse" (Ps. 18:25f.), and "if we deny him, he also will deny us; if we are faithless, he remains faithful" (2 Tim. 2:12f.).

What was said above is closely connected with the way in which the words "righteousness" and "wrath" function in the OT and NT. Especially the concept *righteousness* has been the subject of much discussion after H. Cremer (mentioned on p. 125) again placed it in the context of God's covenantal acts and described it as *iustitia salutifera*. We refer to the biblical theologies. This writer is here and elsewhere in this chapter guided mainly by W. Eichrodt, *Theology of the OT*, I (E.T. 1961) with its lengthy and thorough discussion of "The Nature of the Covenant God" (pars. 6 and 7). See also *TDNT* II, *s.v. dikaiosynē*. Applied to God, the OT words for justice and righteousness (*ṣeḏeq, sᵉḏāqâ, mišpāṭ*) denote what God does as the consequence of the covenant relationship he has entered into with Israel. Directed to the outside it means the defense against and the conquering of Israel's enemies (the earliest use is *ṣiḏᵉqôṯ*, Judg. 5:11); directed inwards it is living up to the covenant promises, especially toward the poor and the helpless, but also when necessary punishing and opposing all who despise their covenant obligations (contra Von Rad, *OT Theology*, I, E.T. 1962, p. 377). Because God's righteousness is thus primarily his active covenant faithfulness, the word occurs *passim* as a parallel of favor, mercy, and the like. In later years the word also (and particularly) came to denote God's covenant faithfulness toward sinful man, especially in Deutero-Isaiah (but see also Ps. 51:16; 143:1), where even the hiphil *hiṣḏîq*, to declare righteous on the ground of the covenant statutes, is applied to people who are declared guilty (50:8; 53:11). After the exile this unity of grace and righteousness was very much lost; God's righteousness was generally conceived of as *iustitia distributiva* which rewards the keepers of the law and punishes transgressors—an element which is not absent from the central witnesses of the OT, yet is secondary in its relation to God's gracious covenant faithfulness. This latter element was not entirely forgotten, as is evident from some of the hymns of the Qumran community (see especially song 8). But not until Paul is Deutero-Isaiah's use of the term resumed and deepened: "For I am not ashamed of the gospel: it is the power of God for salvation to everyone who has faith, to the Jew first and also to the Greek. For in it the righteousness of God is revealed through faith for faith" (Rom. 1:16f.). Interpreters are still not agreed whether Paul's use of "righteousness of God" refers to an attribute of God by which he acts according to justice (genitive of possession) or to something which he gives to man (genitive of origin). In our judgment both are implied. In any case, it is clear that in Paul "righteousness" definitely refers to salvation and redemption. See especially Paul's handling of the word *dikaios* and its derivatives in Rom. 3:21–26. That shows that the element of judgment is not absent, yet that this judgment is turned into grace through Christ's reconciling death and that precisely in this way God's righteousness triumphs (see esp. 25f. and beside it passages such as Rom. 4:25; 8:3; 2 Cor. 5:21).

As such the word *wrath* lacks this positive covenantal ring (see the extensive discussion in *TDNT* V, *s.v. orgē*). But in Israel's mature religious consciousness its meaning was quite different from that in other religions where the wrath of the gods indicates arbitrariness which can be countered by magic and sacrifices. Wrath may not be confused with hatred; it speaks of a violation of the covenant, and it is an expression of the injured love of God. False prophets sought to appease the people with a cheap divine grace. Therefore the true prophets had to confront them with the wrath of God (Amos 9:10; Isa. 5:18ff., and *passim*). Yet that is never their final word. Hosea, Jeremiah, and Ezekiel, who can speak so incisively about God's wrath, also know that God's final word, the word which best expresses his deepest nature, is love. "But, though he cause grief, he will have compassion according to the abundance of his steadfast love" (Lam. 3:32). "For his anger is but for a moment, and his favor is for a lifetime" (Ps. 30:5). "In overflowing wrath for a moment I hid my face from you, but with everlasting love I will have compassion on you" (Isa. 54:8). However, this cannot be made into a closed theory, as certainly as this is the articulation of a free favor, a holy love. Therefore for those in Israel and among the surrounding nations who permanently resist Yahweh there will be a judgment of wrath which will be a final word. The NT speaks similarly about wrath, but with this difference, that the wrath of God is removed from everyone who trusts in the atoning sacrifice of Christ. Here, too, it is not a theoretically closed case. The NT speaks of an eschatological judgment of wrath upon unbelievers and of a hell for those who have known Christ and consciously rejected him (Matt. 25; Rom. 2:8; 1 Thess. 2:16; Heb. 12:25–29). But then wrath is still as it were something that is forced upon God as the reverse side of his (spurned) love. See also John 3:17f. and 36: "He who believes in the Son has eternal life; he who does not obey the Son shall not see life, but the wrath of God rests upon him."

In the course of the church's history many have thought about the relation of love and justice in God. Under the influence of Roman law which interpreted *iustitia* distributively, as *suum cuique tribuere,* the Middle Ages interpreted the word *righteousness* for the most part one-sidedly along this line. This made it a fearful word for Luther, until Rom. 1:16f. opened his eyes and made him see its saving meaning. By itself this might have led Luther to emphasize the oneness of God in his judgment and grace. Such did not happen, however, because of Luther's permanent dread before the majesty of the *Deus absolutus* who, for him, stands in a relation of great tension to the *Deus revelatus, absconditus sub contrario.* See on this par. 19. The tension between transcendence and condescendence is so great in Luther that he often moves on the edge (even going over it) of a duality and contrast in God: on the one hand the God of majesty, of the creation order, the law, the *iustitia distributiva,* the *opus alienum,* the rule of the world; on the other hand the God of love, reconciliation, the gospel, justification, the *opus proprium,* the Kingdom of God. Yet Luther, too, knew of a final unity in which love embraces both wrath and the gospel, much like a good prince who needs weapons and armor-bearers because of his enemies. "But in his hall and castle are nothing but pure grace and love, though the other is necessary for what lies outside. . . . So also in grace there is no wrath and displeasure, and his heart and his thoughts are nothing but pure love" (sermon on 1 John 4:16ff.). But that is a final perspective. We are urged to flee from the angry to the gracious God.

Protestant Scholasticism has not maintained this tremendous tension and deep concern in Luther. What remained was a juxtaposition in God of *iustitia* and *misericordia.* Despite Luther's discovery the concept *iustitia* is again used entirely in the traditional sense of "demanding justice." Well known is the definition from the Lutheran Quenstedt: "It is the highest, unchangeable rule of the divine will, exacting from the rational creature what is right and just" (S p. 80). In the wake of Calvin, the Reformed were more careful in contrasting justice and mercy, but this was without practical significance because, like the later Calvin, they shifted the dualism in God to the doctrine of the eternal decree. Typical of this dualism is the definition of Hottinger (H VIII): "It is predestination of men by which out of the whole human race to be created and about to fall God foreordained some to life eternal, others to death eternal." Note also in H VII Beza's scheme with respect to the decrees. Both these theologians are supralapsarians. But the infralapsarian Belgic Confession is no improvement when, in art. 16, it ascribes the salvation of part of mankind to the mercy of God and the fact that God passes by "others" to his justice. Even more than the Lutherans, the Reformed through their doctrine of predestination have eternalized the duality in God. That has caused much uncertainty and has robbed many Christians of the joy of the Christian faith.

Sooner or later Luther's rediscovery of the biblical usage had to cause a reaction. It came late and, in turn, was one-sided. Ritschl was the one who saw the revolutionary significance of the fact that in the Bible justice and grace often coincide. This led him to eliminate every notion of retribution from the idea of righteousness and to make it coincide with God's forgiveness. Yet he could not completely eliminate the idea of God's wrath: he left it, however, only an eschatological function: those who resist God's will of love to the end will be destroyed. See his main work *The Christian Doctrine of Justification and Recon-*

ciliation, esp. II (E.T. 1902) on righteousness, pars. 14 and 15; and on wrath, pars. 16–21. Today the one-sidedness of Ritschl's presentation is generally recognized. In contrast to this exclusive emphasis on love, the orthodox Lutheran doctrinal tradition tends to systematize the duality in God which Luther so deeply experienced. A striking example is R. Prenter, *Creation and Redemption* (E.T. 1967), esp. pars. 17 and 32.

Lutheran theology is inclined to think from the duality which one experiences in God to the unity. Reformed theology is more inclined to do the reverse. Calvin wrestles with this question in connection with the relation of justice and love in the reconciling work of Christ (*Inst* II,xvi and xvii). Is God apart from Christ an angry God and only since Christ a gracious God? That is impossible. His love for us is from eternity. "Indeed, because he first loved us, he afterwards reconciles us to himself" (xvi,3). There is a disagreement, but not in God himself, but between his righteousness and our sin: "perpetuum et irreconciliabile dissiduum inter iustitiam et iniquitatem." To remove this, reconciliation in Christ is necessary. Only in this way can God's eternal love reach its goal. Here we are in a different climate than with Luther. On account of these pages which start from the unity of God as love, the Lutherans have opposed him, Socinus has supported him, and Calvin later by way of clarification added II,xvii, without, however, changing his standpoint. Yet nothing has come of this insight of Calvin and, as we saw, it also remained barren in later Reformed Scholastic theology, because his doctrine of the eternal double decree of election and reprobation (*Inst* III,xxi–xxiv) introduced a duality in God which is much more open to criticism than that of the Lutherans, since one can flee from the angry to the gracious God but not from the one eternal decree to the other.

In the Reformed tradition Barth has tried to continue from Calvin's starting-point and maintain the unity of God, also where it concerns his eternal decree, as the unity of holy love. See with respect to the doctrine of God esp. *CD* I, par. 30,2: "God's Mercy and Justice." Barth wants to maintain the unity of both without all too easily identifying them in the fashion of Ritschl. Due to God's holiness there is also a *iustitia distributiva,* wrath and judgment upon sin. God remains faithful to himself and to man by taking this judgment upon himself in Christ. Since then this judgment is for us a matter of the past. All preaching of judgment in the Bible is meant to make us aware of the judgment we had deserved but from which we have escaped through Christ. That is how Barth attempts to incorporate the duality of God toward us in the unity. But in order to do that he closes off what remains open in the NT; there the judgment is borne by Christ, yet it is not a finished matter because it remains a future reality for all who reject his sacrifice.

Starting from opposite directions, Lutherans and Reformed wrestle with the same problem. They need each other. God is not indulgently lenient, but not schizophrenic either. He is one. "But this unity . . . is not a unity which can be rationally expressed in a consistent concept of God" (Prenter, *Creation and Redemption,* p. 420). If anywhere, we are aware here how much we are still on the way and can only be engaged in *theologia viatorum.* We live yet in the *dissiduum.* God cannot yet be fully himself toward us in the harmony of his being. But we are on the way toward it. For God as unambiguous holy love is also the source of the whole work of redemption.

Everything we have said in this paragraph makes it imperative that we now speak about God as a person. In modern studies of the faith a separate paragraph or chapter is often devoted to this theme. In our case this would result in a repetition of much that was said before. Yet it is necessary that we specifically take up this subject, more or less as an appendix to the previous subject, because precisely the rejections, the vacillations, and the arguments around the statement "God is a person" shed a clear light on the problems with which the doctrine of God is burdened, especially in our modern times. What we shall say about the application of the word *person* to God is entirely based on what we said in paragraph 14 about the symbolic language of revelation.

We know God through meeting him. This word is derived from the world of personality. God may be infinitely higher than we are, but when we meet him he gives himself as a person to persons. In whatever way he may be more than what the word *person* suggests to us, there is no way that he can be less, and in everything in which he is more he can in no way be different.

Assuming this, further reflection leads, however, to difficult questions which we cannot avoid. For what, exactly, do we understand by "person"? For centuries person was defined as "individual." But God is not an individual among others, each with his individual limitations. Later *person* was preferably defined as the "I" or the "awarensss of self." But the "I" is aware of itself relative to what is not the I. God, however, is not a person relative to something else. A similar objection can be raised against the designation "subject" on account of its polar relation to the concept "object." In our age we emphasize especially that a person is a "being of dialogue" and that man becomes a person only in being addressed, in being listened to and responding. But of God we cannot say that he becomes a person only through his relationship to us. These considerations make it understandable why many philosophers and theologians are inclined to deny personality to God; all the more so when we think of the propensity of children to personify whatever they do not understand—which might seem to indicate that intellectually mature people would also have to rise above this stage in the God concept they hold.

Precisely this reminder of the tendency to personify, however, must urge us to be careful here. Children personify whatever holds a secret and is off limits for them. When one matures, the area of things which are personified shrinks until only real persons remain. In that case God belongs as such to the world of persons. For he is pre-eminently the sovereign and free one whom we cannot appropriate for our own ends. Therefore to use impersonal designations for him would be to misapprehend the essence of his deity as this comes to us in the revelational encounter. Because the language of this world is the only one we have, we have only "it" and "he/she" words, which are derived, respectively, from the world of things and of persons. Neither of the two is adequate, but in distinction from the first group the last-named category may be regarded as "analogically adequate," as we have called it in par. 14. This implies that God is infinitely more than what we know of human personality, but also that we may correctly ascribe to him whatever in the world of persons is more than the world of things: self-consciousness, freedom, the ability to enter into fellowship with others; in brief: being a subject.

If this is so, we may no longer say that we are persons in the real sense and God only in a kind of figurative sense. This thesis will have to be turned around. God is subject in a divine and absolute sense. As created in that image, we too are subjects, in a derivative, creaturely way. We are not subjects in the absolute sense. We do not even know what that is. Our subjectivity is dependent on other persons and limited by the objective world in which we are rooted and of which we are a part with our psychosomatic existence. Thus the belief in the personality of God shows us where we stand as persons. This is at the same time a liberating and encouraging faith. If we had to think of God after the analogy of the "it"-world, our personality would be an anomaly in an impersonal universe, a happenstance result of a blind evolutionary process. We may, however, believe, on the basis of a personal and personalizing revelation, that our personality answers an eternal purpose and that we are destined for encounter, dialogue, and answerability.

More than once the thought has been expressed that it was Christian thinking (Christology, the doctrine of the Trinity) that provided the stimulus for the concept of "person," and that it was only through the relation with the personal God that man's personality was discovered. The beginning of this discovery would then have been Augustine's *Confessions,* and ever since it would have remained an inalienable part of Western culture. How far this thesis is tenable in its cultural-historical perspective needs closer investigation. For centuries the definition given by the Christian philosopher Boethius (ca. 500) was the generally accepted one: "A person is an indivisible essence endowed with a rational nature." In this definition the person is still very much the expression of the general genre of that part of nature which possesses the gift of reason. The Middle Ages expressed the personality or subjectivity of God with two characteristic words: *aseitas* (God is *a se,* his own ground, unconditioned subject) and *actus purus* (in Aristotelian language God is pure actuality; there is no unrealized potentiality in him). Not until and after Kant and Romanticism did the concept of the (human) personality *(Persönlichkeit)* come to stand central as the self-conscious opposite of the objectifiable world of things. As regards the concept of God, one could go in two directions with this perspective. Following Spinoza's "omnis determinatio est negatio," German Idealism regarded the concept of personality as inapplicable to the deity, which was conceived of as absolute Reason. This line was also followed by theologians like Strauss, Biedermann, and Lipsius (who were especially influenced by Hegel). In contrast, for the majority of theologians the ascription of the personality concept to God became precisely the shibboleth of good theology over against Idealistic-pantheistic thought on the one hand and naturalistic-atheistic thought on the other. In the Netherlands this was especially the stance of so-called ethical theology; see J. H. Gunning, *Spinoza en de idee der persoonlijkheid* (1876).

Under different names, this contrast continues in the 20th century. The idea of autonomous man who is free, has come of age, and has manipulative ability cannot be harmonized with the idea of an absolutely free Subject; that would threaten our subjectivity, if not destroy it. Particularly in Existentialism (Sartre) a divine and a human self are seen as competitors.

In theology it is especially Tillich who, though on different grounds, does not want to see God designated as a person. For if God is Being itself, he transcends "the polarity of individualization and participation" (and "personality includes individuality"). Therefore, "the polarities of being disappear in the ground of being, in being-itself." Yet we cannot do without the symbol of a "personal God." "It means that God is the ground of everything personal and that he carries within himself the ontological power of personality. He is not a person, but he is not less than personal" (*ST* I, p. 245). On Tillich's views in this regard see also par. 14.

Diametrically opposed to this stands the personalistic (Jewish) theology of Buber. His great influence has been especially through his *I and Thou* (E.T. 1937). Among the Christian theologians in the Netherlands in this century we mention P. Kohnstamm, who stands in the tradition of ethical theology and who wrote *De heilige* (1931), and the moderately liberal G. J. Heering who wrote *De christelijke godsidee* (1945). Brunner is also a theological personalist, especially in his programmatic *Truth as Encounter* (E.T. 1964). That God's being-a-person does not threaten or exclude our personhood but instead presupposes and makes it possible is, following Buber, elaborately defended by H. Ott in *Der persönliche Gott* (1969).

There is much to be said against calling God a person. There is even more to be said against not doing it. With however much reluctance as concerns one's own point of view and with however much appreciation for the opposite position one takes a stand here, a choice must be made—not making a choice is a choice too—because it concerns the faith and theology in their totality. At stake is nothing less than whether one meets God as the one who loves in freedom (Barth) or experiences him as Being itself (Tillich).

Besides the literature already mentioned we refer to Barth, *CD* II,1, pp. 287–297 (with a detailed and critical discussion of the use of the concept of the personality of God in the 19th century); Althaus, *CW* par. 25; Brunner, *Dg* I, pp. 121–123, 139–141; *RGG* V, *s.v. Person* (by Pannenberg); H. Gollwitzer, *The Existence of God as Confessed by Faith* (E.T. 1965), pp. 183–201; H. Thielicke, *The Evangelical Faith,* II (E.T. 1977), ch. VII; and G. Ebeling, *Dogmatik,* I (1979), par. 9 B III.

22. THE DEFENSELESS SUPERIOR POWER

AFTER THE PREVIOUS PARAGRAPH, which is to be regarded as central in the discussion of the being of God, it is traditional to proceed to a longer or shorter treatment of the regular attributes, such as omnipresence, eternity, wisdom, and omnipotence. But most of these do not derive their reputation and position in the study of the faith from the fact that they suggest themselves to us by the encounter with the God of Israel, the Father of Jesus Christ; their background is rather the influence of a philosophical and one-sidedly transcendental concept of God which was abstracted from revelation. We are grateful that the theology of this century, particularly under the influence of Barth, tries to pour biblical content into these abstract concepts, or at least tries to bring them into relation with the biblical experience of revelation. But even then the strange provenance of these concepts remains noticeable. This tempts the dogmatician to go to strange territories. With the omnipresence of God he feels compelled to construct a philosophical conception of space, and with God's eternity to do something similar with time. With other attributes (wisdom, goodness, glory) he may in contrast easily repeat what was said elsewhere about God. For these reasons we do not regard ourselves as a priori obligated to discuss the traditional content of the doctrine of the attributes.

This does not, however, give us the right to set aside this entire content without a critical examination. Perhaps some of the terms that have been passed on raise questions which are of great significance for our relationship to God. The reverse is very well imaginable too, that because of the Greek philosophical orientation in the doctrine of the attributes some crucially significant virtues of God are generally not discussed; to that possibility today's theologian will also have to devote his attention.

As I see it, there are two regularly discussed divine attributes which may not be forgotten, and another two thus far barely discussed which deserve their own place. The first two are the omnipotence and the unchangeableness of God, and the other two, the defenselessness and the changeableness of God. It will be noted that taken as pairs they contradict or seem to contradict each other. This contrast is needed to bring out the content and the limitation of each concept.

We begin with the set, omnipotence and defenselessness. The general and popular idea is that in the biblical witness concerning God the emphasis is on God's omnipotence. But that is a great mistake. On the contrary, the first impression one gets from the biblical account of revelation is that of God's impotence, of how man has taken the initiative away from him, of what we shall call here his "defenselessness." By this we understand that attribute by which he leaves room for his "opposite" and accepts and submits himself to the freedom, the initiative, and the reaction of that "opposite." It has to do with the passive and receptive, the enduring and the suffering in God. The traditional doctrine of God had no place for this aspect, not even in the discussion of the patience or long-suffering of God, though it is very prominent in the Bible. We do not call this attribute the "impotence" of God. That would be a logical contradiction of the omnipotence of God. Defenselessness does not as such exclude an active exercise of power; it concerns the very special way in which God makes his power felt.

We meet this defenselessness already in creation. God steps back as it were by setting a world opposite himself. He gives it its own laws and dynamics, which he accepts with all its consequences. That is even more true in the case of man. He is created by God in his image, which implies at least that, analogical to God, he has the freedom to love and to exercise power. He can respond, be a counter-player, take the initiative, in fact on behalf of and under God even exercise dominion over a part of creation. In creating man, God as it were recedes (is it really "as it were?"—more about this later) to make room for another. That room is needed because the other is to be a partner whom God wants to meet and have fellowship with. One cannot be a real partner without having one's own area of freedom and initiative. In giving this room, with all the attendant consequences, God relinquishes some of his power and makes himself more or less dependent.

How drastic this surrender of power is, also for God himself, is shown when man prefers to use his freedom to withdraw from the intended encounter and fellowship with God. That is *sin,* that man demands for himself the God-given room. Man becomes God's competitor instead of his partner. In the God-given space a life develops which is no longer determined by God's communion and authority. Here a definite limit has been put to the power of God. If he should be present beyond that boundary, he is present as the one who is hidden or angry or provoked or unrecognized, in a manner which we have called defenselessness. That is how we see him present in Israel, which he had chosen as the experimental garden of mankind. God's history with Israel is to a large degree the history of a God who sees his plans fail and who repeatedly must react to the hostile or at least disobedient initiative of his partner, without apparently having (or wanting to have) the power to force that partner to his will.

In accentuated form that defenselessness becomes visible when Jesus, renouncing all earthly power, becomes the victim of the indifference, the dislike, and even the hatred of his environment. This defenselessness reaches its nadir on the cross where he is unable to save himself, where God is silent, and where free and rebellious man triumphs over God.

But even after that the problematic of defenselessness continues. For as the Holy Spirit God must work with defenseless means, with the means of proclamation and persuasion. The Spirit, too, goes the way of the cross, because everywhere he is resisted and grieved. And where he wins human hearts for himself, there by sanctifying them he also molds them into the defenselessness of not avenging themselves, of turning the other cheek, of the preparedness to suffer.

We can think of so much in the OT that everything cannot possibly be mentioned here. God's defenselessness is the presupposition which pervades both the somber writing of history (especially of the Deuteronomist school) and the continual and usually futile calling and pleading of the prophets. Think especially of the laments of Yahweh in the prophets (e.g. Mic. 6:1–5; Mal. 1:2f., 6; 2:6; 3:8f.) and the bold expression that God "repented" of having created man (Gen. 6:6). In the NT this defenselessness is still more deliberately set forth: in several parables which picture God as a man who has gone on a journey and who is thus absent (Matt. 24:50; 25:14; Mark 12:1), in Jesus' refusal to establish his Kingdom by force (Matt. 26:51f.; Luke 22:38; John 6:15; 18:36), in his powerlessness and God-forsakenness on the cross (Mark 15:31f., 34), in man's power to resist the Holy Spirit (Acts 7:51, with a quote from Isa. 63:10) and even to quench him (1 Thess. 5:19), and in the exhortation to the believer never to avenge himself (Matt 5:38–42; Rom. 12:19–21; 1 Pet. 2:19–23). Recall also Jesus' powerless lament over Jerusalem (Matt. 23:37), the manner in which Paul pictures him as a powerless slave (Phil. 2:6–8), and the book of Revelation which presents him as a stranger who stands at the door and knocks (3:20). That is apparently how God is.

In the history of the church this element has had all too little influence, and in the history of theology it has been even less. The deepest cause is likely that this image of God does not satisfy our urge for security, and that the concomitant image of man does not satisfy our urge for maintaining ourselves. It was aided by the unfortunate circumstance that the Apostles' Creed mentions only one attribute of God, the "almighty." This one-sidedness works through till the present day in liturgy and catechesis. Moreover, especially with respect to theology, we should recall again the fatally one-sided emphasis on God's attributes of majesty at the expense of the attributes of condescendence. Even then, however, it remains puzzling why in the discussion of God's omnipotence during the Middle Ages so little thought was given to the limitation of God's power by the rebellion of man, while there was endless discussion about such abstract questions as whether God would be able to do everything he wants to (e.g. change 4 into 3, or make the past undone as if it had never happened) and how his unlimited power is related to what he evidently decided he wanted to do. Characteristic, also for many following centuries, is Thomas, *ST* I, q. 25: "De divina potentia." Thomas and the tradition after him do indeed know of a limitation: next to the *omnipotentia absoluta* there is, since the beginning of creation, an omnipotence of God which is partly determined by that creation, a *potentia ordinata* or *conditionata* (q. 25, art. 5, ad 1). At the end of the 16th century, when under the influence of the Renaissance and humanism man's freedom and autonomy were strongly asserted, this led, till far into the 17th century, to great tensions on the subject of the relation of God's omnipotence and human freedom. The Jesuit Molina came with his doctrine of the *scientia media,* which holds that God's foreknowledge is also determined by human initiative; this teaching was welcomed in Lutheran theology and, strangely, at first also found acceptance among the Reformed. On this teaching see Barth, *CD* II,1, pp. 567–586. The Pope ordered the controversy about it stopped in 1607. In Reformed theology a fierce conflict arose between Remonstrants and Counter-Remonstrants. The main point of dispute was whether or not man's free will can resist the grace of God. The Remonstrants affirmed this, appealing to Acts 7:51 (*Remonstrantie,* art. 4). Their view was condemned in the Canons of Dort III/IV, esp. 10–12. In both controversies (as in other disputes, e.g. around M. Amyraut) the problematic was of very limited scope, though far-reaching. For the question is whether, relative to God's election to salvation, there is room for independent initiative on the part of man.

Since the Enlightenment man's autonomy and being-of-age has come to receive an even stronger emphasis than it did in humanism and the Renaissance. This led a number of theologians to a more radical probing of the question of what was then sometimes called the "self-limitation of God." In Germany and England the so-called Kenotics (after Phil. 2:7, *heauton ekenōsen;* among others, G. Thomasius, F. H. R. Franck, C. Gore), who with respect to the incarnation and the human consciousness of Jesus taught such a self-limitation of God. This led them occasionally to strange speculations, while they did not always avoid turning the self-limitation into a kind of self-obliteration, thus missing what they were after. On Kenotic Christology see P. Althaus, *RGG* III, *s.v. kenosis,* and the thorough exposition in F. W. A. Korff, *Christologie,* I (1940), pp. 270–291. We also refer to F. D. Maurice (mentioned in par. 21), who regarded self-sacrifice as expressive of the fact that God is perfect love. In the Netherlands similar ideas were developed by ethical theology; see D. Chantepie de la Saussaye in *Ernst en Vrede,* III (1855), pp. 437–447, and J. H. Gunning in *Blikken in de openbaring,* II (1868), esp. III and IV on "The Majesty of God." In my judgment the purpose of these theologians was in principle correct. The criticism of their ideas often stemmed from the familiar, traditional one-sided concept of God. They themselves, however, occasioned misunderstanding because of the narrow scope of their concepts and their as yet unclear perception of the unity of being and revelation. In the 20th century these lines of thought were continued by such thinkers as Kohnstamm, in *De heilige,* and L. Ragaz, in *Die Botschaft vom Reiche Gottes* (1942; see the twelfth conversation). Ragaz' defense of the notion of a "world in becoming" is found back in the Roman Catholic *New Catechism* (E.T. 1969), which links the confession of omnipotence and that of a suffering and struggling God in a sinful world in process of becoming (pp. 492–500).

One might think that precisely Barth would have come with a profound reformulation of the doctrine of omnipotence on the ground of the union of power and powerlessness which we see in Christ. Remarkably this does not play a role in his long discussion of omnipotence (*CD* II,1, pp. 522–607) until nearly at the end. From the outset he works with the omnipotence concept of traditional Scholastic theology, which he finally qualifies and corrects from the perspective of the concept of love (pp. 597ff.), and which in reference to the crucified one (1 Cor. 1:24) makes him underscore reconciliation but not God's powerlessness and defenselessness (pp. 606f.). In contrast, H. Vogel dared to relate omnipotence and powerlessness dialectically to each other, though he worked it out insufficiently; see *Gott in Christo* (1951), pp. 359–361. In his prison letters Bonhoeffer went much further, even going so far as to present God in Christ as the victim of our autonomy and having come of age; recall the often-cited words: "The God who is with us is the God who forsakes us. . . . God lets himself be pushed out of the world on to the cross. He is weak and powerless in the world, and that is precisely the way, the only way, in which he is with us and helps us . . ." (*Letters and Papers from Prison,* E.T. 1971; letter of July 16, 1944). Next to Bonhoeffer, particularly the process philosophy of A. N. Whitehead and the process theology built upon it have carried forward this line of thought, from the conviction that God himself is participant in what happens in the world with all its ups and downs. Whitehead called God "the great companion—the fellow sufferer who understands" (*Process and Reality,* 1929, p. 488; see all of pp. 484–497).

So everywhere in revelation we meet a God who retreats to give us room in our rebellion against him. He is like the father who gives his possessions to his rebellious son (Luke 15). That is what we tried to say in the word *defenselessness.* Yet we have to say that this cannot be the final word, though it can be a first. It can provide an adjective, but not a noun. God would not be God, and we would not even have encountered him in the space which he has created for us and which we have reserved for ourselves, if his defenselessness would have been the defenselessness of powerlessness. The opposite is the case. The defenselessness is the expression of his superiority. He can yield because he knows that he will win. Therefore yielding is only the first visible sign of a movement which is rather the opposite of a retreat: a new and hidden active presence.

The creation of man means freedom for man and delegation of authority from God. But God keeps accompanying man as his sustainer and lawgiver. When man has fallen into sin, God does not abandon him but goes after him with his invitations and warnings, his favors and his judgments. In Israel he enters anyway into a covenant with man who is estranged from him, a covenant which man continually breaks through his disobedience, but which God in his faithfulness permanently maintains. This disobedience does, however, compel God to be present differently than was his intention. But he is never absent. He is present in his judgments when he allows his unfaithful covenant partner to walk his self-chosen path all the way to the bitter end. But when man has reached that end and stands there with empty hands, he discovers that God is there waiting for him as his redeemer. Therefore the whole Old Testament is full of praise for the "Lord of hosts" and for his mighty, redemptive acts.

In the life of Jesus, too, the aspects of power are certainly not lacking. On the one hand we think of the "authority" in his teaching which made a deep impression on his hearers, on the other hand of the "mighty works" which he did in healing the sick and driving out demons. Especially, however, in Christ's resurrection the superior power of God's presence manifests itself in the face of sin and death. And in the light of the resurrection the cross is shown to be not only the confirmation of man's power over God, but also and much more the opposite: the expression of a divine must and a sign of the power of God which was reconcilingly active in it.

Finally, the Holy Spirit in his own defenseless way is active with superior power. No matter how stubborn the resistance of the human heart, the Spirit is able to make of antagonists children of God through the power of forgiveness and renewal, and to give them a new birth unto faith, hope, and love. And no matter how worldwide the resistance may be, the Spirit is able to gather a people of God out of all nations and races and to make the gospel a leavening influence, also in secular culture.

All these experiences combined lead us to speak of God's defenseless superior power. If we look at his defenselessness in the world, we would almost call it impotence. And if we look at his superior power in the world, we would almost call it omnipotence. But when we look at how they relate to each other, we see that both terms are to be avoided. Unfortunately, however, the church, under the pressure of a wrong concept of God, has been on its guard against the first side but not against the other. She has emphatically taught the omnipotence of God and has thereby become responsible for far too much unnecessary acquiescence, rebelliousness, doubt, and unbelief. In the Bible the term "almighty" occurs only a few times and then in eschatological contexts. For the present we cannot use it. But we cannot do with less than the term "superior power." The legitimacy of this word cannot be derived from a weighing against each other of positive and negative phenomena in human existence. We dare to use it on the ground that the crucified Jesus is also the one who arose. Therein we meet the superior power of God's holy love. The consequence of that belief is the hope, that is, the certain expectation that some day this love will melt away all resistance and will then be almighty, because then our God-given power will fully put itself into the service of this love.

We have to go one step further yet. If some day in his fellowship of love with us God will be the almighty, then such is possible only because he is already in himself and from eternity the almighty. He does not rise from little to much power all the way to the top, as we see that in earthly powers. Only he can become almighty who in his essence is such already. Being almighty in his love, God has decided to make within it room for man and his power. He decided to lose power to gain fellowship. His powerlessness is a gracious unwillingness to be almighty without us and against us. And so he has involved himself in a history with us in which, for the sake of the genuineness of this covenant partnership, he hides his superior power and manifests it in his defenselessness, to give us the room we need to become ourselves; but in that defenselessness he maintains his superior power to keep us from choosing eternally against him and therewith against ourselves. Therefore we pray in word and deed:

> Thy kingdom come,
> Thy will be done,
>   On earth as it is in heaven!

Barth has given little or no attention to this defenselessness of God's omnipotence; he does, however, provide good overviews of the references to superior power in the OT (*CD* II,1, pp. 600f., 603f.) and in the NT (pp. 605ff.). "Almightiness" (omnipotence) is a word for which there is no equivalent in the Bible. The word "almighty" seems to occur rather frequently. But the OT has *'El Šadday* in the Hebrew. The precise meaning of that name ("the highest God"?) is a disputed question. The Septuagint translated it in Greek as "the almighty" (*pantokratōr*), the same term which it used for "Yahweh of hosts." In that faded meaning it is used in 2 Cor. 6:18. For the rest it occurs only in Revelation, which is precisely the book that directs our eyes to the future. The popularity of the predicate "almighty" for God finds absolutely no basis in biblical usage. There it is just the aspects of power and defenselessness which are often strikingly combined, e.g. in the word "must" (*dei, edei*) which denotes the necessity of Jesus' suffering; it must be done because it is forced upon God and because in his superior power he makes it part of his plan. Cf. also Acts 4:27f. For the OT we refer to Gen. 50:20 and Isa. 10:5–20. See also par. 28. For the convergence of both aspects in the NT see also e.g. Rom. 8:18–39 and 1 Cor. 1:18–25, and the beautiful image in Rev. 5:6: in the center of the throne stood the Lamb, looking as if it had been slain.

Against this background it becomes necessary not only to criticize the generally held notion of omnipotence, but also the understandable reaction that we can detect in and since Bonhoeffer's letters from prison. Defenseless remains an adjective qualifying superior power. A purely powerless god is no God. For that reason, too, we should be careful in speaking of the suffering of God, as many have done since the publication of K. Kitamori, *Theology of the Pain of God* (Japanese 1946; E. T. 1958). Then one points to the suffering of Jesus. However, it is not God who was crucified, who died, and who was raised. Otherwise not only theologically but also christologically we end up on a wrong track (see par. 33). In the suffering of Jesus, God is no powerless victim (Rom. 8:32), but the one who suffers along with. That is another form of suffering, but not a lesser suffering. H. Wiersinga, *Verzoening met het lijden?* (1975), ch. 3, is good on this.

23. THE CHANGEABLE FAITHFULNESS

IT IS CUSTOMARY in the study of the faith to devote some attention to the attribute of God's unchangeableness (immutability). This is correct if one means by it the unchangeableness of God's faithfulness. God is not unreliable or capricious. He adheres to his purpose and does not forsake the work of his hands. To believe means, as such, to believe in such an unchangeable God. But in the centuries of theological discussion, this faith has been so much abstracted from the living contexts to which it belongs and so much been combined with alien philosophical thought patterns that it lost its luster and power and came in conflict with other elements of the faith which are equally important. In connection with the latter we think especially of the circumstance that in his revelation God manifests himself in the first place as a mobile God who repeatedly changes direction and who renders earlier initiatives obsolete through new starts. He manifests himself new in ever-new situations. That is inherent in the fact that God wants to meet us. All the time he has to adapt himself anew to man who searches for him and yet always avoids him. Is that only a change in the appearance of God which does not touch his being? That is a most important question. The obvious thing to say seems to be that God's being remains unchangeable amid the changing encounters.

But in that case already creation causes us difficulties. The creation of a world outside himself is the greatest change which God has made. But by making this change God also experienced it himself. From the time of creation God was changed. He had now become a creator and sustainer. He had received an "opposite": a finite existence beside his eternal existence. And when he created man he changed again. He created a center of freedom and initiative over against himself. He obtained a recipient for his revelation and a partner for dialogue. And when he entered into a special relationship with Israel, he became the commanding and gracious, the disappointed and tenacious covenant partner. In Christ he again experienced a profound change when the Word became flesh and he came very close to us in the love and obedience of one man. But this man must die on the cross and shout out the pain of his God-forsakenness. Does this go on without God being involved? Then, however, in the resurrection a no less radical change takes place. And this liberation, in which God emerges from the resistance against his presence, continues and widens itself in the work of the Spirit in which this God goes out to the depths of human hearts and the breadth of the earth; and that happens in order that God may once more, in the fulfillment, bring about a change which in its radicality can be compared only with that of creation.

Pondering this only a little, we become impressed with the measure in which changeableness is a part of God's association with his world. That this has found so little echo in the study of the faith, however, is not only due to foreign influences, but is in the first place due to the fact that in the Bible change is never connected with capriciousness but is always an expression of God's faithfulness. Not in spite of but precisely in his change God follows a straight line. Precisely because of the constant change he remains himself, and always stays the same with respect to us. After all, in his holy love he is himself. But love can remain itself only if it continuously reckons with its object. Therefore love is the fusion of changeableness and unchangeableness. Therefore the prophets see God as remaining the same in his covenant faithfulness, also in and after Israel's great catastrophes. Therefore Jesus did not come to abolish the law but to fulfill it. His cross and resurrection are the final consequences from the lines that become visible in Israel's preceding history. In him all the promises of God find their "Yes" (2 Cor. 1:20). And in the Holy

Spirit, the new era, already foreseen by the prophets, begins to realize itself—the completion of which will bring the fulfillment. Hence everywhere in the Bible are sung the praises of God whose faithfulness endures forever.

After the significant introductory words: "God's *aseitas* implies his unchangeableness. Yet this appears to find little support in Scripture," Bavinck offers a succinct description of the convergence of change and unchangeableness in the Bible (*GD* II, no. 193). We refer to some examples of this convergence in the OT: the divine name in Ex. 3:14 both indicates that man will not be able to comprehend or control God in his changes, and in these changes God will manifest himself as the faithful one who fully deserves the trust of his people. In the vision in which God called him, Ezekiel sees, above the heads of the living creatures, "as it were, a vault glittering like a sheet of ice, awe-inspiring" (Ezek. 1:22 New English Bible); for a moment the reader may think that this is the symbol of the unchangeable God, but it is only his throne; however: "seated above the likeness of a throne was a likeness as it were of a human form" (v. 26) which charges the prophet to accompany the coming changes with his word (v. 28c; 2:1ff.). The prophecies of Deutero-Isaiah are filled with the tension between change and unchangeableness; God-fearing people rebel against the thought that God, completely deviating from what he used to do, will now give deliverance through a heathen prince (Cyrus; see esp. Isa. 45); through the prophet God calls to them: "Remember not the former things, nor consider the things of old. Behold, I am doing a new thing" (43:18f.), but at the same time this new thing is pictured as being of the same order as the crossing of the Red Sea (43:16ff.; 48:20f.; 52:12). (In our judgment, Von Rad in the twofold division of his *OT Theology* has rightly underlined the change—Isa. 43:18f. forms the motto of his second volume—but underestimated the continuity in it.) In this connection the *repentance* of God, as the expression of the change in his relationship to man, plays a special role. That is one of the emphases in the little book of Jonah; see further Gen. 6:6f.; Ex. 32:10–14; Judg. 2:18; 1 Sam. 15:11; 1 Chron. 21:15; Ps. 106:45; Amos 7:3, 6; Joel 2:13. This repentance has so little to do with caprice that it creates much rather the impression that it could serve in Israel's creed as denoting the faithfulness of God (Joel 2:13; Jonah 4:2). For that reason the Bible writer can simply say next to it that God, unlike fickle man, does not repent (compare 1 Sam. 15:29 with 11 and 35; Num. 23:19; Ps. 110:4; Zech. 8:14; Mal. 3:6), for what is called repentance means precisely that God in relation to man will act in agreement with his being.

In the NT too, which speaks of enormous changes, these are nevertheless regarded as stemming from the firm promises of God, "with whom there is no variation or shadow due to change" (Jas. 1:17). Impressive is the blending of change and unchangeableness in Rom. 9–11 where Paul speaks of God's changing relation to Israel, but precisely therein reaches the conclusion: "For the gifts and the call of God are 'without repentance' " (11:29 AV).

See further the biblical survey in Barth, *CD* II,1, pp. 495–499; and L. J. Kuyper, "The Suffering and the Repentance of God" (*Scottish Journal of Theology,* Sept. 1969).

After what was said in the previous paragraphs about the development of the doctrine of God, it can cause no surprise that in the history of the church the unchangeableness of God has, as a rule, been developed one-sidedly and at the expense of the changeableness of God. The decision of the Septuagint translators to render *'ehyeh 'ᵃšer 'ehyeh* in Ex. 3:14 with "He who is" *(ho ōn)* was certainly also motivated by the desire to show to the Greek intellectuals that their concept of the one, high, and unchangeable deity could already be found in the OT. This decision has had an enormous influence on the doctrine of God. The first to thoroughly continue in this line was Philo of Alexandria (B.C. 25–A.D. 42). To reconcile his concept of God with what is said about the repentance of God in Gen. 6:6 he wrote the tract *Quod deus immutabilis sit (hoti atrepton to theion),* in which he asserted that if the wise man is above all caprice, then God, of course, infinitely more so; the word "repentance" is meant pedagogically to make our sins frighten us; fortunately God does not drop his creation. Philo's thoughts do not deserve the quick rejection which they often receive today. Here resounds, in contrast to the fickleness of the Greek gods and the vicissitude of earthly events, the belief in the dependability of God. The same is true of the church fathers. Aristides chides his contemporaries for their belief in perishable and changeable *stoicheia;* but the true God is both imperishable and unchanging, while at the same time he alters and turns the world according to his will (*Apologia* 4). That is correct. But we sense a foreign element when it is also said that God is thus "above all passions and shortcomings, anger, forgetting, ignorance, etc." (anōteron pantōn tōn pathōn kai elattomatōn, orgēs te kai lēthēs kai agnoias kai tōn loipōn, *Apologia* 1). Here dependability becomes impassiveness. The doctrine of God's unchangeableness has always retained this ambivalent character in the church fathers. Dependability always included *apatheia.* See on this E. P. Meyering, *Orthodoxy and Platonism in Athanasius. Synthesis or Antithesis?* (1968), II B and IV, esp. pp. 134–142. It should be added that the struggle against the so-called patripassianism of Sabellius made the church fathers even more sensitive to anything that ascribed changeability to God. The Middle Ages, under the influence of Aristotle, saw a hardening of this teaching. According to Aristotle every movement is one from less to more perfection or the reverse. Movement thus implies imperfection. In his doctrine of God, Thomas therefore starts with Aristotle's definition: "the unmoved prime mover." The *immutabilitas* becomes almost *immobilitas* (see *ST* I, q. 9). God begins to resemble the enormous sheet of ice which according to Ezekiel he surely was not (1:22). Right up to our century this concept of God has ruled Roman Catholic dogmatics.

The Reformation dropped the authority of Aristotle, but on this point did not go further back than to the fathers and Philo, that is, it limited the validity of the statements about God's changeableness to his revelation; these were statements about God's relation, not about his being. See Calvin on the repentance of God according to Gen. 6:6; he calls it a "mode of speaking" accommodated to our capacity which describes God for us in human terms. "By the word 'repentance' is meant the fact that God changes with respect to his actions"; it does not say how "he is in himself, but as he seems to us" (*Inst* I,xvii,13). No wonder that on this point, if possible with less constraint even than elsewhere, Protestant Scholasticism continued the tradition of medieval Scholasticism: "Immutability is the perpetual identity of the divine essence and of all its perfections, denying any motion at all, either natural or ethical" (Quenstedt, see S p. 79). Korff is to the point when he writes: "The doctrine of the immutability of God has in its favor that in theology it has thrown up a dam against a pagan fading of the concept of God. But it has only been able to do this by introducing in the God concept an equally pagan rigidity" (*Christologie,* I, p. 257). Molinism and Remonstrantism did indeed oppose this rigidity out of a desire to do justice to the initiative and freedom of man (see e.g. C. Vorstius, *Tractatus theologicus de Deo,* etc., 1610, par. 34f., p. 306: "the will of God is in some way changeable"), but this opposition was too tentative and it was fiercely attacked as synergistic heresy. Very remarkable is Bavinck's train of thought as, not without resistance, he gives in to the classical doctrine of immutability: "Though unchangeable in himself, God lives as it were [! H.B.] the life of his creatures, and is not indifferent to their fluctuating circumstances" (*GD* II, no. 193). And he ends with the strange sentence: "God's unchangeable 'being' is itself the cause of the distinct existence and manifestation of all those things which 'become', and more particularly, of their existence according to an altogether distinct law and order" (p. 148). See for the traditional view and a critique on it also H. M. Kuitert, *De mensvormigheid Gods* (1962), esp. III and VIII A.

The 19th century brought a shift. Not yet in Schleiermacher, who could not use a changeable God as the "whence" of the "feeling of absolute dependence" (*CF* par. 52, Postscript). It did occur in those circles which can broadly be called "mediating theology," which, encouraged by the combination of God and history in German Idealism, raised other related biblical elements, without immediately rendering them powerless through a separation of being and revelation. We think of the Kenotics, mentioned in par. 22, who, referring to Phil. 2:7, ventured to speak of a change in God in the incarnation in the sense that the eternal Son of God subjected himself to a radical self-limitation. In the Netherlands ethical theology thought along the same lines; see J. H. Gunning in *Blikken in de openbaring,* II, esp. ch. IV. See also Kohnstamm, *De heilige,* par. 81, with the title: "The 'immutability of God' and its correlates in conflict with Scripture and especially with the proclamation of Jesus Christ" (p. 377), containing an attack on "the colossus of the Aristotelian God concept" (p. 388). But the most penetrating was I. A. Dorner in his rightly famous study "Über die richtige Fassung des dogmatischen Begriffs der Unveränderlichkeit Gottes" (published 1856–58 in the *Jahrbücher für deutsche Theologie,* later part of his *Gesammelte Schriften,* 1883, pp. 188–377). He seeks to locate the unchangeableness in the love of God. And precisely this implies change. "God restricts his activity precisely for the purpose of maintaining Himself and the unity and unchangeableness of his ethical purpose over against a free and changeable humanity, as it is demanded by the prevailing condition of man."

Barth has consciously continued in the line of Dorner (*CD* II,1, pp. 491–522). Therefore he does not speak of unchangeableness but of God's constancy, namely in his loving-in-freedom. ". . . the pure *immobile* is—death. If, then, the pure *immobile* is God, death is God. . . . And if death is God, then God is dead" (p. 494). "It is in and by virtue of His constancy that God is alive in Himself and in all His work" (p. 495). Does change then also belong to his being? Barth says: "But it is not the case that only in His relation to the creation and man, in His revelation of grace, does it all become a reality which it is not in God Himself"

(p. 499). But the main line is much closer to traditional thinking: "He Himself does not alter in the alteration of His attitudes and actions" (p. 498).

After Barth we observe, in divergent theological traditions, the tendency to emphasize one line of Barth and to posit change as being inherent for God as well. The post-war outlook on life consciously or unconsciously had a great influence here. In a world which is experienced as being essentially static, change could only be regarded as inferior and dangerous. Now that the world is experienced as a dynamic process of evolution, the reverse happens. A God who is essentially a stranger to change becomes essentially strange to us. For that reason the philosopher Whitehead, besides attributing to God a "primordial nature," also attributed to him a "consequent nature," as (in part) the result of an unpredictable process of becoming. For that same reason, process theology that was influenced by him began to speak of a changing God. See C. Hartshorne, *The Divine Relativity* (2nd ed. 1964); J. B. Cobb, *A Christian Natural Theology* (1966), ch. V; D. D. Williams, *The Spirit and the Forms of Love* (1968). Williams, p. 128, expresses their basic thought as follows: "Causality without involvement is incompatible with love." From an entirely different direction (but not without parallels with the school of Whitehead) came Teilhard de Chardin; groping to find his way he spoke about God's being incomplete in the evolutionary process and so he raised all kinds of questions among Roman Catholic theologians about the changeableness of God, especially in connection with the incarnation: "he who is unchangeable in himself can *himself* become subject to change *in something else*" (Rahner, *Theological Investigations,* IV, p. 113, cf. pp. 112–115). "For God is—we stammer—absolute Newness. . . . In a way which we cannot imagine our history must be meaningful not only for us but also for God" (E. Schillebeeckx, in *Tijdschrift voor theologie,* 1966, pp. 132f.). "God's real relations with us imply the recognition that there must also be change, genesis, and becoming in God, be it in an entirely divine manner" (P. Schoonenberg, in *idem,* p. 302).

Given the fact that the unity of God's being and revelation, his changing himself and unchangeability, are to be regarded as equally belonging to him, we may at the end not back off from the difficult final questions which arise here. The easier road of classical theology, which denied any change to God, is no longer open to us. Precisely in his revelation God is himself. His entire being is involved in it. God defines and involves himself completely in the encounter with us; else it would not be a real encounter. There is no other God behind the God who participates with us in a history. It would be blasphemous to say that this history would leave him unmoved. But it would also be blasphemous to say that, together with us, he would be controlled by this history. In that process he is what we are not: "the Rock whose work is perfect." But he is not that in a distant and stark eternity, but as our covenant partner on the way through time with all its fluctuations and surprises.

Our approach here should be the same as in paragraph 22 where we saw in what way God's omnipotence is connected with his defenselessness. Then we must say: In his sovereign love God has made himself changeable. He has decided to be together with us involved in a process, a process which includes Gethsemane's anguish and Calvary's God-forsakenness. He allows himself to be made a victim. Note: he allows it to be done to him. He enters into it and at the same time stands above it; not half in it and half above it, but totally the one and totally the other. This is not self-contradictory. For the more one controls a situation, the more one can allow. For the sake of the unchangeableness of his eternal purpose God can participate in and suffer through the process which he has initiated himself. And we cannot avoid the conclusion (why would we do it anyway?): this struggle of God with his estranged image-bearers does something to him, too. He, too, is enriched, with reborn sons and daughters. After the return of the lost son the father, too, is (not a different father, but) different. That is why later, in paragraph 38 ("The Covenant as 'Tri-(u)nity'"), we must again deal with the doctrine of God.

The love of God entails both faithfulness and changeability, but in such way that the second is an adjective to the first. For centuries the changeability was misconstrued. Now this threatens to happen with the sovereign faithfulness (see the small type above). Very easily one falls into the Scylla of the Hegelian God-concept (the absolute Mind realizing itself in the world), even as theology has for centuries succumbed to the Charybdis of the Aristotelian God-concept. The Czechoslovakian theologian J. Trojan, in *Entfremdung und Nachfolge* (1980), consciously searches for a third approach. From the vantage point of the eschaton he dares to speak of the "not-yet-being-fulfilled of [God's] existence" and of his "enrichment of predicates of being" in salvation history. But at the same time he says: "Only in this way does God authenticate (*bewährt*) himself as universal ground, in which man and his history are also constantly involved" (pp. 66–70). Particularly Barth with great intellectual prowess, yet not without uncertainty, seeks the narrow channel between the two rocks. He does not want to see the changes in history as changes in God himself. But not as changes outside God either. He wants to locate the transcendental possibility of this change in the being of God. In *CD* II,1 he speaks in this connection of the liveliness of God. He takes a big step further in *CD* IV,1, pp. 192–204 by assuming in God's being a polarity of Father and Son, of majesty and service, of commanding and obeying. This eternal secret makes it possible for God to humiliate himself in time without changing himself. In other words, the changes are eternalized in God. But earlier he had taken one step further yet, when in *CD* II,2 he incorporated God's election and God's command in the doctrine of God proper. In that case revelation is no longer the reflection and expression of God's being but is itself part of it. "It is part of the doctrine of God because originally God's election of man is a predestination not merely of man but of Himself" (p. 3), and it "is a relation in which God is self-determined, so that the determination belongs no less to Him than all that He is in and for Himself" (p. 7). But Barth has not drawn the consequences from what he says in these opening pages. Hence Gollwitzer, in *The Existence of God as Confessed by Faith,* could appeal to Barth when in his reaction against the school of Bultmann he sharply distinguished between God in and for himself and God for us, between God's being and God's will (pp. 186ff.). From the perspective of the other line in Barth, E. Jüngel rightly protested this separation in his *The Doctrine of the Trinity* (E.T. 1976), but he could get no further than seeing in the revelation a repetition of God's being. "God's being as self-relatedness is a being in becoming, and in view of that nature it can repeat itself" (see pp. 89ff.). In his *Gott als Geheimnis der Welt* (1977) he takes a definite step beyond that. Here revelation is said to be essential for God: "God's being exists in his coming" (par. 25). That is at the same time a step in the direction of Hegel. Gollwitzer and Jüngel indicate the two directions in which Barth impels us to go beyond Barth. A good survey of how theologians wrestle with the concepts of "unchangeability" and "changeability" in the doctrine of God is given by H. Küng, *Menschwerdung Gottes* (1970), pp. 611–670.

Creation

24. GOD AS CREATOR

THE GOD WE MEET in the revelation to Israel and in Christ is the creator of the world. To some this confession sounds self-evident, to others blasphemous. To many it sounds self-evident, because the world of God and the gods as the expression of the absolute as such transcends our reality and is the ground of that reality; the terms "God" and "ground of the world" are thus identical. This identification causes no difficulty as long as one can think of the godhead as being just as ambiguous and capricious as the world it has produced. This becomes quite different if one's experience of God and that of the world clash with each other. That has happened in Israel and it continues in the Christian faith. God as holy love with his acts and promises did not agree with what the world was like. For the most part the world does not reflect his love but clashes with it. Revelation, therefore, holds the promise of rescue, of deliverance from existence as we know it. This, of course, makes it far from obvious to say of the revelational God of holy love that he is also the creator of the world.

Yet it is being said and it must be said. Though the God we meet in revelation is in conflict with the world, he is that in such a way that it is clear that it is his own world, in fact that he clashes with it precisely because it is his own creation. The rescue which he seeks is not a deliverance out of this existence, not a writing off of the world, but the deliverance of this world and of this existence. Salvation means purifying this world and raising it to a higher level, not its denial and rejection.

It is clear that this identification of creator and redeemer evokes great tensions for faith and great problems for the intellect. It is just as clear that dropping this identification creates much greater tensions and problems or, putting it more correctly, it would mean that we would deny the essence of the redemptive encounter itself and would thus abandon the Christian faith. But belief in the creator is certainly far from self-evident. As the term itself implies, it is a matter of belief. "I believe in God the Father, the creator of heaven and earth." As with the entire content of the Christian faith, so here it is a confession that conflicts with what is daily experienced. We insist that this world of sin, of suffering and death, is created by the Father of Jesus Christ. With that insistence the Christian faith takes over again the belief in the self-evidence of creation as this is found in religion, though now it is made non-self-evident by revelation, to incorporate it, corrected, into the context of a new redemptive faith.

For the history of the belief in creation in the Christian church, see Brunner, *Dg* II, pp. 36–39; *RGG* VI, *s.v. Schöpfung IV a,* and *MS* II, ch. VII 2.

It is not accidental that very soon after the NT era, ideas denying that the Father of Jesus Christ could have created the world became widespread in the Christian church. We think of Gnosticism and Marcion, both of which taught that creation was the work of the demiurge, a lower and imperfect god. Those ideas were opposed especially by Irenaeus *(AH passim),* who asserted the oneness of creator and redeemer as the basis of the gospel. Yet the dualistic conceptions have remained, in the Manichaeans, Albigenses, and Cathari, up till our modern times. There have always been many, and one still finds them, who cannot reconcile the God of love they learn from the gospel with the God of blind force they learn from creation. Luther could rightly say: "The article of the creation of all things out of nothing is harder to believe than that of the incarnation."

Yet dualism has never been more than a heretical sidetrack in Christian thinking. The main line was always the one which held to a self-evident identification of the redeemer God with the creator of the world, and this God was regarded as knowable apart from revelation. A favorite proof text was Rom. 1:19f. It was therefore natural for Christian thought to take its starting-point in this belief of the self-evidence of creation and to proceed from there to the belief in redemption, all the more so because, since the 2nd century, theology tried to find a point of contact in the religio-philosophical ideas of Graeco-Roman culture. Already Aristides (ca. 140) began his *Apology* with the demonstrability of God from creation: "Therefore I say that he is the God who holds together and supports all things" (ch. 1). So it has remained. For Thomas the knowledge of God as the creator and first cause of the world are insights which are accessible to human reason (e.g. *ST* I, q. 44, art. 1). In his wake Protestant Scholasticism reckoned the doctrine of creation as belonging to the *articuli mixti* which, unlike the *articuli puri,* can not only be known by faith but also by man's natural insight (S, R, and H, see indices). The Belgic Confession regards "the creation, preservation, and government of the universe" "as a most elegant book" (art. 2) from which the relationship to the creator can be known. And Vatican I, with an appeal to Rom. 1:20, declared: ". . . God, the beginning and end of all things, can be known with certainty from the things that were created through the natural light of human reason" (though in "the present state of the human race" this is often accompanied with error; D 3004f.). On this point the church and the Enlightenment agreed; for the latter, too, the belief that a perfectly good and wise God had created the world was self-evident (though the 1755 earthquake which destroyed Lisbon gave a severe jolt to this belief).

Only after the unexpected catastrophe of the First World War did the belief in creation begin to lose its obviousness. Barth consequently derives it strictly and exclusively from the revelation in Christ which proves that neither God nor man is alone and that God rules over this world and it is rightly his (*CD* III,1, par. 40). An even greater tension between belief in creation and belief in redemption is found in O. Noordmans, *Herschepping* (1934); note the headings: "The Father more hidden than the Son," "Belief in the Creator as such does not produce a childlike confidence but terror," "To create is not to form but to separate," "The cross stands in the center of creation" (pp. 80–83). In these circles and in this period one liked to point out how the Heidelberg Catechism bases belief in creation strictly on revelation: "What do you believe when you say: 'I believe in God the Father, almighty, maker of heaven and earth'"? Answer: "That the eternal Father of our Lord Jesus Christ, who out of nothing created heaven and earth and everything in them . . . is my God and Father because of Christ his Son" (Q. and A. 26).

In this climate, too, the biblical studies became interested in the relation of the knowledge of salvation and the knowledge of creation. Especially the OT proved a fruitful field of investigation, and was particularly studied by Von Rad. See his *OT Theology,* I (E.T. 1962), esp. "The Place in the Theology of the Witness," with the noted formulation "Creation is part of the aetiology of Israel." This looks like Barth's doctrine of creation (creation as the external basis of the covenant; *CD* III,1, 1945). But in contrast to Barth, von Rad saw increasingly in the OT views on creation that were derived from the environment and that were separate from the main line of salvation history (e.g., Job 38–40; Prov. 8:22, 31). See especially his *Wisdom in Israel* (E.T. 1972). This duality was worked out by A. S. van der Woude in his article "Genesis en Exodus," *Kerk en Theologie* (January 1969), with an appeal to the two sources of revelation in Art. 2 of the Belgic Confession; and even more by C. Westermann, *Commentary on Genesis* (1966ff.), pp. 89–97, 240–244, who speaks of two faces of primeval history, whereby the second, the specifically Israelite, exerts a demythologizing influence on the first (pp. 91f.). In *Theologie des AT in Grundzügen* (1978), pp. 75ff., Westermann speaks of four traditions in P, who gives a dominant place to creation through the word and thereby "admits (*gibt*) that there is no absolutely right view of creation" (pp. 76f.). E. J. Beker and K. Deurloo, *Het begin in ons midden* (1977), remain entirely in the line of Barth: the creation faith as the "unfolding" of the center of liberation (Exodus).

For our own conclusion we refer to the last sentence of the larger-type part of the preceding section. From a religious-historical perspective it is highly improbable, and dogmatically very forced, to hold that the belief in creation was purely an extrapolation from the belief in redemption. But it is not true either that ideas from elsewhere concerning the origin of the world were simply taken over. They were inserted in accordance with the redemptive experience; in line with that experience the creation faith was on the one hand divested of its self-evidence and on the other hand (on new grounds and in a new form) confirmed.

God is thus (also) creator. We ask: what does knowing this mean for our knowledge of God? And the answer must be: in his holy love God has decided to live with a reality outside himself, a reality which as created is of a totally different order. It has pleased him to make this reality share in the glory and love of his own being. The act of creation is an act of condescension. The creative act thus bears the same stamp we discovered in the revelational encounter as originating in the very being of God. To create means that God stoops down, that he limits himself, that he provides living and breathing space for the other which as such is imperfect and will even be rebellious.

We said that God decided this, that he wanted it. Between God and creation lies a decision of the will. God's will is not something arbitrary; it is the expression of his being as holy love. But as the will of God it is at the same time irreducible. "For thou didst create all things, and by thy will they existed and were created" (Rev. 4:11)—that is the hymn of praise sung by faith, yet at the same time it is a hard problem for the mind. Here we stand before a wall. Existence cannot be traced back further; from our perspective it rests on contingency and not on necessity. We cannot make transparent why there is something and not nothing.

But this stumbling block for the mind becomes much greater yet when we are faced not only with something irreducible, but with an irreducible break, a discontinuity in existence, a jump of the infinite into the finite. The created world is an imperfect world, a reality happening in time. It comes from the perfect and eternal God. How can we ever trace back to him that which is temporal and imperfect? True, we can say that God is "above" the world and eternally existed "before" it, but the above-and-under, the before-and-after are also created by God. We can think only in the categories of space and time, which implies that we cannot comprehend what it means that God is the ground of our existence. We cannot penetrate this mystery, we can only make it our starting-point. "The existence of a creation cannot at all be grasped by the intellect . . . nor has any man been able to think of creation in this way" (Fichte).

For that reason thinkers, also religious thinkers, have through the centuries tried to get away from the unthinkable idea of creation; instead of conceiving of the relationship between creator and creation as discontinuous and dualistic they have tried to see it as continuous and monistic, as a relation of essence and appearance, of ground and development, of a river and its source, and in terms of evolution, emanation, correlation, or polarization. The result is that creation is regarded as eternal and co-existing with God. Mindful of the "in the beginning" with which the Bible begins, the church has, on the whole, fiercely opposed these ideas. There is, however, more to it, something which has not always been realized. If creator and creation are to be thought of as together involved in one process, then the possibility of facing each other in a personal relationship is excluded. For a personal relationship is based on discontinuity. A God who forms a continuous and co-existing unity with his world cannot as a person and with his will stand opposite the world and the other. And man is then not God's partner but only his product. One who takes his starting-point in the revelational encounter, by which the Christian faith orients itself, cannot think otherwise about the world and its origin than in terms of creation, person, will, leap, duality. Not doing that, he is sawing off the very branch on which he sits. The idea of creation is indeed the limit of our thinking, but only if we willingly accept this limit as an intellectual crux are we able to make a new start, and can we do justice to the secularity of the world, the personality of man, and to God as the God of the encounter and the covenant. Then we shall no longer try to avoid whatever other breaks and discontinuities we may find in our reality and in God's association with us. Here it becomes clear, too, what the meaning is of the two statements which Christian thought has always conjoined to its confession of God as creator and strongly emphasized, namely that God created the world through the Word, and that he created it out of nothing. God's creation of the world *through the Word* was based on a number of biblical passages, with the purpose behind it to bring out, through the identification of the Word with the eternal Son, the connection between creation and re-creation. Here we are to realize also that especially in the Old Testament the Word is *the* means by which God brings about and maintains the revelational encounter. By repeatedly and emphatically saying that the whole created reality came into being through this speaking of God, one confesses that the world is meant for the encounter and communication. By also saying that the world was created *out of nothing,* one confesses that in this encounter God and man do not come from two different directions and meet each other as equal conversational partners, but that our partnership in the encounter (and thus the encounter itself) is based on and depends on God's initiative and on nothing else. Else, if our existence would depend on other elements besides God, there would be other gods and powers whom we would have to fear. Therefore we may not with a show of profundity explain the expression "out of nothing" as if God, for example, might have created us out of "the Nothing" as out of a dark and chaotic power which keeps threatening our life. Out of nothing simply means: not out of anything. The world has one ground, the will of God who is holy love.

For that reason the confession of our creation, both in the Bible and in the church's hymns, so often takes the form of a hymn of praise. If created reality, which can enrapture but also frighten us, has its sole source of being in the initiative of the Father of Jesus Christ, then, in spite of everything, it must be a good thing. Creation is good because the creator is good.

The conception of creation as divine self-limitation, and as such analogy and prelude of the *kenosis* (Phil. 2:7), was especially developed in the 19th century, partly under the influence of German Idealism. In the Netherlands this notion is particularly found in the ethical theology of Chantepie de la Saussaye, Sr. and Gunning. Brunner, writing on creation, says: "Now we begin to see what a large measure of self-limitation He has imposed upon Himself, in order to realize this aim (namely, to glorify Himself and to share Himself), to achieve it, indeed, in a creature which has misused its creaturely freedom to such an extent to defy God. The kenosis, which reaches its paradoxical climax in the cross of Christ, began with the creation of the world" (*Dg* II, p. 20). Therefore: "The two ideas, creation and self-limitation, are correlative" (II, p. 172).

Down the centuries the doctrine of the eternity of the creation can be found in religiously inspired philosophy (Aristotle, Stoicism, Origen, Duns Scotus, Bruno, Spinoza, Hegel, etc.). At the time of Thomas Aquinas this doctrine was the measure of the extent to which one was influenced by Aristotle and Averroës. What the connections of this doctrine with the whole of the faith are is clearly noticeable in a systematic thinker like Schleiermacher. He does not see man as standing in a relationship of dialogue to God but in a one-sided absolute relationship of dependence. With that conception of the continuity of dependence fits, on the one hand, Schleiermacher's weak defense against Pantheism (*CF* par. 8, Postscript) and, on the other hand, his tendency (he does not venture any further) to think of creation as being eternal, because it is difficult to conceive of "a transition from willing to doing. In contemporary process theology the reverse seems to happen when it posits the co-temporality of God with his creation, in order thus to anchor God's relationship and cooperation with his creatures in his being. See S. M. Ogden, *The Temporality of God* (1964). But in both cases this leads to a pantheistic effacement of the boundary between God and his creation, undermining the covenant relationship.

The relationship of creation and time has always caused theologians a great deal of perplexity. Yet Augustine already has given the only right answer to the question "What did God do before He created the world?": "At no time, therefore, did you do nothing, since you had made time itself" (*Confessiones* XI.14, cf. 11–13); "truly the world was made with time and not in time" (*De civitate Dei* XI.6; cf. XII.16). Kant provided the philosophical complement to this line of thinking with his argument that time and space, being the a priori conditions of perception, cannot be applied to what transcends the limits of sense perception and leads to antinomies. Barth has criticized Augustine's thinking insofar as he feared that it could lead to a contrast between eternity and time: "What is the meaning of *cum tempore* if it does not mean *in tempore*. . . . His eternity is itself revealed in the act of creation as his readiness for time, as pre-temporal, supra-temporal (or co-temporal) and post-temporal, and therefore as the source of time, of superior and absolute time" (*CD* III,1, p. 70). Barth argues correctly here that what constitutes an intellectual crux and break from the perspective of our world, faith regards as ultimately grounded in a continuity. See also Brunner, *Dg* II, pp. 14–17.

For the doctrine of creation *through the Word* the passages regularly appealed to are: Gen. 1:3, 6, 9, 14, 20, 24, 26; Ps. 33:6; 148:5; Isa. 48:13; John 1:1ff.; Heb. 1:3; 11:3. By way of the conception of the Word as the second person of the Trinity, a connection is then usually made with incarnation and redemption. From a biblical-theological standpoint such a direct connection may not be made. It is better to start from the function of the Word in the history of salvation.

For centuries it was assumed as self-evident, with an appeal to Rom. 4:17; 2 Cor. 4:6; Heb. 11:3, that God created the world *out of nothing*. Nowadays this obviousness is (again) disputed, partly out of biblical and partly out of philosophical considerations. The biblical problem is that most of the creation traditions in the OT do not know of a creation out of nothing and that it is not explicitly mentioned until 2 Macc. 7:28. We will come back to that in the next par. The philosophical problem lies in the ambiguity of the word "nothing," which in the history of philosophy was often (think of the *mē on* of Plato and Platonism, and of the *hylē* of Aristotle) not a *nihil negativum* but a *nihil ontologicum.* Since Heidegger it has again acquired that kind of ontological meaning in our popular-philosophical speech. In Augustine the "nothing" out of which we are created is the reason that we are subject to a *privatio essentiae,* and thus to a *privatio boni,* and therefore to the possibility of sinning *(De civitate Dei* XII.2–5; *Enchiridion* 11–15). We are also reminded of that in Barth when he writes about created reality: "It is not nothing but something; yet it is something on the edge of nothing, bordering it and menaced by it, and having no power of itself to overcome the danger" *(CD* III,1, p. 376). In *CD* III,3 these thoughts are elaborated into his teaching of the "Nothing" as "That which is not is that which God as Creator did not elect or will, that which as Creator He passed over, that which according to the account in Genesis 1:2 He set behind Him as chaos, not giving it existence or being" *(CD* III,3, p. 73). This what-is-declared-as-nothing exists by virtue of its rejection by God. "Nothingness is that which God does not will. It lives only by the fact that it is that which God does not will. But it does live by this fact. For not only what God wills, but also what He does not will is potent, and must have a real correspondence. What really corresponds to that which God does not will is nothingness" *(CD* III,3, p. 352). One sees that in Augustine as well as in Barth these speculations serve to locate the possibility of evil in God's good creation. In that context we will return to it later. Barth has thus done everything possible to ban the threat of dualism. But the result is that his "Nothing" becomes a nondescript sort of thing in between a *nihil negativum* and a *nihil ontologicum.* See *CD* III,1, pp. 370–388; III,3, par. 50, and IV,3, p. 178. He reasons, however, in an entirely different manner when in III,2, pp. 152–157 he explicitly discusses the *creatio ex nihilo;* there it is a christologically founded *nihil negativum. Creatio ex nihilo* means nothing less, but nothing more either, than that God is the sole ground of our existence, "that God assumes complete and sole responsibility for the existence of the world, and moreover it does not excuse the fact that it is finite, by suggesting the existence of a 'nothing', an uncreated *hylē,* a *mē on,* which—unfortunately—also played an anonymous part in the process, and is the reason for the imperfection of the world" (Brunner, *Dg* II, p. 10).

The doctrine of the "Nothing" has not prevented Barth from developing more strongly than any theologian before him the view that creation is a benefit. See *CD* III,1, par. 42: "The Yes of God the Creator" (pp. 330–414). This thought is of great importance. All too often creation is discussed as something neutral. It is, however, the work of the same God who subsequently in that creation encounters and saves us. Creation stems from the same purpose and happens in the same style. True, this leaves the question concerning the relation between creation and salvation unanswered. That question will be addressed in the next par.

25. THE WORLD AS CREATEDNESS

FIRST WE CONSIDERED what it means for our knowledge of God that he is related to the world as its creator. Now we ask what this means for our knowledge of the world. For centuries this was hardly a question because the answer seemed readily available. For the authority of Scripture was taken to mean that whatever the Bible says about the creation of the world, and of course especially in Genesis 1 and 2, was regarded as divinely given information about the origin and existence of the world, information essentially similar to the results of natural science or philosophical convictions. Hence under the heading of creation many dogmatics offered all kinds of information about stars and animals, angels and man, body and soul, the origin of the soul, and similar subjects.

That tradition has now come to an end. Successively it has been undermined by the Reformation, the historical-critical study of the Bible, and modern science; Kant's philosophical dualism contributed much to this process. In our century this tradition has entirely collapsed.

For centuries the subject of this par. was preferably dealt with in the form of an exposition of the account of the creation of the world in six days (Gen. 1). Such an exposition was therefore called a hexahemeron. On the history of this genre see Bavinck, *GD* II, par. 35, no. 271. It is worth noting that the theologians did not limit themselves to exegesis but incorporated the biblical data into the view of the universe current in their days. "All these works are written from the standpoint of the Aristotelian-Ptolemaic view of the world" (Bavinck). A classical example is Thomas' doctrine of creation (*ST* I, q. 44–119), which successively takes up: the act of creation, the angels, the demons, the creation of the earth, the work of the six days, the soul, the unity of soul and body, woman, the image of God, the state of rectitude, preservation, the interaction and function of the angels, fate, man's deeds, the origin of the soul, and the origin of the body. Printed in modern book form, the whole covers some five hundred pages. Even if one eliminates the doctrine of man, the state of rectitude, and preservation (but that Thomas also discusses elsewhere), a big textbook on cosmology remains.

The Reformation meant an enormous reduction of this material. This was due to the fact that this movement consciously interpreted the truth in a way that made it personally and existentially relevant. This is strikingly evident in Luther's Small Catechism, which begins its exposition of the Apostles' Creed with: "I believe that God has created me and all that exists," and ends with: "for all which I am in duty bound to thank, praise, serve, and obey him." Calvin too, who was more systematic and objective, devotes only one chapter (*Inst* I,xiv) to the doctrine of creation proper (that is, apart from anthropology, to which he devotes a separate chapter). The title already suggests that he aims to further the knowledge of God, not to give information about the structure of the world: "Even in the creation of the universe and of all things, Scripture by unmistakable marks distinguishes the true God from false gods." Therefore: ". . . it is not my purpose to recount the creation of the world"; to read about that the reader is advised to go to Moses himself and to others (xiv,20). The belief in creation concerns on the one hand the "powers of God in the creation of the universe" (xiv,21), and on the other hand its significance is that we might "bestir ourselves to trust, invoke, praise, and love him" (xiv,22). The Belgic Confession in art. 12 has only this to say about the created world (apart from what is said about the angels): "giving unto every creature its being, shape, form, and several offices [we would say "functions"] to serve its Creator." For the Heidelberg Catechism, which expresses itself more in the spirit of Luther, see p. 157. In Protestant Scholasticism, which in several respects was a return to Catholic Scholasticism, the *locus de creatione* again had the tendency to swell with all sorts of cosmological information. Yet it did not yield to that tendency beyond what was considered responsible exegesis of Gen. 1. The Reformational reduction was only partially undone. A return to the Aristotelian-Ptolemaic conception of the world was out of the question. This was also due to the fact that this view had become an embarrassment since the time of Copernicus and later Kepler and Galileo (despite the official rejection of their theories by the churches). See on this R II, pp. 170f. For the discussion of the locus see S par. 20; R par. 20,2; H IX.

Earlier, however, than the natural sciences, the modern study of the Bible has contributed to the steady reduction in the doctrine of creation. Historical-critical investigation discovered several sources and layers in the OT historical narratives. The creation account could not be from Moses. Eventually students became convinced that its source (P) is one of the later ones and is to be placed in or after the exile. Conceptions of creation, differing considerably from Gen. 1, were now being discovered in other layers and other books. All were now viewed primarily as human faith testimonies. The following may be regarded as the most important statements about creation in the OT: Gen. 1:1–2:4a (P); 2:4b–7 (J); Job 26:12f.; 38:8–11; Ps. 74:13f.; 89:10f.; 104:5–9; Prov. 8:29; Isa. 27:1; 51:9–11. Most of these statements give the impression that the world originated out of a struggle between Yahweh and a primeval sea monster which he overcame. This representation is also found in the Babylonian creation account *Enuma elish* in which the god Marduk, with the help of the evil wind Enlil, slays Tiamat, the salt-water power, and forms heaven and earth by splitting her body. A Ugaritic myth speaks of Baal who wages war with Yam (the sea, the primeval sea) and with "L-t-n, the fleeing serpent." We cannot help but be reminded of the primeval flood (*ṯ^{e}hôm*) and the *rû(a)ḥ* which came over it (Gen. 1:2), and of Yahweh's struggle with "Leviathan the fleeing serpent" (Isa. 27:1; cf. 51:9). Mesopotamian cosmogonies are behind these Israelite creation representations. But nowhere is there a direct borrowing of material. Yahweh's uniqueness made that impossible. The existence of a primeval counterpart, something like an equally forceful chaotic water power, beside and over against Yahweh could not seriously be imagined. Most of the texts suggesting that are of later date and give the impression that they make a poetic use of old fairy tales. There must, however, have been an earlier period in which Israel still thought in terms of this dualistic pattern and had to wrestle with it. A certain amount of dualism was acceptable because creation was seen not only as analogous to the creation myths of the surrounding nations, but also as analogous to the experience of Yahweh's struggle and deliverance in their own history. The history of creation was thus also viewed as an extrapolation from salvation history. This is clearest from Isa. 51:9f. (a late text with old material); cf. also Ps. 74:12ff. in the entire context. Gen. 2:4b–7 occupies a separate place. Here there is no longer a demonic counterpart. Yahweh does find stubborn (but evidently created by him) matter over against him, namely a still dry and uncultivated earth. Creatively he gets at it, so long as it does not rain, by watering it with a flood, a vapor, or a mist (Heb. *'ēḏ*). Out of the now pliable *'ᵃḏāmâ* Yahweh fashions *'āḏām,* from *humus* he makes *homo.* This is the creation narrative of farmers whose fertile land is surrounded by a barren desert. This story views the dearth of water as the antagonist, while Gen. 1 and most other views, in contrast, start from the demonic flood. The latter agrees with the experience in Babel. The Yahwist in Gen. 2 speaks against a Palestinian background. Creation is painted using the colors of one's own experience of the world. But this experience is for Israel at the same time an experience of salvation: the transition in Gen. 2 from the dry desert to the well-watered garden of Eden is an extrapolation and (viewed from the other perspective) a prefiguration of Israel's transition from the dry desert to the land flowing with milk and honey.

With Gen. 1:1–2:4a (P) we are in yet another climate. This is not the language of myth but of scientific reflection—"for here is spirit from your Spirit" (Gunkel). Here we notice, too, that dualism has been overcome: Yahweh creates solely through his word, so that here there is *creatio ex nihilo.* But v. 2 does not appear to fit; it speaks of a "without form and void" *(ṯōhû wāḇōhû)* and of a *rû(a)ḥ 'Elōhîm* (Buber: *Braus Gottes;* a "terrific storm"?) which *mᵉraḥepeṯ* (hovers, flutters) over the *ṯᵉhôm,* the primeval flood. This verse is a "foundling from a distant time" (W. H. Schmidt), "an erratic block" (Kuitert), and therefore a "*crux interpretum*" (Barth). The explanations for it are legion. In my judgment we look here deep into the heart of Israel, which cannot break herself free from the fear of the dark powers which cross Yahweh's plans, and which nevertheless, rising above her own fear, confesses that there are no other gods before the face of Yahweh, who created the world good out of his own goodness.

In the NT, also, this final remnant of dualism has disappeared. At the same time creation is put in a new light here: it is the work of the Word (John 1), of the Son (Heb. 1), that is, of the same Christ who reconciled us through his cross, who arose from death, and who is the head of his church (Col. 1:15–20). According to a very early confession, cited by Paul, we have "one Lord, Jesus Christ, through whom are all things and through whom we exist" (1 Cor. 8:6). The creation faith has here become entirely a function of redemptive faith. We will return to that later. But here, too, faith is expressed with the use of available non-Christian concepts: John 1 uses the Logos concept and Col. 1:16 describes creation as structured by the ancient powers of that time, "whether thrones or dominions or principalities or authorities."

The critical study of the Bible has rid us of an exclusivistic and authoritarian use of Gen. 1 in the doctrine of creation. It has opened our eyes for the variations and the growth of the belief in creation, and for the connections with the *Umwelt* on the one hand and one's own experience of salvation on the other. As a consequence we have come to view the biblical ideas of creation as belonging to a secondary level. They do not belong to the inner circle of the faith. To that circle *does* belong the belief that the God of revelation has created the world. But the how and the what are expressed in terminology and insights derived from elsewhere and which change with the times. That makes it impossible for the systematic theologian to make direct use of any biblical statement on creation for the construction of his doctrine of creation.

Usually natural science is regarded as the real power which has undermined the belief in creation as expressed in Gen. 1. That seems (to us) more so than is (historically) the case. Of course Copernicus and the increasingly mechanistic view of the universe led to an ever greater distance from Gen. 1; it became more and more difficult to read this chapter in a naive and literal manner. But that did not lead to a crisis. A direct attack on the belief in creation was not made until the rise of the theory of evolution of Charles Darwin. Initially, however, this theory was so mechanically and deterministically conceived that very few Christians felt compelled to revise the current conceptions of creation. Rather it was felt that one had to choose between two world views: creation *or* evolution. For a variety of reasons it seemed difficult, between the two world wars, to maintain the theory of evolution. But after the Second World War it was promoted with new strength of vision and arguments, so that now it is so widely accepted that few serious theologians are left who care to deny it with an appeal to biblical "information." It is wrong to say that natural science has started the process of reduction; one may say that it has completed it.

After all this it does not surprise us that, relative to earlier centuries, the leading figures of the 19th and 20th centuries say a lot less in their doctrine of creation. Yet as concerns the systematic theologians, this is not only due to the above-mentioned reasons; it is at least as much due to the philosophical dualism which has became a part of European culture since the Renaissance. Descartes introduced the strict separation of *cogitatio* and *extensio.* This had its sequel in Kant's separation of pure and practical reason. In our century many start from the separation between human existence on the one hand and the world of nature or what is objectifiable on the other hand. It is clear that if, with many post-Kantian theologians, faith is localized in the practical reason which alone can give man a full and authentic existence, faith statements about the (objectifiable) world and its origin are regarded as of little or no significance. Hence Schleiermacher notes with satisfaction: "The New Testament passages quoted above lead us to reject any more definite conception of the Creation" (*CF* par. 40,1). Whereas he wants to develop the doctrine of providence positively, he is of the opinion that the doctrine of creation should primarily be developed negatively, "with a view to the exclusion of every alien element, lest from the way in which the question of Origin is answered elsewhere anything steal into our province which stands in contradiction to the pure expression of the feeling of absolute dependence" (*CF* par. 39). For Ritschl the idea of creation is important only because it leads to "the purpose of man and the restoration of his religious and ethical fellowship with God" (*Unterricht in der christlichen Religion,* par. 12). In our century Bultmann stands in the same tradition of reduction; according to him a concept of creation that goes further than Luther's "that God has created me" is hardly significant (see J. M. de Jong, *Kerygma,* 1958, III A and B). In Barthian theology, too, the tendency toward reduction is clearly evident, notably in his favorite statement that the Bible is not a handbook for cosmology. Barth himself, however, in *CD* III,1, started a new tradition which must still be discussed. Noordmans also goes very far with the reduction; in his *Herschepping* he defines "create" as "to separate," and in the statement that God once created the world he detects especially a judgment by which to gauge the depth of our present alienation from God.

If it is true that faith is not able to make independent statements about the origin and structure of the world, can it then say anything of significance about our reality? Does it have to content itself with the confession that God created this reality, without adding to it some pronouncement about this reality itself? But putting it this way would be to suggest a wrong alternative. Indeed, an enormous reduction has (rightly) taken place which excised all sorts of (pseudo-)information. What remained was the confession of the relationship which the Father of Jesus Christ has with the world as its creator. But precisely this relationship, which is of fundamental significance for the world, implies that basic information is given about it. The contrast is not: information or no information, but: information from the center of the faith or from other sources.

Under the following points we want to outline the knowledge we have of the world insofar as this is implied in the Christian knowledge of redemption.

1. The createdness of this world implies that it and everything in it is structurally good and important. Nothing is evil, nothing is appearance, nothing is inferior.

"And God saw everything that he had made, and behold, it was very good" (Gen. 1:31). "For everything created by God is good, and nothing is to be rejected if it is received with thanksgiving" (1 Tim. 4:4). It is not necessary here to set forth the decisive significance of this vision on reality. Outside the Israelite-Christian tradition this vision is found only by way of exception. Many religions and world views regard the world as having originated from a chaos; in that case the final secret of reality is not one which is good and favorable, but threatening. According to other, more dualistically-oriented world views, part of reality is good while another part is evil and dangerous, e.g. matter and the body. In India, reality is experienced as something that veils *(maya)*. It is clear that each of these conceptions leads to a different life-style and a different culture. The dominant position of what is called Western culture is to a large extent connected with the biblical belief in creation. The foundation for that was laid when the church rejected Marcion and Gnosticism.

2. Createdness not only means that everything is good, but also and for that reason that nothing is absolute. Nothing is less than a creature of God, but no more either. The world has no pivot in itself, not in matter which is eternal, not in the course of nature, not in a world-soul, not in an

absolute spirit. The world is not divine, and where it is treated as sacred it needs to be de-deified from the perspective of the belief in creation.

Much has been written in an earlier period about the convergence of Christian faith and the secularization of the world. See F. Gogarten, *Despair and Hope for Our Time* (E.T. 1970); H. Berkhof, *Christ the Meaning of History* (E.T. 1966), and A. T. van Leeuwen, *Christianity in World History* (1964). Israel's struggle with Baalism was against the religious sacralization of the forces of nature. Because of its rejection of idol worship and emperor sacrifice, the fledgling Christian church found itself involved in a struggle in which its enemies accused it of being "atheistic." After centuries of a more or less dormant state, these foundations of the Christian faith surfaced again, this time in opposition to the Hitler regime with its glorification of the Teutonic race, its blood and its soil. "For although there may be so-called gods in heaven or on earth—as indeed there are many 'gods' and many 'lords'—yet for us there is one God" (1 Cor. 8:5f.). The cultural consequences of this belief are clear, too. In contrast to the worship of nature, it makes room for natural science and the mastery of nature; and in contrast to the sacralization of the state and the societal order it makes room for democracy, change, and, if necessary, revolution. By implication it also excludes Oriental monism, which views the world as the manifestation of a divine cosmic life.

3. The createdness of the world implies the fundamental unity of the world. More basic than the diversity of nations, races, and cultures is their unity. And more basic than the difference in matter and spirit, body and soul, nature and existence, is their oneness.

The cultural consequences of this insight are far-reaching and clear, certainly in an age in which a strong desire for global unity is intersected by the formation of power blocs and by the contrasts between races and between rich and poor countries. But this faith also means taking a stand against the dualism in Western thinking since Descartes and Kant, for human freedom is no absolute novum. Insofar as the modern reduction of the belief in creation stems from that dualism, it must be resolutely rejected. In a sense this was the life work of J. M. de Jong; see his *Kerygma* and the posthumous *Voorrang aan de toekomst* (1969).

4. Createdness implies parts, plurality and variety. And that variety is real. If the world had its ground in itself, the variations, being only surface phenomena, could be reduced to that ground. But creation means that all phenomena are irreducible, because the world has its ground outside itself in its creator. Everything forms a unity, but within it everything also has its own place and character: spirit is not "really" matter, a plant is not an animal, and an animal not a plant. The variety is just as real as the unity, and the unity exists precisely as the composite of the diverse parts.

According to Gen. 1 God created all plants and animals according to their own kind (vv. 11, 12, 21, 24, 25). The belief in creation can stand the tension between unity and diversity. Now the one element, now the other requires emphasis against derailments in human ideas and practices. In our time each is alternately needed. A widespread misunderstanding with respect to the popularized idea of evolution often leads to the world view which has been called the "nothing but": man is actually "nothing but" a higher animal, thinking nothing but a movement of brain cells, animal life nothing but a form of more mobile plant life, life nothing but a more complex form of the inanimate, and this globe nothing but a revolving speck of dust. With these kinds of reductions one jumps lightly over the question as to the nature of the differences and how it is possible that a particular form of existence can break through its own limits. The merit of the much-disputed *Philosophy of the Cosmonomic Idea* of the philosophers Dooyeweerd and Vollenhoven (Free University) is that, from the perspective of the belief in creation, it puts such a strong emphasis on the variety and plurality of the various levels of existence, and points out the confusion that results from the failure to discern the laws which hold for those different levels. Modern science tends to focus particularly on the fluid and always imprecise transitions so as to trace the more complex forms back to the simpler. That reminds us of the unbreakable unity of reality, but it may not make us forget that fluid boundaries are also transitions to other forms of existence.

5. Createdness by the God of holy love, who is faithful amid his changeableness, means that the world is dependable. It is not a haunted house or a bizarre fairy tale. We can depend on it. We can orient ourselves in it, feel secure in it, and make plans for its and our future. Its habitability depends on its knowability, and this knowability is that of a universe governed by law.

In the OT the covenant faithfulness of Yahweh is repeatedly related to the firm hand with which he directs the course of nature. See Gen. 8:22; Ps. 104:5, 9, 19, 20a, 35; 147:4, 6, 15, 16, 19; 148:6 and 14; Jer. 31:35–37. Nor is it accidental that Gen. 1, as the prelude to redemptive history, emphasizes the order in creation and the fact that it is good. This belief in the fixity and predictability of existence is of course not the same as the modern conviction of causality and natural law. But both are even less in conflict with each other. The idea of such a natural causality could not arise in the primitive nature religions since the natural phenomena were regarded as the expressions of capricious deities. Only the convergence of the Israelite belief in creation and the Greek belief in the rationality of reality could produce the modern idea of natural law. In several of its first proponents this idea has a definite religious background; Kepler and Galileo regarded the laws of nature as a conversion of God's creative thoughts into mathematical formulas. This background has become more and more vague. Eventually the deterministically understood concept of natural law became an enemy of the belief in creation. For that reason Christians welcomed the replacement of the deterministic concept of natural law in nuclear physics by that of a static concept (Bohr, Heisenberg). The behavior of the individual atom proved unpredictable. But with the increase in number the probability and predictability of their behavior becomes greater. The dependability of the course of nature is thus not affected by this change (or modification) in the concept of natural law.

6. Createdness by the God of holy love, who is changeable in his faithfulness and who works toward his goal along ever-new ways, means that our dependable world is at the same time open to surprises and changes. It is not a haunted house, but not a bunker either. Creation by *this* God means not only natural causality, but also room for miracle.

All of God's work in revelation, encounter, and redemption breaks open our reality toward the future. However, there is no opposition between revelation and that reality. For in creation we can detect all sorts of opening-up processes at work, whereby the given natural causalities are integrated into higher relationships with a greater measure of freedom. The redemptive work of God is the highest power, and it allows nature no rest but continuously propels it forward with new impulses, driving it toward a goal.

Hence the Bible likes to speak of the "signs and wonders" which God performs in the world (Heb. *ōtôt umopᵉtîm,* Gr. *sēmeia kai terata;* other terms are Heb. *niplaôt, pᵉlaôt,* Gr. *dynameis).* The essence of these is not the miraculous and the unnatural, as e.g. in Ovid's *Metamorphoses.* The Greek word for miracles, *thaumasia,* occurs only once, as judgment against Jesus' opponents (Matt. 21:15). In fact, the gospel and the desire for miracles are at odds with each other (Matt. 4:5–11; Mark 8:11–13; Luke 11:16, 29; 23:8; 1 Cor. 1:22). Miracles are performed by all kinds of people (Ex. 7:11f.; Matt. 24:24; 2 Thess. 2:9). The essence of the central biblical miracles is that they are signs of the Kingdom which makes itself manifest in the visible world. They have their focus and norm in Jesus' appearance and especially in his resurrection. He himself is the outstanding sign that God does not resign himself to the closed circle of our existence but breaks through it and opens it up toward his future. Yet, or rather, exactly for that reason the biblical miracles can only be recognized by faith. That does not, however, make them subjective, for what faith recognizes is a reality which precedes faith. This tension is especially noticeable in the Gospel according to John with its deliberate use of the *sēmeion* concept. The problem is complicated by the fact that the Bible was written in a time in which reality was so much experienced as "open" that an aureole of miraculous legends could form itself around the wonderful acts of God. If anything, it is surprising that this aureole is so small compared to other literature of that time. The question concerning the authenticity of some of the biblical miracle stories requires careful investigation with the tools of literary criticism. For the biblical concept of miracle see, for the OT, W. Eichrodt, *Theology of the OT,* II, pp. 51ff.; and for the NT, *TDNT* VII, *s.v. sēmeion* and A. Richardson, *The Miracle-Stories of the Gospels* (1941); further Barth, *CD* IV,2, pp. 209–264. Brunner, *Dg* II, pp. 160–170, offers a more elaborate dogmatic exposition. In another context we shall come back to certain miracles, particularly the resurrection.

In the history of the church Augustine's definition has had great influence: "A portent, therefore, happens not contrary to nature, but contrary to what we know as nature" (*De civitate Dei* XII.8). Mainly along the same line is Thomas: "Thus the works God does surpassing any cause known to us are called miracles" *(ST* I, q. 105, art. 7). The rise of the mechanistic-deterministic world view made this belief in an open and ungraspable universe very difficult. Modernism rejected the idea of miracle. Orthodox supernaturalism assumed the same world view but maintained miracles as inorganic and incidental divine interferences, in other words, Augustine notwithstanding, really *contra naturam.*

In our century the conflict about miracle has subsided somewhat. Physical science concentrates on the duplicable and predictable aspects of "physical reality"; the historical reality thus lies outside its purview, let alone the redemptive reality. Sciences like biology, biochemistry, and genetics which operate with the theory of evolution tell us how organic nature, in contrast to the disposition toward disorder in nonorganic nature, evolves into ever more complex forms, giving rise to more and more "levels of freedom" (molecules, cells, organisms). In the causal pattern of nature an increasing measure of freedom of choice becomes available. We do not experience the world as a bunker but as a surprising and becoming reality. What is possible in it can be known only from what happens in it. Amid the changing views on the relationship of determinism and freedom, the believer, from the standpoint of the belief in creation, will hold to both: that the God of our salvation has put us in a reality which is dependable as well as full of surprises. For more information on this subject see G. D. Dingemans, *Wetmatigheid en wonder* (1974).

7. Createdness by the God of revelation also decides the purpose of existence. To begin with, it tells us that the world was purposely made. It is not a chance result of a blind process of accidental evolutionary happenings. That belief is a return to the passive resignation of the nature religions which regard the chaos as the final secret of the cosmos. One who believes that the world was intended by God will say, in the first place, that reality has its purpose in itself. God created it for the sake of creating it, in order that it might exist and develop. Next we should recall that this creator has begun a history with man, in fact that in a human he has wanted to meet us humans, because he has a further purpose with us. The realization of that purpose begins to happen wherever man no longer seeks only himself, but seeks his purpose in fellowship with and obedience to God. One who lets himself be guided by that purpose experiences, however, that he lets himself be guided by a God whose purpose is precisely man and his salvation. Putting all these successive points of view on one denominator, we can say that the purpose of the world is the Kingdom of God, as the full realization of human existence through fellowship with God.

In order to determine the purpose of creation we thus choose man as the final goal. One may call this "anthropocentric." But in the preceding chapter we saw that in revelation we meet a God who happens to be surprisingly anthropocentric. The Bible is a pervasively anthropocentric book, because everywhere it invites man to turn around, with the motivation that only so will man obtain his own salvation. And in the center stands the man Jesus as the great sign of God's *philanthrōpia* (Tit. 3:4).

But two derailments are possible here and must be avoided. We may certainly say that the nonhuman earthly reality is intended as the basis and climate for man's life. This "for man" should then, however, be understood in its full breadth and depth. Otherwise we end up in the bourgeois cosmology of the physico-theological literature of the early Enlightenment which tried to demonstrate how the structure of all of nature was such that it served the good of man. The relationship of man to nature has many aspects. Nature is our mother, our companion, and our servant, and also that which threatens as well as feeds us. See *God in Nature and History,* Faith and Order Paper, no. 50, 1968, pp. 16–19. The exploitation of our natural environment and its resources in this age has painfully taught us our dependence on nature and the difference between managing and dominating it. In its very depth this character of nature in its relatedness to man is unfathomable. That is what Job 38–41 intends to say: its unfathomableness points us to the unfathomableness of God. But it is nature that refers us to it; and through this reference nature is serving us. We should, moreover, realize that the nonhuman creation everywhere, and especially in the infinite space of the interstellar world where there are no humans, has its own for us inaccessible relatedness to God. That must keep us humble. God made the Leviathan, apart from us, "to amuse himself with" (Ps. 104:26).

More dangerous and easier to succumb to than erring to the side of nature is that to the side of God. It takes only one step and we regard and treat God as our servant, as the help and guarantee of our drive for happiness. This urge to manipulate God lies deep in the heart of religious man and has through the ages colored empirical religiosity, including the Christian. The strongest defense against it is found in Reformed Protestantism, which views everything, creation too, as happening "for the greater glory of God." Calvin begins his Catechism of Geneva by saying that the purpose of our life is to know God (1), "because He has created us and placed us in the world in order that He may be glorified in us" (2), and one has the right knowledge of God "when one knows how to honor Him" (6). This strong theocentric tone is found in all his writings. According to the Belgic Confession God created everything that it might "serve its Creator," and he upholds everything "for the service of mankind to the end that man may serve his God" (art. 12). But here Reformed Protestantism takes on an inhuman hardness because it seems to forget that God's glory, his *doxa,* lies in the happiness on earth of men on whom his favor rests (Luke 2:14), and that therefore there is great reward in the service of God (Ps. 19:11). Precisely when we are Christ's everything is ours (1 Cor. 3:21–23). Lactantius has given a beautiful summary of the dialectic of the purpose of creation: "The world was made for this reason, that we should be born. We are born, therefore, that we should know the Maker of the world and our God. We know Him that we may worship Him. We worship Him that we may gain immortality as a reward for our labors, since the worship of God rests on very great labors. Therefore, we are rewarded with immortality that, made like the angels, we may serve the Father and Lord Most High forever and be an everlasting kingdom for God" *(Divinae institutiones* VII.6.1). Irenaeus expresses it even more pointedly: "For the glory of God is a living man; and the life of man consists in beholding God" (*AH* IV.20.7).

8. These last points brought us close to making a statement about created reality in its relation to salvation. Now we will have to say that if this world is the handiwork of Israel's God, the Father of Jesus Christ, it must bear the imprint of the holy love of this God and must be intended for the loving encounter with him. The historical-critical investigation of the biblical traditions of creation has made us aware how often these traditions look upon creation as the first of the series of God's redemptive deeds and how they describe it as analogous to it. This means for us as New Testament believers that we confess our belief in creation with an eye to Christ. We believe that from the appearance of Christ we can learn the final purpose of creation.

That same scientific study of the Bible which has taught us to understand the confession of creation as connected with the confession of salvation has also—precisely through its "reduction"—afforded a deeper insight into the four statements in the NT in which creation is seen as the work of the Word (John 1), of Christ (1 Cor. 8:6; Col. 1), and of the Son (Heb. 1). Traditional dogmatics heard in these passages information about the role which the second person of the Trinity, who later became man, already had in the work of creation. It has not been able to do much if anything with this because of its rule that the outgoing works of the Trinity are one; creation is thus just as much the work of the Father and of the Spirit. But these statements have nothing to do with the Trinity problematic. They do, however, make a close connection between creation and the work of the historical Jesus Christ. Without a distinct transition the four passages speak of the one Christ who created the world and brought about redemption. Here, from the perspective of redemption, the same extrapolating mode of speaking is used as in the OT when it speaks about creation in the colors of Israel's passage through the Red Sea (e.g. Isa. 51:9–11). F. Mussner writes correctly about this connection of creation and salvation in Col. 1: "The eschatological salvation is projected back into the creation to the extent that it was done 'for him'" (*MS* II, pp. 460–461). Barth was the first to see the dogmatic significance of these passages and to draw radical conclusions from them, in *CD* II,2, par. 33 and *CD* III,1.

This is indeed a matter which has far-reaching consequences for the study of the faith. In the history of the church, dogmatics has most of the time based itself on a reading of Gen. 1 and 2 which regarded these chapters as containing divine information about a past which is inaccessible to us. Thus they could easily support the idea that creation was a closed event, one which produced a static and perfect result: a completed world in the "state of rectitude." This approach agreed very well with the generally accepted Aristotelian-Ptolemaic world view. After a short while the human race and nature lost this paradisaical state through Adam's fall. Later, however, the second Adam came to restore this state. Salvation thus serves the order of creation. Therefore that order itself cannot be described in terms of salvation, grace, Christ, etc. Influenced by Bullinger's federal theology, Reformed Scholasticism began to speak of the situation in Paradise as a covenant of works (especially since Cocceius). See H XIII. The original perfect state was regarded as the counterpart of the state of grace in

Christ; in the covenant of works man could earn eternal life by his obedience to the commandment. It was only due to the fall that God had to open up an entirely different way to eternal life, in the covenant of grace.

Historical criticism has put an end to this type of thinking. We know now that older traditions of creation lie behind the two creation stories (P: Gen. 1:1–2:4a; J: Gen. 2:4b–25) and that both are intended as a preamble to the historical books about God's relationship with Israel that describe creation in a manner that fits the "style" of God's association with Israel. This noncontrasting but introductory relation of creation to salvation is found in all biblical designs of creation, including those in the NT.

This conception has not been entirely unknown, though, in the history of theology. Already Irenaeus came up with it (but beside it he mentions the idea of restoration). For him Adam is not the perfect man, but the novice who by making the right choice is to attain to a higher degree of fellowship with God (*AH* III.32; IV.61–64). God could immediately have given perfection *(to teleion)* to man, but newly born man *(arti gegonōs)* "could not possibly have received that, or even if he had received it, could he have contained it, or containing it, could he have retained it. It was for this reason that the Son of God, although he was perfect, passed through the state of infancy in common with the rest of mankind, partaking of it thus not for his own benefit, but for that of the infantile stage of man's existence, in order that man might be able to receive him" (IV.38). This line is preserved in the school of Antioch, in Greek Orthodox and Anglican theology, and (as a thin side line) in other traditions. For traces of it in Roman Catholic theology see H. U. von Balthasar, *Karl Barth* (1951), pp. 336–344, and H. Küng, *Justification* (E.T. 1964), chs. 22 and 23. Further H. Berkhof, "Schepping en voleinding" (1961), in *Bruggen en bruggehoofden* (1981), pp. 37–49; and J. Verburg, *Adam* (1973), ch. III. In Western theology, however, this elevation line has on the whole been displaced by the restitution line.

Barth introduced a change with his twofold thesis: "Creation as the external basis of the covenant—the covenant as the internal basis of creation" (*CD* III,1). Particularly Roman Catholic theology has spun this thread further, connecting it with Teilhard de Chardin's doctrine of evolution. Out of an abundance of literature we mention: K. Rahner, "Christology within an Evolutionary View of the World," in *Theological Investigations,* V (E.T. 1966), pp. 157–192; A. Hulsbosch, *De schepping Gods* (1963); H. A. M. Fiolet, *Vreemde verleiding* (1968); and E. Schillebeeckx, *Tussentijds verhaal* (1978), pp. 121–140. From the Protestant side see A. Szekeres, *Christuswaarheid en wordende schepping* (1971).

There are, however, voices which strongly contradict this relation of creation and salvation and which, with nuances, want to maintain the traditional line. Especially Lutheran theology leans toward that because, analogous to and on the basis of the contrast of law and gospel, it aims at a contrasting relationship between creation and salvation. Creation is then the voice of law, of the perfect order intended by God which the sinner is unable to fulfill. Only one who fails in creation can through justification in Christ receive a new access to God. See R. Prenter, *Creation and Redemption,* esp. pars. 15–19. In *God in Nature and History* (1968), too, which follows more closely the elevation line, the more Lutheran countervoice of the restitution line has been included under the title "Creation, New Creation, and the Unity of the Church" (pp. 133–140).

In the theology of the Dutch Reformed Church this opposite point of view was defended by A. A. van Ruler, for whom Christ is indeed "central" but not the "central concern," because Christ is the "emergency measure" through which God brings creation back in line. See especially his 1961 art. "De verhouding van het kosmologische en het eschatologische element in de christologie," now in *Theologisch werk,* I (1969), pp. 156–174. For the *logos asarkos* (who later became man for a totally different purpose) he sees only a mediatorial function in creation. His conclusion is: "The redemptive work in Jesus Christ only happened in order that the creation would again be able to exist before the face of God; it is thus only a moment, an emergency measure in the one counsel and the one work of God; the beginning and the end are more real than what is in the middle; they are therefore also different, both as concerns content and structure." He therefore argues "for a reverse relationship of purpose between redemption and creation" (p. 165). The evangelists and apostles in John 1, Col. 1, and Heb. 1 "easily become somewhat lyrical in their tone." "A dogmatician is a bit calmer. At times he has the feeling that things blend too much in this lyricism. Especially when he reads Col. 1" (p. 159).

Consciously we take our starting-point in the view that creation is the preamble of and pointer to salvation. In our judgment those who reject this do not take the results of biblical-theological investigation sufficiently seriously. We can understand their resistance: they fear that this conception may lead to an evolutionary view in which it is no longer possible to do full justice to sin as rebellion and to salvation as deliverance from lostness. Whether this fear is justified will become clear later in this book.

9. If Christ with his life and life-surrender, his resurrection and exaltation, as the firstfruits of a new humanity, is the pattern of existence for which creation is intended, the question must arise to what extent this purpose is written into the structures of creation and can be learned from them. In any case, this implies that two fundamental statements have been made about creation: on the one hand the confession concerning its goodness which we dealt with above and which was presupposed in the preceding discussion, and on the other hand its provisional and unfinished state. In the eyes of faith, in the combination and the tension of goodness and provisionalness creation itself is a witness to its christological-eschatological purpose. But exactly this second element was until very recently almost completely ignored in the study of the faith. For everything that lies at the basis of that statement, especially the presence of suffering and death in God's good creation, and furthermore the catastrophes and the struggle for life in nature, all those things dogmatics treated for centuries under the rubric "the consequences of sin." It was assumed as a matter of course that the good creation corresponded to the static Greek ideal of perfection in which such dissonants did not fit. Whatever was unharmonious had to be ascribed to the great disruption of sin. From that viewpoint it was natural to think that all this was a punishment in which man had to acquiesce.

Today we know that this represent a representation of the facts is untenable already for this reason, that struggle, suffering, death, and natural catastrophes were already a fact millions of years before man appeared on the scene. We also know that these negative phenomena are not purely negative, because they hang inseparably together with the positive good of the continuation of life. Through the food chain, animals which devour each other maintain a biological equilibrium whose disruption would turn the earth into a desert, a jungle, or a slaughterhouse. We know, too, that man, biologically considered, is a highly complex animal, and that therefore also for him pain and calamities, suffering and death, are an integral aspect of created existence. This holds even for phenomena which at first sight appear clearly connected with sin; we think of the disposition toward aggressiveness, inherited from the animal world, which we must learn to control, yet which we can never do entirely without as a stimulus for the development of life.

As humans we stand in a dual relation to this negative side of creation: on the one hand we accept it as an integral part of existence; on the other hand we experience it as an abnormality and rebel against it. This is seen in our medical, hygienic, and social care activities, and in our unceasing attempts to ward off natural calamities, crop failures, epidemic diseases, etc.

Man, both male and female, is a kind of being who does not acquiesce in existence as it is, and in that respect differs radically from the non-human creation (insofar as we can understand it). As the only creature that is in principle dissatisfied, man rebels against existing reality, and so presupposes the existence of another kind of reality of which it dreams, but without experiencing it. Man is created with what can alternately be called nostalgia, rebellion, longing, idealism, illusion, and utopia. He or she cannot just be what they are. They run ahead of themselves. One can also say: man "is" precisely that which he is not (yet). His authentic existence lies above and ahead of him—as a promise or as a mirage? Faith says: as a promise; the creation is intended to be elevated and to become a world which is centered upon and which serves a radically new form of humanity, in conformity to the image of the glorified Christ. The believer knows of this secret and therefore will not be found in the company of those who like to acquiesce in the present world, but among those who actively long for another world.

With that we acknowledge that the world contains a tragic element. It is incomplete, unfinished, defective. There is much happiness, true, but even that is not without the awareness of its imperfection. There is much sorrow for which no one can be blamed. There is much suffering which no one can remove. We know that all this is part of God's good creation, yet also that it will be eradicated from the new world as this is re-created in Christ. Therefore, if necessary, we can acquiesce in it, and wherever possible fight against it. What we cannot do is explain it. Why has God (provisionally) wanted something which nevertheless (ultimately) he does not want? The only answer we can give is no answer: apparently it was never God's purpose to call into existence a ready-made and complete world. He evidently wants his creation to go through a history of resistance and struggle, of suffering and dying. If this is the will of him whom we have come to know as holy love, we may believe that some day it will become clear that all the pains of childbirth and growing up of this world in process of becoming cannot be compared with the glorious outcome.

Various writers in the Bible, from different perspectives and out of their own experiences, have pondered the vexing negative aspects of the creation. Traditional dogmatics has made too limited a choice out of these aspects, whose elements, moreover, it often pulled out of their context. It has especially operated with the curse in Paradise in Gen. 3:17–19 and with Paul's reflection on sin and death in Rom. 5:12–21 (cf. 6:23). In both cases there is suggested a causal connection between sin and physical evil. In our judgment this was the way in which both writers, using the world view with which they were familiar and the language they had, tried to articulate the inseparable bond between man and his environment; for man who is alienated from God suffering and death become total enemies which ultimately he has to face alone and defenseless. That we must be careful not to harden these notions into dogmatic theories becomes evident when we consider how the same Yahwist in Gen. 2:7, and even more emphatically in 2:19f., asserts man's affinity with and dependence on the lower creation; and when we see how the same Paul in Rom. 8:18–22 and in 1 Cor. 15:44–49 speaks about physical evil apart from sin. More about that later.

The statement that the world was created good (*ṭôḇ*), even very good (*ṭôḇ m^{e}'ōd*, Gen. 1) was wrongly taken as evidence of perfection; good, however, means here primarily "suitable for its purpose," namely communion between God and man. In dogmatics, the book of Job, which is a sustained and intense protest against the linking of sin and suffering (and not the only protest—see Luke 13:1–5; John 9:3), has never received the emphasis it should in the canonical choir. In the appeal to Isa. 11:6–8 (peace in the animal world in the messianic kingdom) the poetic language was not recognized and, moreover, it was erroneously concluded that this was a restoration of an original paradisaical state. The healing miracles of Jesus have often been regarded as a removal of the consequences of sin; yet their real purport was to erect signs of the coming Kingdom from which suffering is banished (Matt. 11:5, a citation from Isa. 35; cf. Matt. 12:28). Revelation 21 and 22 picture a perfected world which is not at all a restoration of the situation in Gen. 2: "He will wipe away every tear from their eyes, and death shall be no more, neither shall there be mourning nor crying nor pain any more, for the former things have passed away" (21:4, an allusion to Isa. 65:17–19). According to v. 1 the *ta prōta* are in general "the first heaven and the first earth," and "the sea."

Paul speaks even more directly about this provisional state of the world. In 1 Cor. 15:44b–49 he contrasts Adam and Christ quite differently than in Rom. 5:

the "first Adam" was made of the dust of the earth, as "soul," "natural" *(psychikos)*, "of dust" *(choikos);* the "second man" is not soul but life-giving spirit, not out of dust but from heaven. In God's order the lower comes first, "then the spiritual." They are related as seed and plant (v. 44). Rom. 8:18–25 speaks of "the whole creation" which groans (*stenazei*) as it longs for imperishableness; the world is in a state of "eager longing" which can be compared to the "pains of childbirth." Is that condition a result of the fall into sin? That is how many expositors look at it. Nevertheless, in my opinion the formulation and the context point in another direction. See v. 20: it is precisely without and against its will *(ouch' hekousa)* that the world is subjected to futility *(mataiotēs)*. Why? Because this happened to be the decree of God *(dia* + accusative). But that is not God's final word. He also has given it hope *(eph' elpidi)*. Therefore its groaning is meaningful. In connection with all these NT statements one should realize that they have been written after and against the background of Jesus' resurrection through whom, as a beginning, the basic human problem of death received a solution.

In the history of the church, man's powerless longing for what he is not has been deeply fathomed by Pascal in his *Pensées* (e.g. "Know that man infinitely surpasses himself," ed. Brunschvicg, fr. 434; though its description stands entirely in the restoration perspective). That tradition is continued by Vinet and the ethical theologians. But the rise of the theory of evolution put this restoration framework into a crisis, forcing a rethinking of the ambivalent character of existence. Bavinck thought he could solve the problem by positing that God, foreseeing the fall, already took it into account in the ordering of creation *(GD* III, par. 43, no. 340, end). Stranger yet is the fact that Brunner opposes this idea, though with greater hesitation (*Dg* II, pp. 131f.).

Interestingly, it is precisely Barth who, apparently without ascribing any theological relevance to the results of physical science, has nevertheless forcefully developed the doctrine of the provisional character of the creation. In *CD* III,1 he explicates, on pp. 372–376, the doctrine of "the shadow side of existence." Because this doctrine was not clearly distinguished from the doctrine of the "Nothingness," Barth expounded it again, in *CD* III,3, pp. 295–299. Creation is indeed "also in its negative aspect bordering on nothingness"—it is, as it were, the vulnerable side of existence which is turned toward the "nothing": "On this shadow side the creation is contiguous to nothingness" (p. 350)—but the creation praises its creator also with its shadow side, its poverty, darkness, fear, deprivation, and death. As creation with its bright side shows itself worthy of its creator, so with its dark side it shows itself dependent on its creator. With these two sides together it points to its redeemer and perfecter, the crucified and risen Christ. "God created man to lift him in His own Son into fellowship with Himself. This is the positive meaning of human existence. But this elevation presupposes a wretchedness of human and all existence which His own Son will bear and share. This is the negative meaning of creation. Since everything is created for Jesus Christ and His death and resurrection, from the very outset everything must stand under this twofold and contradictory determination" (p. 376).

A strong emphasis on the provisional character of creation is found in Roman Catholic literature, e.g. Hulsbosch, *De schepping Gods*, esp. X, the pastoral constitution *Gaudium et spes*, esp. 10 and 22, and *The New Catechism* (E.T. 1969), among others on pp. 259ff. In his article "God en de chaos," in *Theologisch werk*, V (1959), ch. III, A. A. van Ruler presents an entirely different approach; he seems to regard the shadow side (including guilt) entirely as the positive and definite will of God. See further the various contributions to this theme in *Wending* (July/Aug. 1962) under the heading "Het bittere raadsel van de goede schepping," *God in Nature and History*, esp. VII; J. Trojan, *Entfremdung und Nachfolge*, pp. 51–70. On the relation of tragedy and guilt, see H. J. Heering, *Tragiek* (1961), esp. XI-XV.

Why has God wanted it thus? One can point to the necessary and painful process in which the many need to grow into a unity (Teilhard de Chardin). With Van Ruler one can note that a cosmos without a chaos is unbearable and that the chaos is God's play. One can say that it is "exactly through this trial" that God "gives us the opportunity to achieve freedom for ourselves" (Hulsbosch, p. 156). With J. Hick one can believe: "What now threatens us as final evil will prove to have been interim evil out of which good will in the end have been brought" (*Evil and the God of Love*, 1967, pp. 399f.). But these answers have no more than individual and speculative significance. Quite different is D. Sölle, *Leiden* (1973), who sees suffering as especially caused by (social) guilt. We get no further than the conclusion of the book of Job where suffering is only and entirely traced back to the incomprehensibility of a God who calls us yet to trust him (38–42:6). See H. Wiersinga, *Verzoening met het lijden?* (1975). The last sentence of the larger type above is an allusion to Rom. 8:18. In my judgment we can say no more than is done there by Paul. The plus of the future over the creation marks our interim existence as provisional.

10. As concerns the doctrine of creation, the historical-critical study of the Bible and the hermeneutics based on it has, quantitatively, taken away much information, but qualitatively given back much more (see under 8). One important insight derived from this investigation has already been mentioned but requires further consideration: the conceptions of creation in the Old and New Testament, a fruit of extrapolation-to-the-beginning of experiences with God in redemptive history, were always, naturally, expressed with contemporary insights of nature and contemporary conceptions of the origin and existence of the world. Way back one spoke of a struggle between Yahweh and the Leviathan, later of the creation and watering of the world desert, still later of a creation out of nothing by the creative word of progressively higher forms of existence, and in the Hellenic period of a creation through the logos and a creation of "powers" or "elements of the world." It is senseless and impossible to harmonize all these representations. In fact, their multiplicity constitutes a challenge to following generations always to articulate afresh the belief in creation in contemporary views of the universe.

For our age that implies the task of articulating the belief in creation in terms of the evolutionary view of the universe. That seemed impossible in the previous century because Christian thinking was still attached to the (one-sidedly understood) creation account of Genesis 1, and because traditional deterministic Darwinism seemed to exclude the idea of creation. Both mutually impeding presuppositions have now fallen away. Contrary to the universal law of entropy, on our planet the evolutionary process has again and again lifted existing forms of reality over their own thresholds and led to results of the greatest improbability: a marvelous and capricious process which has nothing of a determined course but which should much rather be termed *évolution créatrice.*

Connecting the Christian belief in creation with this world view is certainly no more difficult than connecting it with the ancient Babylonian or the Aristotelian-Ptolemaic world view. In fact, we must even say that it is easier to link it to the notion of evolution than to the static Ptolemaic world view. After all, the doctrine of evolution makes a great historical process of what we call nature, a process leading to the phenomenon man, and so continuing in man, leading in a new way toward a new and open future. In the Bible creation and history are similarly connected. In Genesis 1 creation is set forth as a historical process taking six days—we would say taking the form of an evolutionary process—and so prefigures the history of redemption which reaches toward the eschatological future. This does not mean the obliteration of the difference between belief in creation and the theory of evolution. The creation faith contains as such no information about the manner in which God called the world into existence. And, conversely, the theory of evolution has no answer to the question as to the sense and purpose of that turbulent process which billions of years ago likely began with a massive, chaotic gas cloud. The believer who accepts the evolutionary view regards it as the description of the phenomenal outside of the creation event—for the time being, for later it may turn out that other models are needed with which to speak about the origin of the universe. The vocabulary of the creation faith can as such be connected with all kinds of scientific vocabularies which can underline, concretize, and illustrate it; but what this faith speaks of remains independent of all these modes of expression.

On the relation of faith and natural science in Gen. 1, see Von Rad, *OT Theology*, I, p. 148, where he ends with the sentence: "In the scientific ideas of the time theology had found an instrument which suited it perfectly, and which it could make use of for the appropriate unfolding of certain subjects—in this case the doctrine of Creation." On creation and evolution, see Brunner, *Dg* II, pp. 39–42.

Purposely we referred to evolution as a theory, a doctrine, a vision. A handy summary is found in Publication no. 38 of the Nederlands Gesprekscentrum, *Evolutie* (1970), which clearly indicates the facts on which this theory is based. There are enough facts to make it unwarranted any longer to speak of a hypothesis (a term with which Christians used to dismiss evolution), but not enough to regard it as proven fact (as is currently suggested in popular science). This booklet emphasizes that the vision preceded the investigation and its results: "Before the facts there was the myth of evolution, before the theory of evolution the idea of evolution" (p. 4). Just as unwarranted as the earlier rejection is the current tendency on the part of many Christians to canonize it in a way that is reminiscent of the Christianizing of the Ptolemaic world view.

Meanwhile it is clear that the insight into the coherence of creation and redemption (see under 8) had to lead to the discovery of converging lines with the theory of evolution. One could ask the naughty question whether perhaps men like Barth and Von Rad made their hermeneutical discoveries due to the influence of evolutionary thinking. Such is not the case, however; they were led onto this track by the historical-critical study of the Bible, in a time (between the two world wars) when the theory of evolution had a period of disrepute. The search for a synthesis between creation and evolution had, however, happened much earlier, in Anglican theology. See Lewis B. Smedes, *The Incarnation: Trends in Modern Anglican Thought* (1953), and A. M. Ramsay, *From Gore to Temple* (1960). On the European continent this type of thinking gained entrance through the enormous inspiration given by the posthumous work of Teilhard de Chardin (d. 1955). This Jesuit biologist has not had many direct followers among theologians. That was impossible since an uncritical extrapolation from his biological-anthropological categories could not possibly have done justice to the great realities of sin and reconciliation. But in Roman Catholic theology his vision has had the effect of putting all of theology in a different key. See the literature mentioned under 8 and 9. Following the line of Barth, Protestant theology could have favored a division of territory between faith and science, or, following Brunner, a modest link which would be limited to the doctrine of creation. Furthermore, the two volumes *Geloof en natuurwetenschap* (Dippel, De Jong, and others, 1965 and 1967) are very reserved on this point. See also Dippel's criticism of Hulsbosch's book (referred to above) in *Kerk en theologie,* July 1965. A much greater assimilation of evolutionary thinking from the Protestant side is defended in S. M. Daecke, *Teilhard de Chardin und die evangelische Theologie* (1967); by the biologist-theologian G. Altner in *Grammatik der Schöpfung* (1971); and by A. Szekeres in "La pensée religieuse de Teilhard de Chardin et la signification théologique de son Christ cosmique" in the symposium *Le Christ cosmique de Teilhard de Chardin* (1969), where he shows the convergence between Teilhard de Chardin and the new hermeneutics. For the pros and cons of a separation, see *Kerk en theologie* (October 1983).

Theology derives its insights from the gospel and not from current scientific and ideological views. Yet we believe that the truth does not contradict itself. What is experienced as truth in other areas of reality may shed new light on what the gospel tells us and thus can contribute to the ongoing articulation of the gospel. In any case, we are familiar with the negative reverse and know how difficult the coupling of revelation with an antiquated world view has made it for many to hear the gospel. In this task of passing on the gospel, theology must not be an obstacle but serve as an interpretive aid. This is not too difficult with the doctrine of creation on account of the convergence between the new hermeneutics and the vision of evolution. That convergence might also work fruitfully in other areas. An impressive (Anglican) example is A. R. Peacocke, *Creation and the World of Science* (1979).

11. Most handbooks on dogmatics include a section on angels in their discussion of creation. For the Bible speaks repeatedly of such "ministering spirits," sinless inhabitants of a world in which spirit is not hampered by matter but uses it freely, without limitations; at the same time they are creatures who, in spite of and with their senses of a higher order, serve the cause of the redemption, protection, and direction of earthly humanity. What can one say about these beings in a study of the faith? Faith is based on the encounters of God and man within the context of our earthly reality. Humans may make the discovery that in special cases God uses the mediation of extraterrestrial beings for such encounters. One who cannot speak from experience about such mediation does well to refrain from passing judgment on the credibility of those who maintain that they do know such experiences. But one cannot expect of him that he develops a doctrine of angels, an angelology. By far the great majority of systematic theologians of our time are not ready for that. From that it by no means follows that they are on the wrong track. For no matter how often the Bible may speak of incidental appearances of angels, there is hardly any reflection on it, and one finds no basic outlines of an angelology.

Nevertheless, the accounts of angels are based on a threefold assumption which is certainly closely related to the Israelite-Christian faith. The appearances of angels give expression to the belief that (a) God's world, including those beings who are consciously subject to him, is far richer than what can be seen on our planet; (b) outside this provisional and alienated world there are other realities which already now are fully and perfectly filled with his glory; and (c) these worlds do not look down with contempt on our darkened planet but possess a genuine willingness to be used in the service of God's love for man to help our world reach its destination. It is worth considering whether the belief in the "eternally rich God" does not point us in the direction of this threefold insight, even though we know that nothing can be proven here. One who is convinced that man is the only rational creature in the universe and that God has nowhere yet reached his ultimate goal would attach a narrowness and importance to the redemptive events on earth which is in conflict with the bright and wide expanse of sky under which these events take place. A generation like ours which assumes (without proof), in its theories and science-fiction literature, the existence of conscious beings on other planets who are interested in this earth can hardly find the belief in angels strange. But theology can do more than suggest such lofty, faraway, and yet helping nearby beings.

From the Bible no angelology can be constructed. See *TDNT* I, *s.v. angelos.* The "messengers" or "sons of God" function in widely varying contexts. The biblical givens can hardly be put on one denominator: the Angel of the Lord in the Pentateuch, the heavenly royal court in Job, the princes of the nations in Daniel, the heavenly choir on Christmas night, the "powers" in Col. 1, the angels of judgment in the Apocalypse. In the NT a prominent group of believers, the Sadducees, does not believe in angels (Acts 23:8). This makes it problematic to what extent the belief in angels was indigenous in Israel, or whether it was a foreign element. Yet all too easily on inadequate grounds it is assumed that on this point Israel has been strongly influenced by the outside. In the primitive polytheistic religions the belief in spirits and demons functioned entirely differently than the belief in angels in Israel, so that the difference is much greater than the similarity. The angelic figure belongs to a faith which views the one God as being beneficially related to his earthly creation; the angel is a creature, a ministering creature. The belief in angels has been stronger at one time than another. In the last two centuries before Christ it became very strong, likely because Greek philosophical influences led to a belief in which God was more and more removed. The NT contains some traces of a later coloring of redemptive events by this belief. We think not only of the Lucan protevangel or the insertion in John 5:4 but also of the fact that while Mark sees only a young man sitting by the opened tomb, the other evangelists speak of angels.

In the history of the church, the church fathers up to and including Augustine generally spoke with reserve about the angels. The great influence of Pseudo-Dionysius the Areopagite quickly changed that; in his *De caelesti hierarchia* (ca. 500) he grouped the angels in a descending series (three times three "choirs") as mediators between God and men. Since then the *locus de angelis bonis* became very elaborate in Scholastic and Counter-Reformation theology. See Thomas, *ST* I, q. 50–64 and 106–113. The Reformation introduced a radical moderation in this locus. But Protestant Scholasticism broadened it again through biblicistic combinations of texts. Schleiermacher put an end to that. He treated the angels in an Appendix (*CF* pars. 42 and 43). His carefulness and soberness in discussing this subject have much to say to us. His conclusion about this particular approach is: "It can, therefore, continue to have its place in Christian language without laying on us the duty of arriving at any conclusion with regard to its truth" (par. 42). Most present-day theologians are brief, reserved, or hesitant on this subject. An exception is Barth, *CD* III,3, par. 51 (pp. 369–418), since he assumes that also in these statements the Bible is authoritative. But according to him one can speak about these beings only in the form of *Saga.* He aims to give a christological foundation to angelology and rewrite it from that perspective. As a result he puts all the emphasis on the ministering function of the angels in the redemptive events. They become strictly functional, almost devoid of ontological contours. This part of Barth's work has had less influence than any other. Deriving it from the doctrine of the devil (see Brunner, *Dg* II, p. 146) or from the authority of the belief of Jesus (so among others Althaus, *CW* II, p. 69) has not been convincing either. Our empirical age is not conducive to making pronouncements in this area. It now appears strange to us that a man like Van der Leeuw could so passionately defend the presence of these heavenly servants. How we as moderns can visualize the relation of higher spirits to the earth is not the kind of subject one can read about in systematic theologies. For that one should consult books like C. S. Lewis's *Out of the Silent Planet* (1938). For the history of angelology, see Barth, *CD* III,3, pp. 369–418.

It is customary also to speak about heaven in connection with the angels. In the Bible the word has three distinct yet confluent meanings: (1) the visible starry firmament; (2) a higher created reality, inaccessible to human observation, where God is praised and served; (3) the sphere, the space of God's being itself. In the context of our subject our concern is with the second meaning, for it seems to coincide with the significance of the angels. Up to a point this is indeed so. But the concept of heaven includes more. The word *heaven* belongs to the figurative language of the faith, to a language which, precise though it may be, points to real though shadowy distances which loom up when we encounter God. The earth is not alone. It exists as the opposite of a higher created reality where God's will is continuously and perfectly done. This reality is not only the counterpart of the earth, but also the partner which surrounds it with blessings, and the end for which it is intended. Not that the earthly life, as that which is inferior and no longer useful, will be cast off; it will be made heavenly, glorified. The goal is: "Thy will be done, on earth as it is in heaven." Everything that serves that purpose may be called "heavenly." Christ comes from heaven, we receive a heavenly calling, heavenly gifts, and a heavenly blessing, and we expect a heavenly inheritance, a heavenly city, and a heavenly country. Faith looks beyond, and its horizon is wider than our world in its present state. Hence we conceive of the angels as in that heavenly world, yet that world itself is more comprehensive. It is also the exemplar and emblem of the earthly creation. Salvation means that heaven is active in penetrating the earth. That belief is the opposite of world flight. Speaking about heaven we say that our world still exists in a lower stage of development, and that we expect that God's work on earth will lift the earth to a higher level of existence, in harmony and fellowship with a mode of existence which is fully permeated with God, of which we surmise that for a long time already it is blessingly and invitingly embracing us.

See *TDNT* V, *s.v. ouranos.* Further K. Schilder, *Wat is de hemel?* (1935), an eschatology with much emphasis on the redemptive-historical function of heaven. Barth's conception is found in *CD* III,3, par. 51, esp. 418–450. In this spirit G. C. van Niftrik wrote his *De hemel* (1968); the subtitle "Over de ruimtelijkheid van God" is indicative that the third meaning of heaven is the starting-point and main concern here, and that that heaven is also man's future expectation.

Does heaven, via process theology, receive a new place in theological cosmology? So in W. Welker, *Universalität Gottes und Relativität der Welt* (1981), esp. chs. IV and V.

26. MAN (I): LOVE AND FREEDOM

THE WHOLE CONCERN of the study of the faith is man. With just as much right we can say that the concern is God. For its concern is their encounter and relation, the common history in which both are involved. Therefore we ought to be aware of what we are doing when we offer a separate doctrine of God and devote one or more separate paragraphs to man. In the previous chapter we sought to derive the contents of the doctrine of God strictly from the encounter, as the supposition of the history in which he has involved himself with us. Now that we begin to speak about man we need to presuppose that here within the framework of the doctrine of creation we look at man from a very limited perspective. Here the concern is not yet man in the history in which he is involved with God, but the phenomenon man which is the presupposition of this history. We are thus not concerned with real man but with an abstract formula, with "man as such." One might ask of what use this theme is in the study of the faith. Provided the proper limits are kept in mind, abstraction and formalization can contribute to greater elucidation and depth, which is what we are after. In a world like ours in which man, on all the fronts of his knowing and erring, his achievements and failures, curiously or bewildered asks himself who he really is, the Christian faith must also know what answer to this vital question it receives from revelation.

By putting it like this we introduce at the outset a decisive limitation. The study of the faith does not pretend to offer a comprehensive anthropology. It does not devise a total picture of man. Theology can do this no more than psychology, sociology, or anthropo-biology. It only asks: what can be learned from man's history with God about man himself? At the same time it assumes that this history is so central and so disclosing as concerns the being of man, who he really is, that here fundamental discoveries can be made, without which we would not really get to know ourselves.

In the history of the church there has for many centuries been an extensive theologization about man in the framework of the doctrine of creation. This was possible because the Bible was regarded as a source of supernatural information about all kinds of themes, among them the theme of man. That expressed itself in an eagerness to combine biblical statements about the being of man (as a rule the starting-point was Gen. 1:26), about his composition (body, soul, spirit), and about his origin (is the soul a product of procreation or an immediate creation?—traducianism versus creationism). The results varied considerably, based as they were on selected passages from the Bible, a selection, moreover, which—usually without being aware of it—was determined, limited, and filled with traditional or contemporary concepts of man. By studying how systematic theologies have poured meaning into Gen. 1:26, one could write a piece of Europe's cultural history.

Thomas has a very elaborate anthropology. In *ST* I, q. 75–102 he discusses: soul and body, their relationship, the faculties of the soul, intellectual faculties, the faculties of will and desire (with a complete epistemology), procreation, the situation in Paradise, etc.; he defines the image of God as *intellectualis natura,* which includes primarily: "aptitudinem naturalem ad intelligendum et amandum Deum" (q. 93, art. 4). On this point, too, the Reformation has effected a radical reduction. In Luther man's being is concentrated entirely on his relationship to God (*coram Deo*) as a lost and justified sinner. Calvin has one chapter on man as a created being *(Inst* I,xv). His anthropology is much more limited than that of Thomas, and at the same time, in contrast to Thomas' Aristotelianism, clearly Platonic in character: the immortal soul is the more noble part of man *(nobilior pars),* consisting of intellect and will; it is separate from the body *(a corpore separatum),* for the latter is only a perishable house of clay. Calvin's doctrine of the image of God, which has a christological basis and which he sees as consisting in the right relationship with God, has only a tenuous connection with this fleeting psychology. In Protestant Scholasticism the study of man as he was in creation, also called man in the state of integrity, is expanded once more, again with Aristotelian concepts (see esp. R II, par. 20 4 B). Later Descartes' dualism becomes influential. And in the dogmatic anthropologies of the 19th century the influence of (German) Idealistic thinking is everywhere noticeable, especially that of Kant and Hegel and later of the dominant faculty psychology. So through the centuries Christian anthropology has been a combination of biblical and contemporary thought patterns—in which, according to the designers, the first element was dominant, but as later generations saw it, the second.

For a number of reasons we cannot continue this tradition. First of all, because in the 20th century we have discovered how limited the denominator of all these designs was. Not counting exceptions, they were all based on a static-idealistic-individualistic conception of man. Man was regarded as an independent spiritual being. That picture of man we have mainly inherited from the Greeks, and this legacy has distorted or displaced the biblical notions. Since Heidegger's *Geschichtlichkeit* and the emphasis on the changeableness of man, he is no longer seen as a static being. And Marx, Darwin, and Freud have put an end to the Idealistic and individualistic approach. Humanness is now defined as fellow-humanness and viewed first of all as it is related to and differs from animal existence. For these reasons the traditional Christian conceptions of man with their "Greek" style have become foreign to us. In the entirely different conceptions of phenomenology, existentialism, and neo-Marxism we find all kinds of elements which can help us to rediscover the biblical proclamation regarding man.

But now one could ask what there is against making in our age a conscious combination of biblical and contemporary anthropology, formally similar to the way this used to be done unconsciously. In the process of articulating the gospel for our age there is certainly room for that. But the study of the faith is not the place for that. Having become aware of the unconscious combinations made by earlier centuries, it is rather the task of dogmatics strictly to ascertain what the authentic and indispensable evangelical aspects in anthropology are. Precisely this restriction enables her to exercise a salutary critical and inspiring function in the tangle of existing pictures of man. The fact that the time is past in which theology and philosophy together had a monopoly on anthropology forces her even more into this reducing role. Especially in recent decades a whole spectrum of sciences studying man has arisen: psychology, sociology, anthropobiology, pedology, andragology, cultural anthropology, and others, and most of these with several branches. Each has its own specific approach to man which determines the method and limits the results. Theological anthropology cannot act as if this historically grown methodological state of affairs is nonexistent. We are rightly asked what our source of knowledge, our point of view, and our method are. Border crossings are permitted only if good grounds can be adduced for that. Also for that reason, in dogmatics we cannot go back to earlier combinations with ideas derived from elsewhere.

In our time there is still another factor. Less than ever before do we have the courage to construct comprehensive pictures of man. The second technical revolution drags us along toward an unknown future. In the time between our grandparents and us more changes have taken place in man and in his environment than in many previous centuries taken together. Year after year we are surprised at the new discoveries we make about ourselves. We have the feeling that we no longer and not yet know who we really are. We are still on the way toward our full identity. As Christians this does not frighten us. For we know that our real identity is hidden with Christ in God (Col. 3:3) and that it has not yet been revealed what we shall be (1 John 3:2), or how God ultimately viewed and intended us when he created us.

Finally, we point again to the historical-critical way of reading the Bible and the hermeneutics based on it. The Bible is no more a textbook for anthropology than for astronomy or biology. In the Bible, people in diverse situations and using different concepts articulate what they think of man in the light of the encounter with God. The Yahwist in Gen. 2 has a more "Aristotelian," the Priestly Codex in Gen. 1 a more "Platonic" approach. The picture of man of Ecclesiastes is quite different from that of Ps. 8, and the one of Deuteronomy very different from that of Paul. But even more striking is that in the Bible man-in-himself is only rarely a separate theme. So from all sides we are pressed to practice strict moderation in our theological doctrine of man. We do not regard that as a loss. We are rather confident that we can make some contribution if in the discussion about man we adduce only and fully those perspectives which we have received in the revelational encounter.

The first thing we will then have to say is that man is apparently a being who is made to encounter God, to respond to his Word. Man is a responding creature. One is inclined to quickly replace this word "responding" by "responsible." But that would be a restriction. That would one-sidedly put the relationship within the frame of command and duty. The elements of offer and surrender are then excluded from the outset. Conversely, "responding" implies too much. For it is not said that man will accept this word-offer. What it does imply is that he is made to do it. Therefore, I want to describe man as a "respondable" being. It does not seem likely that we shall ever be able to tell precisely where the borderline between man and animal lies. From the point of view of theology it must be said that man had only become fully man when he became aware of God's presence and learned to pray.

By describing man as "respondable" we delimit him from the outset in his maturity and autonomy. The first word does not come from him. He is made man by an initiative from the outside and from above. His creativity is based on re-creativity. And no less important is that with this description we have found that man's essence lies in a relationship, namely the relationship with God. From the standpoint of the Christian faith it is out of the question to regard man as a self-contained being who later happens to enter into relationships with other beings. Man is that creature who is made to live with God. We do not imply thereby that man is only this relationship, and not even that he is only relationship. He is a being who only in the relationship becomes himself. But, of course, he must exist in order to enter into a relationship. Therefore we must distinguish between his being and his relationships. But from the start we have to say of this being that he is made for relationships, and in theology that he is made for the relationship with God. Further theology cannot go. It has no means of its own to develop a doctrine about the essence of man. It possesses no information about the relation of body and soul, the conscious and the unconscious, heredity and nurture, soul and spirit, intellect and will, individual and community, etc. It will have to leave theorizing on these matters to philosophy or the special sciences that deal with it. Its own insight into man's respondability-to-God does, however, give it a criterion for critical judgments. From the outset it will have to reject concepts of man which leave no room for this insight. Incidentally, faith's view of man can be connected with all kinds of views of man, modified or corrected or not, as is evident from church history. But in the study of the faith we are not concerned with such connections, but with the constants in terms of which every Christian conception of man needs to be constructed, because they are an inherent datum of the revelational encounter itself.

In Gen. 1 the world is created through the speaking of God. That is also how man is created. But he alone is not made "according to his kind," but "in our image." This is a comprehensive expression. Because so far in the passage God has been pictured only as a speaking God, "in his image" must *inter alia* mean: one who like God can speak, the only creature that can perceive and respond to the creative word.

In dogmatics not much thought has been given to man's relation to the animal. For ages a Platonic-Idealistic view of man prevented such an interest. In the Genesis creation stories this is altogether different. After the aquatic animals and the birds are created on the fifth day, the land animals and man are made together on the last day of creation (Gen. 1:24f.). According to the second account man is in the company of the animals until he becomes aware that this does not satisfy his need for fellowship (Gen. 2:18–20). Elsewhere the OT strongly emphasizes the common lot of man and animal, while fully recognizing the profound differences. For that reason already the Christian church should not so fiercely have rejected the evolutionary connection of animal and man in biology and zoology since the previous century. The investigation of the difference between animal and man in modern ethology and anthropo-biology is also for the Christian a fascinating concern. Does the uniqueness of man lie in his ability to make fire, to make tools, in his naked skin, his language, his erect posture, his poverty of instincts, his helplessness, his disharmony and incompleteness? The theologian will want to take these (relative) differences between man and animal into account as additional factors that serve to make man's respondability possible.

By putting the relation central, theology is in line with present-day phenomenology, which has also greatly influenced psychology, psychiatry, sociology, and pedagogy. Besides Barth's fresh anthropological approach, in *CD* III,2, it is especially the influence of phenomenology that has freed theology from a sterile partnership with a static, individualistic conception of man, and has opened our eyes to the prime significance of relation in the Bible, though we may not forget that this relation presupposes the existence of a person's self, which does not coincide with the relation.

Meanwhile, by labelling man "respondable," we have given only a formal description. He is made to respond to the Word of God. But the content of that Word is the holy love with which God beneficially turns to his human creatures. Man is not made just for responding-as-such, but for responding to this Word, that is, to God's love. Love can only be responded to with reciprocal love. Man is made for *love.* He cannot do without that nurturing love from the outside, nor without responding to that love. In his love God created this entire world. But he created man as a being who could understand that love, and enjoy and respond to it. And that not as just one characteristic among many: in this relation of receiving and giving love, man heeds his most central calling and actualizes his true essence. In love, man becomes himself. Therein he flourishes, and therein his abilities answer to their purpose. Only a life which is nurtured by the certainty of God's love and is thus inspired to all kinds of reciprocal love, is a life which (to the extent that such is possible now) has reached its destination and goal. We know that from the manner in which and the purpose with which God approaches man as well as from what he desires of man.

In this context we are not concerned with the content of the concept of love, but with its central place as indicating the core of what it means to be man. This central place is evident in the Bible. It follows from the covenant relationship of man with a God whose essence is holy love. Very explicit statements in this regard are found in Deut. 6:5; Hos. 1 and 2; the great commandment, Mark 12:19–31; John 21; the "song of love," 1 Cor. 13; Rom. 13:10; Gal. 5:6; Eph. 5:2, and 1 John 4:7–21.

Love as the highest, or at least a very high, value in life has, under the influence of Christianity, so much become a matter of course in our European-American culture that we tend to forget that it is not natural at all to rank it so highly. There are many views of man and cultures in which it has little or no role at all. In the Oriental religions man is made much more for spiritual self-realization (Hinduism) or for losing himself in Nirvana (Buddhism). Elsewhere man is only a building block for the community: tribe, people, or state. In Nietzsche's teaching of the will to power and in his conception of the anti-Jesus Zarathustra we see a view of man in which love in the Christian sense has no role. And for the practice of life it holds for a great many that love is a beautiful word, but that when it comes to the crunch man is made for standing on his own rights and enjoying himself (assuming that the term "made for" does not already intimate too much of meaning and purpose). There are, however, enough other facts that indicate that this cannot be a last word. It is especially in psychopathology and psychiatry that we learn that a human life devoid of love becomes very much deformed. The Christian faith makes us understand these experiences as indications of what it basically means to be man.

If man is made to respond to God's love and to reflect it, this implies that *freedom* is essential for man in a manner and in a measure in which such cannot be said of the rest of creation with which we are familiar. For a response is in principle something else than an echo, since it is voluntarily given and formulated. And love is the highest form of voluntariness. Forced love is an inner contradiction. Love is the highest form in which our free will realizes itself. Therefore the Christian faith excludes every conception according to which man is finally only a product or a plaything of strange forces that are extraneous to him. At the same time we want to intimate with the word "finally" that man is not pure and absolute freedom. He is not God. He is situated and rooted in a world which both determines and limits him, and which is ruled and shaped by him. The relation of lot and freedom in man is one of the most difficult philosophical problems. This problem is directly related to the no less difficult relation of body and soul or spirit. The study of the faith is in no position to offer a theory about that. Faith is certain that this duality exists in man, and also that the freedom is so real and so great that we can genuinely decide and respond and are capable of real love and responsibility. Faith possesses no information about the how. It is bound, however, to reject any view of man which either attributes absolute freedom to him or restricts him so much that no room is left for his freedom. Man is not an angel, and not an animal either.

Freedom means that man, in contrast to the animal, is an unfinished being. Man is created as potentiality; his identity does not lie *in* him but *before* him. Therefore man lives in the sphere of history. By means of the freedom with which God endows him and the love to which he calls him, God begins a journey with him and involves him in a hazardous adventure. In the doctrine of God we observed already that thereby God also involves himself in an adventure. For by creating somewhere in the cosmos a free being, God limits his freedom to make room for daughters and sons as partners and counterplayers.

For the above-mentioned reasons it is neither necessary nor desirable to bring up again the age-old problem of the freedom of the will in philosophy (determinism versus indeterminism). The less so because in this area philosophy nowadays has to give the floor first of all to those sciences which move on the borderline of man and animal, of freedom and lot: biochemistry, genetics, ethology, anthropobiology, *et alia.* It is certain that man lives from a double fundamental experience: he knows that he is determined by the physical world and by his own corporeality; at the same time he knows that, nevertheless, he can, within limits, make decisions to act in this way or that. An explanation which does not try to do justice to both fundamental awarenesses, but explains one of the two away, does not deserve to be called explanation. Present-day biochemistry seeks the solution in a freedom which increases as the molecular connections in the organisms grow more complex. The higher the forms of life, the greater the freedom in the system of causality. Of theologians of this century particularly Tillich has reflected on this problem. He regards "freedom and destiny" as belonging to the ontological polarities of being man: "Destiny . . . is myself as given, formed by nature, history, and myself. My destiny is the basis of my freedom; my freedom participates in shaping my destiny." "The word 'destiny' . . . points not to the opposite of freedom but rather to its conditions and limits" (*ST* I, p. 185).

Illustrative is the difference in accent in the two creation accounts in Genesis. In J the togetherness comes first: man is made from the dust of the earth and begins his life as a companion of the animals; but the tree of the knowledge of good and evil awakens in him the awareness of his freedom of choice. In P man is created on the same day as the land animals, yet as a totally different being: he is created in the image of God so that he can have dominion over the rest of creation; the image of God thus implies freedom.

In the history of the church the concept of freedom has had a difficult time. An exception is the Eastern tradition; since Irenaeus it speaks openly of the freedom of the will. This is not the case in the West since Augustine emphasized man's lostness and the doctrine of predestination. The freedom of the will as inherently a datum of creation leads Roman Catholic theology to attribute a cooperative factor to the actualized will in the work of redemption. Conversely, Reformation theology was and is inclined, for fear of the latter, to minimize freedom as a created structure. Both sides are in danger of forgetting that sin can exist only as a result of (misused) freedom, and that the power and risks of freedom are so great that freedom is even free to destroy itself. A strong emphasis on freedom as an integral aspect of man does not prejudice in any way what may happen to that freedom in the history which it inaugurates. Except that man remains responsible in everything, also when he forgets or denies his responsibility.

Finally, we must note that freedom, as the infrastructure of love, is always means and never purpose. For the modern Western spirit freedom often seems to be its own purpose. The Christian faith cannot agree with that. It must view the misuse of freedom as being just as bad as the lack of freedom. With Paul (Gal. 5) it insists that Christ sets us free *from* the law and *for* love. "Freedom to serve God" (Augustine).

On p. 184 we said that we must limit ourselves to the constants out of which every Christian view of man is constructed. We have tried to indicate what these are. But we are not done with that so long as the impression remains that these elements, which the Christian faith discovers in the revelational encounter, might have validity only within the limits of this encounter. For man is an indivisible unity. And in the encounter with God he does not act with some aspect of his being, but as man who in his totality responds and acts from the center of his existence. Therefore what we discovered as being essential for the encounter with God is also fundamental for the totality of being human. If with respect to God man appears to be made for existence-in-relationship, then that is his real nature. If man is evidently made for the giving and receiving of love, then this holds also for other personal relationships. If evidently man is for that purpose endowed with an exceptionally high degree of freedom, then it must be possible to find that freedom back in the exceptional manner in which man acts everywhere in the cosmos. In this sense faith cannot help coming with the pretension that it does more than make just one contribution, among many, for the construction of the view of man. If it is the very nature of man that he is called to be-with-God, then he must also realize that nature as a being-with-his-fellow-human-being. For the other person is also one who is called to relate in love to God, to whom I have to pass on God's love, and vice versa; since he is created, like me, in the image of God, I am called to relate analogically to him. And in the cosmos around us, with which we cannot primarily have a relationship of love, the other element of our nature, that of freedom, must particularly come to stand out. Freedom means that we lift ourselves above the common lot we share with the cosmos (partially, but increasingly more) and take it into our own hands. With the same freedom with which we are called to respond to God's love, we must have dominion over the world, managing and ruling, cultivating and transforming it with our technology and culture. So the Christian vision of faith contains a number of elements which are decisive for our entire view of man, because they do not touch just one aspect but the essence itself. Saying that, it may, however, not be forgotten that the essential does not coincide with the totality, any more than the heart with the body or the center with the circle. Biology and the science of human behavior can enrich our insight into man with many new aspects. And the progressive evolution of man as the subject and object of so many startling discoveries and inventions may yet lead to further great surprises. But we believe that whatever can enrich and surprise us will, in the long run, always underscore and elucidate what we in the encounter with God discovered as being the core of man's nature: our respondability, our love, our freedom.

The reduction which we felt compelled to introduce in Christian anthropology thus turns out to be the opposite of a depreciation; it compels us much rather toward the perspectival center.

One may differ on how the mutual interaction of the three relations in man—child of God, neighbor to his fellowman, and lord over the world—is to be construed. In any case, they are of equal weight. None of the three is only a means with one of the others as purpose. What can be said is that the three relations of lord, neighbor, and child, in that order, open up steadily more comprehensive perspectives within which the earlier relation(s) is (are) taken up. In the larger print above it was emphasized that all these relations show the same "style." If theology had discovered this much earlier, it would have been able to contribute much more to the development of those ideas of which she now often needs to be reminded by the secular sciences, ideas such as freedom, relationality, fellow-humanness, technical mastery of the world, the meaning and limits of the manipulation of nature.

For a further consideration of the three relationships and for the relevant biblical data, see H. Berkhof, *De mens onderweg* (1960), pp. 7–59.

At this point we want to raise a question which has to be asked somewhere: are we to conclude from the revelational encounter that earthly man is a unique creature in the universe? Only now, in the space age, has this become a very meaningful question. The Christian church used to approach this question from the standpoint that the incarnation of the second person of the Trinity was a unique event, not capable of repetition here or elsewhere. We can hardly think in those categories any more. The question which we can ask is: could God create elsewhere similar beings, who are free and made for love, and associate with them in a history which is similar to or entirely different from the history of mankind on planet earth? Formulating the question like that, the answer can hardly be anything else than "yes." This is certainly true if, as we observed in our study of the doctrine of God, the condescendence is essential for the God who has created our universe.

Finally, a remark about the methodology used in this par. It is not the traditional-biblicistic one which is still used a great deal (also to some extent in my above-mentioned booklet). The anthropology is then constructed especially on the basis of an exegesis of the image of God in Gen. 1:26. This definition of P is, however, the reflection of only one witness. Even though there are hardly any other definitions in the Bible besides it, this does not mean that therefore it can be declared the dogmatic foundation. (For that matter its poly-interpretability makes every dogmatician read into it his own views.) Barth (*CD* III,2) introduced the christological method: from the fact and the manner in which God became man he tried to find out how man was intended. This method opened up surprising new perspectives. But it also meant an overloading of Christology and therefore it remained somewhat artificial. Here and in what follows we try to combine the best of both methods by keeping in mind the totality of the divine encounter in the redemptive history of OT and NT and by searching for its anthropological presuppositions.

27. MAN (II): GUILT AND FATE

AS ALREADY NOTED, man was created as a risky being. A creature grounded on love must possess the freedom, that is, the possibility to refuse love or to give it to someone or something for whom it was not intended. According to the Christian faith, with the creature man this possibility has become the "normal" reality; and this reality is so dominant and so fatal for man's destiny that God's revelation of salvation, as we know it, is a continuous reacting of God to this abnormality in his creation, a continuous struggle to banish sin and to carry out his purposes in the face of the power of sin.

In the study of the faith, man as creature and man as sinner are usually dealt with in two separate chapters. That hangs together with the manner in which for centuries Genesis 2 and 3 were separated from each other. Genesis 2 was read as containing information about a shorter or longer period of human perfection and bliss in Paradise; the fall into sin in Genesis 3 rudely disturbed this idyllic situation, resulting in a radical change in man and his environment. Yet neither the purport of the Yahwist's narratives of the origin of man and the world, nor our knowledge of man's primeval history gives us grounds to assume two such successive phases in the history of mankind. Concretely we know no other man than the one who is a sinner. Therefore what we said in paragraph 26 does not refer to a past condition of mankind, but it describes the structure which God as creator has given to man; therefore we said repeatedly that man is "made for" love. That does not imply that he corresponds to it or used to. Yet this structure is permanent and indestructible. Without this structure there would be no sin; after all, there would be nothing to sin against, as in the case of plants and animals. But owing to his freedom man is called functionally to fill this structure; the gifts he has from God he is to use in a specific direction; the *humanum* as potentiality demands actualization. And we know no other man than the one who mysteriously goes against the purpose of his existence.

Therefore in the one chapter on creation we consider in two paragraphs immediately following each other *man as creature and as sinner*. Thereby we say that sin was not just a regrettable wrong step of our remotest parents, but is deeply rooted in the creaturely structure of the risky being called man. It is also our judgment that it is so closely related to what we have discussed in paragraph 25 (9) as the "provisional state" of the creation that phenomenally it can often hardly be distinguished from it.

Yet we feel that creation and sin should be discussed in two clearly separate paragraphs. For sin does not belong to created reality and does not issue from it. On the contrary, it is unnatural. It is not a tragic fate put on our shoulders against our will. Then sin would no longer be sin, no expression of freedom; then we would not be responsible for it, nor guilty, but only to be pitied. Creation and sin do not coincide. Between them lies the leap of (misused) freedom. Sin is no incident—therefore it is discussed in the same chapter as man. Sin is not a creative given—therefore it is discussed separately after man.

For ages the study of the faith has distinguished between the state of integrity and the state of corruption. Yet there have been several theologians who under the first rubric have not given a description of a remote past but have limited themselves to a description of what we have designated here the creaturely structure of man. This is especially true of those who, following Irenaeus, did not think of the state of Paradise as a state of perfection, but as a pristine beginning in which man's freedom was as yet unactualized. According to Irenaeus, Adam was *infans* and *infirmis;* only through the exercise of his free will could he become fully human and so be made to share in the divine glory (*AH* IV.61–64). We hear a similar idea of Paradise as potentiality in the well-known distinction of Augustine; according to him, in Paradise man was *posse non peccare,* whereas now, because of original sin, he is *non posse non peccare,* and when he has obtained salvation in eternity he will *non posse peccare* (cf. *De corruptione et gratia* XIII.33). The Western church has always tried to guard against two deviations, against Manichaeism which regarded sin as inherent in the creation and against Pelagianism which regarded it as an incidental act of man's free will.

One may say that already the Yahwist, in his impressive story of creation and the fall, was driven by this twofold concern. It must not be overlooked that there is no break between Gen. 2 and 3. Together they are the prelude to the narrative of the earliest humanity (Gen. 2:4b–11:9), which in turn constitutes the introduction and background to God's election of Abraham and Israel. In Gen. 2 man hardly does anything as yet; God is still preparing his needed environment. Only in Gen. 3 does man begin to do something, and that involves that right away he becomes guilty. This becoming guilty is repeated in Gen. 4 and again in Gen. 6 and 11. The writer wants to say two things: sin is as old as humanity, and yet it is not inherently part of the creation. Or: man sins of his own free will, and yet there is no one who is prepared to use his freedom in another direction. In J Adam is the first man as well as man in the generic sense.

Much has been written about the concept of "sin" in the Bible, especially in the OT. See the various works on Biblical Theology and the literature they cite. Furthermore, of course, the art. *hamartanō,* in *TDNT* I, which also has some pages on Gen. 3 (pp. 281–286).

In passing we referred to pre-history and therewith to the results of natural science in general. Later we will come to the relation of sin and evolution. Here we observe only that the human and anthropoid fossils which have been discovered, seen in their chronological order, nowhere point to an earlier stage of higher development; on the contrary, they suggest a descent from the animal. The Yahwist, I think, would not have been surprised at this result!

Now we have to enter more deeply into the *nature of sin.* We have noted that sin is the misuse of freedom. We are so made that we need to find the anchoring of our life in the holy love of God by seeking our security in him and by being obedient to him. Sin is the refusal to find our anchoring there. This sounds too negative to serve as a definition. But sin can only be described in negative terms. It is not a "something," it is the *act*-ual negation of the core around which and the direction for which our existence was created.

When man chooses this negation, an infinite number of other possibilities open up; one can focus one's existence on a thousand other cores and go in a thousand other directions. Therefore it will not do to label one or a few cores and directions as specifically sinful, more so than others. It can be said, however, that this wide gamut of possibilities moves between two extremes. For we stand in the triangular relation of God–I–the world. Refusing the anchoring in God, one may try to find it in the world, or unanchored choose for one's own autonomous I. In the first instance man seeks his fulfillment in the world around him to which he gives himself. In the second instance he is his own point of reference and his goal is self-affirmation and self-realization. In the classical doctrine of sin, the first attitude is that of desire *(concupiscentia),* the second that of pride *(superbia).* One glance, however, makes it clear that these extremes are not really opposites; they are rather the two sides of one fundamental choice which realizes itself in innumerable variations. For in his enslavement to one of the innumerable aspects of what we call the world, man's aim remains self-affirmation. And where he makes himself consciously the center of his world, being that center he cannot do without that circumference for nourishing his self-realization. The picture becomes even more complicated because the relationship to God usually continues to assert itself in the sinful estrangement; the relationship to God does not disappear, but becomes an isolated element beside life's large priorities or is used to achieve these priorities. All these considerations make it impossible to localize sin, whether psychologically or anthropologically. Sin expresses itself in commission and in omission, in a base gratification of lust and in a strict observance of the law, in a calculating egotism and in an enthusiastic devotion to people and powers.

Here we come upon yet another decisive reason why sin cannot be defined. To be able to sense and describe the all-pervasive atmosphere of sin, we would need to be able to take our stand outside sin's territory, that is, we would have to step outside ourselves. That we cannot do. The conclusion would then have to be that we can make no statements about this all-pervasive fact of our existence. If we think we can say something, we must give an account of that in the consideration of the question how we arrive at a knowledge of sin.

In the history of the church both conceptions of sin, as *superbia* and as *concupiscentia,* have, alternately or combined, played a large role. Especially Augustine spent his whole life pondering the nature of sin. For him *humilitas* was the basic virtue of the redeemed life, and therefore *superbia* the cardinal sin. He likes to quote Sirach 10:13, "Pride is the beginning of all sin." However, as the punishment for Adam's pride the life of his descendants became suffused with *cupiditas* and *libido.* Augustine develops this doctrine of sin especially in *De civitate Dei* XIV. First he distinguishes *multae variaeque libidines,* among which is the *libido dominandi* (which thus comes very close to *superbia,* XIV.15, end).

But immediately following (XIV.16, beginning), with an appeal to the usual meaning of the word *lust*, he narrows the *libido* to "the lustful excitement of the organs of generation." Sexual desire is sin par excellence. It is therefore always accompanied with shame. In Paradise it must have been the case that the sexual organs were not spontaneously aroused by certain stimuli but were made to function by an act of the will, as we still do that with our hands and feet (XIV.21–24).

This narrowing of (original) sin to sexuality has had enormous consequences up till the present day. Yet this teaching has never received the stamp of ecclesiastical approval. On the contrary, in 1341 the Pope condemned the error "quod concupiscentia carnis est peccatum at malum" (D 1012). And Trent (D 1515) included in *concupiscentia* much more than the area of sexuality and did not label the inclinations of the flesh sin but the fuel for it ("tinder of sin . . . because it is from sin and inclines to sin"), and at the same time a stimulus to fight against in the power of Christ. The Reformers took issue with this torturous way in order to avoid the sexualization of sin while retaining the element of concupiscence in sin, and with an appeal to Rom. 7:7 saw it as a weakening of the consciousness of sin. Both sides lacked a clear and common definition of sin as concupiscence.

Thomas already reduced concupiscence (he calls it: "the inordinate longing for some temporal good") to love of self: "The inordinate love of self is the cause of all sin" *(ST* I, II, q. 77, art. 4). This brought him again close to the *superbia*-line of Augustine. It is mainly Protestant theologians who have continued that line. It is worth pondering that in Latin, Roman Catholic, frolicsome southern Europe sin was and is especially viewed as desire, while in Germanic, Protestant, and "Faustian" northwestern Europe and North America it is especially regarded as pride. An example of this second conception is J. Müller's monograph, *Die christliche Lehre von der Sünde* (1839; see esp. in the "Neue Ausarbeitung" of 1844, Bd. I, pp. 369f.). Another example is Brunner (*Dg* II, chs. 3 and 5). A still clearer example is Reinhold Niebuhr, *The Nature and Destiny of Man* (1941); see Vol. I, esp. ch. VII: "Man as Sinner": man is deceived by his freedom to try to overstep the limits of his finiteness and to become like God. "Biblical and Christian thought has maintained with a fair degree of consistency that pride is more basic than sensuality and that the latter is, in some way, derived from the former" (p. 198).

There is yet another line in Protestant theology, especially in liberal theology, in which sin is understood more as desire and worldliness, because of the refusal to subject a lower level of man's evolutionary ascent to the higher one. Schleiermacher understood it as sensuality, as the flesh waging war against the spirit. In the Netherlands it was especially the father of Modernism, J. H. Scholten, who developed the view that sin is "merely natural life," "life which is not yet ethical," the animal part in man which becomes sin only through the awakening of moral freedom (see e.g. *De leer der Hervormde Kerk,* 4th ed., 1861, II, pp. 533ff.). The modern evolutionary thinking in theology since Teilhard de Chardin has given new relevance to this view; in another context we will return to it. As a result the old accentual differences between the Roman Catholic and Protestant doctrine of sin have become less important. See also the drastic reinterpretation of the concupiscence concept in K. Rahner, in "The Theological Concept of

Concupiscence" (*Theological Investigations,* I, E.T. 1961, pp. 347–382), who argues for a more "Protestant" view. Very important in this connection is the way in which Barth develops the doctrine of sin, by successively viewing it from three perspectives: as pride, as sloth, and as falsehood (*CD* IV,1–3). Especially the new aspect of sloth has proved to be fruitful: sin is not only doing what is wrong, but also failing to do the good and refusing to accept responsibility for the consequences (see Harvey Cox, *On Not Leaving It to the Snake,* 1968).

The age-old tension between the conceptions of sin as pride and as concupiscence is thus coming to an end. It belongs to a time which thought mainly in terms of substances and hardly in terms of relations. Sin had to be localized somewhere. But a broken relationship cannot be localized in just some aspect of man. As a matter of fact localization had already proved to be very difficult for this reason, that the desire for what the world has to offer, as well as the love for self and the drive for self-realization, is as such and to a degree not objectionable. They are thus not able to provide a description of sin. Hence theology has repeatedly turned to a negative and so to a more comprehensive definition of sin. Again it was Augustine who was the most penetrating. For him sin is a separation from true being, a loss of being, *privatio boni;* sin is a *nihil positivum.* Later, in Protestant Scholasticism, this striking definition is made: *privatio actuosa,* a negativity which (nevertheless and for that reason) develops a terrific force. Barth has summed up these ideas in his doctrine of the *Nichtige:* sin is what is rejected by God and due to this rejection exists as a real threat (*CD* III,3, par. 50). Can we get beyond these negations? If there is more to say, then it must be what the Reformers said who defined sin as *infidelitas* or *incredulitas,* thus regarding it as the reverse side of the *sola fide.* See Luther, "The Freedom of a Christian," sections 11 and 24, and the beginning of his exposition of the first commandment, in The Larger Catechism. For Calvin see *Inst* II,i,4. Cf. Rom. 14:23. Sin is doubting God's holy love (Gen. 3:1–5!). By putting it this way, sin's enigmatic negativity is not explained, only articulated. The vacuum created by this doubt is then filled by the combination of pride and desire.

Looking back from the perspective of church history, where does the Bible stand in this dispute between pride and desire? The narrator of Gen. 3 intentionally puts the two accents side by side: on the one hand man wants to be like God (v. 5), on the other hand he succumbs to the tree which is desirable, a delight to the eyes (v. 6). In 1 John 2:16 sin is characterized in three descriptions: "the lust of the flesh, and the lust of the eyes, and the pride of life." Paul characterizes sin as "flesh" (*sarx*), but this word includes not only "immorality, impurity, licentiousness," but also "jealousy, anger, selfishness" (Gal. 5:20). Roughly stated, in the OT sin manifests itself especially as the allurement of the deified life (Baal worship), and in the NT especially as man's attempt to justify himself. For a further development of the doctrine of sin we must, therefore, also point to the next chapter (Israel). In virtue of God's special revelation to Israel, this people particularly has representatively manifested the true nature and depth of sin.

Our thinking about the nature of sin thus directs us to the question concerning the *knowledge of sin:* how will we ever be able to get a good focus on sin if it cannot be localized but permeates our entire existence?

The question may seem abstract. For awareness of sin is a universal fact of experience. There is no culture or language without some vocabulary to designate man's guilty failing. Everything seems to favor taking the knowledge of sin as the vestibule and point of contact for the gospel, which would then give the answer to this universal problem by speaking of forgiveness and grace.

Yet it is not that simple. True, people everywhere are aware of culpability, but their idea of the what or the one before whom they are guilty varies immensely; and in line with that the nature and content of man's failure are equally varied. One can fail in heeding the oracles of the gods, but also in listening to one's own conscience. Wrongs can be made in the bringing of sacrifices, but also in the association with the neighbor. And in between these two extremes there lies an enormous range of possibilities. The substance of sin varies with the value system against which one sins. For that reason one cannot appeal to an awareness of sin which is common to all men. Common is only the formal awareness of a distance between commandment and conduct, between ideal and fact, a gap which certainly is not or cannot always be bridged by man. This consciousness hangs together with the earlier-mentioned fundamental anthropological fact that man is still incomplete, reaches beyond himself, and anticipates himself. This fact as such is most important. But it does not itself give information as to what is sin and what is not, and as to what is more and what is less sinful in the sight of God.

For the Christian faith, too, it holds that what specifically must be regarded as sin is to be derived from the value which is sinned against; at least if we make the concept of "value" comprehensive enough. For at stake is the encounter with the holy and gracious God who chooses Israel, judges her, and takes her back, Jesus Christ who died for our sins and was raised for our justification, and the Spirit who transforms men by his judgment and renewal. The acts of this God presuppose our existence as humans, and in these acts we are unmasked as lost sons and daughters, alienated from the Father, rebelling against his Kingdom. That is a terrible and entirely unexpected discovery. We would not know of it without the representatively radical place of Israel in the encounter with this God, and without the cross of Jesus in which this history climaxed. For whatever else the cross may tell us, it certainly proves that we cannot stand God and that he must be eliminated if he comes too close to us. Those who took the initiative in that felt that they had to condemn Jesus precisely in the name of God. It was not criminals who did this, but men of high moral and religious convictions. For one who sees God acting in Jesus, this is precisely the evidence of our radical and total alienation from God. Since the cross it is no longer possible to think optimistically about man and to expect salvation to come from his own good potential and abilities.

That we have some knowledge of the atmosphere of sin in which we live is thus because in the encounter with God we have been handed a criterion from the outside. Knowledge of sin is faith knowledge. What God calls sin goes infinitely deeper and is infinitely more comprehensive than what we can dig up out of our own "heart," even with the most merciless introspection. For in that case we are still engaged in comparing ourselves with ourselves: our deeds with our conscience, our conduct with our ideal of what we would like to be, our "lower I" with the moral law in us. In our association with God it is announced to us that also and specifically with "the higher in us" we affirm our independence over against God.

The fact that the knowledge of sin comes from the outside does not mean, however, that it remains external to our life. In the encounter with God we learn to agree with him, also in his radical judgment upon us. Not that this indictment can ever become fully internal. We would not be able to bear that. It would drive us to utter despair; or we would have to be so holy that we could identify ourselves with God's evaluation of us, without perishing under it. Moreover, everything we can now already know and surmise of God's judgment upon our life would only paralyze us, if this knowledge were not accompanied with and if it were not the reverse of our knowledge of God's grace. God sees through us and yet he loves us. Graciously he tells us the truth. Standing in the sunlight of his grace, we can bear to look into the impenetrably dark abyss of our guilt.

In the light of this knowledge of sin, whatever other knowledge of sin there may be in the world is not thereby made worthless. All that knowledge is now the manifestation of a deep-seated human awareness of a continuous failing and erring. That awareness is affirmed and deepened by the Christian knowledge of sin. But at the same time it is being limited and, measured by the standard of God's judgment, disclosed as an unconscious attempt to escape the ultimate seriousness of God's verdict of guilty over us. This is true both where sin is only a cultic wrong, rectifiable through ritual acts, and where sin is profoundly experienced as a doom that lies heavily and unremovably upon mankind. This is, of course, not to deny that, psychologically speaking, manifestations of a genuine and deep awareness of guilt are also found outside the Christian experience of God. We may not even limit this to the psychological. For—we repeat—the knowledge of God in Christ is not exclusive; it is normative. But this normative character makes it inadvisable, in our conversation with the nonbeliever, to find a common basis in the knowledge of sin. For what we understand by it here is a very special knowledge derived from the encounter with God.

The phenomenology of religion provides insight into the great variety of conceptions of sin and the value systems of which they are the expression. See the handbooks and other literature (mentioned e.g. in *RGG* VI, *s.v. Sünde und Schuld*

I). Particularly important is P. Ricoeur's phenomenological treatment of sin in his *La symbolique du mal* (1963, 2nd vol. of *Finitude et culpabilité*). He distinguishes between sin as *souillure* (defilement), as *péché* (transgression), and as *culpabilité* (guilt). Significant for the combination of phenomenological and theological points of view is H. J. Heering, *Over het boze* (1974).

The question how and what knowledge we can have of sin became especially relevant in and after the Reformation. For Luther this was an intensely personal experience: the *Deus absolutus* or *nudus*, the *Deus maiestatis*, the demanding God, is the angry God who crushes us under his law. There is therefore a *duplex cognitio Dei*, of which the first can also be called *cognitio generalis* because it is obtained *per rationem et per legem* (see T. Harnack, *Luthers Theologie*, 1862, I, par. 6). The knowledge of sin thus derives from a different source (viz. the law) than the knowledge of grace (which derives from the gospel).

Modern Lutheranism, elaborating these thoughts, usually regards the knowledge of sin as a result of God's universally accessible revelation in creation, which is in fact, owing to man's failure to live up to the creation mandate, a revelation of wrath. Hence Lutheranism preferably pays attention to the evidences of frustration and pessimism in human life and culture, in order that it may then respond to these needs with the gospel of forgiveness and grace. "Through his assent to the judgment and through his longing for redemption man is true man. And only if he is first a true *man* can he later become a *Christian*" (R. Prenter, *Creation and Redemption*, p. 281). Cf. Althaus, *CW* I, par. 4; but also Brunner, in the Reformed tradition, *Dg* II, pp. 119–121. In our judgment this separation on the one hand overemphasizes man's understanding of his own existence (as if man would know of himself what God means with sin, anger, and judgment), while on the other hand the gospel is robbed of its dimension of judgment and turned into pure grace. An overview of the positions and discussion within Lutheranism is found in the symposium *Gesetz und Evangelium* (E. Kinder and K. Händler, ed., 1968). See beside it the critical questions raised by Barth, *CD* IV,3, pp. 370f.

In Reformed Protestantism the so-called "Further Reformation" followed the same dualistic direction, though not as far, because it did not connect the knowledge of sin from the law with general revelation, but found the source of that knowledge in a peculiar illumination by the Spirit which preceded grace. So it abandoned the common human and cultural context of the Lutheran position but maintained the duality in the work of God. On this tradition see J. de Boer, *De verzegeling met de Heilige Geest volgens de opvatting van de Nadere Reformatie* (1968).

Calvin followed a different route. He regarded the knowledge of sin and the knowledge of grace as opposites, as the double reaction to the one (judging and liberating) gospel—whereby the *fides* and its knowledge of grace are logically prior to the *poenitentia*. ". . . we mean to show that a man cannot apply himself seriously to repentance without knowing himself to belong to God. But no one is truly persuaded that he belongs to God unless he has first recognized God's grace" (*Inst* III,iii,2; see the whole of III,iii, which bears the heading: "Our regeneration by faith: repentance"). A good survey of this problematic, with a solution in the line of Calvin, is offered by G. C. Berkouwer, *Sin* (E.T. 1971), chs. 6 and 7.

Continuing Calvin's thinking, Barth has his own radical standpoint. Starting from the idea that the law is nothing but the form of the gospel, he expounds the doctrine of sin after he has dealt with Christology to indicate that man comes to know his sin exclusively through the confrontation with Christ. In the light of Christ's humiliation our existence is revealed in its pride (*CD* IV,1), in the light of Christ's exaltation in its sloth (IV,2), and in the light of Christ's disclosure of truth in its untruthfulness (IV,3).

The biblical passages which are usually adduced to find a separate source for the knowledge of sin, namely the law, are Rom. 3:20 and Gal. 3:19–25. The second passage speaks, however, of the redemptive-historical function of the law as the precursor to Christ. Rom. 3:20 reads: *dia nomou epignōsis hamartias* (RSV: "through the law comes knowledge of sin"). Paul is saying here: through the law we become "acquainted with" sin, that is, it awakens our resistance and we begin to transgress the law. Cf. Rom. 7 where this statement also has a redemptive-historical background: through its confrontation with the law Israel fell into sin, instead of being sanctified as was God's intention. See also Berkouwer, *Sin,* ch. 6.

In the encounter with God as holy love, knowledge of sin and knowledge of grace always go together in principle, though in the religious experience they may be separate and follow each other. Law and gospel can only (and must) be distinguished as two aspects of *one* revelation, but they cannot be juxtaposed to or follow each other as two revelations, each with its own contents. The law then becomes grace-less and the gospel sweetly sentimental, and so both obscure the knowledge of God which together they were to mediate.

It is correct to say that with the consideration of the two themes of the nature and the knowledge of sin the most important points have been made. Yet the study of the faith has never left it at that. It has also raised the question of the *origin of sin.* For a number of reasons: thinking itself cannot avoid this deepest question, there are certain biblical passages which seem to suggest an answer, and especially the persistent question about the why: why did God permit sin? why so much hatred and envy, all those conflicts and cruelties?

But this question about the origin is as dangerous as it is unavoidable. Suppose someone would know an answer, what function would it have except to serve as an explanation, to make sin transparent, and so extenuate man's guilt? An explanation puts the subject in a more or less systematic and rational context. May we ever do that with sin, which as such does not fit anywhere? There is one thing we know about sin: that it is reconciled and forgiven, and so is being removed. Does one not undermine the seriousness and the joy of this heart of the gospel if one first of all wants to know where sin comes from and how it could happen?

Such is not necessary, however. One who, horror-struck, notices the reality of sin, and then asks how it is possible, may also say thereby that he refuses to be satisfied with a vague awareness of this horrible fact but instead wants to have an even deeper and clearer view of it. The more we discover what sin is, the more we are astounded that man and the world could be so foolish and reject God's offer of love. Then we are amazed, too, that God permitted it and still puts up with it. Why? Perhaps there is no answer. But it must be possible, nonetheless, to consider this question without the hidden motive of minimizing sin and justifying oneself.

At this point we differ with Berkouwer in his study *Sin.* He argues that one cannot at the same time profess sin and explain it. I find this a forced alternative. As a matter of fact, however, by what Berkouwer calls explanations (the dualistic and the monistic conception), he understands and rejects something which in our judgment must indeed be rejected *(Sin,* chs. 1–6). But there is another alternative, as will hopefully become evident from what follows.

If God is the arch-enemy of sin who will not rest before he has driven it from his creation, it seems natural to look for the origin of sin in a cosmic power which is hostile to God, a sinister opponent whose aim it is to thwart the power of holy love wherever he can. This dualistic solution is widespread in the history of religion, and down the centuries has also fascinated many in the Christian church because it seemed to make it possible to explain the awesome power of sin without having to make God responsible for it. Yet in the official tradition of the church this dualism has never had a chance (see also paragraph 24). The Christian faith could not and would not pay the price that had to be paid for this solution, the price of having two gods who challenge each other's power, the price of a conflict which is inherent in the created universe. Then the God whom we know would not hold this whole world in his hand. And what would then be the guarantee that at the end of the cosmic duel he would be the winner and not the loser?

Especially early Christianity felt a strong attraction to this dualism—witness such movements as Gnosticism, Marcionism, and later Manichaeism. No less than Augustine was under the spell of this last-named movement for years. After he had broken with it, the rest of his life he searched for a better answer to the vexing problem of the origin of sin. Modern man thinks less metaphysically-dualistically than was done in those days. But many Christians of today do not get much further than a practical dualism: between the God of holy love and the powers that seem to dominate the world. On dualism see Berkouwer, *Sin,* part II.

Courageous and intellectually deep-probing thinkers have therefore not shrunk from looking at the alternative that perhaps the origin of sin might in one way or another be in God himself. The awareness of the true contents of the word *God* drives one as it were in this monistic direction. From him and through him and to him are all things. Could one of the greatest "things," sin, fall outside of that confession? Would it have had even the least chance of existence if he had not in one way or another wanted it? But rightly we also shrink back from this idea. How could God ever combat sin and fulminate against it if he, in whatever way, wanted it? The more we give in to this last idea, the more the central gospel dialectic of sin and grace is bound to become a farce.

Reformed Protestantism has ventured the furthest in this monistic direction, driven by its strict theocentrism. And it felt itself supported by a number of biblical statements which seem to intimate that sin, too, was ordained by God, such as the passages about the hardening of Pharaoh's heart (Ex. 4:21; 8:15; Rom. 9:17), about Saul (1 Sam. 16:14), and about Judas (Matt. 18:7). For other texts which were adduced to support this conception, see H XII, pp. 274ff. and Bavinck, *GD* II, par. 39, no. 306ff. This led Calvin to make strong and occasionally questionable statements: "For the first man fell because the Lord had judged it to be expedient; why he so judged is hidden from us. . . . Accordingly, man falls according as God's providence ordains, but he falls by his own fault" *(Inst* III,xxiii,8). Especially in his doctrine of providence he wrestled with this theme; typical is the heading of the chapter on this subject: "God so uses the works of the ungodly, and so bends their minds to carry out his judgments, that he remains pure from every stain" *(Inst* I,xviii). This sounds like a contradiction. In any case, Calvin could not or did not want to be consistently monistic, and Reformed Protestantism after him has always detested and rejected the idea which it insinuated, that God might be "the author of sin." When Maccovius, a professor in Franeker, argued that God ordains man to sin, he met with general disapproval, and the Synod of Dort in its session of May 4, 1619 admonished him to be more moderate. We will deal further with this Reformed position under the discussion of providence.

Others, more subtly, have looked for the origin, or rather the possibility, of sin in the fact and the nature of created reality. After all, what God creates and thereby places outside himself as another reality, can never have the same perfection that he himself has; creation as such is bound to be imperfect. Not that this imperfection is itself sinful, but it does render creation vulnerable, susceptible to sin. This argumentation is attractive but just as dangerous. There is only one small step between it and viewing sin as inherently part of creation as its tragic aspect; that would give man a splendid excuse for the fact that he cannot repair that weak spot in the creation. Unless this weak spot would precisely and fully be connected with man and his responsibility. Then we are back where we began: with human freedom.

Several of the greatest thinkers have sought an answer in the direction here indicated. First of all Augustine must be mentioned. We refer to what was said in par. 24 about his doctrine of creation out of nothing. Man possesses being which has its origin in God, who is both *summa essentia* and *summum bonum*. But God created him out of nothing, the nothing, the Platonic *mē on*. That makes him changeable and imperfect. This expresses itself in the freedom of the will which makes it possible for man to cling to a supreme being, but also to turn away from it and so condemn himself to a loss of being. See especially *De civitate Dei* XII and XIV.

A different line of thought is found in Thomas. To avoid, on the one hand, making God the origin of sin and, on the other hand, giving to sin its own independent existence over against God, he seeks the solution in the pronouncement: "God is the cause of evil by accident." Sin is an unintended by-product of a good creation in which beside the first cause secondary causes are operative. Not that they can create anything themselves, but their failures can have a wrong effect on the good creation: "Whatever there is of being in a bad action is reduced to God as the cause; whereas whatever defect is in it is not caused by God, but by the deficient secondary cause" (*ST* I, q. 49, art. 2; see all of q. 49).

Barth's manner of putting the problem came up twice when we mentioned his doctrine of the Nothing. See especially the end of par. 24. Creation borders on the Nothing, from which sin as that which God declared to be nothing (and as such possesses reality) exerts its influence. The creation is not sinful as such, but it is threatened as such.

In yet another direction goes Tillich (*ST* II, pp. 19-96: "Existence and the Quest for the Christ," esp. pp. 29-44: "The transition from essence to existence and the symbol of the 'fall' "). Our essence is the divinely given potentiality which must necessarily be actualized by the leap into freedom, and which is at the same time the leap into guilt. Is sin then an ontological necessity which can be traced back to God? Would it thus be tragedy instead of guilt? On p. 44, Tillich summarizes his answer as follows: "Theology must insist that the leap from essence to existence is the original fact—that it has the character of a leap and not of structural necessity. In spite of its tragic universality, existence cannot be derived from essence." It is, however, necessary to add that according to Tillich the fact of the leap itself is of "structural necessity." One should also read pp. 44–59 to judge whether Tillich avoids concealing the element of guilt in sin behind the ontological-tragic element (estrangement).

Reinhold Niebuhr charged Tillich with a "coincidence of creation and the fall." He himself tried to steer clear of it through his doctrine of finite freedom. Simultaneously possessing freedom and being a finite creature, that is the task before which man is placed in his createdness. Sin is his inability to bear this tension and his desire to use his freedom to transgress his creaturely limitations; contrary to that, the highest use of freedom is that one recognizes its limits. See Niebuhr, *The Nature and Destiny of Man,* esp. I, chs. 7 and 8.

One notices that sooner or later all these thought patterns begin to circle around the mystery of human freedom. An exception here is Barth, who tries to reach further and thrust through to God; but, as we see it, with his thesis that "not only what God wills, but what He does not will, is potent, and must have a real correspondence" (*CD* III,3, p. 352) he lands in the vacuum of empty speculation. On the problem as a whole, see also Ott, *AG* art. 19; and John Hick, *Evil and the God of Love* (1966), a broad overview with an optimistic solution.

Must we thus find the origin of sin solely in man, in a mysterious misuse of the freedom given to him? All indications seem to be that there is nothing to be discovered beyond this answer. Yet before we draw this conclusion, we need to begin by realizing well what we say when we make man solely responsible for his rebellion against God. He is meant for fellowship with God. How then did he get the terrible and fatal notion of the opposite? Entirely from himself? so that sin is purely the result of a "spontaneous ignition" (Brunner)? That would give man's sin a demonic character. But the striking thing in the biblical presentations of sin is that, while it is indeed described as an incomparably great culpability and calamity, it is precisely this demonic which is lacking. In the Bible man is a debtor, yet a victim at the same time. He evokes God's anger, yet at the same time his compassion. That he sins is his own fault; yet there is also something in it of being overpowered, which in the Bible is variously designated as "God," "our being 'dust,' " "slavery," "the powers," or "the devil."

Here we must first of all come back to those "difficult" texts in the Bible in which God is presented as causing man to sin or leading him further into sin. Besides what is said about the hardening of Pharaoh, Saul, and Judas, we can think of strong statements such as in Josh. 11:20; Ps. 105:25; Isa. 6:20; Ezek. 14:9, which clearly suggest that God makes man sin. But elsewhere in the OT sin is viewed as the result of man's being flesh and dust, and this is regarded as a mitigating circumstance which evokes God's mercy (Ps. 78:39; 103:14). In the NT, especially the apostle Paul speaks of such an overpowering force beside man's guilt. Sometimes sin is depicted as an extra- and suprahuman power which makes us its captives (Rom. 6:12–23; all of 7). Then, too, the law can be depicted as such a seducing power (Rom. 7:5–11). Elsewhere it is the powers, the *exousiai* and *stoicheia*, which so much control men's actions (Eph. 2:1f.) that the struggle against sin must as it were be fought in a supramundane realm with these mysterious powers which manipulate man and society (Eph. 6:12).

Also from this perspective, the story of the fall in Gen. 3, where man does not spontaneously become disobedient but is seduced by the serpent, deserves special attention. The narrator did not intend a disguise of Satan, as later church doctrine had it (most likely the Yahwist was not acquainted with the Satan idea), but literally an animal (3:1a), a representative of that world with which man *qua* origin is closely related (2:7, 9a), but to which he is *qua* his destiny nevertheless a stranger (2:20b). From that strange yet familiar world an influence comes to man which seeks to alienate him from his calling and to which he succumbs (3:6).

But the most important picture which the Bible uses to indicate that man is such a "victim" is that of Satan or the devil. In the OT it can still be seen how this picture was dialectically separated from the initial notion that God himself can allure man into sin. That idea was difficult to harmonize with the belief in the saving purposes of God. In 1 Kings 22:19–23 we see how this function is taken over by a "spirit" who belongs to the heavenly court. In Job 1 and 2 he is called *śāṭān,* that is, accuser, where apparently he is already a figure with a definite name and function. In vain he tries to seduce Job to fall away from God. In Zech. 3:1–3 Satan tries to convince God of the guilt of the high priest, again in vain. In 1 Chron. 21:1 we read: "Satan stood up against Israel, and incited David to number Israel." Striking is the omission of the article with Satan; at that time he became a generally known figure. More important is that with this information the writer intends to make a correction on the writer of 2 Sam. 24:1, who asserts: "Again the anger of the Lord was kindled against Israel, and he incited David against them, saying, 'Go, number Israel and Judah.' " Here we see clearly that the picture of Satan was used to avoid making God the origin of sin. With this meaning Satan occurs, however, in the OT only in these three passages. In the intertestamental period the picture of a satan becomes much more important; now he is increasingly viewed as the arch-enemy of God, though the view in Job is not absent altogether. In this period arises also the idea of Satan as a fallen angel (whereby sin is traced back neither to God nor to a counter-god). There is, however, no unity of conception.

In the Septuagint *śāṭān* is translated as *diabolos* (opponent). In the NT the terms *satanas* and *diabolos* are used interchangeably. It takes up again the picture in Job that Satan in his role of accuser belongs to the heavenly court and that he tries to sift believers as wheat; but what is new is that through the coming and the work of Jesus Satan has lost this juridical position and with it his power over the world (Matt. 4:8–11; Luke 22:31; John 12:31; Rev. 12:7–12). Of central significance is Jesus' announcement: "I saw Satan fall like lightning from heaven" (Luke 10:18). Jesus must have viewed his life work primarily as a struggle with this evil power, above the heads of the people and for their sake (Mark 3:27). He came to break this relentless force which they themselves could not cope with (Heb. 2:14; 1 John 3:8). That struggle is now in principle decided; it has deprived Satan of every legitimate relationship with God and has limited his power. How such an opponent could be possible in God's creation is hardly ever asked. Only in 2 Pet. 2:4 and Jude 6 is this opposition traced to a fall in the angelic world (erroneously some have also tried to find this in John 8:44, but there the correct reading is *ouk estēken,* not *ouch' hestēken*). Paul refers to Satan repeatedly, mostly in connection with personal or church problems; but when he deals with the power of sin in general (Rom. 6–8; Gal. 4 and 5, and other passages), he does not underscore it with the Satan conception but with other concepts mentioned earlier: law, sin as a power, *exousiai, stoicheia.* For the conception of Satan in the Bible, see especially *TDNT* II, *s.v. diabolos* and VII, *s.v. satanas.*

In the history of the church the concept of the "devil," as expressing the overpowering threat to which man is exposed, has dislodged all the other above-mentioned designations. This is not surprising, considering its metaphorical and direct force. Christian art in particular has promoted this. For ages the idea of a satan has deeply influenced the Christian mentality. This makes it all the more remarkable that it has had only a marginal or isolated function in the study of the faith. The great exception is Luther; but in his thinking, the powers of sin, death, and the law play at least as large a role, beside the devil, to express the relentless force of evil. In Berkouwer's book on sin Satan has no function, because Berkouwer fears that this could only be a denial of guilt (see *Sin,* ch. 4, e.g. p. 112: "There is no relentless force, except that which is actualized in the *modus* of man's own culpability").

By speaking of Satan as a picture and by putting it on one line with a number of other biblical pictures that express the relentless force of sin, we make a specific hermeneutical and theological decision. We regard the Satan image as belonging to the third of the four circles we spoke about in par. 17, pp. 97–98; the circle which includes those images which, varying with the concepts available to a culture or age, underscore the primary content, or articulate or picture it. Our motiviations for taking this stance are implicit in the above discussion. This view, however, obligates us to ask specifically what in this (and other) image(s) is binding for faith and the study of the faith.

With the term "freedom" the last word has thus not been said about the mystery of sin. Then we would no longer see the limitations of that freedom. The freedom whereby we choose to rebel against God and our own nature is not spontaneous and automatic, not absolute and unlimited. Man is no devil. Beside the dimension of guilt, there is in his sin also the element of what we nowadays call the tragic: guilty man is also man who is blinded, foolish, and deceived. That is what the biblical concepts and pictures which describe sin in extra- and suprapersonal categories mean to say. Guilt has roots which go far deeper than man's personal and conscious will. Particularly the picture of Satan is meant to express that; one who rejects or demythologizes it will have to verbalize in another way the insight that lies behind it, an insight that has its source in the encounter with God. That is the insight concerning the "higher power" to which man is exposed, yet without absolving him from his responsibility. With this formulation we indicate a tension which we can barely endure in our life and mind. We can stress the tragic so much that it becomes a cowardly excuse for our sin; there are many who like to take refuge in the irresistible power of their nature, heredity, or environmental factors. Conversely, it is also possible that we stress the guilt factor so much (in this case mostly not our own guilt but that of others!) that mercilessly we demand what in certain situations cannot possibly be done and have no eye for the "guiltless guilt." The tension between guilt and the tragic, between freedom and destiny, is difficult to bear; we break it all the time and then fall into either fatalism or optimism. As a matter of fact, demanding too much of man and despairing of man are easily transmutable, especially the first into the second. The Christian faith has always, correctly, uncompromisingly maintained both man's responsibility and his helplessness. It is open to question, however, whether this has always been done in the right manner. Here we touch on a concept which we must now further investigate, that of hereditary sin.

It is a persistent misunderstanding to think that the doctrine of Satan was meant to explain sin. For it explains nothing, but only shifts the problem partly into a suprahuman sphere. We have seen that in the Bible this transposition happens along several lines. All imply a (partial) lightening of human responsibility, so that what remains can and must be fully accepted as man's own guilt. The serpent beguiles man and therefore receives the heaviest punishment (Gen.

3:14f.); but when the Lord has so dealt with the serpent, man is given his responsibility and punishment (vv. 16–19). The fact that Satan is pictured as a *person* underlines, together with man's beguilement, his responsibility: sin does not originate through an attack on man, but in a "dialogue" in which man comes with his own "input." Very remarkable are the three NT passages which speak about sin against Christ as acting in ignorance (Luke 23:34; Acts 3:17; 1 Tim. 1:13). From the context it is clear that this ignorance delimits man's guilt, yet in that delimitation sharply defines it. Those who do not know what they do, need forgiveness nevertheless. Note also the emphasis with which in the Wisdom literature and other passages sin is pictured as "folly": man does not sin for the sake of sinning, but to make gains for himself, and he fails to see that instead he is hurting himself (see also Gen. 3). When this element of folly or blinding falls away and man sins against his own better judgment, he becomes demonic. The statement about "the sin against the Holy Spirit" (Mark 3:28f. and parallels) refers to that borderline possibility. Therefore in John 8:44 it is said of the devil (in contrast to sinful men who have to learn it from him, their "father"): "When he lies, he speaks according to his own nature" *(ek tōn idiōn)*.

There are a few writers who have noticed and assimilated the significance of this difference between human and satanic sin. Bavinck quotes from (Bernhard?) Weiss: "Either one devil outside humanity or thousands of devils in human form," which he prefaces by: "the belief in the devil maintains simultaneously the awesome seriousness of sin and the saveability of man" (*GD* III, par. 43, no. 342). For that same reason G. K. Chesterton spoke of "the happy doctrine of the devil." Particularly Brunner has taken this insight into account in the doctrine of sin (though connected with a one-sided conception of sin as pride): man is not ingenious enough to invent sin himself. "Sin as the result of spontaneous ignition" is the act of Satan. "Human sin thus presupposes a tempting power, otherwise sin would be devilish" (*Dg* II, p. 108; see also chs. 3 and 10, and ch. 5, pp. 138ff.). In the Netherlands, ethical theology has touched on these lines of thought. They are particularly developed by F. W. A. Korff in his book *Advent* (1928), pp. 23–28, which also contains many other insights pertaining to the doctrine of sin. On the question of the relationship of guilt and the tragic, see also Heering, *Tragiek,* esp. XI–XIII.

As a rule the handbooks on dogmatics do not deal with the doctrine of hereditary sin at this point but somewhat later, not under the origin of sin but as part of the consequences of sin. We depart from this rule because we feel that the doctrine of hereditary sin is untenable in its traditional forms and that the truth which it tries to articulate is to be dealt with differently, namely in the context we are now concerned with. This doctrine aims at a systematization of a passage in Paul, namely Romans 5:12–21. Speaking about the decisive significance of grace, Paul introduces there an antithetical analogy between the far-reaching consequences of Adam's sin and that of the still further-reaching bearing of Christ's salvation: through Adam's sin death came upon the whole human race because in Adam all share his sin and condemnation. The nature of that participation is not further described. The theories of hereditary sin vary in their perception of that participation. Those theories thus make central something which for Paul was only marginal or unimportant. Moreover, they misjudge the function of this passage. Both the wider context and the immediate setting (vv. 11 and 21) prove that Paul's purpose with this passage was to illustrate the superiority of grace over the power of sin. Whatever is said in this passage itself about the power of sin is stated figuratively but also literally in subordinate clauses (vv. 12, 15, 17, 18, 19, 21). To isolate these statements about sin from their context and intention for the purpose of systematizing them is to do violence to them. There is also the further consideration—one which is, apart from what has been said so far, decisive for us—that we cannot regard this reflection of Paul, expressed in terms of the exegetical insights and methods of his time, as in itself authoritative. Its authority inheres in the elements of Paul's encounter with Christ, which is here the subject of theoretical reflection, not in the reflection itself. Paul's aim here is to relate grace and the reality of sin. Both are stronger than man; but grace is also stronger than sin. Relative to the doctrine of sin, we thus have the same theme here that occupies us in this whole discussion. Beside the personification of sin, bondage, the powers, and Satan, we find here yet another avenue along which Paul articulates the overpowering force of sin, what we have called its "tragic" aspect. To isolate and to extend this particular approach, ignoring others and forgetting that we must tackle the problem of systematization for our own time and with our own modes of thought, inevitably lead to the self-contradictory idea of hereditary sin. The nature of sin is, however, precisely that it is man's misuse of his own freedom, and as such nontransferable. If we emphasize "sin" we must weaken the hereditary, and vice versa. Both are realities, but they cannot be captured in one word in such a way that the "original" (hereditary) is also marked as sin. Then we have not mentioned yet the flood of fatalism and despair which has been the result of the ecclesiastical teachings about hereditary sin, and which has obscured the heart of the gospel. These considerations compel us to search for a different solution to the problems that are rightly raised here.

The literature on this theme, particularly in Roman Catholic, but also in Protestant theology, is overwhelmingly large. This is due to the difficulty of combining the original and the guilt. Until the present day the attempt has not succeeded. Good orientations are given by Berkouwer, *Sin,* chs. 12–16; P. Schoonenberg, in *MS* II, ch. X,4; U. Baumann, *Erbsünde?* (1970); K. H. Weger, *Theologie der Erbsünde* (1970).

In his story of the sin of the first human beings, the Yahwist wanted to express the universality of sin in space and time. The story does not imply that through Adam's sin mankind was burdened with a hereditary fate, and is in fact even unlikely considering how the fall is, as it were, repeated in Cain, in Noah's days, and in the building of the tower of Babel (the parallelism with Gen. 3 is striking in Gen. 4:3–16 and perhaps intentional in v. 7). Elsewhere the OT never refers to Gen. 3 to explain sin. (If there is an allusion to Adam in Job 31:33 and Hos. 6:7—which is highly unlikely—then it is only a first example of sin.) Only after the closing of the canon, when Gen. 3 came to belong to its introductory chapters, did it again become theologically important in the intertestamental period. See M. Boertien, "De joodse achtergrond van de parallel Adam/Christus in het Nieuwe Testament," in *Gereformeerd Theologisch Tijdschrift,* 1968, pp. 201–220. This is the background against which Paul's passage in Rom. 5 is to be read.

Here we do not offer an exegesis of Rom. 5:12–21. We only point to two problems which have played a large role in the dogmatic discussion. First to the words in v. 12: *eph' hōi pantes hēmarton,* which by way of the Vulgate *in quo omnes peccaverunt* were taken to mean: in whom (that is, in Adam) all have sinned. So this text could serve as a major witness for the traditional doctrine of hereditary sin. From the 16th century on it was realized that this translation is incorrect; *eph' hōi* means: on the ground of, because. Then it seems to say precisely the opposite of the traditional doctrine, namely that everyone dies because of his own sin. But that makes it a strange element in this context (see already v. 14). Do we have to insert after the last words in v. 12, "in Adam"? The meaning of the last words in v. 12 can only be: because in Adam all had sinned.

This brings us to the second problem: how do Adam's descendants share in his sin? One can think of biological transmission or a juridical imputation. Without a doubt the second is much more congenial to Paul than the first. And only in that case is Adam the antithetical analogy with Christ with whom we, according to Paul, are connected through a forensic declaration of justification. Paul is then extrapolating backward toward Adam the imputation relationship and the corporate personality concept. H. N. Ridderbos, in his commentary *Aan de Romeinen* (1959), par. 12, also defends this widely held view. Berkouwer, *Sin* (see esp. pp. 497–502, 509, 524), opposed it, however (together with many others). Following the renderings of Luther and the Dutch Bible Society, his view is that juridically it overburdens the *katestathēsan* in v. 19, and he concludes that "at the decisive point the 'transfer' in the Adam-Christ parallel remains obscure" (p. 502). Cf. Verburg, *Adam,* pp. 36–57 and pp. 245f. n. 241, who likewise rejects the juridical conception and concludes from the end of v. 12 that for Paul it is precisely personal sin which is of greatest importance. In our judgment it is clear only that Paul, utilizing the Adam theology of his time, sought to articulate the overpowering force of sin.

It is understandable that after the Enlightenment, owing to the growing awareness of man's freedom and responsibility, the contradiction of hereditary sin became increasingly intolerable. For J. M. Hasselaar, *Erfzonde en vrijheid* (1953), esp. XIII, the current doctrine of hereditary sin is therefore "theologically unacceptable." He recognizes only personal sin. The same is true of Barth in his brief passage in *CD* IV,1 (pp. 499f.) on *Ursünde.* Also for Berkouwer, *Sin,* ch. 9, hereditary sin is no more than a term indicating the common, the total, and the "overpowering" characteristics of personal sin. In Roman Catholic theology especially Schoonenberg has gained prominence through his reinterpretation of the doctrine of hereditary sin (see esp. *MS* II, ch. 5). He construes hereditary sin as "the sin of the world," the sinful, collective pressure of the situation upon us.

So he comes very close to what we have called the tragic dimension; this is really something quite different from the sin of a first human being. In the same spirit on this subject is the *New Catechism,* pp. 259–270. But the passage in question is rejected in the Vatican corrections. Among Protestant thinkers, O. Weber, *Gl* I, pp. 667–677, stands very close to Schoonenberg's view. See also Ott, *AG* art. 18. The sharpest distinction between the actual situation and sin as the wrong response to it is made by H. Wiersinga in *Doem of Daad. Een boek over de zonde* (1982). But his one-sided view of sin as deed misconstrues the gravity of the problem: "If sin is a deed, we do not coincide with our sin. We can 'take off' sin, the way we take off clothes" (pp. 83f.; see also ch. 6).

Now that there is a widespread consensus about the incompatibility of sin and hereditary transmission, the time is ripe for a new appreciation of the truth of the latter. In our judgment one does not yet do justice to it by making it an aspect of personal sin, as communality and situationality. It has less of a bearing on personal sin, but precisely because of that it has its own unique import.

Sin as the mysterious misuse of freedom is intensely personal, but at the same time it is embedded in a world of infra- and suprapersonal powers which, on the one hand, drive (not force) man in the direction of sin, while on the other hand they link the sinful deed to consequences that far exceed the individual offense. We have observed that in the Bible this tragic element is variously designated. Our question now is, with what concepts can and are we to designate this? For an answer, where it concerns the infrapersonal, we are in our time very much helped by the insights of the evolutionary view of the world. The study of the faith cannot canonize such insights, yet we can accept them as an aid toward a more intelligible formulation of certain elements in the Christian faith. We know that evolution consists of an increasing mobility of the molecular connections. In the phenomenon man this mobility assumes the shape of freedom. This freedom arises within a large totality of factors that are inherited from the pre-human world. According to his zoological descent, man is socially a primate of prey. From the animal kingdom he inherits his attachment to an individual or social territory, his mechanisms of defense and aggression, his individual or collective urge to maintain himself. In the animal all this is natural and morally neutral. But in man this inheritance is linked to a new possession: freedom. Thereby God makes him responsible for how he uses his inheritance. He may not and cannot divest himself of his inheritance. He is called to subdue it, to weave it into and to make it fruitful for the calling of his freedom, in other words, to the love he owes to God and his fellowman. He needs this inheritance for his existence as man. At the same time it is a heavy burden which pulls man away from his responsibility. What is inherited is not sin. But if man's freedom does not control it, but instead allows itself to be led astray and controlled by it, the result is sin. Sin is the unnecessary, divinely forbidden, and therefore guilty yielding to the gravitational force of our natural background. Sin is a possibility which comes with freedom. Animals cannot sin. The frightful possibility of sin arises only with man as the culmination of the evolutionary development. Sin is not a fall from a higher form of existence, but the refusal to rise to the higher form of existence of loving fellowship with God. Sin is contrary to nature precisely because it is a yielding to the pull of our inherited nature. Man falls victim to it if he does not in confidence, in surrender, and in obedience open himself to the call from on high as it invites us to join unconditionally and with his whole being in God's venture of a joint history with man. We are nourished from below and called from above. We are threatened and loved. We become guilty if we allow ourselves to be directed more by the first than the second. And yet that is what we, humans, do all the time and everywhere. Therefore God must regularly mobilize fresh forces of love to pull us away from the temptation.

We have looked for the origin of sin. Creation referred us to the freedom of man, and that referred us back to the overpowering sinister elements around us. Sin is still as mysterious as before: a senseless and mortally dangerous rebellion against the purpose of God. But it is not an ingenious and demonic idea arising purely within man himself. Its roots lie deep in the structure of our reality. This idea, which in a particular sense we rejected above (namely as a possibility to excuse ourselves), we must now use after all, namely as an elucidation of the *nature* of our guilt. And even the in itself blasphemous idea that *God* is the author of sin now appears to contain a truth: he has caused us to come forth out of a world in process of becoming as threatened and challenged creatures. Could he not have made us different? But then we would not have been humans in this world. He has wanted us to have this provisional kind of life. That therein we have turned in the wrong direction is a greater sorrow for him than it can ever be for us. But that he yet continues with us is our guarantee that his love will some day triumph over all our failures. Then, and not before, will our pondering of the mystery of sin cease.

The mythological language of Gen. 3, having sin come from the animal world, is strikingly close to that of modern thinking! Yet there remains a reluctance in theology to connect the doctrine of sin with the evolutionary view of the world. This is because this combination has usually resulted in a view of sin as a not yet, a standing still on a lower, "sensuous" level of evolvement. This objection can indeed be raised against Schleiermacher, J. H. Scholten, various Anglican theologies, and also against Teilhard de Chardin. Yet lately there is, rightly, a growing insight that concepts like evolution, animal background, natural aggression, and freedom do not need to weaken sin but can instead underscore and concretize its nature and seriousness. Especially the more recent Roman Catholic theology shows much interest in this theme. As I see it, in Hulsbosch, *De schepping Gods* (chs. II and III), the danger of weakening sin has not yet been overcome; this is not the case in Fiolet, *Vreemde verleiding*, ch. 8. Protestants are very hesitant to link the doctrine of sin and the modern view of the world. A clear exception is P. J. Roscam Abbing, *Actuele uitdagingen aan de christenheid* (1967), esp. pp. 146–152. See also the Faith and Order Study, no. 50: *God in Nature and History* (1967), VII: "Nature, Man, Sin and Tragedy." A theological consensus appears to be growing in this area. This can receive additional support from what we noted above about the manner in which Augustine, Thomas, Tillich, and Barth relate the possibility of sin to the nature of created reality. Despite the speculative aspect of Barth's doctrine of the Nothing, the manner in which he combines sin and "superior power" can be fruitfully and correctingly connected with modern evolutionary thinking.

In the preceding we have pointed to fate (the inherited) as the subpersonal background of guilt. But there is still another fate aspect. Man's guilt does not only arise from fate; it, too, produces factors which sooner or later assume the nature (suprapersonal) of fate. The traditional doctrine of hereditary sin can be regarded as a (mistaken) combination of both fate aspects and a (futile) attempt to subsume them under the concept of sin.

Sin involves consequences which have the character of fate. After all, we do not sin all by ourselves. We grow up in a world and we participate in a societal structure which is not congenial to what we are meant for, namely love. Our society is based on the motive of (personal or collective) self-interest, which, depending on circumstances, in the form of greed, ambition, party interests, competition, nationalism, etc. determines the relationships and modes of conduct, and it is held in check and tempered only by the insight that one can hardly ever safeguard one's own interests without more or less reckoning with those of others. In such a world we are born and grow up. Example and formation of habit drive us in the same direction. Sin is a cumulative process or a contagious disease. We cannot get away from this pull, and we do not want it either. Voluntarily we go along and participate. Guilt and fate go hand in hand. Because of the way which Jesus went in this world, the way of consistently loving God and man, the way of keeping one's life by losing it, we know how differently life should be lived, but also the superhuman power that requires, and particularly the price one must be prepared to pay for that in this world.

Beside this aspect of the consequences of sin, which we could call the *interpersonal* aspect because it is based on mutual influencing, we must distinguish a *suprapersonal* aspect, which is based not so much on the mentality of persons as on the driving force inherent both in the institutions of our established society and in the anonymous powers of current codes of behavior, taboos, traditions, or the dictates of fashion. Of course both aspects hang together. First personal sin broadens itself, assuming an interpersonal shape, and then, continuing, it concentrates or institutionalizes itself in suprapersonal magnitudes. It is the experience of those who manage to wrest themselves loose from being blinded by interpersonal forces, to take up the challenge of love, that individual goodwill seems to accomplish little or nothing against all those forces which inexorably dictate to individuals a certain pattern of conduct: the state, the business, the interest of the party, the needs of society, custom, fashion, public opinion, the ideology (Western or Eastern), etc. One who tries to do something against it is usually thrown aside or gets crushed under the wheels. Very few possess the strength and the courage to take this risk. The vast majority do not even begin with it, also because they have so much identified themselves with these powers that they are blind to their inhuman influences. In this respect, too, we have to be made cognizant of the manner in which Jesus disarmed the "powers" (of religion and state, of law and tradition) and "made a public example of them, triumphing over them by the cross" (Colossians 2:15).

Above we have given no more than a cursory indication of how the contemporary study of the faith would have to approach and develop the theme of "the consequences of sin." The first aspect, the interpersonal, which concerns the contagiousness and the spread of sin, has as a reinterpretation of hereditary sin been extensively dealt with in the newer theology since Schleiermacher (*CF* pars. 70–72). See particularly the study of Schoonenberg, referred to above, in *MS*, especially the importance he assigns in the doctrine of sin to the "situation" and the fact of "being in a certain situation." In contrast, the second aspect, the suprapersonal, has thus far hardly received attention in dogmatics. Possibly, life in an earlier time may have given less occasion for it, but that has changed entirely in our modern society in which structures and institutions, powers and ideologies, play such a decisive and often disastrous role. It is time for this aspect to receive consideration. For that the theologian can find a surprisingly direct point of contact in the manner in which Paul articulates this suprapersonal aspect in his teaching about the "authorities and powers" and the "basic principles of the world" (*stoicheia tou kosmou*). He regards these as belonging to the structure of creation, but apart from Christ they come in between God and us to estrange us from God and from ourselves. See Rom. 8:38f.; 1 Cor. 2:8; 15:24–26; Gal. 4:1–11; Eph. 1:20f.; 2:1f.; 3:10; 6:12; Col. 1:16; 2:8–3:4. For an actualization of these lines of thought, see H. Berkhof, *Christ and the Powers* (E.T. 1962), and K. Barth, the posthumous volume of *CD* IV,4, par. 78,2. As far as I know, the most incisive discussion of the activity and influence of the supernatural powers is found in the theologian of the Social Gospel, W. Rauschenbusch, in *A Theology for the Social Gospel* (1917), chs. VII–IX; this book is still very worthwhile reading.

Traditionally, something entirely different was discussed under the heading "the consequences of sin," mainly, following Gen. 3:17–19, misery and suffering, death, and the corruption of nature. This was also called the punishment of sin. See on this theme Bavinck, *GD* III, par. 43. We perceive these elements as an indication of the provisional character of our creation and refer to the discussion of it in par. 25 under 9. This is no implicit denial that sin has also altered our relation to these elements. This is especially true of death: outside of the covenant bond with God it is the irrevocable end of a life which is alienated from him, and the sign that God cannot immortalize this existence. Only the belief in Jesus' resurrection sheds a new light on the provisional nature of our life, and with it on our death. On the various aspects under which death can be viewed in the Christian faith, see P. J. van Leeuwen, *Het christelijk onsterfelijkheidsgeloof* (1955), esp. III B–D.

Our sin is thus everywhere surrounded by our fate. But it does not coincide with this fate. The Christian church has always so emphatically emphasized the latter statement that it has found it very hard to fully recognize this fate dimension: it has constantly tried to bring it back to the guilt dimension by subsuming the elements of fate under the rubrics of "original sin" and "punishment for sin." That has often lent an unwarranted hardness to Christianity in its evaluation and treatment of the tragic aspects of life. Yet this was the counterpart of taking man's maturity and accountability with the utmost seriousness. In the Christian faith man is not addressed as a victim but as a doer. He is not pitied but accused. Up to the present day this has had enormous consequences for every segment and aspect of societal and cultural life. Nothing does more for the humanization of man than addressing him as one who is fully accountable relative to God and his neighbor. If we give up this "hard" language, we give up the Christian faith itself. But this language also discloses radical failure, our persistent refusal to go along with God's purposes for us. And this coalescence of being-held-accountable and being-accused is bearable only because God has taken it up *for* us and therefore *against* us to rescue us from this dead-end road. The Christian doctrine of sin is uncommonly hard and radical. One can endure it only because its epistemological source is the message that God comes to us forgivingly and renewingly. But, conversely, this message can be understood only if we are willing to accept how radically we need forgiveness and renewal.

Note Paul's argumentation in Rom. 5:12–21: mankind's radical condemnation in Adam is pictured as analogical to the justification in Christ, of which it is said that it not only compensates for the effect of sin but exceeds it. A clear difference in thinking exists in contemporary Dutch theology as to the measure in which room is to be given to the element of the tragic beside that of guilt. Berkouwer, *Sin,* is the most negative toward it. Furthest in the other direction (following C. A. Mennicke and Tillich) goes P. Smits, "Zondebesef en zondebegrip" (*Nederlands Theologisch Tijdschrift,* Aug. 1958). An in-between position is taken by Heering, *Tragiek.*

28. THE PRESERVATION OF THE WORLD

WITH THIS TERM we want to indicate that activity of God by which he does not abandon the world which creatively he called into existence, but takes care of it in such a way that it is and remains on the way to the goal which he has in mind. The study of the faith uses different words to designate that work: preservation, government, providence, and others. Later it will be seen that none of these really articulates what concerns us here. The much-used term "providence" certainly does not do that; it suggests a harmonious relationship between God's love and the course of the world which simply does not exist. The term "preservation" is very vague; but that may be an advantage. A disadvantage is that it suggests a one-sided relationship, as if the world would be no more than a passive object; it does not do justice to man's own role in respect to God and the world. Hopefully we can remove this suggestion, and with that in mind we prefer to make this vague word our starting-point.

Much has been written about the question whether preservation is indeed a separate theme after and beside creation. In paragraph 24 and especially in paragraph 25 much was said already which refers as much to preservation as to creation. Apparently it is difficult to draw a dividing line. For ages preservation has also been denoted as "continuing creation" *(creatio continua)*. After all, every new plant, animal, or man means the origination of something new. Especially the theory of evolution has fostered the idea that creation continues, first in the origination of continually new varieties of plants and animals, and later—from the perspective of an evolutionary process of millions of years only a short while ago—in man's appearance, and more particularly through the manner in which he is active to bring about an entirely new era: the product of evolution is now becoming its leader. For all these reasons it seems advisable to let creation and preservation coincide.

But some of these arguments can be assessed entirely differently. Precisely *man's* emergence as the crown of creation meant an enormous break. It drastically changed God's position as creator. God grants him the secret of his own being: the duality of freedom and love. So in the world man becomes God's partner as well as his steward. Man becomes co-creator, co-preserver, co-ruler. This could have meant that God would have withdrawn from his creation to leave the responsibility for it entirely up to man. That has not happened. But after the creation of man the situation has entirely changed. There is yet another, directly related reason for speaking of a sharp break: not only has man come in between, but with man also *sin*. The steward tries to seize the power. The partner becomes a rebel. This could have meant the banishing of God from his own creation. That did not happen. But the dual factor of man and sin makes it impossible for God to keep, as it were, happily going with creating new things. His relation to the world now becomes an entirely new one. For that we must look for a second term beside "creation." To my knowledge, this is also what the study of the faith has generally done.

It is to the honor of Protestant Scholasticism that terminologically and materially it has wrestled with this problem. It used three successive terms to elucidate the question from various angles: preservation, concurrence, and government *(con-*

servatio, concursus, gubernatio). Concursus referred to the mode of interaction of God's and men's work. Barth has taken over this division in his extensive treatment of this theme in *CD* III,3. The tension between God and sin does, however, not come out in these words. For that other words were introduced under the theme of *gubernatio,* such as: *permissio, impeditio, directio, determinatio.* See S par. 21, III; R par. 20,5; H XII. What follows will make clear why even these concepts could not do justice to the problem. For the critical connection between the classical Protestant approach and modern questions, see Beker-Hasselaar, *WK* II, pp. 53–113.

The doctrine of preservation, of God's permanent relatedness to the world he has created, is the most popular part of the study of the faith. Regularly one can hear people say that they are firmly convinced that "there is something," "that God has a hand in everything," "that everything must be the way it is," "that we are all in God's hands," "that nothing happens by chance." For many this conviction seems to be the whole of their faith. The hymnals of most churches also contain an abundance of songs extolling preservation. But for a large and growing number of people this most popular part of the study of the faith is precisely the most impossible aspect. To them it is absurd to think that God would concern himself with the details of this puny planet, and the notion that God could, for example, have anything to do with Auschwitz they regard as blasphemous. We have here a direct parallel with the contradictory feelings that are evoked by the idea of creation (paragraph 25). What is self-evident to the one is unthinkable to the other. The Christian faith must reject both positions. At the same time their contradictory merging compels the Christian faith to examine carefully the basis and the nature of its confession that God preserves this world.

Beginning with the basis, how dare we believe that God concerns himself with our small, absurd, and sinful world? The answer must be: exactly for this reason, that God comes to us in his revelational encounters in this world and so involves us in his struggle with and for this world, for this shows us that what happens to this world is a permanent concern of God. In one way or another he is involved in what happens in his creation, on planet earth.

By saying "in one way or another" we are also faced with the question concerning the nature of preservation. We have no direct knowledge of that nature. We know God through the path he goes with Israel, with Christ, and in the Spirit. That path makes us speak of revelation. In the second chapter we saw how relative that revelation is. The real revelation is still to come. Yet we dare to speak of revelation if we compare the experiences we gain on that path with the knowledge of God's work and purpose which we pick up outside of it. Outside this path we can certainly become deeply impressed with the law structure, the grandeur, marvelousness, power, abundance, vitality, multiformity, etc. of our world, so that with Paul we can see an "eternal power and deity" operative in it. At the same time the product of this working is in many respects so ambiguous, senseless, or cruel that we cannot harmonize it with what we have learned about God from his revelational path. Everything would be much easier if we had not come to know God as holy love, but as a capricious God who is the reflection of this capricious world. If, as in many religions, god or the gods are viewed as the world raised to the level of the divine, it is easy enough to deal with preservation as a self-evident matter and as a central conviction. But that is not possible in the Christian faith. The confession of the preservation of the world by *this* God is the confession of people who do not see and yet believe. This world and God's path through it cannot (yet) be harmonized.

Is this only a matter of lack of insight? Because we, insignificant and shortsighted people, happen to be unable to perceive that everything answers precisely to God's purpose? That cannot possibly be the only reason. For on the path of revelation we have at least learned that this world and all that is in it does not agree with God's will and purpose. It is thus not only a question of insight, but first of all of the nature of the preservation itself.

In the Hellenistic world in which early Christendom made its appearance, the belief in preservation and providence was widespread due to the great influence of Stoic philosophy. This philosophy spoke of divine *pronoia* (Latin *providentia),* which were very pantheistically and fatalistically conceived. (On this teaching and its difference from the Christian view, see Brunner, *Dg* II, p. 5.) The influence of this conception on pristine Christianity is noticeable already in Acts 17:28 where Paul, addressing an intellectual audience, appeals to the words of a Stoic poem: *Tou gar kai genos esmen:* "as even some of your poets have said." With minor variations the quotation is found both in Callimachus' famous hymn to Zeus and (later) in a didactic poem about celestial phenomena by Aratus. What serves only as a convenient apologetic introduction in Acts 17 has become a graphic, semi-Stoic, semi-Christian *pronoia*-teaching in the Apologist Theophilus (ca. 180; in *Ad Autolycum* I.6). Since then the doctrine of preservation and providence has for many centuries been an *articulus mixtus,* a conviction one could also arrive at without the Bible, on the basis of one's own observation. Only in our century has this synthesis been broken, on the one hand through a clearer insight into the nature and function of the biblical belief in preservation, and on the other hand through a broader and more sensitive reaction to the absurdity of all that happens in the world.

The Bible does not have nearly the same interest in preservation or providence as later Christian piety and doctrine. One did, to be sure, connect the word *providentia* with what Abraham said when he offered Isaac, according to the Latin translation of Gen. 22:8: *Deus providebit.* But at the most that statement says something about what is called *providentia specialissima:* God's special care for believers. That subject will be dealt with later in a different context. In the OT we think especially of the so-called nature psalms and various passages in the

Wisdom literature which poetically describe the wisdom and beauty of the world. But to this literature belongs also the remarkable 28th chapter of Job with its complaint that wisdom—the divine secret that upholds our existence—cannot be found in the created world. The book of Daniel portrays preservation with the picture of angels who rule over certain people and who live in conflict with each other (10:13 and 20; 12:1); a similar image likely lies behind Deut. 32:8 if the Septuagint reading "sons of God" is correct. The most important reflection on our theme is the story of the covenant God makes with Noah (Gen. 8:20–9:17). The writers of it extrapolate Israel's covenant faith and relate it to the whole world: the continuing existence of the world is a miracle that rests on a covenantal act of God. Despite its sin, he decided to let the world continue, because by means of later covenants with Israel he wanted to bring it to full salvation (Gen. 12:3). In the NT, too, preservation is a marginal theme: God allowed all the nations to go their own way, and they live by the forbearance of God who gives them all they need in order that they would seek him (Acts 14:6f.; 17:25–27; Rom. 3:25). In this connection reference is often made to Matt. 6:25–34; but here the fertility and abundance of nature is parabolically employed to urge us to make the concern for daily living secondary to the seeking of God's Kingdom. In my judgment, the only somewhat intentional reflection on our theme lies in what Paul says about the powers and the *stoicheia tou kosmou* (see also the previous par.). In this connection one should think especially of Gal. 4:1–11 and Col. 1:16. God maintains the world by means of specific structures which rule it in his name. These structures have a preserving and uniting function. They are means, not purpose. They must lead us to Christ and become the expression of his love. Failing to do that, they can become idols and make separation between God and us. As in the covenant with Noah, we notice here too how closely preservation (as a means) is linked to salvation (as purpose). Preservation refers back to creation, but no less forward to the salvation in Christ and the consummation. It is a miracle which can be understood only in the light of redemption (for which in a sense it lays the foundation).

On the path of revelation we come to know God as the one who accepts man as his partner, who is grieved by his rebellion, who wrestles with him, who lets himself be beaten; but who is also repeatedly, though never definitively, stronger than human resistance, and who is able to bend this resistance and its consequences in a direction which suits his purposes; who is even able by his Spirit to renew men unto voluntary obedience to him. If this is how we come to know God through his revelation, we know that God must act similarly in all of his preserving concern with the world. Then we do not think of the preservation in nature, which was and is the usual interest of dogmatics. We discussed the nature of the physical world and its provisional character when we dealt with creation (paragraph 25 under 9). The real problematic of preservation does not concern nature but history. God preserves the world with and in spite of his rebellious partner. The elements we noticed a moment ago in the history of salvation—the wrestling between God's will and that of men,

God's suffering under our disobedience, but also his resistance to, his thwarting and bending of fatal human intentions—all these things, too, must be genuine aspects of God's active presence in history.

Preservation is often erroneously presented as a static state of affairs. In reality it is filled with tension and drama. Considering how we have come to see ourselves in the light of revelation as opponents of God's saving purposes, we can imagine what would become of this world, which is permanently hovering near and over the edge of the volcano, if the strong hand of God's holy love were not operative in it. This world is entrusted to man as God's steward. As created human beings we do carry out this mandate. But because of our sin, at the same time we contravene what we do: through our egotism as individuals, groups, races, and nations, through our slowness in being concerned for others and those coming after us, through our grabbing and plundering of the earth's natural resources. There has hardly ever been one period at any time in which sensitive spirits were not justly very much concerned about the future. And yet in and after the greatest of crises, life continued restored and renewed. That, too, happened through people. Sometimes these people had noble intentions, but often they acted from cool calculations or out of definite self-interest. Whatever the motives, faith perceives in the purpose and effect of their labors the working of God's Holy Spirit. Due to this human work the world does not plunge into the volcano but remains on the edge of it, or is even pulled slightly away from it. Faith sees in this the miracle of preservation. God's Spirit sees to it that with our sin we do not run his work into the ground and defeat his saving will, but preserve and develop the world entrusted to us. He remains faithful to what he has begun, because he wants to save and complete it. Each day that life continues is to the believer a sign that God still sees something in it and has a purpose for it. We designated this "preservation." We see now that this word evokes a much too sweet and static picture, as of a pensioner who takes care of his garden. But we can also hear the word differently: this human world threatens to disintegrate, to destroy itself, to fall. But God stops its fall. He holds his hands under it. That is how he upholds (preserves) it.

Of the generally used traditional terms we thus avoid not only the *providentia* (which we want to reserve for God's relationship to believers, in the spirit of Rom. 8:28), but also the *gubernatio*. God's relation to his world is not to be compared with that of a king to his country but with that of a king to a riotous province. Faith perceives God's kingship and looks forward to its eschatological disclosure. See the so-called royal psalms, 93 and 96–99, and Rev. 11:17f.

The Bible is full of examples of the dramatic and at the same time hidden manner in which God is active in the world: Joseph (Gen. 50:20), the Pharaoh (Ex. 9:16), Assyria (Isa. 10:5–19), Cyrus (Isa. 45:1–7), Judas (in the light of Matt. 18:7), the instigators of the crucifixion (Acts 4:24–28). From these and others

Protestant Scholasticism has correctly deduced the earlier-mentioned concepts *permissio, impeditio, directio, determinatio.*

Even so, traditional dogmatics has unfortunately not done justice to this biblical dramatic. Western thinking was so much in the groove of the subject-object scheme that it could not bring God and man together as two (cooperating and opposing) subjects. In this conceptual scheme, that kind of *concursus* always amounted to competition. Thus one had to assume that God is the subject of all that happens and that man plays an instrumental role in it. Thomas *(ST* I, q. 22: *De providentia Dei)* finds a place for man in the *executio* of the *gubernatio* as one of the *causae secundae* with God as the *prima causa.* He asks (art. 2) "whether anything can resist the rule of divine government." The answer is "no." There is indeed man's rebellion, but "even sinners have good intentions." And one can "resist the rule which is from some secondary cause, but not the rule that comes from the cause of the entire universe." In the final analysis every *inclinatio* is an *impressio a primo movente;* the arrow may seem to be self-directed, yet it is entirely guided by the archer.

Luther constructed his doctrine of God's activity in nature and history on the concept of the *larvae Dei:* the whole of reality is simultaneously God's mask and his instrument. Both in his personhood and in his function man is a disguise through which God speaks. W. J. Kooiman offers an impressive portrayal of this aspect of Luther's thinking in *Gods maskerspel in de theologie van Luther* (1955), also found in *W. J. Kooiman 1903–1968,* pp. 115–145.

Particularly Calvin has wrestled with the problem of God's activity in the world because he found that it agrees so little with our expectations, so little in fact that somewhere he drops the remark that the things God does are only "inchoate and incomplete" (*Inst* I,v,10). The last three chapters of the first book (xvi–xviii) are on the problem of providence. If there should be something that is not subject to God's rule, we would be nowhere. Of course sinful people act against his will. But that, too, he uses for his purpose. Calvin rejects the idea as if God would "permit" evil. For whatever "we conceive of in our minds is directed to his own end by God's secret inspiration" (xviii,2). Does God then bring about the evil which he himself forbids? Answer: "And indeed, unless Christ had been crucified according to God's will, whence would we have redemption?" But that is something which we cannot grasp (xviii,3). Does not that excuse man? No, for God and man may want the same but do not act from the same motive (xviii,4). The sun's rays make a corpse stink but do not stink themselves (xvii,5). Hence the heading of xviii, "God so uses the works of the ungodly, and so bends their minds to carry out his judgments, that he remains pure from every stain." With an appeal to Prov. 21:1 and other passages, Calvin also ascribes man's sinful inclinations to God's activity, but then refuses to draw the consequences that God would be the author of sin, seeking refuge in God's incomprehensibility. This line of thought with its near total consistency received much opposition. It was feared that man's responsibility was not given its due. But on the common ground of regarding God and man as respectively primary and secondary cause, it was difficult to find a better construction. The counter idea of Roman Catholic, Lutheran, and Remonstrant theologians always amounted to a delimitation of the active *prae-destinatio* by a more passive *prae-scientia* in which God is led by his foreknowledge of what his free creature will do. But this conception was difficult to harmonize with the other conception, accepted by all, that God is the almighty who everywhere and always does exactly what he wills. The competition-framework offered only the two possibilities: God is either an almighty tyrant or a powerless spectator. Neither of the parties was prepared to adopt these consequences for itself, but they did accuse each other of it.

Only in our century, due also to the influence of phenomenology, personalism, and existentialism, has it become clear that the commonly held conception of God's omnipotence and the competition-scheme implied in it, cannot resolve the centuries-old problem of the relationship of God's omnipotence to man's free will. The Bible calls the relationship of God and man a "covenant." That term does not suggest a subject-object scheme; it intimates much rather the concept of "inter-subjectivity." Yet even that term is not adequate because we do not deal with two subjects that are on the same level, but with a Subject who in sovereign love makes room for other subjects and allows his actions to be determined and limited by them, yet without thereby losing anything of the sovereignty of his own subjectivity.

The power which effects this inter-subjective relationship between God and man, we discover and designate in salvation history as the Spirit of God (Rom. 8:16). We perceive that same Spirit in God's work of preservation. Cyrus, too, is called God's anointed, that is, anointed by his Spirit, even though he does not know him (Isa. 45:1–5). It is noteworthy that the OT several times relates the Spirit to preservation (Ps. 104:30; Job 34:14f.; Isa. 28:26; 42:5, and other passages). The study of the faith has taken little notice of that. Favorable exceptions are Calvin, *Inst* I,xvi; II,ii, and other chapters, and A. Kuyper, *The Work of the Holy Spirit* (E.T. 1900), I, ch. II. We must now pay for this traditional neglect because many want to think of the work of the Spirit as primarily that of the preservation and development of the world. Nowhere, however, can we separate this work of the Spirit from the work of regeneration and renewal which that first work is meant to serve. We may connect the Spirit, and that with great caution, only to such activities and developments as serve the true liberation of human life in agreement with biblical standards. The terrible mistake made by the German Christians who saw Hitler as an instrument of the Holy Spirit is an abiding warning. At the same time it needs to be said that Christianity has often resisted the Spirit by its opposition to all kinds of emancipation movements. See par. 54 and my *The Doctrine of the Holy Spirit* (E.T. 1976), pp. 94–96, 100–104.

The question how this work of God is related to that of the free and disobedient creature is humanly unresolvable. We may not (in extreme Protestant fashion) speak of the "sole activity" of God; then we are in danger of eliminating man and his responsibility. Nor may we, however (in a Thomistic Roman Catholic manner), soften this concept to mean "whole activity"; then, too, man is in danger of being reduced to an instrument. We may thus not, as classical theology used to do, place God's concern with the world over against chance on the one hand and fate on the other. The elbow room of the creation is so great that chance and fate too, though not having the final say, are certainly realities in it, even though as elements within a totality which ultimately is fully in God's hands. That is also true of human freedom. We could picture it as a circle which is enclosed by the larger circle of God's sovereign free power. But that mathematical picture misconstrues the dialectic which we have here. This is how we must see it: God creates for himself a partner and allows himself to be limited and resisted by the freedom of that partner. But all of salvation history guarantees that ultimately he will not lose his grip on the world and will not rest until he has—no, not conquered and subjugated but—led his human opponent to the true freedom of the sons of God. In his association with the world he is so great that he can remain present in it when he is cast out, and active when he is resisted.

With the word "can" we say too little. For we derive this certainty from his history with us, in the center of which stands the cross. The cross is the climax of our resistance and hostility toward God and therefore the nadir of God-forsakenness. Here free and guilty man seems to have the final and only say. Yet this God-forsakenness is enclosed by an unfathomable presence of God whereby the God-forsakenness becomes the way leading to a new and reconciled communion between him and man. Since this has happened we know that even the greatest horrors do not happen apart from God. He does not want them, but they cannot thwart his purpose and must ultimately serve it.

It is hardly necessary to say that the above-designed picture of a dynamic and dialectic upholding is everywhere presupposed in the Bible. The static picture of a preservation by a first cause using secondary causes stems mainly from the Greek conception of the universe as a harmoniously organized cosmos. In support, reference is sometimes made to Jesus' words about the sparrow and the hairs on our head (Matt. 10:29ff.), but the subject there is God's special care for his children, not that of general preservation; the combination of these two themes has caused much confusion. Incidentally, it is to be noticed that it does not say (as in the RSV and as read by the Heidelberg Catechism) that no sparrow falls "without your Father's will," but with greater reserve and depth: "without your Father." In these simple words we could summarize the whole of the belief in preservation. In this connection one could also refer to several parables, such as that of the sower, of the vineyard and the evil tenants, of the royal banquet, of the prodigal son, of the talents, all of which picture the strange, oftentimes seemingly powerless and always dramatic manner in which God is related to this world. The first Christian community experienced the cross first of all as the work of sinful men (see Acts 2:23, 36; 3:14; 4:10). But in the light of the resurrection, the early Christians knew that in and behind the undiminished subjectivity of sinful men, God himself was present in the crucifixion as the active subject: he did not spare Jesus but gave him up for us all, so that precisely the cross is the wisdom and power of God (Rom. 8:32; 1 Cor. 1:18; 2 Cor. 5:21; also Acts 2:23; 4:28).

Therefore we can perceive in preservation, beside and subject to God, a tangle of all sorts of forces. He is the ultimate subject of this whole chaotic process. Classical theology has rightly maintained that. But because of this ultimate fact it proved unable to make room for the penultimate facts. Its philosophical presuppositions made it impossible to give due weight to the independence of the secondary causes. Only in the 19th century, in the Netherlands especially in ethical theology, did the search for other concepts begin. See J. H. Gunning, *Blikken in de openbaring,* II (1867), of which the final chapter has the characteristic title: "Providence, or: God the Creator of Freedom."

Contemporary dogmatics has generally broken with the pure instrumentality of secondary causes. Among modern thinkers, Barth *(CD* III,3) remains closest to the traditional doctrine of the "whole" activity of God, by the use he makes of the traditionally accepted three parts, by the fact that only after that he presents his doctrine of the "Nothing," and by his emphasis on the powerlessness of sin. Good discussions of this theme are found in Brunner, *Dg* II, ch. 6; Weber, *Gl* I, pp. 554–580, and Trillhaas, *Dg* pp. 152–162. With many others they are aware that we can put the problem differently and hopefully better than our predecessors, but that this does not mean that we can resolve it. Brunner speaks of the "impenetrable mystery" (p. 175), and Weber says: "The belief in providence did not have its origin in an interpretation of events and does not lead to such an interpretation either" (p. 563). On this theme see also G. C. Berkouwer, *The Providence of God* (E.T. 1952), and *MS* II, ch. VII, par. 2,6. In *Reaping the Whirlwind* (1976). L. Gilkey offers his own unique approach to the doctrine of providence as the center of the faith, by a combination of classical and modern insights, especially process theology. The latter also brings up the question whether we must perhaps analogically view nature and its determinativeness as relatively independent over against God; thus G. D. J. Dingemans, *Wetmatigheid en wonder,* esp. ch. XIV.

Under the name "theology after Auschwitz," we have in recent years become more intensely conscious of the problem of God's preservation of the world and the role of man in it. The horrors denoted by the term have first of all unmasked man in his demonic autonomy. After Auschwitz (and after Hiroshima!) the doctrine of sin has acquired new dimensions. Against this background the non-self-evidence and the contradictory nature of God's upholding of the world become even more pronounced. But principally our confession of God's preservation is today no different from the way it is expressed, e.g., in Ps. 93 and in Art. 13 of the Belgic Confession.

Finally, we point out that the rubric of preservation often included a discussion of creation ordinances or preservation ordinances through which and within which God accomplishes this work. The reference was then primarily to such institutions as the family, the state, labor, society. We have left out a discussion of such ordinances. A dynamic conception of preservation requires a dynamic conception of these and other forms of life and societal structures within which preservation takes place. The number of such forms is much greater than was suggested by the traditional doctrine. And the patterns of state, family, etc. are subject to so much change that in the framework of a systematic theology little that is worthwhile can be said about them. By picking out some and making them the object of God's care, we would shortchange many others, giving these few an established character which they do not have in God's preserving work. Moreover, this would only promote an attitude to life on the part of the believer which is oriented to the past, something which is precisely opposite to the direction which God has given to his world and his work in it.

Israel

29. ISRAEL IN THE CHRISTIAN FAITH

WHAT IS CALLED ISRAEL here is by and large discussed as the Old Testament in the Christian church. It contains the first and by far the largest part of the Bible. Therefore, it is self-evident that everywhere in the Christian churches it should have an important role. In this chapter we shall constantly speak about the Old Testament. But deviating from usual practice, we make this name subordinate to the name Israel. For here we are not concerned with the book as such, but with the faith and the history of the people of Israel to which this book bears witness. By recognizing this book as a source of revelation, the Christian church professes its belief that God pursues a unique course through history, and that the appearance of Jesus Christ was not an isolated epiphany but a decisive phase on a way which had begun ages ago, a way which took the shape of an electing, guiding, judging, and saving concern with one special people.

The Christian church has off and on, sufficiently or insufficiently, been aware of that. Sometimes she has regularly related the New Testament to the Old, but at other times (unfortunately, more often) she has read the New separate from the Old. In some respects she is intensely concerned with the Old Testament; think of the important place Israel has in her instruction or the Psalms in her liturgy. In other respects she seems to forget Israel almost completely and not need her at all. The latter is especially the case in the creedal statements and systematic theology handbooks. An example is the structure of the Apostles' Creed: the confession jumps directly from the Creator to Christ. This happens especially with an unhistorically vertical trinitarian mode of thinking; beginning with the Father who is the creator, one continues with the Son who is the redeemer. In the study of the faith this can never be consistently maintained, for in between creation and redemption one must assume the fact of sin. But usually one proceeds then directly from the doctrine of sin to Christology. There is hardly room and interest for God's history with Israel. The impression is given that after a long period of divine inactivity, Jesus drops out of heaven. There are, however, not only vertical incursions from eternity, but there is also a horizontal course of God with us through time. From the second perspective, God's centuries-long association with Israel as the Old Testament describes it assumes great theological significance.

Of course, this importance has hardly or never been denied in the study of the faith. Yet often this has been regarded as a purely historical circumstance in the sense that Jesus Christ happened to be born from the people of Israel and thus can be understood only against the background of its history and holy books, just as a knowledge of the antecedent evolvement of Greek culture is necessary to understand Plato. But in the case of Jesus the historical setting points to a much deeper connection: in the Old Testament he found the God whom he began to call "Father" in a special sense and whose way with his people Israel he wanted obediently to walk to the end. Therefore one cannot be a Christian without accepting in one way or another *with* the authority of Christ also that of the Old Testament. We say "in one way or another," because it is clear that it is impossible to put Christ's relation to the preceding way of Israel on a common denominator. We have to do justice to at least two fundamental realities: (1) that Jesus knew that he had been sent by Israel's God and wanted to be obedient to the Old Testament; (2) that Jesus was rejected by leaders of the people of Israel because they regarded his claims and actions as being in conflict with the Old Testament. This duality recurs in Paul's speaking about the Old Testament as on the one hand the book which prophesies of Christ and his grace and on the other as the law that kills and the "ministry that brought death." Whether and how these two approaches can be brought together will have to become clear in later paragraphs. But both presuppose that there is an intrinsic connection between Christ and the Old Testament, and that we cannot understand Christ unless we understand God's way with Israel, regardless whether Christ is the continuation or the radical turning of that way. The assumption of the entire New Testament is that Israel's way and the way of Jesus Christ are together the *one* way of the *one* God. Furthermore, if one calls Christ the fulfillment or the end of Israel's way, this is based on the presupposition that his significance depends on the experiences and results of that preceding way. Unless the Christian church in her faith and reflection regularly experiences that way, she cannot understand the import of Jesus' work and lot; then, as we see happen all the time, she interprets him in categories imported from elsewhere, and so misunderstands him.

In the first century, when the gospel entered a world permeated by Hellenistic, Gnostic, and syncretistic ideas, many soon came to feel the relation to the OT as an obstacle for a truly contemporary interpretation. Marcion (ca. 150) cut the knot and ascribed the OT to a lower creator God who could act only according to the law of retribution. He himself is proof of the impossibility of separating the

Testaments: of the NT he could use only the epistles of Paul and an expurgated Luke; the rest came from falsifications made by adherents of the creator God. A strong Marcionite church continued to exist as late as the 4th century. But the catholic church has resolutely rejected Marcion. In our age, Harnack, who twice wrote a book about Marcion, has again tried to put the church before a decision. Familiar are his words: "to reject the OT in the 2nd century was an error the church rightly resisted; to maintain it in the 16th century was a destiny the Reformation could not escape; but still to preserve it in the 19th century as one of the canonical documents of Protestantism is the result of religious and ecclesiastical paralysis" (*Marcion, das Evangelium vom fremden Gott,* 1921, pp. 248f.). The background of his view was an extreme-Lutheran separation between law and gospel (see pp. 248–255). The church has not followed Harnack any more than it did Marcion. A few years after he wrote these words, National-Socialism emerged and in its wake the German Christians, many of whom wanted to be done with the OT as being a Jewish book and tried to construct a "Nordic Christ" from the gospels. Now, too, the OT, acting as a brake on contemporary interpretations, proved to be the safeguard for the uniqueness of the NT (and therewith for its own contemporary critical relevance), as the struggle of the Confessing Church demonstrated.

In our time a certain tendency in Christian theology in India deserves attention. It wants to see Christ as the fulfiller of Hinduism's ages-long religious search. From this some draw the consequence that the preparation in Israel is rather quite accidental, principially interchangeable with preparations in other religious traditions, so that in India the Veda can more or less take over the role of the OT as the introduction to Christ. See R. H. S. Boyd, *An Introduction to Indian Christian Theology* (1969). The danger is not imaginary that the Christ of the NT (preferably the Johannine) loses his concrete redemptive function and becomes a general cosmic principle. That is not what the theologians from India want, but in our judgment it can be prevented only to the extent that the non-exchangeableness of the OT is accepted.

It is interesting to see what place is given to God's way with Israel in various dogmatic handbooks. At the beginning stands Irenaeus, who ascribes great significance to the OT in his struggle with Marcion and Gnosticism. See especially *AH* IV, first half. All the emphasis is on the continuity and organic connection with the NT toward which the *oikonomia* of the OT grows as toward its fulfillment: "But one and the same householder produced both covenants, the Word of God, our Lord Jesus Christ, who spoke with both Abraham and Moses, and who has restored us anew to liberty, and has multiplied that grace which is from Himself" (IV.9.1). It took centuries before this emphasis on the unity of the Testaments was again asserted and strengthened. That was done by Calvin in *Inst* II,vi–xi; see esp. chs. x and xi in their sequence: x. "The similarity of the Old and New Testaments"; xi. "The difference between the two Testaments." Because of its thoroughness, Calvin's discussion of this problem is of lasting significance. Central is the thought that the "covenant made with all the patriarchs is so much like ours in substance and reality that the two are actually one and the same. Yet they differ in the mode of dispensation" (II,x,2). The so-called federal theology, which began with Bullinger and culminated in Cocceius (ca.

1660), developed its own theory about the connection of the Testaments; it constructed a redemptive-historical theology on the basis of a series of covenants. See H XVI, especially G. Schrenk, *Gottesreich und Bund* (1923), and for the Anglo-Saxon sequel to it A. D. Miller, ed., *A Covenant Challenge to Our Broken World* (1982), esp. pp. 130–155. The Lutheran tradition had much less interest in the OT than the Reformed, due to its greater emphasis on the antithesis between the Testaments than their continuity, in accordance with the contrast of law and gospel.

Except for Irenaeus and the Reformed tradition there are, in all these centuries, hardly any examples of a systematic interest in the way of Israel. Thomas, Schleiermacher (*CF* par. 132), Tillich, and Althaus do not discuss it. Trillhaas is very negative about it (*Dg* ch. 6). Until far into the 20th century only Reformed theology (and then with many exceptions) seems to present a more positive picture. But of how little significance this often is, is evident from Bavinck, *GD* III, par. 44. Weber (I, III, 2, par. 3) offers a more thorough discussion, but within the overly narrow limits of the doctrine of Scripture. Brunner, going back to the traditions of Irenaeus and Calvin, constructed an economy of salvation of the Testaments with a deeper analysis of the law and the phenomenon of prophecy (*Dg* II, chs. 7 and 8). Very original and still insufficiently studied is the threefold manner in which Barth deals with the way of Israel in his *CD*. First in I,2, par. 14,2: "The Time of Expectation" (p. 71: "Revelation in the Old Testament is really the expectation of revelation or the expected revelation"); next in II,2, par. 34: "The Election of the Christian Community" ("Israel is the negative side of the Christian community, mirror of judgment, a form that passes away"); finally in IV,3, par. 69,2: "The Light of Life," pp. 53–72 (p. 65: "In and with the prophecy of the history of Israel there takes place in all its historical autonomy and singularity the prophecy of Jesus Christ Himself in the form of an exact prefiguration. . . . It is a true type and adequate pattern." These three approaches appear contradictory, yet are not. They are all based on the same christological approach to the OT. Broadly speaking they can be distinguished as: the OT as preparation, as antithesis, and as identity. These three lines are found everywhere in the NT and in the history of the church. It is regrettable that Barth has not more closely related them to each other.

Fortunately, in theology today the interest in the way of Israel has become an ecumenical concern. Particularly conspicuous is the Reformed (formerly OT scholar) systematic theologian H.-J. Kraus, who devotes more than a third (pp. 131–336) of his *Systematische Theologie* to this theme. For Lutheran theology see R. Prenter, *Creation and Redemption,* pp. 51–105 (especially antithetical with the NT) and H. Thielicke, *The Evangelical Faith,* III (E.T. 1982), pars. 9–11 (much more nuanced). For Roman Catholic theology, see P. Schoonenberg, *Het geloof van ons doopsel,* II (1956), and esp. *MS* II, ch. 12,3 and III,1, ch. 3 (with two different angles of approach). Yet Roman Catholic theology, more than the other two mentioned, is inclined to treat the OT especially as a lower and preparatory phase, whether in a positive or a negative sense. Reformed theology is particularly interested in emphasizing that for the correct understanding of the NT we are entirely dependent on the experiences and concepts of the OT. A good illustration of this difference is the contrast between the *New Catechism* (E.T. 1969), pp. 34–63, and the publication of the Synod of the Dutch Reformed Church, *Klare wijn* (1967), esp. III. A survey of a number of modern concepts of the relation OT–NT is found in Ott, *AG* art. 3.

30. THE WAY OF ISRAEL IN THE OLD TESTAMENT

The method

OUR CONCERN is now to give content to the repeatedly used term "the way of Israel." That does not seem difficult to do, for the New Testament rests on the Old and in numerous statements it elucidates the Old. In the New Testament, especially in Paul, we are given the Christian vision of God's way with Israel. The picture we receive is, on the one hand, that of a futile attempt to obtain salvation through the law and, on the other hand, that of a way on which there is a growing expectation of the coming of Jesus Christ who would give sinners the salvation which the law was unable to give to them. That is how the New Testament speaks about the Old, and that is how everywhere in the preaching, liturgy, and catechesis the Old Testament was and is applied. And because this book seemed to resist this kind of application, one could apply to it the classical methods of allegory and typology with the use of which one could still find in it the basic christological truths.

In the study of the faith we cannot simply take over this direct route from the New to the Old Testament. As the consequence of the appearance and the resurrection of Christ, the writers of the New Testament began to read their Holy Scripture with new eyes. Everywhere they discovered in it the relationship to Christ, which they articulated with the exegetical methods of their own time and generation. There was considerable variation in their methods and the insights into the Old Testament they obtained with it. The Christian church cannot pin itself down on *one* of these, let alone on all taken together. She looks upon these interpretations as an invitation to following generations to seek in faith the connection between Christ and the way of Israel, using contemporary methods of exegesis. This means for us who live after the Reformation, and especially after the Enlightenment, that we begin with the Old Testament itself, and thus ask in the first place what the Old Testament writers themselves mean with what they say. Thus we do not begin with reading the Old Testament as a witness to Christ. Therewith we do not set our faith in Christ aside. We believe that Christ was God's next and decisive step as a continuation of the way he had gone with Israel before. To know the meaning of his appearance it is thus necessary that we know that way first. Conversely, we must derive the meaning of Israel's way from the appearance of Christ. Both directions are needed and supplement each other. Christ is both the "result" and the "principle" of our reading of the Old Testament. He is both in *this* sequence. First we need to know the Old Testament to be able to know him, and then vice versa. In this paragraph we deal with the first, in the next with the second.

The different ways in which the OT is quoted in the NT can, as I see it, be subsumed under eight headings: (1) as authority for our life with God; (2) as preparatory revelation; (3) as the revelation of the law which stands in contrast to the gospel; (4) as a prophecy of the age of salvation; (5) as a prophecy of the messiah Jesus; (6) as a prophecy of the dispensation of the Spirit; (7) as a prophetic description of the resistance against salvation; (8) as a prophecy of the eschaton. Rubric 5 is by far the largest. Exegetically it causes the most difficulty, especially because the writers use certain OT texts as directly prophetic of Christ. The christological interpretations of OT passages such as we find e.g. in Matt. 1:22f.; 2:5f., 15, 17f., 23; 8:17; 1 Cor. 10:4f.; Gal. 4:21–31, and others, may seem very spiritual or profound, and indirectly we may even regard them as true; yet as an explanation of the intention of these passages they have no more meaning for us. This was not the case in the NT age itself because the writers followed the current hermeneutical methods as we find these in the rabbinic writings, in Philo, or in the Qumran documents. What was held to be profound insight then, we now regard as unallowable playful freedom with respect to the text. But that reading of the OT as a book of "messianic predictions" has had its time.

Beside this reading of the OT as directly prophetic of Christ, much christological interpretation of the OT by the NT can be characterized as typology: earlier events and persons are regarded as a "foreshadowing" of Christ and his life. In this way a christological perspective is obtained on Adam, Melchizedek, Moses, the serpent in the wilderness, the manna, the worship in the tabernacle, David, Jonah, etc. This method as such need not violate the OT because, exegeting *e mente auctoris,* it only puts it in a new context of which the original author had no knowledge. See on this L. Goppelt, *Typos. Die typologische Deutung des AT im NT* (1939).

Allegory is a different matter. It cannot be precisely distinguished from typology, yet generally speaking it attaches little or no value to the historicity of OT persons and events; it regards these as bearers of "higher" "spiritual" "truths." As distinct from typology, the danger is much greater here that the literal meaning of the text is violated and that the OT is made the mouthpiece of a message which is foreign to it. The allegorical interpretation of the OT was introduced by Philo of Alexandria (ca. A.D. 30); he used the allegorical method to show the affinity of the OT with Plato and Stoicism, and so tried to win his contemporary Hellenistic intellectuals for the Jewish faith. The NT contains only traces of allegory (1 Cor. 5:6–8; 9:9; 10:4; especially in the Epistle to the Hebrews which in several aspects breathes a "Philonic" atmosphere: 3:6; 7:1ff.; 10:20; 12:22). But very soon afterward, under the influence of Philo, this method became dominant in the church, beginning with the Epistle of Barnabas (ca. 140) which also uses the allegorical interpretation of the OT cultic laws to brand the Jews for their literal (sensuous) understanding of these rites. It is not accidental that allegory and Hellenization of the Christian faith went hand in hand. Allegory reached its peak in Alexandria in the 3rd century in Clement and Origen. The latter places above the literal meaning the psychical or moral, and above that the pneumatic or mystical sense; with this "threefold sense of Scripture" he became the champion of the allegorical method which through and beyond the Middle Ages was *the* means to harmonize the stubborn OT with the doctrine of the church. (Augustine tells in his *Confessions* V.14 how Ambrose's allegorical exegesis of the OT made this book acceptable to him.) Their views differed as concerns the value of the literal meaning of the text. The school of Antioch (4th and 5th century, strongly opposed to allegory) and Jerome (ca. 400) defended it and so helped preserve its respectability. After Irenaeus and the men of Antioch it was combined with a strong emphasis on typology. The Middle Ages, certainly the second half, have not been nearly as one-sidedly allegorical as is often thought. The literal interpretation was strongly championed by Nicolas of Lyra (ca. 1325), who used as one of his arguments that "from the literal meaning alone and not from the allegorical can an argument be construed to prove and to clarify anything doubtful."

The Reformation and Humanism pushed allegory radically into the background. The exegesis *e mente auctoris* was given the central place, often, following the NT, combined with a typological elucidation. The humanistically trained Calvin was the most consistent in his concentration on the *one* meaning of the texts as this is found in their literal reading. His successors and even more his Roman Catholic opponents inclined more toward the plural sense of Scripture.

With the Enlightenment an entirely new period arrived for which the Reformation and Humanism had paved the way: together with allegory now also typology loses its standing as an element in a scientifically respectable exegesis; from now on the intention of the writers of the OT is basic for its interpretation, and no longer the NT or the dogma. This is not to say that after that there were no more allegorical and typological approaches to the OT, but in order to be taken seriously they must be able to hold their own before the bar of historical-literal exegesis. In the case of typology this could still be done (in Von Rad, H. W. Wolff, and others), but not with allegory. On this whole theme see L. Diestel, *Geschichte des AT in der christlichen Kirche* (1861), and as its continuation H.-J. Kraus, *Geschichte der historisch-kritischen Forschung des AT* (1956). For a summary of the many similarities and differences between the OT and the NT, see P. J. Roscam Abbing, *Inleiding tot de bijbelse theologie* (1983), pp. 141–203.

Here we come upon a new problem: the relationship between the history and the book. Thus far we have used the terms "Old Testament" and "the way of Israel" more or less interchangeably. But if we take the "way" purely historically, the two concepts do not coincide. Israel's religious history is much broader than what comes through of it in the Old Testament. It can be compared to a tree whose roots are found deep in

Babylonian-Egyptian-Canaanite soil and whose branches reach all the way to Hellenism. To this religion belong also: the religion of the nomads, polytheism, magic, the cults of the high places, bull worship, ritualism, nationalism, Baalism, even the worship in the temple of the Babylonian nature deity Tammuz (Ezekiel 8:14). The Old Testament is an elucidation of this history from the standpoint of what religio-historically can be called radical Yahwism, the choice for the one, image-less God introduced by Moses, preached by the prophets in opposition to the will of a large segment of the population, and whose worship in and after the exile gained the upper hand over Baalistic, semi-Yahwistic, and other traditions. What now is to be regarded as "the way of Israel": her varied but normless history or what was accepted as valid by the unifying canon? Putting it differently: is the way of Israel to be determined historically or theologically, descriptively or normatively?

We cannot assume that we face an absolute contrast here. If God comes to us in history, we cannot separate what he has put together. Therefore our concern must be the history that lies behind the canon. But this history is in itself diffuse, contradictory, and normless. Beside all that was derived from elsewhere, the Yahwistic faith was the new and original component in it which persisted against all opposition. Its victory in and after the Babylonian captivity, when Israel was brought low and could come to its senses, received shape in the formation of the canon. The canon itself is thus a decisive element in the way of Israel. Therefore we understand by "the way of Israel" the struggle of the Mosaic-prophetic beginning of the faith in Yahweh with the idols, the traditional forces of naturalism and nationalism, and the victory of that faith, which consisted herein that Israel, contrary to its natural religious impulses, in the canon once and for all recognized and established the norm for its religious beliefs and life.

In the 19th century a contrast developed between those who dealt with the way of Israel as "the history of Israel's religion" and those who treated it as "biblical theology of the OT." Slowly the insight has gained ground that this contrast, also in terms of the criterion of scientific description, is untenable. Precisely the canon informs us about all the forces that opposed Yahwism, and it has included all kinds of Extra-Yahwistic material, especially in the Wisdom literature and in the legal codes. And *nolens volens* the religio-historical approach must concentrate on what was original in Israel in its struggle *with* and victory *over* or integration *of* its traditional religious heritage. The earlier-used model of an evolvement from the tradition to an "ethical monotheism" is not in agreement with the drama of the facts. It is becoming increasingly clear that relative to results it makes little difference whether one starts from the religious development of Israel or from the content and purport of the books of the OT. For this controversy and its development to the present, see H.-J. Kraus, *Die biblische Theologie* (1970).

With that we face a third and the most difficult methodological problem: Is it possible to give a description of this way of Israel in terms of its content? The Old Testament in its perspective and statements is as broad and varied as life itself. Moreover, if for a moment we disregard those aspects which are evidently not central but are situated somewhere around the center—the creation traditions, the laws, the cultic precepts, the Wisdom literature—can those aspects which are considered central be put on a common denominator? Can centrality be deduced from regularly recurring features? Does the way of Israel have a recognizable structure with definite landmarks and a clear direction?

To find the answer the study of the faith has to turn to the disciplines of hermeneutics and the theology of the Old Testament. As everywhere in science, here, too, we find widely varying answers from which we have to make our own independent choice, provided of course we reckon with the current state of research and orient ourselves especially to what the different theories happen to have in common. In this we are helped by the structure of the Old Testament canon. The Jews speak of "the law and the prophets" (the New Testament does this too) and officially recognize the threefold division: law–prophets–writings. The Christian editions of the Old Testament likewise have this tripartition, with this difference that in it the writings comprise a smaller group and stand in between the law and the prophets, while the law is there expanded to include the historical books from Joshua up to and including Esther (of which the larger part, according to the Jewish enumeration, is included in the second group as the "former prophets"). More important than these differences are the similarities: first come the law, the *Torah,* the story of God's gracious coming to Israel in deliverance and law-giving and in the establishment of the covenant. Then follow the prophets (*n*^{e}*ḇî'îm*), the story of what has happened to this covenant in history, a story of judgment and grace, of apostasy and accusation, of human faithlessness and faithfulness, and new promises from the side of God. In the writings (*k*^{e}*ṯûḇîm*), the core of which are the psalms, we hear the voice of man as he relates himself to the God of the covenant in confession of guilt and thanksgiving, in doubt and exultation, in meditation and lament.

Covenant and history—these are the two integral constituents of the way of Israel. Covenant means: encounter with Yahweh, experiencing his deliverance, promise, threat, and commandment. The people as a whole and the individual must respond to these. The positive response we find in the writings. In the prophetic books the failure of the people and the judgment of Yahweh dominate. Yet he remains faithful, opening a new vista on the future. Rightly, therefore, the frequent statement: "I will be your God, and you shall be my people" is regarded by many as the core and common denominator of Israel's way. Therefore Israel's way can be summarized as covenant history, for it concerns a covenant which makes history in being realized, failure, and expectation; and it concerns a history which lives from a constant accompaniment which exceeds human powers to make history.

We use the term "covenant history" to summarize a wide variety of hermeneutical traditions. W. Eichrodt, *Theology of the Old Testament* (E.T. 1961ff.), built his theology around the concept of covenant; along the same lines is T. C. Vriezen, *An Outline of OT Theology* (E.T. 1977), who employs as a framework the "relationship of communion" and the "association" between God and man; G. von Rad, *OT Theology* (E.T. 1962ff.), who gives the central position to history; W. Zimmerli, *Grundriss der alttestamenlichen Theologie* (1972), who groups everything around the self-presentation of Yahweh; and C. Westermann, *Theologie des AT in Grundzügen* (1978), who puts divine revelation at the center and connects history and the human response with it. The tension between self-revelation and ongoing history comes out especially in the question whether the OT has a "center." On that see R. Smend, *Die Bundesformel* (1963) and *Die Mitte des AT* (1970). Around this center and yet connected to it are several entirely different entities, such as the blessing (see Westermann), wisdom, nature, and the land. In recent times these elements have again received attention.

Under the headings which follow we shall draw some of the major lines of this covenant history. For supplementation and deepening of the picture to be devised here we refer to what was said, phenomenologically, in paragraph 3 about Israel's faith, and to the exposition of a number of categories in paragraphs 7–18 under the heading "Revelation."

Covenant and law

Through all of Israel's history runs the awareness that it was covenantly related to its God. Although covenants were quite common in the ancient Orient, the relationship to the gods was not seen as a covenant. For that the relationship between the gods and men was too much determined by the forces of nature, people, state, and society. Yahweh's relationship to Israel was, however, not a natural given; it depended on a free act of his will. Therefore its closest analogy in the world of humans was the covenant relationship. Yahweh was best compared to a sovereign who promises his help and protection to his vassals and reciprocally counts on their loyalty and obedience. Of course there is more to the encounter between him and Israel than can be expressed in the term "covenant." Hence that relation is also articulated in other images which show Israel as a steward, servant, child, wife, etc. Yet the picture of a covenant obtained and kept a dominant place because it brought out several essential ideas.

"I will be your God": that means, to begin with, that God takes the *initiative*. In his grace he turns to a group of nomadic tribes and makes them Israel. The covenant rests on his free favor. Some of the traditions within the Old Testament have correctly used the term "election" for that. The covenant rests on election. As regards its origin it is so much unilateral that in certain traditions "covenant" means something like "divine disposition."

God takes the initiative for deliverance and protection. The covenant is first of all a promise which points—backward or forward—to deliverances on the basis of which Israel is invited to trust in the promise. The reverse of these deliverances is often that other nations which threaten Israel or stand in its way will be defeated.

As divine pledge the covenant is always (also) directed to the future. Yahweh guarantees that in the future he will show the same grace and great power as he has done thus far. History is and remains a battleground, but God will repeatedly, and some day definitively, have the final word, for the benefit of his people.

Though concentrated on Israel, the covenant nevertheless has a universal purpose. The God of the covenant is at the same time the God of the whole world. He also acts in and through nature. In addition, the history of the other nations does not happen apart from him—though, by way of exception, that is transparent only in the case of Israel. And when Yahweh's triumph over the hostile powers will finally be complete, then it will be seen that his special concern with Israel also served the purpose of eventually including *all* people in his redemptive work. But that grand perspective was visible only sporadically and at certain peaks.

One more characteristic of God's covenantal activity must be mentioned: the covenant passes through several stages of history. It expresses itself first in the life of semi-nomads, next in that of a primitive agricultural society, then in combination with the state and the Davidic royal house. It comes to stand in the context of social and international relationships; it goes through a process of individualization and becomes a dynamic concept. More and more it also becomes a critical concept, a high standard by which the conduct of the nation and the single individual is judged.

Thus far we indicated how *God* acts in this covenant. But the covenant cannot function without man who responds to it; "you shall be my people." The covenant is unilateral in origin but bilateral in purpose. That is what is emphasized in most Old Testament traditions, particularly in the book of Deuteronomy. God asks trust and obedience from his covenant partner. In the course of history that commandment is regularly spelled out in new pronouncements. Many of these are connected in the Torah with the establishment of the covenant at Sinai, which in turn is viewed as the sequel to the great redemptive act of the exodus out of Egypt. The central and basic form of the law is the "ten words," the decalogue, the first half dealing with the relationship to God and containing some commandments without parallel outside Israel, and the second half comprising commandments for the relationship to fellowman, as these were formulated more often in the Near East. All kinds of laws were later added to the decalogue.

The law is the instrument of the covenant. Precisely through its negative formulations ("you shall not . . .") the commandment invited Israel to stay with its deliverer, in the safety of the covenant promise. As regards its intention the law is thus not at all threatening, rather admonishing and primarily inviting. Therefore the law begins with the reminder of the deliverance from the Egyptian house of bondage.

This does not mean that the law of the covenant is not a demanding law. It demands absolute trust and obedience. This is already evident from the first commandment: whereas other nations cover themselves against the risks of life by simultaneously having a variety of gods, Israel must stake everything on the *one* deliverer, who as a jealous God tolerates no rivals. And whereas other nations capture and multiply their gods in the form of images, so as to have them at their disposal at all times, Israel, according to the second commandment, is forbidden to make an image of Yahweh: it may not try to manipulate him but has to wait for his words and deeds. Consequently in the third commandment Israel is forbidden to use the name of her God after the manner of ancient religions, as a magical formulary or charm. He will come to help his people where and when and how he wills. Confidently they are to wait upon him. Israel must give up all her own securities, listen to him, and follow his voice.

Such an attitude goes right against human inclinations. And yet it is absolutely necessary if man is to find in the covenant his life and his happiness. Therefore the law, in spite of, or, more correctly, owing to its inviting character, is accompanied with a threat to all who withdraw themselves from its grip. For them the covenant partner changes into an opponent. Precisely his faithfulness obligates him to be a jealous God.

From the outset covenantal obedience concerned specifically three areas: the cult, ethics, and law. For, as is already evident from the composition of the decalogue, it concerns here a dual relationship: to God and, for his sake, to men. In the course of the history of the covenant these three spheres of life became much developed and refined. The cult aimed at articulating, affirming, and renewing the covenantal fellowship between Yahweh and his people. The initiative for this is from God. Increasingly the emphasis begins to fall on the removal of sin by means of sacrifice. In the cult reconciliation, grace, and gratitude receive shape. The moral law is in the first place concerned with behavior toward other members of the nation, yet there is a growing emphasis on the suppressed groups: widows, orphans, slaves, the helpless, strangers. Even as Yahweh delivered an underdog people from Egypt, so also his covenant partners must defend and care for the weak. Israelite law, which aims at equal justice for all, equal distribution of the land, and the fight against poverty, fits in with this.

Next to the covenant promises and the covenant commandments, the covenant signs spell out in concrete forms what the covenant is about. These are especially the land, the sabbath, and circumcision. Canaan as the promised, given, threatened, taken away, and regained living space is the great "sacrament" of the covenant which has been of fundamental significance in all periods of Israel's history. That is also the case with the sabbath, an institution without parallel outside Israel, whose 6 + 1 rhythm differs from the rhythms in nature, for instance those of the moon. Herein Israel offers part of her time to God, and receives it back as a blessed gift of rest and refreshment. Circumcision, which Israel had in common with many nations, is less characteristic; in Canaan it came to function as a sign of inclusion in the covenant, setting the Israelites apart from the "uncircumcised," and after the exile and in the dispersion it became even more important.

In the covenantal life the king came to have a central place. David's royal house was in charge of the cult in Jerusalem. The king became the covenant mediator between God and the people. He himself was thus the first who was obligated to keep the covenant law. There was no room for an absolute monarchy within the framework of the covenant. And Deuteronomic history writing, as we have it in the books of Kings, has made sure that the kings of Israel and Judah are only or mainly remembered for their deeds of covenant faithfulness or covenant unfaithfulness.

With the above elements we have briefly indicated what it meant for Israel to live in a covenant with Yahweh. This life embraced everything, from the outward structures to the inner life of the individual. In view of these structures Israel's covenantal life is often called a *theocracy:* law, the cult, social relationships, politics, morality, custom—all aim to express the great truth that Yahweh is Israel's God and that Israel is his people. But this relationship is all-comprehensive, covering the innermost recesses of each individual life: "He has showed you, O man, what is good; and what does the Lord require of you but to do justice, and to love kindness, and to walk humbly with your God?" (Micah 6:8).

The term *covenant* and its reality are likely rooted in Israel's earliest history, and since then, with interruptions, have remained characteristic for Israel's faith. Experts disagree about the etymology, content, history, and translation of the word *b^erîṯ*. The content appears to vary: it is an obligation assumed by the one party, an obligation imposed on the other party, or a mutually assumed obligation. Often, too, the meanings are combined. See for the first Gen. 15, for the second Ex. 24:1–11, and for the third Gen. 17. That alternation is typical of a relationship of two unequal parties. Dogmatics must make sure to keep the various emphases together. See W. Zimmerli, *Grundriss der alttestamentlichen Theologie,* par. 6, and Jenni–Westermann, *Theologisches Handwörterbuch zum AT, s.v. b^erîṯ, Verpflichtung* (E. Kutsch).

A close connection exists between covenant and *law* (Ex. 19:5f., all of Deut.). On the basis of Paul, in the study of the faith the law in the OT has for centuries been viewed as "killing." As Torah it is, however, intended as gracious "Weisung" (Buber). But that intention does not alter the fact that the law is binding and threatening to the disobedient. That element is already present in the Sinai narratives (Ex. 19:16ff.; 32), and it is dominant in the prophets (see W. Zimmerli, *The Law and the Prophets* [E.T. 1965]).

In the preceding part we gave a brief picture of the covenant structure of Israel's way which, though not only there, is found in the first place in the narratives and laws of the Torah. Now we turn to an aspect which particularly occurs in the "writings" (*kᵉṯûḇîm*): the personal response of the believing Israelite to this covenantal encounter. There was, to be sure, more to it, for it also concerned the response of the people as a whole and of the people as such (about which we hear more in the third section, the prophets), but this response came through the yes or the no as it was given either by many or by representative individuals. The writings preserve for us the voices of such representative poets and thinkers whose yes to the God of Israel was regarded as normative by later generations. Besides this, many utterances of such personal faith are found in parts of the law and the prophets. The most important of these are, however, found in the Psalms and in the Wisdom literature (Job, Proverbs, Ecclesiastes).

The believer's relationship to Yahweh is expressed, particularly in the Psalms, in a wide diversity of verbs: to love, know, call upon, confess sin, praise (think of the many hallelujahs), seek, give thanks, contend with, accuse, rejoice, walk, trust in, listen to, wait upon, honor, etc. For the heading we selected two of these: to walk and to wait, because together they express the attitude to which the covenant and the law aim to bring man. The covenant with its redemptive deeds and its laws is, on the one hand, a firm and safe order which tells man clearly how to live; that clear path is the statutes of Yahweh. But at the same time he is the God whom man cannot get in his grip and to whom he has to surrender his life in full confidence. Thus stability never becomes something that can be taken for granted; all the time man must look for new indications of his saving presence, that is, wait upon Yahweh. The stability of the covenant in which one can walk does not exclude the waiting, but is precisely what makes the waiting meaningful. In the practice of the life of faith this duality of walking and waiting includes a wide spectrum of situations and attitudes, from despair caused by God's hiddenness to ecstasy on account of the deliverance he gave, from a deep awareness of guilt to boasting in one's own keeping of the law, from quietly resting in his protection to crying out because of the taunts and suppression of the adversaries.

A frequently used term which captures this duality in Israel's faith is "the fear of the Lord." The term suggests distance and subjection, but it also implies trust and surrender. It intimates a relationship which embraces both humility and intimate affection.

Of many psalms we know or surmise that in their present form they were (also) used as songs for the temple cult, either because they were found to be suitable for that or because they were specifically composed for it, or because they were made suitable through additions. This tells us that the bearers of Israel's covenant structure saw the Psalms as being more than expressions of individual piety but regarded them as normative expressions of the faith: the great and profound words of the Psalms held before Israel how she *ought* to believe.

Wisdom literature generally speaks an entirely different language than the Psalms. It gives us peculiar difficulties. Much of what we find in the book of Proverbs is common ancient Oriental wisdom which hardly seems to bear the stamp of the uniqueness of the covenantal association with Yahweh, let alone that it is directly inspired by it, such as can, for example, be seen in a great many psalms. Using non-Israelite insights, the attempt is made here to relate all of the many facets of daily life to Yahweh, and to show that walking in his ways leads to prosperity and peace, while rejecting this life leads to destruction. But what is obvious to the writers of the book of Proverbs is, however, not in the least so to the writers of Job and Ecclesiastes. For the latter God is far away and his government of the world a mystery. In the book of Job this is particularly so with respect to the problem of suffering as that underscores even further the capricious obscurity of the whole creation; God is present, but as the hidden one who gives no account of his deeds. We thus have extremes here: a recognition of God's presence in the daily course of events in contrast to the experience of his complete hiddenness. And in both cases it is not clear what relation, if any, there is between this piety and the central facts of Israel's faith: Exodus and Sinai, the deliverances in history, kingship, the cult, and the expectation of the future. And then we have not said anything yet about the mysterious Song of Solomon. It does not look as if we shall be able to make the piety of the "Writings" transparent, not with respect to their mutual unity and not as concerns their relation to the center of the covenant and the law. The actual history of the covenant runs from the law to the prophets. Both for the synagogue and for the church this is the main line. The writings constitute a sideline; they were included last in the canon and their precise scope has never been definitely established. The presence of the writings tells us that Israel's collective answer, which is expressed predominantly in a negative way in the law and the prophets, was not the only answer. There was also much genuine piety in the daily life of individuals—a line that continues uninterruptedly, especially via the Psalms, both in later Judaism and in the Christian church, and again and again has resulted in mutual recognitions.

It is interesting to observe the different accents that are made in a variety of OT theologies as they address themselves to this theme. Eichrodt, *Theology of the OT,* places everything against the background of "the strong sense of the permanent gulf," though beside this fundamental common feature he detects many other accents (Vol. II, ch. XXI). Vriezen in contrast sees OT piety "characterized in many respects by exuberance," and he emphasizes the "element of the joy of living," the "appreciation of earthly goods," though he feels constrained to let this regularly be followed by opposite accents (*An Outline of OT Theology,* IX,iv). Von Rad discusses piety under the heading "Israel's Answer" (*OT Theology,* Vol. I, end) and thus seeks especially the relation it has with covenantal history; with the Wisdom literature he could no longer do that, as he clearly stated later in *Wisdom in Israel* (E.T. 1972).

Here we do not address ourselves to the history of the growth of piety. To present an outline of this history we would have to answer the question whether one can speak of a legalistic rigidity of piety after the exile. Certainly as a blanket statement this frequently heard assertion is untenable. Ps. 119, the great hymn of praise to the Torah and its observance, is far too wide and too deep, and particularly too suffused with intimacy and humility, to be interpreted in that way. In the later writings, especially those from the interim period, one can, however, notice tendencies toward an increasingly transcendent God concept and correlate with it an increasing hypostatization of the Torah. Before the Babylonian exile the struggle was against naturalism. After the exile the faith was threatened more by moralism. But in the OT there is not yet a clear front against this second threat. It is difficult to indicate the borderline between genuine affirmations of faithfulness to the covenant and work-righteousness. Not until Paul is there a clear front and a strong stand against moralism, comparable e.g. with the situations of Elijah and Hosea in their opposition to Baalism.

Prophecy and rejection

Prophecy in Israel has been a very varied phenomenon, with a long and diverse history, and in its best forms without parallel in any other religion known to us. Its origin lies in the primitive and confused period between the exodus and the rise of kingship. In that period we hear of individuals and groups who called themselves "seers," who worked themselves into a state of ecstasy through stimulating music so as to obtain the spirit of Yahweh. We also hear of fortunetellers, miracle workers, preachers of repentance, and wise counselors. Usually several of these functions were united in one person. At the same time there were great differences in personality and in the religious and cultural context. Some of the greatest of these seers, later called prophets, were Samuel, Nathan, and Elisha. From the time of Amos and Hosea in the eighth century we possess written traditions of many prophets. In this period of the "writing prophets," which extends to the fourth century, ecstasy recedes to make way for a patient listening and prophecy comes to stand against the background of a worldwide socio-political horizon. The Jewish canon contains yet a third group (which the Christian church considers part of the historical books together with the Torah), the historical books of Joshua, Judges, Samuel, and Kings, called the "former prophets" (*nᵉḇî'îm rišônîm*); they follow upon the Torah and tell the story of what Israel has done with the covenant. Like the prophets, the intention of these books is to give a critical assessment of Israel's behavior from the perspective of the covenant and to pinpoint without reserve the powers which estrange Israel from her God. Prophecy indicated chiefly five such powers: nature, the state, the cult, prosperity, and international relationships. They have also emerged in approximately this historical sequence, with a new threat never displacing the earlier one but always becoming combined with it. First there was the temptation to pray to the fructifying heavens and to the fertile earth by preferring Baal to Yahweh or by depicting the latter as a force of nature (for instance, a bull). Then there came the monarchy in Jerusalem and later in Samaria as well, which also took charge of the temple worship, whereby Yahweh became the symbol and guarantee of Israel's national and political power. The cult, through the prescribed sacrifices and ritual acts, became the guarantee that one could compel Yahweh to be on one's side, also without conversion and obedience. Growing prosperity brought along a feeling of independence which led many of the well-to-do to despise God's law and to exploit and suppress their poorer neighbors. Particularly in the seventh and sixth centuries Israel, and then Judah, get caught up in the power politics of larger kingdoms and the people are tempted to preserve their existence not by trusting in Yahweh, but by cleverly playing the game of international relationships.

Relentlessly the prophets exposed the sins of naturalism, nationalism, ritualism, and individual and national egoism. Whereas in earlier years the prophets were often thought of as predicters of the future, nowadays the vogue is to regard them as preachers who sought to warn Israel and call her to repentance. But this picture, too, is one-sided. There were only a few cases in which the prophets warningly put the people before the choice. We think, for example, of Elijah or of Amos and Jeremiah, and especially of the book of Deuteronomy which sounds a prophetical warning in the garb of a historical narrative, and which has also had considerable influence on prophets like Jeremiah. But for the most part the pronouncements of the writing prophets assume that the opportunity for a choice is past and that God's judgment upon the disobedience is imminent. Openly and concretely they pronounce the curse which, as we have seen, was part of the law of the covenant for those who refused to live by that law. They do this with a great aversion. Regularly we notice some flickerings of hope that the people may listen after all. But just as regularly those flickerings are smothered by the facts. For these prophets the God of the covenant has become the enemy of his own people because, barring exceptions, they have forsaken him. Hence God now comes to be pictured in totally new and provocative images: as a moth, a stranger, a stumbling-block, a trap, a roaring lion. In the covenant the opposite was promised: God would be Israel's covenant partner and therefore the enemy of her attackers. But Israel did not want the gracious unity of covenant and law. She refused to walk quietly with her God and wait upon him. She ignored or manipulated her God. While willing to look to him for comfort and protection, she refused surrender and obedience to him. Therefore Israel's rejection by her God is an accomplished fact.

That is how it is in Amos and Hosea, in Micah and Isaiah. And shortly before the Babylonian captivity this preaching of rejection reaches its climax in Jeremiah (possibly the change in his book comes between 36:7 and 36:31) and among the first group of exiles in his younger contemporary Ezekiel. Particularly the latter depicts Judah's guilt and rejection in frightful and repugnant images (16, 20, 23). Prophecy is the announcement of the total failure of the saving covenantal experiment which God had begun with this people.

For prophecy and its function relative to the way of Israel, see the excellent exposition in Eichrodt, *Theology of the OT,* I, par. VIII; furthermore H. Berkhof, "Het openbaringsgebeuren," in *Geloven in God* (1970), pp. 133–149 and the literature cited there. The prophetic announcement of the failure of covenant and law is elucidated by E. Jenni, *Die a.t.-liche Prophetie* (1962), and Zimmerli, *The Law and the Prophets.* Von Rad, too, emphasizes this very much: "Israel only encountered the law in its function as judge and destroyer at the time of the preaching of the prophets" (*OT Theology,* I, p. 196). See *OT Theology,* II, pp. 136f., 182, 213, 225–230, 267–272, esp. D: "The Law." (This "first" has been attacked by Zimmerli, for he finds this function already in the preaching of the law itself.) We thus reject the idea that the prophetic announcement of judgment was in essence conditional; this contra M. Buber in, among others, *Sehertum, Anfang und Ende* (1955), pp. 49–74, whose conception is often unthinkingly repeated in theology and religious instruction. The conditional functions in the earlier period of the writing prophets (Amos 5:14f.; Isa. 1:27) and in the earlier phase of Jeremiah (26:1–19, not however in 18:1–17 to which Buber appeals). The proclamation of failure is most radical in Ezekiel. The vision in chs. 9 and 10 in which God forsakes his own city and even his temple is of unparalleled force and horror. In Ezekiel we even come across the thought that the God-given covenant statutes were already in themselves a judgment since Israel could not live up to them (20:25). What reaches its climax in Ezekiel can be found everywhere in the preceding writing prophets. Going back still further, the certainty of the failure of the covenant is implied in the earlier narratives as well. We think of Israel's continual disobedience in the wilderness and in the period of the judges. At the covenant renewal in Shechem, Joshua says to the people: "You cannot serve the Lord" (24:19–22). The most telling is the story of the golden calf which follows immediately upon that of the enactment of the covenant and ends in a terrible judgment over Israel; from the very beginning Israel refuses obedience (Ex. 32).

It is difficult to say whether we have here a true recollection of an earlier event or a Deuteronomic historicization of a prophetic indicting message. For our purpose this is not important; in any case, the historical books of the OT already depict the way of Israel as an irreversible way from the establishment of the covenant to the failure of the human covenant partner. I know of no people that has presented so critical a picture of its own history, its outstanding persons not excluded.

God: faithfulness and future

What we wrote above about the prophetic proclamation as announcement of Israel's rejection is only half of the truth. None of these prophets believed that this would be the final word of the great covenant partner. Perhaps Amos is an exception to this rule. His collection, too, ends with the expectation, not that men will do better, but that God himself will graciously bring about a change in the lot of his people (9:11–15). These concluding verses, however, are likely from a different author. This concluding passage brought it into harmony with the fact that all the other prophets, pre-exilic and exilic, despite their radical proclamation of judgment, at the same time spoke of a new and gracious return of God after the judgment. "In that day," "after that," "in the last days" (that is, after a long time), in "the day of Yahweh" it will come to pass that the same God who had to reject and punish his covenant people will change their lot. The ground for that will not be repentance or a more God-fearing life, but solely and entirely the faithfulness of Yahweh, who once entered into a covenant with them and who is determined to fulfill his promises, the breaking of the covenant by the people notwithstanding. In and through the catastrophe the "yes" of Yahweh remains, in order that some day he may fully overcome the "no" (from the people toward him and therefore from him toward the people). The *one*-sided faithfulness of the great covenant partner triumphs over the unfaithfulness of his partner. The motive and nature of this expected new beginning of the covenant are nowhere more strongly expressed than by Ezekiel, who hears God say: "It is not for your sake, O house of Israel, that I am about to act, but for the sake of my holy name, which you have profaned" (36:22). It is remarkable that reference is not made here to God's love but to his holiness: the uniqueness and exaltedness of his deity make it impossible for God to make his gracious purposes ultimately dependent on man. This is marvelously put into words in Hosea where God says: "I will not execute my fierce anger, . . . for I am God and not man, the Holy One in your midst, and I will not come in wrath" (11:9).

What will the future in which this faithfulness of God will triumph be like? The answers to this question vary considerably and are partly dependent on the situation from within which the prophet looks toward the hoped-for future. Alternately and in combination the following arise as elements of the expectation of the future: a radical amnesty of the sins of the people, inward renewal, return from the land of captivity, restoration of Jerusalem, union of Judah and the northern kingdom, construction of a grand new temple, great fertility of land and people, restoration of David's dynasty, and the rule of a just and merciful king from the family of David, and all that as the center of a blessed order in which ultimately all nations of the world will share.

Thereby the prophets did not think of "eschatology" in the customary sense of the term. They saw all this happen in history, as the continuation and completion of what God had begun with Israel. And they expected this realization when the judgment, which they thought was imminent or saw already happening, would reach its God-determined end. As some saw it, this might still be a long way off, according to others it was already taking place, and for most of them it was shortly to be expected. But more important than the varying suppositions and expectations as to the time was the undergirding certainty shared by all that an age of salvation was coming, solely on account of the faithfulness by which God unilaterally stands by his promises.

Above we have briefly summarized what in the ecclesiastical tradition was by and large regarded as the primary subject of the OT and was mistakenly designated as the so-called "messianic expectation." It is better not to use this term because by no means everywhere was the prophetic expectation of a new age centered in a person (and certainly not in a king), and where this was the case the official name *māšî(a)ḥ* was never or almost never applied to him. The concentration on one messianic person stems mainly from the period between OT and NT.

More than once the impression has been given that Israel's expectation of the future was born purely from need and despair, as wishful thinking, as a draft on the future which would render the present bearable. But the roots of this orientation to the future are already found in the "Abrahamitic adventure" which lies at the basis of Israel's history; it was broadened by the illustrious experiences of the Davidic dynasty; it was deepened and purified through the experience of guilt and judgment. This purification even went so far that the prophetic announcement of rejection had to mean a denial of the current expectation of salvation to come: "Woe to you who desire the day of the Lord! Why would you have the day of the Lord? It is darkness and not light" (Amos 5:18). This denial was necessary before the expectation of a new age of salvation could again be posited—solely on the basis of Yahweh's faithfulness.

This leads to the more general question whether and to what extent the renewal of the covenant and the expectation of salvation as proclaimed by the prophets can be seen as the continuation of the blessings and redemption accomplished in the exodus, at Sinai, and in Yahweh's earlier victories over Israel's enemies. Von Rad speaks of a complete break in the tradition and of a new creative act, this with an appeal to Isa. 43:18ff. which serves as the motto for his second volume of *OT Theology*. But already in view of the sequel to this text (vv. 19f.) he is forced to speak not only of a break with but also of an analogy with the first exodus (II, 246). Von Rad's thesis has therefore been much disputed. It all depends on how one views the first covenant: as strongly conditional and bilateral (then there is a complete break) or primarily as the expression of God's grace and faithfulness (in which case its purpose is fully disclosed only in the crisis).

Here it is important to recall once again the plural meaning of "covenant" (see p. 237). It can be both a contract with conditions and a one-sided disposition. That second meaning becomes prominent again in P (in the exile). Therefore the Septuagint did not translate *b^{e}rîṯ* as *synthēkē* (contract) but used *diathēkē* (testament). It has had this unilateral element from the beginning. But that characteristic fully surfaced only in the crisis which resulted in the exile. Meanwhile, after the crisis the fact remained that the covenant is unilateral in origin, bilateral in purpose. This bilateral character will be our next topic.

Particularly difficult is the question whether or to what extent the words about a blessed future to come are really from the great prophets of doom from Amos to Ezekiel. In Amos they are likely a later addition. On the ground of stylistic and other considerations a case can be made for maintaining that in some sense such is also the case with the other prophets; the assumption is then that later readers, from the time after the exile, added to and concretized these statements on the basis of the fulfillment. This implies, however, that there were already prophetic messages of hope which lent themselves to such additions and concretizations. They have nothing to do with inconsequence or wishful thinking, let alone with clairvoyance or political farsightedness; they rest entirely on the deep conviction of the prophets relative to the lasting faithfulness of Yahweh. Significant utterances of this are Hos. 2:15–22; Isa. 1:24ff.; 9:1–6; 11:1–9; Jer. 31:31–34, and Ezek. 36 and 37. For further data and details see Eichrodt, *Theology of the OT,* I, par. XI; Vriezen, *An Outline of OT Theology,* XI B; Von Rad, *OT Theology,* II, part one, G, esp. 2.

Man: hope and despair

In both previous sections we dealt especially with the exilic and pre-exilic prophets. In their preaching the dominant note was judgment; yet they knew that beyond the rejection there would be a new and gracious return of God to his people, for he remains faithful to his covenant. Partly by these men themselves, partly by their followers, the return from captivity was seen as the fulfillment of the promises of salvation and the affirmation of God's faithfulness. Deutero-Isaiah writes during the great change. In his prophecies, amazement and joy stand central; the return of the captives to their land is the beginning of the new age.

But when the people are back in the land, once promised and now given back, and when life gets going again, it becomes steadily clearer that the new age has not yet arrived. The cause cannot lie in unfaithfulness on God's part. A covenant, however, is only then being realized if both parties live up to it with equal dedication and faithfulness. Therefore after the exile the question becomes pressing where man stands who by his covenantal obedience is to give shape to God's faithfulness.

This does not mean that the earlier prophets were not aware of this question. With them already we find answers to which later centuries would refer back. One such answer is the thought that a remnant of the people will survive the judgments and become obedient; that thought occurs from Isaiah and Zephaniah to the time of the apocalyptic writers and Paul. But others, such as Jeremiah and Ezekiel, kept cherishing hope for the whole nation and expected this to come from a radical inner renewal to be effected by God himself. But already shortly after the return Haggai and Zechariah had to observe the fact that this had not happened. They then fall back on the objective signs of God's new and lasting presence in the rebuilding of the city and the temple; Trito-Isaiah (Isaiah 56–66), too, puts great emphasis on that city, even as Chronicles emphasizes the temple with its cult and hymns of praise. In addition, the Priestly Code (Leviticus) and the final vision of the book of Ezekiel (40–48) accentuate the cult, but here the emphasis is particularly on the reconciliation that is made for the many sins that the people keep committing. Yet owing to the dangers of ritualization signalized by earlier prophets, this could not be a final answer either. Therefore others look for an anchor for the covenant as it functions on earth, not to an institution but to a person. Isaiah, Micah, Jeremiah, and Ezekiel had partly pinned their hope on a faithful king from the house of David; that expectation was continued by Zechariah, but the post-exilic political constellation no longer offered any support for it. Deutero-Isaiah saw salvation come from an entirely different direction, as is evidenced by his mysterious songs of the servant of the Lord who through substitutionary suffering achieves salvation for Israel and the people. But to which person or group did the prophet allude? This was soon an enigma to the readers, and it is still that to us.

We referred here to witnesses from the sixth century or earlier. The witnesses from the fifth century speak of energetic attempts to forge Israel into a theocratic community, yet of despairing of the possibility of achieving this goal. Typical in this respect is the book of Nehemiah. We read there of Ezra confronting the people with the law of the covenant and how, initially, this leads the nation to an awareness of guilt; yet in the end (ch. 13) everywhere around him Nehemiah finds transgression of the law and in his loneliness pleads to God for help. Trito-Isaiah, too, is full of such somber pictures of post-exilic Israel (Isaiah 57–59, 66). The same notes sound in Malachi, which sees a new judgment approaching and in view of that calls once more for repentance.

Is, then, God's faithfulness not unconditional after all? But Trito-Isaiah and Malachi believe that there will always be a remnant that will be saved. Especially Trito-Isaiah with his sharp alternation between hope and despair wrestled with the question how God's faithfulness could triumph over human unfaithfulness; he saw no other solution than that God would rend the heavens and come down and interfere himself (59:15ff.; 63:7–64:12). But neither in him nor in later prophets do we read anything that looks like a fulfillment of this expectation.

Eventually the tension became still greater, because Israel after the exile, when she was at the mercy of the great powers, became much more conscious of the universal purport of her faith. Since Deutero-Isaiah, all the nations are being related to Israel's God. The covenant problematic is thus not something which concerns only Israel, but in Israel it concerns all men. Precisely because the covenant is a matter of worldwide concern, it is so much more serious that it does not seem to be able to land anywhere in the world.

From later centuries we have literature which reflects on the problems referred to above and which seeks the solution in a new framework in which some of the earlier answers are combined. We think in the first place of the final chapters of Zechariah (12–14), usually attributed to a third writer and therefore called Trito-Zechariah. According to the writer (he refuses to call himself a prophet) the great day of Yahweh is near. That day will bring a terrible judgment upon the nations who oppose Israel as well as upon Judah and Jerusalem. Of both groups only a remnant will be saved in the judgment. Jerusalem will pierce one of God's representatives, but that murder will be followed by a wave of repentance over the people. Then God will pour out his Spirit upon the people for reconciliation and renewal. And then the survivors from the nations will acknowledge Israel's God, go up to his temple, and find security in his protection.

These chapters place us on the threshold of a genre of literature that began to appear in the second century B.C.: apocalyptic. In the Old Testament it occurs only in the form of its oldest specimen, the book of Daniel. The genre flourished until the end of the first century A.D., and with so many, often bizarre variations that it is difficult to tell what belongs to it and what not. It does, however, have a number of salient features, some of which are important for our context: the expectation of the imminent destruction of this evil world and its replacement by the coming aeon of the Kingdom of God; universalism, to the extent that the coming change is a matter not only for Israel but for all nations and kingdoms; particularism, for only a small number of that large whole is actually predestined to the Kingdom. The vision in Daniel 7 particularly has had a great influence: the world powers are beasts emerging from the sea of nations but perishing in the world judgment; then God gives dominion to a (son of) man who is the symbol of oppressed faithful Israel. In the Qumran documents this Israel is limited to the members of that community who are the heirs of the internal covenant of Jeremiah 31 in virtue of their strict fulfillment of the law. Those centuries really had a multiplicity of answers in which pious thinkers tried to combine their trust in God's covenant faithfulness toward man with what they saw human life, also in Israel, was like and as it filled them with despair.

They saw the horizon, the union of heaven and earth, recede, as they saw Israel's way continue; and yet they kept believing in this union.

This course of Israel's way induced Von Rad to deny that the OT has a center, "for, as we have seen, Israel was hardly ever really at rest in her relationship with God. She was always being driven forward by his constant new promises to constant new moments of fulfillment" (*OT Theology,* II, p. 363). R. Smend has opposed this denial of a center; see *Die Mitte des AT* (1970). If in our thinking about the covenant we make our starting-point the faithfulness of God, Smend is right; if we look at the fact that this faithfulness cannot "get on the ground," Von Rad is right.

For the remnant idea see Isa. 1:9; 7:3; Zeph. 3:12; *TDNT* IV, *s.v. leimma.* Thereby we should remember that this concept embraces both hope and despair and that "rest" means especially: after the judgment there will again be a future.

Whole libraries have been written about the servant of the Lord, the *'eḇeḏ Yahweh* in Deutero-Isaiah. Does the name stand for a group of faithful people or does it refer to a single individual? And if an individual, is he then a prophet, a teacher, a priest, or a king? Or are a number of these aspects to be combined? A more or less commonly accepted answer has not yet been given. All we can say is that in this figure Deutero-Isaiah saw the covenant "get on the ground" in someone or some people, and so saw God's promise of faithfulness concretely and actively take shape.

Apocalyptic, as a special genre of believing reflection on the problem of the covenant, has often and wrongly been treated in step-fatherly fashion in the biblical disciplines. Even Von Rad hardly manages to say a positive word about it see *OT Theology,* II, pp. 301–308, and the more nuanced treatment since the 4th edition—in German—pp. 315–330). By way of contrast see D. S. Russell, *The Method and Message of Jewish Apocalyptic* (1964), and P. von der Osten-Sacken, *Die Apokalyptik in ihrem Verhältnis zu Prophetie und Weisheit* (1969). There is no consensus yet on the question concerning the biblical-theological and dogmatic significance of apocalyptic. See the contrast between K. Koch, *Ratlos von der Apokalyptik* (1970), and W. Jaeschke, *Die Suche nach den eschatologischen Wurzeln in der Geschichtsphilosophie* (1976), pp. 154–180.

Israel as experimental garden

Israel's way, as exhibited in the Old Testament, has neither a climax nor an end. It does not run dead either. It ends in a multiplicity of vague tracks which stand in contrast to the canonical documents of earlier centuries in which the drama of the relationship between Yahweh and Israel was so clearly evident. The cause of this difference lies partly with the composers of the canon: it is simply a fact that one detects the broad lines more easily in the more remote past than in a more recent or still continuing period. But the deepest cause of this course of events within the Old Testament lies in the covenant theme itself, as this was posited in the Torah and disclosed by the prophets in its full problematics, and which had not been brought to a solution. In and after the exile there was a much deeper awareness of the wonder of God's covenant faithfulness toward a guilty people than in previous centuries, yet the way in which this faithfulness could also make the human partner faithful had not become convincingly clear. Out of a mixture of fear and expectation all sorts of solutions were proclaimed which were no real solutions or did not touch reality. This provisional end-result might lead to a negative evaluation of the entire way of Israel in the Old Testament. But that this cannot be done becomes obvious as soon as we call to mind what is a fundamental presupposition of this entire way, namely that Israel in going this way acted vicariously for all mankind. In the history writers and the prophets, the covenant with Israel stands between creation to the one side and the vision of the coming glorious new age for all nations to the other. It arises out of the world situation and is meant to become a blessing for the whole world. But this also implies that Israel, in her refusal to follow God on his redemptive way, bears vicariously the guilt of all men and the condemnation upon all and is vicariously driven into this impasse.

For this calling and role we use here the term "experimental garden." In the first place because it conveys fairly accurately to modern readers the ultimate purpose of Israel's way; in an experimental garden the soil and what can be done with it are tried out, so that other fields, to which these experiments are applicable, may benefit from it. An additional reason for using this term is the fact that in the Old Testament, Israel, in distinction from other nations, is more than once pictured as a specially cultivated and tended vineyard, from which might thus be expected a greater yield, but whose unproductivity arouses the greater anger of God.

Probably only at times was Israel aware of this vicarious service, and then only in a small minority. It finds expression, on the one hand, in the fact that the great history writers describe Israel's history against the background of creation and the earliest history of mankind, and on the other hand in the fact that prophets and psalmists regard Israel's salvation to come as being of decisive significance for the whole world. From this wide perspective, backward and forward, also the present time regularly exhibits signs which point to this election to service for the good of the whole world.

Here we meet the word *election.* Though this term is consciously used only since Deuteronomy, the concept itself forms the presupposition of the entire way of Israel. This people was elected to know God, to be saved by him, and to show him love in return in the cult and songs of praise and by obediently walking in his ways. Election is thus a favor as well as a mandate; and the mandate involves the calling to live from the love of this sovereign God in all areas of life. In the midst of the nations, this gave Israel both an exceptional advantage and an exceptional burden. It became increasingly obvious how much Israel was overburdened by it. Election meant for Israel that vicariously she clashed with the law of God and came under his judgment. "You only have I known of all the families of the earth; therefore I will punish you for all your iniquities" (Amos 3:2). And we who are witnesses of this way know that Israel is no better or worse than the other nations, but that her guilt and fate disclose the way of the whole human race. The abiding relevance of the Old Testament is that the experimental garden Israel has shown once and for all how unfruitful we humans are in our faithfulness to God and our neighbor; and then, too, how unimaginably faithful God remains to mankind which ever and again seeks life apart from him.

Occasionally one can still hear it said, wrongly, that the universal purpose of Israel's way is an insight which arose only in the later prophets, since Deutero-Isaiah. Note the comprehensive pre-history of the human race which the Yahwist gives as the background of Israel's history (Gen. 2–11). Then in Gen. 12 the scene suddenly and radically changes: instead of the world there is the tent of a wandering Aramean. But the theme stays the same, for the goal is that in Abraham "all the families of the earth will be blessed" (v. 3). Approximately the same can be said of the Priestly Code (Gen. 1, its treatment of pre-history, and the table of nations in ch. 10) and perhaps also of Chronicles, which begins with the name Adam. And in the Elohist, as the motivation for Israel's election, we read the striking words: "for all the earth is mine" (Ex. 19:5); both likely mean: election is out of the world and for the world. This eye on the future of the nations recurs in accentuated form in Isaiah (2:1–5; 11:1–10) and later in Zech. 12–14. The most eloquent testimonies in this respect are Ps. 87 and the end of Isa. 19 (whether or not from Isaiah himself). In Ps. 87 the nations merge in the covenant with Israel, in Isa. 19:24 Israel is cast in the role of a humble "third" after Egypt and Assyria, who are also directly loved by God. See further how in many psalms the nations are directly involved in the fortunes of Israel (e.g. 96, 97, 98, 117). In several of these and similar passages the line between future and present becomes vague. How much the nations are involved in the way of Israel becomes clear from the role of figures like Melchizedek, Ruth, and Bathsheba, and from the story of Jonah in Nineveh. In this connection we must also refer to the second prophecy about the servant of Yahweh in Deutero-Isaiah (49:1–7), where he is given a calling reaching further than just to Israel: "I will give you as a light to the nations, that my salvation may reach to the end of the earth." All these statements point to the positive side of Israel's function as an experimental garden. They make it very clear that Israel's failure disclosed the failure of all of humanity, but only in the NT are we made clearly and consciously aware of it.

Having come to the end of this theological sketch of the way of Israel, it is useful to compare our result with that of other designs. We discovered in the OT a covenant structure with an intensifying and never-ending dialectic: the faithfulness of the great covenant partner over against the unfaithfulness of the small covenant partner. Comparing this with what other contemporary authors (for names and traditions see the end of par. 29) have written on the way of Israel, there is, on the one hand, a great unanimity with respect to the elements that must be taken into account, yet on the other hand a wide diversity as to the emphasis to be placed on the several elements. In broad lines we can depict the situation as follows: Roman Catholic theology is inclined to accentuate the positive of the history of the covenant, strengthened by evolutionistic categories: in the course of history the love of God becomes increasingly more visible, reaching its highest revelation in the appearance of Christ. Lutheran theology is inclined to set the OT as the period of law and judgment over against the NT as the period of grace; the major accent here is on the judgment function of prophecy. Reformed theology tends to put the positive side of the covenantal relationship first and to include therein the negative as a retarding moment. In this category are found theologians like Vriezen who is favorable to the idea of development as this dominates Roman Catholic theology (esp. *An Outline of OT Theology,* II–IV), and Brunner who tries to incorporate the Lutheran antithesis of law and gospel. Noordmans, too, lays all the emphasis on the negative side. See his essay "Het OT en de Kerk" (1939), in *Verzamelde Werken,* II, 16–26. He sees the covenant idea as central: "Well, this relationship is such in the OT that everyone who comes in contact with God's statutes becomes a sinner" (p. 19). In his own unique way, against a Lutheran background and with the help of Heidegger's existentialism, Bultmann has written about the OT as a "history of failure (*Scheitern*)." See his 1948 article "Weissagung und Erfüllung," now in *Glauben und Verstehen,* II, pp. 162–186. Characteristic is his statement: "For man nothing can be promise, except as the failure of his way, as the realization of the impossibility of getting a direct hold of God in his own history within this world and of directly identifying his history in this world with the acts of God" (p. 184). His vision is almost generally rejected because with him this *Scheitern* is based on the idea—one totally at variance with the OT—that authentic existence is nonhistorical, not part of this world, and a purely individual happening. An extreme in the opposite direction is Van Ruler, who sees the OT as proclaiming the good creaturely life to which Christ and the Spirit later lead us back. While not denying the negative, "Israel and the Old Testament are at least to the same degree a mirror of the positive side. They reflect what the living God has in view for man and the world: his kingdom, his image, the law, theocracy" (*The Christian Church and the Old Testament,* E.T. 1971, p. 29). But this approach to the OT cannot do justice to the fact that through the prophetic critique (if not earlier) guilt and reconciliation have become the central themes of the OT, as later of the NT. Van Ruler's conception reminds us somewhat of that of Judaism wherein, from the Talmud to modern liberal Judaism, the prophets remain in the shadow of the Torah, as in the *Tenach* readings in the synagogue. Judaism does not read the OT as an irreversible way. It sees the covenant and the law as the center to which man must and can always turn in repentance and conversion; in contrast, the prophetic preaching of judgment and the Deuteronomic view of history are secondary and incidental, not disclosures of a universal bankruptcy. The radical difference between the Jewish and the Christian faith lies first of all in this different reading of the OT (see also par. 4). Or may the convergence between the Old Testament studies of Buber and those of von Rad and his followers give hope that in the future there will be a greater consensus relative to the basic hermeneutical lines in the OT?

The divergencies in the understanding of the OT in the Christian churches and theologies are both to be explained from and will eventually have to be overcome through the insight into the theme and problematic of the covenant concept. The covenant is a gracious disposition from God, yet involving two parties who relate to each other as subjects and whose attitude and behavior are always mutually co-determinative. Grace and judgment, faithfulness and unfaithfulness are always mutual reactions to the other in the covenant relationship. Therefore Israel's way in the OT can never be subsumed in one category but will have to be described dialectically.

To conclude this paragraph, one more aspect needs to be pointed out, one about which we could say little in the foregoing context. We used the phenomenological-historical method, that is, we looked for the structures of Israel's relationship to God and their developments in history. Only so could we track down the theological core of the OT. But no more than life itself can the OT be fully described with *one* method. It can and must e.g. also be elucidated from a socio-economic and political-sociological perspective. One who begins to see the development from nomads to small farmers and then to prosperous citizens, or from tribal federation to monarchy and later to being a province of an empire, discovers all kinds of developments in the OT which could greatly enrich and broaden the sketch presented here. In our opinion they would not, however, alter the basic theological lines. The same cannot be said so easily of the cultural-historical approach to the OT. Its disregard by a wrong doctrine of inspiration has caused much confusion and misunderstanding. After all, in those thousand years Israel also greatly developed socially, culturally, and ethically, partly under the influence of the high cultural level of the surrounding nations, partly as the result of the uniqueness and power of Yahwism, which at first used all sorts of borrowed customs and ideas and only later changed or rejected them. We read of God revealing himself in stones and trees or through the casting of the lot with the Urim and the Thummim, and of appearing on mountains or making his voice heard in the thunder. Initially the cult of this God resembled that of the nomads, later that found in the temples of the surrounding civilized nations. At first Israel thought of the wars she had to wage against her neighbors as simply wars of Yahweh. In accordance with Oriental ethics, Israel saw herself obliged to devote captured cities to Yahweh by means of the "ban," that is, by massacring the inhabitants. For ages her thinking was wholly or mainly collective; only the people as a whole is important, and the individual only as a part of that whole. Therefore sin could be punished in an entire (innocent) group or in the descendants to the third and fourth generation. Another consequence of this collectivism was that the OT almost nowhere speaks of a glorious future for the individual after his death. In its views on marriage, too, Israel began on the level of other nations; Abraham's polygamy and Solomon's harem belonged to the common cultural pattern of their environment. Many more examples could be added. Israel has given shape to its faithfulness to Yahweh within the cultural traditions of its environment and times. As such this is nothing unusual; we do the same. The normativity of the OT (the same holds for the NT) does not lie in its forms of expression but in what these forms were meant to express, or, more correctly, in what these expressions pointed to, namely God in his acts. The demise of the forms we mentioned, and many more that could be added as the association between Yahweh and his people proceeded, makes it clear that the purposes of this God came through inadequately in these forms: the God of the mountain and of thunder appears, as time progresses, not to be localized in one place; he is not even tied to his temple. Oracles must yield to the prophetic word. Those wanting to identify Israel's national and military aspirations with the will of Yahweh are later called false prophets. In Ezek. 18, by order of Yahweh, retribution to the third and fourth generation gives way to personal responsibility. The Yahwist who reports Abraham's polygamy knows only monogamous marriage as the will of God (Gen. 2:21–24). And still later the awareness breaks through that if Yahweh is stronger than death, even dying does not terminate the covenant relationship with the individual.

There is no unanimity as regards the extent to which these shifts and developments are due to Yahwism, to immanent cultural factors, or to foreign influences; nor do we in many instances possess sufficient information to reach such unanimity. With these illustrations we do not intend to say that later developments possess as such a normativity which we deny to earlier ones. Normative for us, in the sense of being a decisive disclosure, is the *way* Israel had to go with her God and what she learned on the way about him and about herself. That way and those experiences we must make our own spiritual possession and express them afresh in our world.

Realizing that, one will stop drawing wrong conclusions in one direction or the other from the time-determined character of Israel's way. It will not do to conclude that the OT preaches a bloodthirsty and immoral God and that therefore it must be rejected. It will not do either to canonize, for instance, the wars of the Lord or the casting of the lot (and why not then polygamy?). Nor will it do, from our own cultural height, either to despise those conspicuous time-determined elements or to explain them away. All these attitudes stem from regarding the Bible as an inspired communication of eternal truths, and not reading it historically as a record of the way God has gone with Israel by which he also shows and readies for us the way to fellowship with him.

31. THE WAY OF ISRAEL IN THE NEW TESTAMENT

The method

ALREADY IN PARAGRAPH 29 we pointed out that the Old Testament has been and often still is seriously neglected in the study of the faith. Christ is made the center and starting-point, and from there one looks back on the Old Testament, with the result that it can no longer speak for itself and that the hermeneutical approach to it does not measure up to the requirements for a scientific study of the Bible. Therefore in paragraph 30 we tried to let the Old Testament speak for itself, without bringing in Christ. The reader might expect that in paragraph 31 we would now elucidate the Old Testament from the perspective of the New. But continuing the direction we took in paragraph 30, we want to do the opposite: elucidate the New from the Old.

Methodologically this is possible and permissible. If between the Testaments there is both a connection and a break (paragraph 29), both must become visible regardless of the direction from which one looks at their relationship. But that implies that there is much to be said in favor of looking from the Old Testament to the New before we do the reverse, since this has been the factual order of redemptive revelation, the factual and irreversible direction of God's way with Israel and mankind. Jesus was the child born out of Israel as the mother (Revelation 12). He also understood himself first of all as a son of this people, as sharing and taking part in its way. Therefore he tried to find his own way using the Old Testament words as his guide. If one does not come to it from the Old Testament, Christology (which is the subject of the next chapter) is given a slanted perspective. Not until we have approached Christ from the Old Testament are we in a position (further in this paragraph) to determine his significance for the study of the Old Testament.

OT and NT belong together in such a way that they mutually elucidate each other. They are as it were each other's hermeneutical horizon. This mutuality has seldom if ever been taken seriously in the study of the faith. The least in the Greek Orthodox, Roman Catholic, and Anglican traditions; more so in the Lutheran because it relates OT and NT (one-sidedly) to each other in counterpoint fashion as law and gospel; the Reformed tradition has done the most to take this mutuality seriously, yet it has not done enough. In the more Lutheran-oriented approach of Bultmann as well as in Barth who is more in the Reformed tradition, the OT is Christocentrically read and evaluated, while the opposite line hardly gets a chance—notwithstanding the fact that the NT on nearly every page implicitly or explicitly refers back to its OT presuppositions. An exception to this rule in church history are the Anabaptist and anti-trinitarian groups in the 16th century who regarded the books of Moses as the center of the Bible (especially the "Sabbatarians"), from whose midst groups even converted to Judaism; but those have been only borderline phenomena without influence on dogmatics in general. A theologically important exception in our century is Van Ruler with his often quoted statement of 1940 that "the OT is the real Bible, also for the Christian church, and the NT so to speak is no more than its explanatory glossary in the back" (*Religie en politiek,* 1945, p. 123). This "no more than" is debatable. In *The Christian Church and the Old Testament* Van Ruler attributes much more of an independent value to the NT relative to the OT (cf. p. 251).

The unfortunate consequences of this one-way traffic did not fail to materialize. Detached from Israel's way in the OT with its enormous tensions and drama, the NT could be forced and distorted into all kinds of other hermeneutical schemes, and the way was open to misinterpret it Gnostically, mystically, spiritualistically, individualistically, otherworldly, existentialistically, etc. Then one begins to discuss the *Vorverständnis* (mindset) of the NT without seeing that this is implied in Israel's way in the OT. Apart from the OT the NT becomes a pale booklet, "cheap grace," a matter of course.

In this connection we have to refer particularly to K. H. Miskotte, *When the Gods are Silent* (E.T. 1967), especially the part: "Witness and Interpretation."

Like Van Ruler in his shortly earlier booklet, he wants to let the OT, as well as the NT, speak its own unique and distinctive language (see esp. III, "The Surplus"). While this leads Van Ruler to exaggerate the contrast between OT and NT, Miskotte, in the spirit of Barth, wants to relate OT and NT as being respectively the period of expectation and the period of recollection, as an equal and twofold witness to the exclusive revelation, that is, to "God himself as he unrepeatedly and irrevocably unites himself with human life in Jesus Christ at one point in time" (p. 111). But the definitiveness of the Christ revelation does not in our opinion deny, but rather presupposes, that it is preceded by a real history which is real revelation, and not just as words of expectation pointing to the future. (The book itself provides impressive testimony that this is the case, despite its one-sided Christocentric concept of revelation.)

John the Baptist

In the New Testament God's way with Israel begins with the ministry of John the Baptist. He is the forerunner of Jesus the bringer of salvation. That is more than a matter of historical sequence. John points to the stronger one to come; Jesus begins with John and points to him. Apparently Jesus cannot be understood apart from John's preaching. The reason is that John sums up the whole of Israel's way in the Old Testament and brings it to a climax. All the elements we discovered in the law and the prophets are found back in him: God's law covering all of life, the awareness of Israel's radical failure, the call to repentance and conversion, the belief in the nearness of God's Kingdom, of the judgment, and of the outpouring of the Spirit, guaranteed by a messianic figure, and with a view to these things the offer of forgiveness and cleansing. There is again the great tension of the covenant: how can God's faithfulness carry through in spite of man's unfaithfulness? John's prophetic preaching had an eschatological edge: a great number will perish in the coming messianic judgment; he who comes, comes especially as judge. But unlike the apocalyptic sects of his day, John offers his proclamation of grace as the final chance to all the people, and he does not believe that outward marks can save from the wrath to come.

Sooner or later John came to recognize in Jesus the stronger one who was to come. But when he languished in prison, awaiting his death, and Jesus failed to bring in the world judgment, he did not know what to think of it anymore. For it was precisely the apocalyptic elements in John's preaching, the imminent end of the world and the irrevocable judgment upon it, to which Jesus failed to correspond. Jesus himself was aware of this discrepancy; unlike John he was not a preacher of repentance, yet he recognized this preaching of penitence as coming from God and as the necessary background of his own ministry. For Jesus saw himself as the fulfillment of Israel's way as this way was summed up in John's preaching of repentance. Only against the background of this summary could his preaching of the new age that had come be experienced as a liberating event.

It is possible that the NT may give a somewhat slanted picture of John's person and ministry in that his specific and explicit pointing to Jesus (as esp. in John 1:29–34 and Acts 13:24f.) may also have been written as a polemic against the sect of the Johannine disciples (cf. Acts 19:1–7). In that light, however, the historicity of John's disappointment (Matt. 11:2–6) can hardly be doubted, because this story could only play into the hands of the Johannine sect. In Mark, John is especially the eschatological prophet; in Luke, the one who concludes the OT period; in John, Jesus' forerunner and herald. Modern studies emphasize rather one-sidedly John's links with apocalyptic at the expense of his affiliation with the great prophets, pre- and post-exilic. Historically it is likely, as is generally agreed, that there are links between John and the Qumran sect but that these do not help explain what is peculiar in his preaching. See *RGG* III, *s.v. Johannes der Täufer* (Vielhauer); H. H. Scobie, *John the Baptist* (1964); and L. Goppelt, *Theology of the New Testament,* I (E.T. 1981) and II (E.T. 1982).

Jesus began his public ministry by having himself baptized by John, thereby declaring his solidarity with John's preaching on the one hand and with the sinful people on the other hand. Eventually the second solidarity modified the first, without however eliminating it. Typical are statements like "among those born of women there has risen no one greater than John the Baptist" (Matt. 11:11), and "The law and the prophets were until John" (Luke 16:16); see also the parable of the children who failed to dance and mourn (Matt. 11:16–19). But in all three instances what follows brings out the difference as well: John's preaching of repentance is now followed by the glad tiding of the Kingdom that has come with its gifts of grace. Both proclamations belong together, however. In a very remarkable way this is made clear from the dispute about Jesus' authority in Mark 11:27–33: that authority can only be discerned by those who acknowledge John and his baptism of repentance and conversion as coming from God; only those who with John walk the way of Israel to its climax of total confession of guilt can understand the change made in Jesus as a miracle of divine grace and vice versa.

Jesus the bringer of salvation

Despite a final sign of God's faithfulness, John saw the covenant event between God and Israel ending in a great judgment. But there Jesus saw it as his calling to play a unique and definitive role, namely to intervene on God's behalf and to resolve the conflict between divine faithfulness and human unfaithfulness. As the background of his ministry we should bear in mind what was discussed in paragraph 30 under the heading "Man: Hope and Despair." Jesus saw himself as Israel's representative, as the obedient man in whom the covenant would be made firm. He knew himself chosen by God for that purpose—more than that, expressly sent by him. In him Israel's way is now being fulfilled and so the blessed rule of God breaks its way through the world.

This mission of Jesus has a divine background and a human foreground, and these are the opposite of each other. The divine background consists in his being sent, in Jesus' unique bond with God who in him manifests his faithfulness to his people. This is indicated by the titles Jesus gave himself or which those around him or later the Christian community gave him: the son or the son of God (in the Old Testament Israel is called the son, but Jesus addressed God with a new and very intimate name: Abba); the son of man (man par excellence, the figure from Daniel 7 symbolizing the remnant of Israel); the servant of the Lord (the one in whom the figure of the suffering servant in Deutero-Isaiah is being fulfilled); the messiah (Israel's anointed king, the good shepherd to come in the end-time). All these names are reminiscent of the prophetic expectation of a person or a group who vicariously and on behalf of guilty Israel will realize the covenant.

In his faithfulness *God* gives this man. He gives him to his unfaithful *people*. Therefore with the divine background there goes the human foreground: Jesus comes on behalf of God to the people, to the lost sheep of the house of Israel. With the glad message of the coming Kingdom he comes precisely to those who totally despair of sharing in it themselves: the violators of the religious and moral norms, those for whom these norms are too demanding, the crowd who does not know the law, the poor, the beggars, the sick, the demon-possessed—all who are outside the rules of conduct of covenant and law that promise entrance into eternal life.

The divine background and the human foreground belong together. Here appears, on God's behalf, the messenger of salvation, spoken of by Trito-Isaiah: "The Spirit of the Lord Yahweh is upon me, because Yahweh has anointed me; he has sent me to bring good tidings to the poor . . . to proclaim the year of the Lord's favor" (Isaiah 61:1f., quoted as fulfilled in Luke 4:18f.). Therefore in Jesus the Kingdom of God has "come near," in fact already "has come upon you." It is breaking through in Jesus because he came to "fulfill" "the law and the prophets," that is, he came to complete God's way with Israel through a supreme gesture of love and reconciliation from the side of the covenant partner who had always remained faithful—a gesture consisting in the sending of a human partner who vicariously confirms the covenant for the people and brings the Kingdom near.

The above as well as what follows necessarily anticipates the next chapter on Christology. Here we have to anticipate matters which only there can be explicitly taken up and given further consideration. This anticipation is necessary because only from the perspective of the way of Israel, as it runs from the OT to the NT, can we find the proper framework within which justice can be done to the person and work of Christ. We must break radically, also methodologically, with a mode of thinking that approaches Christ apart from Israel, for the result is almost always that he is put in frameworks (ethical, idealistic, existentialistic, futuristic, revolutionary, etc.) that are familiar to us but which do not fit him. Therefore the titles of Jesus that we mentioned in the large type are all derived from the OT. New Testament scholars are not agreed on which ones were used by Jesus himself, and with what meaning, and which ones were attributed to him by followers and onlookers, or were later put into his mouth. It could also be that Mark 8:27–33 represents the real situation, namely that Jesus' names were the topic of discussion between him and his followers. There we see, too, how they seize upon the OT royal title "messiah" and how strongly Jesus rejects its use: it was too politically loaded and left no room for suffering. But no title acquired sole rights, because Jesus also transcended the OT expectations and showed himself as "the man who fits no formula" (see E. Schweizer, *Jesus* [E.T. 1971], pp. 13ff.). For centuries the church forgot that Jesus was entirely rooted in the OT. The church may not forget either that his way of humiliation and exaltation became an unpredictable synthesis of OT expectations—making it impossible for many to recognize him from the OT.

The rejection

In Israel this highest affirmation of God's covenant faithfulness met with an equally firm rejection. Jesus was found worthy of death by those who at the time were the religious representatives and leaders of Israel, and who therefore were regarded as acting on behalf of all Israel, as the kings had done in earlier centuries. Decisive for their judgment of Jesus must have been his threefold radicality: that of his unique relationship to God as "the one sent from the Father," that of his boundless grace also for those who did not fulfill the commandments, and that of his relativization of the commandments from the perspective of the twofold love commandment. All this stemmed from his awareness that he was fulfilling the Old Testament expectations of salvation, and was thus more than Moses. Those who rejected all this could not but view it as blasphemy (*the* sin to the Jews), or as a dangerous claim to authority (*the* sin to the Romans), or both. The representative leaders were unable to view Jesus as fitting the Old Testament expectations, and therefore they felt compelled to reject his actions as undermining tradition and authority. In contrast, Jesus and his followers understood this rejection as being in the line of the entire Old Testament history of unfaithfulness: as there was no place for the righteous of whom the Psalms speak, and even as Amos and Jeremiah were rejected, so also the Son of man had to be rejected.

Until the present day these two interpretations of Jesus' ministry have kept Judaism and Christianity apart. The first gives a central place to Moses as lawgiver and views the commandments, which are given concrete expression in the Talmud and subsequent rabbinic teaching, as the way of salvation to which Israel has been elected. The second views Moses and the prophets as leading up to a radical grace that renews man and commandment.

The sharpness of the dispute is tempered somewhat by the fact that Judaism understands the revelation to Moses as intended only for Israel. Through the covenant with Noah the nations have their own relationship with God, and why would not the revelation in Jesus be intended for that by God? On the other hand, Christianity is aware of the connection between Israel and the nations precisely because it knows of Israel's character as "experimental garden." In its rejection of Christ this nation also acted as God's elected representative of the "no" with which all of humanity is inclined to respond to the radicality of this God. The representatives of Israel who reject Jesus are at the same time the representatives of all of humanity. One who accuses the Jews of having crucified Jesus does not yet realize what really happened then and there. Therefore the New Testament also regards Pilate's participation in sentencing Jesus to death as symbolizing the role of the nations after and beside the role of Israel.

Jesus was condemned by the Sanhedrin (*synedrion,* session, council), a college consisting of priests, experts in the law, and prominent citizens ("elders"), which since the Persian era exercised the rights of the former kings, be it in sharply curtailed fashion because of the occupying powers. It was the highest legislative court and governmental body. See *TDNT* VII, *s.v.* (Lohse). In the Sanhedrin there were often conflicts between the priests and the experts in the law (see Acts 5:17, 34ff.; 23:6ff.), but nothing about that appears in the accounts of Jesus' trial.

Especially in the sixties an intensive discussion ensued among NT scholars on the part played by the Sanhedrin and by Pilate in the sentencing of Jesus. For it was not at all imaginary that the evangelists, writing primarily for non-Jews, exaggerated the role of the Sanhedrin, slanting their accounts in favor of the Roman governors. D. Flusser, *Jesus* (2nd ed. 1969), goes very far in that respect, seeing in Mark an anti-Jewish distortion of the report of Luke. For a thorough and balanced consideration, see R. Pesch, *Das Markus-evangelium,* II (1977), "Exkurs der Prozess Jesu" (pp. 404–424). In general the picture presented by the evangelists of the relationship between the Sanhedrin and Pilate agrees very much with that of the relationship between the representatives of the people and the occupying authorities in the Roman empire, and especially in the province of Judea. See S. Safrai and M. Stern, eds., *The Jewish People in the First Century,* I (1974), esp. pp. 315–324.

With these historical notes nothing has been decided yet about the *theological vision.* From the Jewish side Jesus' claims of authority and his relationship to the *halakah* remain decisive grounds to reject him. See the sharp statement by F. Rosenzweig in a letter to E. Rosenstock: ". . . that we have crucified Jesus and, believe me, would do it again, we alone in the wide world . . . ," namely, on account of his blasphemous pretension to be the Son of God (*Gesammelte Schriften,* I, 252). By contrast many Jewish thinkers are able to accept Christendom in the light of the covenant with Noah, and (since Maimonides) as a "praeparatio messianica," a being-on-the-way of the nations to the true faith in God, by participating in the Torah and the messianic expectation (Zeph. 3:9). From the side of Christianity,

Paul was the first to reflect on the rejection of Jesus by his people and has probed it most deeply. Behind that happening, too, he sees God at work, and he is even able to think of it as a saving event, because otherwise salvation would not have come to the nations. And the turnabout of Israel is to be expected from their becoming envious of the riches of the faith among the nations (Rom. 11:11–32). Unfortunately, the Christian church not only has remained far behind this vision, but for centuries its thinking has even gone in the opposite direction, blaming the Jewish people exclusively for the crucifixion of Jesus, apart from its representative character, and apart from its own inability to represent the riches of its faith to Israel.

The breakthrough

The extraordinary events after Jesus' death, happening first in the small circle of his immediate followers and later in ever-widening circles, led Jesus' followers to the discovery that all these things were happening according to the Scriptures and that Jesus' crucifixion had not been the frustration of the expected new age, but instead the way leading to it. Jesus' resurrection meant that God's faithfulness overcomes the unfaithfulness of his people, and that in its representative Jesus as the "firstfruits from the dead" the resurrection to come as promised in Hosea 6:1–3 and Ezekiel 37 is opened up to this people. Many were brought to repentance and conversion through this coming of the "last days." Therefore, yet another promise pertaining to the age of salvation received fulfillment: the Spirit was poured out and began an extraordinary work of conversion and renewal, in which the promises of the new covenant, written on the hearts, and of the working of the Spirit in the end-time were given fulfillment (Jeremiah 31:31–33; Joel 2:28–32; Zechariah 12:10, and other passages). Soon this work of the Spirit spread beyond the borders of Palestine and in new languages and forms continued among the many peoples of the Graeco-Roman world. With that a third prophetic expectation began being fulfilled: through the work of missions the nations of the world were being included in Israel's salvation. All this implied, as we noted earlier, a new understanding of Jesus' suffering. This was no sign of failure, but the vicarious and reconciling suffering of the servant of the Lord of Isaiah 53; not only an expression of man's guilt but especially its removal, the radical and definitive cancellation of debt which was expected as a condition for and as an element of the messianic era.

That is how those among Israel who read the new events in the light of the Scriptures saw the new age as now having fully made its entrance. They were in the midst of the last days. The only thing still to be waited for was the completion and climax of all this: the kingdom of perfect peace that is going to embrace the whole earth, with Israel and her messiah at the center. But in this expectation all the emphasis was nevertheless on the joy over the present which appeared to guarantee the early realization of this future.

The delay

Yet after only a little while it became evident that Israel as a whole did not join in. The great majority, in Palestine as well as in the Dispersion, refuses to take on its task of being the bearer of the messianic renewal movement. The refusal to accept Jesus perpetuates itself in the rejection of the message of the resurrection. In Acts Luke tells us how Paul, following the order of the new age, begins everywhere in the synagogues, but after a longer or shorter period is forced to stop his preaching there, and then finds an unexpected fruitful field of labor in the Hellenic-Roman marketplace.

The age of salvation has arrived, the signs are present, but it does not carry through. The nations flow into it but Israel stays out. She perseveres in the old line, the attitude she had displayed toward the earthly Jesus, and before that toward Moses and the prophets. We cannot be fully certain as to what were the decisive historical, psychological, and religious reasons for that in the years 30 to 50 of our era. Major factors appear to have been: the fact that someone who had suffered crucifixion did not fit the promises, the relativization of law and temple in early Christian (Hellenistic-Jewish?) circles, the "easy" entrance requirements on which Gentiles were accepted as full members, as well as the fact that the movement of the messiah Jesus did not fit the nationalistic aspirations. But the Jewish-Christian community saw behind it the continuation of the unfaithful partnership written about in the Old Testament.

The new age has arrived. But it turns out to be defective. An obstruction gets in the way. The course is being altered. All this came without prior warning and unforeseen. While the peoples are flooding in, God's covenant lawsuit with Israel remains even now undecided. And again, after so many times, the horizon of the kingdom of peace recedes. The fulfillment has come in the resurrected Jesus and his Spirit. But the consummation cannot come so long as the ways of Israel and that of the body of Christ, composed of Jews and Gentiles, remain separate.

Thus Jesus, the bringer of the end-time, remains provisional, "precursory," the great precursor who by his obedient humanity, his sacrifice and resurrection, breaks open the way to the future. Nothing less, but no more either.

There are no indications that this delay caused a crisis in the Christian community. Apparently the things that did happen made a deeper impression than those not yet happening. However, instead of a crisis eventually something began to happen which was certainly no less serious: the community began to write off "the Jews." She saw herself as the terminal point of all God's ways. The pain over the incompleteness of the situation was felt less and less.

What should have been and in principle was the order of the new age as concerns the relationship of Israel and the nations is clearly shown in Eph. 2:13–22 (cf. Rom. 11:16–21, a passage already reflecting, however, the situation of dissociation): through Christ the Gentiles are incorporated into the (Spirit-renewed) people of Israel. There is an allusion here to the eschatological visions of Trito-Isaiah and Deutero-Zechariah (esp. Isa. 57:19 and Zech. 9:10). See also Ps. 87.

Here we touch on what is theologically called the problem of the *Naherwartung* (early expectation), as it is called in theological literature. Usually the problem is discussed only or especially in connection with the earthly Jesus, and the question is then: did Jesus expect the early coming of the Kingdom of God? But then it is overlooked that such an expectation was a part of the religious life of Israel at least from the time of the return from the Babylonian exile (see e.g. Trito-Isaiah, the second half of Zechariah, and Daniel). In this expectation they were regularly disappointed. Jesus and the earliest Christian community shared both that expectation and its disappointment; they were thus entirely on the way of Israel. From Acts 3:19–21 and 25f. we get an insight into the early community's awareness how her *Naherwartung* was dependent on Israel's conversion. That perspective, too, is almost totally neglected in the discussions about the *Naherwartung*.

The delay caused by Israel's disobedience led to anti-Jewish sentiments in the Jewish-Christian community (see Matthew, the role of "the Jews" in John, and 1 Thess. 2:14–16). This should not be called anti-Semitic, for then the OT prophets would have been that too. (It did not become that until non-Jewish Christendom took over this charge, contra Rom. 11:20f.!) Paul has deeply probed this mysterious delay. To him the attitude of the majority of his own people was one of being blinded (2 Cor. 3:14f.), of refusing to abandon their self-righteousness and to live from grace (Rom. 10). But he believed, too, that this mystery served a positive function in the progress of the new age: Israel's temporary hardening makes room for the conversion of the Gentiles (Rom. 11:11–24).

Looking backward: the Old Testament

The study of the faith commonly gives the impression that the Old Testament begins to look entirely different in the light of the messianic new age that made its appearance in Jesus, and that it speaks an entirely different language than if it is viewed by itself—though it is added that this being "different" precisely discloses God's real intentions with the Old Testament. The impression that a distinction is to be made between the Old Testament "by itself" and "in the light of the New Testament" is natural, considering the apparent or seeming directness with which the New Testament writers discover Christ in the Old Testament.

Yet that impression is not correct in our opinion. In contrast we would hold that precisely in the light of the new age of salvation the basic lines of the Old Testament are confirmed. Actually we discovered three basic elements: the faithfulness of God, the unfaithfulness of man, and the expectation that some day the former will triumph over the latter. In that light we began to read the New Testament. Now going the opposite route, what we discovered in paragraph 30 is not being corrected or augmented with entirely new additions, but confirmed and deepened. We are aware that this is also because as Christians we have from the start approached the Old Testament from the perspective of the New. To that extent there is circular reasoning here. But we feel that an attentive and close reading does in fact confirm these basic lines. We see here one continuous way of God with man.

The community of the resurrected Christ reads the Old Testament as the book of the abiding faithfulness of God, a faithfulness which could hold out even against the greatest unfaithfulness. Of that faithfulness, which became man in Jesus, many people and situations in the Old Testament had already been the bearers. These were now read as forerunners, pointers, and types of the coming Christ. At the same time Christ is more than these types: he "fulfills" the meaning of Melchizedek, Moses, David, and Jonah, of the tabernacle, the serpent, and the manna in the wilderness. For these are all testimonies of that gracious faithfulness of God which has spoken its final word in Christ. (See also paragraph 30: "The method.")

At the same time the congregation of the crucified Christ reads the Old Testament as the story of the always continuing unfaithfulness of his people (see in this paragraph: "The rejection"). The latter received so much emphasis, first through the cross and next through the refusal of the majority in Israel to accept Jesus as the risen one, the bringer of the new age, that the disobedience of Old Testament Israel came to stand out all the more for the church. Less than ever before could this now be regarded as a string of incidental and more or less chance deviations. Apparently this unfaithfulness was deeply rooted in human nature itself. And apparently God's revelation of salvation in the Old Testament had been unable to overcome this inability. For that the entirely new beginning of Christ's sacrifice to bring about reconciliation and forgiveness was necessary. And from that it followed that Israel's way in the Old Testament served to prepare for that, by showing man's inability to respond to and live in harmony with the saving covenantal relationship without this radical new divine act. That is how in the New Testament, next to the similarity with the Old Testament, the contrast could also become strongly accentuated as a contrast between law and gospel. Especially Paul has elaborated this contrast.

It might seem that at this point we no longer have a deepening, let alone a confirmation of Israel's earlier association with God, but a change, if not a radical break. That is how many Christians have understood Paul, and consequently they regard the Old Testament as irrelevant for Christians, being a dead-end road, while for that same reason the Jews reject Paul as a distorter of the Old Testament. But Paul does nothing else than repeat, underscore, and place in a comprehensive anthropological framework, in the light of the cross, the radical prophetic preaching of judgment as the one of the two foci of the Old Testament. His witness can approximately be summarized as follows: God could not radically and definitively bestow his grace before its necessity had been historically demonstrated. That was done in Israel as she represented the human situation before God. God gave his salvation in the form of the Torah, which, intended to serve life, in fact evoked man's deeply rooted rebellion against God. But so, too, it had to serve God's saving purposes, as a "custodian" preparing us for Christ. It is not due to a contradiction in God that law and gospel come to stand over against each other as "ministry of judgment" and "ministry of reconciliation," but it is our rebellion which forces him in his way with us through history to expect less and less from us and to descend progressively deeper. That is how Paul elucidates and sums up the way of the Old Testament, and his method is essentially the same as that of, for example, Jeremiah 3, Ezekiel 16 and 20, Daniel 9, Nehemiah 9, or John the Baptist.

This epitome becomes dangerous only if it is handled ideologically by people who themselves do not participate in Israel's way. Then the Old Testament becomes an illustration of the doctrine of man's inability, and apart from this way the New Testament becomes an announcement of cheap grace. The way of Old and New Testament is one and indivisible. Radical grace is understood only in the way of a covenantal association with God, a way in which our radical guilt is constantly disclosed.

To characterize the relationship of OT and NT, Augustine's words, "The New is in the Old concealed, the Old is in the New revealed" (*Quaestiones in Exodum* II.73), are often cited. This formula is, however, much too general to help us along. Worse is its implied suggestion that everything in the OT is found in much clearer form in the NT. So it has promoted the neglect of the OT in the Christian church.

For the specific problems encountered in the Christocentric exegesis of the OT, see par. 30, *s.v.* "The method." For this exegesis the NT has used the Jewish hermeneutical methods of that time. According to our standards, only in the case of Matthew's "formula quotations" (1:22f.; 2:5f., 15, 17f., 23; 8:17) can one speak of an exegesis which is principially forced. For all the other passages it is more a matter of recognition, analogy, new elucidation, and placement in a wider interpretive context as the result of new redemptive facts. Von Rad (*Theology of the OT,* II, part three, A and B) has shown that these typological reinterpretations are already applied by later traditions in the OT to earlier ones and that they belong integrally to the history of redemption and the history of tradition itself. We have gone one step further and have argued above that the NT not only formally does nothing new, but also materially in its understanding of the OT remains in the line of the prophetic understanding of the way of Israel.

Many, especially Jewish theologians, are of the opinion that this is no longer true of Paul. See H.-J. Schoeps, *Paul: The Theology of the Apostle in the Light of*

Jewish Religious History (E.T. 1961), esp. V: "Paul's Teaching about the Law." He speaks of "Paul's fundamental misapprehension" (V par. 6), even while acknowledging many OT parallels, of "an erroneous doctrine" (p. 187). The reason is that Schoeps sees the law of the covenant primarily as separate from the subsequent history of the covenant and the radical prophetic critique based on it. He notes that "Paul does not know the Jewish [not the OT! H.B.] faith in the power of change." His critique stems from his use of a different hermeneutical framework than Paul (more on that later). A much more positive view is offered by Schalom Ben-Chorin, *Paulus: Der Völkerapostel in Jüdischer Sicht* (1970).

Our brief summary above of Paul's view of the Torah and the OT is based especially on Rom. 7; 9:30–10:21; 2 Cor. 3:17–18, and Gal. 3:15–4:10. In our judgment, the main line there is clear. We cannot enter here into the many problems of exegetical detail. It is necessary, however, to say a few words about the special problem of Rom. 7. What one reads there depends on one's view of the "I" who speaks there. In our opinion this I is neither individual-autobiographical nor rhetorical-general but the collective I of redemptive history. From the perspective of the deliverance in Christ, Paul looks back at the way Israel has gone under the Torah and he notes: "if it had not been for the law, I would not have known sin. . . . For apart from the law sin is dead. I was once alive apart from the law, but when the commandment came, sin revived and I died; the very commandment which promised life proved to be death to me. . . . Did that which is good, then, bring death to me? By no means! . . . We know that the law is spiritual; but I am carnal, sold under sin" (7:7ff.). This agrees with the accusatory description by the prophets of Israel's rejection of Yahweh's covenant love. Only Paul stresses more than the prophets usually do, from the standpoint of the deliverance in Christ and the new covenant in our hearts given by the Spirit, beside his unwillingness, man's powerlessness. His choice of words, moreover, is sometimes reminiscent of Gen. 3 (7f., 11), due to which he sees, more than the prophets, Israel in its relationship to God as the representative of all humanity (cf. Rom. 5:12–21). But in both cases he continues the lines already found in the OT. For a further treatment of this subject see Zimmerli, *The Law and the Prophets*.

Particularly Lutheranism lives very much from those Pauline passages which seem to suggest that OT and NT are antithetically related as law and gospel. This leads to the dubious inclination to extend this antithesis to God himself (wrath and grace, left hand and right hand) and the failure to recognize that it does not originate with God but is forced upon him by man's sin. Thereby it is easily overlooked that Paul posits the antithesis on the basis of an existing continuity which is especially evident from the fact that Abraham and Christ belong together (Rom. 4; Gal. 3). Only in that framework do the Torah and the history of the covenant grounded on it get their (death-bringing and therefore saving) function as the way to Christ (cf. Gal. 3:15–25). This antithesis is therefore not in conflict with the fact that the scientific study of the OT has clearly demonstrated the saving purpose of covenant and law. Also for Paul the law is "holy and just and good" (Rom. 7:12), but not able to set free because it is "weakened by the flesh" (Rom. 8:3), that is, its saving operation is being frustrated by the resistance of the human heart, a resistance which can be overcome only by Jesus' obedience and the renewal by his Spirit (Rom. 8:3f.). For the difference in understanding of Rom. 7 between Paul and Luther, see P. Althaus, *Paulus und Luther über den Menschen. Ein Vergleich* (1938).

Present-day Lutheran theologians generally emphasize more the (dialectical) unity of the Testaments. See E. Kinder and K. Händler, ed., *Gesetz und Evangelium* (1968). In addition, we need to be constantly aware that Paul is not devising an ideology but looks back upon and summarizes a historical way. The static adjacency of the Testaments, still dominant in the theologies of all faiths, fails to recognize that the revelation is not primarily a written document, but history—a history in which we through the Spirit must learn to participate.

Looking forward: Israel and the church

If the age of salvation that had arrived had evolved toward its completion, in accordance with the prophetic vision, the way would have been open toward a new world community with Israel as the core and augmented by all who out of the nations would repent and turn to Israel's God. Because the great majority in Israel withdrew from it, the appearance of Jesus, contrary to the intent, has led to two forms and two ways of the people of God. The first form, Israel, continues the old covenant dialectic, and waits for its solution, as if Jesus Christ had made no change in this respect. The second form, the church, which has never lacked a "remnant" out of Israel as a sign of hope, lives from the new covenant, the accomplished work of salvation, and experiences the working of the Spirit everywhere among the nations of the world. Those who are on the one way cannot understand those on the other; and vice versa. That from faith in the same God one could move in two such different directions has occasioned great bitterness and hostility, first of Israel toward the church, but after that, for centuries, everywhere in the world, even more of the (dominant) church toward the Jews in the dispersion.

This proves already that both forms cannot get away from each other. As long as Israel does not recognize Jesus as being first of all its covenant-fulfiller, the church is reminded that her faith is and can be contradicted and that she does not yet live in the consummated new age. Apparently fulfillment and consummation, revelation of salvation and redemption do not coincide. And if the church nevertheless wants to act as if the Kingdom has already arrived, then there is Jewry with its endless sufferings to thoroughly disturb this illusion. And yet the church cannot adopt Israel's conception of the faith. She believes not only in a future, but also in a redemption that has already happened and of which the future will be the unfolding; not only in an end of the times to which we are now restlessly on the way, but also in a center in which we may rest.

Inquiring after the deepest roots of this parting of the ways, we find that it goes back to a different way of reading the Old Testament. Both sides are aware that the Old Testament covenant dialectic can cease only by man's answering God's faithfulness with his own faithfulness. But which man? The New Testament says: the new man given by God, the true representative of Israel and mankind. Judaism says: the people who turn around and follow the good urges in their heart, obey God's will, and so, as co-workers of God, help to usher in his Kingdom. The Jews fear that Christians have a dangerous doctrine of hereditary sin and human inability. Christians fear that the Jews hold to a dangerous doctrine of work-righteousness. Though rejecting the traditional doctrine of hereditary sin (see paragraph 27), we regard the Jewish expectation of man as a covenant partner as in conflict with the prophetic tenor of the whole Old Testament (see paragraph 30).

The church cannot shake off Israel, no matter how often and how cruelly she has tried. Precisely in that cruelty she has confirmed the Jewish truth that the kingdom of peace has not yet arrived. If she writes off Israel on account of her disobedience to God's definitive revelation of his faithfulness in Christ, then by that very fact she also writes off herself: "For if God did not spare the natural branches, neither will he spare you" (Romans 11:21). Because the new age is still incomplete and this incompleteness persists, in spite of the faithfulness of her Lord (in the church, too), the dialectic of faithfulness and unfaithfulness continues. Ezekiel's vision of God forsaking his temple (Ezekiel 9) also threatens her (1 Peter 4:17). Unless she may have hope that God's faithfulness will some day triumph over Israel's unfaithfulness, she has no grounds to hope the same for herself.

The church keeps believing *for* Israel (that the people and its messiah will find each other) and therefore also *in* Israel (that within the way of this people the signs of God's covenant will always and afresh be and become visible). In the era of salvation we live in now, it retains, as the special address of the faithfulness and the promises of God, its own form as a separate people with a separate land and a separate way of judgment and grace, and thus with separate promises for the future (Romans 9:1–5; 11:28f.). This separateness can become a temptation to Israel to a proud isolationism, and an offense to the church because it shows her the limits of her universality. But for both it is a reminder that the present era of salvation is only provisional, which makes us look forward to a future when we will recognize each other and come together on the basis of the messiah Jesus, of which future the Christians out of Israel are through the ages the sign and guarantee (Romans 11:1f.).

The church cannot force that future. In vain she has attempted it by trying to convert Israel or in some other way to get rid of her. Yet it is not God's intention that the church should play only the role of a spectator in this mysteriously obstructed age of salvation. Paul points to a third possibility: as Israel's disobedience brought salvation to the world, so the church by her obedience must bring salvation to Israel by making her jealous (Romans 11:11, 14), that is, through her faithful obedience and its fruits she must convince Israel that in Christ and the Spirit radically liberating and renewing powers, as an anticipation of the consummation, have poured from God into the world. So long as this convincing does not happen on a large scale, it is an indication that the church also fails and resists the Spirit given to her. If in spite of that we do not despair, it is only because we know of the faithfulness of Christ and the power of his Spirit.

On the difference between Judaism and the Christian faith see also par. 4 and the literature mentioned there. To illustrate how the difference is viewed from the modern Jewish side, here are a few quotations. F. Rosenzweig writes to E. Rosenstock, who has converted to Christianity: ". . . we are to you a constant reminder and memorial of your 'not-yet'; for you who live your life in an *ecclesia triumphans* need a mute servant who shouts to all of you, when you think that you have enjoyed God in bread and wine, 'master, remember the very last things' " (allusion to a story of Herodotus; *Gesammelte Schriften,* I, 285). M. Buber says in his well-known discussion with K. L. Schmidt in 1933: "We know . . . that world history is not yet broken down to the very ground, that the world is not yet redeemed. We feel the unredeemed state of the world. . . . For us the redemption of the world is indissolubly one with the consummation of the creation . . . with the realized kingdom of God. We cannot conceive of the idea that the final and complete redemption of the world is being anticipated in some part of it, let us say the soul, which is already now redeemed. . . . We do not notice a break in history. We know of no middle in history, but only of a goal, the goal of the way of God which does not stop on its way" (in *Der Jude und sein Judentum* [1963], p. 562). And very specifically in his address "The Focal Points of the Jewish Soul": "The final unique difference between Judaism and Christianity lies in this, that the God who reveals himself to 'flesh' and meets man in a mutual relationship is not incarnate, and that the history of mankind, directed to the consummation, is in a continual state of crisis." S. Ben-Chorin formulates the same as follows: "The Jew is deeply aware that the world is not redeemed, and within this unredeemed state he does not discern and recognize enclaves of redemption. The conception of a redeemed soul within an unredeemed world is foreign to him, totally foreign, impossible to conceive of from the ultimate basis of his own existence. Here lies the core for Israel's rejection of Jesus" (*Die Antwort des Jona,* 1956, p. 99). These statements touch the heart of the matter, though they are not free from misunderstandings, e.g. the "pietistic" misunderstanding about the redeemed soul in the last quotation. That does not alter the fact that these same thinkers have deeply pondered the distinct God-willed path of the world church. The most profound thoughts about it are found in F. Rosenzweig, *Der Stern der Erlösung,* esp. III,iii (1921). But is there a possibility of a convergence of the two ways? From Schoeps come these remarkable words: "Israel's messianic expectation is oriented to what is coming, the church's eschatological expectation of the return of the one who has come. Both are united in the common expectation that the decisive event is still to come—as the goal of God's ways which in Israel and the church he walks with mankind. The church of Jesus Christ has not preserved a picture of her Lord and

Savior. If Jesus should return tomorrow, no Christian would be able to recognize him by sight. It could well be that he who is coming at the end of time, and who is the expectation of the synagogue as well as of the church, has the same face"(*Paulus,* p. 274). Here we can think, too, of the growing interest in Jesus on the part of the Jews, especially in the state of Israel. Among Christians there is lately arising a strong awareness of Jesus' "provisional nature," especially through and after J. Moltmann's *Theology of Hope* (E.T. 1967). Next to Paul, who lives especially from the redemptive new age that has now come, we begin to listen more to the message of the Epistle to the Hebrews, emphasizing as it does not only the fulfillment, but just as much the unfinished state of the new age and which sees Jesus literally as the forerunner* of a people still on the way to redemption (12:1–3). There is thus a remarkable convergence. But the question whether in the person and work of Jesus God has spoken a definitive word, as reconciliation and as directional signal, keeps the two apart.

From the side of Judaism this separation goes back, in turn, to a different way of reading the OT, as a result of which Jesus comes to stand in an entirely different perspective and Paul is regarded as standing outside the Jewish tradition. The synagogue has three readings from the Torah followed by one reading (less ceremonial) from the prophets. There is no irreversible relationship between the two. No matter how great the apostasy, the way to return always remains open. That is the standpoint from which the Talmud reads the history of Israel's way in the OT. A heavy emphasis falls on the goodness of creation. Gen. 3 describes a reversible event. The weaknesses of the patriarchs are excused; much is made of their merits from which the later Israel is benefitting. The people did indeed sin in the wilderness, e.g. with the golden calf, but Moses could rightly expostulate with God that it was his own fault because he had let them live in Egypt, where they had not learned anything else (exegesis of Ex. 32:11). Many more examples could be added. See R. Mayer, *Der Babylonische Talmud* (1963), the rabbinic explanations found in the series *Zoals er gezegd is over*..; also K. H. Miskotte, *Het wezen der Joodsche religie* (1932), VIII; L. Baeck, *The Essence of Judaism* (E.T. 1961), II; H.-J. Schoeps, *Jüdische Geisteswelt* (n.d.), *passim,* esp. II and III. One must also keep in mind that for Judaism the continuing tradition is of greater significance than the fixed canon of the OT. The urgently needed discussion about the hermeneutics of the OT is thus complicated by the problem of the relationship of Scripture and tradition. For the hermeneutical difference see also H. W. Wolff, "Zur Hermeneutik des AT," in *Probleme a.t.-licher Hermeneutik* (1960), esp. pp. 150–153.

In the NT, Paul is about the only one who wrestles with the problem of the separation within the people of God (one gets the impression that other writers either do not yet or no longer think about it). Actually everything essential that can be said about it from the perspective of the unity of the OT and Christ is found in Rom. 9–11. For centuries only individuals and sectarian groups have seriously concerned themselves with this part of Paul's message. Church and theology viewed it as an isolated discourse and were mainly interested (wrongly) in that part of Rom. 9 which seemed to be important for the dogma of predestination.

---

*The Dutch has a play on words here which cannot be reproduced in English: *voorlopig* (= provisional)—*voorloper* (= forerunner) [S.W.].

Only after 1933 have larger groups in the churches begun to ask themselves what the apparently ineradicable phenomenon Israel may have to say to us, as promise, admonition, soul struggle, correction, and challenge. The reflection on it was and is often obscured by anti-Semitic, philo-Semitic, and anti- or philo-Zionistic sentiments. Moreover, for earlier pietistic and liberal theologies as well as present-day existentialistic and political-ethical theologies, it is hard to conceive that God would maintain concrete relations in history and with nations. Therefore the spirits seem to divide on the question whether, beside the command to Israel to be faithful to the law, the promise of the land as a gift is still relevant. Judaism by and large has no doubt about that. The very least Christians should do is see the land as a "sacrament of God's faithfulness"; in our judgment those who do not, fail to take the way of Israel seriously. One may then be willing to attempt to develop a "theology after Auschwitz" (see par. 27, end), but not a "theology after the return," though in Jewish thinking destruction and return are inseparable. The first is indeed a separate theme in Western Europe and North America, but not for the Jews in Israel. For the place of the land, see the symposium of Jews and Christians, *Jüdisches Volk-gelobtes Land* (1970); the "guide" of the synod of the Dutch Reformed Church, *Israël: volk, land en staat;* and the biblical-theological discussion, with an excellent final chapter on hermeneutics, of W. Brueggemann, *The Land* (1978).

A theological consensus about the relationship of the church to Israel is not yet in sight. For a variety of approaches, see E. Flesseman-van Leer, *Met de bijbel tussen kerk en jodendom* (1982), and F.-W. Marquardt, *Die Gegenwart des Auferstandenen bei seinem Volk Israel* (1983). Two variant approaches to a comprehensive "theology of Judaism" are offered by F. Mussner, *Traktat über die Juden* (1979), and P. von der Osten-Sacken, *Grundzüge einer Theologie im christlich-jüdischen Gespräch* (1982), both with extensive literature.

Jesus the Son

32. IN SEARCH OF THE HISTORICAL JESUS

In the previous paragraph we presented one approach to the way of Jesus as the messiah of Israel. We might call that the approach *from behind:* we see him in the line of redemptive history, how he arises out of the Old Testament problematic, and gives and is the answer to it. But with this approach he does not come fully within our purview. He is the fulfillment of Israel's way precisely because he is more than a small segment of that way, namely a new beginning and a turn made by God. Therefore, to the approach from behind must be added an approach *from above.* In other words, there must be added an approach that starts from the Word, the creative and saving speech of God which in him became "flesh," that is, an historical human life. But because the word became historical in him, a dated life within human history, yet a third approach is possible and necessary, the approach *from below,* whereby we apply to his appearance the methodology of all historical investigation, and ascertain what he looks like in the light of a careful investigation of the sources and within the framework of his own time.

We regard these three approaches as complementary. All three relate to the manner in which eternity unites itself to time in Jesus the Christ. We could think of yet a fourth approach, one *from before,* from the perspective of what he works through the centuries in human hearts and in the peoples of the world. We cannot do without that approach either. In the study of the faith it is usually dealt with under other headings: the work of the Spirit, the church, justification, etc. We shall do that too, but wish to make a clear transition between Christology and the subsequent chapters. In this separate chapter on Christology we concern ourselves particularly with the approaches from above and from below. Thereby it should be noted that through the ages classical dogmatics knew only the first: the man Jesus was seen exclusively as the product of the Word becoming flesh, the "Word" being thought of as the "second person" of the Trinity. As a reaction there arose since the Enlightenment a strong emphasis on the approach from below. Ecclesiastical thinking often fiercely opposed that. Understandably so, because this supposed "purely historical-scientific" approach was often motivated by the desire to prove that Jesus had not been the Son of God, but only a uniquely gifted and inspiring man. Yet that does not as such justify the church's opposition. If in Christ the Word has become flesh, it should be able to stand the test of historical-critical investigation. Precisely from the standpoint of faith, historical investigation is to be left free. In view of the methodological limitations inherent in such investigation, it is not able to uncover the divine secret of Jesus the Christ. But if this secret is there, the investigation will sooner or later in one way or another hit upon it. So it can prepare the way for the other, more deeply penetrating approach.

By putting it this way, we opt for a sequence in which the approach from below comes first. In our world (after the Enlightenment) this could hardly be otherwise. We approach Jesus as an historical figure first of all with our own historical awareness. But we need not argue this sequence only from the standpoint of our own cultural period. The people from Jesus' own time also began by interpreting him with concepts derived from their own world and experience. It was as a consequence of that interpretation that some of them discovered that they had to interpret him differently to do justice to him.

In this connection see the familiar passage Mark 8:27–30 ("Who do men say that I am? . . . But who do you say that I am?"), to which Matthew adds: "flesh and blood has not revealed this to you" (16:17), that is, the essence of the person of Jesus is not grasped with the use of familiar categories.

In the NT there is a plurality of approaches. The one "from behind" comes through especially in Matthew, Luke, and Acts (cf. also Rom. 1:2–4); the one "from below" in Mark, but also in Luke with his appeal to careful historical investigation (Luke 1:1–4); the Christology "from above" we find in Paul (e.g. Phil. 2:5–11) and still more in John (prologue of the Gospel and *passim*).

In the history of the church this last-mentioned approach (with remarkable, but few exceptions) has been one-sidedly followed. This had to lead to a minimization of Jesus as a man living in a particular historical context. The historical-critical search for the "historical Jesus" was a necessary and beneficial correction to that. Unfortunately, from the very beginning it was burdened with an ambiguity which has greatly hampered the progress of this quest. On the one hand the aim was to be purely historical and unbiased, while on the other hand many of these critical scholars were consciously or unconsciously sure beforehand of the outcome: that Jesus would turn out to be nothing more than a man among men. This second element has often obscured the first: the sources were (and sometimes still are) read with a skepticism and suspicion concerning their historical reliability such as is not applied by historians in parallel situations. Over against that one finds, of course, other scholars who close their eyes to clearly critical facts. This inquiry is marked with a nervousness not found in other historical studies, and it demonstrates how much the New Testament proclamation of Christ compels people, also today, to take a stand. This can never be entirely avoided, and may even stimulate the search, if one is aware of it. But most of the

different strands from the tradition, something which does not escape the untrained as well as the trained reader of the Bible. Fine examples of such differences in narration and interpretation are: the depiction of John the Baptist, the apocalyptic discourse (Mark *before,* the others *after* the fall of Jerusalem), the stilling of the storm (the changes Matt. makes in Mark), the parable of the wedding banquet (with entirely different accents in Matt. than in Luke), and the resurrection narratives. In this discipline the danger of splitting hairs is indeed great, as is that of presenting the evangelists (against their intentions) as autonomous creative writers. A sober treatment will throw into sharper relief, beside the redactional revision, what the evangelists have in common, or the separate traditions (*Sondergut*) they have used. See *RGG* II, *s.v. Formen und Gattungen im NT* (by the champion of redaction history, G. Bornkamm), and J. Rohde, *Die redaktionsgeschichtliche Methode* (1966).

A separate question in this connection is: what led to the scriptural fixation of the story of Jesus and why precisely in the second half of the first century? It is a rather generally valid law that the need for writing something down arises when the generation of eyewitnesses is dying out. In this instance the rapid spread of Christendom and the needs of missionary preaching provided an additional stimulus. Perhaps it was also necessary that the proclamation of the ascended Lord be protected against a docetic and gnostic evaporation, through more consciously connecting it with his early life.

The preceding would have looked somewhat different if all Gospels had been written before the fall of Jerusalem, as J. A. T. Robinson argues in *Redating the NT* (1976). But his ideas have found little acceptance.

2. So we are directed to the tradition process which preceded the formation of the gospels. After the First World War, by means of the method of form criticism, scholars have been able to penetrate more deeply into this process than before. We assume now that there existed, beside the more or less coherent passion narrative, small units of sayings, disputes, stories of miracles, etc. which corresponded to the needs of the community for introductions, arguments, and illustrations to be used for preaching, instruction, missions, apologetics, etc. However, on the question to what extent these small units (which are put together in the synoptic gospels) give a reliable picture of Jesus' own ministry, scholars are mainly divided into two groups. There is a more conservative and a more sceptical group. That difference goes back to a different model of the tradition process. The school of Bultmann sees it primarily as a collective, unconscious, and creative process, of which the first Christian community was the bearer, and which was governed by its needs to maintain itself and to spread out. In this way all kinds of contradictions, elaborations, legendary accretions, and the like can be readily explained. But this model does not reckon, or only insufficiently, with four things: the above-mentioned vital importance to the community of the historicity of the tradition, the fact that for many years there were still eyewitnesses who could correct the formation of the tradition, the great care with

which during that same time the Jewish scribes tried to preserve their oral traditions, and especially the picture we get from Paul about the care of the apostles to pass on the tradition intact. For these reasons most scholars not part of the school of Bultmann orient themselves to another model; they regard the tradition much more as a conscious reproductive process, carried on by individuals and directed by the apostles. This conception is much more in agreement with the information the New Testament furnishes here and there about this process. But the strongest point of the first model is the weakest here: following this line it is difficult to find a satisfactory explanation for specific variations of very important statements and stories, for instance of the institution of the Lord's Supper or of the post-resurrection appearances. The reality must have been more complicated than both models suggest. But in my opinion the second of the two models stands the strongest. Moreover, the truth of the first model can be incorporated into the (more complex) second model, but it is difficult to think of the reverse: a consciously directed process will always be attended by unconscious sociological factors, but not to the extent that these factors will necessarily alter or stop the process itself; it is not possible, however, to conceive of individual bearers of authority involving themselves in an unconscious process without changing the nature of that process. As a matter of fact the picture of a community which immediately after Jesus' departure begins to produce words and stories, as if it were devoid of recollection, conflicts with what is humanly and historically likely. With this it is not said that the tradition process did not lead to some loss of depth, a measure of obscurity as well as embellishment, and in general exerted an altering influence. It can be shown that this has happened. (The most important reason for this cannot be dealt with here but will be taken up under the next point.) But that can never be the determining starting-point of the investigation. The burden of proof ought to be on those who deny the historicity of a part of the tradition, not on those who acknowledge it. This is a normal rule for the historical investigation of a tradition only a few decades removed from the event.

Before the First World War, generally four sources were regarded as lying behind the three synoptic gospels: the ur-Mark, the Logia-source, and material unique to Matthew or Luke. The form-critical study of the NT discovered that all these sources were collections of small units previously handed down orally. The dominant book of this approach became R. Bultmann, *The History of the Synoptic Tradition* (1921; E.T. 1963), which is based on the assumption that "The proper understanding of Form criticism rests upon the judgment that the literature in which the life of a given community, even the primitive Christian community, has taken shape, springs out of quite definite conditions and wants of life from which grows up a quite definite style and quite specific forms and categories" (p. 4). This starting-point does not reckon with what the earliest NT writer,

Paul, tells us about the manner in which the *paradosis* is preserved and passed on. See 1 Cor. 11:23–25; 15:1–8; Gal. 1:18–2:10; cf. Rom. 6:17; 1 Cor. 11:1f.; Phil. 4:9; 1 Thess. 2:13; 4:1f.; 2 Thess. 2:15; 3:6. See also Luke 1:1–4 and 1 John 1:1–4. This traditionary pattern can also be observed in the period that followed and led to the formation of the canon, from Papias to Irenaeus. Outside the school of Bultmann the research is, therefore, mainly oriented to the second model. A (one-sided) methodological counterpart of Bultmann's above book is B. Gerhardsson, *Memory and Manuscript* (1961).

3. Meanwhile, the research concerning Jesus is faced with yet a third problem, of a unique and intriguing nature. It is found in the fact that the New Testament offers a twofold picture of Christ. The strange fact is that the other books show hardly any knowledge of or interest in the particulars of Jesus' life as these are told in the gospels. In the epistles and in Revelation the life of Jesus occurs only in much abbreviated perspective, as the introduction to his death and exaltation. The writers see him first and foremost as the now exalted Lord to whom God has entrusted his authority, the one who now in the presence of God intercedes for his people and who in the Spirit is present with them, and whose active presence is evident in the establishment of the church and its spread to the ends of the earth. This Lord was, as the purpose of creation, already before its foundation present with God, he came down from heaven to save us, after completing his work he returned to God, and he will shortly come again, and then he will be revealed unmistakably and fully visible as the victor.

The immediate explanation for this totally different picture of Christ would seem to be that the impression made by the man Jesus was apparently so overwhelming that eventually he was elevated into a mythological being. It is, however, precisely the earliest writings that proceed from the "deified" picture of Christ. Moreover, they refer to still earlier confessional statements from the community which breathe the same spirit. On the other hand, the picture of the historical Jesus in the gospels was, as a whole, not committed to writing until several decades later. It did depend, as we noticed with the second problem, upon a process of tradition going back to the very beginning, but we cannot point to a time, however brief, when it functioned without the image of the exalted Christ. On the contrary, the picture of the earthly Jesus was never more than an aspect beside or in the preaching of the exalted Christ.

It is not surprising that there are always some students who start from the second image and who take as their center of attention the early community (of course the Hellenistic, because one could not expect this of a Jewish community) which gathers itself around a "cult hero" as the center of a mythological, gnostic, or philosophico-religious system; the earthly Jesus is then only the nebulous historical cause of this cult. This conception, however, does so little justice to the historical Palestinian dimension of the gospel that the pendulum as a rule swings back soon. The pendulum movement will not stop, however, if one rejects the explanation given by the New Testament itself, namely the resurrection of Jesus which divides the two phases and joins them into one historical-transcendent progression. The question concerning the credibility of the resurrection will therefore be our fourth and final problem.

The double picture—apart from its explanation—is important because of the light it sheds on the freedom which, next to their faithfulness, the traditionists exhibited. For an important part this freedom had to do with the addressees they had in mind. But it had especially to do with the belief that Jesus of Nazareth is still alive and continues to work as the exalted Christ. The experiential knowledge of Jesus which the community now gains from her belief in the proclamation colors and enriches the recollection of his earthly life. Wherever necessary or desirable, the tradition can put things into the mouth of the earthly Jesus which his Spirit makes clear to the community. A confluence of the two images and phases is, however, no more the case than that of keeping them watertight apart. Most of the time historical investigation is able to trace such backward projections. To faith this is of little interest, but for the historian it is mandatory that the dividing line be as clear and as accurate as possible.

This blending of the images occurs the least in Luke and the most in John. The latter has consciously elucidated the earthly life, including its hidden *doxa* as it was disclosed through the resurrection. John's picture is the least historical and the most real.

The relationship of the two images in Paul is not easy to formulate. Bultmann wrongly supposes (with an appeal to 2 Cor. 5:16) that Paul had no interest in the first picture. For an overview and a more balanced consideration see B. Lategan, *Die aardse Jesus in die prediking van Paulus* (1967).

The earliest confessions, which are all based on the "second image," come through in passages like Rom. 1:3f.; 10:9; 1 Cor. 8:6; 12:3; 15:3ff.; Phil. 2:6–11; 1 Tim. 3:16.

The influence of the second picture on the synoptic historical narrative is variously evaluated: there are maximalists like Bultmann and Conzelmann and minimalists like Cullmann and Jeremias. Generally it is now assumed that this influence is noticeable, e.g. in the passion announcements and in the story of the transfiguration on the mountain. Its total influence cannot be determined with the means we have. In the school of Bultmann this influence on the story is called *Gemeindetheologie* (community theology)—an unfortunate term, because it suggests an autonomous intellectual activity. The problem is excellently formulated in G. Bornkamm, *Jesus of Nazareth* (E.T. 1960), ch. I.

The history of the quest shows a pendulum movement in which one either tries (most of the time) to explain the second picture from the first, or regards the first image as a margin or even historicizing projection of the second. We find these two views already in the contrast between H. E. G. Paulus and D. F. Strauss in the first half of the previous century. See A. Schweitzer, *The Quest of the Historical Jesus*, chs. 5, 7–9. Like Strauss, in the Netherlands G. A. van den Bergh van Eysinga (ca. 1930), under the influence of Hegel, derived the first picture radically from the second. About him and his school see G. Hartdorff, *Historie of historisering?* (1950). In this pendulum movement historical investigation and systematic reflection are continually interacting. This is clearly shown in R. Slenczka, *Geschichtlichkeit und Personsein Jesu Christi* (1967). In our century, Bultmann, partly philosophically inspired by Heidegger, has again taken the second image as the starting-point, after which in the neo-Bultmannians the center shifted again from the kerygmatic Christ to the historical Jesus. On the relationship between the two pictures, see M. Hengel, *Der Sohn Gottes* (1975), and C. F. D. Moule, *The Origin of Christology* (1977).

It is clear that there is a connection between the three problem areas referred to, and thus between the answers that are given. Broadly stated there are two groups: Bultmann and his followers who read the gospels as faith testimonies concerning the kerygmatic Christ, the product of a process of reflection by the Christian community; and many others who ascribe to the first community a much stronger awareness of the historical dimension of her faith. It will be clear that the writer of this book stands with the second group, whereby historical considerations and religious convictions go hand in hand—something which is true of most researchers of this field.

Though there are these two more or less opposite scientific traditions, the one more minimalistic and sceptical, the other more maximalistic and conservative (with numerous in-between varieties), the surprising fact is that the differences in result with respect to the words and deeds of the historical Jesus (since form criticism no one thinks any longer of the possibility of a coherent biography) are much smaller than one would expect on the basis of the opposite starting-points. In broad lines, the following insights may be regarded as the common result.

Jesus was a rabbi, a miracle worker, a prophet, a sage—all these combined because he was more than all this and did not fit any available category. He had himself baptized by John. Like him he announced the early coming of the Kingdom of God and invited people into it. But unlike John, he knew himself specially called by God to proclaim to those who despaired of their right to enter it, the good news of their acceptance by God. Therefore in his preaching and with his healing miracles he directed himself especially to the sick, sinners, the demon-possessed, children, the poor, Gentiles, all who according to the prevailing religious standards could not inherit the Kingdom. He invited them to a life with God which was determined by grace and love, and not based on achievement and reward or the keeping of certain commandments as such. His commandment was therefore simultaneously libertine (see his attitude to the sabbath laws) and radical (see his love for his enemies).

Anyone who by faith in him accepted God's forgiveness might again freely as a child associate with God as his Father, and could find in that new relationship a great inner freedom toward the powers of the state, the law, possessions, vocation, and family. Jesus was thereby convinced that in his offer of grace the Kingdom itself was already present in a provisional form. This conviction rested on a most intimate relationship with God whom he, very intimately, addressed as "Father," and it manifested itself in a speaking with an unheard-of "authority," a declaring of God's will without an appeal to earlier authorities. This unheard-of pretension, coupled with a radical relativization of the established order and his preference for the minus-groups of this order, was bound to lead to great tensions both with the Jewish religious leaders and the Roman authorities. When Jesus came to Jerusalem for a decisive act, banding together they had him put to death for his blasphemous claims and his politically dangerous activities.

On two central points there is a wide divergence of opinion. The first concerns Jesus' self-consciousness. Did he give special names to himself to express his unique relationship to God, such as: the son (of God), the messiah, the servant of the Lord, the son of man? Or did the community afterwards put these titles into his mouth and that of his contemporaries? Difficult historical questions are encountered here. But they are less important than they appear, because those who answer this question in the negative also do not doubt that there must have been in Jesus an "implicit Christology": Jesus simply could not express the uniqueness of his relationship to God in traditional concepts. The second controversial problem is the question whether Jesus foresaw his own suffering and death and incorporated it in his expectation and preaching. Or did the community only afterwards, in the light of his resurrection, ascribe a redemptive significance to his death? In our judgment, those who hold the second at the expense of the first receive much less support from the texts than with the previous point. Decisive here is the question whether it was first the community or whether Jesus already understood his lot in the light of the Old Testament. In the first case one must minimize or deny the historicity of the last supper—much is to be said against that. In that case the continuity between Jesus and his first community comes to hang on a very slender thread. Most likely the community continued to build interpretively on convictions which it had already discovered in Jesus' preaching.

For the similarities between the different designs compare e.g. R. Bultmann, *Jesus* (1926); W. Manson, *Jesus the Messiah* (1943); Bornkamm, *Jesus of Nazareth;* E. Schweizer, *Jesus Christus* (1968); and H. Conzelmann, in *RGG* III, *s.v. Jesus Christus.* For Dutch literature see A. F. J. Klijn, *Wat weten wij van Jezus van Nazareth?* (1962), and M. de Jonge, *Jesus: Inspiring and Disturbing Presence*

(E.T. 1974). It was a remarkable surprise when Bultmann, five years after his *The History of the Synoptic Tradition,* published his booklet about Jesus wherein he displayed so much more knowledge about the historical Jesus than the readers of his earlier book could have surmised. A contribution of its own nowadays also comes from Jewish theology (much more "conservative" than Bultmann!) with its strong emphasis on the tie between Jesus' preaching and especially rabbinic statements. See especially D. Flusser, *Jesus* (2nd ed. 1969), and Schalom Ben-Chorin, *Jesus im Judentum* (1970).

As concerns Jesus' death about the same groups contrast with each other. Jeremias, G. Sevenster, and others oppose the school of Bultmann. For the arguments pro and con cf. Conzelmann's art. (see above) with G. Sevenster in *RGG* I, *s.v. Christologie I.* There are difficult questions here. Every reader of the Bible is familiar with Jesus' refusal of the title "messiah" and with his striking use of the title "son of man" only in the third person. If this last reference is historical, did Jesus refer to himself or did he appeal to a coming heavenly figure (cf. Mark 8:38)? What is the relation between that and the statements in which Jesus expresses his own lowliness in this title (e.g. Matt. 8:20)?

As concerns Jesus' death, almost the same groups contrast with each other. Particularly the genuineness of the tradition regarding the Lord's Supper (1 Cor. 11:23–25) and Mark 10:45b is under discussion. The spuriousness of the passion announcements in their present form and of the (Hellenistic) *dei* is generally accepted. Likewise the core of genuineness in statements such as Luke 11:49–51; 12:49–51, and 13:32f. A thorough discussion, in a conservative spirit, of the relevant texts is given by J. Jeremias, *N.T.-liche Theologie,* I (1970), pp. 264–284.

With both subjects, in addition to the historical questions, hermeneutical, dogmatic, and philosophical arguments enter into the discussion. In the wake of Heidegger, the school of Bultmann can hardly imagine that existing could go together with objectifying oneself or that a decision here and now could be combined with a conscious surrender to and a making oneself part of a divine plan of redemption. Yet that is what the synoptics clearly suggest. Is that thus a reflection of the community? Conjoined with this is the hermeneutical question whether Jesus himself interpreted his work and his fate in the light of the OT or whether it was the community which first did this. For the study of the faith that question does not seem decisive, if it assumes that the community, as it was led by the Spirit, rightly did that. But in that case we have to assume a Jesus who, though fully immersed in the OT, would not have determined his own calling on the way of Israel with the help of the OT. Over against that see par. 31. The neglect of the OT as the background and presupposition of Jesus we regard as the Achilles' heel of the school of Bultmann. This background has been exchanged for an existentialistic presupposition, with the result that Jesus' own concept of existence is as much as possible reduced to actuality and decision.

4. The third problem leads directly to the fourth, the resurrection. All the earlier-indicated questions return here. Yet about this most difficult point, too, there exists a not insignificant measure of agreement. It is generally assumed that the "second image," and the courage to profess the faith and the willingness to suffer that went with it, would be un-

thinkable if the resurrection narratives did not contain a measure of truth. This truth must lie in the fact that someone or a few individuals (Peter, Mary Magdalene, later also Paul) and perhaps even more (see the list in 1 Corinthians 15:5–7) were witnesses of appearances of Jesus after his death. This gave his followers the conviction that Jesus lives and that his violent death was not a failure, but a passing through to his exaltation which was a new phase in the breakthrough of God's Kingdom. The story about the empty grave is quite a different matter. About its historicity there is little unanimity. Those who deny it point out that Paul does not even mention the empty grave in 1 Corinthians 15 and that the story about it can easily be understood as an explanation in retrospect for the appearances; moreover, the stories about the discovery of the empty grave in the four evangelists cannot possibly be harmonized with each other. Counter-arguments are: in 1 Corinthians 15:4 (. . . buried . . . raised) Paul assumes the empty grave, though with the eyewitnesses of the appearances this fact occurred only secondarily; in a legend about Jesus' empty grave, women (who could not act as witnesses in Judaism) would never have become central figures, and in Jerusalem it could easily have been refuted with the facts (see, however, Matthew 28:11–15). In our opinion the counter-arguments are the stronger, except for this point, that they do not provide an explanation for the variety and the contradictory elements in the stories. But that is also true of the hypothesis of an explanatory legend. For the present time, we cannot make further progress with purely historical means. Philosophical and/or religious considerations now decide the question one way or the other.

It is often said that the Christian faith stands or falls with Jesus' resurrection. This is true in this sense, that without a clear liberating event, analogous to the Old Testament redemptive acts, Jesus' way could be seen only as a mistake or a failure. But that this life and death are our decisive hope for the future is something God could have made clear to us in other ways, too. Essential for faith is that God manifests in history that he stands behind the way of Jesus and that this man is therefore for us the way to salvation. On the question concerning the "how," historical research may and must have a voice. But precisely on this point research soon compels one to make a personal choice which need not be unscientific, yet which will always carry one beyond the boundaries of the investigation.

The controversy between Bultmann who started from the "kerygmatic Christ" and some of his followers who began with the "historical Jesus" led in Germany, in the sixties, to a new and intensive study of the resurrection as the transition provided by the NT itself from the first to the second image. The literature on the subject has become overwhelming. A good introduction is offered by B. Klappert, ed., *Diskussion um Kreuz und Auferstehung* (1967), to which are to be added F.

Viering, ed., *Die Bedeutung der Auferstehungsbotschaft für den Glauben an Jesus Christus* (1966), and A. Geense, *Auferstehung und Offenbarung* (1971), esp. ch. II. An interesting introduction to the problems from the Anglo-Saxon side (in a conservative spirit) is from the archbishop of Canterbury, A. M. Ramsay, *The Resurrection of Christ* (revised editions since 1961).

Here, too, one can distinguish minimalists and maximalists. But even Bultmann assumes that the resurrection faith (which is the same as recognizing the significance of the cross) had its historical occasion in visions seen by the disciples (*Theology of the NT*, E.T. 1970, par. 7,3), even if materially that occasion is not important. The neo-Bultmannian G. Ebeling, in *The Nature of Faith* (E.T. 1961), ch. V, went much more deeply into the historical substratum of the resurrection faith, but he, too, is concerned only with the *faith* which later arose in others, including those *without* such appearances. In *The Resurrection of Jesus* (E.T. 1983), P. Lapide takes a much more "realistic" view because of his interest in the Jewish religious world of that time.

The reason that the appearances are such a fixed starting-point is that it is clear that Paul with his list in 1 Cor. 15:3–5 recites elements of the earliest kerygma (and, moreover, experienced an appearance himself). These appearances were at the same time mandates for proclamation. It should, however, be remembered that also in the stories about the empty grave appearances and mandates play a central role. A sharp division, let alone a contrast between reports about appearances and about the empty grave, cannot be made.

A secondary but difficult point is the relationship of the appearances in Galilee and Jerusalem, aggravated by the mysterious (genuine?) word in Mark 14:28 (cf. 16:7). Many students are inclined to locate the original appearances in Galilee and to assume that later a combination was made with the empty grave in Jerusalem. But it is at least as likely that both of the late stories about appearances in Galilee (Matt. 28:16–20; John 21) are legends inspired by Mark 14:28. The earliest report (1 Cor. 15:3–5) does not mention a place.

Historical investigation is unable to come up with decisive answers to the questions we are wont to ask in connection with the resurrection. This is argued correctly by Geense, *Auferstehung und Offenbarung*, esp. II and III. What Kirsopp Lake, in his critical and sceptical book about the resurrection, says with respect to the empty grave can be applied to this entire theme: "The historical evidence is such that it can be fairly interpreted consistently with either of the two doctrinal positions . . . but it does not support either. The story of the empty tomb must be fought out on doctrinal, not on historical or critical grounds" (*The Historical Evidence for the Resurrection of Jesus Christ*, 1907, p. 253).

The last remark brings us back to the question we raised already at the beginning: the significance of historical investigation for the faith. This research has often been viewed and feared as an undermining of the faith. But genuine investigation can only promote the truth. The faith is more than this truth, yet it does presuppose and imply it. Nor can historical investigation lay the ground for faith, for with its limited means and empirical orientation it cannot ascertain that *God* is actively present in Jesus. It can, however, correct, refine, and elucidate faith's presuppositions. The quest of the historical Jesus aims to find behind the testimonies the historical situation from which they arose and to reconstruct it. Its ideal horizon is the "re-enactment" of the original situation. Of course it never gets that far. As a finite human work it never gets beyond provisional probabilities which are always susceptible to correction, partly because its view and the means it must work with are limited, partly because every investigator brings along his own subjectivity as a factor which is both inspiring and disturbing. But this limitation in no way eliminates its value. Genuine results have been achieved. The more penetrating and persistent the questions, the closer the quest approximates the actual situation of the contemporaries and eyewitnesses. And then something strange and surprising happens: the secret of Jesus does not become unraveled, but its mysteriousness becomes even more sharply visible. It becomes evident that the investigation, far from absolving us from the need to make a most personal choice with respect to Jesus, instead irresistibly forces us to it. Then we stand again where the crowds stood, the disciples, the scribes, the poor. And we hear the two questions: Who do men say that I am? And who do you say that I am?

The study of the faith in its own way aims to concur with Peter's answer. Then all the information gained as a result of historical investigation gets a new coherence and perspective. Then we also begin to discover answers where before there were only questions. The Old Testament, John the Baptist, his passion and death, his resurrection, his new mode of existence as the living Lord—everything is joined together in the one continuous covenantal way of God with his people, on which Jesus Christ turns out to be God's great and definitive step toward his future and to us. Standing in this faith we shall now examine his person and life, his death and glorification.

33. THE PERSON

WE SAID that the study of the faith in its own way concurs with Peter's answer. This concurrence is a leap, a decision, which is not implied in the results of the historical research. It is, however, even less in conflict with it. And it is least of all a leap in the dark. It rests on and is justified by the totality of the image which the person and life of Jesus evoke—whereby in the final analysis it matters very little whether with this picture one thinks of the faith testimony of the New Testament writers or of the manner in which it is being sifted and corrected by the historical quest. The concern is the picture in its totality. No one, however, is equally motivated by all the parts of the picture. The one is compelled to faith and obedience by the extraordinary authority with which Jesus speaks and acts, the other by his radical love for people, a third by his discourses and parables, or his inner freedom, or his preparedness even to die, or by the conviction that he is the only one who rose from the dead. In all these cases, when one is gripped by one aspect it leads to the recognition of other aspects. This psychological process as such lies outside the scope of the study of the faith. But it is necessary that we point to it here, because dogmatics must guard the totality of the picture as well as the combination of its parts. In the study of the faith we will have to say that there are three central elements which presuppose each other and which in their combination are decisive for who Jesus is and for the faith that looks to him, namely his ministry with authority, his resurrection, and how his way constitutes the continuation and fulfillment of God's way with Israel. Where one of these three is missing it is no longer clear why we should allow this person to have a radical reorienting influence on our lives.

In the course of time, the church and theology have variously answered the question concerning the ground of the faith in Christ. For centuries not much was said by way of an answer. It was assumed that the ground lay in the authority of the Bible and the church. But Christ does not derive his authority from the Bible; the Bible derives it authority from a history of encounter of which Christ is the center. After the Enlightenment the ground was preferably sought in the person and life of the earthly Jesus, e.g. in "the constant potency of his God-consciousness, which was a veritable existence of God in him" (Schleiermacher, *CF* par. 94), or in "the inner life of Jesus," the oneness of authority and love in him: "Through the fact of his personal life Jesus establishes a certainty of God in us which is stronger than any doubt" (W. Herrmann, *Der Verkehr des Christen mit Gott,* 1866, esp. ch. II), or in Jesus as the New Being, a term which "points to the power in him which conquers existential estrangement or, negatively expressed, to the power of resisting the forces of estrangement" (Tillich, *ST* II, pp. 125–135). Pushed to the background by dialectical theology, after the Second World War this approach by way of Jesus' earthly life gained much in influence. Think of Bonhoeffer's "the man for others," of the "faith of Jesus" according to Ebeling, of his freedom and responsibility for the world according to Gogarten, of his contagious freedom according to Paul M. van Buren, of his ability to play a double vicarious role according to Dorothee Sölle, etc. But in these designs it remains unclear whether in these impressive capacities Jesus only realizes the potentialities which we all in principle possess (so that his authority would be only that of an historical example) or whether he is unique. In the latter case his pretension hangs in mid-air, unless there be a legitimation by God. According to the NT this lies in his resurrection. For this reason others find exclusively therein the ground of faith. The most thorough example of that is W. Pannenberg, *Jesus—God and Man* (E.T. 1968). Here the danger threatens that Jesus' life is one-sidedly seen as anticipation: see esp. par. 6, and even stronger J. Moltmann, *Theology of Hope* (E.T. 1967), esp. III, pars. 1 and 2. Jesus' resurrection, however, is immediately bound up with his life, whose legitimation it is (Phil. 2:9). Both see correctly that the resurrection becomes meaningful only from the perspective of a certain epistemological horizon, which Pannenberg tries to find especially in apocalyptic, and Moltmann, with more justification, in the history of the promises in the OT. So we are directed to the third legitimation element, which though underdeveloped in modern theology is central in the NT: Jesus as the fulfiller of the way of Israel. Thereby we must not only say that Jesus fulfills the promises and expectations of the OT, but that in his person and way he turns out to be God's liberating answer to the covenant problematic of the OT as a whole. A combination of the three conjoint grounds of faith is found in Rom. 1:2–4, a formulation possibly based on a confession-formula of the earliest (Palestinian) community.

Having inquired after the ground of faith, we now come to the main question: what does faith see in this Jesus? Of course, this question cannot be detached from the previous one. But with that question the concern was especially those elements of the way of Jesus, his deed and his destiny, which compel us to faith. Now our concern is the fact that faith thrusts through to the *person.* We know him only in and from his way. But that way derives its unique significance for us from the person whose way it is. "Who do you say that I am?"

According to Mark, Peter answered: the Christ, the Messiah, the bearer of the Old Testament expectations. By way of explanation Matthew adds: "the son of the living God." Apparently this was a central expression for the Christian community of his days. In the New Testament the secret of Jesus' person is indicated with many names (son of man, son of David, lord, word of God, servant of God, prophet, high priest, king, savior, a few times briefly and daringly: God). But it is clear that from the time shortly after the resurrection until today the Christian community senses that the title "Son of God" is the most adequate. We thus start from that.

It is remarkable and significant that this title, which was used to express Jesus' uniqueness, did not have an exclusive sound, either for Hellenistic ears (Stoics) or for Jewish ears, and that more than once the New Testament witnesses use it in a broader sense. Sonship is a redemptive-historical concept. From the outset this must be kept in mind in dealing with the question concerning the person of Jesus. Jesus as the Son of God is not a purely vertical incident *(in-cident,* "intrusion") on the way of Israel and in the history of mankind. In the Old Testament, the heavenly beings around God's throne are called his sons. Particularly of Israel it is said that it is God's son or his sons. And in Israel, in a few statements that have had a great influence, the king is called God's son. In none of these is the reference to a relationship of physical origin. With Israel and its king, sonship is a matter of a covenantal relationship of mutual love and (with man) of obedience. In the same sense, in the New Testament believers are called children and sons of God: "For all who are led by the Spirit of God are sons of God" (Romans 8:14). Jesus' sonship, too, stands in this covenant tradition. He is pre-eminently the obedient and therefore beloved covenant partner. His relationship with

God meets the requirements of the representative purpose with the king and other types of mediators in Israel, as is evident from the narrative of his baptism (Mark 1:11). Through this representation, he becomes as son "the first-born among many brethren" (Romans 8:29), the one who in the age-long procession of God's children leads the way and bears the brunt of the attack (Hebrews 12:1–3). This insertion of Jesus as Son of God into the course of the covenant goes so far that somewhere the title is even defended with an appeal to the Old Testament sonship of all believers (John 10:33–38; cf. Psalm 82:6), because sonship is the same as "doing the works of the Father."

This context, within which the central title of Jesus is used, has been neglected in the study of the faith. If we now consciously avoid that mistake, we may not, by way of reaction, neglect the no less important fact that within this context Jesus' sonship is entirely unique. This Son of God stands and is one with all the other covenant partners before and after him, but that is his place precisely because he stands at the same time and from the beginning and especially opposite them. Only thus is he the liberating sequel and answer to the preceding history of the covenant. For in that history sonship had come to a dead end. The sons are lost sons. "If then I am a father, where is my honor?" God calls out in Malachi (1:6). A new beginning is necessary, and the prophets know that this cannot be expected from below. God himself must provide the true man, the faithful covenant partner. That new beginning from above is called "Jesus." He finally fulfills the sonship. He is the Son *par excellence*. And he is that not as the fruit and climax of human religious and moral purity, but in virtue of a unique and new creative act of God. Therefore, there is between Father and Son not only a covenantal relationship, but also a relationship of origin, a new covenantal relationship based on a unique relationship of origin. Jesus is therefore *the* son, the "only-begotten" Son. It has rightly been pointed out that with "son" the Old Testament never thought of such a relationship. But the prophets did certainly expect a new beginning from God in the form of a man or men. Now this new beginning comes to us in someone for whom God is uniquely the Father and who is therefore the Son in a pre-eminent sense, in whose God-created relationship with God the covenant is renewed and forever established: *Immanu-El,* God with us.

This unique sonship comprises a number of elements. Because it takes place within the context of the covenant with Israel, central to it is the living out of the faithfulness of the Father and responding to it with total obedience, whereby Jesus authoritatively represents God's loving faithfulness. And because this faithfulness is directed to people, Jesus, too, directs himself fully to the neighbor, constantly denying himself, so that he may be the channel for the grace of God to men who are lost in guilt and ruin. Connected with this is the freedom with which

Jesus relates to the established powers and traditions, which are intended to make human life possible as a life of freedom and love, yet so often are opposed to it. With this freedom toward social conditions is coupled a freedom toward and a control of the forces of nature, in particular of the destructive forces of sickness and demon-possession which threaten man's existence.

That man is pre-eminently the Son. And with this man belongs an altogether unique way of life. Person and way are inseparable. In a world of shrewd calculation and self-interest this becomes the way of being a stranger, of growing conflict and suffering, but from his side also of a constant and growing self-denial and the readiness to make the final sacrifice. At last he is thrown out, but even then he holds on with all the power of his love to those who throw him out. At the same time he holds on to God and on God's behalf to them. And then it becomes manifest that it is true after all that only he who is willing to lose his life to God's ultimate purposes with life keeps it, even in the face of death. Then the Son, far ahead of us, enters a new way of human existence, in which the covenant and sonship intended by God will finally reach their full development.

But this unique person and way of life have no relevance for us, can at best only discourage us, unless this sonship has more than only individual significance. That is indeed the case. A few times already we have used the word *representation.* In Israel the king is called by God to represent the people. The weal and woe of the people depend on his attitude. And Israel itself has a representative role in the midst of the nations. A people or an individual cannot themselves take on such a role. One has to be called to it by God. Those who were called regularly failed in their redemptive role. Now there comes one who does not fail, because his calling is based on a new creative act. He, who is the true Son, penetrates with his radical covenantal obedience to the final salvation. So, as our substitute, he breaks open for all of us the way to the future of full salvation.

This brings us back to the question concerning the relation of the Son and the sons. As regards its origin, and thus as regards its representative power, Jesus' sonship is unique. But as regards its content it is that to which all of mankind is called through the covenant way of Israel. Here we see what we, what Israel, what Israel's representatives should have done and are, but in which all have obviously failed. Jesus' sonship therefore concerns us because it is that in which he, exactly in virtue of his uniqueness, wants to involve us. The exclusiveness is here the condition for the inclusiveness. We must become like him, but in virtue of his going-before and in abiding dependence on it. This duality is strikingly and carefully expressed in the New Testament when Jesus is called the "firstfruits" and when it is said that we are not natural but "adopted sons," destined as "fellow heirs with Christ" "to be conformed to the image of the Son."

In passing we touched on the relation of person and work. Which of the two is the main concern of faith? For centuries dogmatics has put the person first: Christ, the God-man, the second person of the Trinity. In his polemics with the Scholastics, Melanchthon strongly reacted against that in the famous words in the opening paragraph of the *Loci communes* (1521): "To acknowledge Christ is to acknowledge his benefits, not, as is sometimes taught, to behold his natures or the modes of his incarnation." Later he had second thoughts about it. But under the influence of Kant's separation of theoretical and practical reason this separation of work and person returned in the school of Ritschl, for whom the confession of Jesus' unique person was only a value judgment or esteem of high importance which was meant to express the uniqueness of his saving influence on us. Along this line Bultmann formulated the problem powerfully and succinctly: "Does he help me because he is the Son of God, or is he the Son of God because he helps me?" *(Glauben und Verstehen,* II, 1958, p. 252).

When the problem is thus formulated, one cannot possibly choose: not theologically, because person and work derive their significance for faith from each other, and not philosophically, because the function abolishes itself without the substance and the substance becomes known to us only in the function. In our cultural situation we cannot go back to the one-sided ontological mode of thought of years ago, yet a purely functionalistic way of thinking leads nowhere. Good on this is Weber, *Gl* II, pp. 17–20. For a survey of the arguments see G. C. Berkouwer, *The Person of Christ* (E.T. 1954), ch. 7; cf. the discussion of G. Foley and H. Berkhof in *Kerk en theologie,* July 1959, pp. 159–165.

On the name "son of God" in the OT see P. A. H. de Boer, *De zoon van God in het OT* (1958), and especially *TDNT* VIII, *s.v. huios* (Fohrer). For the NT see also *TDNT* VIII, *s.v. huios* (Schweizer). These articles also list the many texts that are important here. A number of important passages in the NT which prove how central this title was in the earliest community are: Matt. 4:3, 6; 11:27; 16:16; Mark 1:11; 9:7; Luke 1:35 (cf. this with 3:38!); John 20:31; 1 John 2:23 and *passim* in the Johannine writings; Rom. 1:3; 8:3f.; Gal. 4:4; Heb. 1:2.

It is striking how close together the different titles like son, servant, and anointed are in the OT (in Ps. 89:29ff. they are even used indiscriminately), all as designations of the faithful partner and instrument of the covenant. It is therefore doubtful whether these titles in the NT can so accurately be put into different contexts as scholars aim to do. Whether Jesus himself ever called himself the "Son of God" or "the Son" is doubtful (it depends, among others, on the genuineness of Matt. 11:27). But with an extraordinary familiarity he did address God as *Abba* and on his own authority passed that name on to his followers, without thereby putting himself on the same level with them (cf. John 20:17).

In the study of the faith there has been a great deal of controversy between orthodoxy and heresy about the time when Jesus' sonship began. Did Jesus become son at his exaltation (cf. Acts 2:36), or through the resurrection (Rom. 1:3f.), or at his baptism (Mark 1:11), or with his conception and birth (Luke 1:35), or before (the rest of) creation (Col. 1:16); or was he already son from eternity (John 1:1–17; Rom. 8:3; Phil. 2:6; Heb. 1:2f.)? This variety in time designations in the NT is due to the fact that all the writers want to maintain two things simultaneously: this sonship has its origin in eternity; and it realizes itself in a history of struggle and obedience.

The idea of representation as an Old Testament redemptive-historical category has become generally known through H. Wheeler Robinson, "The Hebrew Conception of Corporate Personality," in *Zeitschrift für die a.t.-liche Wissenschaft,* Beiheft 66, 1936; see further on it J. de Fraine, S.J., *Adam et son lignage* (1959). For the significance of the idea of representation in Paul, see H. N. Ridderbos, *Paul* (E.T. 1975). The study of the faith cannot do without this fundamental thought, yet in our individualistic culture needs to be very precise as to its translation.

On believers as "sons of God" in the NT see *TDNT* VIII, pp. 389–392. Important texts are: Matt. 5:45; Rom. 8:14–17, and Rev. 21:7. On the relation of Christ as the Son to the sons see Rom. 8:29; Heb. 2:10ff., and esp. Gal. 4:1–7. Paul interchanges *huioi* for *tekna.* John, who throughout calls Christ *huios,* uses *tekna* exclusively for believers to indicate the exclusiveness of Christ. On this point see also other passages with a different terminology: 1 Cor. 15:44–49; 2 Cor. 3:18; Col. 1:18, and passages which speak about a (being crucified, suffering, dying, being buried, raised, and glorified) "with" Christ. Despite this clear line in the NT (and its background in the OT), there has been a great reluctance in the history of the church to honor this perspective, for fear that it might detract from the exclusiveness of Christ. At most one was willing to speak of an analogy of function between Christ and us (Luther: the believer is to the neighbor an *alter* Christ; and see the three offices parallelism in the Heidelberg Catechism, Lord's Day 12, Q. 31 and 32). This changed under the influence of Schleiermacher and German Idealism, because Christ then becomes the anthropological archetype and his exclusiveness fades away. In the Netherlands, Modernism was introduced when J. H. Scholten accepted his professorate in Franeker with an oration in this spirit: *Oratio de vitando in Jesu Christi historia interpretanda docetismo* (1840). Naturally, but unfortunately, it caused a polarization on this point (too) between Orthodoxy and Liberalism. It is remarkable that even Barth, who sees the redemptive-historical connection of the sonship, immediately abandons it in the interest of the trinitarian conception (*CD* IV,1, pp. 206–210). In contrast there is the Christology of Gogarten who gives a central place to the sonship as "responsibility for the world," but because of it can hardly see Jesus otherwise than as the first and great believer (*Christ the Crisis,* E.T. 1970, esp. chs. 17 and 18). Pannenberg, *Jesus—God and Man,* pp. 345–347 and 378–390, offers a significant discussion of the sonship of Christ and of us as daughters and sons of God.

Jesus is the Son in virtue of a new creative act of God. What does this mean? We face very difficult questions here. Yet we cannot avoid them, because they are decisive for the ground, the nature, and the perspective of our faith. Jesus is thus more than a man among men, called by God like Moses and the prophets, and adopted as son because of his obedience. In that case the covenant would still not have received a permanent basis. That basis is acquired only because Jesus rests on a new creative act of God. And that newness implies that he does not restore an imaginary, perfect covenant relationship from prehistoric times. History is not turned back, but instead makes its most decisive jump forward. The "last Adam" is infinitely more than the first. What is effected here as covenant relationship is an entirely new beginning, something totally unique, which is at the same time a pointer to and a promise for a future which even now is still unrealized.

Is Jesus the Son thus not really a man, but God? If he were not a man, his way within humanity would be an isolated spectacle, of no concern to us. In the New Testament, nothing is proclaimed about him which would be nonhuman or extra-human. But also very little that is simply empirically-human. Everything is related to human existence as it was intended and promised by God in the covenant. Jesus is man, the perfected covenant man, *the* new man, the eschatological man.

The question is now, however, what these far-reaching words imply. Furthermore, how they fit in with the emphasis with which in the New Testament, Jesus, as the Son, is put on the side of God over against men. Are there then two subjects in him? No, he is not a dual being; "For there is . . . one mediator between God and men, the man Christ Jesus" (1 Timothy 2:5). But that he is able to be the mediator in our alienation from God is based thereon that he is a new start from God, "conceived by the Holy Spirit." So through him God's purpose can land in the world. There are thus not two subjects in Jesus, but his human "I" is, out of free will, fully and exhaustively permeated by the "I" of God; and in virtue of this permeation he becomes the perfect instrument of the Father. This completed covenant relationship signifies a new union of God and man, far beyond our experience and imagination.

This union is, however, not something static; it passes through a history. Jesus starts his covenantal way as the carpenter's son from Nazareth, and finally, after much inner turmoil and struggle, he ends by fully participating in the life of the Father and in his work in the world. The exclusive sphere of God, the "glory" (Heb. *kāḇôḏ;* Gr. *doxa*), passes in Jesus to *one* man. God does not push the human person of Jesus aside, but he permeates it entirely with his Spirit, that is, with himself. So in the obedient and therefore resurrected and glorified Jesus our humanity far transcends what we can imagine and even consider covenantally possible. In that transcendence humanity in its covenantal relationship to God is, however, not obliterated but brought to its highest fulfillment.

In these centuries theology was thrown back and forth between a Christology "from below" which took its starting-point in Jesus' true humanity, and a Christology "from above" which started from his deity. In the first case the suprahuman in Jesus remained underexposed, in the second the humanity he has in common with us. Both types of Christology were rejected by the church as inadequate, in other words, as error. The deviations of the first kind are often labelled Adoptionism, those of the second Monophysitism. In this controversy the formulation of Chalcedon (A.D. 451) became decisive for ecclesiastical Christology; it describes Jesus as "truly God and truly man . . . so that one and the same Christ, the only-begotten Son and Lord, is known in two natures, without confusion or change, without division or separation . . . whereby the two natures come together in one person and one subsistence." The unity of Christ as a person was thus maintained, yet within the unity of the person one found a duality of being ("two natures"). Until today the great majority of Christian churches accept these pronouncements as expressing their belief in Christ.

To that it should be added, however, that until today theological reflection has felt the problem in this formulation and has therefore tried to get beyond it. For though Chalcedon repudiates one-sided solutions when it speaks of two natures which come together and constitute *one* person, it leaves open the question whether this person is to be regarded as standing on the side of the divine or of the human nature, and which attributes belong to the one person and which to the divine or the human nature. That is why after Chalcedon the controversy continued unabated. In the following centuries the official doctors of the church have generally answered the open question in this vein, that it was the second person of the Trinity who assumed the impersonal human nature. This makes Jesus' humanity passive so that, negatively, it possesses no human "I," or, positively, its "I" is the divine "I" (the *anhypostasis* or *enhypostasis* doctrine). With that answer, contrary to the intention of Chalcedon, Christ's genuine and full humanity has been misconstrued for centuries. In addition, the duality of the "two natures," by which the unity of the person is obscured, obstructed the way to the Jesus of the gospels. Consequently, since the Enlightenment, Chalcedon and classical Christology were increasingly put on the defensive in relation to the Christology "from below."

However, the Chalcedonian formula becomes much more intelligible if we remove it from the framework of the static notions of "nature" that governed the thinking of the Greek church fathers and that of many centuries after them. The NT speaks a different language, also when it speaks of the duality of the structure of the being of Jesus' person. It does not speak of the two structures as being found statically on top of each other but as historically following each other. See Acts 2:22–36; Rom. 1:3f.; Phil. 2:8–11; 1 Tim. 3:16; Heb. 5:7–9. The NT shows us a history in which the man Jesus, because of his total obedience even to death, may share in the life and rule of God. In this history Jesus transcends the boundaries of what we understand by the "human." However, he does not lay aside the "human"; but on the way of a progressive obedience and glorification he exhibits more and more new and to us unknown dimensions of the divinely intended humanity. One who wants to express that comes understandably and dangerously close to dualistic-sounding formulations like "God-man" and "two natures."

In the light of this last observation we understand why the controversy between a Christology from above and one from below (both of which are rooted in the NT) has never come to an end. At the same time it makes us aware of the good elements in Adoptionism and in Monophysitism. The first looks at Jesus' way from its beginning, the second from its end. Both want to construct a picture that is valid for all the stages, at the expense of the recognition of the unique and surprisingly wonderful way which the Son must go through the depths to glory.

In the NT we find a broad spectrum of christological statements and designs. Classical Christology had no eye for that. Modern biblical theologies give a good picture of this variety; a useful, recent summary is that of R. Schnackenburg in *MS* III,1, pp. 227–383. All the titles which in the NT are ascribed to Christ have an OT root. Sometimes God seems to be the subject which acts in Jesus, then again the man Jesus seems to stand opposite God. Statements of this kind, which are contradictory in terms of substantialistic thinking, are regularly found in the same writer. Cf. e.g. Rom. 1:3f. with Phil. 2:6f.; Heb. 1:1–4 with 5:1–10; John 10:30 with 14:28. Especially the last two passages caused classical systematic theologians great difficulty. Conversely, it can be asked, however, whether from our standpoint the statements about Jesus' pre-existence do not cause difficulty. That is not the case with John 1:1–14; that passage is about the "word" in Gen. 1, which is again creatively going forth in the coming of Jesus. This is not the case either with Col. 1:15–20, for there it is precisely the man Jesus who, as "the first-born of all creation," has become pre-eminent in everything, and for whose sake the world was made as it is. Heb. 1:1–4 is also about the pre-existence of one who further is portrayed only as the obedient son and mediator (high priest). These texts know nothing of a separate pre-existent life, apart and different from the earthly and glorified life of Jesus. Only Phil. 2:5f. seems to teach that, if this symbolic language is removed from its context and purport. But here, too, the pre-existent one is not God the Son, but the man Jesus. In Jewish and Hellenistic image thinking the category of pre-existence is often applied (e.g. to the Torah, wisdom, the son of man) to indicate the divine initiative *behind* and the meta-historical validity *of* these phenomena. The NT pre-existence statements also aim to extol the divine initiative and the divine condescension in the creation of Christ. See for the "mythical" language of Phil. 2:5–11 G. Eichholz, *Die Theologie des Paulus im Umriss* (1972), pp. 132–154, and J. A. T. Robinson, *The Human Face of God* (1973), ch. 5; and for the roots of Paul's other statements about pre-existence (Rom. 10:6f. and 2 Cor. 8:9) in the speculative wisdom literature E. Schweizer, *Neotestamentica* (1963), pp. 105–109. For the dogmatic aspect see Ott, *AG* art. 26.

Apart from the statements about pre-existence which aim to express the divine initiative in the sending of the Son, the NT has many other statements which place Jesus above and outside our empirical human existence; but equally applicable is the claim: what is solely ascribed to Jesus is at the same time a pneumatological-eschatological promise to us. As regards sonship we have already pointed that out. It also holds true for the resurrection (Rom. 6:4, 11; 1 Cor. 15:21f.; 2 Cor. 3:6; 4:10; Col. 2:12; 1 Peter 1:3, etc.), for the exaltation (Eph. 2:6), for the session at the right hand of God (Rev. 3:21), for Christ's priesthood and kingship (Rom. 5:17; 1 Pet. 2:9; 2 Tim. 2:12; Rev. 5:10, etc.), yes, even for his parousia (Col. 3:4; 2 Thess. 2:10). Jesus forgives sins on behalf of God, in order that we may learn to forgive (Luke 6:35; Col. 3:13, etc.). Jesus performs signs on behalf of God, in order that we may learn to do the same (Mark 9:18f.; 16:17 and 20; Acts 14:3; Heb. 2:4). Jesus exists as the *eikōn* of God (2 Cor. 4:4;

Col. 1:15), in order that we might come to share his *eikōn* (Rom. 8:29; 1 Cor. 15:49; 2 Cor. 3:18). Jesus exists in the *morphē* of God (Phil. 2:6), in order that we might become *symmorphos* to him (Rom. 8:29; Phil. 3:21), *metamorphousthai* after his *eikōn* (2 Cor. 3:18). Jesus shares in the *doxa* of God, in the sphere which is most uniquely God's, so that we also might share in it (e.g. John 1:14; 17:1, 10, 22). Considering this general NT vision, it is indeed justifiable to regard the daring words in 2 Pet. 1:4: "in order that through these [promises] you might participate in the divine nature" as typically Hellenic or marginal, but not as foreign to the purport of the NT. Even as by a new act of God in Jesus as the true covenant partner the climax of the union of God and man is brought about, so likewise on that ground and in dependence on it, our humanity is destined for a union with the life of our divine covenant partner which we cannot now imagine. But does this not detract from the exclusive nature of Jesus' being-God? We must note in the first place that that which is entirely unique in Jesus relative to us is as a rule not expressed with the word "God," but with names like: lord, savior, firstfruits. Can we then, however, still speak of God's becoming man? That, however, is an expression which is not derived from the NT. There the terminology is that of God's *sending* of his son, and of the *Word* (God's creative speaking) which became flesh, and there a few times, on account of the intimate union of God and man in him, Jesus is called "God" (in any case in John 20:28; Tit. 2:13, and 1 John 5:20), but then only for the purpose of capturing in an accentuated formula Jesus' uniqueness and instrumentality relative to us (to which, on our side, corresponds the accentuated formula in 2 Pet. 1:4); moreover, what is at stake in these passages is Christ as "*the* representative of God in the world and in history . . . himself the bearer of the divine office" (*TDNT* III, *s.v. theos,* p. 106). What we have here is a covenantal functionality which only in this way agrees with the numerous statements in which Jesus distinguishes himself from God, or is distinguished from God by the writers. See also the highly remarkable covenantal grounding of the title in John 10:28–38 (v. 35: "If he called them gods to whom the word of God came . . ."); cf. P. Schoonenberg in *Tijdschrift voor theologie,* 1969, pp. 378–385.

In the history of the church, when the biblical encounter thinking was changed into substantialistic thinking, Jesus' two natures came to stand in contrast to each other. Those who started from the oneness in the divine person had to lessen the genuine humanity. Those who began from the latter had to make of Jesus a dual person. This problematic has continued until our century. The idea had to arise that the Chalcedonian formula was more of a hindrance than a help. Barth was still able to reject that idea by ascribing what was always regarded as belonging to the *vere homo,* mainly Christ's obedience and humiliation, to the *vere Deus,* the subordination which is eternally a part of God himself, namely of the eternal Son in the trinitarian being. But this does no more than transpose the christological duality into God himself. It would mean that Jesus represents only one side of God. And Barth too, while he dares to speak of the passion of God, does not dare to speak of the death of God. See *CD* IV,I, esp. pp. 192–205.

Especially after 1960, in a period when thought was (once again) predominantly molded by the desire to start from human experience (see par. 10), many no longer based their Christology on the "Johannine model" but on that of the

Synoptics, i.e., on the earthly, historical Jesus. The first comprehensive treatment in this spirit was W. Pannenberg, *Jesus—God and Man* (E.T. 1967), at least in the first half; in the second half there is a change toward the classical trinitarian treatment: the strict surrender to God by Jesus the Son is the embodiment, on the human level, of God the Son in his most intimate trinitarian communion with the Father. That kind of change from a Christology "from below" to one "from above" has since then been found in many writers, such as D. Wiederkehr in *MS* III (1970), 477–648; J. Moltmann, *The Crucified God* (E.T. 1974); K. Rahner, in K. Rahner and W. Thüsing, *Christologie—systematisch und exegetisch* (1972), pp. 18–78; W. Kasper, *Jesus der Christus* (1974); E. Schillebeeckx, *Jezus het verhaal van een levende* (1974), who only toward the end deals with the problem of the "from below" (pp. 531–545; and Jon Sobrino, *Christology at the Crossroads* (1978), in which the *vere homo* is given its own Latin-American accents. All these can be characterized in the words of Kasper: "The internal divine Trinity is so to speak the transcendental requirement of salvation history, making possible God's self-giving in Jesus Christ through the Holy Spirit" (*Jesus der Christus,* p. 218).

In the same recent era these christological designs are matched, however, by just as many in which the change to the current trinitarian approach is not made, because Jesus as the Son is not only approached from below, but is also viewed as the one who on behalf of God belongs below. The first in this group was P. Schoonenberg in *Hij is een God van mensen* (1969). He advocates a "reverse anhypostasis": Jesus is a human person who through union with the Word makes this Word a person. This union is precursor and promise for that of all humanity. He is the eschatological man. In later publications he speaks of a "mutual enhypostasis" and of a "fusion" of the persons of the Word and of Jesus into one "divine-human" person. He considers neither an eternal Trinity nor a pre-existence of Christ relevant for the knowledge of faith. Whereas Schoonenberg's thinking is especially molded by the concepts and problems of Patristic theology, E. Flesseman-van Leer in *Geloven vandaag* (1972), ch. XI, starting from the OT idea of covenant, rejects the two-natures doctrine and pre-existence, and sees Jesus as the chosen man and the true covenant partner. The New Testament scholar W. Thüsing, in K. Rahner and W. Thüsing, *Christologie—systematisch und exegetisch* (1972), esp. pp. 234–303, reaches in the main the same conclusions. J. A. T. Robinson, *The Human Face of God* (1973), offers a liberal-Anglican variant in which Christology is approached from the perspective of the evolution of an "emergent humanity" in which Jesus appears as a "natural but extraordinary revelational person" who as "pure love" tells us the deepest and final things about God. In a much more biblical manner H. Küng, in *On Being a Christian* (E.T. 1976), also arrives at the conclusion that precisely as man Jesus is the mirror of God's being (without further elaborating it). From the perspective of the Pneuma-Christology, which must have played an important role before the Council of Nicea (see par. 37), G. C. van de Kamp, *Pneuma-christologie: Een oud antwoord op een actuele vraag?* (1983), asserts: "The basic affirmation of Chalcedon is better preserved in a Pneuma-Christology model than can be done in classical Christology." H.-J. Kraus, *Systematische Theologie* (1983), par. 146, expresses himself in the same vein but is less polemic.

There is thus a great divergence between trinitarian and "from below" Christologies. Yet there are also important convergences. As we saw (unlike in previous centuries), the first now find their basis in the story of the earthly Jesus (an exception is Beker–Hasselaar, *WK* III, who do not bother to provide a biblical-theological foundation for their strictly trinitarian Christology). Most of those in the second group start from the perspective that Jesus as the Son is the result of a new creative act of God and thus comes "from above." The great difference lies in a trinitarian-Chalcedonian approach over against one that is based on biblical salvation history.

Is it possible that in some way the two can be brought closer together? A remarkable attempt to that effect is made by A. van de Beek, *De menselijke persoon van Christus* (1980; on the anhypostasis concept), who sees in Christ the unity of a divine and a human person in a manner that makes us think of the later Schoonenberg.

Some in the first group detect only a "functional" Christology in the second group. But in our judgment the majority of this second group rightly contend that there is a tertium between a "substance" Christology (Christ one in being with the Father, *homoousios*) and a purely functional, namely a new covenant, relationship effected by God, which has its own ontological character.

I know of only one example of a direct confrontation between the two groups, namely the discussion between Kasper and Küng in *Grundfragen der Christologie heute* (pp. 141–183), ed. L. Scheffczyk (1975). This discussion also brings out where the hermeneutical difference lies, namely in the question whether the Christology of the Gospel of John must be regarded as the consequence of all earlier NT confessions (so F. Mussner in *Grundfragen,* pp. 77–113) or as one articulation among others, determined by the front against which this Gospel was written (J. D. G. Dunn, *Christology in the Making,* 1980).

From the vantage point of the perspective presented here, three Christologies stand out in history as being especially important. The first is that of Arius, the Alexandrian theologian who was condemned at Nicea (325) and there sharply attacked by Athanasius, with whose Christology the one here developed is often compared. As we see it, Arius's strong point was indeed that he positioned Christ radically on the side of the creature, as created by an act of the divine will. Jesus was thus "changeable" (nowadays one calls it "Geschichtlich"), as is apparent from his temptations and the like. Arius also correctly pointed out that the preexistence statements in Col. 1 and Heb. 1 refer to the earthly Jesus. Athanasius's refutation of Arius's arguments appears artificial to us (see Athanasius, *Orationes contra Arianos).* Arius perceived basic problems that his opponents simply dismissed. But his opponents were right in not accepting his view, because due to his adoptionism and moralism he completely failed to see the saving relationship of Christ to God and the people. Both parties read the OT purely allegorically, and it could not enter their minds to understand the secret of Christ against the background of OT covenant history.

The second to be mentioned is Calvin. His Christology is connected with his discussion of the OT. The emphasis, therefore, does not fall on the person but on the function of Christ, namely as the mediator who represents God with man and man with God, and therewith on the threefold office as he derived it from the OT (*Inst* II,xii–xiv). Typical is the title of the opening chapter: "Christ had to become man in order to fulfill the office of mediator." But because Calvin had to treat this in the framework of Chalcedon, he comes at times very close, particularly in his commentaries, to a separation of the two natures and an almost Nestorian duality in Christ. Cf. E. Emmen, *De christologie van Calvijn* (1935).

The third one who must be mentioned here is Schleiermacher. He has radically abandoned the framework of Chalcedon. He starts from the side of man: Jesus is the archetype, the true human existence as God eternally intended it. Due to the constancy of his divine consciousness one can speak of an existence of God in him. See esp. *CF* par. 94. But Schleiermacher sometimes comes very close to a pantheizing naturalization of Christ, because he does not use the framework of the OT covenant but the categories of German Idealism. The strength and weakness of Calvin and Schleiermacher can still serve as beacons to us.

If Jesus the Son is God's new creative beginning, the real man after his image, then he answers to the final intentions God has with his human creation; and then we cannot separate his historical appearance, neither from the beginning nor from the end, neither from creation nor from the consummation. For the creation this means that with the creation of "Adam" God had in mind "the last Adam," who is therefore in God's counsel "the first-born of all creation" (1 Cor. 15:45; Col. 1:15). And for the consummation it means that "this last Adam" will be the consequence of the new humanity which began in Jesus, when the human world around him is being renewed after the likeness of his image. So he stands at the beginning and at the end of the history of mankind. Only within this cosmic framework can the scope of his appearance fully come out.

Passages in the NT where this cosmic significance of Christ is expressed are: John 1:1–5; 1 Cor. 8:6; 15:44–49; Eph. 1:10 and 22f.; Col. 1:15–20; Heb. 1:1–4; Rev. 3:14. Especially 1 Cor. 8:6 is highly remarkable, because this is the earliest passage and Paul refers here to an insight which he assumes to be present on the part of his readers. It would seem that from the outset Jesus' person and way must have made an enormous impression that he could be so related to the whole creation *(ta panta)*.

Here we must have another look at the concept of pre-existence. In the above-mentioned passages, this does not refer to a trinitarian dwelling of the Son with the Father, but to a co-operating of the historical Jesus with God in the work of creation. (Hence Col. 1:15 can speak of the "first-born of all creation.") In this mythical form (current in the Rabbinic and Hellenistic Judaism of that time) was expressed what we with our Western thinking would call an "ideal pre-existence": God's first and dominant thought in his plan of creation was Jesus the Son. In his doctrine of election, *CD* II,2, esp. par. 33,1, Barth offers a theologically provocative elaboration of this insight. See also the discussion of the doctrine of creation in this book, par. 25, sub 8. The contrast between personal and ideal pre-existence should not be exaggerated. If the man Jesus was from eternity in the mind of God, it follows that as covenant partner he was also from eternity over against the Father.

To conclude this par. something should be said about the virgin birth. Many religio-historical, biblical-theological, and systematic studies have been devoted to this theme. Especially the historians of religions have put forth much effort to trace the story in Luke 1 back to earlier traditions. A first suggestion has been Egyptian and Greek tales about gods who beget divine children with earthly women. But the climate in Luke, in which the child is brought forth *(episkiazein)* in the way of promise and faith, is miles removed from those tales. Is the story then of the order of the miraculous births in the OT (Isaac, Samuel, Samson)? That is the case with the preceding story about John the Baptist. But the young girl, Mary, cannot be compared with the barren Sarah or Hannah; here is a miracle of a totally different order. Is the story perhaps an elaboration of the Septuagint translation of Isa. 7:14 which renders *'almâ* as *parthenos?* But among the OT quotations in Luke 1, precisely Isa. 7:14 is *not* mentioned. (It does occur in Matt., but his use of OT quotations rests on a theological reflection in retrospect.) A convincing source for Luke in earlier traditions has not yet been found. For a survey of the religio-historical arguments, see *TDNT* V, *s.v. parthenos* (Delling). Is the story then historical? But apart from Luke and Matthew none of the NT writers gives an indication of knowing this story, even though such an indication might have been appropriate in some cases (John 1:13; Gal. 4:4). Did Mary, then, later mention it only to a few? But after the resurrection this silence is hardly imaginable in the circle of disciples (cf. Acts 1:13f.). In our opinion, therefore, it seems most probable that it is a later enrichment of the tradition, to give concrete expression to the confession that Jesus, the Son by pre-eminence, could not be generated by man; "born of the virgin Mary" would then be intended as the earthly counterpart of "conceived by the Holy Spirit."

The parallel (among others by Barth) often made with the resurrection or the empty grave does not hold, because the resurrection is central in the very earliest kerygma and in all the traditions, while here we have only one, limited to two obviously later traditions. It is therefore regrettable that in many later summaries of the kerygma, among others in the Apostles' Creed, the virgin birth did receive a central place, thereby making its acceptance until today a touchstone of orthodoxy. That has been rejected not only by liberalism, but also by Brunner *(Dg* II, pp. 350–356), Kohnstamm, Van der Leeuw, and others. For a survey of the arguments *pro* and *con,* see G. C. Berkouwer, *The Work of Christ* (E.T. 1965), ch. 10; and (with opposite conclusion) H. Thielicke, *The Evangelical Faith,* II (E.T. 1977), pp. 407–413. In our judgment wrong contrary arguments have often been used. Decisive for the study of the faith can and must only be the fact that in the NT it does not belong to the kerygma and its *paradosis*. Apparently, faith in Jesus as the unique Son does not depend on it; the converse seems to be the case.

34. LIFE AND HUMANITY

IN THE FOLLOWING PARAGRAPHS the subject is the manner in which the sonship evolves and realizes itself on the way which the Son goes through life. Then we begin of course with his historical life as a man among men. What we call "of course" does not, however, seem to be so at all. We face the strange fact that, while innumerable people through the centuries have first of all been fascinated and gripped by the picture which the evangelists draw of the earthly Jesus, the study of the faith has for centuries hardly shown any interest in the life of Jesus. That has to do with the "double picture of Christ" we spoke about in paragraph 32. As a rule, dogmatics has based itself on the proclamation structure of the epistles, not the story structure of the gospels. That would be correct if we were forced to make a choice here. But the proclamation of the crucified and exalted Christ presupposed and included the knowledge of his earthly life. Without this life, cross and exaltation come to hang in the air. Hence in traditional dogmatics they have often become a sterile abstraction.

This does not mean that in the study of the faith we survey the entire life of Jesus. Our concern is not biblical history, nor the results of historical-critical investigation, nor the theology of the New Testament, but a concretization of the sonship on the basis of the more permanent features in Jesus' words and deeds. Actually we have been occupied with that three times already, in the different starts we made under the three perspectives of paragraph 31 (Jesus the bringer of salvation), paragraph 32 (the results of historical investigation), and paragraph 33 (Jesus the Son of God). Therefore some repetition and some curtailment are unavoidable here.

In the history of theology the life of Jesus has always stood in the dark shadow, on the one hand of the two-nature doctrine, on the other of the doctrine of reconciliation. Nevertheless, Thomas found it possible to consider fairly extensively words and miracles as well as certain events in the life of Jesus (baptism, discourse, temptation, transfiguration) (*ST* III, q. 35–45). In Protestant Scholasticism little remained of that. It distinguishes two natures (God and man), two states (state of humiliation and of exaltation), and three offices (Lutheran: *officia;* Reformed: *munera,* namely prophet, priest, and king). Jesus' life could be discussed with all three, but with the human nature the discussion was primarily about the incarnation, and with the state of humiliation about the work of reconciliation. With the prophetic office only Jesus' proclamation came up for discussion; with the priestly office something was said about his active obedience in the sense of a substitutionary obedience to the law of God (S pars. 34–38; H XVIII and XIX; Bavinck, *GD* III, par. 46). Hence even today in all kinds of orthodox instruction in the faith the impression is given that Jesus came to earth only to suffer and to die. The fact that the Apostles' Creed has no article about Jesus' life, but immediately moves from "born" to "suffered" is also responsible for that.

Yet the doctrine of the threefold office of Christ did and does offer a good opening toward a development of Christology which is more functional, historical, and related to the OT and the covenant problematic. Jesus' work is seen here as the fulfillment of the three representative offices in the OT. He himself is thus approached here as the true human covenant partner. Already Eusebius (*Historia ecclesiastica* I.3, 6–13) pointed out that in Israel three kinds of office-bearers were anointed and that Jesus, according to Luke 4:18, came to fulfill all three. Yet it was not until Calvin that this idea was made fruitful for theology; this he did in *Inst* II,xv; until then he had, with Luther, distinguished only two offices, omitting the prophetic. See J. F. Jansen, *Calvin's Doctrine of the Work of Christ* (1956), who himself advocates a return to the twofold office. Since J. Gerhard the threefold office has also penetrated Lutheran dogmatics, and in the 20th century also Roman Catholic doctrinal pronouncements and theology. This scheme is often criticized as being artificial and as separating what is one. However, on account of the reasons mentioned, it can be a useful distinction. After all, the concern is the three covenant aspects of revelation, reconciliation, and lordship (so Brunner, *Dg* II, pp. 273f., 305–315; cf. Barth's division, *CD* IV,1–3). That this scheme has not lived up to the promise it holds is, in our opinion, partly due to the restraint put on its effect by an anhypostatically accentuated two-nature doctrine. For an historically thorough and critical study of this scheme see Pannenberg, *Jesus—God and Man,* par. 6 I (he sees its beginning in Osiander). For a biblical-theological defense from the Roman Catholic side, see *MS* III,1, ch. 7. See further Berkouwer, *The Work of Christ*, ch. 4.

We do not use the scheme of the threefold office because it easily leads to artificial divisions, and its gain (OT background, representation) can better be realized by a consistently historical arrangement.

With Calvin (see Jansen, *Calvin's Doctrine of the Work of Christ)* and with his successors the prophetic office remained insufficiently developed. On the one hand it included all the proclamation of the exalted Christ through the word and sacraments of the church. And the other offices were hardly, or not at all, seen in relation to Jesus' life. See the critique by Barth, *CD* IV,3, pp. 1–18.

Post-Enlightenment liberal theology could have made a new start here. That did not sufficiently happen. Here, too, Jesus' life remained an abstract something. See Schleiermacher, *CF* pars. 93–98, and (somewhat better) Tillich, *ST* II, pp. 118–138. Also G. J. Heering, *Geloof en openbaring* (1935), II, III, misses his opportunity, through his polemics with orthodoxy.

In our century fruitful beginnings are found in F. W. A. Korff, *Christologie,* II (1941), pp. 123–147; Brunner, *Dg* pp. 275–281; Pannenberg, *Jesus—God and Man,* par. 6 II and III; *MS* III,2, ch. 8,3. Cf. also the *New Catechism* (E.T. 1969), part III. Very remarkable is the broad discussion of the man Jesus in Barth, *CD* IV,2, par. 64,3 (pp. 154–264). Barth, who connects the humiliation with the divine in Christ, puts the human in Jesus entirely, and therefore one-sidedly, under the aspect of the exaltation—cf. the title "The Royal Man"; but within this framework rich material is brought together here.

The first and central element of the sonship in Jesus' earthly life is his love for the Father. This filled his whole life, to the farthest corners. There was between them a relationship of mutual intimacy on which all temptations (the temptation in the wilderness) and all threats (Gethsemane) suffered shipwreck. The source from which this power came must be sought in his constant and intense prayer life. Jesus, who dared to call God *Abba,* knew on the one hand that this relationship was entirely unique, resting on a very special calling, election, mission, even creation, but that on the other hand it was the Father's will that he should make people share as much as possible in the secret of this intimacy. "No one knows the Son except the Father, and no one knows the Father except the Son and any one to whom the Son chooses to reveal him" (Matthew 11:27).

The consequence and reverse of this radical love is the no less radical obedience to the Father. Jesus is not will-less with respect to God. He has a passionate will, whose driving force is to have his own will yield to that of God and to will nothing else than what God wills. "My food is to do the will of him who sent me, and to accomplish his work" (John 4:34).

This element includes the fact that Jesus represents the people before God, because his actions in complete solidarity with the Father are an analogy and an instrument of God's purposes and deeds. "And they glorified God, saying, 'A great prophet has arisen among us!' and 'God has visited his people!" (Luke 7:16).

This representing of God with men implies in the first place the establishment of the covenant order, in the spirit of the law and the prophets. It is the order in which man no longer tries to maintain himself beside and thus over against God—not with his own law-abiding achievements either—but lets himself be totally governed by God's love and reflects and continues that in his deeds. That is the purport of the Sermon on the Mount and of many other commandments in which God's original gracious covenant purpose is placed right within everyday life with an unprecedented radicality. "Love your enemies, and do good, and lend, expecting nothing in return; and your reward will be great, and you will be sons of the Most High; for he is kind to the ungrateful and the selfish" (Luke 6:35).

Jesus was first of all himself the embodiment of this order, the man who completely answers to God's purpose and translates it in his words and deeds. God directs himself with his condescension to a helpless world, estranged from him, which is particularly represented by two groups, by the guilty and the wretched. To the guilty, Jesus comes with the message of radical forgiveness. "For the Son of man came to seek and to save the lost" (Luke 19:10). And to the wretched he comes with the deed of compassion. "When he saw the crowds, he had compassion for them, because they were harassed and helpless, like sheep without a shepherd" (Matthew 9:36). This compassion is shown especially in the many healings Jesus performed. Both forgiveness and healing aim to elevate man, on the basis of God's gracious coming, to the true humanity of being a free and happy child of God. That is why Jesus, in Luke, can sum up his entire coming and ministry in the words of Isaiah 61:1 and 2: "The Spirit of the Lord is upon men, because he has anointed me to preach good news to the poor. He has sent me to proclaim release to the captives and recovering of sight to the blind, to set at liberty those who are oppressed, to proclaim the acceptable year of the Lord" (Luke 4:18, 19).

Immediately connected with this ministry is the freedom to which he calls the people, a freedom which is in the first place the climate in which he lives himself. It is not something which needs to be captured from the people and the circumstances, but which he, from the outset, possesses relative to them on account of his fellowship with the Father: with respect to the temple and the cult, synagogue and commandment, priests and scribes, sabbath and government, mother and brothers, food and clothing, property and money, popularity and the power of the state. In his life all these things became so secondary, temporary, and relative that those around him felt this attitude as an extreme threat to the established order, though it expressed itself in the form of a "calm conservatism" (*gelassener Konservatismus,* Barth). It was the fruit of a strong *carefreeness,* which in turn was born from the absolute priority of the Father and his gracious lordship. "Seek first his kingdom and his righteousness, and all these things shall be yours as well" (Matthew 6:33).

With Jesus this freedom extended even to the nonhuman part of creation, what we usually call "nature," but which for Jesus included chaotic and demonic elements behind which he saw the work of Satan. As the Son of the Creator of this threatening world he lived in it as the lord and master, and he used his freedom to make the love of the Father triumph even in the dark shafts of reality, as a sign of the coming kingdom of peace. "He was with the wild beasts" (Mark 1:13).

In dogmatics all these aspects of Jesus' humanity are often summed up as his *sinlessness.* It is an unfortunate term, too negative, too static, too limited. The situation becomes different if we realize that sin is refusing a relationship, and that sinlessness means total surrender to God and total solidarity with sinful people. The Gospel writers speak about Jesus' temptations, anguish, and struggle. However, they say nothing about failure and guilt on the part of Jesus, about a letting go of the Father or a giving up of the people. Then Jesus would have been no more than one man among all others; then the covenant of God and man would not have been definitely established in humanity and would still be as problematic as ever. But through the resurrection he was "designated Son of God in power" and his life was shown to have been ruled by "the Spirit of holiness" (Romans 1:4). So the Christian faith stands or falls with the belief in Jesus' sinlessness. But like us all, he had to become what he was. A whole world tried to pull him away from his calling. Could he have succumbed to that? In retrospect, in the light of the resurrection, this question may be answered in the negative. But Jesus did not know that in advance and he felt the full impact of the opposing forces. He had no idea of his sinlessness on which he, encouraged by it, could fall back. "We have not a high priest who is unable to sympathize with our weaknesses, but one who in every respect has been tempted as we are, yet without sinning" (Hebrews 4:15).

Instead of the negative "sinlessness," we have in the heading used the word *humanity* to express the core of Jesus' life. It might be objected that this is a worn-out and misused word. By applying it to this unique life we wish to highlight the depth and the breadth of God's purpose for man, about which we spoke in similar vein in paragraph 27. Here is the complete structure of what it is to be man, in his threefold relationship to God, the neighbor, and nature. Here is also the highest quality of what it is to be man, as love and freedom. Here human existence has reached its full maturity and therefore has fully become God's partner and instrument. This kind of humanity is foreign to us. We have no more than an inkling of what it is like and can only recognize some fragments. Lonesome it stands in our human world, as an example we do not follow, and therefore as a constant accusation of our failures on the point of humanity. Yet it stands foremost as an invitation to us to become involved in this new form of being-man, and therefore as a promise that God has something infinitely better in mind for us than what we seek in our own self-chosen ways. But that this humanity spells a liberating and renewing salvation for us, and the how of it, can only become clear if this earthly life is not viewed as an isolated occurrence, but as the beginning of a history, whose course is our concern in the following paragraph.

The reader may have noticed that the eschatological perspective in which we saw Jesus' life in pars. 31 and 32 did not further come up here. As the perspective and the framework it was rightly put first, but in the work of Jesus this framework recedes into the background. The Kingdom of God is the term for the future consummated covenant relationship, but with Jesus all the emphasis falls on the fact that this Kingdom has now "come near" (*ēngiken,* Mark 1:15), "has come upon you" (*ephthasen,* Matt. 12:28), in fact is "in the midst of you" (*entos hymōn,* Luke 17:21). Among the systematic theologians it is especially Pannenberg who, also from the perspective of his anthropology, eschatologizes Jesus' earthly life as much as possible. By seeing Jesus especially as the herald of the nearness of the rule of God he puts this life too much in the futuristic and noetic sphere, at the expense of the fact that Jesus himself is the Kingdom that has come near and that the statements about the future derive their force from that. The expression "realized eschatology" (Dodd) may thus be incorrect; with Jesus the present as "realizing eschatology" does indeed stand central. For that reason Pannenberg, when he begins to speak explicitly about Jesus' earthly life, finds himself forced to introduce all sorts of elements which do not find resonance in the totality of his Christology (*Jesus—God and Man,* par. 6 II).

Freedom as the life sphere of Jesus is only lately receiving more attention. See e.g. P. M. van Buren, *The Secular Meaning of the Gospel* (1963), esp. V: "He simply spoke and acted with the authority of a singular freedom." At Easter "the freedom of Jesus began to be contagious." Since then what Christians tell about

Jesus is "the story of the free man who has set them free." With Van Buren this freedom looks very much like autonomy; the love for the neighbor is only incidentally mentioned and the love for God not at all. Here a modern pathos of freedom is projected onto Jesus. That is done especially where he is portrayed as a revolutionary. On the incorrectness of this see M. de Jonge, *Jesus: Inspiring and Disturbing Presence* (E.T. 1971), IX (with an appeal to Matt. 6:33). By far the deepest and broadest discussion of this freedom and this revolutionary spirit in Jesus is given by Barth in *CD* IV,2, pp. 171–179.

Our existentialistic and positivistic time knows little what to do with Jesus' unique relation to nature. No doubt it contains some legendary material, but there must be an historical core behind it. For a survey of the research of the NT see H. van der Loos, *The Miracles of Jesus* (1965); for the significance of Jesus' healings as "acts of fighting" *(Kampfhandlungen)* see Barth, *CD* IV,2, pp. 209–247; a more systematic treatment is offered by *MS* III,2, ch. 8,3,4. As we see it, the key to the understanding of the healing and nature miracles lies in their connection with the OT expectation of the future (cf. Matt. 11:5).

Much has been written about Jesus' sinlessness. Classical theology understood it statically-ontologically as *impeccabilitas.* Then there is no room for temptation and struggle. That is still fully true of Schleiermacher, according to whom "the constant force of his *(sc.* Jesus') consciousness of God" excluded all inner struggle (*CF* pars. 93,4; 98,1). So for our feelings Jesus becomes nonhuman. As a matter of fact, the NT does not picture him like that. We prefer to speak of a functional *impeccantia* rather than of a substantive *impeccabilitas.* But can those be separated? See Korff, *Christologie,* II, par. 9 IV; P. Schoonenberg, *Hij is een God van mensen,* pp. 138–144. In the NT this theme regularly returns; see John 8:46; Rom. 8:3; 2 Cor. 5:21; Heb. 4:15; 5:7f.; 7:26; 9:14; 1 Pet. 2:22; 3:18; 1 John 3:5. Nowhere is Jesus' sinlessness explained as stemming from his virgin birth, as was later sometimes done. The problem which the study of the faith faces here is largely philosophical in character; it has to do with the relation of being and historicalness, or of essence and existence. Human existence realizes and discloses itself only in a series of choices whose outcome is also for the chooser uncertain in advance, but which in retrospect yields a coherent life pattern. In the Authorized Version the *chōris hamartias* in Heb. 4:15 is rendered: "without sin," and in the Revised Standard Version: "without sinning"; this change has everything to do with a shift from ontological to functional thinking! Against the sinlessness of Jesus, Mark 10:18 has sometimes been adduced; but this humble pointing away from self to God was precisely part of Jesus' sinlessness.

35. DEATH AND RECONCILIATION

JESUS' EARTHLY LIFE led to a death sentence, and to suffering and death. This event and the circumstances leading up to it occupy about half of the gospel narratives. There is thus a very close connection between Jesus' life and death. We may not make an orthodox caricature of it, as if Jesus came to earth only to die. He came to live, but to live in such a way that in this world he could not but perish. For that reason we may in no way regard Jesus' suffering and death as an unfortunate combination of circumstances. In this suffering and death Jesus necessarily and voluntarily took the consequences of the life he had chosen. And only because he took this consequence, his life took on that final seriousness which the evangelists and we sense in his words and deeds. He brought the Kingdom of God near to man, and he was prepared to pay the price for that himself. Only in that sacrifice was the new humanity which he came to bring completed and fully disclosed.

In Mark, which has sixteen chapters, the first announcement of suffering occurs already in 8:31 (the second in 9:31, the third in 10:33f.); but the suffering casts its shadow ahead as far as 3:6. For that reason M. Kähler could call Mark a "Passion history with an elaborate introduction." The other evangelists do essentially the same, John the most.

A (defensible) maximalization of the connection between life and death is given by the Heidelberg Catechism, A. 37: "That during his whole life on earth, but especially at the end, Christ sustained, in body and soul, the wrath of God against the sin of the whole human race." An (objectionable) isolation of the suffering is given by the Geneva Catechism in Q. and A. 55: "Why do you make the transition forthwith from birth to death, omitting all the story of his life? Because nothing is dealt with here, except what so pertains to our redemption, as in some degree to contain the substance of it." Pannenberg, *Jesus—God and Man,* makes an (equally objectionable) separation when he begins the discussion of the suffering as follows: "After the discussion of Jesus' activity, we turn to his fate"; and after having modified this somewhat, he concludes this section: "Nonetheless, his passion and death remain something that happened to him and are not to be understood as his own action in the same sense as his activity with its message of the nearness of the Kingdom of God" (p. 245). Diametrically opposite is the idea of Schweitzer, developed in his *The Quest of the Historical Jesus,* that Jesus wanted to go to Jerusalem because of a "dogmatic" (apocalyptic) conviction, so that there through his death he might bring about the *peirasmos* which would force the Kingdom to come. But this theory is based on a use of a text which has been shown to be invalid by the form-critical method.

Important for the connection between life and suffering are the two authentic words, Luke 12:49 and 50, regardless of the question whether they were spoken on one occasion. Jesus comes to change the course of the world (fire), but he knows that he will himself become the victim (baptism); see *TDNT* VI, p. 944: "Jesus will bring a judgment of fire on the earth in which He Himself will be implicated."

In his person and ministry Jesus came to fulfill the covenant, or (in the language of Matthew) "to fulfill all righteousness" and thus to bring near the Kingdom of God. The feast of the union of God and man had come, and he generously invited people to the royal banquet. But invited Israel, through the mouth of its official spokesmen, refused to participate. Precisely now that God gives the new man, around whom mankind may renew itself, it becomes clearer than ever before that there is no place for God's kingly rule in this world. Men cannot tolerate this nearness. Jesus never doubted that some day God's will would be done on earth too, but he had to discover that his way did not lead directly to the completion of the Kingdom, but that between them there is a gaping abyss through which he himself had to go. Step by step, in fellowship with the Father, he assimilated that discovery, integrating it into his calling to men. Jesus had invited the people into the Kingdom. But apparently that inviting was not enough; God wanted more than that and the people needed more than that. So Jesus agreed to drink the "cup" to the dregs. For "unless a grain of wheat falls into the earth and dies, it remains alone; but if it dies, it bears much fruit" (John 12:24).

What transpires here between God, the Son, and men is, as we see it, most deeply fathomed in John. The words just mentioned are preceded by: "The hour has come for the Son of man to be glorified." And after Judas has left to betray him, Jesus says: "Now is the Son of man glorified, and in him God is glorified" (13:31). And that while precisely the opposite seems to happen. But the "glory" of God, what he is like in the very depth of his being, is: his condescension, his love which stops for nothing. It shines more clearly according as there is less in man to which it can join itself, and according as the loneliness and darkness around it grow deeper. In contrast the true humanity of the Son stands out more clearly according as he puts himself at the disposal of this glory and with his self-denial goes to the very limit. So Father and Son hold mutually on to each other, determined to make the glory, the love, the covenant faithfulness victorious against all human resistance. This resistance cannot break the communion between Jesus and the Father and thus not between Jesus and men. The greater the outward defeat and the inner struggle, the greater becomes the revelation of love, the more the Son is "lifted up" (John 3:14). With the death of Jesus the covenant seems to collapse for good. But the Son holds on to the Father and the people to the very end, and so the covenant did not perish but was fulfilled. The significance of Jesus' suffering and death is his sustained and fulfilled being-one with men for the sake of God and with God for the sake of men.

Jesus knew, or rather *believed* against all appearances, that his path of suffering, too, was a necessary part of God's redemptive way. In addition to knowing the "that," did he also have knowledge of the why and the what for? The traditional-orthodox view that Jesus knew exactly what his suffering was for conflicts with some of the most authentic (because "offensive") facts: his agonizing in prayer in Gethsemane (Mark 14:32–42) and his anguished cry from the cross: "Eloi, Eloi, lama sabachthani" (Mark 15:34). In both we see Jesus as a tormented man who shrinks back from the way before him. In Gethsemane he does not want the suffering, but stronger yet is his desire that God's redemptive will be carried out; so his anguish of soul ends in a new obedience. On the cross he recognizes in his own torment the suffering of the righteous man in Ps. 22. But in view of the Jewish manner of quoting we have to assume that Jesus applied the *entire* psalm to himself; then his anguish of soul ends in a new confidence (see Ps. 22:3–5, 9f., 22–31). We do well, therefore, to avoid speaking about the often-heard theme of Jesus' God-forsakenness. Precisely in these words of anguish of soul, obedience, and confidence the Son (speaking with John) was glorified and the Father was glorified in him. On the quoting of Ps. 22 in the passion history see C. H. Dodd, *According to the Scriptures* (1952; 1965 ed., pp. 97f.), and E. Fromm, *You Shall Be as Gods* (1967), who in the appendix, "Psalm XXII and the Passion" (pp. 231–236), also points out that "It is finished" in John 19:30 may be an intended quotation of the final words in Ps. 22.

With the above we do not wish to say, however, that with Jesus there was absolutely blind obedience and surrender. Guided by the OT he tried to find his path of faith. There he found all the passages that speak about the suffering of the righteous. But there he also found other pointers for his road of suffering, which we find back in the gospels, even though in the gospels we often find it hard to distinguish between how Jesus before and in his passion read the OT, and how the OT after his resurrection began to function for the Christian community.

What did Jesus and (after his resurrection) his followers think of when they believed that the covenant was not abolished through Jesus' suffering and death, but instead confirmed? They thought of the way and the promises of God in the Old Testament. Only in that light could Jesus' suffering be seen and understood. But what elements did they think of? In one of the earliest confessions we read that "Christ died for our sins in accordance with the scriptures" (1 Corinthians 15:3). That reminds us of the tradition about the last meal which Jesus had with his disciples, in which were heard together the words "(new) covenant," "my blood," and "for many." In the Old Testament the covenant with Moses was established with blood (Exodus 24:8). In the same way the new covenant (Jeremiah 31:31) could not be established without surrender of life. But that must then be the sacrifice of the life of a suffering servant of God, who as the representative bears the sins of many (Isaiah 53:12). For those who were initiated into the way of Israel and the experiences gained on that way with God, it was self-evident that Jesus' suffering and death had to be read in this light. The covenant estrangement is so terrible that the representative could bring about reconciliation only at the cost of his life.

We have used the words *representative* and *representation* before. In these words we hit upon the final, solid core of our salvation, and it is very much a question whether this core can be further split or elucidated. The great witnesses of revelation in the Old Testament realized more and more that Israel, in her estrangement from God, needed someone who could reconcile and bring the parties together by representing the people with God and God with the people. Our human world turned out to be incapable of bringing forth this man. In Jesus the Son, God creates this man, as a new and irreducible act in his struggle to save man. The creation of this new man is thus in itself an act of grace and redemption.

His whole appearance is motivated by the fact of covenant estrangement, it is there "because of our sins," and it is thus God's forgiving and reconciling gesture. "God was in Christ reconciling the world to himself, not counting their trespasses against them" (2 Corinthians 5:19). Every part of Jesus' life was marked by that sign. And from this representative, this mediator, must now issue forces which join us to him and so to the Father. "Therefore, if any one is in Christ, he is a new creation; the old has passed away, behold, the new has come" (2 Corinthians 5:17). But that does not come about until the representative has gone the limit in his obedience to the Father and in his solidarity with rebellious and hostile man, and persists in holding on to both and keeping them together when neither of the two would seem to afford him any reason for doing that. That this life is representative and reconciling comes out only in this climax and nadir: death. Stronger than that, it is only at that point that it becomes really effective. So long as the ultimate conclusion had not yet been drawn, the issue had not yet been determined. Therefore salvation can now be summed up in such terms as suffering, cross, dying, blood (that is, surrender of life). In that representative manner the Son stands right and thus righteous opposite the Father. And therein we are made righteous before God. "For our sake he made him to be sin who knew no sin, so that in him we might become the righteousness of God" (2 Corinthians 5:21).

On the cross takes place the definitive encounter between the old man, the new man, and God. Here man is irrevocably disclosed as the enemy of God's ultimate and renewing purposes for his life. But the price of the radical surrender of our life to God and our neighbor, which we refuse to pay for our redemption and renewal, is here substitutionarily paid by the new man. In that act is disclosed the secret of the new and the true humanity: the preservation of life through the loss of it, the bearing of fruit through dying. And so God is here definitively revealed, and once and for all defined as Holy Love, who loves the sinner and hates sin, who has sin carried away to break open the way to the sinner.

From this it follows that the reconciling event is not finished if it does not become reality in a reconciled community and in reconciled people, who themselves are reconcilingly active among themselves and to the outside. As the cross may not be isolated from Jesus' prior life, so it may not be isolated from the history of reconciliation it was to set in motion. But that isolation has also frequently happened, and so obscured the effective power of Jesus' saving work. After the words from 2 Corinthians 5:19 referred to above Paul immediately continues with: "and entrusting to us the message of reconciliation. . . . We beseech you on behalf of Christ, be reconciled to God" (vv. 19 and 20). The advancement of the reconciling work under the guidance of the Spirit will be discussed in paragraphs 37ff.

What is said above is *one* way to put into words the redemptive necessity of Jesus' suffering and death. There are several others in the NT and countless more in the history of the church. (For the various interpretations of Jesus' death in the NT, see R. Michiels, *Binnen het jaar,* 1983.) Fresh attempts are always made to verbalize it, yet it has never led to a theological consensus. There remains an impenetrable haze, making it impossible for us to express in words the decisive connection between death and salvation; and one who thinks that he is able often makes the connection superficial, rational, and all too human. "My thoughts drown in this ocean." The Eastern church has left it alone. As a matter of fact, with her ontological mode of thinking she was much more interested in the person of Christ than in his work. At the great christological councils Eastern thinking dominated; the Western church, in contrast, was primarily interested in the work of Christ. Many theologians have tried to capture that work in more or less understandable theories. This makes it all the more remarkable that this has never led to more profound, universally accepted ecclesiastical pronouncements about the connection between cross and reconciliation. *That* Jesus died for our sins, as our substitute, to remove the barrier between God and us—that has always and everywhere belonged to the essence of the faith. *Why* this had to be precisely so and the exact nature of the connection between cross and reconciliation—whatever the theory, intuitively it has always been found to be inadequate.

The NT itself has large sections in which the saving significance of Jesus' suffering is not or is barely heard. In the words from the cross Jesus is the suffering righteous man from Ps. 22, who in his suffering remembers and holds on to God, his fellow-sufferers on the cross, his mother, and his enemies. In the earliest proclamation of the Palestinian church, which we can possibly find back in Acts (2:23; 3:18; 4:27f.), the cross is especially the sign of human wickedness that is obliterated by God in the resurrection. One can get the impression that Paul was the first to articulate the saving significance of the cross. He was compelled to probe and formulate that saving significance more fully because as a Jew and apostle he was aware of the offense of connecting salvation with a crucified person (1 Cor. 1:18–25; 2:1–5). But he knew that if the resurrection was from God, the crucifixion cannot have happened apart from him. Mark 10:45 (a word from Jesus himself, or otherwise a confession from the earliest Palestinian church), and especially the words of the institution of the Lord's Supper, in which reference is made among other passages to Isa. 53, pointed him already in that direction. He has tried to elucidate that saving significance from the perspective of the covenantal righteousness both demanded and given by God (Rom. 3:21–26), with both lines intersecting in Jesus' sacrifice, which fulfills the OT sin offering (v. 25, *hilastērion*). Mostly he works with a variety of pictures that point to it, derived from the juridical (Rom. 8.3; Gal. 3:13), cultic (Rom. 3:25; 1 Cor. 5:7), financial (Rom. 3:24[?]; 1 Cor. 6:20; Gal. 3:13; Col. 2:14; cf. Mark 10:45; 1 Pet. 1:18), and military (Col. 1:13; 2:15; cf. Mark 3:27; Heb. 2:14) areas of life. The passages mentioned here prove that figurative language is not only found in Paul and that the images are joined together and blend. The writer of the Epistle to the Hebrews greatly elaborates cultic images. While in the OT the cult hardly takes part in covenantal history but appears especially as a timeless stabilizing institution, in the NT in the light of Jesus' sacrifice of his life it becomes *a posteriori* involved in the covenant problematic, as demonstrative of the inadequacy of the temple and its animal sacrifice (Heb. 7:11–10:18). The designation of Jesus as a "lamb" or "lamb of God" may have a cultic background, but it may also allude to Isa. 53:7 (*amnos:* John 1:29, 36; Acts 8:32; 1 Pet. 1:19; *arnion:* in Rev. *passim*). In this connection, the cultic terms *hilaskesthai, hilasmos,* and *hilastērion* are to be mentioned (Rom. 3:25; Heb. 2:17; 1 John 2:2, 4–10). They establish a connection with the concepts *kipper* and *kōp̱er,* important in the OT cult, according to which sin must be "covered" or "wiped out" by the substitutionary sacrifice of a life which God in his grace both gives and accepts. Cf.Lev. 17:10 and *TDNT* II, *s.v. hileos,* etc. It is clear that in the NT precisely this element of the covenant and the cult is generally seen as fulfilled in Christ, though in the prophetic perspective in the OT itself the cult nowhere has this role. The new covenant of Jer. 31, however, necessitated a new and much more radical substitutionary surrender of life than was ever surmised under the old covenant (Mark 14:24; Heb. 8 and 9). In addition to these concepts and parallels one also finds in the NT, however, the entirely different elucidation of John, who understands the cross as the climax of God's love and glory.

Here a few words will have to be added about the concepts *substitution, transfer of guilt,* and *punishment.* The first is frequently used in connection with the cross. It can mean the same as "representation." It results in misunderstanding if we connect the representation exclusively with the cross and see the cross no longer as the sealing of a substitutionary life. Dorothee Sölle, *Stellvertretung* (1965), fears that the substitution which leaves room for the other has in the Christian faith often become the replacement *(Ersatz)* which renders me and my actions superfluous. Without concurring with her conception, one can appreciate her fear. In the NT, however, there is no ground for such fear, because the other side of the substitution is our participation through the Spirit (see par. 37).

The concept *transfer of guilt* is a closer approximation of "substitution." Is it right, however? Our existentialistic autonomous outlook on life rebels against it: "Don't take my last possessions away from me, my sins shall go with me into the grave!" (H. Marsman). Are then perhaps only the consequences of our sin transferable? But such a distinction is foreign to the NT and would rob passages such as John 1:29; 2 Cor. 5:21; Gal. 3:13; 1 Pet. 2:24, etc., of their force. The substitution is total. Guilt is a relational concept. Our debt (guilt) before God is enormous, and representation signifies that in him the relationship is restored, that is, that which from our side obstructed the relationship simply does not count anymore in the light of his perfect love and obedience (2 Cor. 5:19). Indeed, no one has the power to transfer his guilt. But as the covenant representative Jesus is apparently able to assume our guilt. Apparently—again we face the question: why? Why is representation possible? and why does this require the total sacrifice of a life? and how is this sacrifice related to the assumption of the guilt? The NT asserts the "that," but has no answer to the "why" and the "how." That is God's secret. Apparently "it was fitting *(eprepen)* for him that he, to bring many sons to glory *(doxa),* should bring the Pioneer of their salvation through suffering *(pathēmatōn)* to his goal" (Heb. 2:10). The words *dei* and *edei* also intend to convey that, without explaining it. The only explanation they suggest is: the way of the OT went from judgment to grace, from death to life, and according to the will of God Israel's representative will have to walk this way to the very end; only so is there a real substitution, a real assumption of *our* place (Matt. 26:54; Luke 22:37; 24:25f., 44–47; cf. Mark 8:31; John 20:9).

Finally, the concept of *punishment.* Did Jesus bear the punishment for our sins? In Isa. 53:5 this word is used incidentally. The NT does not make use of it, though Rom. 8:3 and Gal. 3:13 come close to it. For Jesus identifies himself with the estrangement from God and all its consequences. But the juridical interpretation and extrapolation of the concept of punishment, as it is found in Western orthodoxy since Anselm (see below), is foreign to the NT. This has put such a burden on the word that it is better to avoid it. Generally speaking, it seems preferable in our time not to interpret Jesus' death primarily and exclusively with Paul's one- sided juridical and cultic concepts (as has been and is being done in Western theology), but also with the Johannine concepts of love, obedience, and glorification (as is tried here).

The theological history of the Western church is saturated with theories that seek to give further elucidation of the connection between cross and salvation. Where they separated Jesus' suffering from his life, and from its OT background as well, they often came with rationalistic or one-sided constructions which lacked both the mysterious depth and the metaphorical breadth of the NT witness. It would carry us too far to discuss the various theories and, moreover, these can be found in dogmatics handbooks and many other publications. We mention only six important conceptions, with which the possibilities within the Western way of thinking are likely exhausted: Anselm in *Cur Deus Homo?* (1098), whose theory has become very influential through its echo in the Heidelberg Catechism, Lord's Day 5 and 6; Anselm's opponent Abelard (ca. 1130), who over against Anselm's "objective" doctrine of atonement developed a "subjective" one in his commentary on the Epistle to the Romans. A deeply thought-out third view is offered by Calvin (*Inst* II,xvi); this caused him to be suspected of Socinianism, which he tried to refute in ch. xvii (which he added to the final edition). Socinianism came with a very astute attack on the objective doctrine of satisfaction; it did not see Jesus' death as reconciliation, but as the confirmation of his teaching and his passage to the resurrection (for description and literature see Bavinck, *GD* III, no. 378). A. Ritschl in his *The Christian Doctrine of Justification and Reconciliation,* III (E.T. 1902), esp. chs. 7 and 8, offered a new form of the subjective doctrine of reconciliation. A conception in which God is entirely active in the work of reconciliation, characterized by some as "Theopaschitic," is offered by Barth in *CD* IV,1, par. 59, esp. 2: "The Judge Judged in our Place." This line is continued in J. Moltmann, *The Crucified God* (E.T. 1974), who regards Jesus "God-forsakenness" as a moment within the trinitarian event in which God receives powerless man; the relation to man's guilt is here much less clear than in Barth.

A classical survey of the major types of the doctrine of reconciliation is G. Aulén, *Christus Victor* (E.T. 1937); a survey of the literature that has appeared since can be found in H. Wiersinga, *De verzoening in de theologische discussie* (1971), esp. ch. 1. The questions which always cause the differences are: Is this sacrifice directed to God to appease his wrath? Or, exactly the other way around, does God seek to move man to respond with love through his sacrifice of love? Is Jesus in his sacrifice God's representative with man, or the other way around? How are wrath and grace, justice and love related in God? One notices how the Western distinctions between God and man, justice and love, and especially subject and object, govern the discussion. The hope that these would rationally clarify the doctrine of reconciliation has been in vain. When we start from the inter-subjectivity in the history of the covenant and the idea of representation as a functioning aspect of it, many of the concepts and alternatives cease to be meaningful. Even the question whether God is the subject or the object of reconciliation can then no longer be put like that. In Jesus he gives the man, in whom he also himself receives reconciliation and peace with men. See E. Flesseman-van Leer, *Geloven vandaag,* ch. XII. But then the existence and the specific character of the representative and of his way are not explained. The rich imagery in the NT invites us to express this mystery time and again in contemporary symbols. H. Wiersinga, *De verzoening,* ch. 6, tries to do this more in the line of Abelard; his opponent, H. Ridderbos, in *Zijn wij op de verkeerde weg?* (1972), more in Calvin's line. An overview of the present-day problems and insights in this area is found in *Waarvoor stierf Jezus?* (Tenminste-Jaarboek 3, 1982).

As an appendix to this par. something should yet be said about the descent into the realm of the dead. In the second half of the 4th century this became an article of faith in several confessional statements; thus it also found its way into the Apostles' Creed. As a result it receives more theological attention than is justified by the structure of the NT kerygma. As such it says that Jesus continued his substitutionary solidarity with us to the very end, into death. He suffered, died, became a dead man. The early church put it this way: descending into the abyss where the dead are gathered together (Heb. *šᵉʾôl;* Gr. *Haidēs*). But because it was he who never forsook God who entered this state, he deprived it in principle of its terror. Very early already, this truth gave rise to ideas of a preaching of Christ in the realm of the dead and a deliverance from it of the OT saints. The obscure passage 1 Pet. 3:19f. (cf. 4:6) seems to suggest still more, namely an opportunity for repentance after Christ's atoning death for those who had died in unbelief. Read in that light, this article would also intend to express the universality of Christ's work. All three elements—the solidarity, the victory, and the universality—are right. But they are already implied in what is professed about Christ's person, his representation, his cross, and his resurrection. Whatever goes beyond that is pious fantasy. Calvin demythologized this article by making it refer to Jesus' so-called God-forsakenness on the cross (*Inst* II,xvi,8–12). This is a profound reinterpretation which has had a great influence, but which historically (it goes counter to the order in the Apostles' Creed) and in our judgment also systematically (see what we wrote above about Jesus' so-called God-forsakenness) is untenable. Excellent historical and systematic discussions about this point are given by F. W. A. Korff, *Christologie,* II, pp. 318–340, and H. U. von Balthasar, in *MS* III,2, cf. 9,4. See also Althaus, *CW* II, par. 46, and Pannenberg, *Jesus—God and Man,* pp. 269–274. A hermeneutical-historical approach is presented by D. A. Du Toit, "*Nedergedaal ter helle. . . .*" *Uit die geskiedenis van 'n interpretasieprobleem* (1971).

36. RESURRECTION AND GLORIFICATION

THE BELIEF IN JESUS as the savior of the covenant and the initiator of the Kingdom of God perished at the cross. His followers fled in despair. It is only due to the appearances of the risen Jesus that despair gave way to a new and unusually strong faith. Therefore the resurrection may be called the decisive redemptive event. Without it, the interpretation which we gave of his path of suffering in paragraph 35 would hang entirely in the air. Why should we ascribe redemptive significance to *one* of the innumerable Roman executions in an occupied territory? Without the resurrection all we have left is the late Jesus of Nazareth, one of the many martyrs who died for a conviction. Then he can only be a teacher and example to us. In fact not even that, because in that case he failed in both respects: he was too much mistaken in his own role to be our teacher, and he put his own person too much in the foreground and covered it too much with divine authority to be an example. Therefore the Christian faith stands or falls with the resurrection. At the same time we have to say that belief in the resurrection cannot be separated from the preceding way of Jesus, nor from God's way with Israel (see the beginning of paragraph 33). Nor can it be separated, as will be seen later, from the active presence of this risen person in subsequent history. It is not accidental that the resurrection happened to this particular man. If ever something like a resurrection would happen to a man, then it would happen to him. What that means for him and for us we shall now set forth in four points.

"If Christ has not been raised, your faith is futile and you are still in your sins," that is, then nothing has changed in our situation of alienation (1 Cor. 15:17). Without the resurrection the entire NT would have remained unwritten. Yet in many a study of the faith the discussion of the redemptive significance of the resurrection is rather meager, because the interest focuses on historical-critical questions concerning the fact and its nature. See e.g. Trillhaas, *Dg* ch. 19, and Weber, *Gl* II, ch. 2, par. 2,4. For the historical-critical aspect we refer to par. 32. The faith rests on a much broader and deeper basis, yet it cannot exist without reliable knowledge of resurrection phenomena after Jesus' death, which the NT witnesses could interpret in the light of the whole of Jesus' way. Brunner exaggerates, and is even incorrect, when he says: "Indeed, we might say: we would believe in him as the risen Lord, even if there were no narratives of the resurrection at all" (*Dg* II, p. 371; see also, however, the restriction that follows).

We speak here of "resurrection." But the NT as a rule speaks of "raising" (*egeirein, egerthēnai, egersis;* see the passion announcements in Matt. and in Luke; further, among others, Acts 3:15; 4:10; 5:30; Rom. 1:4; 4:24; 6:24; 8:11; 1 Cor. 15 *passim;* 2 Cor. 4:14; Gal. 1:1; Eph. 1:20; Col. 2:12). The frequency and the confessional accent which many of these words have show that "raising" was regarded as the most adequate expression for what had happened. "Resurrection" occurs much less (*anhistanai, anastasis;* see the passion announcements in Mark—corrected by Matt.!—further 1 Thess. 4:14 and John 11:24f.; in John the Son is very "autonomous," see 2:19; 10:18). We abide by current usage. We do not forget, however, that Jesus' resurrection was first of all a creative act from God's side. This act did not, however, happen to a random individual, but to someone whose life called for it, in view of the purposes and promises of God. If anywhere, then here synergism has its place; cf. S. Boulgakof, *Du verbe incarné* (1943), pp. 317–320.

An excellent insight into the various aspects of the resurrection, which will be discussed in the following four points, is given by J. M. de Jong, "De opstanding van Christus," in *Geloof en natuurwetenschap,* II (1967), pp. 67–117, and Klappert, *Diskussion um Kreuz und Auferstehung,* esp. pp. 10–52.

1. What we have said so far implies that the significance of the resurrection is first of all retroactive, in that it is the divine validation of the way of Jesus in his life and death. Without this exceptional sign from God we would have no certainty about the exceptional nature of his life and his surrender of it, and that life would only for a limited time have attracted the interest of a small group of people. It is only through the resurrection that we know that *God* was in Jesus.

But this validation concerns not only our knowing, but in the first place Jesus' own existence. In the raising from the dead God validates this life, he declares only this life as valid, as a life in agreement with his design. And this declaration happens in the form of a crowning, an elevation of this life to a higher state (see under 2). This life and only this life is on behalf of God "crowned with success." Only the kernel of wheat that dies in the ground bears fruit.

God was in the *man* Jesus; *one,* only *one* man receives from him the validation which all humanity needs. That fact puts our humanity under judgment. Apparently our present life is meant to be only provisional and intended for the resurrection. But apparently our life does not reach that goal, because we do not consistently follow and want the way that leads to it. "He humbled himself and became obedient unto death, even death on a cross. Therefore God has highly exalted him" (Philippians 2:8, 9). We struggle, individually and together, with and against each other, to preserve our life and to keep it, if necessary at great cost, preferably of much that belongs to others. Our struggle to keep our life leads to the loss of it. In his struggle Jesus was willing to pay the price of his life, and in that willingness he did not primarily think of himself but instead of others. Since his resurrection we know that whoever is willing to lose his life will keep it. But those who believe in his resurrection, too, do not, as a rule, dare to entrust themselves to the law for life which it disclosed. The most we have in our world are vague analogies. Jesus stands alone.

The significance of the resurrection as the validation of Jesus' life and death is expressed in Phil. 2:9, cited above, and it is presupposed in many other statements, particularly from Paul. This validation is so much a new act of God that occasionally it can be said that only the resurrection made Jesus that which he is (for us); through this act of God he was *made* both lord and messiah (Acts 2:36, but see also 2:24: it was simply impossible that God could have done anything else with this man); and he was *horistheis* as Son of God, that is, declared, defined, designated, and appointed (Rom. 1:4; yet "through the Spirit of holiness" who *before* his raising from the dead had ruled his life).

Validation expresses continuity. In our opinion the appearances after the resurrection are also to be seen in this light, insofar as they emphasize the fact that the wounds of the cross were still visible in the resurrected Christ (Luke 24:39; John 20:20 and 27): precisely as the crucified one, that is, because he let himself be crucified, is he the resurrected one.

In particular the schools of Barth and Bultmann have stressed this noetic function of the resurrection relative to what preceded it. Bultmann sees the belief in the resurrection as the articulation of the significance of the cross. His neo-Bultmannian pupils relate this belief more to the life of Jesus, as the awareness that God stands behind this life project (Jesus' faith or conduct); see e.g. Ebeling, *The Nature of Faith,* ch. V, esp. pp. 69 and 70f.; cf. Van Buren, *The Secular Meaning of the Gospel,* esp. V, end. In this tradition the resurrection is regarded so exclusively as noetic that it is not a separate fact, but only a fresh elucidation of preceding facts: a "look," a "perspective" (Van Buren), a "speech event" *(Sprachgeschehen,* Ebeling).

This is not the case with Barth. For him the resurrection is a separate fact; it intended, however, to disclose the meaning of the cross. Therefore his most important section on the resurrection bears the heading: "The Verdict of the Father" (*CD* IV,1, par. 59,3). "The resurrection is marked off from the death of Jesus as a new and specific act of God by the fact that in it there is pronounced the verdict of God the Father on the obedience of the Son: His gracious and almighty approval of the Son's representing of the human race" (p. 354). *CD* IV,2, pp. 140–153, is also governed by this perspective. Then in *CD* IV,3, par. 69,4 (The Promise of the Spirit) the resurrection is much more prominently seen as connected with the Spirit and the parousia. An approach to the resurrection from the perspective of the reconciliation of man's guilt on the cross is offered by Geense, *Auferstehung und Offenbarung,* esp. III.

With Moltmann and Pannenberg this perspective recedes into the background. For Moltmann the resurrection is so much a *nova creatio* that it hardly leaves room for a connection with what precedes and for the "therefore" of Phil. 2:9; see *Theology of Hope,* ch. III, pars. 2–13. This is not the case in Pannenberg, who views the resurrection as the validation of Jesus' claim to absolute authority which expected its confirmation from the eschaton to come (that is how Pannenberg understands Mark 8:38; see *Jesus—God and Man,* par. 3 I). In our opinion this is a drastic narrowing, which misconstrues the fact that in the resurrection Jesus' entire existence and course of life are validated.

2. We noted already that the validation happened in the form of a crowning, an elevation to a higher state. That fact is not the necessary consequence of the idea of validation as such. It could also, and perhaps better, have been expressed in a miraculous return of Jesus to this earthly life, thus in a raising similar to that of Lazarus and a few others as related in the gospels. But here something entirely different happens: no return to earthly life, nor however a continued existence of the soul in a higher world, but something which is best described as a borderline event. We are told of a short period of appearing and disappearing, of absence and of presence simultaneously, in which Jesus is no longer present as before

while yet he is repeatedly present for a few moments in a kind of continuity with the past, in which he appears as someone who walks on the borderline of two worlds. According to Luke, this occurred in a period of forty days (Acts 1:3), that is, in a transition period as they are found more often in the biblical narratives (for instance, Moses on the mountain, Elijah and Jesus in the wilderness). Jesus is still near, but as one who is departing. He disappears ahead of us. He passes on to a new form of existence which is unknown to us. The last person to whom he appears is Paul, who hears him speak in a blinding flash of light.

In the proclamation of the New Testament, this period of the appearances hardly plays a role. It has then served its purpose of being a manifestation that with his resurrection Jesus entered into a new and higher existence. Sometimes this is referred to as "exaltation," but a better term to express the nature of the event is "glorification." In the way of obedience and self-surrender, Jesus' humanity is taken up into the sphere of God, the sphere of "glory" (Heb. *kāḇôḏ;* Gr. *doxa),* which thus far had been the exclusive sphere of God himself. Not that thereby he changes from human into divine, but as man he receives the most intimate union with God, as the capstone of his whole preceding way. The same is meant when it is said that Jesus is in "heaven," ascended into heaven, or was taken up into heaven. This is not so much a designation of place as one of form of existence. The same is intended with his "sitting at the right hand of God," thus in the place of the viceroy, of the rightful representative. And that implies still more: from now on God is essentially united with man and his divine existence is forever inseparable from man. And because God's right hand expresses his exercise of power, Jesus' glorification guarantees that God will rule in the spirit of and after the will of this man. God and Jesus in *one* place, on *one* throne—those bold expressions indicate a reality which had not entered the human heart: the covenant between God and man which had failed for so long, has now in *one* man eternally succeeded.

Resurrection is no return, but the opening act of the "exaltation," a term which more than once is used in the NT to sum up certain things that are distinguished both in the narratives and in the study of the faith as: raising from the dead—forty days—ascension—session at God's right hand. See Acts 2:33; 5:31; Phil. 2:9.

For the use of *doxa* (actually: divine brightness) and *doxazein* in relation to the risen Christ, see Acts 3:13; Rom. 6:4; 2 Cor. 3:18; Phil. 3:21; 1 Tim. 3:16; 1 Pet. 1:11, 21. In John these words are already connected with Jesus' earthly life and his suffering (1:14; 2:11; 11:4, 40; 12:23, 28; 13:31), but their fulfillment and revelation remain as yet future (7:39; 17:5). In the other gospels *doxa* is once by way of anticipation ascribed to the earthly Jesus: at the glorification (transfiguration) on the mountain (Mark 9:2). See *TDNT* II, *s.v. doxa.*

On the symbolical significance of the forty days, see *TDNT* VIII, *s.v. tessares.* According to Barth this is the period of real disclosure and revelation, of the pure presence of God, because during that time the man Jesus was publicly present among us in the form of God (*CD* I,2, pp. 101ff. and esp. III,2, pp. 448–466; cf. also IV,3, pp. 290–318). As we see it, this is saying more than is warranted by the texts. There is more reason to speak with Noordmans of "the cloudy contours of Easter"; see *Gestalte en Geest* (1956), pp. 173–176. Yet that can easily lead to an undervaluation. Therefore, relative to the figure forty, we prefer to speak of a decisive transition in the history of salvation, for Jesus toward his exaltation as well as for us toward a life with the exalted Jesus in the Spirit.

This forward orientation of the resurrection is seen very little by Barth and not at all by Bultmann and his followers. In contrast, for Moltmann, Pannenberg, and their disciples, this "anticipatory" character of the resurrection is its essence. They understand it especially as anticipating the future of man and the world (see under 3); it is not clear how they see the meaning of the state of anticipation for Jesus himself.

After these two, especially H. Küng in *On Being a Christian* (E.T. 1976), ch. V, and in *Eternal Life?* (E.T. 1984), B V, and E. Schillebeeckx in *Jezus het verhaal van een levende* (1974), pp. 270–324 and 528ff., have dealt extensively with the nature and design of Jesus' resurrection. However, amid the many insights they offer, the uniqueness of Jesus' glorification recedes and gives way to a blending with general ideas of immortality and going-to-heaven. For Küng see *On Being a Christian,* p. 359: "Resurrection means dying into God," and for Schillebeeckx see p. 528 e where "new creation" is described as "there is life-after-death." This approach makes it nearly impossible to give substance to the ontological significance of Jesus as the firstfruits in the glorification.

There are two more difficult questions that ought to be discussed here: (a) *What is the significance of the empty tomb?* This is a difficult question because Jesus' glorification excludes a continuation of the old existence, which for that matter, according to Paul, holds also for us (1 Cor. 15:35ff.). Jesus' body which was laid in the tomb could not possibly serve as the somatic instrument of his glorified existence. We can thus not say of the empty tomb that it is redemptively or intellectually required. But no more can we conceive of his glorified human existence as consisting only of spirit or soul, and thus only half-human. Furthermore, the new humanity is the glorification of this concrete earthly existence which was laid in the grave. For Jesus, too, it holds: "this mortal must put on immortality." Therein lies the promise that God will redeem this world in the totality in which he created it. All that is the message of the empty tomb. Of Jesus' transition we get to see only this negative sign: an emptiness; but as such this tells us how comprehensive and radical the transfiguration is. It is no more than a "sign"; yet no less either, for with the appearances alone the idea of resurrection, and thus of a future hope for the earth, would hardly have occurred to us. See Barth, *CD* I,2, pp. 178–183; IV,1, p. 341; Althaus, *CW* II, p. 272; Brunner, *Dg* II, pp. 371f.; De Jong, in *Geloof en natuurwetenschap,* pp. 106–108.

(b) *Where is Jesus now according to his human nature?* We who live on this side do not know what glorification is. In the resurrected Jesus we see only a glimpse and a beginning of it. Thus we do not know what sort of spatiality corresponds to the mode of existence in the glorification. The classical Lutheran theory that Jesus was made to share in God's omnipresence is unacceptable: in his glorification Jesus remains man, one of us; he is God's covenant partner and counter-player, but is not absorbed by God. More we do not know. Nor would that more be relevant for us. It is remarkable and significant that only Paul speaks about the *sōma* of the glorified Christ, but then refers to his church on earth. Here takes place the materialization of his glorified existence, which concerns *us*. Is there perhaps no other? Yes, there is; for as the firstfruits and the head Christ is more than what assumes bodily form in his church. But that more we know only as Spirit, and that is enough. See Brunner, *Dg* II, pp. 376–378.

3. Jesus is the representative. Everything he is, he is in our stead and for our good. His glorification is the ground of our coming glorification. As the first and only one he is at the same time the firstfruits. Here people who had alienated themselves from God and thereby from the future intended for them, receive the future as a gift of grace.

With this great difference: the firstfruits has entered the future ahead of us, but we still live from a promise, on this side of the border to the future. Every imagination as if with Christ's resurrection the union of God and man, of heaven and earth, would have become a universal reality, is an illusion which is rudely refuted by the facts. But in addition we live from a new fact and from a real promise grounded on it. In that light our reality of sin, suffering, and death turns out not to be what we from ourselves thought it was: dependent on itself, tragic, definitive, it turns out to be provisional, marked as passing away through the resurrection of the firstfruits.

Are we able to say what kind of world will sooner or later take its place? We can say no more about it than what can be derived from the humanity and resurrection of Jesus: "It does not yet appear what we shall be, but we know that when he appears we shall be like him" (1 John 3:2); "Just as we have borne the image of the man of dust, we shall also bear the image of the man from heaven" (1 Corinthians 15:49); ". . . who will change our lowly body to be like his glorious body" (Philippians 3:21). This minimum of knowledge points to a maximum of reality, and therefore, despite its soberness, creates room for a wealth of imagery about a banquet to come and a city of gold.

Why did this future not immediately come about as a direct consequence of Jesus' glorification? That is what the first community had expected to happen, though this expectation decreased as the powers of the Spirit began to be manifested more strongly and in an ever widening area. And by now nearly two thousand years lie between Jesus' resurrection and the future to which it points. Indeed, taking the whole of history, not even mentioning evolution, this is a minutely small period, yet that does not alter the fact that the resurrection has not concluded history, but on the contrary has itself introduced and put its stamp on a new phase in history. Why? That is something we do not know. A possible answer is that otherwise the world might have been caught by surprise and that is out of keeping with God's whole method in preservation and redemption. As there has been an ages-long way to the Christ-event, so possibly there must be an ages-long way in which this event can penetrate history, and in which the world grows toward a new "fullness of time" which becomes the threshold of its glorification.

Meanwhile we are not yet that far. We live "between the times." Our representative is no more and not yet here. What is now the present for him is yet future for us. And what is the past for him is still the present for us. We still live under the cross, yet with the prospect of the resurrection. That implies, too, that we may already live from the reconciliation, but that the redemption still lies in front of us. It also implies that in Christ's path of life we have behind us the disclosure of what it means that we are human, but that we are still on the way toward the fulfillment of the meaning of our own existence.

This interim situation gives an "ex-centric" direction to our life in two senses. First of all vertically: our center of orientation and inspiration does not lie in this world but above it, in him who has reached the goal and represents us with God. On the other hand horizontally: the life we expect is not yet here; we still live as in a foreign land, awaiting the moment when God will make all things new. This dual ex-centricity of the Christian life is also reflected in the believer's attitude toward the present: of security and rest because the future is guaranteed through Jesus' session at God's right hand, and of anxiety about and rebellion against what is now after all these years still out of keeping with the new fact. Jesus' being raised from the dead raises our spirits, his rising from the dead arouses in us a spirit of rebellion.

The connection between Jesus' resurrection and ours is implicit in the NT in a variety of terms and lines of thought. See e.g. John 14:2f., the undertone of John 17, the argumentation in 1 Cor. 15 (especially the remarkable logic of vv. 12–16), the beautiful formulation of 1 Pet. 1:3, and the pithy and powerful: "They proclaimed in Jesus the resurrection from the dead" (Acts 4:2; cf. Rom. 5:10; 8:10, 29; 14:9; 1 Cor. 6:14; 2 Cor. 4:14; Col. 1:18; 1 Thess. 4:14; Rev. 1:5). See also the use of *aparchē* in 1 Cor. 15:20. This connection implies incompleteness at the same time: the reconciliation is not yet the redemption (Rom. 6:1–14; 8:23–25); therefore those who say "that the resurrection is past already" "have swerved from the truth" (2 Tim. 2:18). On the distinctive attitude to life which this entails, see Heb. 11:8–10, 13–16; 12:1–3, 18–29; also Col. 3:1–3, which succinctly expresses the dual ex-centricity (which according to all of ch. 3, despite 3:5, is no world flight).

In the wake of A. Schweitzer, far too much has been made of the problem of the delay of the parousia, as if it would have burdened the community with a deep and lasting trauma. Already for Jesus himself this question was likely dislodged from center stage through the presence of the Kingdom in his own ministry; and the same must soon have happened in the community under the pressure of the presence of the Spirit and the challenge it entailed (see 1 Thess., esp. 4 and 5). This raises the question as to the meaning of the preceding history. In an impressive passage (*CD* IV,3, pp. 316–334) Barth has given the answer that Jesus wants to conquer with *us,* and that for that reason he gives man time and opportunity to be not just a spectator but an active participant in the harvest that follows from the seed of his redemption (pp. 331f.). This answer is primarily christological. Pannenberg, *Jesus—God and Man,* gives an anthropological answer: the expectation of the future as the extension of Jesus' resurrection is in harmony with "the ultimate destiny of man . . . for [which] man inquires in the openness of his existence" (p. 243). H. Berkhof, *Christ the Meaning of History* (E.T. 1966), among others on pp. 78f. and 100, offers a christological-pneumatological answer: the history after the resurrection is the period when the analogy of Christ's cross and resurrection is being realized over the whole earth. If God's way with Israel and in Christ is intended to bring about the redemption of all mankind, it is really unnecessary to ask what is the sense of the continuation of history, because the sense of Christ's work requires this continuation and becomes effective in it.

In Germany the new accent on the resurrection has occasionally led to the contrasts of *theologia crucis* and *theologia resurrectionis*. See on that first of all the book, still worth reading but with a romantic-philosophical slant, by W. Künneth, *Theologie der Auferstehung* (1933), pp. 133–139; further Trillhaas, *Dg* pp. 317–320, and Moltmann, *Theology of Hope,* III, par. 9, and *The Crucified God,* ch. 5. From this one can distill an intolerable paradox, unless one realizes that it concerns steps on *one* way which we have not yet walked to its end, but which now already, through the Spirit, makes the liberating power of its goal felt. When cross and resurrection are no longer being related to each other and used to define each other, they are made to be something else than what they are in the communion with Christ. He who sits at God's right hand can also be portrayed as the lamb, standing "as though it had been slain," in the midst of the throne (Rev. 5:6). What the practical and concrete importance of this combination of cross and resurrection is can be seen from 2 Cor. 4:7–11 and 6:3–10.

In the "realistic" West, the resurrection as a central redemptive event has always stood very much in the shadow of the cross, certainly compared with the Eastern church. This is particularly true of all those Protestant churches who have seven weeks of Lent, but usually reserve no more than two weeks for the celebration of the Easter event. A wholesome reaction began with Moltmann and Pannenberg, both of whom understand the resurrection as "anticipation," namely as the "appearance" of a new world for which God has destined mankind. Both are of the opinion that the relation between Jesus' resurrection and our future went by way of Jewish apocalyptic thinking. Moltmann is here much more cautious than Pannenberg. For a critique of their standpoints, see Geense, *Auferstehung und Offenbarung,* V. In our opinion that relation is much rather to be sought in the belief in Jesus as the representative. See Pannenberg, *Jesus—God and Man,* par. 3, and especially Moltmann, *Theology of Hope,* III, pars. 5–14.

4. If Jesus has reached the goal for himself and in that is our representative, it is hard to imagine that the fruit of his representation would only be

future. His session at God's right hand, this man's covenant bond with God, would then have no effect for the present. The opposite is the case. The book of Acts, the epistles, and Revelation, which together form the bulk of the New Testament, are predominantly about the work of the exalted Jesus now in the church and in the world. That work is mainly the renewing work of the Spirit in the hearts and lives of men, by which they are involved in the covenant and prepared for the future. That will be the subject of paragraph 37 and most of the subsequent sections. But the work of the exalted Christ does not coincide with the work of his Spirit in us. Aside from that, he is present himself, and he is there for us and for the world. His influence on God and on history is more than the direct influence of his Spirit on us.

The first community expressed its belief in this fact by calling the exalted Jesus the "Lord." As God's covenant partner he has a managing and ruling function. Precisely he who in his earthly life was willing to be the servant, the slave in the fullest sense of the term, is therefore now active as the Lord. As such, his activity is directed toward God, toward the world, and toward his followers and their bond with each other.

As the exalted Lord his activity is directed *toward God*. He represents us, wandering and failing, suffering and guilty people, before God. He is the guarantee that our covenant bond with God is not being broken. The fact of this saving representation we can only approximate in analogies and symbols, by saying with the New Testament that he is our advocate with the Father, that with the sacrifice of his life he enters for our sake into the presence of God, or that he acts on our behalf. All those words give expression to the belief in his active and saving representation.

As the exalted Lord his activity is also directed *toward the world*. Not as if he would possess a separate ruling power or province beside God. His session at God's right hand means that God, for his work in the world, is bound by this covenant, that he rules in the spirit of Jesus, that he directs everything to the revelation and victory of this covenant. The man Jesus, who gave his life for us, has the final say over the course of world history.

As the exalted Lord his activity is also directed *toward his community*. We do not now refer to the fact that by his Spirit he works in the community, but that as our representative he is the guarantee that the movement he established through his resurrection will not stop, but will always carry on, in whatever form, against all the forces that aim to undermine or destroy it. Moreover, those who are willing to join this movement will not be disillusioned in their faith, but will experience that they are being protected and will keep the upper hand over the temptations and setbacks.

What is ascribed here to the exalted Lord must also, on account of the covenant relationship within which it happens, be ascribed to God and to the Spirit. The nature of this active covenant partnership implies that we can speak of a triune activity. If we start from Christ, it means that we believe that *one* man has overcome for us and that the blessings of that fact must forever remain a part of God's plans and deeds with respect to the world. To say it with the Heidelberg Catechism: "that in him we have our flesh in heaven as a sure guarantee" (A. 49).

A nearly overwhelming amount of literature exists about the *kyrios*-title in the NT and its background. The emphasis on the present function of the risen Christ in contrast to the eschatological function is the work of the Hellenistic congregations (in contrast to the Palestinian). W. Bousset, *Kyrios Christos* (1913), followed among others by Bultmann, *Theology of the NT,* par. 12, heard in the *kyrios*-title the cultic deification of Jesus, as a parallel of the many *kyrios*-cults in Oriental Hellenism. Yet according to the Aramaic liturgical expression "Maranatha" 1 Cor. 16:22) the title has its origin in the Palestinian community. Next to the "liberal" explanation of Bousset there is the "orthodox," which holds that here the divine name of the Septuagint is consciously applied to Jesus; see e.g. W. Förster, in *TDNT* III, *s.v. kyrios.* Bultmann rightly labels this "highly unlikely." For although Jesus was already called "lord" in his earthly life according to the evangelists (this may have been done in retrospect; "lord" was, however, also a common form of address), from the confessional statements which emphatically use *kyrios,* namely Acts 2:36; 5:30f.; Rom. 1:4; 10:9; 1 Cor. 8:6; 12:3, and Phil. 2:9, it is evident that Jesus did not possess this title from the outset, but that it was conferred on him on the basis of his exaltation. Immediately connected with this is the special role of Ps. 110:1 in the NT: Jesus is called Lord as the one who sits at God's right hand (Mark 12:36; 16:19; Acts 2:34–36; 1 Cor. 15:25; Eph. 1:20f.; Heb. 1:3 and 13, and other passages). This would seem to make it natural to see an antithetical connection between the *kyrios*-title, as designating him in his exaltation, and the title *pais* as characteristic of his earthly life and suffering (see also the contrast *doulos-kyrios* in Phil. 2:7–11). All the emphasis falls on his joint rule with God (see also O. Cullmann, *The Christology of the NT* (E.T. 1964; III 1). In the Netherlands during and after the War, this title was heavily stressed to indicate that ultimately we owe obedience only to Christ. That was not primarily what was meant with this title, but it is a consequence of it (1 Cor. 8:6; Phil. 2:11).

For the aspect *toward God* see Rom. 8:34; Heb. 7:25 and 9:24, and 1 John 2:1. For that *toward the world:* Matt. 28:18 (translate with the New English Bible: "Full authority—*pasa exousia*—in heaven and on earth has been committed to me"); Rev. 5:7 (the lamb opens the sealed book, that is, gets history going). For the aspect *toward believers:* Matt. 16:18 and Rom. 8:35–39 (read as the consequence of 34b). The Belgic Confession, art. 27, expresses beautifully how this protection of the church is the other side of Christ's kingship.

Here we face what classical dogmatics summed up as the *munus regium* (S par. 37; H XVIII), whereby precisely the Lutherans emphasized the toward-the-world aspect much more than the Reformed, and distinguished it as the *regnum potentiae* from the *regnum gratiae.* A succinct summary of the Reformed conception is given in the Heidelberg Catechism, Q. and A. 49–51.

In religious experience the living Lord often becomes secondary to God and the Spirit. This is not the case in many so-called Pietistic circles. We have in mind particularly Zinzendorf and the Blumhardts. Barth takes up this theme in *CD* IV,3, interestingly under the *munus propheticum.* Modest later attempts can be found in D. Ritschl, *Memory and Hope: An Inquiry concerning the Presence of Christ* (1967), and Slenczka, *Geschichtlichkeit und Personsein Jesu Christi.* But today the greater interest of theology concerns our points 1 and 3, thus not the relation to the present, but that to the past and (especially) the future.

In par. 33 in an appendix we said something about the virgin birth and in par. 35 about the descent into the realm of the dead; here we will deal with the ascension since it is one of the articles of the Apostles' Creed. Implicitly this has been done already, especially under 2. That Jesus was taken up into heaven is a biblical way of saying that he was glorified, that he was fully permeated with the presence of God. We called that a designation of form of existence, not a designation of place. About the latter the NT provides no information at all. In contrast, much is said about the fact of the exaltation and Christ's being-in-heaven as the fruit of the resurrection; see Acts 2:33f.; 3:21; 5:31; 7:56; Eph. 1:20f.; 4:8–10; Phil. 2:9–11; 1 Tim. 3:16; 1 Pet. 3:21f.; Rev. 3:21; 5:6; 22:1, and especially in Heb., which hardly mentions the resurrection: 2:9; 4:14; 6:20; 9:24. But nowhere do we detect any interest for such questions as: where is that presence of God? how and when did Jesus get there? and how is his exaltation related to his appearances on earth?

The only exception to this rule is the Hellenistic historian Luke. He is interested in periods, breaks, and transitions. Like the other evangelists, he concludes his gospel with the first appearances (assuming that 24:51: "and was carried up into heaven" is a gloss; the RSV relegates it to a footnote). But in his second book he cannot describe the following period, that of the church, without clearly delineating it from the period of the appearances. That he does in Acts 1, where he speaks of the appearances as a period of forty days, thus portraying them as a transition period, to which he gives a definite conclusion with an ascension. But compared to nonbiblical (Hercules) and OT (Elijah) ascension stories, this report hardly deserves that name. It is said in only one sentence: "as they were looking on, he was lifted up, and a cloud took him out of their sight" (1:9). The ancient conception of the world is evident here; but it is not openly said. The cloud not only serves to make the readers aware of Luke's ignorance concerning the sequel, but especially to remind the reader of the other occasion when he had connected Jesus with a cloud, Luke 9:34f., at the transfiguration on the mountain. Now it concerns the glorification itself, the entrance into the sphere of God, of which the high and mysterious clouds are the sign. A period is now concluded; angels elucidate it (1:10f.).

Luke stands alone with this story and also with his inclination to make the exaltation historically visible. In contrast to the cross and resurrection, the ascension is therefore no separate redemptive fact within the framework of the NT kerygma. That does not mean that Luke did not wrestle with an important problem, namely that of the relationship between the brief appearances and the abiding exaltation. Some theologians who do not go along with his conception lean toward another conception, namely that the appearances took place from the sphere of glorification. See e.g. *MS* III,2, ch. 9, 5, 2b. But in that case all appearances would have to be analogous to that of Paul (Acts 9:3; 22:6; 26:13) and the glorification on the mountain. Such, however, is not the case with any of them; it is rather true that Jesus appears as an ordinary human being, even as an unknown and thus unrecognized man (Luke 24:16; John 20:15; 21:4, 12). Luke in fact sees the glorious appearance to Paul as something distinct, separate in time and nature from the forty days (different than Paul himself in 1 Cor. 15:8). Did Luke perhaps think of an advancing from resurrection to glorification? And John perhaps, too (see 20:17)? Boulgakof, *Du verbe incarné,* pp. 323f., is the only theologian I know of who thinks further along that line: the forty days prove the ontological identity of this world with the world to come; this period is "a special path" which "establishes a bridge between the present state of the world, man's physical existence, and the glorified state of the world." An attractive but speculative idea is that stories of the appearances exhibit no inner connection, let alone planned progress. As a single individual Jesus is far ahead of us, lifted up to the new world; we who remain behind lack the categories with which to make that transition transparent. But even if we had them, the answer to the question concerning the "how" would still not belong in a confession of faith. Therefore it is regrettable that the Apostles' Creed, with the trio virgin birth—descent into the realm of the dead—ascension into heaven, includes precisely three of these "how" answers which did not belong to the kerygma and have only marginal significance in the NT, and presents them as redemptive facts that are to be believed. See on this theme and its treatment in the history of theology: F. W. A. Korff, *Christologie,* II, ch. VI; Althaus, *CW* II, pp. 274f.; Brunner, *Dg* II, pp. 372–378; Trillhaas, *Dg* pp. 320–323; *MS* III,2, ch. 9, 5, 2b.

According to the Apostolic Constitution of Nov. 1, 1950, the Roman Catholic Church has felt the need for yet a second ascension, that of Mary, better called Mary's "assumption to heaven," because according to the definition Mary "was taken up body and soul into heavenly glory" (D 3903). Why this need? Because Jesus' glorification functioned insufficiently as the guarantee of ours, since he was too little regarded as a man with and for men. See on this G. C. Berkouwer, *The Second Vatican Council and the New Catholicism* (E.T. 1965), ch. 8, esp. pp. 233–246; cf. Barth, *CD* IV,2, pp. ixf. With the heavy emphasis on Christ's humanity in recent Roman Catholic theology, the need for this newest dogma appears to have virtually disappeared.

37. THE SPIRIT AND THE PARTICIPATION

IN THE PREVIOUS PARAGRAPH, under 4, we were already compelled to say something about the Spirit. Now we address this theme in a separate paragraph as the conclusion of Christology. Even as the previous chapter, on Israel, led to Christology (paragraph 31) and so formed the transition to this chapter, so this christological chapter leads to pneumatology and thus forms the transition to what will be taken up in the remainder of this book, except for the final chapter. With this division, which is at the same time an intentional overlapping, we give expression to the fact that, despite all the turns, we nevertheless deal with one uninterrupted activity of God in history.

We do, however, stand before a turning point here. That is not the great turning point toward the consummation to which the resurrection points. But it is far less a break which announces a vacuum in God's activity. It is a turning point which ensues from what happened before and which prepares for the consummation: from the outset it is impossible that the firstfruits who is going to be the center of a renewed humanity can remain a single individual. It has to become evident that in his person and work he represented us, and that from now on, in virtue of his work, a process toward the renewal of the human race is under way. Therefore the concentration of the representation is now followed by the centrifugal movement of the winning of people, of the spreading of the renewal among people everywhere.

One may say that this movement began already during Jesus' earthly life. What else did he intend with his words and deeds, his parables and healings, but the gathering around him of a community of people who would repent from their sins to celebrate the presence of God's Kingdom? Yet this complementary expansion of his mission never got beyond beginnings. Purposely Jesus did not yet turn to the nations, and hardly even to Israel as a whole. In Israel he did call a number of people "to follow after" him, but by no means did he ask that of all his followers; that meant that a small group would literally have to go with him to be a witness of the way he had to go, so that later, having been eyewitnesses, they could win others for that way. Moreover, that limited intention can hardly be said to have succeeded; when the real suffering began, all deserted him. When he died, there was absolutely no evidence that even one was still with him. Only after and through the resurrection did the complementary counter-movement forcefully and definitively begin. Only then was it really clear what one chose for. It was then, therefore, that the work of missions began.

In the history of the church up to the present, for various reasons a disproportionate emphasis has been put on what is called *akolouthein* in the NT and usually is translated by "follow after." This is not to be confused with *mimeisthai,* which with greater justification can be translated "follow after" or "imitate" and which is significant in that it expresses the relationship of the believer to God, to Christ, and to other believers (1 Cor. 11:1; Eph. 5:1; 1 Thess. 1:6; Heb. 6:12; 13:7; *qua* meaning also in Matt. 5:44–48, and other passages). *Akolouthein* is used exclusively in reference to the small group of disciples who accompanied Jesus, as the rabbinic disciples accompanied their rabbis. But because Jesus went a unique way, this following received a new importance: it involved enormous risks of which one must be well aware. None of the disciples could unfailingly keep it up. Even so, after the purpose of Jesus' life had dawned on the disciples, their apostolate was founded on that special period when they were eyewitnesses. Anyone who still wants to base the faith on this concept should be well aware of the difference. At that time the following had a redemptive-historical function which cannot be repeated. That does not imply that we may no longer use the word if we perceive the difference. After all, the believer is set on a way which will exhibit an analogy with that of his Lord. Cf. 1 Pet. 2:21 (where *epakolouthein* is used). See *TDNT* I, *s.v. akoloutheō.*

In this connection it is significant that all the appearances of the risen Jesus, with the exception of those on Easter morning itself, contain mandates for the work of missions which is now beginning (Matt. 28:19f.; Mark 16:20; Luke 24:49; John 20:21–23; 21:15–19; Acts 1:8), while—note this—the ingathering of the church is only of subsidiary importance in these passages. On the connection of resurrection, future, and mission, of *promissio, pro-missio,* and *missio,* see Moltmann, *Theology of Hope,* III–V; "the *pro-missio* of the kingdom lays the foundation for the *missio* of love in the world."

The moving force behind this turning toward the outside world is everywhere indicated as the (holy) Spirit. That is the third name, which after and next to the names of God and Jesus or Christ expresses the manner in which God involves himself with man. This name denotes God's active presence. God is always and everywhere actively present in his creation. The Old Testament speaks of the activity of God in nature and culture, and also in Israel's kings and prophets. Our whole life, thinking, and acting we owe to that Spirit in which we are created and by which we are supported. But man is not a will-less instrument of that Spirit. He can go against his purposes, and he does that daily. To reach our destination, however, it is necessary that we are permeated and led by the Spirit, so that we become his voluntary servants and co-workers. The prophets noted that such was not the case, but they hoped on the basis of God's faithfulness that some day the Spirit would permeate Israel and eventually all of mankind. That expectation began to be realized after Jesus' resurrection. Through the preaching of what God had done in him, people experienced that God had become present and active in a new and unparalleled manner. They recognized therein the fulfillment of what had been expected among Israel, and they noted that the Spirit which had been promised for the end-time had now indeed been "poured out" and that he was likewise active in crossing Israel's boundaries and reaching the world.

The word for Spirit, Heb. *rû(a)ḥ;* Gr. *pneuma* (the first word is feminine, the second neuter!), referred originally, like the Latin *spiritus,* to the movement of the air; it can be translated "wind," "storm," "breeze," but more often as "life," "vitality," "principle of life," "life in its movement and dynamics." Even in its most "spiritual" significance, that background does somewhat color the meaning, even the notion of wind or storm (see John 3:8; 20:22; Acts 2:2–4). Of God it is said that he has or is Spirit, that with it he animates his creation, and that he gives that Spirit to man so that he becomes a living and dynamic being. On the Spirit in nature and in man see Job 27:3; 33:4; 34:14f.; Ps. 104:30. On the Spirit in culture see Ex. 31:3 and 35:31; Num. 11:17; Isa. 45:1–5; Dan. 1:17; 5:11. The working of the Spirit in redemptive history is experienced in the OT only to a limited degree; this has to do with the fact that the covenant, though present, was present more in offices and structures than in the hearts and lives of men. The Spirit inspired Moses and Joshua, the judges and the kings, and in a very special way the prophets. See J. H. Scheepers, *Die Gees van God en die gees van die mens in die OT* (1960), esp. pp. 312–315. But the time will come when the Spirit will be poured out on all and will dwell in their hearts. See Num. 11:24–29; Jer. 31:33; Ezek. 36:27f.; 37:5, 14; Joel 2:28. The NT statements about the Spirit are to be read against the background of these expectations. This holds also for the often misunderstood statement "God is Spirit," which is to be read in the whole context of John 4:19–26; then one sees that it means: now that the messiah has come, God is actively present and our prayers and adoration can be directed toward that. This new, eschatological mode of being-present is so overwhelming that God's general presence in creation and culture pales in comparison with it. The NT hardly speaks about it. This has caused its neglect in the study of the faith. Wrongly, for the OT does stress it. Calvin certainly had an eye for it; see S. van der Linde, *De leer van den Heiligen Geest bij Calvijn* (1943), pp. 34–57. That is also true of A. Kuyper in his *The Work of the Holy Spirit* (E.T. 1900), part 1, pp. 18–55. Cf. also Barth in *CD* III,2, pp. 344–366. This tendency is much stronger in the newest Roman Catholic theology; see the Festschrift for Schillebeeckx, *Leven uit de geest* (1974). For newer trends in Protestant theology in various directions, see K. Blaser, *Vorstoss zur Pneumatologie* (1977).

Speaking here about the Spirit, we do not refer to his general work in creation, a subject which was at least implicitly raised in paragraphs 24 and 25, but to that very special presence and activity of God which followed upon the appearance and resurrection of Jesus. To be able to understand and articulate its nature and purpose, it is necessary to consider three preliminary questions, which are partly biblical-theological, partly dogmatical in character; not until we have answered these are we ready for a closer delineation of the work of the Spirit.

1. *From what perspective do we gain access to the essence of the Spirit?* The Spirit is God active in the present. It is therefore natural that we seek access to his essence on the basis of his operations in the present. This has mainly been done in three ways. Roman Catholicism preferably defines the Spirit from the viewpoint of his place in the church, whose soul and animating principle he is. In the tradition of orthodox Protestantism his essence is especially determined from his influence in the life of the individual in effecting faith and conversion, regeneration and sanctification. Liberal Protestantism likes to start from the common content and structure of man's spiritual life, and to understand the Spirit as analogous to it. Something can be said in favor of all three. Even more could be said for a combination of all three. But in that case the difficulty

inherent in all three approaches is felt even more, namely that of the jump from the activities of the Spirit to the Spirit himself. After all, the Spirit is more than his activities. The Spirit does not coincide with and is not bound to the church, the converted individual, or the human spirit. He is the Lord. And he blows wherever he wills. We must first know him from a different perspective before we can distinguish in our human phenomena and institutions between what comes from him and what is only human or altogether too human.

For that reason we do not seek access to his essence from his operations, but from his origin, which, as it concerns us, is found in Christ. From Jesus, the Son of God, who is the new man, a wind begins to blow in our life, though he is not the ground and norm of the general working of the Spirit in created life, but of its special accentuation which we experience in the encounter with Christ. The Spirit is no timeless and static phenomenon, but a power which upholds creation, which arises in history and forms history, and which finally in the whole of God's work introduces a new period. This approach is the main line in the New Testament. Only along this line are his operations in the present seen in the proper light.

Typical for the Roman Catholic approach, where the Spirit stands in the shadow of the church, is the encyclical *Mystici corporis* (1943). Yet already the encyclical *Divinum illud munus* (1897) of Leo XIII had invited attention to the work of the Spirit in the individual; that aspect is becoming more and more prominent in recent decades. The orthodox-Protestant approach is formulated in Luther's Small Catechism in the exposition of the Apostles' Creed as follows: "The Holy Spirit has called me through the gospel, enlightened me by his gifts, and sanctified and preserved me in the true faith." Calvin too, in *Inst* III, develops the work of the Spirit along those lines. But Luther continues with: "just as He calls all of Christendom on earth . . . ," etc., and Calvin devotes *Inst* IV to the church. Later, orthodox Protestantism became more individualistic. Liberal Protestantism likes to appeal to, "The Spirit testifies with our spirit" (Rom. 8:16), so as to link the specific operation of the Spirit in the church with his general operations. Examples of this approach are A. B. Come, *Human Spirit and Holy Spirit* (1959), and G. W. H. Lampe, *God as Spirit* (1977).

In the NT the special work of the Spirit is perceived entirely from the perspective of the fulfilled work of Christ. See John 7:39; 12:24; 17; 20:22; Acts 2:33; Rom. 8:3f.; 1 Cor. 15:45; Eph. 4:7ff., etc. The historian Luke has historicizingly expressed this redemptive-historical relationship by having the outpouring of the Spirit take place on the Jewish feast of Pentecost *(pentēkostē)*, the harvest festival celebrated fifty days after the beginning of the harvest (Deut. 16:9); in Luke's time this feast was also regarded as the Sinai feast fifty days after the exodus out of Egypt (the passover feast), which to the Christian Luke means fifty days after the resurrection and ten days after the forty days of the appearances. In John (20:22) this event takes place already on the day of resurrection.

As a result of more recent biblical-theological studies, this christological approach also found its way into the study of the faith. In *CD* I,1 and 2 Barth still approached pneumatology from the classical orthodox-Protestant perspective, but in IV,2, par. 64,4 he made a new opening from the perspective of the risen Christ, and in IV,3, par. 69,4 he even presents the work of the Spirit as a new parousia of Christ. H. Berkhof, *The Doctrine of the Holy Spirit* (E.T. 1976), ch. I, views the Spirit as the activity of the risen Christ; Weber, *Gl* II, pp. 272–291, as the continuation of the threefold office.

Finally this observation: in our judgment only this christological determination of the Spirit can be an answer to the question which has been with us continually since Lessing answered it by: "Accidental truths of history can never be a proof of necessary truths of reason" (in *Über den Beweis des Geistes und der Kraft,* 1777). Whoever (with the Enlightenment) regards the Spirit as an unhistorical entity or (since German Idealism) as expressing itself in history-in-general, attempts in vain to prove the "absoluteness" of the historical fact of Jesus. Intellectually it is not possible to leap across "the nasty big ditch" (Lessing) between general happenings and the historically unrepeatable. We must get away from trying to prove the *possibility,* but instead proceed from the *reality;* in this case, from the Spirit who from Christ comes to us in history and so in *fact* bridges the gap.

2. *How does the Spirit relate to Christ?* There is not only a relationship of sequence. In the New Testament the relationship between them is presented in two ways. On the one hand the Spirit creatively precedes; he is greater than Jesus and controls him. Jesus is the work of the Spirit. On the other hand the Spirit is the work of (the risen) Jesus, interpreting Jesus and being ruled by him. Jesus is the fruit of the Spirit and the Spirit is the fruit of Jesus. In the study of the faith the second aspect has always received due attention, but not the first. The reason was that Christ and the Spirit were not viewed primarily in redemptive-historical perspective, but especially as historical embodiments of their place as second and third person in God's eternal triune being. It is not feasible to have such positions in eternity play musical chairs in time. That problem falls away if in our reflection we do not start from eternity and move toward time, but proceed from time toward eternity. As such, though, we are not yet concerned here with the consequences this has for the study of the faith. All we do here is observe that the New Testament clearly speaks of a twofold relationship, to which the study of the faith thus far has done no or only scant justice.

In the NT it is the Spirit who begets Jesus (Matt. 1:18; Luke 1:35), who descends upon him at his baptism (Mark 1:10), who drives him out into the desert (Mark 1:12), with whom he is anointed so that for that reason he may be called the Christ (Luke 4:1; Acts 10:38), who inspires and guides Jesus (Luke 10:21; 12:10; John 3:34), who is the power through which he brings his sacrifice (Heb. 9:14), and the ground of his resurrection (Rom. 1:4; 1 Tim. 3:16). This emphasis is made especially in the synoptic gospels, though the passages mentioned here show that it is not absent from John and Paul either. Yet in both of these the second emphasis is dominant; for John see 7:39; 14–16; 20:22; for Paul see Rom. 8:9; 1 Cor. 15:45; 2 Cor. 3:17; Gal. 4:6; Phil. 1:19. Nor is it altogether absent in the synoptic gospels (Luke 24:49). A combination of the two emphases is found in John 1:33.

In the history of theology the first emphasis has been pushed aside, as we said before. However, we have to note a remarkable exception in the earliest period, the post-apostolic era. In the *Pastor Hermae* (ca. 140) a beginning toward a Christology along the first line is found. See *Similitudines* V.6 and IX.1 and 12. There the Spirit is the real Son of God, through whom Jesus is created; and later, because of his obedience to the Spirit, Jesus was made "a partner with the Holy Spirit." G. C. van de Kamp, *Pneuma-christologie?* (1983), offers an extensive overview of this Christology as found in Ignatius, Barnabas, 2 Clement, Melito of Sardis, and Pseudo-Hippolytus's *In Pascha.* At least traces of it are found in Tatian, Tertullian, Justin, Lactantius, and others (wrongly regarded by Harnack and Loofs as tendencies toward an Adoptionist Christology). Before Nicea there was still lots of room to regard Jesus as the incarnation of the Spirit, next to or in place of the incarnation of the Logos.

A new interest in this first emphasis is found in A. A. van Ruler, *De vervulling van de wet* (1947), IV, par. 3; see: "The pneuma includes the messiah. . . . He is the Spirit who posits the Christ" (p. 170); in Berkhof, *The Doctrine of the Holy Spirit,* pp. 17–21; in G. J. Hoenderdaal, *Geloven in de heilige Geest* (1968), 7, esp. pp. 114–117 and 130–133; in *MS* III,2, ch. 12; and in W. Kasper, *Jesus der Christus* (2nd ed. 1975).

3. *How are the Spirit and the exalted Christ related to each other?* This question is an accentuation of the previous one. If the Spirit creates and inspires Christ so that he becomes the exalted one and as such now sends the Spirit, can one still distinguish between his actions and those of the Spirit? Is it not so that since the resurrection Christ and the Spirit coincide for us? Here we limit ourselves to the biblical-theological answer to this question. That answer is not univocal. Often the New Testament speaks about the Spirit as a power clearly distinguished from Christ, as "another comforter," "the Spirit of Christ," who leads us to Christ and in us prays for the coming of Christ. But the work of the Spirit is also frequently presented as the work of the exalted Christ himself: "I am with you always," "now the Lord is the Spirit," in the resurrection he becomes "a life-giving Spirit" and therefore he does not leave us as orphans but comes again to us. As a rule this second aspect has been neglected in the study of the faith, because it did not fit the classical trinitarian pattern in which the second and the third "person" remain clearly distinguished. But we will have to learn so to speak about the being and acts of God that this double speaking about the relationship of Christ and the Spirit need not be avoided (nor literally repeated), but becomes transparent in such a manner that we too can use it and pass it on.

On the first line are passages like Luke 24:49; John 14:16; 15:26; 16:7, 13, 26; 20:21–23; Rom. 8:9, 11; 2 Cor. 3:17b; 2 Cor. 13:13; Gal. 4:6; Phil. 1:19; Rev. 22:17. On the second line such passages as Matt. 28:20; John 14:18; 1 Cor. 6:17; 15:48; 2 Cor. 3:17a; also the letters to the seven churches (Rev. 1–3), which are dictated by the exalted Christ and for the most part end with a summarizing admonition to listen to what the *Spirit* says to the churches. In this respect it is also significant that the Pauline expressions *en Christōi* and *en pneumati* are similar in purport (see e.g. Rom. 8:9–11). Immediately following each other it is said in Rom. 8 that the Spirit intercedes for us (vv. 26f.) and that Christ intercedes for us (v. 34). In John 14:16, 26; 15:26, and 16:7 the Spirit is called *paraklētos* (advocate, helper, counselor), and in 1 John 2:1 this is the name of the exalted Christ. These two series of texts show, too, that the two lines cannot be ascribed to two traditions, e.g. a Johannine and a Pauline; they are absolutely intertwined.

Recent years have seen a special interest in the second emphasis, especially through the study of I. Hermann, *Kyrios und Pneuma* (1961), who concludes that for Paul the Lord and the Spirit are identical (p. 140). This is denied by J. P. Versteeg, *Christus en de Geest* (1971). A detailed discussion is given by Lampe, *God as Spirit,* ch. III, who himself advocates a spiritualistic conception.

Three theologians in the Netherlands have each come up with their own specific formulation of this relationship: A. A. van Ruler in "Structuurverschillen tussen het christologische en het pneumatologische gezichtspunt" (*Theologisch werk,* I, 1969, pp. 175–190) puts Christ and the Spirit over against each other in counterpoint fashion: *assumptio* over against *adoptio,* substitution over against reciprocity, etc. (in our view this can be maintained only at the cost of the denial of Jesus' true humanity); cf. his "Hoofdlijnen van de pneumatologie," in *Theologisch werk,* VI (1973), pp. 9–40; Berkhof, *Holy Spirit,* I, who identifies Christ and the Spirit (but does not maintain this in the following chapters); and G. J. Hoenderdaal, *Geloven in de heiligen Geest,* II,6, pp. 114–133, who argues for an "interaction of pneumatology and Christology which mutually include each other" (p. 133) (but is unclear as to the "proper function" of the Spirit apart from Christ). Compare also how much earlier this problem was discussed in Anglican theology, in A. M. Ramsay, *From Gore to Temple* (1960), App. C, esp. pp. 180f.

Having arrived at this point, we must now try to understand and articulate the multiple relationships of the Spirit to Christ. The Spirit is the name for God himself in his activity among us. Due to our disobedience and powerlessness there is no more than a loose connection between the Spirit and the world. This lasts until as Spirit God takes a new initiative to get a hold on his creation, by creating the new man and by inspiring him with his Spirit. In that man the covenant is confirmed and in him the Spirit makes his abode on earth. From now on the Spirit and Christ coincide. As the totally faithful covenant partner, Jesus is the form of the Spirit, calls the Spirit to the earth, and creates room for the Spirit. From now on the activity of the Spirit exists in the mode of the outworking of the absolute covenantal oneness between God and Jesus, and of the new life he has obtained for us in that oneness. Because it concerns here the most intimate union of God and man, what happens here can be approached from two angles: (1) the Spirit creates Jesus *and* Jesus sends the Spirit; and (2) the Spirit is the activity of the exalted Christ *and* a separate activity of God on earth, made possible by Jesus' sonship. Christ and the Spirit are the two poles of the new covenant.

With that we have finally come to the central question of this paragraph: what does the Spirit as he proceeds from Christ do to man? In the title we have purely formally called it "participation"; giving this term its material content will be our concern in the next three chapters. Before we come to that we will here have to outline the basic pattern of this work of participation. We must derive it from the Son's relationship to us, the lost sons. He is the one man who is at the same time the firstfruits. From him as the source, our life outside the covenant with God must be brought into a crisis, our alienation must be overcome, and we must be moved to voluntary surrender and participation, in order that we may become conformed to the image of the Son.

The first step of the Spirit toward achieving that goal is forming a community within which he can work with his healing and renewing power. This community as "the body of Christ" (*corpus Christi*) is the place of incorporation into this field of power. We can support Bishop Cyprian's thesis "Outside the church no salvation," provided we realize that after Paul's conversion there are exceptions to this rule, and that for us "church" includes many incorporating communities. Therefore in a later section we have included first the chapter on "The New Community" (paragraphs 39–42).

But this renewed community intends and presupposes the renewal of the incorporated persons, a work that has many facets and bears many names, such as faith and conversion, justification and sanctification, calling and regeneration (preferably at least two terms are being used). That is the topic of the chapter "The New Man" (paragraphs 43–52) and in a sense, too, the chapter "The Renewal of the World" (paragraphs 53–56). All of these could be described as parts of the work of the Spirit. For he is the subject of all those operations and of their coherence. However, only a separate treatment can do justice to the many perspectives. By opting for that we continue a long tradition (which requires elaboration, however; see below).

All major church groups have their own access to the comprehensive work of the Holy Spirit. The Eastern Orthodox Church puts all the emphasis on incorporation into the church, in which the Triune God dwells and works. In the Roman Catholic Church as well, participation in Christ is closely connected with participation in the church community. There the Spirit is primarily a social event. In our time this has been set forth in great detail by H. Mühlen, also in answer to the growing socialization of humanity. See his *Una mystica persona. Eine Person in vielen Personen* (1964, 3rd ed. 1968); cf. his article in *MS* III,2, pp. 513–544, and as a summary his art. "Soziale Geisteserfahrung als Antwort auf eine einseitige

Gotteslehre," in C. Heitmann-H. Mühlen, eds., *Erfahrung und Theologie des Heiligen Geistes* (1974), pp. 253–272. The strength and weakness of the Protestant churches is their heavy emphasis on personal faith that does not shift the responsibility to an institute but at the same time easily degenerates into individualism. The latter happens even more if the marks of true faith are sought in certain experiences or behavioral patterns (especially among the orthodox) or evaporate into general spiritual experiences (especially in liberalism). In our age each of these traditions (maybe with the exception of the Eastern Orthodox?) becomes aware of its own shortage. In the following chapters we shall attempt to explain how each facet of the work of the Spirit presupposes or evokes the other facets.

If the participation as outlined above is to be described as an event with several facets, then as a consequence the work of the Spirit is to be characterized as an event that participates and intervenes in history in an entirely new way, both in the inner and outer history of the individual and that of mankind as a whole. Participation means that the Spirit, from the exclusive center which is Christ, constantly draws new circles in time and space. Earlier we referred to that work as missions. This concept as used here comprehends everything the Spirit does and effects in his ongoing incorporating activity, including the church, the inner life of the individual, the works of love, and liberation; and what in a narrower sense is called missions as an organized activity of the church or a group of Christians. All this has its place and significance because it is a dimension of the great participation movement of which it is simultaneously both fruit and seed. Separated from this movement, either the institutional church or the religious life of the individual easily becomes a goal in itself. The Spirit is a historical power who touches us, transforms us, and enlists us for service in his ongoing work, a work which in this present world will not be completed, so that whatever he accomplishes here points beyond itself and must always and anew exceed its own boundaries.

At this point the unfortunate consequences of the earlier-mentioned tendency to determine the nature of the Spirit from his work in the church and in the individual is evident. Even apart from its impossibility, one of the evil consequences was that church and individual could easily be regarded as the terminus of the work of the Spirit. Both the Roman Catholic ecclesiastical and the Protestant individualistic conception of the Spirit misconstrued the context in which both have their relative value: the context of the Spirit as a christologically determined power in redemptive history, and therefore a historical power.

The earthly Jesus did not yet think of missions. His concern was the realization of the covenant with Israel, by which this people of itself would become a light to the nations. Yet we noted already that the stories of the appearances stand in the context of missions (and e.g. much less in that of the church). Both in John (20:21) and in Luke (24:47f.; Acts 1:18, and especially 2) the giving of the Spirit and the missionary movement coincide. To the early church, the triumphal march of the gospel through the world must have been a redemptive fact of no less significance than the resurrection of Jesus. When later in the church, until the present day, the redemptive facts came to be regarded as having come to an end with the ascension of Jesus, after which the Spirit only "applies" them, we are miles removed from the vision of the NT which sees the activity of the Spirit as the historical presence of God that builds the bridge from the firstfruits to the coming consummation. Precisely Luke with his historicizing schematization (resurrection, forty days later the ascension, after another ten days the outpouring of the Spirit, then the story of his course through the ancient world) has sought to impress this on our minds. In the NT the Spirit is not primarily an institutional or inner power, but a historical force. To the best of my knowledge, in the handbooks on dogmatics only Barth has thoroughly done justice to this comprehensive vision, be it as the last of his three perspectives (*CD* IV,3). See further Harry R. Boer, *Pentecost and the Missionary Witness of the Church* (1955); H. Berkhof, *Christ the Meaning of History,* ch. V; idem, *The Doctrine of the Holy Spirit,* ch. II. The pneumatology of Noordmans deserves special attention in this connection. In his last book, *Gestalte en Geest,* esp. III and IV 1, he conceives of the Spirit as the creative interpreter who makes a way for himself to the future through the historical forms.

In the above we hit more than once upon the limits of the participative work of the Spirit. Through the work of Jesus he acquires a thus far unheard-of passage toward our world, enabling him to begin a great work among us. But he cannot complete it. No more than Jesus is he the closing horizon of our history. On the contrary, like Christ he opens new horizons. Like the Son, the Spirit is in turn and in his manner a "firstfruits." On many fronts he joins battle with the alienation from God and the self-sufficiency by which man is held captive. But a definite victory is still out of the question. These are only starts, only "a small beginning" (Heidelberg Catechism). Though his work in individuals, churches, and cultures is powerful, it is also fragmentary and continually frustrated by human resistance. These works are defenselessly handed over to depreciation and even denial. Those who themselves share in the participation event experience his activity, yet precisely they experience painfully how much the Spirit is provisional. Whatever he does is a guarantee but at the same time a postponement of the consummation. It is under the guidance of the Spirit that we remain on the way; and on that way we are given enough to keep the faith and our hopes and too little to delude ourselves in a kind of "spiritual fanaticism" that we have arrived.

Paul uses the word *aparchē* for Christ (1 Cor. 15:20) as well as for the Spirit (Rom. 8:23). That the Spirit is no more and no less than a promise is pointedly expressed by Paul with the word *arrabōn* (2 Cor. 1:22; 5:5; Eph. 1:14); it is derived from the Semitic language of commerce and means "first installment," "deposit," "pledge." Here we are given a small foretaste of the renewal which some day will cover the whole world. For the fragmentary and battle-like character of his work see also Rom. 7 and 8 and Gal. 5.

Van Ruler was so struck by the "torso-character" of the work of the Spirit that he viewed the Spirit as he viewed Christ, as an "emergency measure" on account of sin: when the Kingdom comes, the pledge is returned and there ensues a direct relationship between God and man; see *De vervulling van de wet,* ch. IV, par. 2. As we see it, his learned exegetical discourse is not convincing. The Spirit is precisely the greatest directness that is possible in the covenantal fellowship. The eschaton does not mean his abolition but on the contrary his full unfolding (cf. 1 Cor. 15:42–49). For a view which is entirely the opposite of Van Ruler's, see S. Boulgakof, *Le paraclet* (1946), pp. 265–272.

38. THE COVENANT AS "TRI-(U)NITY"

CONTRARY TO COMMON DOGMATIC PRACTICE we did not use the concept "triune" or "trinity" when we considered the being and attributes of God. As we see it, when we discuss God as the source of everything that arises next in the study of the faith, there is no reason to ascribe to him something like triuneness. As the creator of the world, as the establisher of the covenant, and as the one who reveals himself to us, we know him as the *one* God, as a person. In this singleness he is at the same time infinitely rich. It is right to say that his singleness goes infinitely beyond what we call singleness. But from this knowledge there is no way toward a doctrine of God as triune. In traditional theology the discussion of the doctrine of the Trinity next to and following the being and attributes of God is therefore usually little more than an unrelated appendix.

It is a fact that in the larger and smaller type we regularly had to mention the classical doctrine of God as "three persons in one essence," but it was usually done critically to show how this doctrine has saddled us with problems that are foreign to Scripture and indigestible to the believing mind. Only in the preceding paragraph 37 did the concept force itself upon us spontaneously and in a positive sense, after we had spoken about Christ and the work of the Holy Spirit had come up for discussion. Then it became clear to us how the entire Christian faith hinges on this coming-together of God and man, as it takes place in the Spirit who proceeds from the Father to the Son and then in turn proceeds from the Son to human beings. In that event we saw the being of God in action: creating, acting, suffering, and struggling. The name for God in action toward the world is: Spirit. His supreme act as Spirit is the creation of the new man, the true Son, who by his love and obedience prepares for us the way from alienation to fulfillment, and therewith opens the way for the Spirit who wants to unite us with him and conform us to his image. So the combination of the three names of Father-Son-Spirit, or, with equal validity, of Father-Spirit-Son, proves to be the summarizing description of the covenantal event, both as to its historical and its existential aspect. The Father is the divine partner, the Son the human representative, the Spirit the bond between them and therefore also the bond between the Son and the sons and daughters whom he draws to the Father. Can we say then that we have here "one essence in three persons"? No, there is here *one* event that happens from God, thus an event that is performed by the Spirit, one which occurs primarily between two persons, God and Jesus, but in which all the time new persons are being involved. May we then not call the Spirit a person? No, if thereby we put him separately beside the person of God. Yes, if we understand that this name expresses the personhood in God in its outward actions. The Spirit is precisely God-as-person, God-in-relation.

Viewed like this, it is very strange indeed that in the course of the history of the church the Trinity, which was a self-evident confession, changed into a difficult problem, an impenetrable mystery, an intellectual crux, and a cause of age-long conflicts and schisms. The reason was that it was not regarded as descriptive of the structure of the covenant but as a description of the "structure" of the *one* covenant partner, God. That one Person is then presented as a plurality. And with that the problem came: How can God be one and yet three? How can he be a person and at the same time consist of three persons? And how can Jesus regard God as greater than himself if from eternity he is "one in essence with the Father"? So God became a mystery in which his covenant partner, man, does not share. The latter can only adore this mystery; for his faith it has no significance. For he prays not to the Trinity, but to God. He does not pray to Christ either, but to God "through Jesus Christ our Lord." Nor does he pray to the Spirit, but to God *for* the Spirit. So for the believer each of the three names has its particular function in his covenantal fellowship with God. Together they do not constitute *one* being in eternity, but *one* history in time.

With the term Trinity we point to a continuing and open event, directed to man. For we are invited to participate in the trinitarian event because the Spirit conforms us unto the image of the Son. We are made to share in the relationship between Father and Son, without the uniqueness of their relationship disappearing. Particularly the high-priestly prayer (John 17) speaks of the coherence and incoherence of the relationships. "No one knows the Son except the Father, and no one knows the Father except the Son, and any one to whom the Son chooses to reveal him" (Matthew 11:27). For that reason even classical theology could describe the purpose of salvation as: partnership in the Trinity (*consortium trinitatis*). The reason that we keep using the term Trinity (and not "multi-unity") is that even the most intimate human relationship with it still presupposes the distance in essence with respect to God and his Spirit, and the distance as to origin with respect to the "only begotten Son."

With the foregoing we do not, however, wish to intimate in the least that the Trinity is an event that is not part of God. Such cannot be, for his being and his revelation are too closely connected (see paragraph 19). The entire trinitarian event is grounded in God's eternal determination to be a God of blessing, a determination which belongs to his very nature. In this connection we must refer especially to what was said in paragraph 23 about God's faithfulness and changeability (see esp. p. 153): in his sovereign love God has made himself changeable. Together with us he is involved in a process, which also does something to him because as Father it enriches him with sons and daughters. The trinitarian event arises from the very nature (essence) of God and leads to it. In that sense the Trinity is natural (essential) for God. It describes how God, according to his eternal purpose, extends and carries on in time his own life so as to share it with man. The Trinity is thus not a description of an abstract God-in-himself, but of the revealed God-with-us.

A customary distinction in the doctrine of the Trinity is that between the immanent or ontological Trinity and the economic or revelational Trinity. Though this distinction is based on a conception of the Trinity which we reject, we use it wherever it is helpful to clarify points of view. Such is already the case in the NT. In several passages God, Christ, and the Spirit are mentioned in one breath, without a clear reflection that points to a Trinity, because their cooperation spells our redemption: Rom. 5:5ff.; 8:3f., 8–11, 16f.; 1 Cor. 6:11; 12:4–6; 2 Cor. 1:21f.; 13:13; Gal. 4:6; Eph. 4:4–6; 2 Thess. 2:13; 1 Pet. 1:2. Here and there one detects a slight reflection (1 Cor. 12:4–6; 2 Cor. 13:13; Eph. 4:4–6) which has become much more explicit in Matt. 28:19 and in the later interpolation in 1 John 5:7, the so-called *comma Johanneum.* Apart from these last two passages, all others are clearly revelationally trinitarian (or revelationally triadic) statements. But this revelation is grounded in an eternal intention. Therefore the Son can be presented as pre-existent (John 1:1ff.; 3:13; 8:58, and other passages; Rom. 8:3; 1 Cor. 8:6; Gal. 4:4; Phil. 2:5f.; Col. 1:15ff.; Heb. 1:1ff.). See on this pre-existence par. 32, p. 289. In the same way the Spirit can be presented as pre-existent (in the farewell discourses in John 14:16; 15:26, and 16:7, and in Paul in 1 Cor. 2:10ff.). Cf. the line of thinking of the NT scholar W. Thüsing on these pre-existences, in K. Rahner-W. Thüsing, *Christologie—systematisch und exegetisch* (1972), pp. 249–273. He sees the Spirit as the most specific indication of the power of God, with a tendency toward speaking of a "binity" instead of a Trinity in the NT, and he states: "Consistently elaborating on Paul's theology leads to the conclusion that Jesus' pre-existence is in reality that of the Spirit (as the power of God seeking to communicate itself), because the possession of the Spirit is what constitutes Jesus' uniqueness. The Johannine logos (that is revelational) Christology may be a parallel to that" (p. 250). A fine illustration of this is the story of the baptism of Jesus in the Jordan (Mark 1:9–11), which is pictured as a trinitarian event: the Spirit (together with the Word, the voice) links the Father on high with the obedient Son below. As we see it, the NT witnesses to God's saving association with us in Christ and the Spirit, and it traces both types of association back to eternity, without transforming this insight into a doctrine of an ontological Trinity (with the exception of the much later gloss, 1 John 5:7).

The trinitarian controversy is described at great length in many dogmatics handbooks, monographs, and encyclopedias. Here we assume the reader's acquaintance with it. It should not be forgotten that this controversy was not an independent theme, but the sequel to and consequence of the christological dispute. As Christ was more and more identified with God (see par. 33), it became necessary to speak of a two-ness in God. (An analogous consideration of the Spirit did not arise until the middle of the 4th century.) That, however, resulted in a conflict with biblical monotheism (the *monarchia* of God), which appealed so strongly to the Hellenistic world, to the one side, and the clear fact that in the gospels Christ subordinates himself to God, to the other. Eventually the "solution" was found in making the distance between the revelational Trinity in history and the Trinity of essence in eternity as great as possible. On earth Christ can proceed from the Spirit and be subordinate to the Father, but in eternity the Son is "of one substance with the Father" (*homoousios tōi patri,* since the Council of Nicea, A.D. 325; D 125) and does not proceed from the Spirit, but the Spirit from the Father (Eastern church) or from the Father *and* the Son (Western church; the "filioque" controversy [see below]).

This solution led of course to a new problem: how can one conceive of God as one-and-yet-three? The formula "three persons in one essence" did no more than cover up the problem, for the Greek *treis hypostaseis en miai ousiai* and the Latin *tres personae in una substantia* are not the same. See also M. Wiles, *The Making of the Christian Doctrine* (1967), pp. 124–140. For the sake of the unity of God, the uniqueness of the three persons which constitutes the revelational Trinity was as much as possible obliterated in the Trinity of essence. This attempt climaxed in three teachings: (1) the teaching of the *perichōrēsis* or *circum(in)cessio,* formulated by John of Damascus (ca. 745) in *De fide orthodoxa* I.8ff.: in eternity there is a continuous mutual interpenetration of the three persons; (2) the rule: *opera ad extra sunt indivisa,* for which the foundation was laid by Augustine in *De trinitate* I.4: that which in revelation is especially ascribed to one person (creation to the Father, reconciliation to the Son, appropriation to the Spirit) is nevertheless the work of all three together; (3) the doctrine of the *appropriationes,* the reverse side of the preceding: the ascription of a certain work to one specific person is meant figuratively, as *appropriatio* to our minds (since Augustine and Leo I; see Barth, *CD* I,1, pp. 428f.). The effect of these teachings was that the Trinity of essence really had nothing to do anymore with the revelational Trinity. How large the gap had become is best realized when one looks at the first half of the so-called Athanasian Creed, also called *Symbolum quicumque* (6th or 7th century; D 75). This dry summary of trinitarian dogma has been elevated to ecclesiastical confession and as such remains valid in many churches, also Protestant. This is most regrettable because this statement totally ignores the revelational Trinity and does not connect the redemption of sinners (it begins with: "*Quicumque vult salvus esse . . .*") with the history of salvation, but hangs it on an abstract eternity.

If the signs do not deceive, a solution to the centuries-old "filioque controversy" appears in sight (see above) owing to discussions in Faith and Order; see Paper No. 103, *Spirit of God—Spirit of Christ* (1981). Cf. J. Moltmann, *Trinität und Reich Gottes* (1980), ch. V, par. 4, who on the basis of the discussions proposes: ". . . the Holy Spirit, who proceeds from the Father of the Son" (p. 201). But so long as there is a failure to profess the procession of the Son from the Spirit of the Father, the bond with the interaction within the economy of salvation has not been effected, and the abstract eternity of the formula has not been cut through. See also from the Roman Catholic side Y. Congar, *Je crois en l'esprit Saint,* III (1980), pp. 266–278, with the proposal to declare, as a continuation of the Council of Florence, the *filioque* and the *per filium* as being complementary.

The result of this doctrinal development has been that the trinitarian confession does not function in the faith of the church. K. Rahner notes correctly (in *MS* II, pp. 319f.—see all of pp. 318–347) "that the Christians, despite their orthodox confession on the trinity, are in their actual religious life almost pure 'monotheists.' Therefore one may dare to assert that if the trinitarian dogma were to be thrown out as false, this cut notwithstanding, the bulk of religious literature could remain unchanged." And P. Kohnstamm writes in *De heilige* (1931), p. 26: "Not only that the suspicion of tri-theism has made the way to the church unnecessarily difficult for me—and no doubt I share this difficulty with thousands of others in our time—but even as a member of the church I have for many years understood nothing of what is nevertheless regarded as its central dogma."

However, there have been other voices, too. In Irenaeus e.g. the revelational Trinity is central and we come across striking formulations such as (in connection with Isa. 61:1): "pointing out both the anointing Father, the anointed Son, and the unction, which is the Spirit" *(AH* III.18.3); that the saved "advance through steps of this nature; also that they ascend through the Spirit to the Son, and through the Son to the Father" (V.36.2); or still more "theocentric": "the Spirit truly preparing man in the Son of God, and the Son leading him to the Father, while the Father, too, confers [upon him] incorruption for eternal life, which comes to everyone from the fact of his seeing God" (IV.20.5). Particularly Marcellus of Ancyra (middle 4th century) tried to avert the disconnection of the revelational and the ontological Trinity, with his bold but speedily condemned doctrine of the three activities *(energeiai oikonomiai)* of God in creation, incarnation, and outpouring of the Spirit, in which God is extending himself *(platynesthai)*—which, however, is in its turn negated in the consummation. (Thus for Marcellus, too, eternity and time remained separate worlds.) And Augustine, whose great essay *De trinitate* did so much for the further abstraction of the doctrine of the Trinity, nevertheless tried to make this doctrine helpful for the confession that God is love, by representing the three persons as relationships: the Father who loves, the Son who is being loved, and the Spirit who is love itself *(De trin.* VIII and IX).

With the Reformation a much stronger counter-movement announced itself. This was not surprising, since it aimed at a radical restructuring of church dogma in a pastoral and personal direction. For the doctrine of the Trinity this meant a turn in an anti-speculative direction that stressed the economic Trinity. In the first edition of his *Loci communes,* Melanchthon expressed himself strongly against the hair-splitting distinctions in the traditional dogma of the Trinity. But later he spoke again the language of the traditional view and Scholasticism. In general, Luther and Calvin did not attack the tradition on this point; yet their heart was not in it. Having considered the relation of Father and Son in the work of redemption, Calvin continues: "This practical knowledge is doubtless more certain and firmer than any idle speculation" (*Inst* I,xiii,13). And when Caroli, a minister in Lausanne, in 1537 demanded the signing of the three creeds of the early church, Calvin refused; according to him this was a legalistic and traditionalistic demand, and he criticized the Nicene Creed on account of its overly repetitious language (*battologia*). But this did not lead the Reformers to a radical criticism and revision, since they felt they had other, more important issues to deal with. See J. Koopmans, *Het oudkerkelijk dogma in de reformatie, bepaaldelijk bij Calvijn* (1938). The result was that, since the middle of the 16th century, in Protestant Scholasticism the former hair-splitting distinctions about one-and-yet-three and three-and-yet-one could regain their earlier position in dogmatics.

A remarkable counterpole to that was the anti-trinitarianism or Unitarianism which flourished about 1600 in Poland and Zevenburgen. Its criticism of the person concept in the trinitarian dogma (as leading to tri-theism) was to the point, yet too rationalistically inspired and limited, and hence too negative to make a contribution toward renewal of the doctrine.

Not until the 19th century can one speak of a turn toward giving priority to the revelational Trinity, and even then hesitantly and partially. Only a few followed with the same intensity the bold innovation of Schleiermacher. He ends his *CF* with a brief chapter bearing the characteristic title: "Conclusion. The Divine Trinity" (pars. 170–172). The thesis of par. 170 is: "All that is essential in this second part of our exposition is also posited in what is essential in the doctrine of the Trinity; but this doctrine itself, as ecclesiastically framed, is not an immediate utterance concerning the Christian self-consciousness, but only a combination of several such utterances." In other words, Schleiermacher recognizes a revelational Trinity, but regards the doctrine of the ontological Trinity as a rationalizing extrapolation which transgresses the boundaries of our religious field of knowledge; we know nothing "of an eternal distinction within the supreme being." After this the final paragraph comes as a surprise: "We have the less reason to regard this doctrine as finally settled since it did not receive any fresh treatment when the Evangelical (Protestant) Church was set up; and so there must still be in store for it a transformation which will go back to its very beginnings." Schleiermacher regards his rejection of the immanent Trinity as a preliminary step, as a waiting for a better opportunity from the vantage point of the NT statements concerning Christ and the Spirit.

Later, the positive and negative aspects of Schleiermacher were alternately followed. Modern theology has always leaned toward the second aspect, except where in the wake of Hegel it interpreted the Trinity in philosophical-Idealistic terms. Confessional theology maintained traditional trinitarianism. Other schools began to search in the direction that was hesitantly shown by Schleiermacher. As concerns the European continent, we think in this respect of the *Vermittlungstheologie* (mediating theology), the ethical theologians, the school of Ritschl. The combination of the biblical witness and German-Idealistic thinking led to all sorts of attempts to develop the ontological Trinity from the perspective of the personality of God, self-consciousness, the idea of love, and the like. Anglican trinitarian thinking of that period, and Anglo-Saxon theology in general, owing to its tendency toward Empiricism, exhibits a firm attachment to the revelational Trinity and an inclination toward tri-theistic formulations. See L. Hodgson, *The Doctrine of the Trinity* (1943), and A. M. Ramsay, *From Gore to Temple*, Appendixes C and D. Even more important is F. D. Maurice who from being a unitarian turned trinitarian and was bold enough to combine the unity of God with the element of subordination. In his view the self-surrender (sacrifice) and subjection belong to the eternal essence of God himself: "What He was on earth must be the explanation of what He is. . . . If the idea of subordination in the Son to the Father . . . is once lost sight of or considered an idle and unimportant school tenet, the morality of the Gospel and its divinity disappear together" (*Theological Essays*, 1853, 1957 ed., p. 78).

In the 20th century, under the influence of dialectic theology, there was a resurgence of interest in classical thinking on the ontological Trinity. But rightly one could not and would not go back (prior to Schleiermacher's starting-point) to the revelational Trinity. Characteristic is Brunner's position: he derives the knowledge of the ontological Trinity from the fact that revelation is a Person-person encounter; for this to be a real encounter with God himself, it is necessary that in Christ and in the Spirit we meet God himself in Person, and that there thus be an "identity of the Revealer with the one who is revealed"—which for Brunner does not exclude but includes critique of the classical doctrine (*Dg* I, ch. 16). Close to Brunner is K. Rahner in his earlier-mentioned study, in *MS* ch. V, in which he sees the ontological Trinity as grounded in God's absolute determination to communicate himself (as truth and love) and to effect himself the acceptance of that communication.

Barth and his school led the way in an even more forceful and bold attempt to restore the unity of the revelational and ontological Trinity. This is not so much the case yet of the intentional treatment he devotes to the Trinity in *CD* I,1, pars. 8–12, although already there he looks for the roots of the doctrine of the Trinity in the fact that "God reveals himself as Lord" (p. 352). That approach is particularly followed in *CD* IV,1, par. 59,1, where Barth regards Christ's self-humiliation as the Son as expressive of the fact "that in God himself there is an above and a below, a *prius* and a *posterius*, a superior as well as one who is subordinate"; see esp. pp. 192–197, with the Spirit constituting the mediation and union of this above and below; see *CD* IV,2, pp. 330–348. G. C. Berkouwer, in *The Triumph of Grace in the Theology of Karl Barth* (E.T. 1956), ch. XI, regards this as a trespassing of what faith can know in the direction of Theopaschitism. Yet in Germany three great theologians have gone further in this direction: W. Pannenberg in and after *Grundzüge der Christologie* (1964), esp. par. 9; J. Moltmann in *The Crucified God* (E.T. 1974), esp. ch. VI,5, and in *Trinität und Reich Gottes* (1980), esp. ch. V; and E. Jüngel in *God as the Mystery of the World*, pars. 22–25. For all of them the Trinity is the description of a history within and of God himself, with the cross as the center. Hence Hegel with his divine triad is their point of orientation. If the doctrine of the Trinity is not viewed as arising out of the covenant association between God and humankind, one can only regard it as a divine *Inter Nos*.

Even as for centuries a static ontological Trinity was kept far removed from the revelational Trinity, in order that in the spirit of Aristotle God might remain the unmoved first mover, so now there exists the inclination to make the ontological Trinity coincide with the revelational Trinity in such a way that, in the spirit of Hegel, the process of humiliation and exaltation takes place in God himself. As we see it, this is more a speculative way out of the problems handed to us by the trinitarian tradition than a solution which agrees with the covenantal structure of the Christian faith. For also in the modern conception the Trinity remains the description of a relationship solely within God, of a God without people—because in these theologies Christ does not function as the human covenant partner, but as the anhypostatic second person of the divine being. In its NT form, however, the structure of the Trinity describes precisely the fellowship with man, for which God emerges out of himself. We need to return to that intention. We may not let ourselves be held back from it by a tradition, imposing though it may be, which is artificial and in its abstractness dangerous to the faith. See also the related problematic in par. 23, end, small type.

The New Community

39. THE COVENANT AS COMMUNITY

SPEAKING OF COVENANT we speak of community. In that community we are as individuals joined both to God and to other people. Therefore on the way of Israel we find from the outset a covenant community. It is wrong to say that in Israel this *still* coincided with the national community. Precisely its covenant with God made Israel into a nation. It was a conglomeration of nomadic tribes whose center of unity was the dedication to the same God in whom, on the basis of his liberating acts, they put their trust. In paragraph 30 we spoke extensively about the permanent crisis which engulfed this covenant community. "Israel" shrank into a remnant; it became a normative and after that almost an eschatological concept. The coming of Jesus caused such a turn in this crisis that the people of God split in two. As a result the greater part of Israel came to stand over against what we call the church, the community consisting of a very small part of Israel, together with believers from all nations, which follows the way of Christ. About this division in the people of God we spoke at the end of paragraph 31. Here, at the beginning of the doctrine of the church, we need to recall that so as to be able to see the church in the proper perspective. The church is not the only form of God's people. God's faithfulness also watches over Israel. Its extraordinary way of persecution and continuing existence, of exile and return, of destruction and liberation puts us in touch with God's faithfulness in yet an entirely different form. Without reunion with this Israel no one church can appropriate to itself the great marks of unity, holiness, and catholicity. The division in the people of God proves that we are still on the way. This does not mean that it matters little or nothing which part of this people we would want to join. If Jesus is the Son of God, the covenant comes to stand in a new light and we may speak of a partial fulfillment of it, which lends a different character to the entire covenant community. On account of the fulfillment, we may joyfully speak of a new community which is being born out of the way of Christ and the working of the Spirit. Since this fulfillment is only partial (many aspects of ecclesiastical life will show it), our joy must remain tempered by our awareness of guilt and by expectation, and all "triumphalism" is cut off at the root.

It has been suggested that Israel's uniqueness as a covenant people is expressed in the word *'am*, while the word *gôy* would refer to non-Israelite, profane nations. In view of Gen. 12:2; Ex. 19:6, and 33:13 this division is untenable, however. The same holds for the NT translation of both words (*laos, ethnos*); see John 11:50 and 1 Pet. 2:9.

In the NT the church is regarded as the true, obedient Israel, because it chooses for Christ. Thereby the writers have in mind a community consisting of believers out of Israel and the nations. That during those years of separation one would continue to regard the other part of Israel as the people of God is unlikely and cannot be proven from the NT. Yet without hesitation the evangelists continue to apply the OT word to Israel. And in Rom. 11:11–32 Paul comes very close to the conception of a twofold people of God. Ecclesiology has never reckoned with the polar relationship of church and Israel. A beginning is made by Barth, esp. *CD* IV,3, pp. 876–878, and H. Küng, *The Church* (E.T. 1968), pp. 132–150; and even more H.-J. Kraus, *Systematische Theologie* (1983), pars. 196ff. Theology, too, should be much more aware that in countries which leave no room for Israel to be herself (Hitler-Germany, Russia), the church does not get the chance to be herself either.

We noted in paragraph 37 that when we say Spirit we say participation, but also that this can be thought of in more than one way. It could consist in an immediate and direct association of the Spirit with individuals. This is all the more conceivable because faith is an intensely private matter: the peace-bringing encounter of God and man as the foundation of a new life. There are, however, no individuals if by that we mean isolated individuals, completely detached from each other. What does exist, however, is persons, people who realize their humanity in the encounter with others. Humanness is always fellow-humanness. Already for that reason people can fully experience their participation in the covenant event only as incorporation into a community in which they support and mutually enrich each other. A great deal has been written, from all kinds of perspectives, about the relationship of person and community. The conclusion is always that they presuppose and need each other. As regards this mutuality, the emphases may be quite varied in different cultures, periods, institutions, phases, and political systems—which, however, as a rule sooner or later leads to reactions. It would be strange if this polarity and tension, which one finds everywhere in the human world, would not occur in the participative work of the Spirit. Such is demonstratively not the case either—witness church history up to the present day.

This means that that we can either deal first with the individual believer and then with the church, or take the second first. We choose for the latter. Considering what we have said so far, there is no cogent and principial proof for this procedure. Yet there are a number of other weighty and compelling considerations. In the doctrine of God we noticed that God does not want to be all by himself, but seeks fellowship with and wants to be enriched by his creatures (paragraphs 19–23. Jesus invited his followers into his fellowship and therewith to the fellowship with each other. The great commandment points us simultaneously to God and to the neighbor as God's representative for us. The exercise of our faith normally takes place in a communal center: Sunday observance, discussion groups, mutual pastoral care, diaconal help, instruction in the faith. Personal faith, too, is as a rule born out of contacts with others, in nurture, conversation, literature, proclamation, or missions, so that from the start it is oriented to a faith community. Later we shall find still more arguments which prove how determinative this community dimension is for all God's work. Here we wish to point to one more very practical motive for taking up the church before the individual: in the Protestant study of the faith the opposite has usually been done, with the result that community awareness in the Protestant churches is underdeveloped compared to that in the New Testament. For putting the individual first threatens to make of the church, which is discussed afterwards, entirely or mainly an aggregate of individuals and a product of personal faith; while the reverse, the fact that personal faith is a product of the community, then finds it hard to get a hearing.

The interdependence of person and community and the tensions inherent in it, which can lead to different types of life and society, are so much a part of our humanity that it will not do to find a purely theological solution for the ecclesiological problems in this area. Tribal religions are collective, Hinduism and Buddhism individualistic, the ancient religions often primarily nationalistic, etc. Phenomenologically one can perhaps say that the Abrahamitic religions combine a strong emphasis on the individual with a strong sense of community. Both in the OT and in European history influenced by the Christian faith, we observe an increasing individualization, which, however, leads to ever-new attempts to maintain and to renew the community. This could not be otherwise, because implicit in the Christian faith is a conception of personhood (both of God and man) which sees it as a seeking of fellowship.

In the earliest creeds the confession of the Spirit is followed immediately by that of the church and preceded by that of the individual. In the Roman Catholic Church the Spirit, according to a frequently cited word from Augustine, is the soul of the body of Christ, the church (*Sermo* 267,4); the church is then the avenue by which the individual shares in the Spirit. Accordingly, for centuries personal faith was thought of entirely as a *sentire cum ecclesia*. Changes are now in the wind due to the new emphasis on the church as the people of God. The strongly individualistic mood that arose since the 16th century contributed to the formation of an opposite type of church—the free churches—in which the community is seen solely as the fruit and support of personal faith. To this church type ought to be reckoned the Anabaptists, Baptists, Quakers, Remonstrants,

Congregationalists, and later also the Liberal churches. There the Spirit is in principle directly present with the individual, and the church is a human product of this personal work of the Spirit. The churches of the Reformation were born on the borderline between the Middle Ages and the modern period. Up to the present time the theology of these churches bears traces of that. In Luther one can find lines of thoughts that point in a pronouncedly individualistic direction. Calvin consciously puts the relationship of the Spirit to the individual first (*Inst* III). The title of *Inst* IV is: "The external means or aids by which God invites us into the society of Christ and holds us therein." That seems to prove that the church is secondary to the individual. But already the first chapter breathes a different spirit, as is shown by its heading: "The true church with which as mother of all the godly we must keep unity." Calvin speaks in strong terms about this motherhood of the church (i,4); but at the same time the church is said to be an outward help, necessary because of our ignorance, sloth, and fickleness of disposition (i,1). This going back and forth has to do with the fact that the Reformed conception of the church is the daughter of the Roman Catholic type and the mother of the free-church type. Most systematic theologies follow Calvin in moving from the individual person to the community, including Barth (*CD* IV,1, 2, 3) and O. Weber. But there are not a few exceptions in Reformed theology in which the church comes first: John Owen, *Pneumatologia* (1674); W. à Brakel, *Redelijke Godsdienst* (1700); A. Kuyper, *The Work of the Holy Spirit* (E.T. 1900); Brunner, *Dg* III. Lutheran theology shows the same picture: in Althaus the church comes first, in Prenter the individual, while Trillhaas goes so far as to treat the visible church as an Epilegomenon (*Dg* chs. 30–33). From the conviction "that the individual human being emerges by way of communion" (p. 7), the American Presbyterian J. Haroutunian in *God with Us: A Theology of Transpersonal Life* (1965) argues strongly, though with some exaggeration, for the priority of the community in the Christian faith.

By addressing ourselves first to the new community which the Spirit brings into existence before taking up the renewal of personal life, we do not suggest in the least that we regard the latter as a by-product of the former. It is not its by-product, but its fruit. If with a term still used by Calvin but no longer current with us, we call the church our "mother," we stress that the importance of the church lies in that which she brings forth: personal faith. The covenantal encounter becomes reality only in the individual person. In a sense the person may be called the end of all God's ways with the world. Precisely because he is the real concern, he will have to be discussed last, after the community which leads him to Christ. Speaking first about that community, we can then give due consideration to the person. The other way around is much harder. If we should begin by describing the renewal of the individual, more or less detached from the community, it becomes difficult to assign the supra-personal and institutional aspects of that community their organic slot. That, too, is for us an important argument for choosing this order. In our opinion this, better than the reverse, reflects the way of the Spirit in his work of incorporation and participation.

The interposition of the community between Christ and the individual gives us a clear focus on the *mediating* function of the church, and that is part of its twofold character. Mediation means that the church comes from somewhere and goes somewhere, in order to link the beginning and the end. She must bridge the gap between Christ and man. Her first task is thus to confront man with Christ; she must be a place, a space, a home where man is welcomed and led to Christ, where he is nourished, shaped, and renewed. But the consequence of that is that in this house there begins to grow a community of the renewed, people who have become mature through the gracious gifts (*charismata*) with which the Spirit equips them and which he wants them to use for the upbuilding of the community (which is another indication how much the individual depends on the community and only through it becomes himself. The church thus has two faces: she is institute *and* community, fertile soil *and* plant, mother *and* family. And these two are not related in an artificial equilibrium, but so that the first is the foundation and the root of the second and the second is the purpose and fruit of the first—while the second works itself out in a continual renewal of the individual. The relationship in which we stand to the church is twofold: we are in the church, we belong to the church—and together we ourselves make up the church. The second rests on the first; the first misses its goal without the second.

A favorite attempt to clarify the essence of the church is that in terms of the etymology of *ekklēsia*. The word is derived from *ek* and *kaleō* and denotes the assembly of free citizens in the Greek city-states who through a herald were "called out" of their homes to the marketplace. In ordinary usage the word denoted "the people as assembled," "the public meeting." In the Septuagint it is used almost everywhere as the translation of *qāhāl* (also because it sounds somewhat the same?), the "assembly of the Lord" in the OT. Another translation of *qāhāl* is *synagōgē*, which in the dispersion became the name for the Jewish house of worship. Very early already the Hellenistic churches applied the first translation to their gatherings and therewith to their community in general, both local and universal. For them the word connoted in particular that they were the community which in the line of the OT is being gathered by God around his covenantal acts. See *TDNT* III, *s.v. kaleō*, and *MS* IV 1, pp. 38f., 153ff. Brunner's conception, *Dg* III, p. 32, that in *ekklēsia* in the NT the idea of *klēsis*, in the sense of calling to serve the world, is central, lacks all foundation.

This is the place for a brief digression on two common translations of *ekklēsia*: "church" and "congregation." One who thinks especially of the first aspect we mentioned, the place or the institute, will prefer the word "church." In Roman Catholicism this is almost the exclusive designation. Luther started out with a preference for the word *Gemein(d)e*. In the Reformed churches both terms are alternately used, depending on whether one wishes to emphasize the first or the second aspect. The free churches have a marked preference for "congregation," and often choose other designations as well, such as "brotherhood," "bond," or "union." The theology of around 1900 clearly preferred "congregation." The reaction against individualism after the First World War led to a new appreciation of the name "church," especially in dialectical theology. Later Barth came back to the term "congregation." This is the more popular term wherever there is little appreciation for the institutional aspect, as is the case today, when the church is approached primarily in terms of personalistic or sociological categories. We shall use both words interchangeably, while preferably employing "church" when we speak very much in general or deal with the supra-personal and instititional dimension.

Though in our century the number of books about the church is legion, comprehensive discussions of the church are fairly rare. Some important monographs from the Anglican perspective are A. M. Ramsay, *The Gospel and the Catholic Church* (1936), and L. S. Thornton, *The Common Life in the Body of Christ* (1943). From the Lutherans there is E. Kinder, *Der evangelische Glaube und die Kirche* (1958). From the Reformed have come T. F. Torrance, *Royal Priesthood* (1955), and G. C. Berkouwer, *The Church* (E.T. 1976); and as the result of ecumenical cooperation the Faith and Order report *One Lord, One Baptism* (1960), the first part of which is entitled "The Divine Trinity and the Unity of the Church" (pp. 7–44). The Roman Catholic theologian Küng wrote *The Church,* and *MS* IV 1 and 2 (1972, 1973). Küng's book, more than the others, deserves to become the point of orientation for continued ecclesiological reflection on account of its biblical, critical, comprehensive, and ecumenical nature. A Protestant counterpart, and a book with a strong emphasis on the relationship with the world, is that of J. Moltmann, *Kirche in der Kraft des Geistes* (1975).

All these publications are the fruit of a predominant a priori-dogmatic approach (proceeding from "the essence of the church," often using one of the four marks: one, holy, catholic, and apostolic), or of a more biblical-theological and redemptive-historical way of looking at the church. Meanwhile a predominantly sociological approach to the problem of the church is gaining ground. Because of its nature it will not soon lead to comprehensive designs. Eventually, however, it will have to be incorporated into a systematic ecclesiology as a dimension in its own right. For the weakness of ecclesiology until now has been its fairly strong "docetic" and consequently sometimes "triumphalistic" nature. High-sounding statements are made about the church, but without taking the trouble to connect these with the oftentimes quite different empirical reality. At present the dogmatic and sociological approach are still very uneasy with each other. In this chapter we want to reckon as well as we can with sociology and its critique; but what we can do is limited, also because the sociology of the church is still in its infancy and the necessary interdisciplinary thinking has only begun. See P. de Haas, *The Church as an Institution* (1972).

Yet it is not enough to ascertain this twofold character of the church. Broadly speaking, for centuries the institutional aspect has dominated. Only through the Reformation, and even more in the free churches, has the community aspect evolved. After that yet a third aspect began to evolve in the life and in the reflection of the church, first through Europe's colonial expansion and afterwards through the secularization in Europe—the orientation to the world. The church is after all the mediating movement between Christ and his people. The final goal of the church cannot possibly be the individual believer. God wants a whole humanity for himself. In the movement of the Spirit to the world, the church as the provisional terminal is at the same time a new starting-point. Christ is the firstfruits, with a view to the harvest of the church. And that harvest is in turn a firstfruits in its relation to all mankind. The church thus stands between Christ and the world, being as it were equally related to both. We should thus not speak of a twofold but of a threefold character of the church. Only in the successive combination of institute, community, and apostolate does the church as the movement of the Spirit become visible in its full scope and directedness. This suggests the further division of the chapter on the new community: first the church as institute (paragraph 40), next the congregation of Christ as a body (paragraph 41), finally the people of God as firstfruits (paragraph 42).

Only after the Second World War has this third aspect received the necessary attention. A torrent of studies on this subject broke loose. Under the inspiration of H. Kraemer, the Netherlands became a leader in this. Especially J. C. Hoekendijk has penetratingly studied this aspect and so has had a great influence in ecumenical circles and theology. The two reports of the World Council of Churches, *The Church for Others* and *The Church for the World* (1967), became the well-known articulation of this concern.

In this light it is remarkable that the great monographs on the church show little or no awareness of this aspect; also in Küng's monumental work it remains limited to the Epilogue. Apparently much of the study of the faith is still done from the standpoint of an introvert-ecclesiastical situation. The great exception here is Barth, who in *CD* IV,1 discusses the church as instituted by God, in IV,2 as a community of people, and in IV,3 from the perspectives of calling, mission, mandate, and service. Thus far Barth's ecclesiology has not been equalled, also on account of its structure and division, which we find so convincing that we follow it here in our own division.

40. THE CHURCH AS INSTITUTE

FOR MANY CENTURIES the study of the faith started this theme on a high note, in the spirit of: the church is the God-established, Christ-directed, and Spirit-animated institute of salvation. It was conveniently overlooked that "church" refers to many different communities and "institute" to many different organizations. It did not take long before reflection on the church was far removed from everyday reality where the ecclesiastical institutes are found. We do well therefore to begin from that empirical reality. Then the beginning must look something like this: the Christian churches are forms of organization that belong to the genre of the institutes. Like all institutes, their right to existence is based on the interpersonal activities they bring about and maintain. The uniqueness of the churches lies in the nature of those activities. That nature can be described from the perspective of their origin as well as from their goal. Seen from the vantage point of origin, those activities aim to extend through time and space that which has once taken place in history, in Israel, and in Christ. Seen from the standpoint of goal, those activities aim at the renewal of people by means of that history, by bringing them into a relationship with God and Christ and so into a new relationship with each other, to life, and to the world. The concern of this institute is thus participation in the covenantal event, which in paragraph 37 we came to know as the work of the Spirit.

What are the activities which make such participation possible, which are as it were "mediating"? It is clear that such a general question also evokes a general answer. If one were to ask different believers which activities were or are mediating for the origination or building up of their faith, he could expect a wide variety of answers, such as the reading of certain books, the singing of certain hymns, participation in certain groups, and contact with certain persons. The Spirit blows where he wills and the participation is as varied as life itself. Many of these means to pass on the faith are not institutionalized, nor are they susceptible of it. A closer look will usually show, however, that the incidental means, regular or irregular, are also in one way or another linked to and fed by other means of a more constant and institutional character (for example: the songs are found in an ecclesiastical hymnal, the books are written by leading churchmen or other members of the church). In the study of the faith we search for the enduring and institutionalizable means of transmission that are essential to the ecclesiastical communities. Protestant dogmatics usually distinguishes three: the sermon, baptism, and the Lord's Supper. In our opinion these should be augmented by instruction in the faith, religious discussion, and the diaconal task or the ministry of Christian mercy as intentional and indispensable media of transmission. These elements are partly embedded in and partly supported by the regular gatherings of the congregation in the worship services, in which other elements, intentionally or unintentionally, also have a mediating character (confession of sin, proclamation of pardon, song, prayer). To make all these activities happen, people are necessary who hold particular offices. And they, with their functions and responsibilities, together with the whole community, must operate within a clearly defined set of agreements which we call a church order. So we arrive at nine elements that are essential to the church as transmission institute, seven of which are themselves transmission instruments, while the last two are intended to facilitate the work of the instruments of transmission, and for that reason are closely and necessarily linked to them. We thus come to a total of nine institutional elements: instruction, baptism, sermon, discussion, Lord's

Supper, diaconate, worship service, office, and church order. We shall now take them up in this order, though sometimes under different names.

The problematic we deal with here has through the centuries had an important focal point in the word and concept of sacrament, a term under which several means of transmission are customarily subsumed. The ecclesiastical history of this word is complex, has often been described, and is of little importance for our purpose. A good survey can be found in J. Plooy, *De mysterie-leer van Odo Casel* (1964), pp. 161–169, and *MS* IV 2, pp. 70–93. *Sacramentum* was taken to be the translation of the NT word *mystērion* and was used for many elements in the faith and the ritual acts of the church. Already Tertullian employed it as his favorite term for baptism, and eventually it came to be used only for what we now call sacraments. But for a long time, actually up to the present, their number has remained uncertain and controversial. In the early Middle Ages one counted five, seven, nine, twelve, or thirty sacraments. Since the 13th century their number is said to be the sacred number of seven. The Eastern church went along with this (Council of Lyons, 1274; D 860). See further D 1310, 1601, 1864, 2536. Since then the Roman Catholic Church has the following sacraments: baptism, confirmation, eucharist, penance, extreme unction, priestly orders, and marriage. These have in common that they all have a basis in matter or quasi-matter which signifies the substance which they carry, namely sanctifying grace. Despite their fairly large number—to which other rites could be added which were called *sacramentalia*—there is clearly a narrowing of the mediation of grace here. It is conceived of as being "material." Nonmaterial forms of transmission such as the sermon were not part of it and consequently were minimized. This vision, born in the climate of the mystery religions of the first centuries and structured with Aristotelian categories, has remained dominant in the Roman Catholic Church until today. There is now a tendency, however, to view the sacraments more as fruit of the incarnation or as functions of the church as the "ur-sacrament," and to interpret them much more in an encounter framework, thus less substantialistically and more personalistically. See E. Schillebeeckx, *Christ: The Sacrament of the Encounter with God* (E.T. 1963), and K. Rahner, *Church and Sacrament* (E.T. 1974).

The Reformation, due to its personalistic conception of salvation, could do little with the traditional doctrine of the sacraments. It based itself on an experience from the later Middle Ages (the preaching by the mendicant orders), when the proclamation was found to be the central means of transmission. It could as a result have added the sermon to the series as the eighth sacrament. But such was not done. Instead, two other decisions were made. The seven sacraments were reduced to the two which were clearly instituted by Christ, baptism (Matt. 28:19) and the Lord's Supper (1 Cor. 11:23–26). And the sermon was put beside and above the sacraments as a separate means of grace. Therewith the narrowing of the concept of sacrament was not abolished, but precisely confirmed. That objection does not hold for Zwingli (who rejected the concept of sacrament altogether) and hardly for the Lutheran tradition (which used it only sparingly), but very much for Calvin and the Reformed tradition. As much as possible Calvin went back to the church fathers and in particular to Augustine. He did that also on this point and with it he took over some of Augustine's Platonic ideas. The material sacrament is of lesser importance than the spiritual word. See especially *Inst* IV,xiv,3: the promise given in the word does not need such an outward appendix; it is added because of our ignorance, dullness, and weakness; for we are creatures who always creep on the ground and cleave to the flesh. In the same spirit, the Belgic Confession in art. 33 says of the sacraments that God gave them because of "our weakness and infirmities" so that by them he might "the better present to our senses both that which He declares to us by His word and that which He works inwardly in our hearts." There are thus three means of transmission, of which two are called "sacraments" and have a subordinate place.

In the free churches new forms of mediation were discovered, e.g. silence in Quakerism, the hymn in Methodism, and spiritual conversation in other groups. But even now no one thinks of labeling these as sacraments. The traditional sacraments, which were first central, then made secondary by the Reformation, now become marginal or fall away altogether, as with the Quakers and the Salvation Army.

We do well to break with the concept of sacrament. Having long ago lost its comprehensive significance, it combines and sets baptism and the Lord's Supper apart in a way which is not found in the NT (unless one tries to base it on a dogmatically extrapolative interpretation of 1 Cor. 10:2f. and 1 John 5:6–8). Therefore we will have to break with the classical and classically unequal Reformation triad of "word and sacraments." Their biblicistic foundation (instituted by Christ himself) is no longer a convincing argument due to the modern study of the Bible. In the great transmission process as it goes on in the history of the church under the guidance of the Spirit, new instruments regularly emerge that serve in a mediating capacity. This does not imply that the number of mediating forms may be endless. That which is to be transmitted is so specific that, whatever changes may occur in human history and culture, only a limited number of means will be suitable for use in transmission. In principle, however, the series as we have epitomized it should remain open.

One could ask why we have not included the Bible in this series. Is it not uniquely the transmission medium? Even as in Roman Catholic theology the church functions as the ur-sacrament, so in Protestant theology this designation could with equal right be given to the Bible. However, precisely as the Bible it can hardly be regarded as one in a whole series. Within the institutionalized series, the Bible is everywhere the book from which the media derive their content. And when the reading of the Bible is engaged in as an institutionalized activity, we are in the vicinity of the sermon or dialogue as media. Wherever a purely individual reading of the Bible leads people to believe (as often happens), the Bible functions outside the church as one of the noninstitutionalized means we mentioned earlier and which do not belong to the discussion of the church as institute. We discussed the Bible in par. 17; see also the consideration of the relationship of Word and Spirit in par. 12.

I. Instruction

We put this first because the means of grace accompany and shape a Spirit-originated and Spirit-guided process of incorporation, and in the sequence in which we consider these means we would like to reflect, insofar as this is possible, the order of that process. The birth of faith itself from the proclamation of Christ falls outside this process; it is its presupposition. We shall say something about that when we deal with the renewal of man. The church with her institutional means finds the new convert with his awakening or at least presumed faith on her way, and her task is to help this faith grow. Giving instruction in the faith is the first means (logically, but by no means always psychologically) by which the church receives the new convert and guides him along. Since this is done by the church as institute and the aim is the full church membership of that person, the relationship which is effected between the new convert and the church through that instruction is usually heavily emphasized. But the church is not goal but means here—something which holds for all the means of grace. The goal is sharing in Christ, incorporation into the covenant, and only for that reason and out of that fact the initiation into the church. The church is instrumental in involving the life of the disciple in Jesus' way of dying and rising again. She instructs him in the meaning of becoming conformed to his likeness, the likeness of his death and resurrection. This instruction can be done only in words. But these words point to the way of the Spirit and they can be the means by which the Spirit guides the new Christian on this way. This implies that ecclesiastical instruction ought to be something quite different from merely passing on information or an intellectual understanding of the faith, though of course it is based on information. Yet it is also something entirely different from proclamation. Principially, though, it begins with it even as it regularly issues in it. But proceeding from the grace proclaimed, the instruction relates this salvation to the totality of life. It spells out what faith, hope, and love are, what it means to die and rise with Christ, what we are to do with our guilt, what our attitude toward our death, our vocation, our fellow human beings, and the world around us must be, etc. So it leads man toward the decisive choice. Actually the term "instruction" smacks too much of pure intellectualism for this task of the church. We retain it because it has been the customary term for many years, but we prefer the unusual word *initiation.* This also implies that as institutional activity this work has its limits. As soon as the initiated person has made his choice and confirmed this by his profession of faith, instruction in this special sense ceases. As a believer, however, he remains a pupil all his life, but then so that he will come of age and can also pass on to others something of what he has received. The instructional aspect of the involvement of the church must therefore find its sequel in the conversation about spiritual matters, a subject which will be taken up under point 4.

From the very beginning instruction has been a fundamental element of the church's ministry of grace. Never, however, has it received the theoretical recognition to which its significance entitles it. Due to its verbal, nonmaterial character, it fell outside what was commonly understood by a sacrament. Yet the NT lacks all ground for this underestimation. The same text to which the church appeals for the sacramental character of baptism (Matt. 28:19) contains first of all the command to make disciples (*mathēteusate*) and after baptism the teaching-to-observe (*didaskontes autous tērein*). Note also the significance of words like *manthanein, didaskein,* and *didaskalos* in the NT. Jesus' ministry, as the gospels report it, was very much that of a teacher, as of a rabbi to his disciples. The importance of teaching is also evident from the technical terminology as this already begins to evolve in the NT: the originally very general term *katēchein,* meaning little more than "inform," is being used for the instructional situation (see perhaps Luke 1:4, and certainly Acts 18:25; 1 Cor. 14:19; Gal. 6:6). Already in 2 Clement 17:1 it has become an established term. One of the earliest non-canonical writings, the Didache, witnesses to the central place of catechetical instruction (esp. 1–6). For the place of catechesis in the history of the church see *RGG* III, *s.v. Katechetik.* The practice of infant baptism has had a great influence on the nature of the instruction, leading to a situation in which in practice it was mainly given to the under-age members of the church. As a result the element of information became the most prominent. With secularism on the rise this is changing again, a change abetted by the fact that the religious instruction in the schools has a predominantly informative character. This reopens the way toward a strictly ecclesiastical understanding of the instruction. This development, in turn, has, however, led to an understanding of catechesis as being especially an initiation into the *church* whereby to the one side the relationship to Christ and to the other the totality and complexity of life and the world were not sufficiently emphasized.

2. The washing

Here we deal with what is generally called "baptism." That appellation is likely here to stay, but it does not speak anymore. It suggests only an ecclesiastical ceremony, and one does not connect it with a word like "to dip in" or "immerse." (In "Baptist" circles this connection is, of course, more readily made than in churches practicing infant baptism.) Yet in its original New Testament use the word *baptismos* simply meant "immersion" or "washing." The ecclesiastical practice this word denoted was also called "washing" (*loutron*). We go back to that term, because it suggests both "immersion" and "washing" and is a reminder of the substance and purport of this ecclesiastical rite. The concern of this act has always been that of being received as a member of the community, communion with Christ as well as with his church. Almost from the beginning that reception was accompanied by the use of water. Everywhere and always water has meant two things to man: threat *and* refreshment. One can drown in water, and it can be used to quench one's thirst and for purification. Everywhere in the world religious practices are found in which water has this negative or positive function or both. Judaism in Jesus' day, too, had its washings for purification. But with John, who baptized in the Jordan River, the water received a more radical and comprehensive significance: man goes down in it to signify his lostness before God, and he rises up out of it as a sign of God's forgiveness. So man in repentance, forgiveness, and conversion is equipped for the great future to come. Jesus, too, had himself so immersed, and that hour became decisive for his whole life as it moved from the one immersion to the other. From Luke we have his certainly authentic statement: "I have to undergo an immersion, and how great is my distress until it is completed!" (Luke 12:50; cf. Mark 10:38f.). When it was at last fully accomplished, through his immersion into the death on the cross and his rising from the dead in the resurrection, this did not mean that his disciples could now abandon the water symbolism; on the contrary, only then did the double meaning of the water really begin to speak to them. For that reason John's water rite was continued, not only with an eye to the approaching future, but especially as a looking back to the great redemptive event that had taken place, with which believers are connected through this washing. He who by instruction has been initiated into the way of the covenant which issues in the death and resurrection of the new man Jesus, now receives in this water the incorporation into this double event of death and rising again. That incorporation has become the decision of the believer himself. He has himself baptized. But note: he *has* it done to him. He has something done to him, a new beginning which comes from God and into which he is received. He comes as one who is still an outsider, as one who is passive and to whom something is done. Only through and after this washing-event does his active life as a believer begin. Thus it is not for nothing that the images of creation and birth have again and again been used for this washing. It does not express the fullness of the Christian's path of faith, but only the beginning, which is entirely from God and which consists in the salvation that is prepared for us and without us. But it is a beginning which we can never leave fully behind. All the time we must fall back on it as the ground, the center, and the source of our whole life as believers. The water event at the beginning tells us that we live from a redemptive and creative act of God, from imputation and justification. What this involves will be further described in the following chapter.

Through the water that threatens and cleanses us we are bodily and forcefully taken up in the great turnabout of human existence, which happened when the true man voluntarily abandoned himself to the powers of darkness, so rescuing our human existence as it went through its greatest crisis. Rising up out of this water event, we become aware of having been placed on a new way on which we ourselves in dying and rising are being conformed to the image of the Son. And we also become aware that this is the opposite of a private way, "for by one Spirit we were all baptized into one body" (1 Corinthians 12:13). Being incorporated into Christ, we are at the same time incorporated into God's people, to share in its struggle for renewal. Preceding that way is, however, the incorporation through the washing with water. It is the opening of that way, the first encounter between God and the convert-believer within the framework of the covenant. Man stands there on the borderline between being and not yet being a believer. He is still entirely the object of drowning and being rescued. He goes here through the zero-point of his existence. Does this mean that faith is the constituent condition for baptism or absolutely not? The answer must be that in this washing of regeneration life is not made dependent on man's faith, but on Christ's substitution. However, only the awakened faith understands this and therefore can desire this washing. Is it therefore true that only he who consciously believes can go through this washing? However, exactly this washing speaks of a salvation which lays the foundation for faith and transcends faith. Partnership in the covenant is broader than this faith. It also embraces the children, the mentally handicapped, the demon-possessed, the despondent in slums and tenements. In the New Testament people are baptized because they belong to the family, and we even read of people who have themselves baptized for the benefit of those already deceased. In turn, the faith which rests in Christ's substitution can also act substitutionally in the covenantal relationship for those who do not yet or no longer believe. The entry gate to the covenant may not individualistically be narrowed. The encounter between God and man is beyond our intellectual grasp. In any case, according to the New Testament the children of believers are also involved in that covenant. But the gate may not collectivistically be made so wide that the relationship between washing and faith is broken. What is at stake is a genuine mutual encounter between God and man. The rule is that one consciously desires and submits to the washing. But beyond that there are all kinds of other possibilities. The church leaves room for that, provided it is clear that the believing community assumes responsibility for the support of the baptized infant and for its initiation according to its ability into the salvation for which faith is not a condition, but of which it is a fruit.

As little as has been written about instruction as a means of grace, so much has been written about baptism as the washing by which one is incorporated into the church. This is understandable. From the very beginning it was regarded as a sacrament, but because of its physical nature it gives rise to difficult questions, and these questions are made even more numerous by the practice of infant baptism.

As regards the name, *baptizein* as the intensive of *baptein* (immerse, dip in) has especially the negative meaning of: sink down, perish. In its literal meaning *baptein* occurs in the NT in Luke 16:24; John 13:26; Rev. 19:13. In its negative sense *baptizein* in used only twice in the NT, in a statement of Jesus (Mark 10:39; Luke 12:50); for the rest it always has a neutral connotation which is not often found in the Greek world: dip in or immerse in the sense of bathing or washing, particularly of ritual cleansings. That is also how Judaism of that time used it. In the NT *baptizesthai* thus denotes "to wash oneself" (middle) or "to be washed" (passive). Accordingly, the nouns *baptisma* and *baptismos* are to be translated as "cleansing" or "washing" (cf. Mark 7:4; Heb. 6:2; 9:10), with the original meaning of "immersion" always being presupposed. Therefore *apolouein* and *loutron* are used as parallels (Acts 22:16; 1 Cor. 6:11; Eph. 5:26; Tit. 3:5; Heb. 10:22). See *TDNT* I, *s.v. baptō* and IV, *s.v. louō*. Already in the NT *baptizein* is the technical term for the washing of initiation. When the mode of administration shrank to sprinkling, the use of *louein* and *loutron* died out.

Thus far there is no unanimity about the origin of this rite. The regular ritual washings in the Qumran monastery were of a different nature. On the other hand, proselyte baptism, which was administered only once, does resemble our baptism, but that, too, was a self-cleansing, and the earliest testimonies concerning it date from about 80 after Christ. Proselyte baptism could thus have arisen as a form of competition with Christian baptism. The real explanatory background of the latter is the rite of immersion in the Jordan River by John the Baptist; it was done only once, it signified repentance and forgiveness, and it gathered together the congregation which waited for the coming of God, when the baptism with the Spirit according to Joel 2:29 would replace the baptism with water.

Jesus saw his own baptism by John as referring to yet an entirely different baptism (Luke 12:50), for which reason he did not himself administer baptism (John 4:2; contra 3:22). The gospels give the impression that Jesus instituted baptism after his resurrection. But both texts, Matt. 28:19 and Mark 16:16, are so evidently the product of a later reflection that baptism, as a means of grace, cannot be based on a command from Christ. Nowadays the inclination is to base it on Jesus' baptism in the Jordan or on the nature of his saving work (Mark 10:38; Luke 12:50). One could, however, equally well conceive of the likelihood that the coming of the new age in Jesus' resurrection and the outpouring of the Spirit would have given the believers such an intense awareness of the eschatological baptism with fire that no room was left for a baptism with water. But apparently the course of events was different. The need was felt for expressing the experience of the Spirit in an act of immersion and rising up again. John's rite of repentance and forgiveness now took on a new glow and meaning for the early church. Because the Spirit does not exclude but includes the water, the institution of the baptismal washing could be attributed to Christ, for the Lord is now the Spirit.

Even so, the interest in the washing with water is rather marginal in the NT. Often that interest has been presented as much greater than it really is, by finding allusions everywhere to baptism, e.g. in John 3:5; 19:34f.; Tit. 3:5; 1 John 5:6–8, and in expressions like "being sealed," "enlighten," "anointing," "regeneration." Sometimes this is possible, more often it is unlikely, and almost always the text is susceptible of more than one interpretation. The fact remains that the number of passages that speak explicitly about baptism is relatively small. And to these passages belongs even 1 Cor. 1:14–17! That same Paul is the only one who has left to us something like a theology of baptism. Because Eph. 5:26 is an incidental remark and Gal. 3:27 and Col. 2:12 are no more than general references, the whole of Paul's baptismal theology must be found in Rom. 6:3–14. Here we learn what the washing with water means when it is submitted to not so much as anticipation of the eschaton, as in John, but primarily in reference to the accomplished saving work of Christ. Immersion and rising up out of the water are now not primarily linked to repentance and forgiveness, but are viewed as a participation in Jesus' death and burial and in his resurrection, as a sign that sin and death are now in principle behind us and that through grace we have been set free to fight against sin. Backward, Paul connects the washing very closely with the way of Christ, and forward with the way of a new life in his service. We find an example here of early Christian *paradosis*, possibly with the use of the language of the mystery religions (v. 3: *synetaphēmen;* v. 5: *symphytoi, homoiōmati*). Another start toward a theology of baptism is 1 Pet. 3:18–22, esp. 21; but the translation and interpretation is beset with so many difficulties that it is virtually impossible to use in our theology. In the larger type we have given our exposition of what is said in Rom. 6.

The history of the church has witnessed a great deal of discussion and controversy about baptism. This was partly due to infant baptism (see below). But that practice aggravated a typically Western problem (also) in relation to the so-called sacraments. Western thinking likes to operate with the subject-object scheme. As pertains to the washing with water the problem came to look like this: is this act as such the bearer and communicator of grace, apart from the faith of the person being baptized? Or does it derive its efficacy from the faith of the recipient and is it primarily the sign that he has received the baptism of the Spirit? Actually the answer had already been given ages ago, implied as it was in the prevalence of the practice of infant baptism since the 4th century. According to Roman Catholic doctrine, baptism works *ex opere operato* and washes away original sin; the more personal element of the gift of the Spirit is moved to the sacrament of confirmation which is administered by the priest at a later age. When in Europe the accent shifted more and more from the primacy of what is objective to the human subject, there arose increasing opposition to this impersonal and causal perception of the initiatory rite. First the Cathari and Waldenses and later the Anabaptists and the Baptists rejected the baptism of babies. In their Anglo-Saxon form the Baptists grew into a worldwide type of church, with a strong emphasis on a personal decision to accept Christ as Savior. In a new context, the Pentecostal movements continue this conception of baptism. In the 20th century this conception also makes headway in the traditional churches, among other things due to Barth's opposition to infant baptism, now set forth in detail in *CD* IV,4.

The Reformation churches continued to practice infant baptism, but tried to find another, less objective basis for it than is found in Roman Catholic doctrine: in a presumed faith of the small child (the Lutheran *fides infantium*), in the covenant with believers and their seed (Calvin), in a presumptive regeneration (a part of the later Reformed). These conceptions are not convincing. It is a weak position, being the midpoint between the more consistent objective thinking of the Roman Catholic Church and the more consistent personalistic thinking of the Baptist movements.

Yet this weakness is not altogether a loss. The NT does not know our split of objectivism and subjectivism. The washing of initiation belongs to the encounter event which as such is inter-subjective, but of which the initiative lies entirely with God. This is reflected in baptism. As an act within the encounter event it expresses precisely that God is the first and that faith may ground itself on a saving work that transcends our faith. We refer again to Rom. 6, which speaks the language of faith yet in that language points to an event to which one may always relate himself in faith (vv. 3, 6, 11). One who consciously submits to baptism will find it obvious that baptism does not depend on his faith, but the other way around. Yet the test of the validity of this insight depends on the question whether a conscious faith is always essential, or whether the baptism of minor children and e.g. imbeciles is imaginable in certain ecclesiastical contexts. Only if the church consciously keeps these options open does she maintain the right relationship of baptism and faith with respect to adults.

The washing of regeneration marks the boundary between the church and what is not the church. The extent of salvation is wider than the circle of those who consciously and personally believe. The paralytic is healed because of the faith of his friends (Mark 2:5), the servant of the centurion upon the faith of his master (Matt. 8:5–13), the Kingdom of God is promised to small children (Mark 10:13–16), children are sanctified through the faith of their father or mother (1 Cor. 7:14) and are (also for that reason) regarded as sharing in the life of the church (Eph. 6:1ff.; Col. 3:20f.; 1 John 2:12), Christians have even been baptized for members of their family who died in unbelief without Paul preventing such baptism (1 Cor. 15:29). People submit to this rite of initiation together with their whole family, which experiences the consequences of their change (Acts 10:46; 15:9; 16:15, 33; 18:8; 1 Cor. 1:16).

These considerations, while not making it obligatory, do establish the legitimacy of infant baptism. Though we may not say that children "ought to be baptized," we may say that they too may be given the rite of incorporation if they grow up in a community (family, village, institution) in which they are involved in God's salvation. In every instance it depends, however, on a pastoral decision, not on a general dogmatic principle. In principle the incorporative rite is possible at any age, either before a profession of faith or already earlier as a stage on the way within the congregation toward conscious faith. What is not possible, however, is the centuries-old practice of baptizing babies apart from any context of a meaningful and active faith. Due to secularism this practice is now rapidly decreasing. Believer's baptism must be the normal practice. This does not mean, however, that it must be quantitatively dominant. The other incorporation possibilities will prevent adult baptism from being misunderstood as a subjective confession or as a premium on faith. And this in turn will prevent the other possibilities from being used "out of custom or superstition," apart from the context of faith.

Finally, something about the form. In the course of time immersion shrank to watering, then to sprinkling, sometimes to mere moistening. We reject the thought that this could have a bearing on the "validity," but we do deplore this shrinking of the form. For it obscures the relation with the double function of the water, with the baptism of John and with the language of Rom. 6. This, as well as an unrestricted baptizing of babies, has greatly impaired the mediating character of this means of grace. What do we still experience of the working of the Spirit through this means? It may be that the Spirit will replace it by other means that do mediate. The signs, however, appear to indicate a revitalization of the language of the washing (revival movements with massive re-baptism in rivers and swimming pools). This deserves our positive appreciation, because the double voice which mankind has always perceived in the water—perishing and purification—has not for nothing been recognized as pointing to the deepest secret of the world, as this has been disclosed in the turnabout from the cross to the resurrection. For an overview of the aspects of baptism and discussions on baptism, see K. Blei, *De kinderdoop in discussie* (1981).

Out of the superabundance of literature on baptism, we limit ourselves to the following as guides for further study: (1) For the classical Reformed position: G. C. Berkouwer, *The Sacraments* (E.T. 1969), chs. 5–8; G. de Ru, *De kinderdoop en het Nieuwe Testament* (1964). (2) For the classical Baptist position: G. R. Beasley-Murray, *Baptism in the NT* (1962) and the smaller book edited by James Gray, *Studies on Baptism* (1959). (3) For the "neo-baptist" conception of baptism: M. Barth, *Die Taufe—ein Sakrament?* (1951), and K. Barth, *CD* IV,4 (1967). For the ecumenical consensus that has come about, see the so-called Lima report *Baptism, Eucharist and Ministry* (Faith and Order Paper no. 111, 1982), which unites many points of view; e.g., "Baptism is both God's gift and our human response to that gift."

3. The sermon

The third institutionalized medium, after the initiation and incorporation, which mediates and nourishes the participative process is the guidance given to the believer in the regularly recurring sermon. We speak of "sermon" and not of "proclamation," because the latter concept is much broader and our concern is one fixed institutionalized activity: the weekly or sometimes more frequent exposition and application of the Bible in an official gathering of the congregation. In many Protestant churches this is for many the central form in which the gospel comes to them and in which the participative process takes place. It is therefore surrounded with high expectations; but because man plays a larger role here than with other means, it can and regularly does evoke feelings of great disappointment. Thus it is not surprising that much reflection and writing has been devoted to the sermon. We are concerned here only with its mediating character. That character is closely related to the two poles between which it moves. To the one side it is *exposition* of the Bible: it explains the acts and the words of the history of the covenant within their own context and situation. To the other it is, using a traditional term, *application*, transposition into our context and situation. Yet, considered from the perspective of the two poles of the encounter, exposition and application are the same. The exposition is implicitly interpretation toward us, so that God's salvation is brought to bear on our own life. As a consequence our life with all its facets is being related to that salvation. In the sermon the Spirit seeks to bridge the gap between the world of the prophets and apostles and our world. The sermon thus contains elements of the instruction and thus of the initiation. But unlike those two it is related to the history, to the progress of our daily life with all its cares and sins, challenges and temptations. Our whole existence must constantly be related to and involved in the way of cross and resurrection. So the sermon mediates salvation using the mode of relevance for the present, by linking this salvation with the present time.

The word *sermon* derives from *praedicare* (to call out openly), which was the Vulgate rendering of *keryssein.* As concerns its essence the gospel is *kerygma,* message, and appeal in one (2 Cor. 5:20). Therefore it must be proclaimed over and again, and in that act it becomes what it is and wants to be. Kerygma is, however, much broader than the sermon in a congregational context. For it includes first of all missionary preaching (Mark 16:15; Rom. 10:17). From way back a different term, *homilia,* was used for the congregational sermon. The underlying assumption of that term is not a one-sided announcement, but a community of like-minded people. *Homilein* means "to associate with," "to converse." As a technical term the word *homily* comes from Greek philosophy and denotes the personal instruction given by the philosopher to his pupils, in which he plies them with questions and counter-remarks. Very early the church took over this word (cf. Acts 20:11; Ignatius, *Ad Polycarpum* 5). The congregational sermon was given as a form of instruction from the Scriptures, in a personal tone and in a way that the listeners became involved as much as possible.

In the history of the church this communal element fairly soon disappeared. But as late as Augustine's day it was still possible to applaud after the sermon. Through the centuries the sermon reflects rather accurately the different cultures and rhetorical styles. What an enormous difference there is between the first extant homily, the so-called Second Epistle of Clement, the sermons of Chrysostom, Bernard of Clairvaux, the Mendicant orders, Luther, Bossuet, Smijtegelt, Van der Palm, Kohlbrugge, Van Oosterzee, or Niemöller. And that is how it should be if this medium is to maintain its mediating character. That the sermon is monological in form is as such no objection, as is often thought nowadays. This form reflects the fact that salvation is not a product of our own minds but that it has to be announced to us. It becomes objectionable only if the listeners get the feeling that the preacher and his thoughts are no longer mediating but obstruct instead. Something is wrong, too, if the sermon no longer issues in discussion by the church members, in which they themselves, as mature members of Christ's church, continue the application (see under 4). In order to be a genuine homily which genuinely mediates, the sermon should start from the problems and needs of the hearers, bring God's grace to bear upon these matters, and finally issue in questions to the listeners from the perspective of the grace proclaimed, questions to which they themselves personally and mutually will have to find the answer.

A great deal of theoretical and practical difference exists among the churches as to the "sacramental" character of the sermon. In the Roman Catholic Church the sermon is denied such a character. There what is called "sermon" was and is often an instructive, informative, or admonishing address which does not carry the pretension of bringing God's grace to bear upon present needs; that happens in the eucharist. The obstacle here is too narrow a concept of sacrament: the sacraments work *ex opere operato*, the sermon only *ex opere operantis.* Lately remarkable attempts are being made to get beyond this position. But the Vatican constitution *De sacra liturgia* (1963), par. 35,2, continues to distinguish the presence of Christ's mystery from its annunciation in the sermon, and the *New Catechism* (E.T. 1969) is disappointingly vague on this point (pp. 331f.); but see *MS* IV 1, pp. 351–355.

Entirely opposite is the Lutheran conception. Luther himself once made the strong statement: "A preacher must not pray the Lord's prayer, nor ask for forgiveness, when he has preached the word (if he is a true preacher). . . . For it is God's word, not mine, which God ought not and cannot forgive me, but can only affirm, praise, honor, and about which He can only say: 'You have taught rightly' " (*Wider Hans Worst,* 1541). In the Lutheran churches the sermon, as the central sacrament, is understood in terms of consubstantiation: God's word is present in, with, and in the form of human words. P. Brunner calls the sermon "Christus-Anamnese" (in *Leiturgia,* I, 1954, C III C), and G. Wingren describes it as "a blow against the devil" (in *Die Predigt,* German 1955). As much as the sermon is regarded in Roman Catholicism as a subjective utterance of faith, so much it is an objective redemptive event in the Lutheran conception. The Reformed view represents a third possibility. See Bavinck, *GD* IV, par. 56: "The Word as a Means of Grace." For Barth the proclaimed word of God is the first of the three forms of this word (proclaimed, written, incarnate); see *CD* I,1, pp. 98–111. As such it is, however, subject to the critical evolution of the other two forms, so that it does not exclude but includes man's responsibility or failures. This dialectic, in which man's word can become "indirectly identical" with the Word of God only through the Spirit, is impressively articulated in *CD* I,2, pp. 743–758 ("Divine Word and Human Word in the Human Proclamation"), and by K. H. Miskotte in *Het waagstuk der prediking* (1941) (in revised form in *Om het levende Woord* [1948], pp. 219–370). A view leaning more toward the Lutheran conception is found in G. van der Leeuw, *Sacramentstheologie* (1949), pp. 182–190 and 319–326. For the relationship of sermon and liturgy, see under 7.

4. The discussion

The sermon, though monological in form, presupposes (witness its name "homily") the context of the reacting congregation and must therefore issue in a discussion if the gospel in all its relevance is to become flesh and bones in the life of the congregation. The discussion cannot replace the sermon, but the reverse is equally impossible. The discussion is the extension of the sermon, the application as it is continued and elaborated by those who will have to confirm its truth in their daily life in the world. By "the extension of the sermon" we do not mean that every sermon is to be followed by a discussion of that sermon. What we do say is that both institutional activities are to complement each other. If it does not have a sequel in the discussion, the sermon is in danger of evaporating, and without the background of the sermon the discussion tends to remain noncommittal.

Yet in the study of the faith the discussion has never been acknowledged as an ecclesiastical means of grace. The reason is that almost nowhere in ecclesiastical practice does it function or seem to function that way. Nevertheless, it is a common fact of experience that many owe their faith and its growth much more to conversations and religious discussion groups than to the officially recognized ecclesiastical means of grace. The fact is that the Spirit uses this means, and that he does so increasingly in our modern times. For the well-being of the church *and* of those believers whose faith is particularly nourished by the discussion, it is high time that the church acknowledge its "sacramental" character and give it its rightful institutional place.

In the first place, then, the private pastoral conversation must be mentioned. For a long time already this has had a more or less institutional place in many churches. We today, more than our forebears, realize how much the building up and the continuation of the congregation depend on this form of passing on the faith. At the same time this form is itself so much dependent on the questions and needs of the discussion partner that the conversation can by no means always have a "sacramental" character. Often it will be directive or nondirective or just psychologically encouraging. As such these kinds of talks can just as well take place outside the context of the church. In the church they derive their justification from the fact that they take place within the context of the transmission of the grace of God and there possess their own "diaconal" character (see pp. 372ff.). Intentional institutional forms of pastoral conversation in which the application of God's grace to the needs of the conversational partner is primary are therefore necessary.

Another form of discussion is that within the congregation. This type is based on the fact that the congregation is a creation of the Spirit and that he dwells in it. A central revelation of that indwelling is the gifts of grace or charismata which the Spirit gives to believers for the benefit of all. We shall say more about that in the next paragraph. Here we shall make some remarks by way of anticipation, because it is particularly this charismatic structure of the church which constitutes the basis for the mediating character of the discussion in which each serves the other with the insight he or she has received into the grace of God and its meaning for the Christian life. With this last observation we have said something about the content as well. As with the sermon, this will be twofold and the difference is only one of emphasis: on the one hand mutual help to gain a deeper understanding of the salvation of which we read in the Bible; on the other hand mutual help in gaining a clearer idea of the attitude which in view of this salvation we must assume toward the cares, temptations, and challenges we face in life. The form may vary; it may be a Bible discussion group, a religious club, a general study group, or whatever, depending on the purpose one has in mind. There should, however, always be the two poles of message and situation, even as with the sermon. Such groups have been and are widespread in the Christian church. They are by no means always ecclesiastical in character. In fact the churchly character might well have a strongly adverse effect on their mediating effectiveness. In our opinion, such need not happen, however. The institutionalization can and must mean safeguarding the discussion against noncommitment and cliquishness. With the proper structuring, every member is invited to join in the discussions and at the same time obligated to attentive listening and careful speaking. In this way the discussion can be a powerful means toward mutual encouragement and correction, certainly in a time in which the congregation is in danger of losing its sight on its way through uncertainty and polarization.

In addition to the discussion, more private forms of conversation should retain their place as ecclesiastical transmission instruments. All the more so, because these latter often have a different character, informative for instance, or in the nature of personal counseling. A fine interaction can develop between these forms and the more ecclesiastical type, if the ecclesiastical protects the private from becoming noncommittal and individualistic, and the private forms prepare for the ecclesiastical, or supplement or anticipate it. The boundaries will always be fluid. The main thing is that the congregation as a whole should have its own forms of discussion and contact which it uses to mediate God's grace.

Conversation as a means of grace has always played a much larger role than one is normally aware of. Already Jesus found much use for it, in addition to preaching and teaching. And in the earliest church the boundary between sermon and discussion was often fluid, as we can gather from Paul's picture of the congregational gathering in 1 Cor. 14 and from the Berean church which, according to Acts 17:11, was organized as a kind of Bible discussion group. Possibly in this connection we should also think of the "prophets" in the early Christian church, who made known God's will for the present and the immediate future, a phenomenon which evoked the need for critical discussion and the "testing of the spirits." But the rapid evolution toward a hierarchical and authoritarian church pushed these freer forms of transmission to the background.

By its very character the Reformation provided a new opportunity for these forms. Luther, enumerating the means of grace in the Schmalkald Articles (1537), III, IV: "On the Gospel," counts five: the sermon, baptism, the altar sacrament, the power of the keys, "and mutual discussion and comforting of the brethren" (with an appeal to Matt. 18:20). Not until much later, however, did this far-reaching remark become productive. J. Henkys' book *Seelsorge und Bruderschaft* (1970) is a discussion of the significance and effectiveness of this expression. Bucer made a new start with his heavy emphasis on the transmission of salvation by the charismatic congregation; it led him to establish his "Christian fellowships" in Strasbourg, core congregations for mutual love, and spiritual care and discipline (under the supervision of the offices).

Calvin bypassed this element of Bucer, but he did include ecclesiastical discipline, which involved regular pastoral visits of the families by the elders. This official and supervisory form of discussion is something else than what we have here. In later centuries it did, however, develop more in that direction, particularly in the Netherlands.

Generally speaking, it must be said that the Reformation did little more than make beginnings relative to the discussion. The discussion of the sermon (called "prophecy") in the Dutch refugee congregation in London (about 1552) is to be regarded as one such beginning. But the convention of Wesel (1568) rejected this form because it caused quarreling, and replaced it with a college (!) of prophets serving as official interpreters of Scripture. In the free churches, with their emphasis on the maturity of the church, the discussion did see a measure of prominence in the 16th and 17th centuries, but without much of an institutional link; in this connection one can also mention the Quakers with their silent worship, interrupted by inspired testimonies.

The heyday of the discussion began about 1670. Earlier, De Labadie had introduced it when he brought true believers together in small groups for the purpose of "prophetic exercise." In the Netherlands the "Further Reformation" made the so-called "conventicles" or "assemblies" very popular as places for fostering spiritual renewal, something which more than once resulted in tension between the participants and the official church. In 1670 in Frankfurt, Spener organized the *collegia pietatis,* which became widespread through his much-read *Pia desideria* (1675) in which he advocates other "gatherings . . . as Paul describes them in 1 Cor. 14, where not just one does all the teaching, but also others who are gifted with special abilities and insight"—always, however, under the leadership of a minister (pp. 98–100).

So the spiritual discussion became a central form of expression and support of Pietism. Under the influence of the Herrnhuters, in Methodism the discussion received institutional form in the "class-meetings." Since then the discussion has remained an integral component of the religious instruction and training of the churches in Europe and North America, bringing their members to greater spiritual maturity. In the 19th century the discussion took the form of Christian men's and women's societies, student groups, etc. Even today there are many Christians for whom the YMCA, YWCA, SCM, and youth groups have been of greater religious significance than the official means of grace of the church institutes. In our century there are in addition all kinds of Christian brotherhoods and movements, the "sharing" of the Oxford Group Movement, after the War many varieties of Christian training, etc.; and in Japan the "nonecclesiastical movement," the Mukyokai, which is entirely made up of Bible circles (see on that Brunner, *Dg* III, p. 113).

But the institutionalization of this increasingly more prominent form of transmission has thus far been only sporadic. It is done somewhat where the societies and study groups have become a more or less integral part of church life, next to the church services, catechetical instruction, and the program of visiting people in their homes. It is done even more emphatically where the worship services are followed by a discussion or where it is even made a part of the service. Yet both the fact and the content of these activities are thus far hampered by the fact that participation carries little responsibility on the part of the participant.

5. The meal

In most churches other than the Protestant, the primary means of spiritual nourishment is the act which in the New Testament is called "the table of the Lord" or "the supper," and which later was called "thanksgiving" (*eucharistia*). The Roman Catholic Church also uses the term "mass" (after the concluding words of the liturgy: *ite missa est*) and Protestant churches the designation "the Lord's Supper" (in reference to

Jesus' final meal before his death). Its great significance as a means of grace derives especially from the fact that Jesus himself, in having a meal with his disciples, gave expression to his ultimate purposes, and mandated them to keep doing the same after his departure.

Always and everywhere the meal has spoken a language of its own. In particular, festive and happy occasions are preferably celebrated with a meal. At a meal a person can be himself and relax; there he finds acceptance as one of the group and enjoys the fellowship of others who are in the same position. As a communal event the meal is at the same time the affirmation of that communion, not infrequently after such communion had first been broken; in that case the meal is also the sealing of the reconciliation.

The meal instituted by Jesus, besides speaking this general human language, spoke especially the language of the Old Testament. One can say that God's way with Israel was from the one meal to the other: from the Passover meal, the annually celebrated deliverance from Egypt, to the meal of the great future, when Yahweh will abolish death, wipe away all tears, and prepare his banquet of rich fare and aged wines on Mount Zion (Isa. 25).

With Jesus that future had begun as God's surprising, gracious gift precisely to people who had lost all hope. The most apt and startling expressions of that were the meals at which Jesus sat down with tax collectors and sinners. These were really more than meals, they were parabolic acts such as were enacted by the Old Testament prophets, in which God's dealings with man are both portrayed and actualized. Especially the last meal before his death was such a parabolic act, when Jesus added to the regular ingredients of the meal, bread and wine, the new meaning of the separation of his body and blood in his approaching voluntary death. In that death he saw a redemptive significance which is mediated through the meal and which was to be permanently celebrated in the meal. It is insufficiently noted that this meal is not presented as an isolated event or a conclusion, but that in nearly all the narratives about appearances of Jesus and of encounters with him after the resurrection the meal has a prominent place. From now on the way of Christ's church also goes from meal to meal. In celebrating this meal, according to the command of Christ, she anticipates the meal of perfect happiness and fellowship in the consummation, and at the same time looks back to Jesus' way of self-sacrifice and resurrection through which that future was opened up to her. But she does not do that in a vacuous present "between the times," for she knows that her now-exalted Lord remains in the Spirit present as the host of these celebrations as she goes her way from meal to meal.

For those who know what is going on here, this meal is of all the means the most comprehensive expression of God's salvation. For here the entire way of salvation lies before us in concentrated form. What we have here is a regularly repeated renewal of the covenant in which past (the sacrifice), future (the Kingdom of God), and present (the presence of Christ in the Spirit) meet, and in which the fellowship with God in Christ through the Spirit coincides with the fellowship of the members of Christ's body with each other. In this celebration we look simultaneously backward and forward, and similarly upward (to the exalted Lord), around us (to the people), and to what is before us (the table with the signs and the rite which together constitute the celebration). Here the covenant way of cross and resurrection, of repentance and forgiveness, of self-denial and rising up again is continually laid out before us. This makes for a double mood at this table: of a sense of guilt and hesitation, and of liberation and perspective on the future. Yet in virtue of the language of the meal the second has the upper hand over the first. Though aware of the price her Lord had to pay for it, nevertheless on his authority the church dares to celebrate the feast and at the table enact the "play" of the future, the liberty, equality, and brotherhood of the coming Kingdom of God.

In the older churches whose roots go back to a mythical and magical experience of life, the celebration of the holy meal occupies the central position. In the younger churches, beginning with the Reformation, the sermon came to stand beside the meal on an equal footing, and soon overwhelmed it. That has to do with the character of our newer European culture which appeals particularly to the intellect and the will of the individual. But precisely this one-sidedness, to which the sermon caters so much, should warn us to keep hearing and celebrating the peculiar language of the meal. Here we touch on the relation of sermon and meal. We construe this wrongly if we put the one above or below the other. Both represent salvation but they do so from a different perspective and appealing to different aspects of our humanity. The sermon speaks of that grace particularly in its immediate relevance for our daily life. The meal is something we receive physically and engage in communally; it speaks the language of our physical existence and of the image, more than that of the spirit and word. Precisely so it keeps alive the awareness of the unspeakable in God's covenantal association with us. While the churches that make the meal central at the expense of the sermon run the risk of misunderstanding the gospel by objectifying it, if not seeing it magically, those churches where the sermon is central at the expense of the meal are in danger of an individualistic and intellectualistic misunderstanding of the gospel. Therefore the sermon and the meal need to supplement, explain, and correct each other. In the mediation of God's grace they presuppose each other as the two foci of an ellipse.

Everything so far suggests a number of ideas for the practice of the celebration. In this practice both the meal character and the communion with each other as well as the anticipation of the future should come out much more clearly than is now the case in most churches (younger *and* older). Almost everywhere the representation of Jesus' sacrificial death crowds out all other elements, the event has shrunk into a meeting of the individual soul with the Lord, the correlation with the sermon is absent, and the table-character has either been dropped or become an insignificant symbol. Fortunately, everywhere a younger generation begins to ask for a new emphasis on the celebration, on the meal, and on the communal aspect.

Where the meal is understood in its full breadth and strength as representing the grace of God, it turns out that, in spite of its stable conventional form and its symbolic character, it can exercise an incisively sifting function in politics and society. Already Paul warns of the possibility of eating and drinking judgment to oneself in the celebration of the holy meal if one persists with the gap between the well-to-do and the needy and thereby shows that he does not "discern the body" (of the Lord and of the church) (1 Cor. 11:20–34). From the struggle of the Confessing Church under the Nazis we remember how the open admission of Christian Jews to the Lord's Supper became the first test in the clash of the spirits. In our day the meal serves a similar disclosing function in the *apartheid* problematic in South Africa. But it functions as such in ecumenical relations as well; if a church denies to believers not belonging to its particular community access to the meal, it looks at itself, not at Christ as the host, and renders his presence doubtful (cf. Matt. 18:20 and 1 Cor. 11:20).

The theologically knowledgeable reader will have noticed that in the above little or no attention was given to the great problems which for hundreds of years have beset the understanding of the table of the Lord and have led to ecclesiastical conflicts and even splits. For a survey of these problems we refer to the handbooks on the history of doctrine. We shall limit ourselves here to the problems we think are relevant, while we try to indicate why this cannot be said of some others.

The decisive starting-point and criterion is the interpretation of the NT reports about the celebration of the last supper. That interpretation is burdened with great difficulties, the most important of which concerns the divergences in the four reports that have been handed down: Matt. 26:26–29; Mark 14:22–25; Luke 22:14–20; 1 Cor. 11:23–25. To these one could add John 6:51–56; Acts 2:42, and 1 Cor. 10:16–17 as passages to be studied. It hardly can be doubted that Jesus, just before his arrest, had a particularly solemn meal with his disciples which he linked with his imminent death; nor can it be doubted that the participants perceived in this event a permanent mandate for their community. But we may never know exactly what Jesus said. It is worthy of note that even with respect to this climax the early church has been so careless with its tradition. Matthew follows Mark. But Paul presents a considerably divergent tradition. Luke in turn is different from both. Does he offer the original tradition, or only a secondary revision of it? Do the words in vv. 19 and 20 (from "which is given for you . . ." to "poured out for you"), which are not found in the so-called Western text, belong to the original text or not? (Most exegetes think they do.) But the confusing variations should not make us overlook the important facts the

NT witnesses have in common: Jesus distributes bread and wine and relates these elements to his body and blood, the two components of a living human being, whose dissolution spells death. And the blood, the surrender of life, is related to a new covenant which is constituted by that very act, possibly with an allusion to Ex. 24:8 and the covenantal meal at Mount Sinai that followed.

Against this background of what the reports have in common the difference becomes clear: in the Synoptics the Lord's Supper stands in the light of the future meal in the Kingdom of God, in Paul the death of Jesus is central, and Luke combines both tendencies. Both Paul and Luke accentuate the second emphasis, because they have Jesus say that the celebration is to take place "in remembrance of me"; later this expression has often been misunderstood as if it concerns a symbolical commemorative meal here, but the intention is that through the *anamnēsis* that which is remembered is made present anew, is being re-present-ed.

The nature of the identity which the words of the institution bring about between bread and body, wine and blood, has also been a source of much discussion. The mooted word "is" did not occur in the Aramaic original. Only Paul gives suggestions as to the nature of the identification when, in 1 Cor. 10:16, he speaks of our *koinōnia* with Christ's body and blood through bread and wine. The OT and Jewish background of Jesus' words exclude our later Western alternative of either ontic identity or symbolic identification. On the strength of Jesus' words a genuine connection between the sign and the matter signified is effected, such as was also the case with the so-called "parabolic acts" of the OT prophets (see e.g. Ezek. 5:5: "This is Jerusalem"), and also happened at every celebration of the Jewish Passover in commemoration of the Exodus. The words *is* and *anamnēsis* are thus to be explained analogically, namely as indicative of an effective representation for which our Western mode of thinking really has no category; this is the main reason for all the confusion in the Western church in respect to the meaning of the meal, a confusion which, as we see it, can only be removed through a deeper reflection on the operations of the Spirit.

Another problem is the *date* and in connection with it the *nature* of the last supper. According to the Synoptics, the Passover meal happened on the evening of the Passover (Mark 14:12–16, and others); however, according to John the final dramatic events took place on the 14th of Nisan, the day before the Passover feast (13:1f.; 19:14, 31). John's date is the most likely. In that case the final meal was not a Passover meal. However, it does not look like an ordinary Jewish meal either. The arguments pro and con are of about equal weight. Authorities on the subject are inclined toward a solution that contains elements of both views: the day before, Jesus held a meal which stood already as the sign of the approaching feast and which was intended to give it a new meaning.

Another difficult question is the relation of the eucharistic celebration to an ordinary meal. For the clear impression is given that the setting of the table of the Lord was a (regular or special) meal. And in the early church we hear repeatedly of love feasts in a liturgical context, the so-called *agapai*, which were regularly held by the congregation and which were also intended to give a free meal to the poorer members. Cf. Jude 12; Ignatius, *Ad Smyrnaeos* 8:2 (where it is called *eucharistia*), and especially Hippolytus, *Traditio apostolica* 47–52. The obvious assumption is that the sacramental and the social meal were originally one, but as a result of abuses, as already noted by Paul (1 Cor. 11:20ff.), had to be disconnected. In the Didache 9 and 10 they are still one, but the split was unavoidable and the social meals began to die out as the churches grew. This detachment was detrimental to the eucharistic meal, which became less and less a real meal. As with the washing, the symbol language became lost. This is true in particular of the traditional Roman Catholic "mass." But even the restoration of the table in Reformed Protestantism has been only a halfway measure. The desire which has lately arisen, to restore the original unity of the vertical and the horizontal, of *leitourgia* and *diakonia,* is commendable indeed.

We have to come back once more to the two traditions of the table that are already found in the NT. The Synoptic tradition clearly links the celebration with Jesus' earlier meals on the one hand and with that of the eschatological banquet on the other. In Paul the representation of the death on the cross displaces these connections. In general the churches have one-sidedly followed the line of Paul. This is not surprising, since the Hellenistic world was familiar with sacrificial meals by which one acquired supernatural strength through the eating of the sacrificial animal. What was meant by Paul as an antithesis (1 Cor. 10:14–22) led to a competitive parallelism whereby the meal, which was intended as *anamnēsis* of Christ's sacrifice, soon was regarded as being itself a sacrificial rite which secured the favor of God. For centuries, up to the present time, Roman Catholic liturgy, terminology, and theology have through official ecclesiastical pronouncements been burdened with this strange tradition. But even the Protestant churches, which rid themselves of this tradition, keep looking one-sidedly to the sacrifice of the cross at the expense of the meal and the eschaton. We must learn again to combine the two traditions and to have them complement each other.

Also from another point of view both traditions are important to us. Concepts like covenant, covenantal meal, and parabolic act clearly belong to the Palestinian tradition, but in Paul's Hellenistic climate the understanding of the meal became much more substantialistic (cf. 1 Cor. 11:30). That causes E. Schweizer to say: "If the question concerning the elements would have been asked—which is not the real question—then the Palestinian would have given a Reformed and the Hellenist a Lutheran answer" (*RGG* I, col. 18). Traditions which later came to stand over against each other are still happily together in the NT, which also proves that the essence of the meal is not to be sought in one or the other of these points of difference.

The literature on the last supper in the NT is considerable. For a listing of important publications and as an excellent introduction to the problems in this area, see E. Schweizer, the art. *Abendmahl I,* in *RGG* I.

With these last remarks we have pointed repeatedly to the history of the church and its dogmas. In that history the meal has for many centuries been one-sidedly perceived in a substantialistic sense, to which only the teaching of Augustine applied a braking influence. In Aristotelian-Scholastic thinking this resulted in the doctrine of transubstantiation which in 1215 was elevated to official dogma (D 802), a dogma which as recently as 1965 was reaffirmed in the encyclical *Mysterium fidei.* This doctrine fixes Christ's presence in the elements, separate from the fellowship of the meal, detached from the encounter, and having an *ex opere operato* efficacy. In this type of thinking, the conception of the meal as a sacrifice is to be regarded as a complement to this objectivism, for here it is precisely man (the priest) who is the subject who actualizes anew the sacrifice of the Lord as the means of reconciliation for the living and dead. Particularly Trent has shaped this idea of sacrifice (D 1738–1743).

The Reformation broke radically with the idea of a meritorious sacrifice. But when it had to spell out the personal relevance of the grace of God in the "biunity" of Word and faith in reference to the meal, profound differences surfaced. These were due partly to the religious outlook and experiences of the Reformers personally, partly to the lack of intellectual categories with which to articulate an encounter. This happened to be just the time when an ontological mode of thinking began to give way to one which started from the subject-object distinction. Neither of these was suitable for expressing the meal-event. On this point, too, Luther stayed closest to the Middle Ages with his views of consubstantiation and *manducatio impiorum*, underpinned by the Scholastic theory of the *communicatio idiomatum*. But behind all this was his passion to keep grace inviolate, not subject to our subjective moods or soul struggles. In contrast, Zwingli approached the meal from the standpoint of the believing subject who in the meal commemorates Christ's benefits and openly gives expression to his faith. Christ is present only in that union of faith; bread and wine are only symbols, otherwise they would be idols. Calvin looked for a third solution by understanding the meal as a communion with Christ in the Spirit. He came closest to a conception of the meal as organ of encounter. But owing to the lack of adequate categories, his concrete exposition of his doctrine was severely burdened with lines of thought which hampered more than promoted what he tried to express, such as the *distinctio naturarum*, the *finitum non capax infiniti*, the parallelism of a bodily and spiritual eating, the construction of having communion with Christ's heavenly corporeality through the mouth of faith, and the mystical plus of the Lord's Supper beyond what is given in the proclamation. Unfortunately, the classical Reformed form for the Lord's Supper, especially the *Sursum Corda,* is also burdened with such theologisms.

As regards literature, besides *RGG* I, *s.v. Abendmahl* and the books already mentioned, we refer for the Lutheran presentation to Althaus, *CW* II, pars. 57–60, and to Prenter, *Creation and Redemption* (E.T. 1967), par. 38; for a presentation from the Reformed point of view see Van der Leeuw, *Sacramentstheologie,* pp. 287–301, and Berkouwer, *The Sacraments,* chs. 9–14. But all this literature is still very much in the grip of tradition.

Only in our time, the second half of the twentieth century, are the various views and theologies about the meal of the Lord beginning to run on the same track. This is due first of all to biblical-theological research, which is far less burdened with confessional prejudices than used to be the case and has resulted in considerable consensus. There is a fast-growing awareness that the real presence of Christ as the host of this meal is only faultily articulated, or even obscured, by our dogmatic formulations of the "how" of it. We also realize more than we used to that none of the confessions (which often were preoccupied with points of controversy) grasp the fullness of what is happening at the table. Thanks to all the work of Faith and Order for so many years, this consensus is now beginning to bear ecclesiastical and ecumenical fruits. See the Lima report *Baptism, Eucharist and Ministry,* in which the central section, "Eucharist," views the meal from five perspectives: (1) thanksgiving to God; (2) remembrance of Christ; (3) calling upon the Spirit; (4) communion of believers; (5) festive meal of the Kingdom. So the report combines many notions that thus far were not fully heard in the various confessions. The drawback is that the report sometimes too quickly combines and passes over the great historical differences and contrasts.

These differences and contrasts have certainly not disappeared where they concern Roman Catholicism and Protestantism, particularly not where they concern the difference in faith experiences at the table of the Lord to which they lead. In the Roman Catholic experience, the elements stand central; in the Protestant experience the acts do. According to Protestantism the Lord's Supper is all about the self-giving Christ who was sacrificed for us; according to Roman Catholicism the communion of faith to which the sacrifice representatively corresponds also belongs to it.

A good starting point for an approach is that offered by the *New Catechism* (E.T. 1969), pp. 163–168 and 332–347. And if the meal is a representation of the new covenant, in which man is also involved as one who responds, should there not be a place for the role of the congregation (not like that in Trent and Zwingli), more so than is now the case in many Protestant celebrations? On that see from the Roman Catholic side H. A. J. Wegman, "Wij gedenken de dood van de Heer," in *Tijdschrift voor Theologie* (1981), 1, pp. 48–62. But so far the Roman Catholic Curia in Rome rejects such reinterpretations.

More than previous generations, we today have become aware of the impossibility of formulating the encounter with Christ in this manner. We also feel much less the need to know and to say more about it. For the "that" is infinitely more important than the "how." But we do have a great need for breaking through the narrow confines within which this meal could hardly speak its own language anymore: the one-sided emphasis on the cross, the one-sided emphasis on the elements (at the expense of the meal as fellowship), and the individualism which is so clearly at variance with the very character of this means.

In our opinion, the practice is going to be more important than the theology. Calvin took a big step forward when (following Bucer) he reintroduced the table and celebrated at least once a month a service of word *and* table. But though it was possible to combine these two renewals in the small French congregation of Strasbourg, this could not be done in the big services in Geneva. The city council of Geneva decided that the meal would be celebrated four times a year; and that "order" is still honored by many Reformed churches all over the world. It ties in well with the fear of going to the table which arose later. Patient instruction combined with practical renewals will have to give us a vision again of the intention of this meal. For that reason, in the Dutch and German churches the name "evening meal" (Dutch: *avondmaal*; German: *Abendmahl*) needs to disappear as a designation of something that is seldom celebrated in the evening. It is preferable, following the NT, to speak of "meal" or "table," of "the holy meal," or of "the table of the Lord."

6. The diaconate

The means discussed thus far are partly verbal, partly symbolic acts. They mediate the saving word of God, which as such is not "only" word, but word-and-deed (the Hebrew word *dāḇar* signifies "word" as well as "deed"). God's grace is mediated to us not only as an announcement, but also as a renewing power. For that reason the sermon is more than word only and the communion at the table more than what we call a symbol. At the same time this renewing power has more dimensions than can be expressed in our words and symbols. Salvation not only concerns man's heart in its relation to God, but from that center it touches all of his life as well as that of humanity. Salvation is total; it is the answer to man's double estrangement: from God and from himself; that is, it is the answer to man's guilt and to his need. Now that in Christ God's kingship has come near and we are made to share in it by the Spirit, this should also become clear in what happens to the concrete forms of need and guilt of man's existence in the world. Otherwise the comprehensive purpose of God's salvation has still not really become clear. This form of mediating salvation we call "diaconate."

God's work in Israel's history and in Jesus has always contained this comprehensive horizontal dimension. It manifested itself in the liberation from Egyptian bondage, in the rescue out of all kinds of emergency situations into which Israel often found itself through its own fault, the climax of which was the deliverance from the Babylonian captivity. Within Israel this dimension manifested itself in the concern for widows and orphans, for the poor and strangers. And Jesus' work was not only that of preaching; he also dined with tax collectors and sinners, and he healed the sick and the demon-possessed. So he translated into concrete action and brought to bear upon daily life the deliverance from guilt and need and thereby showed that the Kingdom of God had indeed come near. It is only obvious that the Spirit continues this diaconal element in the church. Of the earliest church we read that it took care that no one suffered need, and of deacons who, among others, were charged with taking care of the needy. Through the centuries the churches and their individual members have been concerned with the poor and the persecuted, the sick and retarded, the wanderers and the homeless, the prisoners and the derelicts.

In this area much has been done by members of the church who, individually or in organizations, and inspired by the love of Christ, helped to ameliorate the needs they saw everywhere around them. Later we shall come back to this calling to practice Christian mercy. Here we are concerned with the diaconate as institutionalized means of grace. The task of the congregation in this area needs the stimulating model of a pace-setting institution which shows love and mercy. By that example the congregation must continually be reminded that diaconal service is not an optional application or a consequence of the salvation given her, but that this service concerns salvation itself in its comprehensive material, social, political, and universal aspects.

The institutional diaconate, owing to its mediating and exemplary character, is subject to certain rules by which the less restricted diaconate of the members of the church is not bound. (Already from this it follows that both forms are needed.) God's diaconate seeks to serve man who is totally helpless in his need and guilt. His salvation is mediatingly illustrated when help is given where there is no helper. Many needs are taken care of by the various social and political agencies themselves in a given society. A diaconate which seeks to minister to those same needs is engaged in duplication or competition and does not illustrate God's salvation as it should. But in every society, no matter how efficiently organized, there are the helpless needy and the guilty outcasts for whom everyone closes his eyes. These especially are the objects of God's merciful justice, and in the ministry to them the diaconate receives its true and eloquent shape. This requires a great deal of ingenuity, mobility, courage, and endurance. The love of Christ must be the source from which it springs and is nurtured. That love knows no limits. It goes out to the individual and the community, to the evil and the good, to people and structures, ministering mercy and promoting justice. As a salvation-mediating agency the diaconate is called to be the vanguard of the general work of promoting mercy and justice. So it stands in the world as a silent or far from silent indictment of what is wrong in society and as a challenge to "official agencies." Precisely the institutional diaconate should be the critical societal watchdog. This sounds almost like a contradiction in terms. Therefore it is not surprising that the diaconate has frequently obscured its peculiar mediating character. That happened when it contented itself with healing, in cooperation with the existing powers, individual symptoms, leaving the socio-political root untouched. Though it should be added that even with this all too readily accepted limitation it has been a refuge and a beacon of hope for innumerable people. Its very existence and the financial support which it asks from church members are constant reminders that sharing in God's salvation and acquiescing to poverty and injustice are mutually exclusive.

The diaconate is thus by no means an appendix among the media that pass on God's salvation. Now that gradually our eyes are again opening to that, the opposite danger threatens, that of regarding it as the real and complete representation of salvation, at the expense of other forms. Dimensions exist that elude this diaconal mode. In the diaconate as a segment of human labor for renewal, both the renewal as Christ worked for it in his life and the coming total renewal in the Kingdom of God can only indirectly, as it were in a reflection, be represented. Therefore the diaconate cannot do without the explanation and inspiration from the sermon, the meal, and the other means. But the reverse is equally true: the diaconate must protect these means from the danger of allowing people to do nothing. The witness without the backing of the diaconate remains empty, just as the diaconate without the witness is left without a voice. However, one who is really involved in the diaconal challenge needs this reminder less than one who orients himself primarily to the sermon, the meal, or the discussion. For man's need and guilt are limitless. The more one gets involved in it in the name of Christ, the more one discovers how little one actually accomplishes. To persevere nevertheless, we need the daily comfort and inspiration that come from the belief that God himself has become involved in this hopeless world and will himself someday bring about its radical renewal.

Jesus' ministry was a combination of words and deeds, of preaching, meals, and healings. All these aspects together manifested the nearness of the Kingdom of God. There is a difference of opinion as to how these are related, especially proclamation and healing. A passage such as Mark 1:38 conveys the impression that for Jesus preaching was the most important; in contrast, Matt. 12:28 gives the impression that the casting out of demons was the primary sign. In Matt. 11:5 preaching and healings are mentioned side by side as signs of the Kingdom. More than once Mark 2:1–12 is cited to prove that for Jesus forgiveness was of greater significance than healing; but this episode is to be read against the background of the Jewish belief in the close connection between sin and sickness. For the diaconal task especially Matt. 25:31–46, and in particular vv. 35f., is often referred to; it should not be overlooked, however, that this passage concerns the compassion shown by the "unchurched" to the persecuted church of Christ. In the final analysis the real root of the diaconate lies in the manner in which God (especially in the OT) and Jesus have entered into the concrete manifestations of human need and guilt with deeds of deliverance.

The origin of the diaconate is hidden in obscurity. The term *diakonos* in the NT does not help much (see *TDNT* II, *s.v. diakoneō*). *Diakonein* means "to wait on at table" and "to support" or, in general, "to serve." We assume that in the NT the *diakonos*, beside and relative to the *episkopos* and *presbyteros*, was charged with the more servile tasks and other ministering duties, such as that of serving at the table of the Lord and helping the needy in the congregation; this combination appears to be intimated in 1 Cor. 11:20–22, and perhaps also in Acts 2:44–46. The appointment of the so-called "seven" in Acts 6:1–6 also suggests this combination, but for centuries this passage has wrongly been read as a report of the institution of the office of deacon and the diaconate. The name *diakonos* does not occur there, and further only their work of preaching is mentioned. Likely they were assistant apostles for the Greek-speaking members of the congregation. There can be no doubt that from the very beginning the care of the needy was a primary concern of the church (cf. also Acts 4:32–37 and what Paul says about the collection for the poor congregation in Jerusalem, 1 Cor. 16:1ff.; 2 Cor. 9). But the office of deacon included more than this duty: it also pertained to liturgical and financial matters. In the Roman Catholic Church the diaconal task has become entirely liturgical, in many churches it has been eliminated, and in the Reformed churches it has become totally a ministry of mercy. But even those churches which do not have the office of deacon or use it for a different purpose have seldom lacked a broad diaconal ministry, a labor carried on and supported by local congregations, ecclesiastical organizations, monastic orders, Christian governments, groups of individual Christians, or (especially lately) ecumenical agencies. For the history of this work see H. Krimm, ed., *Das diakonische Amt der Kirche* (1953).

Only in the Reformed ecclesiastical tradition has the diaconate become a more or less clearly institutionalized function of the church. To some extent this was due to what has been called Reformed "biblicism"; it was (wrongly) concluded from Acts 6 that the diaconal office of mercy was one of the offices prescribed by Scripture. This is something we may indeed regard as a blessing in disguise! Particularly Bucer, Calvin, and à Lasco have given theological and organizational shape to this office. For Calvin see *Inst* IV,iii,9 and *Les ordonnances ecclésiastiques* (1954); he distinguishes between those who were in charge of the gifts for the poor, and those who themselves were to aid the poor, the sick, the aged, the widows, and the orphans. In Reformed church polity, until recently, the place of the deacon was somewhat lower and less clearly defined than that of the minister and the elder, even though (note this!) his office was regarded as the representation of Christ's most central, his priestly office. In the static society of the post-Reformation centuries little was done to develop a greater responsiveness to needs as well as ingenuity to meet them and to become more proficient in exposing the sore spots in society; a beginning with that was made in the 19th century with the formation of a great number of Christian organizations of benevolence. The experiences during the German occupation, when many of these organizations were forbidden and many new challenges—which were partly illegal—arose, provided a powerful impulse to the institutional diaconate. The result of that can be seen in the *Church Order of the Dutch Reformed Church* (1951), art. IV-7, which, besides mentioning the traditional duties of the deacons, states that they, "standing amidst the social needs of the people, have the task of serving the church with advice concerning those needs, in order that it can also challenge the government and society to see and to meet its calling to work for social justice." Only after that did the so much greater needs of the Third World come into purview. Since then the diaconal initiative has very much shifted to the agencies of the World Council of Churches. The official diaconate is mostly supporting these agencies and making the contacts between this work and the local congregations. At the moment, many regard what is done in this way for the victims of natural catastrophes, military conflicts, race discrimination, and dictatorial regimes as the most eloquent articulation of God's purpose with the world and as more "mediating" than one of the other means of salvation.

Theoretical reflection on the diaconate after the Reformation yielded little more until in and right after the Second World War, when interest in the diaconal task greatly increased again. But then the danger was that the concept of diaconate became so broad and comprehensive that it left little room for the unique dimensions of the institutional diaconate. Two important works which try to do justice to both aspects are: P. J. Roscam Abbing, *Diakonia* (1950), of which par. 25 deals specifically with the diaconate, and P. Philippi, *Das Christozentrische Diakonie* (1963), esp. par. 11 c. 3 and par. 12.

A separate question is whether, or to what extent, the diaconate has to make the *church* or the *world* its primary concern. At the moment there is a strong shift from the first to the second. "So then, as we have opportunity, let us do good to all men, and especially to those who are of the household of faith" (Gal. 6:10). Because God loves the world, the emphasis in this text can be changed when required by changing circumstances. But in no case may church and world, relative to the diaconal task, be regarded as competitors. In her care for her own members the church should actively testify to her possession of the mind "which is yours in Christ Jesus," and which therefore makes her anxious to move beyond her own confines with deeds of mercy. See A. M. van Peski, *The Outreach of Diakonia* (1968).

Regularly we have maintained that the diaconate concerns itself with *guilt* as well as with *need.* Mostly the diaconate is thought of as related only to need. It is sometimes said that preaching as the message of forgiveness directs itself to man's guilt while the diaconate as the ministry of mercy directs itself to man's need. Relative to that it should be observed that in her preaching the church also speaks comfortingly with respect to needs and prophetically with respect to injustice. At the same time, a most important task of the diaconate is that it practically demonstrate God's forgiveness in its ministry to fallen men and women and those behind bars (see e.g. the Salvation Army). The difference is much rather that the words of the sermon are directed to man's heart and disposition and the deeds of the diaconate to the concrete physical situation. On need and guilt as two mutually irreducible areas of concern of the gospel, see O. Noordmans, *Zondaar en bedelaar* (1946), pp. 9–26.

For a general discussion of the diaconal ministry see Barth, *CD* IV,3, pp. 890–895. For theology and practice together, see D. J. Karres, *De gemeente en haar diakonaat* (1969), and *Handboek voor diakenen in de Nederlands Hervormde Kerk* (1983ff.), esp. ch. 1, "Bijbelse achtergronden."

7. The meeting

Most of the means of transmission we have dealt with so far are naturally a part of the weekly gathering of the congregation. This activity must therefore be regarded as very much a part of these means, and for that reason we take it up here. We should be careful, however, not to think of this meeting as only a convenient organizational combination of the institutional means. For that it is itself too much directly involved in the transmission of God's salvation. It is not so that first there were the means of transmission, and that next they were put together in an official and orderly assembly. The meeting itself is logically and historically equally original as the media that are active within it. It is therefore more than a sum of these and other activities. It is itself a mediating field, an organic whole which exceeds its component parts. Therefore it must be discussed here.

We have opted here for the word *meeting*. Strange to say, this word is not normally used, even though the NT, in the few times that it deals with this matter, employs this or a similar word; see Matt. 18:20 (*synēgmenoi*); 1 Cor. 14:23 (*synēlthen*); 1 Cor. 14:26 (*synerchēsthe*); Heb. 10:25 (*episynagogē*), and Jas. 2:2

(*synagogē*). The official term in much theological literature is *liturgy*, which literally means "rendering of a service" (for the benefit of the community) and which is used in the Septuagint to designate Israel's tabernacle and temple service. The NT uses it for that, and furthermore for various forms of Christian service (collection, intercessory prayer, missions) and once for the work of the government (Rom. 13:6), but never for what we call liturgy; see *TDNT* IV, *s.v. leitourgeō*. Apparently the church service was not regarded as a continuation of the temple service, but rather of the service of the synagogue (but this is different already in 2 Clement 40–44). The usual official ecclesiastical designations for the church service are: *officium*, office, *culte*, service, worship, *Gottesdienst, godsdienstoefening*. The problem with all these words is that they denote exclusively an activity performed by man and, moreover, they tend to suggest that this is a kind of achievement toward God. The word *meeting* is more matter-of-fact and less pretentious. The term "meeting" also implies that God and man meet with each other. Already Heb. 10:25 indicates the mediating character of this meeting together, regarding it as necessary for holding onto the faith and for persevering in love and good works (23f.).

Western theology with its restricted concept of sacrament has never acknowledged the sacramental character of the meeting. This contrasts rather strangely with the importance which the churches everywhere attach to church attendance. In fact, for many Christians church attendance is itself a sacramental event which by itself or in spite of some of its elements (esp. the sermon) can strengthen the faith. This edifying character is fully knowledged only in the Eastern church. There the worship service is experienced entirely as the reenactment and realization of the incarnation. (See e.g. S. Boulgakof, *L'orthodoxie*, 1932, IX.) Eastern Orthodox Christians like to speak of the worship service as "heaven on earth" and to relate how the conversion of Russia began with the fact that delegates from Grandduke Vladimir I of Kiev, having attended a service in the Aya Sophia in Constantinople, reported about it: "We did not know where we were, in heaven or on earth." In the Netherlands, G. van der Leeuw has defended the sacramental character of the church service; according to him it is to be oriented to the "basic form of the contact with God, the incarnation of the Word" (*Liturgiek*, 1940, p. 15; cf. pars. 4–9). He was challenged by O. Noordmans, who saw in the Eastern Orthodox conception with its continuation of the incarnation the creation on an independent cultic space which threatened to choke the free encounter of a gracious God with a guilty world (*Liturgie*, 1939, esp. pp. 128–157). Indeed, as Western Christians we cannot take over the Eastern conception of the liturgy; we would experience it as a flight from reality or as a trance. It has its background in the Greek mysteries and it takes place in a collectivistic experience of life which is not ours. Yet it must make us pause to think that precisely because of the spiritual reserves of this liturgy the Eastern churches have been able to withstand the pressures of Islam, Roman Catholicism, and communism. All the Western forms of meeting (including the Roman Catholic mass) are more matter-of-fact and pragmatic, and at the same time livelier, with a greater emphasis on the pastoral and the personal. Nevertheless, the mass could for centuries be celebrated and attended as an objective event in which the believer was hardly more than a spectator. Here, too, the Reformation meant a greater emphasis on personal involvement. In his often cited sermon at the dedication of the castle church in Torgau (1544) Luther described the essence of the Sunday service in these words: "... that we are to come together... deal with and listen to God's Word, bring to God our ordinary and unusual needs and those of others and thus launch up to heaven a strong, effectual prayer, and also together laud and praise God's goodness with thanksgiving. And of this we know that it is the right service and worship of God, a service which is well-pleasing to him and in which he himself is present." In spite of the last words (and in spite of the regular appeal to Matt. 18:20), the Reformation has never theoretically acknowledged the mediating character of the church service. It is not hard to see why this was not done; the subject-object mode of thinking which was still current at the time and the increasing emphasis, since Luther, on the human subject were not conducive to it. But this is one of the reasons why in our tradition the services lack warmth and enthusiasm and are so little celebration. The many liturgical movements after the Second World War, which are often characterized by carefully stylized responses, etc., have made too little change in this situation. And all sorts of "experimental church services" which are in vogue today are lacking too much in sensitivity for the sacramental to be able to bring about an essential renewal. A good theological beginning is found in *De hervormde kerkdienst. Proeve van omschrijving* (Synode Nederlandse Hervormde Kerk, 1950), esp. thesis II, which begins as follows: "The basis of the meeting of the congregation is found in what is the basis of all of Christian life, namely, in the covenant God has established with His people, in which it pleases Him to reveal Himself to us." How closely liturgy, dogmatics, and ethics are interrelated can be seen in G. Wainwright, *Doxology. A Systematic Theology* (1980).

The mediating character of the congregational gathering consists in the fact that it articulates and realizes the encounter between God and his people. It is the reflection and representation of the covenant event. The Lord and his people are together in a structured whole of Word and response. The purpose of that whole is first of all itself. Everything we know about love and friendship needs articulation on the one hand and nurture on the other. The communion with God in Christ also needs both; and it receives both together in the church service. Therefore all the basic elements, in one way or another, explicitly or implicitly or in symbolic form, have their place in this event. The appointed day for that is "the day of the Lord," Sunday as the day of the resurrection, of the successful covenant partnership. In that gathering Christ stands in the center as the one who invites and brings us together and who wants to be present in Word, meal, and our fellowship with each another. But as a christological event the meeting is also eschatological. As celebration and fellowship it anticipates the day which in the deepest sense is "the day of the Lord," and so it gives us a foretaste of the eternal sabbath. But not in such a way that the future makes us forget the present; for sin and guilt are also central themes, particularly the acquittal which enables us to live again. In this gathering we exercise ourselves in concentrating upon God, in lifting up our hearts on high, and in losing ourselves in adoration. That does not, however, estrange us from each other; on the contrary, it welds us together as a community. Nor does it estrange us from the world outside, because the aim of the meeting is to equip us for service in everyday life. Moreover, as our experience of what the covenant is, it is also intended as an eloquent sign that reaches out to and draws in the world. All the while, none of these aspects in the least crowds out the individual; on the contrary, he or she wants the meeting, often first of all in hopes of finding new strength for faith, heart, and life. So we see all the elements and aspects converge here: reconciliation and expectation, present, past, and future, vertical and horizontal, individual and community, church and world. This is the reason that theoretically the meeting can be approached from many different angles and practically be experienced quite differently. There is nothing against that, provided the differences are seen as radiating from and leading to the one center: the encounter of God with his people.

Generally speaking, one can say that the Eastern liturgy is strongly eschatologically oriented, that the Roman Catholic mass christologically focuses on the sacrifice on the cross, that the classical Protestant liturgy pneumatologically wants to evoke the awareness of sin and absolution, and that the Anglican aims especially at worship. In the Netherlands this last element has been much neglected; by way of reaction, it has received a lot of emphasis in the liturgical movement, especially in its earlier phases; see J. H. Gerretsen, *Liturgie* (1911). After 1950 the emphasis came to be placed on the apostolate (see *The Church for Others,* 1967, pp. 25f.), and after 1970 on secularization (see G. J. Hoenderdaal, *Riskant spel,* 1977). A fascinating discussion of many aspects of the meeting can be found in A. A. van Ruler, *Waarom zou ik naar de kerk gaan?* (1970).

Using the essence and the aspects of the meeting as background, we can now speak about the elements that it may or should consist of. In the light of what we have said so far, we can think of many elements and of even more forms in which those elements can come to expression. Tradition, customs, cultural level, and particular needs vary a great deal according to geographical area and historical period, making for a great diversity in possible and legitimate liturgies. That does not, however, do away with the underlying fixed structure of the liturgy. The encounter character of the meeting implies both variability (God regularly encounters different people) and a certain stability: the point is always the encounter with the same God whom we come to know in Christ through the Spirit. The liturgy is to structure the encounter and therefore must itself be structured as encounter. For that reason the liturgy is everywhere an antiphonal event in which, to the one side, God comes to us in such elements as proclamation of grace, command, Scripture reading, preaching, meal, and benediction; and in which, to the other side, we come before God with our confession of sin, litany, praise, profession of faith, prayers and intercessions, gifts for his work in the church and the world, and hymns of humiliation and adoration, of praise and petition. Even those liturgical practices in various churches and areas which at first sight appear to be quite unlike, at a closer look contain in some measure the same elements of this sacred ritual of word and response. Everywhere one finds the threefold service of word, prayers, and the table. The differences concern primarily the manner in which the relation between preaching and the meal is articulated. In point 5 (the meal) we have argued that in the meeting they belong together as the two foci of an ellipse. Most churches do not explicitly deny that, yet it is seldom practiced. Furthermore, important differences arise from whether the encounter preferably resorts to the spiritual vehicle of the word, or expresses itself in gestures or other forms which are directed to the physical senses of sight, smell, or touch. What to the one is the most fitting expression for contact with God, the other may experience as a great hindrance because he feels it as an impoverishment or a materialization of that contact. Another difference concerns the extent to which the congregation as a whole is actively involved in the service or most of the functions are concentrated in one leader. The latter can make a monological and cold impression, while the former can make the service disorganized and irreverent. Yet the study of the faith may not content itself with relativizing this third point of difference any more than the first. The rule for the meeting of the congregation should be that the leader represents God in all the acts in which he relates himself to the congregation and that the congregation as much as possible expresses her own responses to God, not only in stereotyped formulas of response but also in spontaneous prayers.

The congregational liturgy easily becomes sacrosanct, making it very difficult to introduce changes. As a result, for many worshippers many of the liturgical forms have long since lost their mediating character. The essence of the liturgy as the vehicle and expression of the covenantal communion implies its changeability. Moreover, what is now called a sacred tradition, at one time began as an experiment. And for the benefit of those who are estranged from it and for future generations it needs to be accompanied, enriched, and corrected by continually new experiments.

The earliest description of the meeting is found in parts of 1 Cor. 10, 11, 12, and 14. The "corporate worship" described here was short-lived because of the disorder which apparently attended it (14:33, 40). It is remarkable that Paul in fighting these practices points to the missionary function of the meeting (14:23–25). Unfortunately, with the bath water of disorder the baby of corporate fellowship has also been thrown out. Only a few free churches (Quakers, Salvation Army, Pentecostals, and others) have recovered this element.

The book by D. G. Dix, *The Shape of the Liturgy* (1945), which is now a classic, points out this continuity amid the variety and overgrowth of liturgical forms, and the permanent basic structure of the meeting centered around "synaxis" and "eucharist." In this area, Martin Bucer has performed groundbreaking work for the Reformation through the reformational understanding of misery, deliverance, and gratitude. Early on, however, Reformed liturgy was again much reduced, with the result that the worship services became primarily occasions for listening to doctrinal orations. It was not until and after World War II that other elements again became important, as they were in Bucer and the early Calvin. On the development of the liturgy in the Dutch Reformed Church, see H. Jonker, *Liturgische orientatie* (1962). Later this tradition in the liturgy had to yield to a reaching back to pre-reformational traditions, culminating in the handbook *Onze hulp* (1978).

If liturgy is expression of the covenantal fellowship, it may need and perhaps should incorporate still other elements that we presently recognize little or not at all, such as sublimity, bodilyness, mutuality, and homeliness. The present habit of going back to ancient Christian liturgies promote stylization, but it has a stifling effect on the flexibility and spontaneity of the worship that was characteristic of the early Christian church.

8. Office

With the foregoing seven points we have reached the end of what we wanted to say about the salvation-mediating institutional elements of the church. Nevertheless, we shall add two more points to the list, namely office and church order, because both serve to make the other seven operative. This is first of all true of office. Thus far we spoke of elements, means, channels, or activities. But we should not forget that these can function only if they are administered by people, or, as is mostly the case in our situation, by one person. Though that does not make that person himself sacramental, it does give him an institutional function. He or she is mandated to serve the mediating process. Such people thus have a special task in the church. They step outside the ranks of the members of the congregation, in order that for them they may represent Christ, the Spirit, and the Word. Their separate position expresses that salvation does not arise out of our midst, nor out of the Christian church either. It comes simultaneously from above and out of history. Due to its historical character, we could not conceive of it, and due to the fact that it puts us under judgment and offends us, we would not have been willing to conceive of it. Therefore it needs to be announced and mediated to us. Not only are means needed for that, but people too. They cannot of their own accord assume that role. They must have the confidence and the mandate of the congregation. They are themselves members of the congregation, equally sinful and limited as the others; but because of the mandate with which the congregation has invested them, they are made to stand opposite her, to proclaim to her, on behalf of God, the message she cannot give to herself and perhaps does not want to give either. They are thus not the echo of the congregation, but of the one who leads, inspires, and corrects her. That does not put them in a position of isolation, for all they do is serve the congregation in the mediation of grace. And should the congregation be of the opinion that they are negligent or incompetent in their duties and consequently no longer be interested in their service, she can remove them from their separate position.

The task of the offices is that of carrying out the duties inherent in the seven salvation-mediating elements. People are thus appointed for instruction and for preaching, to administer baptism, to officiate in the meeting and at the meal, to depict the church's concern for the needy, and to supervise and conduct the religious discussion in its varying forms, personal and communal. Moreover, in virtue of this calling, the office-bearers are the people who give leadership to the congregation to guard them in the salvation they have and to equip them for a life of faith, hope, and love.

The office-bearer is thus not himself "mediating." Or is he? For it is a fact that the caliber of the personal faith of many members of the congregation is very much dependent on who their leaders are and on their gifts and abilities to mediate and transmit God's salvation. It can be argued that the office, and therewith the office-bearer, have a mediating and thus sacramental character; but only in a derived sense because and insofar as they participate and cause to participate in the process which the Spirit carries out through his means. But in that capacity they are genuinely important. Without such people who stand opposite the congregation on behalf of Christ, the salvation-mediating process would lose its uniqueness and contours and eventually become indistinguishable from whatever else arises in the hearts and out of the mutual fellowship of the members of the congregation.

Relative to the discussion about office, one must bear in mind that this does not refer only to professional theologians and specialized full-time church workers. The early church and most Protestant churches show a different picture; Paul was a tentmaker, and elders and deacons performed their office only in their spare time. Also, the idea of the office being for life, let alone its having an indelible character as in Roman Catholicism, does not belong to the essence of the office. The office is a specific function, distinguished from all other roles to which a person is called by and out of the congregation, for a shorter or longer period of time, either full-time or part-time. A person is called because he or she possesses a charisma (see the next par. on that) which normally, though not exclusively, can also be effectively used in the discharge of the office.

Speaking in general terms, three views on office can be distinguished in the various churches: (1) the Catholic or high-church type, which regards ordination as a sacrament by which the bearer, in virtue of a special promise of the Spirit, is permanently placed not only opposite but also above the congregation; (2) the classical Reformed type, which positions him not only opposite but also in the congregation, and circumscribes his authority by the general office of all believers; (3) the free church or low-church type, which sees in the office-bearer no more than a functional specialization of the office of all believers, in principle no different from that of the custodian or administrator. These three types have evolved successively. This reflects the development in society from a feudal to an aristocratic to a democratic societal structure, in consequence of which there came about a steady reduction in the authority of the office. As such there is nothing against the fact that the phenomenon of the office is colored by the cultural climate of the times; on the contrary, to a certain extent its mediating function requires it. It does, however, make the question concerning the constant factor in its structure all the more urgent.

Can that be derived from the NT? It is remarkable that all three types (can) appeal to it. The first type appeals to the authority of the apostles (Matt. 10:40; 18:18), which is regarded as having passed on, by means of the apostolic succession, to the later bishops. The second appeals to the principial equality of *episkopos* and *presbyteros* (Acts 20:28; 1 Tim. 3:1f.; 5:17; Tit. 1:5–7) and to the conception of office in Eph. 4:7–16. The third appeals to the large place of the mature congregation and the relative unimportance of the office-bearers in Paul's epistles, and to the picture of the charismatic church in 1 Cor. 12 and 14. Indeed, the NT by no means presents a uniform picture of *the* office (it does not even have a separate word for it). For varying interpretations of this difficult subject see A. J. Bronkhorst, *Schrift en kerkorde* (1947), I and II 4; E. Schweizer, *Gemeinde und Gemeindeordnung im NT* (1959); and Küng, *The Church*, E II 2.

For the study of the faith this variety becomes problematic only if it is assumed that the NT (has to) teach *one* revealed church order. The matter looks altogether different if the variety is traced back historically to a difference in situation (Jewish-Christian over against Gentile-Christian, first over against second generation, *et al.*), and if we then accept it as an invitation to shape the office in our situation in *our* way. *The* office is not to be derived from an assortment of texts, but first of all from the NT character of the church and in particular from the function of her institutional dimension. (See large type.)

The Roman Catholic Church has never appealed only to the NT, but foremost to the direction in which the office evolved in and after Ignatius of Antioch: the picture of the single bishop as Christ's representative, assisted by presbyters to whom every church member owes obedience. Essential to the conception of office in all Catholic-minded churches is the doctrine of apostolic succession. This doctrine holds that the official authority, via a chain of laying on of hands, goes back to the special authority of the apostles in the NT. But this teaching, which did not arise until the 2nd century, had as its purpose to show what the pure tradition was amidst the confusion of the many heresies. In the NT the apostle is the once-for-all eyewitness, personally called by Christ himself. "Apostolic succession" is thus an inner contradiction. The unique witness of the apostles now accompanies us through time in the form of the NT canon. The other functions of the apostles devolved partly on the church as a whole, partly on various offices, such as teacher, prophet, elder, evangelist. The office-bearers are to base themselves on the original witness of the apostles (called *successio doctrinae* since the Reformation); but that is something else than an institutional transfer of authority. Particularly in the Anglican Church, which practices a succession of ordinations, much reflection on and discussion of this problem is going on. For a survey see G. Gassmann, *Das historische Bischofsamt und die Einheit der Kirche in der neueren anglikanischen Theologie* (1964). According to this conception there is actually only one office, that of the bishop; the priests have a derived office. Luther, too, has in principle only one office, that of the local preacher. Owing to its biblicistic outlook the Calvinistic Reformation wanted to restore the offices of the NT, yet it dropped quite a few on the assumption that these were intended only for the first period. As in so many other areas, here too Bucer was the architect. According to him the office of presbyter was the basic office, the office of preacher being a specialized form of it and the diaconate a helping office; relative to this he strongly emphasized the principial equality of the offices. See W. van't Spijker, *De ambten bij Martin Bucer* (1970), esp. pp. 360–365. Calvin recognized as a fourth the office of doctor of theology; for his theology of office see *Inst* IV,iii, esp. 4–9. The plurality of NT traditions made it impossible for this biblicistic approach to come up with all the satisfactory answers, and so the Reformed tradition remained burdened with uncertainties and questions. (A survey of this tradition is given by Bavinck, *GD* IV, no. 506.) The primary problem concerns the relationship of minister and elder, who are alternately regarded as equal or as subordinate to each other. Hence the considerable difference in the structure of the offices in the Reformed churches of Scotland, the Netherlands, Switzerland, and Hungary. Yet by its plurality and collegiality as well as by its practice of appointing nonordained office-bearers, this conception of office, in all the years of its existence, has proven its effectiveness and flexibility, and could serve as a model for political democracy.

A strange element in the Reformed theology of the offices is the desire to derive the three offices (Calvin devised four!) from the threefold office of Christ (see par. 34). The minister is said to occupy the prophetic office, the elder the kingly (directing and ruling) office, and the deacon the priestly office. See, e.g., Bavinck, *GD,* no. 506. This is clearly a forced construction in which the minister would represent the least outstanding office of Christ!

In our judgment the Reformed conception, as via media between the high church and low church conceptions, comes closest to the essence of the office in its dialectical relationship to the congregation, and also leaves the most room for new forms as required by the situation. Precisely owing to this position it also experiences the pressure of high church and low church alternatives, whose advantage over the Reformed position is their nondialectical consistency. For the controversies in the Reformed camp, see the study report of the synod of the Nederlands Hervormde Kerk, *Wat is er aan de hand met het ambt?* (1970), and in contrast a more traditional view in A. F. N. Lekkerkerker, *Oorsprong en funktie van het ambt* (1971).

On the ecumenical church scene the pull is nowadays toward elevating the office. See the Lima report *Baptism, Eucharist and Ministry,* the part on "Ministry." Because here, too, there is a fascination with the number three, while at the same time the (regional) bishop is put first, the office of elder suffers eclipse. Yet this is precisely the office that on account of its terminal character and lesser amount of schooling can satisfy the need to bring the office closer to the congregation. At the present time that need is most strongly felt in certain parts of the Roman Catholic Church (United States, Latin America, Netherlands), where vigorous low church (congregationalist) conceptions of the office emerge and Schillebeeckx' *Kerkelijk ambt* (1980) serves as a guide.

9. Church polity (church order)

In a much more subsidiary fashion than the office, church polity is intended to serve the process of mediating the grace of God. Basically church order is a set of rules and regulations which are designed to facilitate, insofar as this is possible, the mediating task of the church and the work of the office-bearers who are involved in it. A book on dogmatics is not the place to come with a detailed discussion of the many questions that are encountered here; that type of discussion belongs under church law. We are concerned here only with the basic questions of church law which are directly related to ecclesiology.

The main question is then: Can there be such a thing as church law? Is it not a contradiction in terms? After all, in the church the Spirit blows where he wills, and while he makes use of means, his work (inside or outside it) cannot be directed by man. However, matters like law, order, rules, and regulations always refer to: compulsion, higher and lower, outwardness, human authority, rights and sanctions. It is questionable, however, whether the term "law" should be so narrowly defined that by implication a tension is created between it and the Spirit. Protestant churches prefer the term "church order." The Spirit is not something so "spiritual" that he can have nothing to do with order. On the contrary, "God is not a God of confusion but of peace" (1 Cor. 14:33); therefore "all things should be done decently and in good order" (v. 40). The Spirit wants to communicate God's salvation to people who are estranged from God. In a sensitive matter such as this it is important to do the right thing, and love for the gospel and for the people whom we try to reach should make us very cautious. Whatever rules we devise must make room for the work of the Spirit. If we insist on having absolute control we stand in his way. But if we permit anarchy we allow all other spirits the same room we give to him. All church polity should serve the one goal of mediating God's grace and of realizing the covenant. It is the Spirit who ever and again translates and communicates Christ to the people. That fact indicates both the basis and the boundaries of our work in church polity; it obligates us to insure that the christological stability as well as the situational flexibility is preserved.

Implied in the above is that we decline to look for a church order in the NT. Time was that theologians could show that the order of their particular denomination could be found in the Bible, but that is a thing of the past. We today know much more of the variations in the traditions in the NT and of how, then and now, throughout all of church history, the polity of the church was co-inspired and colored by the prevailing laws of the country and the existing social relationships. Since in the church the concern is the mediation of God's grace, this is as such an obvious and good development. This insight has changed the nature of the appeal to Scripture, but it has not done away with it. The appeal is now to the matter that is to be mediated and to the nature of the transmission process; it has assumed an indirect character. Rules are needed to guarantee that the work of preaching and teaching, of the washing and the meal, of the liturgy and of the diaconal and pastoral task will be done as effectively as possible. These rules thus describe the required training and duties of the office-bearers as well as the rights of the congregation. That makes it necessary that through our reading of the Bible we develop a sensitivity for what is right and what is wrong, for what is better and what is less desirable.

In the Netherlands, O. Noordmans has concerned himself in the fullest sense with the relationship of Scripture, tradition, and the modern era relative to church polity. He did this in his conflict with Haitjema and "church restoration" on the one hand, and A. M. Brouwer and a large part of "upbuilding of the church" on the other. See his *Verzamelde Werken,* Vol. I. He spoke of a "pneumatic" and of a "world historical" exegesis of Scripture. An overview of his ideas is offered by F. Haarsma, *Geest en kerk* (1967), VI.

For a long time (in a sense until the present) the discussion about the legitimacy and the nature of church law was dominated by R. Sohm, *Kirchenrecht,* I (1892), whose starting-point and conclusion is the proposition that "church law is incompatible with the essence of the church. The true church, the church of Christ, does not know of church law" (p. 459). A later theologian who shows affinity to him is Brunner. He contrasts the "*Ekklēsia*" as brotherhood with the "church" as a corporate body in a juridical sense; the difference is that, more so than Sohm, he wants to do justice to the social structure of the congregation (*Dg* III, esp. I, II-IV). As is evident from his posthumous *Kirchenrecht,* II (1923), Sohm eventually ended up with the *ecclesia invisibilis,* while Brunner has to acknowledge that the church indeed needs an order, even functions, and somewhat of a hierarchical structure (e.g. p. 66). For a critical discussion of Sohm see Trillhaas, *Dg* pp. 535–538; of Sohm and Brunner, see Barth, *CD* IV,2, pp. 679–686.

Sohm's grip was broken in Germany when the "German Christians" came with their *Führerprinzip* and *Arierparagraph.* The Confessing Church stated in Barmen (1934), and as a consequence of that in Dahlem (1934) by instituting the ecclesiastical "emergency law," that the nature of the church implies specific "Scriptural" rules for a church order. The theologian-jurist Erik Wolf, and following him Karl Barth, have elaborated that insight. See especially *CD* IV,2, par. 67,4 ("The Order of the Church"), which can serve as a starting-point for further discussion. Just as we seek to derive church order from the process of mediation, so Barth derives it from the peculiar event of Christian worship; accordingly he also speaks of liturgical law (pp. 695–710). For a concretization see his six points on pp. 723f.

After 1933 the normative and stable elements came to be central, but in more recent years in our rapidly changing world the flexible and situational aspects of all church polity are again strongly emphasized. Both Noordmans and Barth have made room for that. Barth derives it from the fact that the Lord of the church is the living Jesus Christ (pp. 710–719). But he refuses any input from the situation. However understandable this may be after 1933, the result is that his pages on "church law as living law" remain abstract. "A dynamic from below may have no influence at all on church law" (p. 710). This is at variance with all of church history: the Roman Catholic form of church government is unthinkable without the feudal system, the Lutheran without agrarian paternalism, the Calvinistic without the aristocratic citizenry of Geneva, the free-church type without the rise of democracy in Western Europe and America. Over the years sociology has discovered certain things concerning the function of laws to which all institutions, churches included, are subject. See De Haas, *The Church as an Institution.* It is no use closing one's eyes to that. This awareness is useful if it makes one more conscious of the changeability of church orders and of the continual mandate to express in updated form the relation between what is normative and what is situational. Church orders—certainly in our time—should be loose-leaf!

Three problems in the area of church order may not remain untouched, not in a study of the faith either. The first is the problem of doctrinal discipline. If church polity is to guard the mediating process, it will obviously have to set rules for proclamation and instruction. To begin with, the office-bearers will have to state, in one form or another, the content and the norm which they accept for all their transmission activity. If they become aware that they no longer agree with that, they should resign their office. But what is to be done if they do not feel that way themselves, but the church at large thinks differently? In that case the church can make a pronouncement about the teachings of such an office-bearer to avoid a confusion of spirits and to make clear what she sees as the true gospel. Will such a declaration and a concomitant admonition to the office-bearer suffice? In other words, is it enough to practice a so-called ethical, therapeutic, or judicial form of doctrinal discipline? Or should he also by ecclesiastical sentence be deposed from his office, by what is called juridical or justiciable discipline? A church which is deeply conscious of her high calling and which knows of the distortions to which the gospel, since it is foolishness and an offense to the world, is always subject, will not a priori exclude such a deposition as the final resort. There are situations in which it is all or nothing. That is rarely the case, however, where it concerns the deviating ideas of only one office-bearer. Nor should a possible deposition be automatically considered in case an office-bearer defends views which are rejected by his own denomination but accepted in other churches. As a matter of fact, the lesson of history is that "heretics" have often been people who defended truths that had been lost sight of or who were ahead of their own church in their insights as to how the gospel could best be passed on to a future generation. For these reasons juridical discipline may not be excluded, nor may it become the rule. The truth is only rarely served by acts of force; rather it is promoted by coming with arguments, by a spiritual struggle to see the light, and by brotherly discussion.

In times when a static conception of the truth prevailed, and was maintained by the *corpus Christianum*, juridical doctrinal discipline was the commonly accepted procedure. In the case of the Roman Catholic inquisition it was accompanied, wherever possible, by delivering the heretic into the hands of the government; in other words, the punishment was often imprisonment or death. For the Reformation that remained an exception (Reformed: Servetus; Lutheran: Crell). Social and political discrimination continued for a long time, though. Particularly in the Netherlands there has been a lot of doctrinal discipline, first in connection with the Arminian controversy, but especially in connection with the reorganization of the Dutch state church in 1816 which practically resulted in doctrinal freedom. From that time on the right and necessity of doctrinal discipline became an integral part of all groups holding to classical Reformed teachings. These were co-factors that led to the Secession of 1834 and the Doleantie of 1886. Among those who did not break away from the state church, the "confessionals" argued for juridical discipline and the "ethicals" advocated therapeutic discipline. O. Noordmans has done much to bring their standpoints together. See F. Haarsma, *Geest en kerk* (1967), pp. 231–250, and H. Bartels, *Tien jaren strijd om een belijdende kerk* (1946). This resulted in the *Church Order of the Dutch Reformed Church* (1951), of which Art. X-6 simply says: "The Church opposes whatever contradicts her confession," but in which Ordinance XI, under the heading "Exercise of Ecclesiastical Discipline," in articles 6–13 sets forth a careful procedure which guards against too great haste and the misuse of power. It is remarkable and significant, however, that this church has thus far not made use of the prescribed procedure, but has almost always performed her doctrinal discipline through discussions with church visitors and through synodical pronouncements, without juridical consequences.

From their inception the Reformed Churches have stressed that their great difference with the Dutch Reformed Church is their exercise of juridical discipline in cases of doctrinal dispute. This has led in a few instances to the deposition of some ministers. Best known is the deposition from office of J. G. Geelkerken by the Synod of Assen in 1926. Subsequently that act and its motivation were more and more deplored, eventually even in a synodical decision. Since 1926 these churches have not had a case of doctrinal discipline as such. As regards theory, the Dutch Reformed Church has come very close to the Reformed Churches, whereas in practice the latter have grown closer to the former. See also Berkouwer, *The Church*, ch. 14, esp. pp. 377–390. The question of the appropriateness of doctrinal discipline can likely be answered only in a practical-situational manner. The spiritual damage caused by a juridical process or by a "therapeutic" treatment can be very different depending on whether it is done in a fierce struggle against imposed ideologies or in a secular and pluralistic culture.

A second problem in church government, which should at least be touched on in the study of the faith, is the relation of the local church and the church as a whole. This is a significant topic since it belongs to the essence of the church that in all its components and on all levels it is a single entity, called to transmit to the best of her ability the one, indivisible gospel. A local congregation is much more than a subdivision of, for instance, a national church. And a synod is much more than the sum total of its delegates. In no church is this insight entirely lost, nor, however, is there any church which has adequately worded it in its church order. Likely it cannot be adequately verbalized. Theology will have to content itself with constantly pointing out that the church is one and indivisible. One cannot simply add up all the local churches to get the church. It is not a matter of addition but of multiplication in which *one* times *one* remains *one*. Every form of church constitutes an organic whole. Though it may not be possible to express this insight in a church order, it is possible to approximate it, and in cases of conflict it can serve as a corrective principle.

In the NT *ekklēsia* is the regular designation for what we call a local congregation; if the reference is to more than one congregation the plural is used. However, in Acts 9:31 the singular stands for all the Palestinian congregations combined (but note the variant *ekklēsiai* in the *Koinē* text). And the unity of the *ekklēsiai* was denoted through their relationship to the mother church in Jerusalem. Thus it is not surprising to find the singular used in Eph. to denote all the congregations together. (A similar use is there made of *sōma*, a term which in Rom. and 1 Cor. indicates the local congregation.) That usage eventually became predominant. The local *ekklēsia* then came to be called *paroikia* (parish); the distinction can be found as early as the introduction of the *Martyrium Polycarpi* (ca. 160). The parish, served by a presbyter, becomes a subdivision of a much larger episcopal church, which itself becomes a subdivision of a hierarchically structured whole which in the West became entirely subject to the bishop of Rome. This has led to the death of the spiritual independence of the local church, though it took a long struggle (see F. Heiler, *Altkirchliche Autonomie und päpstlicher Zentralismus*, 1941); nor did it happen without constant eruptions in later centuries, which in recent years in the Netherlands and elsewhere have become extremely intense. The Eastern church, not in practice but at least in theory, has preserved the awareness that the local eucharistic community is the full church (see N. Afanassieff, "Das Hirtenamt der Kirche: in der Liebe der Germeinde vorstehen," in *Das Primat des Petrus in der orthodoxen Kirche*, 1961, pp. 7–65). Yet it was only the Reformation, not the Lutheran but the Reformed, which finally became serious about it. Think of the familiar opening words of the Acts of the Synod of Emden (Oct. 1571): "No church shall obtain primacy or dominance over other churches, nor minister over ministers, nor elder over elders, nor deacon over deacons, but rather each shall guard against every suspicion and occasion of suspicion." Already before Emden (ca. 1550), among Protestants in England, this insight gave rise to what later came to be called "Independentism" or "Congregationalism," a conception of the church which allowed no higher authority than that of the local congregation. In contrast with Rome's hierarchicalism, here individualism, unbounded freedom, sometimes even anarchy threaten to determine what the nature of the church is. See further Weber, *Gl* II, pp. 587–590.

In the Netherlands, unlike elsewhere, Reformed Protestantism has shown a strong preference for "the autonomy of the local congregation"; for that see Voetius' influential *Politica ecclesiastica* (1663ff.). In theory the Reformed Churches (note the plural, also in the names of other Reformed denominations in the Netherlands) have continued to show a strong preference for this local autonomy, in part in order to show their difference from the more centralized system of the Dutch Reformed Church. But eventually it became and always becomes evident that no church can do without binding decisions made "at the top." Conversely, the Dutch Reformed Church (singular) is careful not to impose on its congregations regulations that can lead to conflicts of conscience. Everywhere the church is called to demonstrate by its life and organization that the rule of Christ by his Word and Spirit excludes putting undue restraints on the conscience *and* leaving it purely up to the individual, tyranny *and* anarchy.

The third problem relative to church order, one that goes much deeper yet because it was also one of the factors that determined the West European schism between Rome and the Reformation, concerns the relationship between the personal and the collegial elements in the government of the church. For from the essence of the office it follows on the one hand that it is personally performed by an individual as Christ's representative (in pastoral care, catechetical instruction, and conducting of public worship), and on the other that the individual exercise of the office is constantly being corrected and supplemented, because the policy that is followed, the confessional stance, the molding and edification of the members of the church, and the strategy to the outside on all levels, is carried out by the college or meeting (consistory, synod, or council). The office has had both faces from the very beginning. Eventually the bishop of Rome was able to impose his one-person authority on the Western part of the church. However, in the Reformation mounting opposition to that hierarchical rule resulted in the fact that the center of authority was shifted to a group (congregational meeting, consistory/council, or synod). Eventually, as the opposites became hardened, it resulted in the formation of two kinds of persons. Though everywhere, and certainly in theological reflection, people realize that both elements must be kept together, structurally the two have not come closer together. For the Roman Catholic Church, with its one-person rule on all levels, cannot possibly allow room for the collegial element without undermining the monarchical element. By contrast, churches that start from the collegial element have the opportunity to give much room to the personal exercise of authority.

The conjunction of collegial and personal is seen already in the circle of the apostles; Peter is designated as the leader (Matt. 16:18f.; John 21:15–17), but this does not put him on a higher spiritual level (Luke 22:31–34) or give him a deeper insight as to the course the church is to follow (Gal. 2:11–14). At times it seems as if anarchism holds sway in the earliest church (Corinth); then again the situation appears almost monarchical (Timothy, Titus). Ignatius is acquainted with the crystallized situation of an overseer as leader of a college of elders. As the people in Europe came of age and became increasingly vocal, resistance against the papal drive to rule the church from the top mounted. The conflict reached its climax in the struggle between conciliarism and papalism (14th and 15th century), in which the first principle nearly won, but ultimately the second principle triumphed. Since then the popes, as Peter's successors and Christ's vicars, have regularly been able, also by means of councils, to enlarge their power. At the very last moment the pope was able to frustrate the attempt of the Second Vatican Council to have the principle of the collegiality of the bishops function as a counterweight (1964 Constitution *Lumen Gentium,* last part: "Nota explicativa praevia"). The Reformation was born not so much out of the struggle over justification by faith as out of Luther's refusal to recognize the pope as the highest authority in spiritual matters. This led to Luther's excommunication (1521). We cannot deal here with the very diverse ways in which Protestant churches have separated and joined personal and collegial authority (but see the end of this section). Through their renunciation of the authority of the pope, the Anglican and Old Catholic Church have also been able to create effective connections of episcopal and synodical authority. In the free churches, which arose in the 17th century and became particularly prominent in the United States, the scales tipped unmistakably to the other side: the collegial crowded out the personal, and often even had to yield to the basis (the local congregation). It is obvious that this development in the government of the church in the Western world is a parallel of the development in the political and social realm, which moved from feudal rule via aristocratic government to democratic forms. The government of the church and that of the state have interacted in all sorts of ways, but the churches have always resorted to theological arguments to justify their particular systems. That is especially true of the Roman Catholic Church, where the pope's position as Vicar of Christ is regarded as a divine institution. Therefore the bilateral talks of Rome with the major confessional organizations, such as the Anglican and Lutheran, always get deadlocked on the fact that the papal system is not adjusted in favor of giving some scope to the conciliar. There are, however, a growing number of Roman Catholic theologians who believe that what they preferably call "the Peter office" in the spirit of the NT can and must be defined afresh as a worldwide service. H. Küng goes farthest in *Structures of the Church* (E.T. 1964), *The Church* (E.T. 1967), and *Infallible?* (E.T. 1971). The Lima report offers no concrete way out, but emphatically points to the threefold manner in which the office is to function: personally, collegially, and communally (esp. "Ministry," pars. 26 and 27).

In our judgment an interplay of these three elements on all levels can promote the guiding character of the organization of the church. Therefore I regard it as regrettable that in a great number of Reformed churches in the Netherlands (Hervormde and Gereformeerde) such an interplay exists only on the local level (consistory and minister). In Presbyterian churches, for the most part of the Scottish type, it also exists on the classical level (presbytery and moderator), and often also on the national level (synod and moderator). The classical moderator serves there especially as visitor and *pastor pastorum.* The demand for an interplay of "council" and "pope" becomes relevant as churches around the world more and more become one. In that connection it is significant that Jesus designated Peter, the man who had denied him, as leader with the words "and when you have turned again, strengthen your brethren" (Luke 22:32). That means that an ecumenical church leader will humbly and encouragingly portray the justification of the sinner by grace alone. In our judgment this implies the acknowledgment of his own fallibility and submission to a collegial authority.

We could now conclude the discussion of the church as institute, were it not for the fact that so far we have not specifically considered the most fundamental question, namely the problem of the relationship between the Spirit and the means. We have more or less assumed that the Spirit makes use of these means. But what do we base that on? That requires further exploration. First we must look into the *that* of the connection between the Spirit and the means. Then, immediately following, the question of the *how* needs to be raised. The question is thus two-pronged.

First, how do we know that the Spirit works through these means? For centuries it was assumed that all the legitimate means were instituted by the earthly Jesus or the glorified Christ (in the instructions he gave during his appearances after the resurrection). For the seven Roman Catholic sacraments this was never convincing. But with the present biblical hermeneutics it no longer holds for the washing with water either. At the same time this fiction prevented the recognition of other means except the traditional. From this forced position we can be liberated only by the insight that the glorified Christ is inseparable from the work of his Spirit in history (see paragraph 37). The Spirit derives everything from Christ and so points the way to the complete truth (John 16:12–15). He effects ever-new encounters and for that is able to use ever-new means. In this respect we must be careful to distinguish between the numerous incidental and individual means (a conversation, a book, a television broadcast, etc.) and those which are intentional and now function within a Christian community. Under certain circumstances, the church and theology may recognize and accept the latter as institutional means. Such acceptance hinges on whether they are genuinely mediating or are intended to mediate the gospel. That recognition does not depend on whether they are mentioned somewhere in the Bible, though that may be a help and a pointer. The Spirit adds no new truths to Christ, yet he does set in motion a new, worldwide historical process in which he makes people share in Christ. That ongoing work of Christ must also come to expression in the means. The church and the study of the faith are as it were the divining rods which signal and follow the courses of the Word through the world. That involves a risk. To err is human, and that applies to the ecclesiastical as well. The means may vary, too, from time to time and area to area. The result may be confusion. But that will not last long if on both sides one observes the same Spirit at work. And over against the risk of confusion there has stood for a long time, all too long already, the risk of being in a rut. With the above seven means we believe we have described realities which long since have proven their institutional Spirit-power.

This does not mean, however, that in the case of every person the Spirit works through every one of these means. Our very approach to the problem of the transmission of God's salvation gives us the freedom to admit that something which for the one is like a door giving access to salvation may act like a stone wall to someone else. One's character, experiences, and situation play a part in this, too. To the one, for example, the sermon may be the most important experience, while to another it may be quite meaningless; for that person, instead, the discussion or the celebration of the meal may be the source of spiritual nourishment. Respect for the diversity of ways in which the Spirit can work should promote mutual understanding and tolerance in these matters.

Note how according to the letters to the seven churches (Rev. 1–3) the risen Lord concretely expresses and applies his grace to different situations in the post-apostolic era, and how this is always concluded with the affirmation that this is "what the Spirit says to the churches."

On the question of the origin of the washing with water, see the small print on pp. 356ff.

As a reaction against the Reformation, Trent closed the door on the subject of the doctrine of the means of grace when it declared: "If anyone says that the sacraments of the New Law were not all instituted by Jesus Christ our Lord, or that there are more or fewer than seven . . . *anathema sit*" (D 1601). Today's Roman Catholic theologians can no longer hold to this, or only via the detour of "the church as the ur-sacrament" (Rahner).

The Reformation went a long way in the direction we have moved: by reducing to two the number of the sacraments, by its emphasis on the sermon as the central means, as well as by its freedom in its treatment of the offices. Its biblicism, however, soon restricted this development.

Is it possible for means to die off in the course of church history? Theoretically this cannot be denied. But it looks as if the two of which one might especially expect this, the washing and the meal (because these have their roots in a naturalistic culture), can in updated forms again become very meaningful as vehicles of grace. And the assertion one can hear now and then that the sermon is an antiquated means of communication lacks all foundation. Conversely, one should also be careful with increasing the number. Pneumatological and sociological perspectives do not coincide. Certain forms, e.g. of instruction or counseling, whose aim is only the articulation and exchange of one's own experiences instead of mediating a salvation that comes to man from the outside, cannot possibly be recognized as institutional means. The church must be equally on its guard against a sacralistic hardening and a secularistic evaporation.

All this makes it evident that church and institution are closely related. But this institution is not an unchangeable given. It is an institutionalized process of mediation, and therefore it is preferable to speak of an ongoing institutionalization rather than of an institution. As a matter of fact, the study of the sociology of institutions has shown that this is an insight which, *mutatis mutandis*, is applicable to institutions everywhere. "Man cannot live without institutions. This does not imply that man has to accept the established institutions. He may change them. Without institutions man is like a fish on dry land. His freedom consists of the possibility of swimming from one water to the other" (De Haas, *The Church as an Institution*, p. 27).

The second half of our two-pronged question is: how does the Spirit work through these means? Simplest would be the assumption that these means contain the Spirit and that consequently the users *ipso facto* share in the grace conveyed. But that is contradicted by experience. Exactly he who heavily emphasizes the active presence of the Spirit should also heavily emphasize man's power to close himself to the Spirit, and hence the necessity that the work of the Spirit be supplemented by the cooperation of man—in fact, that only so does that work become effective. But does this not make the Spirit entirely dependent on man and is that not in conflict with his nature and operations? One who reasons like that is inclined to postulate that the Spirit in his sovereign freedom uses these means only (using a classical formula) "wherever and whenever it pleases him." But in that case what reasons have we left for accepting these means in the confidence that the Spirit is actively present in them? The moment we try to get a clearer picture of how the Spirit works, we are in danger of conceiving of God as one who uses brute force, or as powerless, or as arbitrary. That exposes us to the danger of conceiving of the means either as possessing magical powers or as purely symbolic. We have here the same reality and the same problematics we have regularly hit upon before: we describe an encounter, one between two subjects, in which God takes the initiative and is the more powerful, but in which he fully honors man's subjectivity. The outcome of any inter-subjective encounter is unpredictable. If in his grace God comes to a person who is alienated from him, the elements of surprise and unpredictability can only be heightened. A theology that wants to remove these elements kills the encounter. Systematization is elimination. And the price for refusing to eliminate them is the forfeiture of systematic transparency. This is integral to this encounter. An outsider is in no position to speak about it. And the insider cannot contemplate it from God's point of view. He can only speak of an event in which God took the initiative and was the more powerful, and in which he surrendered himself! One who surrenders himself is always fully and actively involved in the event, without ever being able to think of himself as the cooperating (much rather as the obstructing) party, let alone as the decisive influence. He is unable to answer the question why in other cases the encounter turns out to be so different, since that is not his encounter. He will maintain the greater power of God, man's responsibility, and the promise and reliability of the means of grace, without being able to combine these three in one systematic perspective.

The question concerning the relationship of the Spirit to certain means has come up a number of times before; for the sermon see par. 12 and in this par. point 3, for baptism point 2, and for the table of the Lord point 5. There concepts like *opus operatum, manducatio impiorum,* and *finitum non capax infiniti* are mentioned, all of which relate to the problematic we deal with here and were often wrongly discussed in connection with only one means of grace. For us, however, these concepts have for the most part become unusable, because they were designed either in their relation to God or to man, but not in reference to the encounter itself.

In the Bible, the primary and normative witness to the covenantal encounter, apparently contradictory lines of thought are simply set forth and left side by side. The OT mentions means of salvation such as the bronze serpent, the ark of the covenant, and the temple, whose blessed influence appears to be almost magical, but then again are suddenly rendered ineffective by human unbelief and disobedience (cf. Num. 21:9 with 2 Kings 18:4; 1 Sam. 4:6–11 with 1 Sam. 6 and 7; 1 Kings 8 with Jer. 7:14; see also 1 Cor. 10:1–5).

The Roman Catholic Church has tried to maintain both perspectives. The major emphasis has always been—and still is—on the objective saving efficacy of the means. "They contain what they signify. The sacrament is an instrumental cause of grace" (Thomas, *ST* III, q. 62, art. 3f.). But that does not mean an automatic efficacy, let alone that it is magic. The means remain inoperative without the proper disposition in man; the least that is necessary is not to create an obstacle. To counter Reformation views Trent declared: "If anyone says that the sacraments of the New Law do not contain the grace which they signify or that they do not confer that grace on those who do not place an obstacle in the way . . . *anathema sit*." And: "If anyone says that through the sacraments of the New Law grace is not conferred by the performance of the rite itself (*ex opere operato*) but that faith alone in the divine promise is sufficient to obtain grace, *anathema sit*" (D 1606, 1608). In these formulations one can detect the later emphasis of the Counter-Reformation which, for fear of subjectivism, shifted the emphasis from the disposition of the recipient to an objectivistic conception of the means. Only very recently has there come about a change. Now there is the desire to rethink the means as avenues of faith encounter. For that one harks back to the simpler language of pre-Reformation times, in particular to the meaning of *fides* and *signum* in Thomas, who says among other things: "Now sacraments are the sort of signs in which the faith by which man is justified is explicitly attested" (*ST* III, q. 61, art. 4; cf. q. 60–62).

The Reformation tried to cut through the dialectic of subject and object and replace it by the correlation of *promissiones* and *fides*, which according to D 1608 was subjectivism in the eyes of Trent. The Augsburg Confession, however, declared: "For by the Word and Sacraments, as by instruments, the Holy Spirit is given: who works faith, where and when it pleases God . . ." (V) and: "Therefore men must use sacraments so as to join faith with them, which believes the promises that are offered and declared unto us by the sacraments. Wherefore they condemn those that teach that the sacraments do justify by the work done, and do not teach that faith which believes the remission of sins is requisite in the use of sacraments" (XIII).

But later the Lutherans shrank back from the danger of arbitrariness "where and when there is a vision of God." They have always had a great pastoral concern for the spiritually tormented sinner; therefore they put all the emphasis on the certainty of the offer of grace in the means. The Reformed, with their *cum verbo* instead of *per verbum* (see par. 12) in the operation of the Spirit, and with their "sign and seal" and their doctrine of the parallelism between the sign and the thing signified, have in their doctrine of the sacraments tried to avoid the pitfall of objectivism without landing in subjectivism. See Berkouwer, *The Sacraments*, esp. ch. 4.

A satisfactory formulation has nowhere been found. In this century, in the Netherlands we have once again been confronted with the transmission problematic in the conflict about baptism in the Reformed Churches, which was one of the causes of the split into "synodicals" and "liberated." The disputed point can be formulated as follows: Are God's promises in baptism valid on condition that we have faith or is the fulfillment of this condition part of the promises given in baptism? To the one side there was the fear of an automatic effectiveness of the sacraments, to the other side the fear of arbitrariness of the Spirit or that of seeing faith as a condition which man must achieve. The so-called Replacement Formula of the "synodical" Reformed Churches (1946) could not satisfy the objectors. See Berkouwer, *The Sacraments*, pp. 180–187.

41. THE CHURCH AS THE BODY OF CHRIST

IN THE SECOND HALF OF PARAGRAPH 39 we made clear how the church as the mediating agency between Christ and the world has three dimensions. The first, that of institutional mediation, has been elaborated in detail in paragraph 40. Possibly many readers feel that now we have had the essential part of the doctrine of the church. That is a great and widespread misconception. Quantitatively this institutional element is indeed the largest. Moreover, it is the first thing anyone notices when approaching the church from the outside: her buildings, her ceremonies, her activities and functionaries, in brief: her existence as an institution. That is of decisive significance, because this is the way in which men are confronted with Christ and become involved in the renewing work of the Spirit. And that is indeed what it is all about: this institution is the means to bring about a community of renewed people. The word "means" does not say enough. The institution is the womb and the fertile soil out of which this community must constantly be born anew and grow up. This community is what the institution is about. To repeat the formulation on page 347: "The church thus has two faces: she is institute *and* community, fertile soil *and* plant, mother *and* family. And these two are not related in an artificial equilibrium, but so that the first is the foundation and the root of the second and the second is the purpose and fruit of the first." Following Paul, we call that second aspect "the body of Christ." What can be said about that we subsume under three headings: (a) the nature, (b) the members, and (c) the growth of the body.

Roman Catholic ecclesiology has for centuries suffered from a neglect of the community aspect. It regarded the church as almost identical with its institutional form. Accordingly, the Roman Catholic believer experienced his church especially as a mother, as the mother church, and himself as a sheep of a flock which is pastored by shepherds appointed by Christ. The community was not regarded as a mature subject, but as the under-age object of the institutional activity. The church was preferably defined as *societas hierarchica*. After the Second World War this viewpoint was increasingly challenged, due to the influence of biblical studies, the ecumenical movement, existentialism, and secularization. As a result, at the Second Vatican Council, in the constitution *De ecclesia*, the church was especially seen as the people of God (see esp. ch. II). Yet the gains made there are largely lost again in ch. III, entitled: "On the hierarchical structure of the church and in particular the episcopate." A powerful attempt to construct an ecclesiology from the community aspect was made by H. Küng in several publications, especially in *The Church*. The struggle between tradition and renewal is still unresolved.

One can gauge the relationship between institute and communion especially from the measure of acceptance, rejection, or modification of the idea of the sinlessness of the church. A Roman Catholic who finds the essence of the church in the institution agrees with it. In the measure that the communion of the people of God is regarded as the essential aspect, that agreement diminishes. For a survey of this problem see K. Blei, *De onfeilbaarheid der kerk* (1972), ch. III.

The Reformation at first emphasized strongly the community aspect; note the early Luther (who wanted to replace the word *kirche* by *Gemeinde*) and, among others, Bucer. But the way in which the Schwärmer (fanatics) realized this aspect induced Luther and Zwingli to put a heavier emphasis again on the institutional side (whereby, in contrast to the Roman Catholic Church, they thought in particular of the preaching). Typical is the Augsburg Confession, VII: "The church is a congregation of believers in which the Gospel is rightly taught and the sacraments are rightly administered." A further development of the community aspect was also greatly hampered by the distinction between the visible and the invisible church (see below), due to which the visibility was regarded more as an institutional aspect than as inherent in the people. Calvin does that too in *Inst* IV, which opens with the definition of the church as the mother of all the godly, and further is mainly polemically concerned with the elements of the institute and their nature. He does recognize the community aspect by his attention to this supervision of the life of the members of the church, "through which the members of the body hold together, each in its own place" (IV,xii,1), but the supervision (discipline) has floundered in a legalistic, individualistic, and negative practice. More than the other Reformers, Bucer constructed his ecclesiology from the standpoint of pneumatology and the concept of the "body of Christ." Unfortunately, his emphasis on the community idea remained dormant for centuries in the continental Reformed tradition.

In the tradition of the free churches, in particular in America, the community idea did begin to bloom, but there was no deep theological reflection on it, partly on account of the pull of individualism in that same climate. In the Remonstrant G. J. Heering (*Geloof en openbaring,* 1937), ecclesiology is entirely absent. In the Mennonite G. D. Kaufman (*Systematic Theology*), it occupies a distinctive but modest position as "The Community of Love and Freedom" (par. 29) and "The People of God" (par. 31). The most thorough discussion in a more or less free-church spirit I know of is Tillich's *ST* III, pp. 162–172, under the heading "The Spiritual Community."

In the newer Reformational theology the community aspect has in general remained underdeveloped. As regards the Lutherans, following the Augsburg Confession, VII, all the emphasis falls on the means of grace on the one hand and on personal faith on the other. Trillhaas minimizes the other aspects and for that reason puts ecclesiology in the Epilegomena (VIII). Prenter (*Creation and Redemption,* par. 39) and Althaus (*CW* II, par. 51) are better, but too restricted. In Ebeling, *Dogmatik,* III (1979), par. 36, the communion remains in the shadow of the word of justification; and in Thielicke, *The Evangelical Faith,* III (E.T. 1982), despite good beginnings, it remains in the shadow of the means of grace and the office. In the Reformed sector things are little better. Bavinck (*GD* IV, par. 53), however, refers in passing to the concept of "the church as organism" enunciated by Kuyper (over against "the church as institution"). Owing to the sharp contrast, some in the Dutch Reformed Church harshly criticized this concept; it deserves better, however. The main heading in Weber (*Gl* II, X: "Die Gemeinde") promises much, but the exposition offers little (pp. 576–579, 590–596). Here, too, Barth has been the great exception. After having elucidated in *CD* IV,1, par. 62 more (but not exclusively) the institutional side of the church (its gathering), he discusses in IV,2, par. 67 its upbuilding, divided into growth, preservation, and polity. At the same time Brunner took a much more radical and anti-institutional direction; see *Dg* III, pp. 3–133. According to him the church is a visible brotherhood of the reconciled (pp. 21–22) to which everything that is authoritarian and juridical is foreign. Since the middle of the 20th century the Bible and the cultural situation have compelled us to pay more attention to the church as communion. See, e.g., Küng, *The Church,* and G. C. Berkouwer, *The Church* (E.T. 1976), ch. 4. For that matter we are beginning to see many more dimensions of the church; see P. S. Minear, *Images of the Church* (1960), and A. Dulles, *Models of the Church* (1974).

a. The nature of the body of Christ

Because of its biblical significance, the phrase "body of Christ," derived from Paul, has remained influential in the history of the church; and even in circles where it was regularly misunderstood or incorporated into entirely different thought patterns, it served as a reminder that we are not only nor in the first place *in* the church (as an institution), but are ourselves and collectively the church. The study of the faith is under no obligation to make this phrase a basic concept, let alone to reproduce all the aspects and accents it has in the New Testament. Yet in our language and time as well, the phrase is so suggestive in meaning and imagery that we have nothing better or equal to replace it with. Moreover, the phrase recommends itself even more by the fact that already in the New Testament it has more than one meaning: on the one hand, the idea of a human body that needs to be complemented and governed by a head; on the other hand, the idea of a social body, a corporate body which is itself a unity in which all the members supplement each another. In view of these notions we arrive at the following elements as essential for the church as a community:

1. If Christ is the head of this body, this community is first of all determined by the common *communion with Christ*. What this "communion with Christ" involves will be shown in what follows, especially in the next chapter. Here it must first of all be stated that this communion (*communio*) rests on our participation (*communicatio*), through faith, in the way which Christ has gone on our behalf and ahead of us. It is the continuous appropriation of his representative life, surrender to death, and victory.

2. This communion is thus characterized by *grace*. It consists of people who know that with all their sins and shortcomings they are accepted by God in Christ. In this communion we can be set free from our attempts at self-justification and our urge to assert ourselves, and in a new way become ourselves. And that newness must then characterize our communion with each other: the congregation is the place where we must accept each other for Christ's sake and where precisely the "weak," in whom we recognize ourselves, are treated with consideration. How such a community functions can be seen in Romans 14f. and 1 Corinthians 8.

3. We are accepted as we are, but not left as we are. The *communicatio* must also include the collective *obedience to Christ*. We are a body with a head that governs it. We must orient our life to the decisions which through his path through life have been made for us. Grace and obedience belong inseparably together as the inside and outside of the *communicatio* with Christ.

4. This *communicatio* with Christ should now, as we briefly noted, lead to the *communio*, the *communion with each other*. Without this *communio*, the *communicatio* would remain body-less, individualistic, and no more than an inner experience. But without the *communicatio* as its basis, the mutual communion becomes purely that of a religio-social club. Christ does not live apart from his church. And the love to God-in-Christ and that to the neighbor are one and indivisible. The oneness of the love for God and the love for man, for which our humanity is intended, must be modeled in the church by the oneness of the communion with Christ and that with fellow-believers.

5. This communion does not exclude other communions; in relation to these it is to be *exemplary, critical, and complementary*. With the word "body" Paul chose a current term to which he gave a new content. Most communions and corporations which we know are based on oneness of blood, of interests, or of purposes. That makes these communities very restricted; due to their particular nature they exclude many people and areas of life. The Christian communion must prove its distinctiveness by going beyond all these boundaries. In principle it should get all

people involved in it (see 2), including those who are excluded by the other communions: the guilty, the lonely, strangers, the unimportant, the retarded, those without a voice. And in principle it has to make all aspects of life subjects of discussion, also those that are not dealt with by other communions: salvation, the future, sin, the meaning of life and death, the rights of strangers, aliens, and enemies.

6. Implied in all this is that the community of the body of Christ lives in a state of high *tension*. On the one hand it must be all-inclusive, on the other hand all the members must be inspired to act communally through their obedience to the one head. The first without the second results in aimless and inert national churches, the second without the first in intolerant and legalistic sectarian churches. The inclination to release the tension is so great that the true Christian community can exist only as a purely gratuitous gift from the Spirit. For one can endure this tension only if he stands in the love by which central and marginal groups, vanguard and rearguard, extremists and conciliators take each other seriously as members, and thus do not neglect each other.

In recent decades there has been much study of the meaning of "body of Christ" in the NT. This study faces two difficulties: (a) The term *sōma Christou* cannot be traced back to the OT, later Judaism, or Gnosticism. We may rather have to think of a not specifically religious use in Hellenistic Greek, where the word could stand for (as with us) a "human body" and could also refer to a "corporate body" (corporation, totality, organization); a city, the state, an army, and even the world itself could be called *sōma*. In 1 Cor. 12 Paul uses a metaphor which at that time was common enough. He must have preferred *sōma Christou* to the OT "people of God," not only because the latter did not express the unique relationship to Christ, but also because the Christian church in the Hellenistic world did not exist like an organism (as Israel did as a nation) but was more like what we now call an organization, a form which then was often called a *sōma*.

(b) The *sōma*-imagery is differently applied in Rom. and 1 Cor. than in Eph. and Col. In the first-mentioned epistles the believers are together, in Christ, a complete body (Rom. 12:4f.; 1 Cor. 10:17; 12:12–27); in the latter Christ himself is the head of this body (Eph. 1:23; 2:16; 4:4, 12, 16; 5:23, 30; Col. 1:18, 22, 24; 2:19; 3:15). In the first group fellowship with one another is preponderant, in the second fellowship with and obedience to Christ. The designation of Christ as the head (*kephalē*) is often connected with it (Eph. 1:22; 4:15; 5:23; Col. 1:18; 2:19), but also used independently of it (1 Cor. 11:3; Col. 2:18), in which case it means something like "master" or "chief."

The use of this metaphor is even more complicated by the fact that *sōma Christou* can also denote the crucified and resurrected body of Jesus, as well as his body which is given us in the bread of the meal. In a few passages it is possible, or clear, that Paul combines these meanings with that of the church as *sōma* (Rom. 7:4; 1 Cor. 10:16f.; 11:29; Col. 2:9–13). It would seem that the various applications of the *sōma*-image in its relation to Christ can best be grasped in their unity if together they are put on the denominator of the so-called "corporate personality" concept: in Christ as the head of his body happen the decisions from which the church lives. Summarizing studies and lists of literature can be found in *TDNT* VII, *s.v. sōma* (by E. Schweizer), in H. Ridderbos, *Paul* (E.T. 1975), IX, and in Küng, *The Church*, pp. 224–240.

The "body of Christ" concept has become prominent in the ecclesiology of recent decades, especially due to the influence of the Roman Catholic *nouvelle théologie* and of Faith and Order. Before that, Protestants had applied the concept only to the invisible church, and Roman Catholic theologians had avoided it because of its unsuitability to denote the juridical-hierarchical aspect of the church. The Roman Catholic *nouvelle théologie*, however, saw more than an image in it, namely the designation of the church's essence: she is literally, in an organic-ontological sense, the visible outside of Christ, his continued incarnation. Pope Pius XII, in his encyclical *Mystici corporis* (1943), has tried to break the anti-hierarchical thrust of this kind of thinking. It soon became clear, however, that this "biological" conception could not be harmonized with the personalistic use, with the alternation of the bridegroom-bride imagery and the accent on Christ as head (see Eph. 4:15f.; 5:23ff.; Col. 2:19). After Vatican II, in Roman Catholic theology this image was displaced by that of "God's people."

An important Protestant objection against the organic-ontological conception was that it involves imagery here, and that in this imagery the distance between head and body remains. Moreover, some regarded "body" not as organism, but as organ, the instrument through which Christ works in and for the world. Eventually it became clear, however, that this did not touch the real issue. This is not whether or not one recognizes the intimate connection between Christ and his body, but the nature of this connection. Exegetical study made clear that this connection is neither organic nor functional, but corporative: In Christ as the head our death and resurrection happened substitutionarily; through baptism and faith we are incorporated in what he in his body did for us and are ourselves becoming his body. See Barth, *CD* IV,1, pp. 659–668, from which resulted his definition of the church as "the earthly-historical form of existence of Jesus Christ Himself" (p. 661). The Faith and Order report *One Lord, One Baptism* (1960) was evidence that the corporative conception was fast gaining ground ecumenically; cf. Berkouwer, *The Church,* pp. 78–91; and from the Roman Catholic side Küng, *The Church,* pp. 234–241.

In this context we also take up a subject much discussed in previous centuries: the relationship of what was called the visible and the invisible church. The fact is that what presents itself as the community of believers includes many who are not real believers, but at best nominal Christians and at worst hypocrites. The realization of this fact dawned especially when, in the 4th century, the church first became a privileged group and then became a national church, making everyone want to belong to it. Theology then began to view the church as *corpus permixtum*, containing wheat *and* chaff (with an appeal to Matt. 13:24–30). Augustine was the first to concern himself in depth with this problem, forced by his controversy with the Donatists who by means of strong discipline sought to establish a "church without blemish or spot." Familiar is his sentence: "Many who seem to be without are in reality within, and many who seem to be within yet really are without" (*De baptismo* V.38). This implied, also in view of his doctrine of predestination, the advent of the distinction between visible and invisible church. The Roman Catholic Church had less difficulty with the problem because it found the center of the church in the hierarchical institution; according to a famous statement of Bellarmine the church is visible and tangible (*visibilis et palpabilis*) in the same way as "the gathering of the Roman people, or Gallic kingdom, or Venetian republic" (*Disputationes*, 1588, Tome II, III, II). Nevertheless, one had to speak of "two kinds of membership," and most recently there has come a growing awareness that the church of Christ does not coincide with the visible (Roman Catholic) church, and this insight has been incorporated in the doctrine of the *corpus Christi mysticum* and the *votum ecclesiae*. A survey of the problematics can be found in G. C. Berkouwer, *The Second Vatican Council and the New Catholicism* (E.T. 1965), VII.

The Lutherans also regarded the church as visible, according to its institutional side (in word and sacrament), but they added that she is invisible as concerns her result: the true faith. Zwingli and Calvin had much more difficulty with the subject because, following Augustine, they emphasized election on the one hand while they sought (at least Calvin) for the purest possible visible church on the other. Accordingly, in the Reformation the distinction between visible and invisible church became a live subject again, though the idea was to concentrate on the (purification of the) visible church. Bucer was the one who stressed the visibility the most. The spiritualists and pietists did the opposite. For an overview see Bavinck, *GD* IV, no. 448 and 492, and Weber, *Gl* II, pp. 601–605. They themselves prefer to speak as little as possible of an invisible church. This trend has continued in the more recent Reformational theology and now encounters the opposite trend in Roman Catholic theology (see above).

An "invisible church" is a contradiction in terms. What was meant by it either was no church (the *numerus praedestinorum* as such does not produce communion with each other) or was not invisible (the groups of like-minded people in the pietistic movements). Naturally the church, just as for that matter any human institution, has a visible outside and an invisible inside: faith, hope, and love are as such invisible. But the fact that not all church members are believers is a truth which as such is not an ecclesiological concern. The centuries-old problem is more sociological than theological in character. Now that the Constantinian era is coming to an end and the churches everywhere are becoming voluntary, the problem is losing its urgency. We see now that the theologians dreamed of the invisible church as fulfilling all those desires that could not be realized in the national churches.

Another subject which in this connection deserves attention is that of the meaning of the description of the church in the Apostles' Creed as *communio sanctorum* ("I believe . . . the communion of the saints"). Only about the year 400 was this article added to certain editions of the Apostles' Creed. The phrase itself had arisen in the previous century with the meaning of "participation in sacred affairs" (acts, mysteries, sacraments). But almost as old is the meaning "communion with holy persons," namely the saints in heaven, whom we can ask to intercede for us. Both conceptions existed side by side and were not regarded as alternatives, since both refer to blessings of salvation one receives through the church (together with the forgiveness of sins, the resurrection of the body, and the life everlasting). Only since Carolingian times did *communio*, next to participation, come to mean communion with one another, making *sanctorum* a subjective genitive with the meaning: the communion constituted by the saints mutually. The Heidelberg Catechism, in Answer 55, presents a fortunate combination of the older and newer meaning. We owe it to that newer conception, well known in churches everywhere, that by way of innumerable explications of the Apostles' Creed the awareness of the church as a communion was kept alive, also in the most institutionalistic state and national churches—even if only as an accusation and ideal that come from the invisible church. See the art. "Gemeinschaft der Heiligen," in *RGG* II; also the art. "*Sanctorum communio,*" in E. Wolf, *Peregrinatio* (1954), esp. pp. 283–288 (though out of fear for too great an emphasis on the human he does not sufficiently recognize the importance of the mutual bond of the members of the church).

b. The varied membership of the body of Christ

Repeatedly in the New Testament the metaphor of the body is connected with an emphasis on the varied membership the body consists of. This is no playful elaboration of a metaphor, but indicative of the insight that the differentiation is as essential to the body of Christ as the unity, and that the unity and the differentiation presuppose each other. Thus what we have here is a further definition of what we have called the communion with each other. The precise description which Paul gives of this communion in his letters has thus far received almost no attention in the study of the faith nor in the Christian faith itself. The interest was limited to generalities: the members of the church must bear with one another and forgive each other, they must help and encourage one another, show mercy and be patient. That is of course to the point. But from this perspective all the members are in principle alike, as if they had all received the same faith, the same hope, and the same love. Yet at the same time they are incorporated by the Spirit into the community. Thereby he endows them, along with their personal faith, with those gifts (*charismata*) which enable the members individually to make their contribution to the upbuilding of this community. When one receives by faith the personal relationship with God and his fellowman, one receives therein the relationship to the community. And according to the New Testament the latter cannot be reduced to the former—as theology has usually assumed. No one possesses all by himself the fullness of salvation. The community, too, is only on the way toward that fullness. It grows toward it when each believer personally makes his small contribution. That contribution does not coincide with his natural abilities, though it is related to it; through God's grace these abilities are made useful, purified, and given a wider application. The diversity in the abilities and skills which we possess in our created existence is made part of the body of Christ and made useful for the ultimate destiny of our life as humans and as community.

The charismata thus exhibit a great variety, the common denominator being the upbuilding of the body of Christ (for the concept "upbuilding" see point c). Many render unassuming and unselfish service in all kinds of seemingly insignificant yet highly necessary tasks; some possess gifts of administration, of management, of planning; others have the ability to detect and to relieve hidden needs or to point out and to fight outrageous injustice; still others have the gift of admonition and counseling, or of visiting the lonely and shut-ins; some are good at defending traditional beliefs that must be maintained, others in dealing with pertinent questions concerning the future; the one has the gift of making the gospel understandable to outsiders, another can do that for small children, and yet another can do that for teen-age youth; the one has a sharp eye for tasks right on the church's own doorstep, the other for global challenges; to the one has especially been given the hidden communion with God, to the other obedience in social affairs, etc. So working together, each does his or her part toward filling the church with all the fullness of God, as Ephesians 3:19 puts it. In this regard, as seen from the whole, no one does more than a small part. And he or she can do that only because of the small parts of many others who each possess a charisma which he does not have himself. Just as together we are dependent on Christ as the head, so we are also dependent on each other as members.

It is clear that taking the charismatic structure of the church seriously would put an end to clericalism and a church ruled by ministers. It would not, however, be the end of the office; on the contrary, after what has been said in paragraph 40 point 8 about the leadership which the office is to give to the church by its grace-mediating function, it is clear that precisely the charismatic structure highlights yet another function of the office: to it belongs the task of finding and involving the charismata in the work of the church as well as, where necessary, restraining those who possess them so that they indeed use these gifts for the common well-being. Without this activation and putting to work of the charismata, as well as discerning, testing, and controlling them, the varied structure of the church would get lost either in a uniform rigidity or in a multiform confusion.

Emphasis on the varied structure of the *sōma* is found in Rom. 12:4f.; Eph. 4:16, 25; 5:30; Col. 2:19, and in a most elaborate imagery in 1 Cor. 12. In Rom. 12 and 1 Cor. 12–14 Paul employs in regard to this varied structure the term "charisma," which also occurs with this meaning in 1 Pet. 4:10; in addition, he uses it in the more general sense of "(gracious) gift." In 1 Cor. 13 the "general" gifts of faith, hope, and love are clearly distinguished from the *charismata* or *pneumatika*

(14:1). Paul never calls them charismata, but speaks in this respect in Gal. 5:22 of the "fruit" (singular) of the Spirit. ("Faith" as charisma in 1 Cor. 12:9 is something else, probably an extraordinary trust in God's miracle-working power, cf. 13:2.)

The awareness of the charismatic structure of the *sōma* disappeared very early; only a passive "flock" was a fitting complement of the hierarchical structure of office. Striking in this connection is the treatment of a number of charismata (*diversae gratiae gratis datae*) in Thomas, *ST* III, q. 171–178: *prophetia, raptus, linguae, sermo sapientiae, sermo scientiae, miracula*. It remained without effect, however, partly due to the fact that it was set within the framework of an individualistic doctrine of the virtues. The Reformation did not bring about a change either. The only exception in this respect, practical as well as theological, was Bucer; see van 't Spijker, *De ambten bij Martin Bucer*, pp. 333–341. The charismatic aspect was somewhat recognized in the free churches and even more, but one-sidedly, in the sects; without, however, penetrating theology. Only most recently, and then hesitatingly, do we see theology turning its attention to the charismatic aspect; interestingly, this is done the most in Roman Catholic theology. See Küng, *The Church*, pp. 179–191, who makes the concept too vague, however, because even love belongs to it, because it nearly coincides with "service," and because it climaxes in the concept of office (see E II). In the spirit of Küng, G. Hasenhüttl wrote an extensive study on this theme, *Charisma Ordnungsprinzip der Kirche* (1969), to which we also refer for further literature. See also K. Rahner, "Observations on the Factor of the Charismatic in the Church," in *Theological Investigations,* XII (E.T. 1974), pp. 81–97. The concept is also given consideration in the pneumatology of S. Boulgakof, *La paraclet* (1946), pp. 272–326. See further G. Eichholz, *Was heisst charismatische Gemeinde? 1 Kor. 12* (1960).

It is debatable whether in the NT the charismata are regarded as natural or supernatural. In any case, it is not true that all charismata are ecstatic in nature; also in 1 Cor. 12 such is only the case with glossolalia (contra *TDNT* IX, *s.v. charisma*, p. 404), which Paul regards as least in significance, but which unfortunately has become the central charisma in Pentecostalism. There is, for that matter, a real difference between 1 Cor. 12 and Rom. 12. To be sure, the charismata in 1 Cor. 12 generally give the impression that, though not ecstatic in nature, they were at least special gifts; see the enumeration in vv. 8–10; Rom. 12:6–8 mentions, apart from prophecy, much more "ordinary" gifts. The Pentecostal groups appeal particularly to 1 Cor. 12; the churches—if they pay attention to it—to Rom. 12. Still another (more related to the office) enumeration is given in Eph. 4:11. See E. Käsemann, *RGG* II, *s.v. Geist und Geistesgaben 3,* and U. Brockhaus, *Charisma und Amt* (1972).

In 1 Cor. 12, in his elaboration of the image of the body and its members, Paul gives an unsurpassable description of how the charismata are meant to complement each other and their significance for the unity and the totality of the body: the charismata are not meant for showing off; instead, they point us to the other members whom we are to serve with these gifts; so it can happen precisely that the member who has the least to offer receives the greatest honor because he or she is served by so many (vv. 22–26).

Not much of this is found in the institutionalized Christian communities. Likely it is the most prevalent in the free-church type as this has evolved in the

United States, where one tries to get each member involved according to the gifts he possesses. After the Second World War a beginning has also been made in Europe, in theory, and with much greater difficulty in practice. It ought to be the task of the council of the church to search diligently for the charismata and involve them in the upbuilding of the whole.

We have purposely avoided saying that each member has a charisma. In our judgment this cannot be concluded from 1 Cor. 12. On the contrary, as we read vv. 22–27, some members serve the others by their passivity, that is, by providing those others with an opportunity to render service. In our opinion, this is an important consideration, for the practice as well as for the study of the faith. It is allowable that there be people in the church who (seemingly) only receive. Not even in our ecclesiology do we allow for the fact that there may be all kinds of members: initiated and catechumens, leaders and followers, active and fringe members. Within the body of Christ everyone is being liberated from the necessity of putting up a false front. The study of the faith reckons only with first-class Christians. That lends to ecclesiology something unreal, even something docetic. In this chapter we have tried to get away from that, though we feel that even in that attempt we have not sufficiently succeeded.

This perspective sheds new light on the meaning of *office*. On the one hand, it is itself based on a charisma or a combination of charismata (provide leadership, give instruction, discern the spirits, *et al.*); on the other hand, it is needed to prevent the charismata from working at cross-purposes and to make sure that they serve their purpose, namely the "upbuilding" (*oikodomē*) of the *one* body (1 Cor. 14:5, 12, 26; Eph. 4:12, 16). The greater the wealth of charismata, the greater the need for organization, integration, and discipline in the use of the charismata; hence Paul's speaking of *taxis* (order). Connected with this is the need to prevent the wrong use and things getting out of hand; hence the charisma of distinguishing between spirits (1 Cor. 12:10). There is thus a dual task, of activating and guarding against, of making room for and of setting limits. In Eph. 4:8–16 that task is particularly entrusted to what we now call office-bearers. "Do not quench the Spirit, do not despise prophesying, but test everything; hold fast what is good" (1 Thess. 5:19f.).

Its charismatic structure protects the church against individualism and collectivism, against anarchy and uniformity, and makes her a training school and model for every responsible society. To serve that goal, the order and content of the charismata may change with the times and circumstances. The constant is that whatever forms the charismata take, these must be *kata tēn analogian tēs pisteōs* (Rom. 12:6), according to the objective content of and the subjective insight into the faith, and that they must serve the upbuilding and the unity of the *sōma*. A thorough attempt to integrate the charismata into the totality of pneumatology is made by C. Heitmann and H. Mühlen (eds.), *Erfahrung und Theologie des Heiligen Geistes* (1974).

In this context it is appropriate to say a few words about the concept of the general priesthood of all believers. It is based on Ex. 19:5f. and 1 Pet. 2:9; cf. also Isa. 61:6; Rev. 1:6, and 5:10. In these passages the primary concern is direct access to God and surrender to his service. Yet in Ex. 19:5 and Isa. 61:6 and 9 this includes a relationship to the world, which in 1 Pet. 2:9 is formulated as: "that you may declare the wonderful deeds of him who called you out of darkness into his marvelous light." In the Reformation the idea that every believer has in principle direct access to God without a mediating office was very important. The other aspect, the relationship to the world, is only in our century receiving greater emphasis. Neither of these aspects relates directly to the church as community. This latter aspect is what Althaus, appealing to Luther, detected in it, namely the mutual responsibility of the members for each other (*CW* II, pp. 298, 308f.). Most recently it is customary to read in it that the members of the church are of age and entitled to their own input and decisions together with the office-bearers. That is not what is said in these biblical passages, yet it is indeed implied in the charismatic structure of the church. For a detailed and thorough discussion of the general priesthood of believers see Küng, *The Church*, pp. 370–379.

The foregoing is already an indication that the structure of the body and its unity are integrally related. Paul expresses it paradoxically and pointedly: "If all were a single organ, where would the body be?" (1 Cor. 12:19). Unity is thus not another word for uniformity, but rather its opposite. It presupposes the pluriformity and consists in the interaction of its parts. But that being so, from this model of the body comes not only the unity but also the disunity of the church. The charismatic structure is not only the necessary presupposition of the one body, but when something goes wrong also its greatest threat. Oneness is the mark of all God's works. The church is principially a singular: the bride, the temple, the one flock. Yet we face the apparently possible impossibility that the form of Christ in the world is divided. That is because the charismata, which are intended to serve and to build up, work at cross purposes with each other, or in any case are used more for the benefit of the possessors than for that of others. Sin transforms the function of the gifts of grace into its opposite. Here we have the clearest proof of how provisional the work of the Spirit still is and how heavy his struggle against what Paul calls the "flesh."

The church is meant to be multiform. The greater the multiformity of gifts, the richer the one body becomes. But the opposite happens if each regards his own gifts as being more important than those of others. Then the gifts are at odds with each other, resulting in a disunity in which all kinds of communities that call themselves churches rally around one or more charismata: the insight into particular elements of the faith (the "pure doctrine"), the "biblical" form of the church, the true tradition, being "with" the times, the true office, the marks of regeneration, a particular ethic, tongue-speaking, emphasis on sanctification, etc. Moreover, every denomination is convinced that by holding to its particular position it passes on the true gospel, with the consequence that in many cases the disintegration of the charismata appears in the guise of a struggle for the true faith. And that may indeed be at stake if elsewhere the charismatic structure is restricted or no longer under the discipline of the Spirit. Some churches try to counteract the disunity by allowing room for as many charismata as possible—which then come to exist side by side in an unstructured church. To counteract this anarchy, a church may curb the charismata by placing them under strict hierarchical supervision. However, all such forms are substitutes for the one charismatically structured body of Christ.

So the flesh wars against the Spirit. But the opposite happens, too. Time and again believers and the communities to which they belong experience this division as unnatural, and after a longer or shorter period again seek contact with those of different persuasions. Thus there is a double movement: from the unity to the division *and* from the division to the unity. The study of the faith cannot transcend that struggle by devising a theory that would fully explain the dividedness (and so more or less justify it). It can only tell us where we stand in that conflict. That means first of all that we must be prepared, without insisting on our own insights, to "speak the truth in love, to grow up in every way into him who is the head, into Christ" (Ephesians 4:15). That growth is impossible if we are not at the same time prepared to humbly allow ourselves to be served by gifts which we lack. And that is possible only if we are aware that the truth we wish to defend is the truth of the love which surpasses our knowledge and which we can only comprehend in company with all the saints (Ephesians 3:18f.), so that there is no room left for contempt, jealousy, or competition.

This implies that unity as such is not the important thing. The unity in Christ is a qualified and thus a critical unity. It creates as its reverse a break with all movements, parties, or churches to whom we are not joined in Christ. Thus, there exists a division which is legitimate and demanded. Yet in this phase of the work of the Spirit the separation of "wheat and tares" is never final. Regularly it turns out that the Spirit is also at work in what we at first legitimately regarded as tares, and he invites us to humbly cross boundaries which we thought were permanent. There is nothing in this struggle for unity to which we can tie ourselves down. The Spirit does not do that either; and he continues to create out of the welter of confusion the new community of God's future.

On the significance of the unity of God's work in the Bible see e.g. *TDNT* II, *s.v. heis*. It is clear that the frequently cited passage John 17:21 (cf. 22f.) also concerns a unity that is shaped by the communion with the Father and the Son. Furthermore, the admonition *to hen phronountes* in Phil. 2:2 means first of all that together we ought to orient ourselves to the example of Christ (cf. v. 5). The dividedness starts already in Israel. The unity of the twelve tribes was of short duration, yet the prophetic spirit never acquiesced in the break (1 Kings 18:31; Jer. 31; Ezek. 37:15–28, *et al.*). In the NT, however, there occurs another break in Israel, one between the community of Christ and the others. But in the church, too, the unity was threatened from the start, by the tensions between Palestinian and Hellenistic Jewish Christians (Acts 6:1–6) and between Jewish and Gentile Christians (Acts 15; Gal.). For that reason statements about unity stand in the context of prayer (John 17:31) or—mostly—of admonition (1 Cor. 1:10–13; 3:1–7; Eph. 4:1–6; Phil. 2:1–5, etc.).

Especially in 1 Cor. Paul wrestles with the rising disunity. In 1 Cor. 12–14 this discord is clearly and in other passages likely related to the charismatic structure, which caused feelings of superiority or inferiority and led to pride and jealousy. Nonetheless, all the charismata are intended to render loving service; therefore only love can be the integrating force (1 Cor. 13). The alternative is "schism" (12:25). It should be borne in mind that 1 Cor. 12 does not offer a picture of normal church life nor a blueprint of the ideal, but is intended in a situation of conflict to point the way toward a new unity.

Church history is full of such conflict situations. It is an illusion to speak of the undivided ancient church and to speak of division only after the great councils (Eastern church) in 1054, or after 1517 (Roman Catholic). See R. Rouse and S. C. Neill, *A History of the Ecumenical Movement* (1954), pp. 1–24, and esp. for the early church S. L. Greenslade, *Schism in the Early Church* (1953).

Very early the church which called itself "Catholic" began to label the other churches "schismatic" or "heretic." This distinction is no longer usable. For the Roman Catholic Church, since 1870, heresy means breaking with the Pope; conversely, one who breaks with a church will regard the latter as heretical. Later a more tolerant nomenclature arose, as in the Anglican "branch theory" and in Abraham Kuyper's doctrine of multiformity. Furthermore, in particular the doctrine of the "invisible church" has been used to make ecclesiastical division look better than it is.

The dialectic of unity and pluriformity has been very difficult for the churches. The Roman Catholic Church with its centrality of the pope bases itself on the unity, but is able to allow only limited room for pluriformity. Protestant churches often focus narrowly on one or a few gifts, insights, or doctrinal or ethical principles, which makes it hard for them to achieve a broader unity. In the 20th century the ecumenical movement has become the great countermovement against division in many Protestant churches. The so-called "unity formula of New Delhi" (1961), broadened mondially in Nairobi (1975) to "conciliar fellowship," is the starting point for further reflection. See the reports of sections I and II of the successive General Assemblies, and the Faith and Order reports *What Unity Requires* (1976) and *Unity in Today's World* (1978).

A problem that remains is that each church has its own conception of unity. For that of the Roman Catholic Church see *Decretum de oecumenismo* (Vatican II, 1964). For the continuing theological reflection see H. Küng, *The Church,* pp. 269–296, and G. C. Berkouwer, *The Church,* chs. 2 and 3. Many consider such striving for organizational unity irrelevant because supposedly only what churches contribute to a society of peace and justice would be important. However, the body of Christ has more dimensions. And the church's call to the nations to live in peace and harmony with each other has a hollow ring if the church itself fails to model how unity in diversity is possible. There are also those who become impatient with the slow pace of the reunification process. But that is not right either. Starting already with the NT, unity is not a static datum or ideal, but a never-ending growth process against all the forces that seek to drive churches and Christians apart. See Eph. 4:12–16. A church that does not participate in this process, whatever its scope, large or small, is a sect.

c. The upbuilding of the body of Christ

It is not Paul's intention that the body which is so structured should remain stationary. He uses the organic image of "growth" as well as that of mechanical "upbuilding." Here we start from the second image, because it immediately calls to mind the idea of human activity and responsibility. Moreover, it conveys the thought that this body of Christ is still unfinished, is still on the way to its destiny. We are not concerned here with reproducing what Paul says about growth and upbuilding (both words contain all kinds of notions that were dealt with in a and b), but with highlighting the necessity of including this separate dimension in our thinking about the church. The church is the house in which God will dwell with his covenant. Yet this is not by far his definitive dwelling among us. This present dwelling is still provisional, incomplete, partial. That God really dwells in this house is evident from the fact that its occupants find it impossible to be satisfied with the shape of the house of God as they experience it now. They see that it is unfinished and that further building is necessary. In the course of history new bricks must be added all the time, new challenges taken up, and new blueprints drafted. The work of construction must continue—always on the same foundation, continuing what has already been built, yet knowing that what has been achieved so far never coincides with the ultimate goal. It is a continuous work, hence tradition and renewal in one. Or to use the other image: the church is capable of growth, it is still a long way from having reached its full growth. Standing still is always going backwards. To be a church means to be ahead of and to reach beyond oneself, to be restlessly on the move, never satisfied with the present, forever searching for new challenges and tasks.

This growth or upbuilding is twofold, extensive and intensive. On the one hand it is quantitative: the church must grow and expand to the ends of the earth. Her Lord is the lord of the world. Every restriction, whether geographical, social, or political, which is placed upon her life and work, constitutes a challenge to overcome it. On the other hand it is qualitative: at no time is the church more than a broken, if not downright miserable reflection of her Lord. In every period and situation she must open up new insights into the salvation she has received and thereby fresh sources for a life of faith, hope, and love, so that in all areas she can answer the challenges which the Spirit at a particular moment places before her.

An implication is that self-criticism is part of the essence of the church. Living with Christ, who is simultaneously her source and gauge, implies an inherent dissatisfaction. That is, however, the opposite of a fruitless self-accusation. The same Spirit who upholds the church with all her shortcomings, inspires her to take new steps forward. The self-criticism which we ought to have as a church cannot at the same time alienate us from the church; for this room in which the Spirit has set us is at the same time the room within which we learn to measure the church (and ourselves in the church) by standards of which we still fall far short. Therefore it cannot be a question whether the church can be sinning as church. An institution cannot sin, but the community which is being built in and by the church sins all the time relative to what is the ultimate purpose of that upbuilding process. To that we must add that it is precisely in this community within which Christ in the Spirit will dwell with sinners that we really begin to understand what sin is and how much we are sinning by our self-seeking and sloth. Precisely the church ought to be the true training school that makes us see our guilt and teaches us to be critical of ourselves; at the same time it must be the place that puts limits to that awareness of guilt and self-criticism in view of the word of forgiveness we hear there and the preparedness we are given to continue with the work of building.

Finally, it is necessary once more to elucidate the function of *office*. We discovered that the office is the function that serves the mediation of grace (paragraph 40 point 8) and, next, that it serves as the director of the charismatic community (paragraph 41 point b). Now we see it as the agency which must challenge and train the congregation not to be content with the status quo, but to discover and exceed her own limitations. That is the task of equipping the saints, so that growth is not stymied and the edification is not stopped. The office-bearers must, therefore, be the ones who from the perspective of the tradition search for the way into the future and they must do this in continuous dialogue with the congregation, trying to find those who because of their charisma are already moving in the right direction in which eventually the entire community should follow them.

In the NT the images of building and growth occur with some frequency, mostly in Paul. For the notion of "upbuilding" in Paul see Ridderbos, *Paul*, X, pars. 68f. and the literature cited there. For the notion of "growth" in the NT see W. H. Velema, *De geestelijke groei van de gemeente* (1966) and the literature mentioned there. The image of upbuilding is connected with the OT prophetic expectation of the rebuilding of the land, the city, and the temple after the exile, as is particularly demonstrated by J. H. Roberts, *Die opbouw van die kerk volgens die Efese-brief* (1963). But it is also true of the image of growth that it is the result of the "already" and the "not yet" of the era of salvation which has begun but is not yet completed.

The dynamic aspects of growth and upbuilding have received very little attention in ecclesiology. An exception is (again) Barth, *CD* IV,2, pp. 641–660.

In the above, though we did go back to the NT, we put the accents differently. In the NT the images of growth and upbuilding have a clearly triumphal accent, thanks to the quick succession of the resurrection of Christ, the giving of the Spirit, and expansion in the Greek world. This quick spread kept the failures of the church in the shadows, though they did not remain hidden (1 Cor. 3:10–15; 1 Pet. 4:17; Rev. 1–3, and other passages). Living hundreds of years later, we are much more conscious of the negative aspects. Moreover, we relate the NT imagery much more to the laws and problems of the historical character (*Geschichtlichkeit*) of things as we experience this. What sounded triumphal in the NT has not therefore become meaningless; we now hear it as encouragement: the Spirit guarantees that the upbuilding and growth will continue, preferably with our help, yet if need be in spite of us. See also Berkouwer, *The Church*, pp. 99–102 and the striking expression by Weber: "The church in an exciting sort of way is not identical with itself" (*Gl* II, p. 645).

As regards the duality of extensive and intensive, in Paul the interest in the second is predominant, in Acts that in the first. Extensive growth is no excuse for the lack of intensive growth, nor vice versa. Depending on the place or the period, the emphasis may be more on the first or on the second, yet they belong together, and there is good reason to question the genuineness of the one if the other is lacking.

The emphasis on the office as agency of equipment did not really begin until after the Second World War. The text appealed to is Eph. 4:12, a passage which itself is part of the *locus classicus* of the intensive growth of the church (vv. 11–16). Now, too, the practice remains far behind the insight; the congregation finds it difficult to regard its leaders as trainers of experts or even as instructors of soldiers rather than as shepherds of sheep. This perspective of preparing the church for service is certainly not the only one, as we found out before; but without it the task of the office remains incomplete. It is most regrettable that many office-bearers (often under the pressure of a congregation that is conservative due to its own sluggishness) regard themselves primarily as upholders of the status quo and not as pathfinders to what is not yet. They are the ones who will have to construct the bridge from the tradition to the future, or, as the case may be, stimulate the congregation to build that bridge: "Let us continue, following the lines of what we have achieved!" (Phil. 3:16).

This is the proper place, after what we have discussed so far, to spend a few moments on the classical concept of the "marks of the church," the *notae ecclesiae*. This subject became particularly important when it became problematic where the true church was to be found, that is, the question became acute at the time of the Reformation. Before that the *notae* or *indicia ecclesiae* were unproblematically identified with the four attributes in the Apostles' Creed: one, holy, catholic, and apostolic. The Reformation discovered, however, that a church may outwardly conform to these marks without having a vital relationship with Christ. Therefore it came with two additional marks by which to test the trueness of a church: the pure preaching of the Word and the right administration of the sacraments, in agreement with the Bible; this would guarantee the bond with Christ, unobstructed by human devices. Note the classical formulation of the Augsburg Confession, VII: "There is, however, a church, a congregation of the saints, in which the Gospel is rightly taught and the sacraments are rightly administered. And for the true unity of the church it is sufficient to agree with the evangelical doctrine and the administration of the sacraments." This "it is sufficient" was indeed applicable to the first period when the forces were mustered and the spirits had to be discerned. But should these institutional marks not in the nature of the case be connected and augmented with more spiritual marks? Thus Luther in *Von den Konziliis und Kirchen* (1539) spoke of seven marks, among which were ecclesiastical discipline, prayer, and cross bearing, and in *Wider Hans Worst* even of eleven, including the Apostles' Creed, the singing of psalms, intercession, and suffering. This augmentation was not continued, however. The Lutherans pointed out that the other marks stemmed from the first two, which were the source of all the marks; thus there was no need to go beyond the "it is sufficient." That was also Calvin's view (*Inst* IV,i,8–10), although evidently he found it difficult not to devise marks for the congregation of true believers. The Belgic Confession (1561), however, went significantly further by including as the third institutional mark: "if church discipline is exercised in punishing of sin" (art. 29; similar is the even more specific art. 18 of the Scottish Confession of 1560). A few lines further that same creed adds to this the congregational "marks of Christians," such as self-denial, the struggle against sin, and following after righteousness. Here, too, there is the desire to break away from the purely institutional. Yet the Reformed did not follow through on this either, for increase in membership and vagueness unavoidably go hand in hand here. The growing superficiality as well as the increasing multiformity of church life added to the reluctance to formulate strict norms with which to distinguish between churches and individual Christians. In the Netherlands, even in the days of the Secession and the Doleantie, both Bavinck (*GD* IV, no. 494) and Kuyper (*Dictaten dogmatiek*, "Locus de ecclesia," p. 225) resisted the temptation to recognize ecclesiastical discipline as the third mark.

The Roman Catholic Church stayed with the traditional four marks of the Apostles' Creed; after the Counter-Reformation, however, they were no longer regarded as normative points of orientation, but entirely as *proprietates*, as visible and tangible qualities, through which the true church distinguishes itself, for all to see, from the heretics. Vatican I had to acknowledge, however, that the manifest marks could not be recognized apart from internal operations of the Holy Spirit and an efficacious help by a supernatural ability (D 3008–3014). In our century these four marks have completely lost their apologetic force. Already long before that the two Reformation marks had lost their discerning and sifting effectiveness, for each church thinks of itself as having the true preaching. The time that the marks of the church could be used to make important decisions relative to the nature of a church seems definitely past. Moreover, we no longer believe in nor feel the need for so-called objective marks which a denomination can use to justify its own existence or beliefs.

Nevertheless, we too need a continuous reflection on the marks, but then in the sense of engaging in self-examination to determine how we measure up to all the essential elements which constitute the ecclesiastical fabric. Beside the four marks of the Apostles' Creed and the two of the Reformation, we should take into consideration such things as the renewal of life, mutual love, the interaction of the charismata, the growth of the church, and (in connection with this) discipline, the diaconate, the ethos, the concern for justice for the oppressed and the victims of discrimination. Are all these marks operatively present with us? Besides, where it concerns the institutional elements (see par. 40) we will regularly have to ask whether these marks function in such a manner that they truly mediate the salvation of God.

Surveys of this problematic are found in Bavinck, *GD* IV, no. 493f., who accepts only the word which is preached and professed as a mark; Kinder, *Der evangelische Glaube und die Kirche*, as a Lutheran voice, with extensive quotes from Luther; Berkouwer, *The Church*, ch. 1, who in this chapter and in his entire book orients himself to the four marks of the Apostles' Creed as the critical norms; and as the most ecumenical, the Roman Catholic Küng (*The Church*, pp. 319–359), who sees the four and the two marks as complementary approaches, but regards their realization rather than their presence as the important thing. A modern interpretation of the marks which is much to the point is given by J. Moltmann, *Kirche in der Kraft des Geistes*, ch. VII.

42. THE PEOPLE OF GOD AS THE FIRSTFRUITS

WITH THIS THEME we return to what at the end of paragraph 39 we referred to as the third aspect of the church: the orientation to the world. The church, as we said there, is the mediating movement between Christ and the people. As the institute mediates Christ to the congregation, so the congregation in turn mediates him to the world. In this chain the world comes last, yet it is the goal that gives meaning and purpose to the preceding links. Everything that has come before serves this goal, even when it is not deliberately stated. But now, finally, it must be deliberately stated, if all the preceding is not to be misunderstood.

The fact of being church is thus not something static; it is a perpetual movement, a bridge-event. Therefore as it moves along it is itself continually changing. First it is an institution, a totality of activities and agreements. Next it is a community, a totality of personal relationships. Finally it is a totality of influences to the outside, or, in biblical language, salt and leaven. Progressing like that the visibility diminishes: a community is less visible than an institution; and generally the influences to the outside are even less clearly marked. To articulate that fact we choose here, after "institution" and "body of Christ," the term "God's people"; a people is a reality, but the bond that unites those who belong to it is much less visible than that of a society or organization. (We shall consider the second term, "firstfruits," later.) Around the institution a congregation is being gathered, which subsequently is scattered among the peoples of the world as the people of God. Whatever comes before, this final development is the goal. But without all the preceding the latter lacks roots, drive, and force.

For centuries a static conception of the church prevailed. The world-outside-the-church was viewed as a rival or hostile power. A favorite picture was that of the church floating as a Noah's ark on the deluge waters of the world. What was forgotten was that the ark was to land as soon as possible so that the earth could be newly populated and cultivated.

Since the Enlightenment the "evil world" becomes itself an articulate subject from which the church can evidently learn a great deal. A concerned vanguard of the church—the more than once unjustly criticized Pietists in the lead—saw the growing secularization as a challenge to engage in missionary, evangelistic, and social work. Barth has described and critically evaluated this turning to the world, beginning with the Reformation era, in six phases (*CD* IV,3, pp. 18–38). In this process, the influence of theology was most of the time no more than indirect or marginal. There was theological reflection by those concerned with missions, of which the *Evangelische Missionslehre* of Gustav Warneck (1892ff.) has become the classical example; but that did not penetrate to the "official" theology. Moreover, it should not be forgotten that the turning to the world had mainly an aggressive-antithetical stance and was less aimed at the conversion of souls than at maintaining and strengthening the Christian influence.

The necessity of re-studying ecclesiology, in fact all of theology, from the standpoint of the relationship to the world has (only) slowly begun to take hold, mainly through the unceasing harping on it by the nontheologian H. Kraemer; see especially his *The Christian Message in a Non-Christian World* (1938), esp. chs. III and X. His influence was worldwide; but in theology his call was heeded the most in the Netherlands, where the Dutch Reformed Church in its new Church Order (1951) speaks first of the apostolate (Art. VIII) and only after that of the confession of the church (Art. X), and where in the first decade after the First World War the so-called "theology of the apostolate" evolved, partly in a radicalism that went beyond Kraemer. This development was spearheaded by A. A. van Ruler as he attempted to view the church strictly as a means to the Kingdom, and thereby also to the world; favorite pictures he used to illustrate this were that of a flame giving light by consuming itself and that of a wagon which serves only as a vehicle to carry the Word to the world; see especially *Het apostolaat der kerk en het ontwerp-kerkorde* (1948), e.g. pp. 68f., and *Theologie van het apostolaat* (1954). But already in this second booklet he defends much more strongly the church's own place and form in the relationship of Kingdom and world. As intimated in note 20 on p. 18, he was made wary by the radicalism of J. C. Hoekendijk, who thought of the church solely as an instrument; see his collection of essays with the characteristic title *The Church Inside Out* (E.T. 1966), of which part one bears the heading: "The Church as Function of the Apostolate." The study report of the World Council of Churches, *The Church for Others,* breathes his spirit. We shall come back to this controversy later.

Meanwhile this apostolary turning to the world still did not get much of a hearing in theological handbooks and ecclesiastical monographs. That is true even of Küng, *The Church*, who refers to this relationship only in the Epilogue. A hesitant but good exception is the ecclesiological Faith and Order document *One Lord, One Baptism* (1960); see pp. 36–40. At the same time appeared the ecclesiological monograph, written from the apostolate perspective: A. B. Come, *Agents of Reconciliation* (1960). But far above all these towers Barth, *CD* IV,3, published in 1959 (E.T. 1961), in which he comes with a comprehensive and carefully worked out theology of the apostolate; see esp. pars. 71 and 72.

In the developments sketched above new light was also shed on the Bible. There was an increasing awareness that all of mankind is the field and the context of God's saving work. It begins already with the history of the Yahwist which pictures the calling of Abraham against the background of world history (Gen. 2–11) and views it as service to the world. The NT repeatedly emphasizes the relationship of the believer and the church to the world, in attitude, witness, and service. See Matt. 5:14–16; 24:14; 28:19; Mark 16:15; Luke 24:47; John 17:21; Acts 1:8; Rom. 15:16–21; 1 Cor. 14:23–25; Eph. 3:1–10; Phil. 2:15; Col. 1:25–28; Jas. 1:18; 1 Pet. 2:9; 3:15f. Eph. 4:15 should also be mentioned here if we are to take *auxēsōmen* as transitive with *ta panta* as the object, as is defended by Barth, Schlier, and K. L. Schmidt (in *TDNT* III, p. 681): "then we cause everything to grow to him who is the head, Christ." But there is more here than individual statements. The concept of "apostle" (sent one) rests completely on this turning to the world; that makes it not a little strange that later, from the perspective of the apostolic succession, the apostles came to be regarded as static-hierarchical princes of the church. Pentecost (Acts 2) is both the birth of the church and the birth of missions. All of Acts narrates the earliest history of the church as mission history. In Paul *mystērion* is an important apostolary concept (Rom. 11:25; 16:25; Eph. 1:9; 3:9; 6:19f.; Col. 1:26f.; 4:3f.). Later we shall deal with other lines of thought and concepts, such as *aparchē* and *plērōma*.

Next to these and other statements of a turning to the world are found others which just as strongly or even more strongly speak of an antithetical relationship. Alongside of e.g. Eph. 3:1–10 stands Eph. 4:17–24, and beside e.g. Col. 1:15–29 we find Col. 2:20–3:11. Apparently turning toward and antithesis are not exclusive of each other but belong together. How we are to conceive of that is a subject for later discussion.

For the NT foundation of this third dimension of the church see D. van Swigchem, *Het missionair karakter van de Christelijke gemeente volgens de brieven van Paulus en Petrus* (1955), and J. Verkuyl, *Contemporary Missiology: An Introduction* (E.T. 1978).

Having ascertained the fact of the church's orientation to the world, we now face the question of the how. This relatedness can be thought of in different ways. If the church exists in the final analysis for the sake of the world, the church will obviously be viewed solely as an instrument for preaching the gospel and for rendering service. This is indeed how many in our day conceive of the church. This makes her totally and solely a servant, having no importance of her own, and with the obligation to minimize herself as much as possible and to give center stage to the world to which she has to minister. After all, God's real concern is the world, and thus not the church. Stated differently, the apostolate is not one of many functions of the church, but the church is a function of the apostolate of God in the world.

When the church after the Second World War with somewhat of a shock became aware of her great apostolary neglect, these and similar ideas arose as a strong reaction to it. We refer to what we said about an earlier phase of Van Ruler, about

Hoekendijk, and about *The Church for Others*. This book contains the frequently quoted sentence: ". . . it is the world that must be allowed to provide the agenda for the churches" (p. 20). Items on this agenda are: pluralism, the welfare state, use of free time, disadvantaged groups, lack of a voice, racism, depersonalization, etc. (pp. 20–22). "The churches today need to discover and proclaim what is their Lord's will in relation to what is happening in the world at large" (p. 21).

The above quotations indicate that the apostolary turning to the world in the fifties became a diaconal orientation in the sixties. In the seventies in turn this led to an orientation toward the political: the church must first of all witness by acting as a political pressure group on behalf of the oppressed and discriminated to renew the societal structures.

Further reflection shows, however, that this purely apostolary approach to the church is untenable. That kind of witnessing and ministering church can only exist when she is intensely driven by the Spirit. She can give only in the measure that she herself receives. She cannot be the bridge between the covenant-establishing God and his world unless she herself has a firm footing on that first shore. Her first relationship is to her Lord, and this relationship is the inspirational source and the content as well as the standard for her directedness to the world. If the reflection on the church starts from her mission to the world, the danger is that all these things are more or less taken for granted as self-evident postulates and as such are not really taken into account; while if the reflection starts from the other end and takes its inception in God, Christ, and the covenant, we cannot stop there but are inexorably sent on to the world. Moreover, in the first approach the independent significance of the church as a community (and not just as a herald or deacon) does not come out, even though a significant aim of the apostolate is to bring about the incorporation into this new community. It would also be difficult to find a place in this view for the reality of the antithesis which the church experiences relative to the world. All these considerations lead to the conclusion that the apostolary orientation of the church is grounded in her communion with her Lord as well as in that of her members among each other.

Especially from the NT it was bound to become clear that the church cannot be conceived of as a purely apostolary functionality; in that case the letters to the small congregations in a hostile world would have looked entirely different. For that reason, Van Swigchem sees the church not only as the proclaimer of the Kingdom, but also as the provisional result, the foretaste (*Het missionair karakter van de Christelijke gemeente,* p. 249. See also G. Sevenster, in *Woord en wereld. Opgedragen aan Prof. Dr. K. H. Miskotte* (1961), who in his contribution "Het karakter der NT-ische gemeente" concludes "that the church is also something very essential in itself, something unique . . . a peculiar community, in which in a variety of ways something of unique and independent existence around word and sacrament must come to expression. This fact of being church has a significance all by itself . . ." (p. 125).

The church is not apostolary because and to the extent that she sacrifices her being-herself to being an instrument; rather it is precisely her being-herself that is to work in the world in an apostolary way. That can only be done if her being-in-the-world is a being-different-from-the-world. For precisely possessing that character she is a witness to the world. She can direct herself to the world only by virtue of her being-different. Yet even her being-different is no goal in itself, but a witness and invitation to the world. The antithesis toward and solidarity with the world do not compete with each other, but they are the two sides of the same reality. The church may and must be something that is distinct in the world. Yet she will continually have to ask herself whether that is also her character relative to the world, whether the world can still experience her presence as the call of the gospel or whether that presence has become a foreign language no one understands.

The language which the church may speak through her existence is the language of the reality of the new community and that of a renewed humanity. In virtue of the fact of the covenant, these new realities may become visible in worship and service, in confession of sin and forgiveness, in reconciliation and communion, in hope and endurance, in a new fellowship with the neighbor, but also in the attitude toward work, money, the tradition, affluence, etc. This is the way in which the church has her face to the world, namely as the "firstfruits" of God's purposes, as the experimental garden of a new humanity.

There is no doubt that in the NT the apostolary activity is overshadowed by the fact of the church, and where it does stand out it presupposes and draws its strength from that fact. See the above-mentioned studies by Van Swigchem and Sevenster. The church works and attracts first of all by shining as a light in a dark world. A favorite text to undergird more deliberate activity is 1 Pet. 2:9, but a comparison with 1 Pet. 3:2 and 15f. suggests that "declaring the wonderful deeds" refers first of all to the church's Christian walk of life.

Of particular significance in this connection are the highly compressed statements in Eph. 1:22f. According to this passage God has given Christ to the church as the head over *ta panta* (all of still unconverted mankind), so that as his *sōma* she is at the same time *to plērōma tou ta panta en pasin plēroumenou,* which, in our view, is to be rendered as: the domain of him who dominates all of mankind. Church and world are thus intimately related. They live from the same covenant secret, the exalted Christ. The church is the community within which the destiny of the world is already known and being experienced, namely that some day all things will be brought together under Christ as the head (1:10: *anakephalaiōsasthai ta panta en tōi Christōi*). See H. Berkhof, *De katholiciteit der kerk* (1962), ch. II, and I. J. du Plessis, *Christus as hoof van kerk en kosmos* (1962), esp. pp. 69–78.

Another statement relevant to this subject is found in Jas. 1:18: "Of his own will he brought us forth by the word of truth that we should be a kind of first fruits (*aparchēn tina*) of his creatures." The word *aparchē*, which in the NT is used for Christ and the Spirit, is here somewhat hesitantly (*tina*) applied to the church. Both in religious history and in the OT the firstfruits are the guarantee of the fruitfulness of all that is still to come. The church must realize that in her life decisions happen that have a bearing on the whole world. According to Eph. 1:22f. and Jas. 1:18 the ground for the church's existence is that she lives in the sight of the world. She has to be proof and model of God's intentions with his creatures.

In contemporary theology, which no longer takes place within a *corpus Christianum* but in a secularized culture, these ideas are again becoming very prominent. One of the first to work them out, and the most thoroughly at the same time, was Karl Barth. That was already implied in his definition of the church in *CD* IV,2, p. 694, as "the provisional representation of the sanctification of all humanity and human life as it has taken place in Him" (namely Christ). That led in IV,3, par. 72, to a discussion of the church under the headings: (1) "The People of God in the Events of the World," and (2) "The Church for the World"; in both what is at stake is the unique existence of the church as a conscious existence in the sight of and for the sake of all mankind. In the school of Barth this is often expressed as the exemplaric existence of the church—a useful epitome, but also one which can easily give a moralistic impression or even suggest a haughty attitude. For that reason others prefer to speak of *Pro-existenz* (existence for the sake of).

One of our reasons for opting for this approach to the relationship of church and world is the conviction that the functional approach, as described above, can be integrated with it, while the opposite cannot be done. See also Berkouwer, *The Church,* ch. 15; and Blei, *De onfeilbaarheid van de kerk,* pp. 389–395.

Finally a few words about practice. Through the centuries the church has likely owed her capacity to attract members particularly to the unique nature of her own communal life in the sight of the world around her. In general, organized activity will only then draw people if it proceeds from and leads to a community which itself exudes the potential to draw people. All this has for centuries been true especially of the churches in the western part of the northern hemisphere. Nowadays, however, the church's strength to draw people is found especially in the southern and eastern churches. It looks as if outreach and mission may start moving in the opposite direction.

That the church is the firstfruits should not be misconstrued as if it were a silent flourishing existence in the midst of a spectator world. That would clash with the nature of this existence. For through the Spirit dwelling within this new community the members are freed from themselves, and directed to the Lord, to each other, to the neighbor, and to the world. Exactly this community cannot but reach out in word and deed to the world, ministering to and drawing people. Her new being involves her readiness to serve and her availability and willingness to help. It belongs to her very essence to be available for the worldwide plans of her Lord. That can express itself in all sorts of ways, and this can come from the church as an institution, from Christian organizations or action groups, and in activities of single individuals. All these activities together can, however, be summarized under the following four heads:

1. *Intercessory prayer.* In this act the church does representatively for the world that which it does not do itself. She intercedes with God who loves the world, maintains it, and wants to save it. She prays for the penetration of the Spirit in the world, for the conversion of the hearts of men, for changes in societal structures, for reconciliation in conflicts, for wisdom, for concern for people, for vision for those in authority on the various levels of political and social life, and for new hope for all the oppressed, the dispossessed, and the homeless who in their needs may confidently look to God. The church prays for them, well aware that thereby she does not shift her own responsibility onto God—her deeds will demonstrate whether her intercession is seriously meant—but firmly convinced that God's love and power far exceed ours and that we plead for what is his cause first of all.

2. *Witness.* When the church reaches out into the world, the word possesses a logical priority. That which is deepest, most essential, we can only, on behalf of God, say in words. That can, however, be done in a great many ways: in preaching, evangelism, missions, personal conversation, education and training, pastoral care, publications, scientific study. In this matter we can easily fail, by keeping silent as well as by speaking at the wrong time, by being unnecessarily apologetic as well as by forcing our views on others. Yet the failure to the one side by one may not be used by others as an excuse to fail in the other direction. A testimony concerning God's love remains ineffective if that same love has no influence on the moment and nature of that testimony. The testimony must be given institutionally, particularly in missions, but likewise individually and in all kinds of intermediate forms. Ideally, all these forms will supplement, even evoke each other. But whatever the form, all will confirm the Pentecostal fact that the Spirit opens people's mouths and equips them to speak the gospel in and for today's world.

3. *The ministry of mercy.* This was dealt with in paragraph 40 point 6 (the diaconate). There we noted that the church helps where there is no helper. This attitude thus ignores every boundary, including the one between church and world. The church is itself a form of witness concerning the God of mercy and of justice. The verbal witness and the ministry of mercy cannot be pitted against each other. The word becomes eloquent in the deed and vice versa. Yet in this interaction each retains its own character. The aim of the word is to win directly for Christ, whereas the deed is not a means to that goal. In concrete needs concrete help is given, driven by the love of Christ, without even the slightest ulterior motive, be that ever so noble. The strict matter-of-factness of the help is itself the best witness for Christ.

4. *Prophecy.* This can be viewed as an aspect of the witness as well as of the ministry of mercy. But precisely because it borders on both and adds its own dimension to both it requires separate attention. It does not

direct itself to persons with the idea of converting or helping them, but to persons as the embodiment of institutions and situations which perpetuate conditions that are clearly in conflict with God's will for his world. The church must confront the authorities with the preserving and saving will of God for the world, in order that in the light of the coming kingdom they will use their power to further the cause of justice, peace, and freedom. For it is not only people who belong to God, but also their societal structures, and these can hinder as well as promote the humanity God wants. See paragraphs 53–56.

Noting these four areas of outreach into the world does not imply that every believer is to be active in all four of them. Particularly here the charismatic structure of the church (paragraph 41) enters in. The one is good at verbalizing needs in intercessory prayer; another has the gift of finding the right words—whether the spoken word or in print—to communicate; a third is particularly sensitive to hidden needs and possesses the imagination and energy to organize and come with the needed help; and a fourth has the gift of prophecy and of expert insight by which he can make himself heard in the centers of political, social, and economic power. Yet all need each other and should gratefully accept each other's help. Also in this posture to the world the office-bearers are to keep a watchful eye, encouraging people to cross the boundaries to the world in one direction or another.

Though in the NT the apostolary nature of the church (especially in the epistles) is dominant, this is not at the expense of the apostolary activity about which particularly the Acts of the Apostles has so much to say. Most of the epistles were written by the greatest apostle, and on every page they witness to his ceaseless missionary activity (e.g. Rom. 15:15–24). And from the text mentioned earlier it is clear that also the churches established by him were aware of their responsibility, both for the work of Paul and for that in their own area.

We noted that particularly Barth emphasizes the apostolary nature of the church as the "provisional representation of the sanctification of all humanity and human life as it has taken place in Christ." But in *CD* IV,3, where he develops his theology of the apostolate, he modifies this definition as follows: that he (namely Christ) entrusts "to it the ministry of his prophetic Word and therefore the provisional representation of the calling of all humanity and indeed of all creatures as it has taken place in Him" (p. 681). The two earlier-mentioned subtitles of par. 72, which deal more with the nature of the church, are then followed by 3: "The Mandate of the Church," and 4: "The Service of the Church." As forms of this service he discusses (pp. 865–901) the praise of God, proclamation, teaching, evangelism, missions, theology, prayer, pastoral care, personal example, the diaconate and prophecy, and concludes with the community and once again the nature of the church.

We ended par. 41 with a section on the marks of the church. There we also had to refer briefly to this paragraph. For it will be obvious that outreach into the world is one of the indisputable marks of the church. That the Reformers, who still thought in terms of the *corpus Christianum*, did not include it is excusable. But anyone who today, either theologically or practically, still ignores it as a central mark is without excuse.

In the Netherlands after the War, in connection with the fresh outreach into the world, it became a big question whether the church institute or Christian organizations were to be the bearer of this outreach. Experience had taught that inherent in the latter approach was the danger of a narrowing and compartmentalization of the witness, or what can also happen, that the cause one stands for is regarded by other Christians as no more than a hobby of the members of the organization. Hence the rise of a strong tendency toward making all kinds of Christian activity part of the regular work of the church. Meanwhile, we have come to realize that subsuming it under the church is as such no cure-all either. As a matter of fact, new problems appear all the time, which at first are better handled by individuals or small groups. The institution, the group, and the individual need each other. The particular form which is best suited for the outreach of God's people into the world will depend on the situation and the people and will have to be determined in each separate case.

All this could, however, give an entirely wrong impression, as if in the relation of church and world only the church is rich and handing out while the world is only passive and poor. In reality things are not that simple. It is complicated by opposition and boundaries. We note three of these, each quite diverse from the others: (1) the enmity of the world, (2) the wisdom in the world, and (3) the disobedience of the church.

1. *The enmity of the world.* This is a wall which the church, if it faithfully carries out its mandate with respect to the world, will sooner or later be faced with in one form or another. For in the offer of grace and the call to conversion too much is asked of man. Failing to see that here he is offered his own rescue, he will increasingly put up his guards and offer stronger resistance as he feels himself more seriously threatened. For the first Christians this was a normal situation which they regarded as a test of their faith, and therefore were able to endure. But the less we understand this boundary and opposition, the more we will be discouraged by it and try to get around it, thereby running the risk of becoming unfaithful to the cause we are to represent in our outreach. Yet even as Jesus had to suffer in this world, so suffering is integral to the experiences of his followers in their outreach. That is the boundary of the outreach, but at the same time a new form of it.

Suffering as the concomitant of the mandate is found frequently already in the OT, in its picture of Moses and in the laments of the prophets. Von Rad repeatedly refers to this element in his *OT Theology*. In the NT, Paul repeatedly mentions suffering as the other side of his apostolate (1 Cor. 4:9–13; 2 Cor. 4:7–12; 6:4–10; 11:23–27). Note also how matter-of-factly, at times almost cheerfully, the NT relates the suffering of the church in the world (Matt. 5:10–12; 10:34; John 15:18–20; 16:33; Acts 5:41; Rom. 5:3; 8:17; Col. 1:24; 1 Thess.

3:25; Jas. 1:2; 1 Pet. 1:6f.; 2:20ff.; 4:12f.; 5:9). It is also noteworthy how already in the NT *martys* and *martyria* (esp. in Rev.) come to have the additional meaning of martyrdom. See also par. 49.

Though this does not mean that suffering is the necessary consequence of bearing witness to Christ, it could well be a significant criterion for judging the genuineness of our words and deeds. Words that do not cost anything and deeds that are meant to make us popular have nothing to do with the apostolary firstfruit-character of the people of God.

2. *The wisdom in the world.* Here we are confronted with an entirely different and almost opposite problematics. The Spirit instructs and liberates the world through the outreach of the church, but he also instructs and liberates the church through its contact with the world. There is a two-way movement and interaction. The whole world belongs to God and no place or time is devoid of his hidden presence. To the church is revealed the world's salvation. But there is a great deal of other truth and wisdom which elsewhere are coming to light and await the time that they will be brought to bear upon the world's salvation, even as salvation awaits the moment that it will permeate and express itself in that truth and wisdom. What God has to say to us in Christ is continually receiving fresh forms if it merges with the wisdom that is discovered in the world. As a rule the church itself is not the first to discover this wisdom at the right time. That may be due to her disobedience, but also to shortsightedness or even, positively, to the fact that God blesses his world with the wisdom it needs for its continuing existence. That makes the church humble. To her has been entrusted salvation, but she does not have a monopoly on wisdom. What she does have is the calling to bring that wisdom, wherever she meets it, in contact with Christ and thus to show it its place and purpose. This implies that in its outreach into the world the church should not only speak but also listen. And when she speaks, she does so because she has listened first. In the dialogue with the world she is not the only one who may speak, though she may say the final word.

We think here of the place of wisdom in creation, as Prov. 8:22–31 depicts it. Paul continues that in 1 Cor. 1:21, where he also makes clear how this world, surrounded by God's wisdom, in its folly constantly fails to recognize it; only the "foolishness of preaching" opens up that wisdom. That does not alter the fact that wisdom plays a large role in the preservation of the world. The progress of revelation in the Bible is also determined by the wisdom of Egypt, Babel, Persia, and Greece. The theological development throughout the centuries is unthinkable without Plato and Aristotle, and later without Descartes, Kant, and Hegel. The natural sciences and the humanities have helped us to better understand the Bible. And strange as it may sound, it has been the spirit of secularism that has stood up against the witchcraft-hunting attitude of a myopic Christendom, that has insisted on toleration, fought injustice, exploitation, and discrimination, and battled for freedom, equality, and brotherhood, a long struggle which eventually has led to the emergence of free democratic states for which Christians and non-

Christians are equally grateful. The problem is complicated by the fact that it is precisely evangelical values which in this way have overcome the resistance of a traditional Christendom. On that see par. 54. Whatever the case, it does not change the fact that the world has its own input in the dialogue with the church.

For centuries, theology viewed the relation between church and world as a monologue. For a long time this was natural, given the dominant position of the church. But that time is past. However, the theological exploration and evaluation of the interaction we have noted here is still only in the beginning stages. It might seem as if Tillich with "the latent church" (*ST*, esp. III, pp. 152–155) and K. Rahner with his "anonymous Christendom" (*passim* in his *Theological Investigations,* esp. in and after Vol. 4) try to find a place in theology for this wisdom; closer investigation indicates that they are particularly interested in the religious (and its concomitant ethical) dimension. What we have in mind is broader, more secular, and rather related to the Wisdom literature in the OT. In *CD* IV,3, Barth has put his finger on the problem in his famous train of thought about the true words next to the Word of God and about the lights of creation (pp. 109–115). For a foundation and critique of Barth's conception, see H. Berkhof and H.-J. Kraus, *Karl Barths Lichterlehre.*

3. *The disobedience of the church.* Though both boundaries mentioned earlier can occur in purer or less pure form, they are seldom found without the admixture of the culpable tardiness of the church. Therefore the church itself continually evokes hostility because the world is often deeply disappointed by the church's own betrayal of the ideals which she herself has given to the world. And for this reason, too, the church can learn so much from the world, that so often she refused to see her priestly and prophetic task relative to the needs and the guilt all around her.

The right outreach into the world encounters the strongest opposition from within the church itself, which refuses to get out of her lethargy and complacency and rise above her fears. In two ways the church walks away from her calling, through churchism and through worldliness. She does this through churchism when she turns in upon herself as a bulwark in an evil world or, less aggressively, as an introverted, self-sufficient group, which is content with her own rites, language, and connections. She does this through worldliness by becoming as much as possible assimilated and conformed to the world. In either case she does essentially the same thing: she avoids the clash and the offense. The second form is the one of open betrayal; normally this is so evident that sooner or later the faithful will rebel against it. The first form is much more concealed; it may look very pious and respectable, because the church is concentrating on her own nature which, as we noted, is the very source of the apostolate. But here the temptation is also the strongest and the corruption of the best becomes the worst. If the church forgets her calling to be God's experimental garden, she becomes a caricature of the Spirit's purposes with her. This sacralization may create the impression that it enables the church to escape the opposite threat of secularism. Precisely in this way she falls victim to it, because sacralization, put in sociological terms, is nothing else than the most obvious form of institutional self-preservation. In both cases the church itself becomes a part of the world. Then the "flesh" is mightier than the Spirit.

Though the OT does present the firstfruits character of God's people as a calling, yet in that light the Torah as well as the prophets speaks almost exclusively of disobedience. In the NT, Acts and the epistles also speak of the obedience of the church. But then, too, the picture remains ambiguous and often somber (Acts 5:11; 1 and 2 Cor.; Gal., etc.). See esp. the letter to the seven churches in Rev. 2 and 3. On the twofold danger of sacralization and secularization see Barth, *CD* IV,2, pp. 665ff.

To a great extent official church history is the story of the defeats of the Spirit. But he does not stop from venturing onto this battlefield. Continually he stirs people and groups, mostly minorities, into action, so that in witness and service they may do that which the church owes to the world. These get to experience to the full what it means to suffer in the world, but mostly they are made to suffer even more from ecclesiastical institutions and majorities—until a following generation erects monuments in honor of the prophets who had been stoned by their fathers.

What God has in mind with the church is still far from realized. We are no further than a small beginning. But the struggle continues, and the participants know that what is at issue here is the meaning of all of existence and, furthermore, that the continuance of this struggle is a sign of the victory which the Spirit will someday achieve over our recalcitrance. Therefore the church is the place where we are constantly being compelled to step ahead ourselves, and where we learn to want more than the present state of affairs and what has so far been achieved. Precisely on account of all the disobedience and failure that surrounds this calling, by being this battlefield the church is the experimental garden and firstfruits her Lord had in mind. For in order to get this battle going this new community was called into existence.

The Renewal of Man

43. MAN THE PURPOSE OF GOD

THE GOLDEN THREAD which runs through all the preceding, linking the deeds, events, developments, structures, and institutions discussed there, is God's intention to adopt people as his children, to make them his covenant partners. This intention can be individualistically misunderstood (as is often done) as if God's concern is persons as pure individuals. For God there are no pure individuals; nor, however, is there an abstract "mankind." For God sees people as they interact with others in the extensive fabric of space and time, of society and history, of structures, tradition, culture, and nature. We are persons, people meant for fellowship with God and humans because of and in all the structures in which we have been placed. This is such a fundamental fact that before we could speak about the renewal of man we had to deal with the church. But now, at last, the way is clear to do full justice to the fact that God has pleasure in *man*. In all these structures his concern is mankind, people, each as he is, unique, human. In that respect, what we have broadly called the "structures" are secondary or, more accurately, instrumental in significance. Their significance is often neglected in the study of the faith. In the next chapter we shall specifically deal with that significance. But here we must note that their importance lies exactly in their instrumentality. About nature we need to be more reserved. We have no right to say that it exists only for the sake of man. Rather, it is partly our servant, partly our companion. As a creation of God which is different from man, it is largely unfathomable to us and as such a pointer to the unfathomableness of its creator; and that is cause for us to be humble (cf. Job 38–41). In calling man the purpose of God, we do not thereby exclude the possibility that God may have other, entirely different purposes in mind with and for his creation. Yet the course of his acts in history, a course in which we participate by faith and which we probe in the study of the faith, discloses him to us as a God of people whose goal is to enter into an eternal covenant with them. On the basis of our knowledge of that covenantal path we may say that apparently in that unique event man is God's purpose.

In the OT it is not yet fully clear that man as a person is the real theme and purpose. There the renewal is seen especially as a command to be obedient and as an eschatological promise. Moreover, the concern of the OT is much more the people as a whole than the individual. And as regards the present, apart from exceptions, the awareness of disobedience, guilt, and failure prevails. Not until the NT does the perspective change, due to the indwelling of the Spirit in man. Paul has articulated the Spirit-wrought renewal in such a way that it has inspired all the generations after him, though none has ever reached his depth and breadth.

In the history of the church (at least in the mainline churches, not in all sorts of sects and movements) one clearly notices an attitude of reserve on this central point. Typical is the Apostles' Creed, which only in the words "I believe in the forgiveness of sins" touches on the theme. The interest is mainly in the objective facts of salvation. Why? From a feeling of impotence, because so little can be seen of the renewal? Out of pastoral wisdom to keep people from engaging in fruitless self-reflection? One should, however, not generalize here. There have been times when the interest in the relationship of God and man was primary. We need to think only of Augustine, Bernard of Clairvaux, the preaching of the mendicant orders, and medieval mysticism. All that is, however, overshadowed by the Reformation. In its deepest intentions, it was not a protest against evils in the church, nor a renewal of doctrine, not even a "rediscovery" of the gospel, but a radicalization of the personal relationship of man to his God. That climaxed in the slogan of "justification by faith alone," which was not aimed against genuine "good works," but against an impersonal and commercialized relationship of man to God. Precisely the subject of this chapter has been deeply probed and elaborately developed by and after the Reformation. That holds especially for the period which is marked to the one side by Luther's *The Freedom of the Christian Man* (1520) and to the other side by the so-called Canons of Dort (1619). In dogmatics, particularly in Protestant Scholasticism, this reflection led to a series of concepts such as: calling, justification, sanctification, conversion, regeneration, illumination, and renewal; in the Lutheran camp, moreover, it gave rise to the doctrine of the mystical union, and among the Reformed to that of the perseverance of the saints (see S, H, and Bavinck, *GD* IV, pars. 49–52). But among the Reformed the simpler and more existential division of misery–redemption–gratitude of the Heidelberg Catechism (1563) has had much more influence.

In the 19th century, this entire arsenal of concepts was, if not abandoned, at least drastically reinterpreted by tying it in as much as possible with psychological and anthropological ideas or even grounding it therein. Where this was accompanied by an aversion toward the objective elements in the faith and an emphasis, instead, on what was called the "moral," "ethical," or "psychological," there was a dissociation from the Reformational encounter thinking in favor of a concentration on man as religious subject. Barth's *Epistle to the Romans* ([2]1922) marked the beginning of a sharp reaction with a radical swing toward the divine side of the encounter. The aftereffects of this reactive swing are still so powerful in theology that many a modern book of systematic theology says very little about the subject of the renewal of man because it is pushed aside by the broad discussion of the objective fact of salvation. This is particularly true of Trillhaas,

Dg, and Prenter, *Creation and Redemption* (E.T. 1955). Exceptions are Brunner, *Dg* III; O. A. Dilschneider, *Gegenwart Christi,* II (1948), pp. 9–181; and especially Barth, *CD* IV,1–3, pars. 61, 63, 66, 68, 71, 73. On the point of the appropriation of salvation, Roman Catholic theology, which used to lag behind, is now actively engaged in trying to catch up. For a radical transpositon of the traditional doctrine of grace into the categories of encounter and social experience, see L. Boff, *Liberating Grace* (1976). See further *MS* 4,2, esp. chs. 12 and 13, and *MS,* chs. 1–5. A difference with the Protestant pattern concerns the closer conjunction with the sacraments, especially baptism, confirmation, and confession.

The expression "man the purpose of God" has an unusual, even provocative ring in the tradition of theology. It gives the impression that we are misunderstanding the Christian faith and giving it an anthropocentric twist. Should we not say the opposite, namely that God is the purpose of man? That is, however, not the opposite of the first statement, only its reverse. For a covenant implies the orientation of the one party to the other. For the creature, man, a covenant with his God can mean nothing less than a radical orientation to him who in this covenant radically orients himself to us. But it does imply for man who is alienated from God a radical reorientation and about-face. God wants a covenant relationship with man as he is; yet for the sake of that relationship he cannot possibly leave him as he is. God's gracious turning to man is correlated from man's side by his turning to God. In this turning man bows before him who intends his salvation. Hence that about-face is not man's alienation from himself, but rather his home-coming, his reaching his destiny.

It is often assumed that on this point of the goal there is a difference, even a contrast, between Luther and Calvin. For Luther the central question would be: "How do I find a gracious God?" His approach to salvation would then be soteriological or even anthropological. For Calvin, in contrast, the central concern would be *soli Deo gloria.* His approach would supposedly be theological and strictly theocentric. This contrast is, however, a theological construction and the result of the failure to see the radical encounter thinking of both Reformers. For Luther see J. T. Bakker, *Coram Deo* (1956), *passim.* For Calvin see his Catechism of Geneva (1542), where he says that the chief end of man is to know God (1), to honor him (7), describing this honoring as "to place our whole confidence in him" (7), and "that each of us should set it down in his mind that God loves him, and is willing to be a Father, and the author of salvation to him" (11). For the *doxa* of God demonstrates and realizes itself in peace on earth, in his favor which rests on men (Luke 2:14). Cf. Irenaeus: "For the glory of God is a living man; and the life of man consists in beholding God" (*AH* 20.7).

However, to attain this goal it is necessary that there be what we called "change," a "turnabout," or in classical language "conversion." Though very much neglected in present-day experience theology (see par. 10), precisely this experience (once for all and continuously) is fundamental to the faith. Thanks to the Spirit, people can be changed. Reflection on this subject is found especially in Wesley and in Anglo-Saxon revivalistic circles. See G. E. Morris, *The Mystery and Meaning of Christian Conversion* (1981). While conversion stands here especially at the beginning, in *MS* 5, 2, III, 2 it is treated entirely as something that happens within the church as the continuous answer to the grace given in baptism, as "Wieder-Zukehr." However, the latter seems more properly to belong to the theme of sanctification.

We cannot state this, however, without reflecting on the purpose God has in mind for man. If in the covenant man is God's purpose, the implication is that God also has in mind a purpose for man. That is not yet stated in words like renewal, about-face, or conversion. On the contrary, they receive their contents from the purpose to which they lead. So the question is: What is the goal of the renewal? That question used to be, and still is, answered in a wide variety of terms in the Bible and in different churches, periods, and spiritual movements. We choose what we regard as the most substantial and concrete answer: conformity with Christ. In him, after all, God's true covenant partner has appeared in our midst. It must be God's purpose that we (as Paul preferably expresses it) "become conformed to his image." Man's potential and future we see before us in his glorified life as he lives it in the presence of the Father, in a loving fellowship with him which also embraces his church and humanity.

That goal seems far away now. Hence the way to the goal is no less important. For the present the expression "conformity with Christ" not only spells out the purpose, but the way as well. As the true covenant partner, Jesus went his way to this goal ahead of us, in order that he might open the way for us. Our way to the goal consists now in participation in his way. Participation means that we follow him and thus implies distance as well. We are not Christ himself. We are dependent on what he has done for us before we can follow after him. Our way, unlike his, is first of all one of repentance and forgiveness. Thereby we are, however, being incorporated into his way of death and resurrection. These few indications must suffice for now; the details will be worked out in the following paragraphs.

This conformity with Christ as the goal and the way implies at the same time our participation in the way of Israel, as that way is depicted in the Old Testament. For that way and the one of Jesus are an unbreakable whole (see paragraphs 30 and 31). Israel's way shows us where we stand and it makes us ask what the question is to which Jesus' way became the answer. One who wants to understand the answer must also make the question his own. We say "also," not "first," because the actual incorporation into the historical covenant event through surrender in faith does not happen according to chronological laws. But the experiences we gain on the way of the covenant are appropriated by participating in it through personal faith: confrontation with the calling from God, the refusal to obey, wrath and forgiveness, death and resurrection. These we make our own through repentance, faith, and the willingness to obey. What this means for man can be described in a variety of terms: conversion, illumination, regeneration, renewal. What is at issue is the consequence of the covenant event for man as a person. And this consequence is at the same time the goal of this event: man as God's child and partner.

It is remarkable how rarely the question concerning God's purpose in the renewal of man has been explicitly discussed in the study of the faith. Its attention was focused on the renewal itself; its results were preferably called "fruits," and so the goal-problematics was by-passed. An important exception in this respect was Methodism, particularly its founder, John Wesley. He characterized the goal as Christian perfection, basing it on Scripture passages such as Eph. 4:13; Phil. 3:12–15; Col. 3:14; 1 Thess. 5:16; Heb. 6:4; 12:14; 1 John 3:8ff.; 4:18; 5:18. He conceived of perfection as living totally from the love of Christ, which drives out all sin. From these texts he concluded that this perfection was obtainable already in this life. He summarized his convictions on this subject in his *A Plain Account of Christian Perfection* (1767); cf. the Methodist *Christliche Glaubenslehre* of A. Sulzberger (Bremen, ²1886), esp. par. 87. See also H. K. La Rondelle, *Perfection and Perfectionism* (1971). Theologically this position of Wesley deserves to be taken more seriously than is usually done. One could at least acknowledge his goal-problematics and try to find an alternative.

For us the concept of "perfection" is unusable, however, if only because of the connotations it has in current usage and which differ so much from those in the NT; see P. J. Du Plessis, [*TELEIOS*]. *The Idea of Perfection in the NT* (1959). To us the term is suggestive of the hard work by which an individual achieves his full potential, or perfects himself.

In Paul we find a group of words that say precisely what is at issue here. These are the words *morphē, morphousthai, metamorphousthai, symmorphizesthai, symmorphia, symmorphos*. Being in the form of God, Christ assumed the form of a slave (Phil. 2:5–11), in order that he may now be formed in believers (Gal. 4:19), so that they may become like him in his death now and later be made like him in his resurrection (Phil. 3:10f., 21). For God's purpose for them is that they be made like *(symmorphos)*, conformed to, the image of his Son (Rom. 8:29). For the important thing is that we, who now bear the likeness of the first Adam, shall bear the likeness of the last Adam (1 Cor. 15:49). See especially 2 Cor. 3:12–18, a central passage in this connection, with its climactic ending in the last two verses; it is clear that we become involved in a re-creative process so that our nature, too, will possess the freedom and the glory of the pneumatic Christ.

We noted already that in these terms Paul links the goal with the way leading to it: conformity with the exalted Christ can come about only through conformity to the way of the suffering Christ, by participating in it by faith. See Phil. 2:1–7; 3:10, and further Rom. 6:1–14; 15:1ff.; 2 Cor. 4:7–11; 6:4–10; Eph. 5:2.

The NT uses many other words to describe the renewal, such as "adoption," "sanctification," "perfection," "regeneration," "glorification," and once even "participation in the divine nature" (2 Pet. 1:4). Different confessions and traditions have each their own preference. Eastern Orthodoxy preferably speaks of deification, the Roman Catholic Church of sanctification and exaltation, Lutheranism of justification, Pietism of regeneration, Methodism of perfection. "Calvin's ideal Christian is a servant of God, Luther's a child of God, Wesley's a perfect man in the full stature of Christ" (P. Schaff). In what follows we shall try to show to what extent the concept of conformity with Christ can embrace the others and do justice to them.

44. JUDGMENT AND REPENTANCE

ISRAEL CAME TO KNOW GOD as the gracious founder and the faithful partner of the covenant. But, as we have noticed (paragraph 30), this covenant was deadlocked in endless conflict situations between God and his unfaithful people. In these situations the love of God could express itself only through its apparent opposite. By his sin man forces God to act as his adversary. God now judges and condemns man. That becomes evident in two respects: on the one hand in that Israel becomes stuck in the dead-end alley of her self-chosen ways, and on the other hand in that the prophets interpret this dead-end alley as the judgment of God. The people as a whole did not accept this prophetic elucidation of its deeds and experiences. Consequently, the alienation from God continued. It would have been removed if the people had acknowledged their guilt in repentance before God. Then there would again have been room for communion. For God wants to be near those who are obedient, but also near those who "weep" and are "contrite in heart" (cf. Isaiah 57:14–21). Yet this repentance, which was institutionally portrayed in the sacrificial cult (sin and guilt-offerings), was really manifested by only a few individuals (see the so-called penitential psalms), and by the people only as they looked back on the waywardness of the fathers. On the way of Israel in the New Testament, the judgment situation is brought to a climax when Jesus is crucified, making the break between God and his people wider and deeper than ever before.

When the Holy Spirit makes a person share in the way of Israel and of Christ, that person learns to recognize himself in disobedient Israel and to acknowledge that God's judgment upon Israel is also God's judgment upon him. Hence that participation always has in it the element of repentance. Repentance is the shocking awareness of a radical failing which cannot be undone and the admission that God is just in his judgment. Repentance thus means our awakening to sin. Sin as a topic in itself is not the issue here; for that see paragraph 27. Our concern here is man's awakening to it as a fundamental element in the renewal process initiated by the Spirit.

We call this repentance. But this common term, which is applied to so many psychological conditions and social relationships, may therefore fail to express what repentance really is. It concerns our relationship to God, or covenantal knowledge. This is a knowledge in which man knows of the love of God against which he has sinned, yet keeps hoping for that love. Repentance is much more than and entirely different from regret. Regret deplores the consequences and to that extent the deeds that caused them. Repentance deplores the deed itself that disturbs the love relationship. Repentance means that unconditionally we assume the blame ourselves, take full responsibility for it, without coming with excuses. Repentance is thus entirely different from depression, self-hatred, or masochism. In repentance we are not busy with ourselves, but with God: "Against thee, thee only, have I sinned" (Psalm 51:6). If we are busy with ourselves we are involved in a dialogue with ourselves, and as a rule have some ground left under our feet, even if only the "better I" by which we condemn ourselves. That ground is here pulled from under us. We know that our repentance cannot make up for anything and that it falls far short of the guilt to which it relates. And yet, this repentance is not despair. That same covenant which awakens and induces repentance is also the covenant which holds on to man in his repentance and puts him back on his feet. The difference between repentance and despair can be seen in the difference between Judas and Peter after their denial of Jesus. That difference is not a matter of emotions and moods, but it lies in the fact that the despairing person lacks the vision of God whose love he has violated. Repentance does not obliterate the knowledge of God, it presupposes it. But the reverse is also true; for the giving God is at the same time the asking God, who with his love to us seeks to elicit our response of love to him, thereby making us aware of our utter failure with respect to that saving command.

The knowledge of grace and the knowledge of sin go together; they presuppose and reinforce each other. Without repentance all the notes of the Christian faith are off-key or fall silent. Then the gospel is changed from a marvelous message of liberation into a more or less self-evident ideology of cheap grace. If repentance falls away, the amazement and joy over God's free *grace* also fall away. For that reason repentance is not just a passing mood at the start of the road of renewal, but the abiding undertone of all of the Christian life, a tone which is expressed in the churches, Sunday after Sunday, in a liturgical confession of guilt.

There seems to be only one step between this insight and the idea that repentance is the condition for grace. But this overburdening of repentance is equally as disastrous for the gospel as the disregard of repentance: grace would no longer be grace if by our repentance we could earn it or automatically bring it about. True repentance totally denies any idea of ability and meritoriousness on man's part. In the depth of his heart man knows that the reason God comes to the penitent sinner is that he can only be fully himself when man no longer puts any obstacles in his way, neither with his disobedience nor with his pretensions and achievements. Only in this sense is it true that the covenant cannot continue without repentance.

The OT (and likewise the NT) does not have a separate word for "repentance." It does contain many terms which carry that notion, and in which it sometimes even dominates. But in that case these words also refer to e.g. concrete sins or cultic acts or a return to a new obedience. The Hebrew words *šûḇ* and *tᵉšûḇâ* and the Greek *metanoein* and *metanoia* come closest to repentance. But these words are not so much about repentance as about actively breaking with a sinful life, in other words about conversion. That should warn us against an isolationistic experience of and reflection on repentance. The Bible does not even have a term for repentance without conversion. See *TDNT* IV, *s.v.* (*meta-*)*noeō* and the conclusions in W. L. Holladay, *The Root šûḇ in the OT* (1959), pp. 156f. In the OT, the prophets frequently call for a turning around and for repentance. Actual confessions of guilt, however, are much less frequent and mainly from the post-exilic period. We think first of all of the so-called penitential psalms: 6, 32, 38, 51, 102, 130, 143; and further of Ezra 9, Neh. 9, and Dan. 9. See the biblical theologies and J. J. van As, *Skuldbelijdenis en genadeverkondiging in die OT* (1961).

In the NT especially Paul has articulated the fact that the revelation of the covenant in the Torah exposes our radical failure, and even evokes it. In his union with Christ, Paul had begun in a new way, with all of his being, to participate in the way of Israel. Movingly he verbalizes in the Epistle to the Romans the knowledge of sin and the repentance to which this participation awakened him, first in more general terms in ch. 2 and 3:1–20, and then in a very personal self-accusation in ch. 7. In this self-accusation he looks back on the OT way of his people. This retrospection in no way means that the Christian no longer has anything to do with this self-accusation; precisely when we are in Christ Israel's experience becomes our own. In 2 Cor. 7:8–11 Paul uses quite different words in speaking about repentance; here he uses the term *lypē* and distinguishes the true repentance, *lypē kata theon,* from the *lypē tou kosmou.* According to the context the distinguishing mark of the first is that it does not lead to despair or hardening (that is how *thanatos* in v. 10 can be interpreted), but to conversion (v. 9: *metanoia*) and new obedience (v. 11). Actually, in these and other passages Paul does nothing else than express in more abstract and intellectual language what is said about repentance in the unsurpassed imagery of the parable of the lost son (Luke 15:17–19; cf. 18:13f.). In all these passages repentance takes place entirely within the covenant and out of the knowledge of grace.

In church history, repentance became a more prominent factor as faith took on a more personal character. Successively it appears under the names *contritio* (Roman Catholicism), *poenitentia* (the Reformers) and *resipiscentia* (Protestant Scholasticism). In the Middle Ages, the repentance problematics arose especially in connection with the sacrament of penance, with its triad of *contritio cordis–confessio oris–satisfactio operum.* The question arose whether genuine contrition was absolutely necessary or whether, on account of the working of the sacrament, attrition (feeling sorry out of fear of punishment) was sufficient. Trent ascribed to attrition a preparatory significance (D 1676–1678). The controversy between those who were strict and those were more flexible, between contrition and attrition, lasted until 1667 when Pope Alexander VII declared the issue undecided and practically forbade it (D 1070). Present-day Roman Catholic theology regards the controversy mostly as senseless (so K. Rahner, *s.v.* "repentance," in *Sacramentum mundi*).

The Reformation was born out of the controversy about repentance. The practice of selling indulgences, linked to the prevailing moralism, had aided attrition and abetted a superficial view. Luther attacked the hawker of indulgences, Johann Tetzel, in his ninety-five theses, which opened with: "Our Lord and Master Jesus Christ, by saying 'repent', intended that the whole life of believers should be repentance." The classical Lutheran exposition of the concept of penitence is found in the *Apology* (1531), art. XII. In agreement with medieval thinking, its drafter, Melanchthon, assumes that the law evokes repentance, but then he links both closely with the gospel, faith, and forgiveness. Otherwise repentance would lead to despair. This starting from the duality of repentance and faith, which corresponds respectively to the *opus alienum* of the law and the *opus proprium* of the gospel in God himself, has remained characteristic of Lutheranism. Calvin, on the other hand, reverses the order *(Inst* III,iii,1–10): only he who knows the gospel can be repentant. Hence the heading of the third chapter: "Our regeneration by faith: repentance." He even says very strongly: "There are some, however, who suppose that repentance precedes faith, rather than flows from it, or is produced by it as fruit from a tree. Such persons have never known the power of repentance" (iii,1). No less significant is that Calvin subordinates repentance entirely (following the biblical mode of speaking) to conversion (iii,5), with the upright life as the goal. The *Apology* keeps the two separate. In a later development the Lutheran conception gained ground. In the 17th-century climate marked by individualism, emphasis on the inner life, and introspection, repentance came more and more to be viewed in isolation. In the Canons of Dort I,12, "godly sorrow for sin" is mentioned alongside "true faith in Christ" as a proof of one's own election, a sorrow which believers "observe in themselves with a spiritual joy and holy pleasure." The appeal here to 2 Cor. 13:5 is unjustified. All of this received strong reinforcement in the Further Reformation, in Methodism, and in Pietism insofar as it followed A. H. Francke with his "spiritual struggle" *(Busskampf*). As in Lutheran thinking, a concomitant of this isolation was the idea that it is the law which evokes repentance (even as the gospel "after that" evokes faith; a chronological element is now added).

The answer to the question whether repentance comes from the law or from the gospel must be that the giving and commanding God is one and the same. Paul can say in quick succession that it is God's kindness which leads to repentance (Rom. 2:4) *and* that the gospel does not nullify the law, but rather upholds it (3:31). At the most we can make a distinction here: faith orients itself first of all to God's giving, while repentance arises primarily from the gap that exists between what God commands on the basis of his giving and our failures in doing what he commands. Glossing over the accusing function of the law (a present-day tendency) is as reprehensible as the isolation of that function (the Lutheran and Pietistic tendency). See on this theme also par. 27, and G. C. Berkouwer, *Sin* (E.T. 1971), chs. 6 and 7. The problem is put very well in the Heidelberg Catechism which, in Lord's Day 1, begins with our "only comfort," that is, the gospel, and then proceeds to point to repentance as one of its three elements; moreover, the source of that repentance is, according to the Cathechism, particularly the confrontation with the law, but then the law as in the summary of the great commandment. Sin is thus a lack of love.

A final remark arising out of everything that has been said so far is that the psychology of repentance is a subject in itself. Our interest is the structural theological connections. When, how, how strongly, and why a particular person becomes repentant depends on many factors. Something which with one person is a psychological fact may not be imposed upon others as a psychological law.

45. JUSTIFICATION AND FAITH

JUDGMENT IS NOT GOD'S FINAL WORD. Therefore repentance does not have to be man's final word. Structurally speaking, both are first words, words that are followed by amazingly different words, namely "justification" and "faith." In the blending of the first as God's creative act and the second as man's receiving act, the great change in our life takes place from which acts issues whatever else can be said about renewal.

a. Justification

This word is derived from the language of law. The tremendous change it seeks to express can also be denoted in words derived from the language of other fields. For the same event the New Testament also uses such terms as "reconciliation," "forgiveness of sins," and "adoption as children." Paul used juridical imagery extensively because he developed the gospel from the perspective of the rabbinical-Jewish question: how is man justified before God? If this question in this particular form has lost much of its relevance, it may be worthwhile to ask whether the concepts that were useful at that time are not to be replaced by others. Jesus, after all, did not use this terminology either. The Apostles' Creed speaks of "the forgiveness of sins." Does not that way of putting it speak more meaningfully to us? At the same time, however, it is also less specific, more negative, less comprehensive. In paragraph 44 we spoke of "judgment"; its necessary opposite is "acquittal" or "justification." We were thus already using juridical imagery. This sort of metaphor is very suitable to denote what is at issue here: the rights and duties of the covenant relationship, being guilty and receiving mercy, to pronounce a sentence and create a new relationship. In the term "justification," the juridical mode of thought is first followed and then completely altered. Hence after Paul this term has regularly been used, and particularly the Reformation has made it a key-word. It has established for itself a firm place in theology. The same is not true in preaching and church life in general. And theology may not exclusively work with this juridical terminology either, which, after all, does not leave enough room for love, the inner life, and the surrender which are an integral part of the covenantal fellowship. Hence further on we shall also use other words. But none of these is as comprehensive as the term "justification."

Even as repentance as the consciousness of judgment is the other side and the personal accentuation of God's way with Israel, so faith as the consciousness of justification and acquittal is the other side and the personal accentuation of the change which is brought about in Israel's way in the person and work of Jesus Christ. Justification is the human-personal reverse side of what in the section on Christology (paragraphs 34–36) we described with the triad humanity–reconciliation–glorification. By going that way, Jesus acted substitutionarily for us as the true covenant partner. What for him was substitution is justification for us.

On account of the work of the substitute, in this transaction we are called by God what we are not: righteous (just), children of God, partners in his covenant. Therein a new mode of existence is imputed to us. Whereas an earthly judge can only declare him righteous who was already righteous in himself, we are declared to be what in ourselves we are not. We are given a new name, because the Spirit unites us with the true sonship of Jesus by putting to our account, in the way of "imputation," his glorified humanity. The norm remains fully valid, but the condemning judgment is annulled. In the Son, God adoptingly stretches out his hand to lost sons and daughters. The first time this event happens is when by faith they accept this hand. But it is also a constantly recurring event. This is no phase which we can ever leave behind us. All the time, through our failures and repentance, we are thrown back on this starting-point, this turn in the judgment of God, in order to start anew from there.

As regards our personal life, the source of our renewal lies in justification. In our repentance we receive the courage not to take flight from ourselves, but to identify ourselves with our guilty past. In our justification we may say farewell to what we are in ourselves and our deeds. We no longer need to prove or justify ourselves at the expense of others. God justifies and accepts us apart from our "works." So we are set free before God, with respect to other people and for the future. Justification imparts to us an unheard-of invulnerability, which at the same time is a source from which we derive strength to fight against sin, to endure, and to serve (see Romans 8:31–39).

Is justification an event which we consciously experience? In a broad sense, everything that concerns us and happens to us belongs to our conscious experience. But the origin lies outside us, in Christ. In the Bible and in the interpretation of the church this event comes to us as a "message," a "word." It does not arise out of ourselves. That is excluded by the notion of acquittal and imputation. Hence in our faith (see under

b) we step outside the world of our experience. We receive the opposite of what we experience. In the face of an entirely contrary experience, we need to be *told* this ever and again. But where we allow ourselves to be told, it enters our experience as a sense of liberation, joy, release, and security.

The reality of the justification of the sinner, from the outside, through the acquitting word, appears repeatedly already in the OT. We can point to Ex. 32:9–14 and other stories from the journey through the desert, the rite of the Great Day of Atonement (Lev. 16), the sin offerings and the meaning of *kipper* (reconciliation as a covering), Ps. 32; 51; 103; 130; and in the prophets to Isa. 6:5–7; 53:11; Jer. 31:31–34; Ezek. 37:1–14; Hos. 1:6, 8f.; 2:22; Zech. 3:1–5. The verb "to justify" also occurs a few times (hiphil *hiṣdîq;* Septuagint: *dikaioun),* but then in the sense of: to declare innocent, prove someone's innocence, make justice prevail; the Pauline usage of the justification of the godless is still a long way off.

In the NT the matter is clearly present in the words and the parables of Jesus, especially in Luke: 14:15–24; all of 15; 18:9–14; 23:39–42, but also in Matthew in the parable of the two debtors (18:23–35) and of the workers in the vineyard (20:1–16). The centrality of the forgiveness of sins is also evident in the words of the institution of the Lord's Supper and in other statements (e.g. Mark 2:1–12; John 8:1–11). We should likewise think here of Jesus' association with tax collectors and sinners. As a matter of fact, there is not a single NT book in which reconciliation and forgiveness are not either central or the starting-point.

But nowhere do we have a deeper theological probing and terminological elaboration of this event than in Paul, especially in Rom. and Gal. For that we refer to the biblical theologies of the NT, the studies about Paul, and the literature mentioned there. We must, however, pause here for a look at the moot concept of *dikaiosynē theou* in Rom. 1:17; 3:5, 21–26; 10:3; 1 Cor. 1:30; 5:21, and Phil. 3:9. Is this a subjective genitive (the righteousness which is an attribute of God and by which he acts) or a genitive denoting the object, cause, author, or relationship (the righteousness which God gives to man and which makes man righteous before God)? In other words, is it a characteristic of God or of man? The Reformers answered, "Of man" (Luther: "the righteousness which is valid before God"); this notion can appeal to the context and to Paul's argument with the rabbis about the question how man can be justified. In the present century, noted expositors (A. Schlatter, C. H. Dodd, E. Käsemann and his school) are inclined to think that Paul speaks of the justice-establishing work of God by which he restores the sinner; this notion has the backing of the OT idea of the righteousness of God, particularly in Deutero-Isaiah (45:21; 46:13; 50:8f.; 51:4–8; 53:11). Indeed, to understand Paul we must begin with the "theocentric" aspect, and then from there, as the new element in Paul, discover how he extends this righteousness of God to (sinful) man. God's justice triumphs in a new covenant relationship in which man is clothed with his justice. Or to say it with Barth: "The right of God established in the death of Jesus Christ, and proclaimed in his resurrection in defiance of the wrong of man, is as such the basis of the new and corresponding right of man" (*CD* IV,1, p. 514.).

Directly related to the fact that in justification we are clothed with an alien righteousness is the implication that for Paul our righteousness is thus an "imputation," a value judgment, or, as Ritschl put it in Kantian terms: not an analytic judgment *a posteriori* (which notes what is there), but a synthetic judgment *a priori* (which adds what is not there). For that see especially Rom. 4. The term *logizesthai* used there indicates an acquitting judgment which, according to 2 Cor. 5:19 (note the *mē logizomenos* there), is the reverse side of the work of reconciliation in which Christ has our sins imputed to himself (5:21; cf. Gal. 3:13). This imputation is anything but an empty and external word; it is a judgment which really renews man, as we shall see shortly.

Yet as early as Paul's own time the paradox of the imputation was misunderstood; it was taken as a license to go on sinning (Rom. 6:1; Jas. 2:14–26; 2 Pet. 3:16). The morally blameless man considers it offensive that his righteousness before God should rest totally on the righteousness of Christ. This is the reason for the early demise of these thoughts of Paul in the history of the church, without leaving much of a trace behind them. But time and again there have also been brief periods when they reasserted themselves as eruptive protests of the gospel against the moralizing spirit of Western European man.

The first strong protest came from Augustine in his struggle against Pelagius, which became a struggle against the widely held semi-latent synergism of the early church. There is, however, a disagreement on the question whether Augustine with his stand really reached back to Paul's doctrine of justification (A. F. N. Lekkerkerker, *Studiën over de rechtvaardiging bij Augustinus,* 1947, denies it; G. de Ru, *De rechtvaardiging bij Augustinus,* 1966, affirms it; see also the careful intermediate position of W. Joest in *RGG* V, *s.v. Rechtfertigung,* cols. 829f.). It is a fact that Augustine's conversion experience, mode of thinking, and confrontation with Pelagius drove him to view justification especially as *sanatio,* as an inner process of healing and cleansing. In this connection it is to be noted that in the Western church Paul's terms *dikaioun* and *dikaiōsis* were translated into Latin as *iustificatio* and *iustificare;* literally, *making* (to make) righteous. Augustine even writes: "For what else does the phrase 'being justified' signify than 'being made righteous'—by Him, of course, who justifies the ungodly man, that he may become a godly one instead?" *(De spiritu et littera* 26, 45). Though Augustine does not deny the imputation, all the emphasis for him (unlike Paul) is on the inner renewal that rests on it, thus on what we are accustomed to call "sanctification." This has become the common meaning in Roman Catholic theology.

The second strong protest against moralism (this time in its late-medieval form), theologically much more radical and ecclesiastically much more consequential, came from Luther. He fell back to Augustine, but then struggled his way to the real meaning of Paul's forensic-imputative doctrine of justification. On this subject there is an enormous amount of literature. But what it was all about can be summed up as follows: in the period 1512–1518 the major emphasis shifts from the *sanatio* to the *imputatio,* from the Christ-in-us to the Christ-for-us. Yet Luther has never denied the *sanatio,* but maintained that this gift of effective grace rests on imputed grace. Thus there arose a new spiritual and intellectual climate in which the "powers of grace," which the church has at its disposal and with which the faithful are sacramentally to be nourished, give way to a personal relationship between God and man, a relationship that is effected on the one hand in the acquitting word and on the other hand in the liberating faith.

But the later ecclesiastical and theological shaping of the doctrine of justification is due not so much to Luther as to Melanchthon, particularly as the drafter of the *Apology* (1531). He was so afraid of the danger of attributing even the least ground for salvation to man that he removed all *sanatio*-elements from the concept of justification, lest the pangs of conscience return again. See *Apology* IV *passim.* But in this way Luther's great discovery was altered from being a dominant perspective into a small dogma, locked in between a repentance entirely oriented to the law on the one hand (see par. 44) and the fulfillment of the works of love which "cannot happen unless after being justified by faith and born again we receive the Holy Spirit" *(Apol.,* art. IV) on the other. A reaction had to come: the Lutheran theologian Osiander (about 1550), calling the current doctrine of justification "colder than ice," went back to the *sanatio*-elements of the early Luther, but unfortunately in such a way that the freedom through the *imputatio* was again pushed back by a substantialistically perceived indwelling of Christ in the believer. In the Formula of Concord (1577) (II, part III) his doctrine was sharply rejected and the line of Melanchthon just as sharply affirmed, but without the awareness that the second was bound to evoke the first. The cost of this development was that in Lutheran Scholasticism, as it now followed, the doctrine of justification could no longer perform the role of hermeneutic key for the liberating understanding of the whole of Scripture, as Luther had come to see this doctrine. Next to it, the problem areas of cooperation, free will, good works, and mystical union began to be independent entities in the 16th and 17th centuries. And in the middle of the 17th century, the doctrine of justification through the imputation of Christ's merits apart from any righteousness in man is regarded as belonging to the secondary fundamental articles of the faith, which may not be denied, but which need not be known either (R I, p. 143)! For this development see H. E. Weber, *Reformation, Orthodoxie und Rationalismus,* I (1937), II (1951), with the thesis: "The doctrine of justification becomes the fate (*Schicksal*) of orthodoxy" (I, p. 64).

For Calvin, justification has never been as much the kind of article with which the church stands or falls as it was for the Lutherans. While they considered the new life as the consequence and by-product of justification, Calvin spoke of a twofold grace (see par. 47). He too taught strictly a justification by imputation (see especially *Inst* III,xi–xviii), but instead of sharply delineating this from repentance to the one side (see par. 44) and sanctification to the other, he endeavored to see these moments as a unity. Consequently, unlike Luther, he was more inclined to follow Augustine and speak about the appropriation of salvation in terms suggestive of a process. Reformed Protestantism remained a stranger both to the Lutheran joy of the discovery of this doctrine and its later constriction. Lutheran orthodoxy had no feeling for Calvin's conception; it detected legalism, work-righteousness, and a *theologia gloriae* in it.

At the Council of Trent the Roman Catholic Church sharply rejected the Protestant doctrine of justification (D 1520–1583), on the one hand from the perspective of an Augustinian *sanatio* conception, "whence man from being unjust is made just and from an enemy into a friend" (1528; cf. 1561—canon 11), on the other hand from that of a synergistic emphasis on the *preparare, disponere, assistere,* and *cooperari* of man with his *liberum arbitrium* (1525f., 1554–1559); this emphasis is so strong that it normally makes certainty of salvation an impossibility (1553f., 1540f., 1563–1566). Another reason the imputation teaching of the Reformers was unintelligible is that what they taught as happening in preaching, Rome sees as happening in the sacraments of baptism, confession, and the Eucharist. The constitution is balanced; the canons on the other hand are one-sided and polemic. Therefore H. Küng has dared to argue in his sensational *Justification* (E.T. 1964) that there is no real difference between Trent and Barth's doctrine of justification; in respect of Trent he speaks of one-sidedly polemical accents and of a misunderstanding of the Protestant position. Along this line J. Feiner and L. Vischer, eds., *Neues Glaubensbuch* (1973), conclude "that the doctrine of justification . . . no longer poses an opposite view that can rend the church apart" (p. 644), such in contrast to ecclesiology. O. H. Pesch goes still further in his very thorough study in *MS* 4,2 (1973), ch. 12, by responding to the question "unanimous in the doctrine of justification" with "comforted we say Yes!" (p. 913). Equally important, however, is the question whether the "imputed righteousness" *already* lives in the way faith is experienced in Roman Catholicism and whether it *still* lives in Protestantism.

We spoke of the eruptive reassertions of Paul's doctrine of justification. Something like that happened again when in 1738 John Wesley was converted after reading Luther's preface to the Roman epistle—a conversion which provided the impetus for the evangelistic outreach of Methodism. In the 19th century, too, such eruptions took place on a larger or smaller scale, sometimes as a rediscovery of Luther, sometimes of Paul. In this connection we think especially of Germany, first with its revival and later its confessional Neo-Lutheranism. But also of A. Ritschl, who helped to open our eyes to the imputative nature of justification, though because of his Kantian-influenced consciousness theology he could not really articulate Paul and Luther. His dogmatic design *The Doctrine of Justification and Reconciliation* (E.T. 1902)—note the sequence of the two concepts—induced the alternative design of M. Kähler, *Die Wissenschaft der christlichen Lehre* (1883), one of the very few systematic theologies built around the doctrine of justification.

Remarkably, however, the most radical return to the proclamation of imputed righteousness was not in Lutheran but in Reformed Protestantism, namely in H. F. Kohlbrugge and his school. Kohlbrugge (1803–1875) experienced his "second conversion" in his preparation for a sermon on Rom. 7:14, which threw him totally back on the imputed righteousness of Christ. As an influential preacher, working in Elberfeld, he emphasized the justification of the sinner so much that other aspects of the faith were neglected or (notably sanctification) were absorbed. See *Hoogst belangrijke briefwisseling tussen dr. H. F. K. en Mr. I. da Costa over de leer der heiligmaking* (1880), a collection which also includes the sermon on Rom. 7:14. His school produced two important studies on justification: E. Böhl, *Von der Rechtfertigung durch den Glauben* (1890), and A. Zahn, *Über den biblischen und kirchlichen Begriff der Anrechnung* (1899). Böhl also wrote *Dogmatik* (1887), which, despite the strong emphasis on Christ's humiliation and reconciling work and on our justification in him, is largely traditional in its design and execution.

In the 20th century, after the First World War, a new explosion followed; not in the so-called Luther-renaissance of K. Holl who aimed to interpret the *imputatio* of the later Luther in the light of the *sanatio* of the earlier Luther, but in the second edition of Barth's *Commentary on Romans* (1922). In that bombshell of Barth it was precisely the imputation, the "new proclamation" granted to sinners by the Word of God, which became the liberating message to a generation confused and bewildered by the War. Later Barth wrote theological expositions of many more aspects of the gospel than he was able to do in the beginning, but he always remained true to the imputative nature of justification as the central moment in the gospel, as evidenced by his thorough and elaborate discussion in *CD* IV,1, par. 61.

The story goes that Luther, at the end of his life, referring to the doctrine of justification, said: "Soon after our death this doctrine will be obscured." That has indeed happened, not only then, but after each subsequent explosion, also in our century. To live as a sinner from the faith that salvation is purely God's free gift is something which in the long run proves too demanding. At the time that we are writing this book, justification no longer commands this central interest in theology (and to a large extent not in preaching either) but is again pushed to the periphery by other accents, particularly the emphasis on sanctification. That brings us to the problem of the centrality of justification. Lutheranism calls it the article with which the church stands or falls. Its own doctrinal development proves, however, that one should not too hastily repeat this sentiment. True, here lies the decisive turning point. But it is a turning point which consists only in and by virtue of the great turning point of the substitutionary work of Jesus as the true Son of God. Both together, as constituting the turning point, may also be called the center of the faith, but then literally as the perspectival center from which the entire circle of God's activities, all the way to the farthest periphery of creation and consummation, becomes visible. The doctrine of justification, far from pushing the other aspects aside, makes visible their true coherence. See on this Barth, *CD* IV,1, par. 61,1.

At the end of the large-type section above we referred to the relation of justification and experience. Justification is related to condemnation and repentance (par. 44). Though far transcending our experience, they become part of our experience as well. In that way they compel us constantly to seek our salvation in justification. Melanchthon was right—only the shocked conscience takes hold of the message of justification. Then this message, which as such contradicts what we feel about ourselves, produces in us a new experience of liberation and joy. Apart from the shocked conscience, however, this message is only an excuse for the person who wants to remain as he is. By putting justification central, Lutheranism directs itself to the tormented and despairing sinner; Reformed Protestantism, with its emphasis on sanctification and the struggle against sin, also has a direct message for the slow and the careless. For a different view on the role of experience, see H. R. Mackintosh, *The Christian Experience of Forgiveness* (1927); the end of ch. X contends, however, that forgiveness, while bringing about experience, is not in itself experience.

b. Faith

In the justified person, the correlative of that justification is faith. We discussed the meaning and content of faith extensively in paragraphs 3 and 4. Hence we refer to those paragraphs. But a mere reference is not enough, because there "faith" is not quite the same as here. Here we understand by "faith" the answer that is expected from us and that corresponds to the word of justification in which the message of the radical change in Christ comes to us personally. Only in this answer does the great change become operative in man's life. Hence "faith" is the central term for man's role in the constitution of the covenant relationship.

In its use in the Christian church, this central term naturally became the comprehensive term for the whole of the encounter of God and man. In that comprehensive sense it is used in paragraphs 3 and 4, as in the title of this book. Here we are concerned with its central and specific usage in connection with justification. This is not just an aspect of its more comprehensive usage; it is the essential meaning of the term, from which the whole of the Christian confession becomes visible and by which the general usage is justified.

Faith as response to the acquittal is an act in which we as it were step outside ourselves, turn our back upon ourselves and all our experiences, to look to the promise that is made to us from the outside and from above. "I believe" is formally an activity on my part, but materially it indicates one's surrender to a new reality: I believe the justification in Christ. "I" is then the subject and "justification" the object, but materially the "I" is first of all the object of this justifying event.

Penetrating still further into the content of the act of faith, we can designate that act with a variety of terms: surrender, heed, accept, acknowledge, trust. Especially the last two words have been used a lot. They have also been contrasted as alternatives, particularly if "to trust" was preferred, and "to acknowledge" was regarded as too formal and too intellectualistic. Trusting, however, always includes as its presupposition that one knows and acknowledges the one in whom he trusts and the matters or promises relative to which that trust is given.

If we want to speak even more materially about the faith, we say that it is an act of humility and boldness in one. One who accepts the imputed righteousness despairs, on the one hand, of his own ability ever to bring about the right relationship with God, while on the other hand he dares to live, contrary to all that he feels in himself, with the acquittal that has been handed to him.

For all these reasons, faith is an act and an attitude which touches the totality of our existence. The wearisome attempts, particularly in the nineteenth century, to localize faith in one of the "faculties of the soul" only narrowed and obscured faith. It is "I" who believe, not just with my intellect, my will, or my emotions, but that "I" in its totality, that is, in such a way that it decisively touches my intellect, will, and emotions.

Faith is, therefore, also that act by which I, as a human being before the face of God, obtain the attitude for which my humanity is intended. In the act of believing surrender man finds his ultimate destination, his true personhood. In that act man comes to himself, in the way that God intends it.

Faith is thus an act of great certainty. The man who believes, believes out of the midst of his doubt and distrust; yet in the act of faith he reaches for a new, in fact the highest certainty. The Christian use of "I believe" is thus on this point the opposite of everyday usage. In the latter case "I believe" means as much as "I don't know for sure," whereas faith in the Christian sense stands for a definite knowing, be it a special kind of knowing, a personal appropriation of God's gracious turning to us.

Faith thus includes certainty. But due to its central and total character it also includes a series of other aspects. The passing into the covenant relationship with God includes the passing from subservience to the powers of the world to freedom, from self-assertion to self-denial and love, from autonomy to obedience, from being the captain of one's life to being hidden in God, from living by what is now to hoping for what is not yet, etc. These aspects will be taken up later. Here we are interested in a precise conceptual definition; the elaboration of all that is implied in this central aspect follows.

"To extract from the NT the true understanding of what faith is, is the most important task of theology" (Brunner). On the meaning of the term "faith" in the Bible see the literature in pars. 3 and 4, esp. *TDNT* VI, *s.v. pisteuō,* and, further, Brunner, *Dg* III, ch. XII. Recently we have become more sensitive to the differences among the Synoptics, John, Paul, James, and Hebrews. Broadly speaking, in the Synoptics faith is especially concerned with the earthly Jesus and his miracle-working power, in John with the person of Christ as the one sent from the Father, in Paul with his work of reconciliation, in Hebrews with the future which is guaranteed in him, while in James the basis is a polemically narrowed-down concept of faith in the sense of accepting-something-as-true. Paul's is the deepest and most comprehensive conception.

Already in the later traditions of the NT still another meaning of "faith" emerges, namely as the content of faith (1 Tim. 3:9; 4:6; Jude 3, 20), a meaning which has also become very common with us. To avoid confusion, a distinction now commonly made is that between *fides qua creditur* (the act of believing) and *fides quae creditur* (the content of faith). This is a necessary but dangerous distinction; it threatens to tear apart as "subjective" and "objective" what in the covenantal fellowship belong together as the two sides of the one event.

In the history of the church, the Pauline conception of faith soon slipped into oblivion, and it was replaced by a conception in which faith meant accepting as true the biblical and ecclesiastical tradition, an act of the intellect which is to be augmented and completed by love and works. For centuries James pushed Paul aside. The Middle Ages made the intellectualist view of faith even more emphatic through linking it with Aristotelian philosophy. See Thomas, *ST* II, 2, q. 2: "On the Act of the Inner Faith," where faith is described as an act of the intellect, a *cum assensione cogitare* (art. 2 and q. 4, art. 2), an act which may be termed meritorious because of the voluntary submission that goes with it (2,9). Without the act of the will, the *caritas,* there is only the *fides informis* (Jas. 2:17) which is being perfected and formed by love, making it a *fides caritate formata* (Gal. 5:6) (4,3f.). Through the centuries this remained the official Roman Catholic conception of faith; see the definition of Vatican I: "The Catholic Church professes that this faith, which is the 'beginning of man's salvation', is a supernatural virtue whereby, inspired and assisted by the grace of God, we believe that what He has revealed is true" (D 3008).

The Reformation, which announced itself to the world in a conflict about the nature of repentance, was born in the quietness of the discovery of the nature of faith in the Pauline sense, when Luther in his study of the Bible began to understand the meaning of Rom. 1:17. For him faith then became an act of the whole man and primarily an act of trust and surrender. The Augsburg Confession (1530), art. XX, confesses that faith is no neutral knowledge of history ("which may be in the wicked, and in the devil"), but "a trust, which doth comfort and lift up disquieted minds," because it directs itself to this, "to wit, the article of remission of sins; namely, that by Christ we have grace, righteousness, and remission of sins." Beside it we mention Calvin's careful definition: "Now we shall possess a right definition of faith if we call it a firm and certain knowledge of God's benevolence toward us, founded upon the truth of the freely given promise in Christ, both revealed to our minds and sealed upon our hearts through the Holy Spirit" *(Inst* III,ii,7). Calvin, as we see here, does not put the trust *(fiducia)* first, but the knowledge *(cognitio);* however, as an act which through revelation touches our minds and through sealing by the Spirit, our hearts. Assent and trust thus go together in the one act of acknowledgment *(re-cognitio).* There is a difference in emphasis here from the Lutheran statements, but no more than that, and certainly not if we put beside it the description in the *Apology* (1531), IV: "faith . . . is to assent to the promise of God, in which he freely, for the sake of Christ, offers remission of sins and justification."

A remarkable shift occurs, however, in the famous definition of the Heidelberg Catechism (1563), which in Answer 21 describes faith as "not only a sure knowledge *(certa notitia),* by which I accept as truth all that God has revealed to us in his Word, but also a firm confidence *(certa fiducia)* which the Holy Spirit works in my heart by the Gospel, that not only to others, but to me also, remission of sins . . . [is] freely given." Here the two aspects are separated and there is even talk of two kinds of faith: an acceptance as true of the whole content of the Bible on the one hand, and a Spirit-inspired confidence on the other. With that the road was opened to the fatal split into "objective" and "subjective" which dominated Protestant Scholasticism, the Further Reformation, and Pietism in the 17th and 18th centuries. From now on one can have a "general," "intellectual," and "historical" faith, yet knowing that more is necessary, namely the certainty of salvation which one does not yet possess with this faith. So the question arises: how do I know that I possess *true* faith? According to the Canons of Dort (1619), "true faith in Christ" is one of "the infallible fruits of election" which the elect "observe in themselves with a spiritual joy and holy pleasure" (I,12). For many this constant spiritual introspection led to a great uncertainty concerning their salvation. Faith, however, points entirely away from itself and is as such an act concerning which we can at the most only *afterwards* detect some consequences and fruits in our deeds or feelings (*syllogismus practicus* or *mysticus*). Here the Reformation, which started as the discovery of the certainty of salvation through faith in contrast to the prevailing moralism, turned into its opposite: uncertainty due to introspection. The distinction between two kinds of faith and the treatment of the certainty of faith as a climax to be reached put Protestantism again right in the vicinity of the Roman Catholic concept of faith. See on this development C. Graafland, *De zekerheid van het geloof* (1961), and J. de Boer, *De verzegeling met de Heilige Geest volgens de opvatting van de Nadere Reformatie* (1968).

The theology of the 19th and 20th centuries occupies itself, relative to the concept of faith, with entirely different questions. Yet it carries on in the same line, insofar as the subjectivizing and individualizing view of the faith continued. Now the particular form of the problem was dictated by Kant, who removed faith from the realm of pure reason, and therewith, in the eyes of many theologians, forever banished the knowledge-element from faith. The question now became: if faith is not located in the mind, in what faculty is it found? Schleiermacher tried to find for faith "a province of its own in the consciousness," namely in the "feeling of absolute dependence." The followers of Hegel, and in the Netherlands especially J. H. Scholten, tried yet again to locate faith in man's reason. Ethical theology in the Netherlands and, in a different way, A. Ritschl located faith, following Kant, in the practical reason, in the distance between what man ought to be and what he is (*Sollen* and *Sein*), of which man becomes aware in his conscience and which is bridged through forgiveness and faith. The existentialist theology of our century also stands in this tradition. Particularly Ebeling has studied the essence of the faith: in our accusing conscience we are struck by the word-event which proceeds from Christ, and that induces in us the attitude of trusting faith, in which and through which we attain to our authentic human existence. See especially Ebeling's small dogmatics *The Nature of Faith* (E.T. 1961), in which the word "faith" occurs in the heading of each chapter; and *Dogmatik,* III (1979), esp. ch. 10, pars. 34 and 35.

In this whole development, faith as man's act is strongly emphasized, at the expense of its relation to that from which it lives and to which it directs itself. The latter aspect was retained, however, in those theologies that were more resistant to the dominant anthropocentric approach. For the 19th century we think especially of Kohlbrugge and his school, with their definition of faith as "to accept God as a Man of his Word." For the 20th century we think of the many noted theologians, but especially of Barth, *CD* IV,1, par. 61,4 and par. 64, who links himself with Calvin in his definition of faith as acknowledgment (*Anerkennung*).

Roman Catholic theology remained with the Jacobite-Scholastic concept of faith. Hence Trent condemned the Reformational concept of faith by declaring: "If anyone says that justifying faith is nothing else than trust in the divine mercy which forgives sin, or that it is by that trust alone that we are justified, let him be anathema" (D 1562). But that "nothing else" is exactly what the Reformers had not said. Here a substantialistic and a relational mode of thinking clashed. The Reformers did not yet possess the philosophical concepts to support their religious insight. Contemporary Roman Catholic theology, as a result of the study of the Bible and its appropriation of, among others, phenomenological philosophy, has left behind the traditional arsenal of concepts. Hence Vatican II speaks of "the obedience of faith . . . by which man freely commits his whole self to God, offering 'the full homage of intellect and will to God who reveals Himself' and freely assenting to the revelation granted by Him" (*Constitution on Divine Revelation* 5). Here the whole person with his intellect and will is involved in the act of faith. Cf. the *New Catechism* (E.T. 1969) on faith: "Faith is the gift of the Spirit which enables us to give ourselves entirely to him who is greater than we, and to accept his message" (p. 289). See also Paul Surlis (ed.), *Faith: Its Nature and Meaning* (1972), which on the one hand strongly emphasizes faith as personal response and on the other hand stresses the anchorage of the faith-act in the totality of man's existence; the first reminds us of the Reformation, the second of the 19th century. Can we still say of the *sola fide sine operibus legis* that it is the dividing line between Protestantism and Roman Catholicism? The Roman Catholic O. H. Pesch hands us the formula: "Man, as he is, accepts that God accepts him as he is" (*MS* 4,2, p. 849, italics).

c. Justification by Faith

God's justification establishes a new communion which man accepts by faith. However, trying to give a closer description of this relationship between justification and faith, we face great difficulties. For is it not true that faith directs itself to the prior word of acquittal? Must we thus say that we were already acquitted prior to and without that faith? In that case faith and repentance, surrender and obedience would neither add nor detract from our justification, and that justification would be a fact apart from our faith and even from our knowledge. That would, however, be an objectivistic misconstruction of the great encounter between God and the sinner which we are trying to define. Particularly Paul says constantly that we are justified "by" or "through" faith. Faith is apparently an indispensable element in this encounter. Without faith there is no justification. Should we then perhaps say that it is faith itself which justifies, in this sense that it is our act of faith which actually brings about the acquittal? But in that case justification would be the reward for our faith and our salvation would again depend on our spiritual achievements or emotions. That would, however, be a subjectivistic reversal of what the proclamation of justification intends to say. That too would be an emasculation of faith, for it would no longer direct itself to the priorly offered justification.

The problem becomes more difficult as one's thinking follows the objective-subjective duality and misjudges the inter-subjectivity of the covenantal encounter. Taking our starting-point in that encounter, we

will more easily than our fathers from the post-Reformation generations allow for a decisive role of man in the covenant; otherwise it would not be a real covenant. But it is a covenant with *God:* out of grace he grants us that decisive role. That role is, for that matter, not one of our own initiative, but a response, induced by the word of God which creates the blessing of the encounter and the freedom for dialogue—and does that over and again, even if there is no response from us. But acquittal does not reach its purpose until the Spirit inspires us to respond with the answer of faith.

This makes it clear why we must speak about the faith in two apparently contradictory ways: faith is on the one hand purely instrumental, no more than a receiver, but on the other hand, by virtue of the acquittal which it receives, it is also a source of inspiration, a center of creativity. Exactly because it is a channel toward God, it is a source toward "the depth and the breadth" of our life and his world. This, too, caused our fathers much difficulty as they reflected on it. For us it may well be easier to clarify it with an analogy drawn from psychology: so long as a person feels that he must prove and justify himself in the relationships of his life, he obstructs the possibility of communication and freely given love, and thus becomes unfruitful; only in forgetting himself does his "self" become creatively active.

In opposition to Judaistic moralism, Paul speaks liberatingly about justification and (not works, but) faith as belonging together. He also speaks unproblematically about what would later become a problem. See especially Rom. 3:21–4:25 and Gal. 3, where it is said that we are justified *pistei, dia tēs pisteōs* or (most often) *ek pisteōs*. Of particular importance is his appeal to Gen. 15:6 (Rom. 4:3ff.; Gal. 3:6): "Abraham believed God, and it was reckoned to him as righteousness." In Judaism this faith of Abraham became a work which God reckoned to him as a merit, since it also comprehended his works, which made it an anticipatory fulfillment of the Torah. See already Jesus Sirach 4:20–23 and 1 Maccabees 2:52. Paul polemicizes against that conception (Rom. 4:4ff.). As he understands this passage, it proves that only God's grace and not our works are determinative for his relation to us; faith is simply our acknowledgment of that fact. (Likely that is also the meaning of Gen. 15:6.) See also *TDNT* IV, *s.v. logizomai.*

Against the attacks of Roman Catholicism, the Reformation needed a sharper definition of the relation of justification and faith. If, e.g., on the one hand Matthias Flacius calls faith purely the empty hand of the beggar *(manus mendica)* and on the other hand Luther regards faith as a forsaking of our idols and thus as the fulfillment of the first commandment and therewith of all the commandments, such an apparent or real contradiction required clarification. Unequalled in finding the right accents are the formulations of the Heidelberg Catechism, Lord's Day 23; see especially Question and Answer 61: "Why do you say that you are righteous only by faith?" Not "that I am acceptable to God on account of the worthiness of my faith, but because only the satisfaction, righteousness, and holiness of Christ is my righteousness before God, and I can receive the same and make it my own in no other way than by faith only."

But as the age of Descartes drew nearer and the subject-object split gained ground, such formulations satisfied less and less. The Remonstrants emphasized faith as an act of man, indeed based on grace, but on a grace which man can resist, abandon, or ignore (see *The Five Articles of the Remonstrants* of 1610, arts. 4 and 5). Despite its rejection of the Remonstrants, Reformed Protestantism, too, remained interested in the believing subject, not so much in regard to the problem of cooperation but more in connection with the experiences of the inner life: without signs of such a life no man may call himself elect or appropriate the justification (the so-called *syllogismus mysticus*). An example is W. à Brakel, *Redelijke Godsdienst,* I (1700), ch. XXXIV, pars. 27f., which depicts justification as God's approving judgment of the preceding process of faith in man. Against this tendency, A. Comrie endeavored to maintain that faith looks to justification and not vice versa; to that end he construed the steps of "justification from eternity" and the "faculty of faith" so that in yet another form the actuality and the wonder of the encounter of God and man in acquittal and faith were frozen over. See from Comrie especially his *Brief over de rechtvaardigmaking des zondaars* (1761). A. Kuyper continued in his line; see *E Voto Dordraceno,* II (1893), pp. 333–346.

Berkouwer, on the ground of his correlation thinking, says correctly: "It is not hard to see that it must be possible to bury the controversy once and for all" (*Faith and Justification,* E.T. 1954, p. 158; see all of ch. 6). Beside it see Woelderink's book, written in a kindred spirit, *De rechtvaardiging uit het geloof* (1941). Both want to get out of the 17th-century problematic and back to the interaction as the Reformation had it. See Woelderink, pp. 204f., 215f., 221, and Berkouwer, *passim,* especially the italicized statement on pp. 188f.: "The marvelous fact is this, that the way of salvation is the way of faith just because it is only in faith that the exclusiveness of divine grace is recognized and honored." Before him, Bavinck had already wrestled himself free from the scholastic tradition on this point; see *GD* IV, esp. no. 475.

In the modes of thought of the 20th century, these scholastic problems hardly ever occur any more. We do not feel the need to go beyond the precision of the Reformation (we *do* feel the need to say the same in contemporary terms). See especially Barth, *CD* IV,1, par. 61,4: "Justification by Faith Alone." Our final conclusion from all of this can be succinctly formulated as follows: *sola gratia* and *sola fide* do not exclude but include each other; they are complementary.

46. GUIDANCE AND SECURITY

IN THE BIUNITY of justification and faith a relationship is established between God and man. Therein something actual, something *act*-ual, happens. The terms "justification" and "forgiveness" are inadequate to describe that actuality. For acquittal and forgiveness state mainly negatively that from which man is being set free, namely from his guilt and the doom of his past. But that liberation is the reverse side of a positive event, namely our entrance into a new relationship to God, whom we may now call "Father," and we may know that we are and may conduct ourselves as his children, his sons and daughters. Central to Jesus' preaching was that his followers might address God with the same familiar name of father *(Abba)* which he himself used. Paul called that the "adoption as sons." With the individual, too, God now establishes a bond, and this bond is really his ultimate goal. Man receives a covenant partner, a savior, a saving Opposite. In the final analysis he is now no longer alone, all by himself. There is Someone who cares for and guides him, and he may have the assurance that ultimately he is safe and secure. So we may believe that whatever happens to us is part of this guidance. And in all these things we may know that we are being upheld by an ultimate security.

In the study of the faith this has usually been called the "providence" of God, and it was then regarded as a particular instance of God's general guidance of the world which we dealt with in paragraph 28. We separate these two subjects; though they border on and are closely related to each other, they are nevertheless faith statements with a different origin and character. The belief in God's general guidance of the world stems (directly) from the belief in his saving operations in history and the belief in creation connected with it. But the belief in the personal union *with* and guidance *by* God is the other side of the covenant relationship into which the believer enters through justification. That belief, having its own origin and character, requires its own theological reflection. The more so because of the important place it has in the life of many, while for many others it is a very difficult belief. And that, in turn, is connected with the many caricatures and misconceptions one finds especially in relation to this subject.

In those periods and circles in which the belief in God's personal guidance plays a central role, this belief is often subject to two misunderstandings: first of all, there is the notion that God will be there to satisfy all the wishes, great and small, of the individual believer, and, secondly, there is the idea that as a rule his guidance can be shown in the course of events. So there arose an individualistic and often small-minded caricature of this faith, to which a reaction had to come. Hence, many people, particularly in our day and age, no longer dare to link God with what happens to them personally, or at the most dare to say that their faith in God gives them a different perspective on the events in their life; they see them now especially as calls to a new obedience. One may say that the first is an objectivistic misunderstanding, the second a subjectivistic.

But what we have here is an actual covenant, a covenant with a two-directional actuality. Its actuality is first of all that man in repentance accepts the acquittal and so acknowledges God's authority over his life. In this activity God becomes the goal of man, of man who now learns to submit his thoughts and plans to those of God. At the same time he knows that with God becoming his goal, he himself becomes God's goal and is made a part of his thoughts and plans. One who gives priority to the petition, "Hallowed be thy name," may later also pray for bread and for protection against temptations. God takes the side of those who take his side. And it is an integral feature of this covenant that he stands up much more for us than we for him.

This, too, like everything else, is a matter of faith and not yet of sight. God's care for us comes to us in the midst of a provisional and guilty world, a world full of capricious events which we call chance and full of determinism which we call fate. God has not yet abolished all these things. He is not yet almighty (on his omnipotence see paragraph 22). But through this world he blazes a trail in which he manifests his superior power. We may believe that he makes everything in our life serve his purposes, and this includes our salvation. Fate and deed are redirected, and that new purpose may be all kinds of things: blessing, comfort, training, nurture, mandate, challenge, chastisement. "We know that in everything God works for the good of those who love him, who have been called according to his purpose" (Romans 8:28).

"For the good," that is, for carrying out the purposes of the Spirit, with us as well as with the world at large. As a rule we have no insight into those connections. For us it is enough to know that in all life's circumstances, on the heights, in the valleys, and on level ground, we are securely in the hand of God. Yet that "knowing" of which we speak here is so much a part of what we experience that this faith does not exist apart from confirmations in the events in our life. It can happen that in these events we seem to detect something of God's purposes with us. Thankfulness may then compel us to make mention of it. But later it may turn out that we were mistaken after all. Then the interpretation falls away, but the faith remains. And without such interpretations faith knows that it is always being upheld and given deliverance.

One could ask whether this special guidance and security is a privilege of believers only or whether it pertains to all men. That question can only be answered by saying that the covenant relationship with God has its own promises and rules. Whether these have any bearing on a situation where this relationship is not experienced, we do not know. For whatever can be said about God's care for all people, see paragraph 28.

The awareness of security brought about by the union with God is a decisive element in the renewal of man. The outsider often thinks that this faith makes man passive. The fact is that only he who has first put himself at the disposal of God may know that he is secure in him. Then, however, this knowledge implies that we may take distance from our own cares and grief, and from our bitterness about people and conditions around us. Security is the source of an increased ability to endure, of being free to think more of the needs of others than of our own, and of courage to dare to do things in the name of God.

In the Bible this theme is often only in the background, but there are also passages where it is so much in the foreground that its true significance clearly stands out. To begin with, there are the stories about Abraham who in his migration dared to put his trust in a strange God from whom he expected guidance and security and who did not disappoint him. The faith of the "father of believers" began with his belief in providence. See H. Berkhof in *Geloven in God* (1970), pp. 101–118. In the OT in particular the book of Psalms is full of this faith; see Ps. 1, 4, 23, 33, 37, 73, 77, 91, 103, 107, 112, 113, 116, 118, 121, 138, 139, 145, 146. Elsewhere this faith is often overshadowed by the interest in God's deeds for the people as a whole, especially his acts of judgment. Note, however, also a passage like Hab. 3:16–19. Important in this connection is also the story of Joseph as this is elucidated in Gen. 50:20. For the NT we think in the first place of Jesus' message not to worry, a message that seems strangely out of place beside his eschatological message of the Kingdom; see Matt. 6:25–34; 10:29–31. Some other passages that witness to God's guidance and security are 2 Cor. 1:3–11; 4:8–10; 6:4–10; Phil. 4:6f.; Heb. 12:4–11; 13:5f., and 1 Pet. 5:6f. But the climax is Rom. 8:12–39 with which Paul ends his lengthy discussion of the doctrine of justification. This passage, and the others as well, are proof how much of a difference there is between the belief in God's guidance and its later caricatures. In Paul it has nothing to do with seeing; for in one breath he says that we do not live by what we see but by what we hope for (vv. 24f.) and that we do not know how we ought to pray (v. 26). Guidance does not put an end to the powers that dominate life (v. 38), nor to suffering (vv. 18, 35f.). But the bond with the love of Christ does not break (vv. 34, 39), so that we know that God causes everything to work for good (v. 28), and knowing this can triumph over all adversity (v. 37). And this section begins with the call to self-denial and obedience (v. 14 is preceded by vv. 12f.). The context of the other pericopes is the same: Matt. 6:25 with *dia touto* refers back to the admonition not to serve two masters (v. 24); Matt. 10:29–31 is a message of comfort in a piece about persecutions, as are Heb. and 1 Pet.; and particularly in 2 Cor. 1 "comfort" is God's response to oppression. We should, moreover, bear in mind that Paul uses the same word for comforting and challenging, namely *paraklēsis, parakaleō.* When we lift the belief in security out of this context, as so often happens, we turn it into a lie. "Likely none of the great thoughts of Christendom has so thoroughly been rationalized and secularized as the idea of providence" (Banning).

This can be illustrated with many examples from church history, but curiously not from the official theology. On this point it has practiced a reserve which seems almost strange, compared e.g. with the exuberance in the church's hymnology (in Luther, Paul Gerhardt, Charles Wesley, and their many lesser followers) and with the functioning of this belief in providence, particularly in European Pietism and Anglo-Saxon evangelical, revival, and Pentecostal movements—even with offshoots in an Enlightenment-like natural religion. A major reason for this reserve is that the belief in "general" providence which functions only marginally in the Bible, as a Stoic legacy was elaborately developed by the church fathers and continued and reinforced by medieval Scholasticism (see par. 28). The belief in security as a special and practically marginal instance of it was simply subsumed under that broader topic. As a result the accents and structures came to be totally different from what they are in the Bible.

On this point, too, the Reformation seemed to inaugurate a break with tradition. Luther in his Small Catechism (1529) begins his article on God the Father with: "I believe that God has created me and all that exists"; but that personal start immediately switches over to the belief in a general providence. Succinctly but forcefully the Augsburg Confession (1530) says: "Now he who knows that the Father is merciful to him through Christ, this man knows God truly; he knows that God cares for him; he loves God and calls upon Him; in a word, he is not without God as the Gentiles are." Calvin placed general providence first (*Inst* I,xvi–xviii), but within it he presented a thorough and marvelous section about God's guidance in the life of the believer and its fruits for our conduct (xvii,6–11); and in his treatment of renewal he returned separately to this last topic under the heading "On the denial of ourselves unto God" (III,vii,8–10). The strongest voice is that of the Heidelberg Catechism. Already Question and Answer 1 place the theme in a broad context; next in Answer 26 the belief in a general providence is given a personal application, and in Answer 28 the meaning of this belief is formulated as follows: "That we may be patient in adversity, thankful in prosperity, and with a view to the future may have good confidence in our faithful God and Father that no creature shall separate us from his love, since all creatures are so in his hand that without his will they cannot so much as move."

But Protestant Scholasticism pushed this whole theme back into the shadow of the doctrine of a general providence. The Lutherans regarded the world as the general object of providence and the pious and the faithful as the special object (treated very briefly); see R par. 20,5, esp. pp. 219f. In H's mention of the Reformed parallel, this special object is not even referred to (XII). In Bavinck, *GD* II, par. 39, and in Berkouwer, *The Providence of God* (E.T. 1952), as in several other dogmatics, that meager treatment persists. That had its bright side too, however: the individual believer, who since 1600 thought himself increasingly more important, in theology found himself entirely embedded within the great saving acts of God. Yet it is likely that precisely the silence in the study of the faith has contributed to the excesses which apart from it arose in the churches since the end of the 17th century.

There are exceptions, however. The belief in security plays a stronger role in A. Ritschl ("the belief in God's fatherly care is the Christian view of the world in abbreviated form"), but there it is Kantianly narrowed and has become the expression of the religious awareness of "lordship over nature"; see *Unterricht in der christlichen Religion* (1875), par. 60, cf. par. 62. A good treatment, detaching general providence, is given by Althaus, *CW* II, par. 64, in spite of the unhappy title: "Sinngebung der Schicksale" ("Making Sense of Fate"; he corrects it himself on p. 446). Barth pays attention to this theme only in passing, mainly as a segment of the doctrine of general providence, under the heading: "The Christian under the World Rule of God the Father" (*CD* III,3, par. 49,4)—a masterful section, which, however, deals mainly with prayer; see further *CD* IV,3, pp. 644–646 and 670–673.

Nor have our modern times produced much that contributes to a better understanding of this topic. It is certain that the restraining influence of the dominant empiricistic and positivistic outlook on life has much to do with that. That is the reason that many, subjectivistically, regard the belief in security as nothing more than a religious interpretation of one's fate, devoid of objective validity.

47. JUSTIFICATION AND SANCTIFICATION

JUSTIFICATION AS ONE'S APPOINTMENT to be a son and daughter of God in and through the true Son has, where it becomes an actual and thus active faith, an impact on all aspects of life. In paragraph 46 we spoke first of the fate dimension of our life and how we know that God has taken it into his own hands. Now we must speak about the deed-dimension and how that is being renewed in virtue of our adoption. Unlike the previous theme, this is a subject in which church and theology have through the centuries, and particularly since the Reformation, had a great deal of interest. There are so many aspects to it that we need no less than four paragraphs to deal with it. In this paragraph we use for it the time-honored traditional term "sanctification." For modern ears this is, however, not the best term. For one thing, because its first component, *sanctus* or saint, suggests the idea of "sinless" or "perfect"; in this context it definitely does not mean that. Secondly, because the term, particularly on account of its Latin derivation, suggests a work that has to do with the individual and what he does for his own perfection. Together with the equally prevalent synonym "good works" it gives the impression that it concerns an egocentric activity. But the opposite is the case. In his sanctification man is freed from his egocentrism and renewed to an ex-centric life, oriented to God, his neighbor, and the world. In the following paragraphs we shall for that reason avoid the term "sanctification" as much as possible. But here we cannot do it because until the present time this particular subject has been discussed under this heading.

Not everyone uses the term "sanctification" *(sanctificatio)* for the renewal of our active life. In the Roman Catholic tradition the customary designation is justification *(iustificatio),* in the literal sense of *iustum facere.* That caused much confusion in the discussion with the Reformation, which returned from the Augustinian meaning to the imputative sense it has in Paul. For the designation of the renewal of man's active life the Lutherans preferred the term "*renovatio*"*;* as such that was a fortunate formulation, but we prefer to reserve it for the totality of the renewal aspects. The Reformed preferred "*sanctificatio*"*;* whatever can be said against this term (see above), it is based on biblical usage.

In the OT the root *q-ḏ-š* (verb *qāḏaš*, niphal *niqdaš*, noun *qōḏeš*, adj. *qāḏōš*) refers to the sacral divine world as distinct from the ordinary profane world. God is holy and is to be hallowed by us; there are holy cultic objects, days, and acts, and relative to these, people are either holy or made holy; finally, the word also has an ethical thrust: by their way of life the people and the individual must show that they belong to Yahweh (the people—Ex. 19:6; Deut. 7:6; 28:9; Isa. 62:12; Dan. 7:27; the individual—Lev. 19; Ps. 16:3; 34:10). The NT employs *hagios, hagiazein, hagiasmos, hagiotēs,* and *hagiōsynē* in a similar way, yet with a most significant shift in accent: the concepts are now also applied to Christ, they are being used less for God and more for man, and with respect to man especially for his ethical activity. The language for man's cultic "objective" sanctification is now also being used to designate what we called justification (1 Cor. 1:30; 6:11; 7:14; Heb. 10:10, 14)—a usage to which Kohlbrugge and his followers like to appeal in their desire to make sanctification almost identical with justification. But next to it the ethical meaning assumes a growing importance (Rom. 6:19, 22; 2 Cor. 7:1; 1 Thess. 3:13; 4:3–7; 1 Tim. 2:15; Heb. 12:14; 1 Pet. 1:15). The dogmatic usage is based on that. Of course, the NT also uses many other words to speak of man's ethical renewal. See *TDNT* I, *s.v. hagios;* and because in this area particularly Paul has drawn the major lines, see also K. Stalder, *Das Werk des Geistes in der Heiligung bei Paulus* (1962), and H. Ridderbos, *Paul* (E.T. 1975), VI and VII. A brief but significant survey of the word usage is found in Barth, *CD* IV,2, pp. 513–518.

Roman Catholic theology so far treats sanctification mostly as the self-perfection of the believing subject; the manner in which the concepts "good works," "reward," and "merit" intermesh in the ecclesiastical tradition force that theology in this direction. Lately attempts are being made to break that grip, mainly through reinterpretation of the traditional concepts. See *MS* IV.2, chs. 10–12.

The Reformation began with a conception of sanctification which was altogether different from the externalized pursuit of merit of the late medieval tradition. Sanctification is man's spontaneous response of gratitude, not egocentrically directed but ex-centrically to the honor of God and the good of the neighbor. See Luther, *On Good Works* (1520) and *On Christian Liberty* (1520). But the Heidelberg Catechism, in addition to mentioning God and the neighbor as motives for good works, says: "that each of us may be assured in himself of his faith by its fruit." What is here the second motive comes first in the *Synopsis purioris theologiae* (1625), Disp. XXXIV.16: "The purposes of good works are three. The first pertains to us, namely as a testimony of our gratitude to God, by which we are at the same time confirmed in our election and calling." This is the so-called *syllogismus practicus,* that is, the conclusion drawn from one's deeds. This motive, which in Calvin initially had only a limited and incidental role (*Inst* III, xiv,14, 18–20), is now more broadly developed, and that leads to an interest in man himself as needing sanctification and as sanctified, an orientation which is at variance with the ex-centric nature of sanctification. The ground for the joy of the fellowship with God is then again sought in man—but never found. Particularly Kohlbrugge reacted against this conception of sanctification; rightly he directed man to the justification which has happened, outside of us, in Christ. Yet for him sanctification was almost the same as justification. Actually he had no other message than the call to faith in the accomplished work of Christ. He was well aware that Paul also called for concrete ethical decisions, but then he pointed out that for that aspect Paul likes to use the imperative of the aorist, which

Kohlbrugge translated as: "Have then put on (the new man)," "Have then put to death (what is earthly in you)," etc., that is, presume that all that has already happened in Christ. (Wrongly, for this aorist imperative does not have this meaning, but emphasizes the inception, actuality, and incidental nature of the act.)

The main stream in the thinking on sanctification goes, however, in the opposite direction. The use of the term "sanctification" promotes the above-signalized individualistic and egocentric reduction of the concept. In more recent years, the younger generation of Christians in churches everywhere has stressed afresh the challenge to active obedience, now especially in larger ethical contexts. They did so without knowing that they were engaged in what theology calls "sanctification." In this term they did not hear the call to work ex-centrically for the well-being of the neighbor and mankind. Yet that is an integral aspect of what this word stands for in the Bible and tradition.

The first, in a sense decisive, and hence often-discussed question is: how is this renewing activation of man, his efforts in the service of God, related to the relaxation granted him in justification? Is that relaxation which is involved in the acquittal not the real and decisive thing that happens between God and man? But why should that person then follow it up by again putting forth effort? Thereby he can add nothing to his justification; instead he runs the risk of practically denying it by his own activity! Or should we say the opposite, that justification, though it is the foundation of our life as a Christian, is not its goal? Is the essential thing then the ongoing renewal which is realized in the deeds of the believer? Is our right relationship to God thus partly dependent on what we ourselves do, activated by our acquittal? In answering these questions, Bible and church, preaching and theology are as it were walking a tightrope. If to the one side or the other we misconstrue the relation of justification and sanctification, we contribute to the obstruction or disruption of the process of renewal.

Wanting to do justice to both, one has the choice between two models of thought with which theology operates until the present day. Mindful of what is said in Matthew 7:18, "A good tree cannot bear bad fruit," one could maintain that sanctification is the organic and thus natural consequence of justification. In that case the believer may rest solely and totally in the comfort of forgiveness, in the confidence that that will make him produce fruits of gratitude. The truth in this train of thought is that the work of renewal is one and indivisible and that justification is its permanent center. Yet in the long run this model does not satisfy. A human being is, after all, not a tree. At every step along the path of renewal his own will is helpingly or obstructingly involved. That which from God's point of view constitutes an organic whole, looks entirely different as seen from the perspective of our responsibility. Man cannot just leave his own deeds to a process. Then he becomes too passive and too careless. That can lead to self-delusion. In that way too little is made of the exertion to the honor of God and the good of the neighbor.

If justification cannot be a quiet resting place, how about viewing it as a jumping board? Then we get a second thought model. Justification is then the starting-point to which we may return whenever we fail in our sanctification, but it is not the goal itself. That which God without us and from the outside begins in us must enter our lives and take concrete shape in us, if it is to be fruitful. Here man's will and responsibility are taken seriously; here life is not a process of growth, but a training school. Yet eventually this model does not satisfy either. It undermines the radical significance of justification as the permanent resting point of our heart. By nature we are moralists. Before we are aware of it the roles are reversed and we have to renew ourselves, be it, of course, "with the help of God's grace" (in other words, of justification).

We will have to use both models in conjunction and let them serve as each other's corrective. The man who is relaxed because of what God has done for him will through that relaxation lose his preoccupation with self and forget himself, and be prompted into fruitfulness for others as an instrument of the love from which he may live himself. It is precisely the relaxation that inspires to effort. Yet those efforts will show again and again how much he fails and how far his love falls short of God's love. That must lead either to despair or to a grim determination to continue, unless he falls back on the acquittal by grace alone. That will not do away with his efforts; instead it will purify them, because he knows that in those efforts he need no longer affirm, prove, and justify himself. Only he who no longer needs to serve himself with his works is able, since he is now free from himself, to do really "good works," works that mean something for the Other and the others.

The Christian faith always stands poised on the sharp edge between anti-nom(ian)ism or libertinism to the one side and nomism, legalism, or moralism to the other. Wherever justification by faith is proclaimed in all its radicality, there the question which already confronted Paul arises: "Are we to continue in sin that grace may abound?" (Rom. 6:1). And James in his epistle had to oppose those who felt that they were exempt from works on account of their faith (Jas. 2:17–26). Luther, too, had to contend with this caricature. The antinomianism which he and Melanchthon had to challenge in Agricola, their supporter, concerned, however, especially the function of the law in bringing about repentance. Likewise the Lutheran Von Amsdorf, who would later call good works harmful for salvation, meant only to resist an unwholesome interest in and a dependence on them. It is questionable how much real antinomianism, let alone libertinism, there has been in the history of theology. However, people liked to accuse each other of it, and warnings against it were constantly sounded; the latter rightly so, because in the practice of the Christian life it is always and everywhere a great danger. But nomism was just as great a danger, and theologically an even greater one. It is not easy to live for long in the tension of justification by faith. Immediately after the NT period Paul's teaching on justification seems virtually forgotten, and the forgiveness of sin is valued only as the door to a life of good works.

The two thought models described above had become distinct realities in the Reformation as early as about 1530. The first model is the Lutheran. Particularly in Melanchthon's *Apology*, especially in "On justification" and "On the delight and fulfillment of the law," everything is removed from justification that might detract from Paul's "without the works of the law"; hence the fulfillment of the law in love is viewed as a necessary consequence of justification while yet strictly separate from it: "first by this faith we are accounted righteous because of Christ, which (faith) we seek and make a law, even if love follows as a consequence." The second thought model is in particular the free-church type (Baptist, later the Anglo-Saxon free churches), but also the Reformed type, at least in the eyes of the Lutherans who even today charge their brethren in the faith with a tendency toward legalism. One should, however, bear in mind that the two thought models involve two different types of people: the Lutheran directs itself to the man who endeavors to justify himself but is thereby brought to despair and inner turmoil; the second model concerns the spiritually carefree and lethargic person who likes to benefit from a cheap grace, and thereby considers himself exempt from the struggle of the faith. For that reason, too, it is inadvisable to pin ourselves down, confessionally and theologically, on one of the two models.

Nor can the Bible be used to support the one over against the other. Everywhere justification and sanctification are presented as being integrally related. For the proclamation of Jesus, see on the one hand especially Luke (particularly the parables in chs. 14–18) and on the other hand especially Matthew (particularly his version of the Sermon on the Mount, and the parables on watchfulness in chs. 24 and 25). But the integral relationship is never something that always and naturally happens, because the transition from the first to the second always requires admonition and exhortation. According to the parable of the unmerciful servant (Matt. 18:23–35) and of the man without wedding clothes (Matt. 22:1–14), what naturally happens can also *not* happen. And Paul, the great proclaimer of justification as the ground, likewise proclaims conformity with Christ as the goal (Rom. 8:29; 1 Cor. 15:49; 2 Cor. 3:18; Gal. 4:19; Phil. 3:21). Though relating the indicative and imperative so very closely to each other, he too knows all too well, as we see in Rom. 6:15–23; 1 Cor. 3:12–15; and Gal. 5, that their integral relationship is not something that is there as a matter of course.

In our judgment the most careful theological probing on this point is in Calvin and Barth. Calvin prefers the term *duplex gratia.* In *Inst* III he starts with faith in the promises of God (ii), next he discusses repentance, and in vi–x he takes up the sanctification of life; then in xi–xiv he goes back to ii with a lengthy exposition of justification, after which xv–xx deal again with good works and the life of gratitude. This zigzagging between justification and sanctification makes a confusing impression, until one sees why Calvin had to put the relation of relaxation and effort in the faith like that. Note his own explanation in xi,1 why he put the second grace first, to return from there to "the main hinge on which religion turns," namely justification. With great congeniality Barth has shown the logic in Calvin's composition, in *CD* IV,2, par. 66: "Justification and Sanctification" (pp. 509–511). He himself summarizes this vision as follows: "This would mean that both answers have to be given with the same seriousness in view of the distinctive truth in both—intersecting but not cancelling one another. In the *simul* of the one divine will and action justification is first as basis and second as presupposition, sanctification first as aim and second as consequence; and therefore both are superior and both subordinate" (p. 508).

48. FREEDOM AND LOVE

THIS AND THE NEXT PARAGRAPHS are concerned with the description of the nature and content of "sanctification": what does this relaxed effort to which our divine adoption inspires us consist of? The same Paul who has probed the justification event deeper than all other witnesses is also the one who has articulated its consequences for the practice of life in concepts which have remained both understandable and irreplaceable. Here we orient ourselves to two key concepts which in Paul are intimately related: freedom and love.

a. Freedom

The freedom which plays such a fundamental role in the Christian life differs from other conceptions of freedom in two respects. On the one hand it is the reverse of something which seems to contradict it—the bond of total subjection to God which Paul goes so far as to call "slavery"; and on the other hand it is a freedom which results in a bond with one's fellowman. Between these two bonds hardly any room seems left for genuine freedom. Hence it is not surprising that in dogmatics it has often been very meagerly treated, despite Paul's entirely different treatment. Nevertheless, unless there is freedom we cannot properly understand the two bonds which surround it.

The adoption unto covenant partnership with God means security with respect to heaven and therefore inviolability with respect to earth. If God is more powerful than our guilt and the fate that threatens us, if neither height nor depth, neither the present nor the future can separate us from his love, then life receives a new face and the powers that used to rule our actions lose their ultimate control. Then we no longer expect our happiness from that side, nor do we allow fear to force us into submission to them. For the bond with God has become the most important and decisive fact for us. The many other bonds we have may be either beneficial or neutral; what these relations cannot do is make or break our life. A distance is created between them and us, the distance of freedom. The bond with God has shifted the center of our life so that it is now above; and that means that these powers that used to determine our life have now in principle lost their power. Neither their acknowledged strength or violence, nor the safety they offer, nor the vengeance they threaten with, are then decisive any longer. In the lives of many this may for a long time remain something that is purely an inner religious freedom. But the moment may come that this inner freedom asserts itself, when we must go against commonly accepted practices and beliefs, because we search for new directions or begin to see that the present state of affairs is in need of drastic change. That assertion of our freedom is the beginning of our following of Christ who, standing in the love of the Father, was so inviolate that the tradition, public opinion, and the accepted standards of conduct had no hold on him. "Where the Spirit of the Lord is, there is freedom. And we all . . . are being changed into his likeness" (2 Corinthians 3:17, 18).

This freedom is not just an ideal to strive for. It is a reality that goes with the security one has in God. This is not to deny that analogical feelings of freedom can also come from other sources, for instance from the demands of conscience, or the awareness of the rights of the individual, or from a deep insight into the corruptness of our ties. As a matter of fact, in this chapter on renewal we should constantly bear in mind that because of the preservation of creation on the one hand and the penetration of the Spirit of Christ on the other, everywhere elements and rudiments of humanity as God intends it can be found. The origin of this freedom, namely the bond with Christ, is entirely different. Whether and to what extent this also changes its nature will have to be shown in each particular instance—assuming that this is something which can be shown.

As regards its nature, this freedom is as such not programmatical, that is, it does not mean that the believer will always pursue this or that ideal or oppose certain specific situations and structures. But it is impossible that it would have no consequences for personal life, politics, and society. These consequences may take the form of incidental conflicts, creative plans, patient persistence, or martyrdom for a cause. It will depend on the times and the circumstances whether this freedom will also take on a broader and more permanent societal- or cultural-critical shape. It will, however, never be identical with a particular shape because there will always be new fronts and areas where it needs to assert itself in struggling, suffering, or creative activity.

In the OT this notion of freedom hardly occurs; Israel's liberation from Egyptian bondage is indeed the backbone of the OT, but it is that as a fact which Israel through its obedience to Yahweh was unable to live up to; the result is that, in passages where the theme of freedom could emerge, accusation and the call to repentance are found. Apart from Paul, in the NT this concept is only marginal: Jas. 1:25; 2:12; 1 Pet. 2:16; 2 Pet. 2:19; however, a loaded statement such as John 8:36 proves the crucial place of freedom.

Whether or not in confrontation with the Greek ideal of freedom, only in Paul does this term have a central place. Moreover, his use of the concept exceeds that of the term itself; witness his struggle about the validity of the law in the Epistle to the Galatians, and what he says in passages like 1 Cor. 4:11–13; 15:30–32; 2 Cor. 4:8–12; 6:8–10, and Phil. 4:10f. about his own freedom. More reflective statements are Rom. 8:37–39; 1 Cor. 3:21–23, a variety of elements in his train of thought in 1 Cor. 7–10, and further Gal. 4:1–11; 5:1–16; Col. 2:8–3:11. Bear in mind, too, that Paul's usage of the concept of "freedom" is wider than ours. It is first of all freedom from sin, from the law and its curse, and from death (Rom. 6:18, 22; 7:1–6; 8:1f.). Pauline studies have one-sidedly emphasized this "vertical" and "inner" freedom at the expense of the "outer" and "horizontal" dimension. See *TDNT* II, *s.v. eleutheros* (Schlier), which virtually ignores this second aspect; and R. Bultmann, *Theology of the NT* (E.T. 1951), who deals extensively with freedom from sin (par. 38), the law (par. 39), and death (par. 40), but devotes only one page, at the end, to freedom from the world and its powers. He who neglects this aspect also underestimates the first aspect.

The revolutionary power of this faith is thereby also underestimated. It is often pointed out (approvingly or disapprovingly) that Paul in his Epistle to Philemon does not advocate the abolition of slavery. What is overlooked is that Paul put Philemon in an impossible position in respect to his slave; the master-slave relationship is not abolished from without but undermined from within. That Paul was not afraid of the societal-structural consequences of such insights is evident from his opposition in the Gentile Christian congregations to the validity of Jewish laws.

Paul does not stand alone in that. The gospels point in the same direction, especially the Synoptic narratives that speak about Jesus' attitude to the law, the sabbath, the temple, the scribes, "sinners," the established order. Barth has given a fine epitome of the Synoptic traits of this "revolutionary character" of Jesus' ministry under the heading "The Kingly Man" (*CD* IV,2, pp. 171–179). Paul's understanding of freedom should also be seen as a consequence and elaboration of the practice of freedom which was demonstrated in Jesus. A one-sided but nevertheless impressive picture of the freedom dimension through the whole NT is found in E. Käsemann, *Jesus Means Freedom* (E.T. 1969).

From Käsemann's essay we also learn of the great threats to which this astounding freedom was already exposed in the time of the NT. That became still worse in the history of the church. It took only a short while before freedom was hardly considered any more in Christian thinking. The church, fearing libertinism, did her utmost to make herself look loyal in the eyes of a suspicious Roman government. And the Middle Ages with its feudal-authoritarian structure of society and its hierarchical-authoritarian church brought no change. Yet freedom remained alive, if only in the great numbers of martyrs of the early church and in many nonconformist groups in the Middle Ages.

The Reformation may be seen as the reawakening of Christian freedom over against the ruling powers. That is how Luther thought of it in his important essay *On Christian Liberty* (1520) in which he posits as the first of two basic theses: "A Christian is the most free lord of all, and subject to none." However, when the peasants in their revolt in 1525 appealed to this slogan, Luther sharply pointed out to them that he meant this freedom in a purely inner sense and that it did not apply to the order and obedience that are necessary in the worldly realm.

While in Lutheranism freedom was almost completely conceived of as freedom from sin and law (thus as a term for justification), Reformed Protestantism, with Calvin (*Inst* III,xix: "On Christian freedom"), continued to relate it somewhat to sanctification, as a freedom from human traditions, freedom of conscience, and freedom to use earthly goods. But that, too, was never more than a marginal note to a conformist ethics. It was in the free churches, broadly speaking, that freedom became significant, beginning with Thomas Müntzer, the Anabaptists, Coornhert, and the Spiritualists. But while in the official churches freedom was stunted, here it evaporated in the direction of the individual conscience with its individualism and autonomy.

In the second half of the 20th century a new awareness of freedom has arisen. It has derived strong support from the worldwide emancipation movements of our time. The theology of P. van Buren in *The Secular Meaning of the Gospel* (1963) is almost totally built on the concept of freedom. The same is largely true of R. Alves, H. Cox, J.-B. Metz, D. Sölle, and many others. But almost always the Christian content and the relation with security and obedience are minimal. It is simply assumed that everyone agrees that freedom consists of the possibility of developing our natural humanity. A better understanding of the basic role of the freedom concept is found in the studies of F. Gogarten; see among others *Christ the Crisis* (E.T. 1970) and *Die Frage nach Gott* (1968).

Theologically more significant, however, is the renewed interest in the idea of freedom in Roman Catholic theology, an interest that is strengthened through the conflict which many are embroiled in with the authoritarian hierarchy. That compels a number of them, as with Luther years ago, to read the relevant passages in Paul with new eyes. See e.g. J. Blank, *Das Evangelium als Garantie der Freiheit* (1970), and especially H. Küng, *The Church* (E.T. 1976), ch. II.1: "The New Freedom" (pp. 150–161), which in general provides a good survey of the problem.

b. Love

Even as freedom is the reverse and consequence of the bond with God in Christ, so also freedom and love can be regarded as each other's reverse. In the process of renewal they belong inseparably together. For that matter, the same is true of our view of man in general. Note what we said at the end of paragraph 26. That is certainly reasonable, for in the renewal God, by his Spirit, seeks to work in us the kind of humanity which he had in mind in creation. He desires free men; but freedom exists for the sake of love, and love is made possible through freedom. The purpose of freedom is to awaken love. And if it should not be love that is awakened, that freedom is apparently something else than what God means by it. He understands it as the ability, in communion with him, to take an independent stance toward the world, which enables us to pass on to the world the renewing power of love which we receive in that communion with him.

We tend to have difficulty with this relation between freedom and love because consciously or unconsciously we operate with a different concept of love: freedom as the possibility for self-realization without being hemmed in or hampered by demands put upon us by God, other people, and the world. From this perspective, freedom and love are entirely different things; if they do not exclude, they at least limit each other. That is another reason why in the church and in theology evangelical freedom has not been taken more seriously.

But if we participate in God's way with Israel and in Christ, then particularly in Jesus' ministry we are confronted with a man who freed himself from the demands of powers and of people, in order that he might be fully free to minister to others with the love of God. A statement like "The sabbath was made for man, not man for the sabbath" (Mark 2:27) is typical for the oneness of freedom and love in him which we may imitate. What we said of freedom holds also for its reverse, namely love: Jesus is the great example of it, and Paul is the man who has best articulated the relation between that love and freedom.

For the unity of freedom and love in Paul we think of course in the first place of Gal. 5. Beside that see Rom. 6:15–23; 1 Cor. 6:12; 10:23f., and especially those passages where Paul warns against using freedom in such a way that it is no longer a channel for love but an obstacle: Rom. 14:13–23; 1 Cor. 8:1–13; 10:25–33. A Synoptic illustration here is the story of Jesus and the temple tax (Matt. 17:24–27).

The love at issue here is the love to the neighbor. It is not the love to God. That love logically precedes our freedom. It is also of a different character than the love to the neighbor, for it is our spontaneous reaction to him who has loved us first. It coincides with faith or—if one wants to make a distinction here—is a constituent part of faith. The love to the neighbor is as such definitely not a reaction to someone who gave his love to us first. The cause of this love is not what the neighbor does to us; its cause is our reaction, our *second* reaction to what *God* does to us. If God loves men, and with me the whole world that is disobedient to him, then I cannot love him without at the same time committing myself to his service. The love to the neighbor is thus the consequence of the love to God. But the word "love" does not mean the same in both instances. To love God implies first of all my grateful and spontaneous response of love. To love the neighbor means that I take his side and help him in whatever way I can. We do that as imitators of God and of Christ. In the Christian faith the love to the neighbor thus has something indirect about it, certainly compared with the love toward God. This may seem to make this love cold and aloof, a weak basis for genuine dedication. The opposite is true, however. If we should serve the neighbors only because and insofar as we find them "loveable," we would soon reach the limits of our readiness to serve. Then we can certainly not, like God, love our enemies. We can do that only if our ultimate motivation does not come from the neighbor but from God. In paragraph 21 we argued for seeing God's love not only as *agapē* (giving itself away), but also as *erōs* (satisfying itself). That certainly holds for our love to him. However, our love for the neighbor involves an act of the will on behalf of God in which *erōs* can enter only as an unsought premium.

Our freedom is thus to realize itself in the commandment "You shall love your neighbor as yourself." In Matthew 22:37–40 this is called "the second commandment," which, relative to the first, the love to God, is said to be "like it." That means that it is inseparable from it and of the same importance. The preceding context shows that this does not mean that it is of the same character and motivation. There is thus no identification. Making the two the same, we minimize both.

In the Bible it is clear that the two go together, e.g. in Lev. 19 where God with his "I am the Lord" solemnly warns Israel not to harm the neighbor in any way, in the parables of the good Samaritan (Luke 10:25–37), poor Lazarus (Luke 16:19–31), and the two debtors (Matt. 18:21–35), and in statements like 1 John 2:9 and 4:20. The difference is shown here too, however; furthermore, e.g. in Matt. 5:43–48, which of course does not view the love to the neighbor as analogous to our love to God, yet does view it as the analogy of God's love to us, a love which does not ask whether we deserve it. Remarkable in this connection is Col. 3:23f., where the readiness to help others is grounded in the fact that we do our task "as serving the Lord and not men" and that we "are serving the Lord Christ." The extra-human motivation is here the foundation for being human. Nevertheless, some are of the opinion that the identification of the love to God and to Christ with that of the love to the (needy) neighbor does occur in the NT, namely in Matt. 25:31–46, where the Son of man is saying in the last judgment: "I was hungry and you gave me food," etc., for "as you did it to one of the least of these my brethren, you did it to me." While it does prove the intimate connection, this is no identification, however; moreover, this passage is not about love to the neighbor as such, but about the attitude of "all the nations" (v. 32) toward the persecuted flock of Christ.

It is remarkable, however, that the Bible speaks relatively sparsely about the love to God; it receives the most emphasis in 1 John 4, a passage which is, however, mainly concerned with pointing out its unbreakable connection with the love of the brother. In contrast, in the NT "the" love often refers only to love of the neighbor: Matt. 19:18f.; John 13:34; Rom. 13:8ff.; Gal. 5:14; cf. Jas. 2:8.

In more recent systematic theology the relationship between love for God and love for other human beings is often sparsely dealt with. Yet already Ritschl had said: "The love for God has no room within which to act outside that of the love for the brothers" (*Unterricht in der christlichen Religion* [1875], par. 6). After the Second World War and the discovery of the tremendous need and misery found throughout the world, theology quickly developed an interest in the subject of love of the neighbor. Thereby it threatened to become detached from the love for God, and so to become a law instead of a sign of received mercy. Furthermore, the idea of love for the neighbor proved insufficient to catch the worldwide and structural dimensions of the neighbor-problematics. For that reason, in the reflection on the problem since about 1970, the biblical term "the poor" was substituted for that of the neighbor. Rightly so insofar as it captures biblical notions (see especially Luke's portrayal of Jesus) that have a bearing on the worldwide problem of poverty and oppression. The gospel is good news for the poor, and for the nonpoor only insofar as they identify themselves with the poor. See J. de Santa Ana, ed., *Towards a Church of the Poor* (1979), and the publication of the World Council with the more cautious title *Towards a Church in Solidarity with the Poor* (1980). However, from the perspective of dogmatics and the pastoral-ethical concern it is regrettable that the multi-faceted biblical term "poor," which stands for a combination of material and spiritual helplessness, now for the most part is narrowed to material exploitation and therefore no longer connects with the biblical message of liberation.

It is not necessary here to deal extensively with the nature and the manifestations of the love for the neighbor in which freedom realizes itself. That belongs to the area of Christian ethics. Our concern is the theme of renewal. This renewal becomes visible in the fact that a person's security in God frees him from constantly having to prove himself, so freeing his time and energy to use the divinely received love for the benefit of the neighbor—in word and deed, in witness and service, in availability and aid. So in his renewal man is freed from himself and becomes ex-centric in two directions.

It is necessary to consider for a moment the repeatedly used term "neighbor." It does not refer to "everyone," not to the person who in some way is close to me, for instance as a relative or one who lives close by. It is rather the person who stands in my way, who irritates me by his animosity or who appeals to me by his need for help. The neighbor is thus the person who on the one hand disturbs me, and on the other hand reminds me that my relationship to God is analogous to his or her relationship to me. The encounter with the other is a challenge to me to act as the representative of God's love by making his or her needs my concern. What a particular encounter will be like and how to deal in a given situation cannot be anticipated beforehand. In one way or another the neighbor and I will be together in a common situation. That situation can be as narrow as belonging to one family or sharing an office, and it can also be (especially nowadays) as wide as the world. The neighbor can be a single individual, but also a whole group of people, a race, or a nation. We are in danger of overlooking the neighbor who is far away for the sake of the one nearby, and vice versa; of remaining blind to the collective and structural powers of which the individual is the victim and, vice versa, of overlooking the human being due to a preoccupation with these problems of structure. The parable of the good Samaritan shows how easily we walk past a situation in which we meet the neighbor, failing to recognize him by our apathy or callous unconcern. This happens especially when the neighbor, who in the

Bible is predominantly the person who is poor, in the mind of the Christian church often one-sidedly becomes the person who is spiritually poor.

Wherever we recognize the neighbor, we become aware how much we ourselves, either as rebel or victim, need divine deliverance and help, and that we cannot possibly plead with God for the mercy we withhold from others. So thinking of ourselves, we forget ourselves and start thinking of the good of the other, of how we can concretely help him. We begin to love the other as ourselves. We may thus also accept ourselves. That choice is even the norm for the love of the neighbor, even as that love is the boundary of our love for ourselves. In that continuous limitation and pruning, our "self" is not suppressed but renewed, and in the communion with God and man it becomes fully itself.

In the Bible, in the OT, the neighbor is called *rēʿeh,* the companion, the person one associates with. Usually the neighbor is there said to be a member of one's own people. As a rule such is indeed the case (the nation was the horizon of the Israelite), yet significant exceptions (Ex. 23:4f.; Lev. 19:33f.; Deut. 10:19; Prov. 25:21) prove that this was not at all meant in a nationalistic and limiting sense; and Ps. 87, Isa. 19, and the book of Jonah point to horizons that are much farther still. The Septuagint rendered *rēʿeh* with *plēsion,* an accusative noun with adverbial sense; *ho plēsion* is "the one from nearby." In Jesus' days the scribes debated the extent (limits) of the concept of neighbor (see *TDNT* VI, *s.v. plēsion).* In contrast to the restrictions that had been placed upon it, Jesus does not make "everyone" the neighbor; rather, due to the boundless love of God the neighbor is precisely the person who hinders and irritates us.

The neighbor whom we meet as the needy fellowman is in particular illustrated in the parable of the good Samaritan (Luke 10:25–37), and as the guilty fellowman we find him especially in the parable of the two debtors (Matt. 18:21–35). This second parable has still another peculiar feature: when the first debtor fails to cancel the debt of the second, his own earlier remission of debt is cancelled. The new relationship to the neighbor is the fruit of the relationship to God; but if that new relationship fails to materialize, it has a bearing on the relationship to God. The same implication is found in Luke 6:36–38 and in the petition, "Forgive us our debts, as we also have forgiven our debtors" (Matt. 6:12). That has nothing to do with good works as a condition for receiving grace. The presence or absence of consequences in the visible interhuman relationships is the indication whether something has really happened between God and man. That is how a continuous interaction is brought about between divine love and human love. Matt. 5:48 points to the same thing, when from 43–47 it draws the conclusion that the heavenly Father is "perfect," that is, unambivalent, consistent, acting only out of grace; hence we must be like that too, not wanting to have it both ways, pleading God's grace for ourselves while treating the neighbor according to what he deserves.

The "neighbor" concept has hardly been dealt with in theology. Its absence in *RGG* is typical. A classical exception is Kierkegaard's *Deeds of Love* (1847), esp. I. Barth twice discussed it in his *CD,* both times in rather different ways, and in our opinion in neither attempt very successful. In I,2, par. 18,3, Barth is so afraid of a legalistic and non-christological approach that he presents the neighbor as our benefactor who reminds us of the helpless Christ; in IV,2 the neighbor is the one who either actually or potentially is a member of the church (pp. 802–824). In our judgment, in the NT the neighbor is the focal point of the love with which God in Christ gives himself to us and the world.

With our remarks on "as yourself," we challenged both the notion, which has been widely held since Augustine, that one can derive from it a self-love as a sort of "third commandment," and also the notion that this addition would imply a condemnation of self-love (Barth, *CD* I,2, pp. 386f., 450–454). This formulation of the second commandment is far from innocuous. It entails far-reaching social and political consequences; looking after one's own interests and those of others should thus go together. For the love of the neighbor in general, see also S. J. Ridderbos, *Ethiek van het liefdegebod* (1975), chs. I–IV.

49. DYING AND RISING

Repeatedly we have illuminated man's renewal from the perspective of his participation in God's way through history. The renewal is grounded in this participation and bound to it. In paragraph 43 we saw that the aim of this participation is "conformity" with Christ. Paragraph 48 showed how this conformity is related to Jesus' earthly life. We do not become "little Christs" ourselves; in comparison with that truly new man, we remain far too deeply rooted in our former existence. Even the term "imitation" cannot be applied to us with the meaning it has in the gospels, and therefore it should always be used with great caution (pp. 325–326). Even so, the renewal will always come to expression in a kind of analogy between us and him. We have seen how this analogy with Jesus' earthly life is concentrated in the concepts of "freedom" and "love." But if there is this conformity with his life, then a certain conformity with his suffering and death is also unavoidable. For the other side of this conformity is "nonconformity" with regard to the powers on which the world pins its hopes for salvation. Sooner or later conformity with Christ will thus evoke the hostility which leads to oppression and suffering. For the world does not lightly tolerate it that its ways are crossed by that way.

Renewal involves suffering, but it is a unique sort of suffering. It may not be identified with the general suffering in the world. The provisionalness and alienation that mark our human existence unleash a flood of misery in which the whole human race involuntarily shares. By comparison, Jesus' suffering and death in which believers share from a distance are voluntary and intentional. The sorrow over one's own sin is also something else. Likewise the anguish and perplexity of soul caused by the hiddenness of God. And the same holds for what we call the dying to ourselves, the self-denial which is to be ever and again an integral dimension of our life as our new nature battles the old; we will speak about that in paragraph 50. Jesus' death and our dying with him is a dying to the world that has its ground in the conflict between us and the world which is caused by our participation in the new way.

Yet this necessary and sharp distinction cannot mean an absolute division. In his totally unique suffering and death, Jesus also shared in the general misery of the world and experienced the anguish of the hiddenness of God. And every believer will in his clashes with the world first of all ask himself to what extent this clash is not due to his faithfulness, but rather to his unfaithfulness to the Lord. But that does not alter the fact that what we here call "dying" is a separate category. Identifying or blending it with other categories leads only to confusion. Much is said about the "cross" and "cross-bearing" that has nothing to do with the uniqueness of Jesus' cross. Both for the reflection on the faith and for the experience of the faith and pastoral care, that creates only a harmful misunderstanding. For that reason, here we focus entirely on the (neglected) theme of the peculiar rising and dying relative to the world which is an element in the believer's participation in the way of his Lord.

Dying means here at least that the full development of the believer's new life, and sometimes of his natural life as well, is resisted by forces from the outside. Dying means the surrender of life. This surrender, like any surrender of life, is involuntary; yet insofar as it is an extension of the voluntary choice for Christ and his way of freedom and love it is not involuntary. The most conspicuous form of this death is of course martyrdom. Any form of Christian abstinence, however, belongs to it, if it is a withdrawal, for the sake of the faith, from the powers that dominate our world; that can express itself in denying oneself certain pleasures, in teetotalism, in conscientious objection to bearing arms, in political protests, in spending a considerable amount of our income on philanthropic concerns. To some extent all this can still be a direct expression of our life in freedom and love, but almost always it brings with it increased pressure from the outside, so that it involves an arduous rowing against the stream. That is even more the case if it results in smaller or bigger conflicts with the environment; and particularly if it makes the Christian community suspect in the eyes of the state. But this surrender of life and oppression can assume more subtle forms as well, as in our Western late-capitalist and pluralist society with its intense secularism, where the Christian faith is regarded as only one (quite unlikely) possible way of looking at life and the world and where there is no room for many of the priorities of the Christian ethos. In such a world the believer must very often feel himself a stranger. Many try to avoid this oppression by adapting as much as possible or by apologizing for their beliefs and attitudes. That stance contains this kernel of truth, that we are always in danger of confusing certain peculiarities of the Christian faith with obedience to the gospel. But one who is aware of that faces the opposite danger of overlooking the fact that the way of Christ will regularly lead to oppression and that we must be prepared to accept that oppression, even to be grateful for it, since it is a sign that we are still in his way.

That last statement intimates that the counterpart of this dying, in a distant analogy with that of Jesus, is our rising with him. But we do not share in his resurrection in the same way that we share his suffering. Jesus arose ahead-of-us, and as individual firstfruits he entered a new world which for us is still future. Therefore for us the resurrection is first of all a future reality. Yet it is a present reality as well, as surely as Jesus arose in *this* world and works in it with his Spirit. Those who share in this death experience already know something of the resurrection to come, and that in three ways. (1) In the certainty, sometimes even the joy, of being in the way of the Lord, thus on the way to the resurrection; (2) in the experience that oppression and suffering do more than frustrate life, that in fact in a marvelous sort of way they contribute to the growth and the deepening of the new life; (3) in the signs which the oppressed believer receives, standing as he does in the covenant relationship of guidance and security (see paragraph 46), that God also puts limits to the hostility of the world and makes all things work for good to those who love him.

The question could be asked whether this radical aspect of the process of renewal is generally valid, or whether it is limited to a few special individuals. Do we not speak here about matters that are too high for "ordinary" Christians? In answer to this question, we have to distinguish and combine various points of view. To begin with, it must unfortunately be said that just in this area the cowardice and conformity to the world of Christendom and the churches are often painfully evident. Much of what goes by the name of Christian and church are but (religious-)worldly affairs, covered by a false flag. Even as Israel's prophets and later Jesus got the strongest persecution from the side of the religious institutions and officials, so through the centuries ecclesiastical institutes have functioned as focal points and instruments of the world's persecution of individuals who sought to follow Christ. No wonder that for many dying and rising with Christ become unintelligible jargon.

Without detracting from the preceding, we also need to note that certain individuals have often more or less vicariously borne oppression. Personally Paul was strongly aware of that role and calling, and he was glad that in this way he could lighten the load of others: "Now I rejoice in my sufferings for your sake, and in my flesh I complete what is lacking in Christ's afflictions for the sake of his body, that is, the church" (Colossians 1:24). This principle of substitution has been operative until the present day through the whole history of the church. The "only" thing then asked of those not oppressed is that they by their intercession, testimony, and service manifest their solidarity with the oppressed.

Finally, the gamut of recognized and unrecognized forms of oppression is as broad as life itself. Perhaps we need to help each other much more in this art of recognition. Then resentment and feelings of inferiority can give way to acceptance, perseverance, and thankfulness.

At first sight it may seem that we are dealing here withy the *mortificatio–vivificatio* theme, familiar from the Reformation. Yet such is not the case. The Lutherans used this phrase as the parallel of condemnation–justification or repentance–faith. In Calvin (*Inst* III,iii,8f.) and the Reformed it was particularly used in the doctrine of sanctification as an indication of the conflict between flesh and Spirit; this point of view will be dealt with in the next paragraph. But as a result, the Reformers and their followers did very little with the context in which "rising" and "dying" function particularly in the NT.

This theme is already a subject of reflection in the OT; on the one hand in the suffering of the righteous, mentioned often in the Psalms, and on the other hand in the suffering of great servants of God, like Moses, Jeremiah, Ezekiel, and the suffering servant. Especially G. von Rad, *Old Testament Theology,* I (E.T. 1962) and II (E.T. 1965), has pointed to this perspective of suffering in the OT.

But only in the NT, after Jesus' death and resurrection, is this theme thoroughly developed and explored around such terms as *thlipsis, lypē, oneidismos, paideia, pathēmata, peirasmos, potērion, stauros.* On this point, too, Paul is far ahead of the other witnesses. See the penetrating thoughts which he reveals in passing, as in Rom. 5:3; 8:17; Gal. 6:14; Phil. 3:10, or intentionally develops, as in Rom. 8:35–39; 2 Cor. 1:8–11; 4:8–11; 6:4–10; 11:23–12:10—thus especially in 2 Cor. Once Paul even makes the strong statement that he always carries in his body the *nekrōsis tou Iēsou,* the "putting to death of Jesus" (2 Cor. 4:10), and once he speaks of the *stigmata tou Iēsou* (Gal. 6:17), the wounds incurred from mistreatments which he bears, as constant reminders that what he stands for is the truth.

Actually there is no level of tradition in the NT which is without this theme. For the epistles see Jas. 1:2; 1 Pet. 1:6f.; 2:21–23; 4:12–14; Heb. 12:2f., 5–11; for the Synoptics Matt. 5:10–12; 20–23 and the statements on cross-bearing (Mark 8:34–38 and parallels; Matt. 10:38; Luke 14:27; the reference is primarily to the participation in Christ's rejection by men); for John, see 12:24–26 and 16:33; for Acts, 4:23–30; 5:41; 7:54–60, and *passim.*

It is important to note the function of the resurrection within this *theologia crucis.* Sometimes it functions in the form of a reference to Christ's victory (John 16:33), sometimes as a reminder of the victory which we already experience through the Spirit (Rom. 8:37), sometimes as the proof that suffering is evidence of being sons of God (Heb. 12:8; 1 Pet. 4:14), more often as a pointer to the resurrection to come as the final victory (Matt. 5:10–12; Rom. 8:17; Phil. 3:10; Heb. 12:2f.; 1 Pet. 4:13), and often also as a pointer to the blessing of perseverance and character which lies hidden in suffering (Rom. 5:3f.; Heb. 12:11; Jas. 1:2; 1 Pet. 1:7). Paul's perspective of the resurrection is still wider, especially in 2 Cor. 5, where he sees the evidence of the power of the resurrection on the one hand in his own repeated rescues and on the other hand in the benefits which his conformity to the way of Christ have for the upbuilding of the church and the advancement of the gospel.

In the history of the church, these NT passages have often been meaningful only in periods of persecution. In addition, the literature on martyrs and saints is to be mentioned. In the *Martyrdom of Polycarp* (from the year 156) the martyrs are called "disciples and followers of the Lord" "of whom we too may become participants and fellow-disciples" (17). In this literature, the emphasis on conformity with Christ has resulted in great uniformity and often pushed aside individuality; see e.g. C. W. Mönnich, *Reidans der heiligen* (1962).

In theology this theme has remained underdeveloped; as a rule theology happens to be a concern of established churches and settled people! But Roman Catholic asceticism and martyrology have at least kept the memory of this theme alive. For Protestant theology see Calvin, *Inst* III,viii: "Bearing the cross," and Barth, *CD* IV,2, par. 66,6: "The Majesty of the Cross"; in both, however, there is a blurring of the lines between this and common suffering, and in Calvin the latter even displaces the uniquely Christian suffering. In our judgment, the best treatment of this theme is in Barth *CD* IV,3, par. 71,5 under the heading "The Christian in the Oppression." More than many others, Kierkegaard has been a witness to this unique suffering, in his own person as well as intellectually, especially in his conflict with Bishop Martensen. See especially the nine issues of *The Moment* (1855). That this suffering was caused by the established church is something that makes one stop and think.

50. STRUGGLE, PROGRESS, AND PERSEVERANCE

IN THE PRECEDING PARAGRAPHS of this chapter we have tried to capture in words the moments of the process of renewal. We could group them around three centers: condemnation–justification–sanctification, repentance–faith–freedom–love, or despair–relaxation–effort. But we are not yet ready to close the discussion. For it so happens that when we look over the whole theme once more, questions arise which we cannot avoid: is this indeed a "process," and if so in what sense? Is there progress in it, so that man would thus be perfectible? But what then must we think of sin that remains in us? Is it perhaps possible to remain stationary? Is backsliding or falling away not also possible? But what then does it mean that the Spirit is in control of this process? Does that mean that there is genuine progress after all? Is that something visible, however? How can we be sure of our renewal? The centuries after the Reformation have extensively pondered these questions, more than we are inclined to do. We shall therefore be much briefer on these questions than is usually the case in the tradition of the Protestant study of the faith. But we do not ignore these questions, simply because that would mean that we would ignore ourselves. Our renewal does mean that we lose our egocentricity, but that implies also that we dare to look at ourselves again in the light of our relationship to God.

The tripartite division of the renewal, as presented above, agrees with the classical division of the Heidelberg Catechism: misery–deliverance–gratitude; see Q.

and A. 2, cf. Q. and A. 115. We repeat that this order is not meant to be chronological or psychological, but only logical, even as in the Heidelberg Catechism (as is evident from Q. and A. 1). This catechism is constructed entirely from the standpoint of renewal. With that it marks the transition to a period of growing self-reflection, in philosophy (Descartes) and in the matter of piety (the mysticism arising in all the churches) as well as in theology. Ecclesiastically and theologically speaking, this period did not really come to an end, though, beginning with late 17th-century Pietism, it assumed a different form; up to and including 20th-century Existentialism, self-reflection remains characteristic of the Western spirit. In recent decades, the interest has shifted to society, politics, the development and future of mankind. How deep that interest is remains to be seen. But it does not look as if theologically the inner life of the believing subject will again be abstracted as happened in all sorts of controversial questions and publications from 1550–1750.

In Reformed theology, this strong interest in the process of personal renewal was greatly stimulated by the Synod and the Canons of Dort (1618–1619). A tradition arose which was preserved in particular by Scottish and Dutch theologians. Unfortunately, we still do not have a comprehensive theological-historical survey of this tradition. Good surveys are found in Bavinck, *GD* IV, pars. 49–52.

a. Struggle

We begin with the most salient problem, one which in no period can be shunted aside as of less importance: how must we picture the renewal relative to the sinfulness that remains a force in the life of believers? For we have to admit that renewal takes place in the face of enormous resistance and that this resistance exerts a determinative influence on the process of renewal, in fact so much so that this "process" takes on the character of a struggle. In paragraph 49, too, we noticed that renewal leads to a situation of conflict. There it concerned the conflict with the world which the believer sooner or later gets involved in, to a greater or lesser extent. Here it concerns the conflict the believer gets involved in, right from the start, with his own self. After all, renewal means becoming loose from one's own self, and thus—since that self does not disappear—an estrangement from that self, and consequently a kind of inner split in our life. The only remedy for that split is that we fight against the claims of that self in the power of our covenant partnership with God, and thus begin to do battle with ourselves. The character of that struggle is thus one of self-denial. Therefore this struggle can also be described as a dying, as in the classical term *mortificatio* (literally: putting to death). Yet this term describes no more than half of the truth. For this self-denial happens in the power of the Spirit, who transforms and renews our "self" in the way of relaxation and security, freedom and love, and carries this out precisely in self-denial. Consequently, what looks like dying from the one angle is from the other a renewal of life and growth, or as the classical term puts it, a quickening (*vivificatio*). Self-denial through the Spirit is the opposite of self-destruction—it is a crossing of the boundaries which we, in our egotism and addiction to the world, have imposed upon ourselves. Self-denial is thus in reality self-enlargement—we become ourselves again as God wanted us to be in the first place.

In this life this is a never ending struggle. To the last moment it remains undecided. For we are part of a world and participate in a history in which the powers of God have not yet overcome. The renewal does not get beyond a struggle with an inconclusive end. So this struggle is the glaring sign of the unsavedness of our existence. At the same time, however, this struggle signifies that God does not acquiesce in our estrangement from him. This conflict-causing indwelling of the Spirit is, in the light of the way of the new man, Christ, on whom we may always fall back, the guarantee of the coming great renewal and the proof that that renewal is being worked out. The Spirit, far from ending the struggle in our life, causes it to begin. For this life it remains true: "righteous and a sinner at the same time" (*simul iustus et peccator*); what no longer applies is nevertheless still there; and what already applies has not yet fully come.

The result is the formation of a peculiar type of person. The renewal creates no harmonious man, but disturbs a natural harmony if that existed before. One becomes a citizen of two worlds, and therefore a split person. This split implies no equilibrium, and certainly no schizophrenia. It indicates a conflict situation, in which man alternately stands on either side, yet with the scales always tipping over to the side of the new. For the peace on the other side has been disturbed for good, and on this side a peace is always given that passes all understanding.

As regards this aspect of the faith, too, Paul more than anyone else guides our thinking. All his admonitions to persevere in the faith, to put to death the old man, etc., implicitly presuppose struggle. He speaks explicitly about it especially in Rom. 6:12–15; 8:12–14; Gal. 5:17–26; Eph. 4:22–24; Col. 3:9. One could conceivably also include Eph. 6:10–17, although there this theme blends with that of par. 49. Paul makes considerable use of a dual symbolism: the "old man" versus the "new," our still-being-in-Adam and our already-being-in-Christ; and "flesh" versus "spirit" (*sarx* versus *pneuma*). In Paul these terms, directly in contrast to the then current meaning, signify our sinful, alienated-from-God existence versus that which is worked in us by the renewing power of the Spirit. Sometimes Paul uses very triumphant language, and then again the hard struggle comes through clearly; he has "the double viewpoint of battling on the basis of victory and of gaining the victory on the basis of the battle" (H. Ridderbos, *Paul*, p. 267).

Usually, especially Rom. 7 is cited as the most poignant articulation of this struggle. Paul speaks here, however, in terms of salvation history (see p. 265). Ridderbos therefore concludes that in principle Rom. 7 does not recur in the renewed life, only incidentally (p. 270). But if precisely as believers we participate in the way of Israel depicted there, we no longer need such a distinction; see G. C. Berkouwer, *The Church* (E.T. 1976), pp. 347–351.

We already touched on the twin concepts *mortificatio–vivificatio* in par. 49. Calvin used it in connection with sanctification to characterize the conflict within renewed man himself; see *Inst* III,iii,3, where he states, in a veiled polemic against the Lutherans and especially Melanchthon, who applied the terms to repentance and the consolation in justification, that the twin concepts mean "rather, the desire to live in a holy and devoted manner, a desire arising from rebirth; as if it were said that man dies to himself that he may begin to live to God." For a more complete description of these words in Calvin, see *Inst* III,iii,8 which uses bold language such as: "we are not conformed to the fear of God and do not learn the rudiments of piety, unless we are violently slain by the sword of the Spirit and brought to nought." This usage has become widespread in the Reformed tradition through the Heidelberg Catechism, Lord's Day 33 (which connects it, however, with the Lutheran meaning). Apart from this usage, Calvin speaks at greater length about the aspect of struggle in III,iii,9ff. under the concept of repentance, and in III,vii under that of self-denial. Barth (*CD* IV,2, par. 66,4: "The Awakening to Conversion"), while agreeing with Calvin's use of the words, criticized him for not sufficiently recognizing the substance and greater power of vivification in comparison with the power of mortification (pp. 574–576).

The formulation *simul iustus et peccator* and its variations comes from Luther and is first found in his *Lectures on Romans* (1515–1516), *inter alia* at 4:7; 7:25, and 12:2. Taken in conjunction with other statements from Luther the formula could be read in a quietistic and antinomian sense, as if it wants to say that man happens to be unchangeable, always remains sinful, and is only righteous in his God-given imputation. Hence Roman Catholic theology for centuries fiercely rejected this formula; it is accustomed to speak much more optimistically about the struggle of renewal, owing to a weaker view of sin and a great confidence in the sacramental powers of grace and the cooperation of man's free will. Protestant theology has often viewed this formula in terms of a static equilibrium or a dialectic state of suspension, which led to somewhat of an extenuation of sin. Barth (*CD* IV,2, pp. 570–577) has emphatically pointed out that it is a battle formula and that it expresses a "falling-out" (*Auseinandersetzung);* the *peccator* is the *terminus a quo.* That is also the spirit in which the newest Roman Catholic theology has now accepted the formula (as a weapon against traditional triumphalism); see H. J. Kouwenhoven, *Simul iustus et peccator in de nieuwe rooms-katholiek theologie* (1969) and Berkouwer, *The Church,* pp. 345–347. Rightly understood, this formula is simultaneously confession of guilt and of grace: in the courage of grace, man dares to admit his guilt and to do battle against himself.

b. Progress

The conflict in which man is involved as he strives for conformity with the image of Christ seems to result in an impasse. The struggle is so fierce that it may seem to impede the progress. It is a real question whether in these circumstances it is warranted to speak of progress, let alone of improvement. One could, of course, console himself with the fact that the believer's acquittal in the judgment of God remains inviolable amid all the ups and downs of his own spiritual life. But the reflection on the faith cannot be content with that; for through the pardon God wants to open for us a new way on which we may and must walk to his goal. The same Paul who speaks so much about struggle knows also of a growing, a going forward, a pressing on, a straining toward what lies ahead, a growing stronger. Some passages in the New Testament even seem to say that in this life conformity with Christ lies within the believer's reach.

Struggle and progress apparently do not exclude but include each other. The progress happens amid the struggle, and apparently the struggle does not lead to stagnation, but to steady progress. The question arises, how are we to conceive of this progress in this conflict situation? In our opinion, we are to look in four directions. (1) Only in the brokenness of the conflict does the believer really get to know himself in his opposition against God; so long as that opposition remains unchallenged, it may seem to lie dormant and can easily be underestimated; the struggle is thus an advancing in self-knowledge. (2) Consequently the struggle also implies progress in living from the acquittal; the better we get to know ourselves, the less we expect from ourselves, and the more we fall back on God's grace as the decisive foundation of our life. (3) But precisely this growing relaxation inspires to fresh and greater efforts, making the struggle more intense. (4) And coupled with that, the conflict spreads to more and more areas of our life; for all the time we discover new areas of conduct and thought which so far were not yet involved in the process of renewal and where new opportunities await us, for example, in the use of our charismata for the upbuilding of the church, in respect to our political insights, in fresh conciliatory approaches to our enemies, in changes in how we spend our income, in the struggle against discriminatory practices and situations.

Paul speaks about progress in the Christian life in such a way that rightly the question is often being asked whether he may have thought it possible to achieve perfection already in this earthly life; see beside the lengthy passage Rom. 6:1–8:17 also 2 Cor. 7:1; 9:8; 10:15; Eph. 5:27; Phil. 1:10; 1 Thess. 5:23; 2 Thess. 1:3. Of particular significance in this respect is Phil. 3:9–16, where it is very clear that perfection consists in living radically from imputed righteousness (v. 9), and that Paul knows that he has not yet reached this radical limit (v. 12), so that his life moves between the poles of having-been-taken-hold-of and taking-hold-of himself (12f., 16). In other writers as well this progress is assumed as a normal aspect of the Christian life (e.g. John 15:6; 2 Pet. 3:18). A special problem is posed by the first epistle of John, which on the one hand speaks of sin as something from which we are never free (1:5–10) and on the other hand of the sinlessness of the believer (3:4–10); see on this M. de Jonge, *De brieven van Johannes* (1968), pp. 155–159, who sees the "logical contradiction" as "a way to express life 'between the times', life between the two 'revelations' of Jesus Christ" (p. 158), determined also by the conflict with Gnosticism. Apparently, according to Paul and John, the possibility of a life completely controlled by Christ is what provides the justification and inspiration for a constant struggle against sin.

In the history of the church, this tension out of which Paul and John write has as a rule been too much to keep up for long. Generally, theology and pastoral work in the established churches adapted themselves to the lower spiritual level of the average member. Even so, the Roman Catholic Church with its emphasis on the so-called "saints" has tried to impress on its members the possibility and importance of making progress (even though according to Protestant feelings this was too much misunderstood as meritorious self-sanctification). In Protestantism, Calvin stands out as he emphasizes not only the struggle but also the progress that can be made. "*Magis ac magis*" (more and more) is a favorite expression with him. See e.g. the strong ending of *Inst* III,vi ("The life of the Christian man"), where he makes statements like: ". . . with continuous effort striving toward this end: that we may surpass ourselves in goodness until we attain to goodness itself" (vi,5). The nature of the progress which is possible and commanded here is succinctly and eminently articulated in the Heidelberg Catechism in Answer 115 (which summarizes three of the four progress aspects we have mentioned). At the same time Answer 114 states that "in this life even the holiest have only a small beginning of this obedience." According to H. Ridderbos (*Paul,* pp. 271f.), this is clearly below Paul's expectations of the new life. Yet Ridderbos' own conclusion: "He [Paul] speaks of a *posse non peccare,* not of a *non peccare* and still less of *non posse peccare* as the picture of the Christian life" (p. 272) does not seem to do justice to Paul's clear language. Only various kinds of free churches and sects, in the more modern era beginning with the Baptists, have really begun to take this emphasis in Paul seriously; we think especially of John Wesley; see p. 431 and the literature cited there. As the national churches are more and more becoming voluntary churches, they will increasingly be confronted with the question how to understand and how to promote this growth and progress of the spiritual life, without it leading to work-righteousness and a grim determination to succeed.

The fact that the Christian life is indeed a matter of goal and an advancing towards it, is bound to bring up the question concerning the relation between sanctification and salvation. Can we still maintain that it is totally and solely the acquittal by which we are adopted as God's children? Is that adoption not also partly dependent on, to say the least, how well our relaxation inspires us to greater efforts? But may we then still say that we are saved by grace alone? Must not we then at least cooperate with grace?

Indeed, something like that should be said. One has to be very precise here, however. Therefore a word like "cooperate" is no more than just beside the point. Our works add nothing to the accomplished grace on which we depend in faith. We do not cooperate with grace, but faith makes grace effective; the presence of grace is seen in its effects. Only he who by faith loses the grim determination to "works" and "sanctification" can do something that gives fruitfulness and progress to his life with God and the neighbor. That often happens in the face of so much struggle against his own "self" that the believer notices primarily his own failures in it, while giving thanks to God for the power of his grace for whatever little he may detect by way of progress and fruit. Faith involves its own activity, but it can never rest in its effects. God's grace for us far surpasses its own effects. We may always fall back on that. One who does that, not carelessly (that cannot and may not be done), but in faith, wants nothing else than that this falling-back realizes itself in his life as progress.

The same Paul who radically asserts that we are not justified by works but by faith, can also say that in God's judgment we will be judged according to our works; see Rom. 2:9–11; 1 Cor. 3:13; 4:5; 2 Cor. 5:10; Gal. 6:7–9; Col. 3:23f. (This same line is found in Matthew's gospel; see 12:36f.; 16:27; 25:31–46). Yet he says nowhere that we are justified by our works. 1 Cor. 3:10–15 shows how Paul conceives of the relationship: if faith produces mainly worthless fruits, man receives no "reward" (elsewhere: "praise"), though he himself is being saved, though only as one escaping through flames (v. 15). Very likely the intentionally strange formulation in Eph. 2:8–10 is also meant to create a distance between faith and works: the believer puts on the works as a garment already made for him. See also 1 Cor. 4:5 and Phil. 1:11. Cf. Stalder, *Das Werk des Geistes in der Heiligung bei Paulus*, pp. 455–469.

The Reformation wrestled intensely with this problem; as a matter of fact, it was forced to it by Roman Catholic polemics which sought to undermine the *sola fide* by appealing to the necessity of good works. Its first answer was that, though only faith justifies, such a faith never remains alone. We can understand Melanchthon's fear in the *Apology* II and III, where he strictly separates faith and works to eliminate from faith all grim determination, work-righteousness, and the terrors of conscience. Calvin did not seek separation, but combination; his solution of the problem is found especially in *Inst* III,xvii,8–10, where he states "that man is so justified by faith that not only is he himself righteous but his works are also accounted righteous above their worth" (9). In his spirit the Belgic Confession (1561) says in art. 24: "In the meantime we do not deny that God rewards good works, but it is through his grace that he crowns his gifts." In this train of thought there is something that does not seem right, and which is not found in Paul. The apostle knows of genuine good works, really done by people themselves; though not decisive in life's ultimate crisis, they are the normal blossom of a life of faith. In our own formulation we have been guided more by Paul (1 Cor. 3:10–15) than by the Reformers.

But the other side of this is that faith cannot be indifferent about its effectiveness in life. For with that effectiveness the believer desires to praise God, to serve the neighbor and, in the end, would also like to find in it for himself some confirmation of the genuineness of his faith. Here we face the question concerning the ascertainability and the ascertainable marks of faith and its progress. On pp. 437–438 we pointed in passing to the double relationship of faith and experience: faith contradicts experience in order that it may then realize itself in experience. The fruits of faith are such that they can be visible to the believer himself and to the outside world. Otherwise faith would be ineffective, unreal. That the fruits are to be visible to the outside cannot very well be contradicted. But should the believer himself be able to see them? It depends. Hopefully, many of these expressions of the faith are spontaneous or unintentional; as such they are not noticed by the believer himself. There are also other expressions, those which come only after an inner struggle and hard decisions; as concerns these, the believer is often gratefully surprised about the grace that overcame his stubborn "self." One who is a total stranger to such experiences may well ask himself whether he *act*-ually believes. But in order to have such an actual faith he should radically turn his back upon himself and turn to the message of adoption. For faith does not arise from and is not built on experience. We can and may, however, sometimes encourage each other and ourselves with our experience, or admonish for the lack of it; nothing more and nothing less. Our psychical and social experiences are as such always ambiguous: they can easily be explained differently (and so explained away). And progress and growth (in other words, an accumulation and coherence of experiences) are even empirically verifiable. In the midst of the struggle we may be confident, however, that God himself will make sure there is progress. But if there should be no experience at all of security and effort, freedom and love, struggle and victory, this may be a hint that faith itself is absent. Therefore in religious life there is at least a place for the kind of self-examination that inquires concerning the presence or absence of faith. Moreover, as soon as we are really concerned whether we believe, we believe already.

For "experience" see also par. 10. Here we deal with the third meaning mentioned there. According to the NT the renewal process is full of empirical aspects. The tree is known by its fruits (Matt. 7:15–20) and the lamp is put on a stand so that its light is visible to all, "that they may see your good works and give glory to your Father who is in heaven" (Matt. 5:14–16). But does this also pertain to the believer himself? Passages like 1 John 2:3; 3:14 and 24 as well as Heb. 10:32–34 and 2 Pet. 1:10 do indeed suggest that the presence of certain moral qualities and deeds, or their absence, can become a meaningful sign to the person concerned.

Reformed Protestantism, which had a special interest in this matter, also on account of the question concerning the marks of election, referred to this self-examination as *syllogismus practicus;* by that is meant: a syllogism, an argumentation which bases the genuineness of the faith on the experience of our obedience. The classical articulation of it is given in the Heidelberg Catechism, which, in Answer 86, mentions as one of the motivations for good works: "that each of us may be assured in himself of his faith by the fruits thereof"—with an appeal to 2 Pet. 1:10; Matt. 7:17; Gal. 5:6, 22f. What is stated here in one sentence, Calvin discusses very carefully in *Inst* III,xiv, 18–20, where he speaks of works as in some way evidencing the presence of grace, "so far, that is, as these are testimonies of God dwelling and ruling in us." Therefore, "we do not forbid him [the Christian man] from undergirding and strengthening this faith by signs of the divine benevolence toward him" (18), provided these signs always drive us to the grace that exceeds these signs. Notwithstanding this definite restriction, Max Weber in his famous study *The Protestant Ethic and the Spirit of Capitalism* (E.T. 1930) promulgates the thesis that the rise of capitalism is due to the fact that the Calvinist regards his success in business and industry as a sign of God's election and favor. For that he cannot appeal to Calvin for support, but can only go as far back as Richard Baxter and English Puritanism in the second half of the 17th century. For a more nuanced view see R. H. Tawney, *Religion and the Rise of Capitalism* (1926). The *syllogismus practicus* has functioned no more than marginally in classical Reformed theology.

It was soon displaced by what, analogically, we would call the *syllogismus mysticus*. In the 17th century, also in theology, the inner religious life of the individual believer became a matter of great interest. For proof of the genuineness of faith one began to look especially to inner feelings and experiences. The classical formulation of the *syllogismus mysticus* is found in the Canons of Dort (1619), where it is said that the elect attain the assurance of their salvation (election) "by observing in themselves with a spiritual joy and holy pleasure the infallible fruits of election pointed out in the Word of God—such as, a true faith in Christ, filial fear, a godly sorrow for sin, a hungering and thirsting after righteousness, etc." (I,12), so that "they are enabled to believe with the heart and to love their Savior" (III–IV,13). To support this argument an (invalid) appeal is made to 2 Cor. 13:5. This led in the 17th and 18th centuries, especially in the Dutch "Further Reformation," as well as in other groups up to the present, to a continuous self-examination *(Dauerreflexion)*, in which the inner experience with its "marks" is put central. The facts are there to prove that assurance of salvation is not obtained along this way; experience offers no assurance, for it can only be had if we seek it in something that transcends experience. Theologically and pastorally the *syllogismus mysticus* turns out to be a dead-end road, for on that road one loses precisely what one seeks to find (and what the Reformation sought in the Word), namely the assurance of salvation. See J. G. Woelderink, *De gevaren der doperse geestes stroming* (1941). Particularly Kohlbrugge strongly opposed this experiential concentration on the believer's inner life; in his *Vragen en antwoorden tot opheldering en bevestiging van de Heid. Cat.* (n.d.), he asks, pointing to the "miserable marks" the believer finds in himself, "Which little word is your final ground when you don't seem to find one mark of genuine grace in yourself any more and you are deeply depressed on account of it?", and he follows with the answer: "The little word 'yet'."

c. Perseverance

The more the believer, prompted by his security in God, ventures the life of new obedience, the more he needs, as he struggles along, the certainty that God's faithfulness and Christ's substitution will carry him through. Justification tells us that we stand on an unshakable foundation on which we can always fall back. But who guarantees that we, as we struggle and stumble along, and even suffer defeats, will not slide off this foundation? The more we fight, the more we sense fearfully how great the resistance in our heart is to surrender ourselves to God and to remain faithful in the struggle. Then the question concerning certainty and security arises anew; this time not as a question regarding the foundation but one that concerns the horizon. The question is not: am I really a sinner received in grace? but: will this adoption be permanent and show its effects in my life? Who can guarantee that? The question is also: who, without such a certainty, can avoid succumbing to despair and keep up the courage to continue to fight?

This confronts us with the doctrine which is known in church history as *the perseverance of the saints*. It is a doctrine that articulates a fundamental insight. Paul, whose Epistle to the Romans is entirely devoted to the renewal of man, starts with justification (chs. 1–5), speaks next about struggle and progress (chs. 6–8), and concludes the train of thought of the first half of his epistle by affirming his conviction that believers will persevere and overcome (8:28–39). That could not be otherwise. Our wavering faithfulness is upheld on all sides by God's unwavering faithfulness. That faithfulness is not dependent on our faith; instead, our faith depends on that faithfulness of God. "For I am sure that nothing will be able to separate us from the love of God in Christ Jesus our Lord" (Romans 8:39).

The believer may and dares to believe that he will persevere in that faith and that nothing will snatch him out of God's hand. Nevertheless, here again we come across what we have noticed so often in questions about the faith, namely that its systematic reflection poses great intellectual problems. We cannot imagine that a believer would doubt his perseverance, on the mistaken assumption that ultimately it would be dependent on him; in that case ultimately all of salvation would be dependent on him, and that would mean that it is no longer a matter of saving grace freely given. Yet we cannot imagine either that a believer would dare to assert with a quiet and unruffled confidence that he will lifelong persevere in the faith; such an assertion would border on recklessness and be as much at variance with the faith as the fear that one will not make it. The same Paul who wrote Romans 8 issues many exhortations to struggle on, lest we lose the victory and should find ourselves disqualified in the end.

One who intellectually detaches himself from the faith (a danger particularly to the student of theology) feels himself compelled to a choice in which either God guarantees the faith and to that end manipulates man, or man, on account of the decisive character of his cooperation, is totally dependent on the power and permanence of his own faith. God and man are not locked in a competitive struggle, however, and do not so limit each other. Instead, they meet each other in a covenant in which God elicits our responsibility and cooperation and at the same time helps us in our weaknesses. His faithfulness also consists in the fact that he creates and seeks our faithfulness and realizes his faithfulness in and through our faithfulness and so causes it to triumph. We do not persevere, but he perseveres, by constantly calling us, disturbing us, inspiring us. So we learn to persevere and receive the assurance that "he who began a good work in you will bring it to completion at the day of Jesus Christ" (Philippians 1:6).

In the Bible, especially in the NT, we regularly find this witness of certainty and perseverance, not as the manifestation of human steadfastness but of divine faithfulness. In the discussion of the perseverance of the saints, its defenders always pointed to Luke 22:32; John 6:37, 40; 10:27; Rom. 8:29f., 34, 39; Phil. 1:6; 1 John 2:19 and 3:9, and to the Johannine concept of "remain" *(menein).* Those who were opposed pointed, however, to all those passages in which believers are warned against a possible falling away or which presuppose such a possibility, such as Ezek. 18:24; Rom. 11:20; 1 Cor. 9:27; 10:12; 2 Cor. 13:5ff.; Gal. 5:4; Heb. 6:4–8; 10:26–31; 2 Pet. 2:18–22. Other examples are apostate Christians like Alexander and Hymenaeus, and Demas (1 Tim. 1:20; 2 Tim. 4:10; cf. 1 Tim. 4:1). David's and Peter's deep fall also come up in this respect; but their life could also be used as an argument by the supporters of the doctrine of perseverance.

Augustine, a thinker with a passionate concern for God's work of renewal in man, dealt specifically with perseverance in *De dono perseverantiae* (429). His starting-point was that though a believer could lapse *totaliter,* he could not lapse *finaliter.* In a fine way of getting at the subject, he dealt with perseverance first of all as the presupposition of the six petitions of the Lord's Prayer (chs. 2–7).

But it was not until the Reformation that these questions received broad and thorough attention. Soon significant differences announced themselves. The Lutherans put the main emphasis on the assurance implicit in justification, in comparison with which the struggle in sanctification remained in the shadows; consequently, they felt far less the need for the assurance afforded by the doctrine of perseverance. By contrast Bucer, emphasizing much more the progress in the renewal process, wrote of perseverance as based on the "divine seed" which the Holy Spirit had put in believers already at their birth as a religious potential (cf. 1 John 3:9). Calvin dissented; he did not believe in such an innate goodness; the elect "do not differ at all from others except that they are protected by God's special mercy from rushing headlong into the final ruin of death" (*Inst* III,xxiv,10). He wrote a balanced, careful, and pastoral presentation of perseverance (esp. III,ii,15–28 and 38f. and III,xxiv,6f.), in which he tried to provide a basis for certainty *(certitudo)* while warning against false security *(securitas).*

Nevertheless, he could not prevent the rise, since Beza, of a rationalistic systematization. Hence the Remonstrants could doubt perseverance and eventually even deny it; in the alternative they proposed they came close to the Roman Catholic dialectic of cooperation plus "assistance of divine grace." The Synod of Dort (1619), (mainly) by going back to Calvin's position, stood in a strong position against this dubious Arminian standpoint. See J. N. Bakhuizen van den Brink, *De Nederlandse belijdenisgeschriften* (2nd ed. 1976), ch. 5 of the Canons (pp. 266–277), the fifth point of the Remonstrants (p. 289) and the "Views of the Remonstrants concerning Article Five," esp. points 4 and 8 (p. 293).

Pastoral concerns, too, played a role in the differences. The Lutherans and the Remonstrants feared that the doctrine of perseverance would make people careless and indifferent. Calvin sought to comfort the fearful with it—a comfort which according to the Lutherans was fully offered in the doctrine of justification. A fine dogma-historical and dogmatic discussion of this theme, in the spirit of Calvin, is offered by G. C. Berkouwer in *Faith and Perseverance* (E.T. 1958) and by J. Moltmann in *Prädestination und Perseveranz* (1961). In both one can also read about the controversy since 1561 between the Lutheran Marbach and the Reformed Zanchius, which led to a sharper demarcation of the positions. Berkouwer contends that perseverance is a confession of *faith,* one that is possible only through listening to the Scriptural admonitions and the contemplation of one's own ups and downs. "Apart from faith nothing can be said here, but all thought will entangle itself in contradiction" (p. 106).

This is the place to say something about the concept of the *ordo salutis* as this is current in Reformed dogmatics. On the basis of Rom. 8:29f. (sometimes Acts 26:17f. is cited as well), attempts were made to introduce a kind of sequence in the renewal process, e.g. faith–justification–calling–illumination–regeneration–mystical union–renewal (so S pars. 41–48), or calling–justification–sanctification–perseverance (so Bavinck, *GD* IV). That easily led to "categorization," thereby turning the way of salvation into a psychological process. Already the aorists used by Paul, even for designating *future* "phases" (so: *edoxasen*), prove that that was not what he had in mind, but that his concern was the unity of the aspects in the process of renewal as these exist in God's eternal gracious purpose for man. But precisely that unity means that in the study of the faith various aspects must be distinguished. Aspects are logical distinctions; they do not suggest a chronological sequence, let alone a psychologically observable evolutionary process. Yet renewal means participation in a way of God through history, and such a way has at least a logical before and after. Barth, looking to Hollaz, is too negative on this point (*CD* IV,3, pp. 505–507); his volumes IV,1–3 prove, however, that he too needs a kind of logical order. Misuse should warn us, but it does not abolish its use. A. König, *Heil en heilsweg* (1983), offers a correction and renewal as well.

Meanwhile in our study of the concept of perseverance we have come in the vicinity of another concept closely tied in with it, one which through the centuries has received much theological attention, namely election. It is correct to say that what is called "perseverance" from man's perspective, is from God's point of view "election." But this is also a term with which we cross the boundaries of the renewal process and its problematic. For "election" is not only the final resting place of the heart in the ups and downs of the spiritual struggle, it is also the basic word, which is as comprehensive as salvation itself because it characterizes the totality of God's dealing with his people, his church, his world. Everywhere we meet a God who for and often against man takes the initiative to establish a saving fellowship and carries it through despite our opposition and apathy. He supports us, despite ourselves. That is how we came to know him on the way of Israel, in the life of Jesus, in the working of the Spirit, in the upbuilding of the church, and as he calls, blesses, and equips people. And we shall get to know him fully when, despite all our resistance, he makes all things new.

Our favorite term to designate God's fellowship with us has been "covenant." But we have also regularly pointed out that this differs from a human covenant in which the two partners are equal. That difference is expressed in the word "election." We are elected to this strange covenant in which the One not only calls the other, challenges and involves him, but also precedes, supports, and cares for him, because the Faithfulness of the One is ultimately not dependent on the faithfulness or unfaithfulness of the other.

This makes it understandable that there are people for whom election is the center and foundation of their faith and their reflection on the faith. But in this study of the faith we do not follow them. The reason is that the confession of election is rooted in a covenant fellowship which is not comprehensively characterized by the word "election." For the word only states what God does. It expresses his unilateral initiative by which he makes specific people and groups the objects of his grace and calling. In election, Israel, the church, or man is only object. In the covenant, however, man is given a subjective standing. The covenant also involves man in his responsibility, his guilt, his conversion, his obedience. All that is not contained in the word "election." Yet it is only the person who knows of all that and who is burdened by his own failures as a covenant partner, who can and may fall back on the one-sided Faithfulness by which he knows himself to be upheld. Election is the first word in God's activity and the last in the confession of believers. It marks the horizon which surrounds and makes the covenant arena possible.

Lifting the word out of the covenant context from which it arises causes accidents, as is abundantly proven in church history. When election is made into an isolated subject, is one-sidedly applied to the individual and his eternal destiny, and no longer is confessed but intellectually analyzed, it evokes a series of questions that are absolutely unanswerable, because they are out of (the covenant) order; questions such as: Why, years ago, was only Israel chosen? Why is Christ our savior and not some other savior figure? Why is the church sometimes spread all over the world and then again a diminishing minority? Why have many never heard the gospel? Why do some hearers believe and many others do not? With those questions we no longer take our stand on this side of the covenant fellowship, but on the side of God and eternity. That is not our side; therefore we are unable to ask the right questions and receive no answers. The penalty is a fatal choice: *either* we have to believe in a god who is arbitrary and fickle, *or* in a god who is powerless and thus totally dependent on the initiative of man himself.

The mystery of election, far from detracting from whatever is to be said about the doings and the failures of the human covenant partner (free will, resistance, conversion, obedience), presupposes and establishes it. How? That we do not know; we are not God and therefore do not know how it is possible that his divine sovereignty does not detract from our human freedom, but instead evokes it and makes it possible. We do not fathom *how* it can be done, but experience and confess *that* it happens.

Purposely we discuss the word "election" at the end of this paragraph which is full of our human responsibility, a responsibility which again and again proves too much for our limited strength. What keeps us from despairing is the certainty that we persevere because God in his election perseveres with us. But it is to be remembered that this comfort is only for those who keep struggling.

For an extensive survey of the concept and the words for "election" in the Bible see *TDNT* IV, *s.v. legō (eklegomai, eklogē, eklektos)*. In the OT the concept is in turn applied to the people of Israel, the patriarchs, kings, priests, the remnant, the servant of the Lord. Here the focus is on election to the service of God and in him to the people, the neighbor, and the world, In the NT the concept is in turn applied to Christ, the apostles, sinners and outcasts, the church, and the individual. Here the main focus is election unto sons of God and to eternal salvation (which includes election to service; cf. Eph. 1:12; 1 Pet. 2:9). We mentioned already how Paul in Rom. 1–8 structures the process of renewal, culminating in the perseverance of the saints. In integral relation to it Paul mentions election (8:28–30), which then in 9–11 is extended beyond the boundaries of the church and the individual and applied to Israel and the nations of the world.

As a fundamental term election can come up for discussion with a variety of subjects: in connection with God, his counsel and good pleasure; in connection with sin which makes it impossible for us to save ourselves; in connection with Christ, the chosen one, in whom we are chosen; in connection with the Spirit who alone can create faith; in connection with the chosen church, and in connection with the individual who within the church ventures to believe in his personal election. Always, however, election stands in the context of doxology and gratitude.

Not until Augustine did election become a permanent theme in the history of the church. In his thought this doctrine is closely interwoven with the doctrine of original sin and man's inability to save himself. It is noteworthy, too, that the above-mentioned *De dono perseverantiae* forms the second half of a tract of which the first half is entitled *De praedestinatione sanctorum* (428). The history of the doctrine of predestination is described in many handbooks and monographs. Here we mention only some of the highlights. Luther, who in his *On the Bondage of the Will* challenged Erasmus, boldly presented predestination from the perspective of God's total sovereignty as this is implied in his existence. But later he did not repeat those thoughts. In Lutheranism, predestination became of secondary importance; it did not really need the doctrine for the same reason that it could virtually do without the doctrine of perseverance. Calvin and Calvinism moved in an opposite direction. Initially the doctrine was not much emphasized; in the first edition of the *Inst* (1536) and in the Catechism of Geneva (1542), it is only incidentally mentioned in connection with the doctrine of the church (viewing the church, in Augustinian fashion, as the *numerus praedestinorum*). In the final edition of the *Inst* (1559) it was taken up as the conclusion of the renewal process described in III (xxi–xxiv), now much more in detail and with a polemic thrust. Next to beautiful pastoral passages (for Calvin predestination was on the one hand a humiliation, on the other a comfort), we come across these sentences: "... since election itself could not stand except as set over against reprobation ... those whom God passes over, he condemns.... From this it follows that God's secret plan is the cause of hardening" (xxiii,1). So election threatens to become an abstract principle and God an arbitrary God; which leads Calvin, convinced of his faithfulness to Scripture at this point, to make the painful statement: "The decree is dreadful indeed, I confess" (xxiii,7).

At this point emerges what is called Supralapsarianism, the doctrine according to which God already in his decree of creation, irrespective of sin, differentiated between elect and non-elect. Yet in the Heidelberg Catechism election is mentioned only in passing in connection with the church (Answer 54). And the Calvin-inspired Gallican Confession (1559) in art. 12, and the similar Belgic Confession (1561) in art. 12, did not follow Calvin's strict logic but the Infralapsarian line according to which God in his just judgment "leaves" people, because of their sin, in the perdition to which they have condemned themselves, while saving others from it solely out of grace. The Canons of Dort speak in similar vein about predestination (I,6). But there was something inconsistent about this whole approach. Hence Calvin's successor, Beza, developed the Supralapsarianistic doctrine, making it into a system (see H VII and VIII and particularly the scheme on pp. 147f.). This detaches predestination from the doctrine of renewal and puts it back in the doctrine of God, the *locus de decretis Dei.* Many regarded this consistent system as deterministic and rejected it. Remonstrantism countered it with the doctrine that God does not elect to faith, but on account of faith (*Remonstrance,* art. 1); however, the ultimate decision was again man's. Generally, Reformed Protestantism has opted for the Infralapsarian position and accepted its weaknesses and consequences along with it. Evaluating these controversies from our (ad)vantage point of historical distance, we must say again (as earlier on other points) that the feeling was that one had to choose between God or man as the subject, and that they lacked the theological categories with which to grasp the uniqueness of the biblical-covenantal (inter-subjective) mode of speaking.

That is not to say that it is easier for us to solve the problems they faced, only that we who view them from the perspective of different intellectual categories are better able to see how insoluble they are. We are more aware of our limitations in formulating theological concepts. Two worthwhile attempts at reformulating the classical problems and placing them in a biblical framework are: J. G. Woelderink, *De uitverkiezing* (1951), and G. C. Berkouwer, *Divine Election* (E.T. 1960). These publications stress the pastoral tenor of election and oppose an extrapolation that turns it into a deterministic doctrine. Another attempt (polemic in design) at restructuring the doctrine of election along more biblical lines is James Daane, *The Freedom of God: A Study of Election and Pulpit* (1973).

Going the other way, Barth has tried to break through the classical impasse in *CD* II,2. Handling election as a basic term, he treats it as comprehensively and Supralapsarianistically as Beza; with this great difference, that he knows of no double predestination, because election in Christ is solely and totally grace. "The doctrine of election is the sum of the Gospel" (opening sentence, p. 3). But then, too, many questions arise, particularly in reference to the force of man's "no"; is man's resistance still taken seriously here? Barth has not convinced us that we should make election the basic theological term. See also K. Schwarzwäller, *Das Gotteslob der angefochtenen Gemeinde* (1970), who, however, goes back to Luther's *On the Bondage of the Will*. An extensive and thoughtful discussion of the classical questions is offered by Weber, *Gl* II, pp. 458–562. Unlike him, however, we preferred in the preceding chapters to include wherever relevant the discussion of the elective dimension of all God's work, using a terminology that fitted the particular topics, and to place the explicit formulation of the concept of election at the end of our discussion of man's renewal (just as Calvin did in *Inst* III).

51. THE COMPLETED RENEWAL

WHATEVER PROGRESS AND IMPROVEMENT there be in the believer's life, the ultimate goal of the renewal—conformity with Christ—still lies far ahead of us. So far that it may seem unattainable to us, due to our own sin as well as to our being a part of a world that is subject to sin, misery, and death. In this respect, particularly death is the power robbing us of the hope that total renewal might be within our reach. And not just the death that comes prematurely, but every death. Precisely the "normal" death makes us aware that this life is meant to be finite. Indeed, until the very last moment man may develop more of his inherent potential, and in general it is true that each phase of man's life expresses in its own way the inexhaustible mystery of human nature, of what it means to be "man." That implies, however, that it is incorrect to speak of an evolution in man's personal life; what may be done is to speak of the kind of progress in which man continually makes discoveries, which, however, tend to displace earlier ones. When someone dies at an advanced age, we usually have a feeling that he had reached the end of his potentialities, or even—considering modern medicine—that he outlived his potentialities. That, however, is particularly the experience that goes with our modern "northern" civilization. Before our time and around us, millions of people, perhaps the majority, have died too early, because famine, illness, war, and natural catastrophes prematurely cut off their potentialities. But close to us, too, every day thousands are dying, whose life, due to circumstances beyond their control, illness or whatever, never came to real fruition. Further pondering this, one could ask whether anyone ever realizes more than a fraction of his potential. So death always evokes in us contradictory feelings; it is necessary and good for man as well as for the history in which he plays his role (how else would subsequent generations get their opportunity?), yet all the time it also cuts short possibilities by withholding from that man and his history the realization of these possibilities. Out of an indestructible longing for much more of a realization than this earthly life offers, mankind's hopes and beliefs have therefore through the ages reached beyond death. But is that anything more than wishful thinking?

That does not mean that we should not be able to obtain new insights about death by looking at it from the perspective of entirely different areas of human experience. Such is certainly the case when we look at death from the viewpoint of the Christian faith. We have been placed on a new way, the way of God's covenant faithfulness, a way that begins with Israel and on which we meet God as the God who with all his heart works for his lost mankind; who therefore in Jesus creates a new human existence which through death attains to resurrection and glorification, and who in Jesus is at work with his Spirit to involve people in that new way of life. That salvation is so great that it cannot possibly be realized within the confines of this present provisional and sinful existence which is now our lot. Therefore death cannot be the end of God's way. That becomes especially clear from the theme of this chapter: if the Spirit wins people for God and imparts to them in struggle and pushing forward a renewal which is no more than very fragmentary, then God will have to finish beyond death what he started here—or death would be more powerful than God and thus the real god and the ultimate, chill mystery of human life. On the ground of this alternative or, rather, in virtue of the encounter with this faithful God, the Christian believes in what is called, using traditional language for it, a "life after death." We believe in the completion of the renewal.

The Christian church is thus not basing this expectation on, for example, scientific discoveries or occult experiences. She does not even appeal to the widespread feeling that somehow this fragmentary human life must be able to come to full unfolding after death; as such that feeling could very well be "wishful thinking" or rash self-affirmation. Faith is not confirmed by this feeling; on the contrary, this feeling is confirmed by faith or, better stated, by God who is moved by our frustrations and our groaning (Romans 8:18–22).

Meanwhile, we are not to think of this hope in the face of death as a more or less rational inference, nor as a more or less irrational leap. It is not so that the believer on his way of renewal suddenly happens on the wall of death, and then, those cliffs notwithstanding, yet keeps believing in the completion of his renewal. Death is not a surprise event, but one which, in other forms, he has met more often already on the way of renewal. Death is included in the renewal process as a fermenting element. Four times so far we have come across it: (1) in Jesus' death as the necessary consequence of his obedience, a death which became the doorway to his exaltation (paragraph 35); (2) in our dying to ourselves as the counter side of our justification (paragraph 44); (3) in the dying we experience as we meet the hostility of the world (paragraph 49); and (4) in death in the form of our constant self-denial in the renewal process (paragraph 50). In all these forms of death a dissolution of man's self occurs, which will at the moment or in retrospect prove to be the counter side of liberation and renewal. Hence the believer knows that on the path God goes with his people, death and renewal do not exclude, but include each other. The natural death which comes to all men as a biological necessity does indeed seem entirely different from the preceding forms of death. But in Christ's death the two have been linked to each other. What is established between them is the link between creation and redemption. As concerns its provisional character, creation is meant to be dissolved. Man's created nature is such that he can only reach his destination through the dissolution of his selfhood. His sin is that he refuses this self-surrender and in self-affirmation resists death. So long as he does that, he is bound to experience death as a defeat; a defeat which, from the perspective of faith, is "the reward of sin." But through our participation in salvation we come to understand death in relation to its divinely designed purpose, namely not only as the confirmation of the provisionality of this earthly existence, but also as its abolition and therewith as the gateway to the perfection of this life.

It remains difficult to tie this faith in with our negative experience of dying and death. After all, the principle of life which integrated and animated the organism is completely gone. Man who was taken up into a covenant with God apparently or seemingly no longer exists. However, God, who entered into this relationship with man, is still there. With the "guarantee" of his Spirit he guarantees this relationship, and thereby that the person with whom he entered into covenant will persist in his new life. More we cannot and need not know on this point.

It is unusual to discuss already in this context what is called "personal eschatology"; normally this is done at the end, as an aspect of eschatology. The major concern is then the consummation of the world and of history, while the destiny of the individual after his death remains a more or less unrelated subject alongside of it. Then we get this question: Where "is" man in the interval between his death and the consummation of the world? When the question concerning an intermediate state is formulated like that, faith has no way of giving an answer, because we transpose our personal life to a strange context, lifting it out of its primary context: this earthly life in which our faith, hope, and love are no more than fragmentary, clamoring for perfection. Only out of this background can we in a following chapter speak meaningfully about the context of the world and history. As a reaction against an individualistic eschatology, we are today in danger of forgetting that the core of all expectation and the climax of God's covenantal saving work is the perfection of *persons.* The tendency not so long ago to relate the consummation primarily to the future structures of society remains below the level of the Christian expectation. It makes those who have died before "fertilizer on the fields of the future." See Hans Grass, "Das eschatologische Problem in der Gegenwart," in *Theologie und Kritik* (1969), esp. pp. 217–229. For the design which we have followed, see E. Flesseman-van Leer, *Geloven vandaag* (1972); see XV: "De toekomst van ons leven" (the future of our life).

In the course of the seventies (the "me"-generation) the interest within and outside the church shifted (again) to the personal "hereafter," now reinforced (scientifically based or not) by testimonies of reincarnation and by experiences of heaven of dying people in the twilight zone (so-called "extrasensory perception"). Because of that the modern idea that our self is totally dependent on the body, and therefore simultaneously dies with it, is not as firm as it used to be. That can be a gain. The fact is, however, that the testimonies of reincarnation point neither to a heightening of humanness and of communion with God, nor to greater insight into the human situation; they only satisfy the desire for repetition, the hope that this life can be perpetuated. However, since this life is unrepeatable, it is meant to be taken seriously. Therefore in our consciousness there is no recollection of earlier lives. "Extrasensory perceptions" often happen, but on this side of death. They point to an enlargement of the human consciousness, and no one knows how much truth there is in them relative to the hereafter. Both ways know of a "self," but hardly or not at all of a personal relationship with God. Theology has also become newly interested in what may await the individual after death. See J. Hick, *Death and Eternal Life* (1976), who tries to relate the Christian expectation of the future with that of Buddhism and Hinduism, by means of the idea that the individual is perfected only by surrendering to the vastness of the totality. He thinks of many vertical reincarnations of the one earthly life. For a summary see his *The Centre of Christianity* (2nd ed. 1977), ch. V. Beside this book with its universal-religious and speculative-synthetic method is H. Küng, *Eternal Life?* (E.T. 1984), who bases himself exclusively on the resurrection of Jesus and is much more reserved in his statements. But because he conceives of Jesus' resurrection as a form of immortally going-to-heaven, he detaches the personal expectation of the future from the history of mankind and its future in the Kingdom of God. (On this second aspect see par. 58.)

Inevitably the question arises why the OT says so little about man's personal future. One can refer to Isa. 26:19 and Dan. 12:2, and possibly to Ps. 16:9–11;

49:16; 73:25f. Very likely all those statements are from a rather late phase of OT covenant history. At first the individual person was only a part of the nation as a totality, and only gradually did he become detached from it. Until the NT era, the promises concerning the individual person remained a matter of dispute (Matt. 22:23; Acts 23:8); the decisive answer was only given in Jesus' resurrection (1 Cor. 15:12–22). The protracted silence of the OT serves as a warning not to think of the otherworldly perfection of the individual as God's sole purpose; he is also concerned about the present, society, the world and its structures.

However, anyone who after Jesus' resurrection would still regard the perfection of the person as *quantité négligeable* should note how in Matt. 22:29 and 33, 1 Cor. 15:34, and Phil. 1:6 this perfection is directly related to God's own reality and nature: the living God requires the living partner.

In the NT, the words *zōē* and *thanatos* have more than one level of meaning; see *TDNT, s.v.* Hence it is customary in the study of the faith to distinguish between spiritual, temporal, and eternal death. The distinctions we are required to make here are so much one subject in the Bible that in passages like Gen. 2:17 and 3:19 and Rom. 5:12–21 and 6:23, the biological normality of "ordinary" death is ignored. 1 Cor. 15:45–49 shows, however, that Paul was aware of a death that occurs apart from sin. But for sinful man's concrete life and death this is an abstraction devoid of essential significance; only for faith does it make sense to make such distinctions (the statement in Rom. 6:23 about death as the wages of sin is, in light of 6:15–22, to be regarded as a phase which by faith we have left behind us). For the NT see J. N. Sevenster, *Leven en dood in de evangeliën* (1952) and *Leven en dood in de brieven van Paulus* (1954).

A much-discussed problem is that of the continuity and discontinuity between our earthly life and the life that awaits us. Already Paul grappled with it and used the metaphor of the seed and the full-grown plant (1 Cor. 15:35–38). On account of God's faithfulness also in and beyond death, the continuity must have the first and the last word in our faith and in our thinking. It is indeed only by virtue of that faithfulness that he graciously bridges the rupture of death. For centuries, church and theology have sought the anthropological correlate of this faithfulness in a Platonically conceived "immortal soul," which naturally survives purely physical death. That is definitely not the view the NT takes; on the contrary, it asserts that only God possesses immortality (1 Tim. 6:16) and that in the resurrection we will be *clothed* with immortality (1 Cor. 15:53). As a reaction, this has led many in our century to deny every anthropological continuity; see e.g. G. van der Leeuw, *Onsterfelijkheid of opstanding?* and P. Althaus, *Die letzten Dinge* (revised after 4th printing, 1933), ch. IV.2. But that detracts from the covenant relationship: God's faithfulness holds on to us even in death and guarantees our identity even in discontinuity. From the perspective of this side of death we are unable, however, to determine what that identity is. Bavinck writes: "What that is we do not know and can never find out" (*GD* IV, no. 573). But God guarantees that I, or my "self" (whatever that may be), will be kept and renewed. See F. W. A. Korff, *Onsterfelijkheid der ziel of onsterfelijkheid der Godsverhouding?* (1946); P. J. van Leeuwen, *Het christelijk onsterfelijkheidsgeloof* (1955), and G. C. Berkouwer, *Man: the Image of God* (E.T. 1962), ch. 7.

Yet lately there are thinkers who again take their starting-point in an anthropological continuity. One of these is Karl Rahner, who sees death primarily as an act of the immortal person who so brings himself to maturation. See his *On Christian Dying* (E.T. 1971). This view is widespread among present-day Roman Catholic theologians, but attacked, among others, by Schillebeeckx (in *Tijdschrift voor theologie,* 1970, pp. 418ff.). It misjudges the hard discontinuity of death and ascribes to man at this point a self-determination which he does not possess. Later Rahner became more "dialectic"; see *MS* 5,5, 1 and 2, esp. pp. 476–492.

The relation of continuity and discontinuity is a very precise one; it will not do to play off the one against the other or to detract from the one at the expense of the other. The continuity of the Spirit's work from beginning to end requires the radical demolition of so much, of everything in our life that is opposed to God's total claim upon us.

Only now, finally, can we raise the main question of this paragraph: What can we know by faith about the content of the perfection on the other side of the boundary of death? In any case, that knowledge is limited to what we, in virtue of the coherence between this side and the other side, can derive or surmise from our experience of the faith. We know that Christ's Spirit, who here takes possession of people and partially transforms them, on the other side completes that process in this sense, that we, using a few New Testament designations, "shall be with Christ," "shall be made like his image," so that "God may be all in all." All that lies so far beyond our present experience, also beyond our faith experience, and it is so unimaginable, that we are inclined to think of it as being the product of an instantaneous re-creative act of God, so that from death man suddenly awakes to a totally changed life. But then we detract from the close tie between life on both sides of the death crisis. The same New Testament speaks about the completion as "fruit," "harvest," and "wages" of the sowing and struggling in this life.

That tie has first of all a negative consequence: on the other side, in the light of the all-exposing light of God's presence, we shall become aware of our culpable failure in respect of his covenant faithfulness as we never did or could within the confines of our earthly existence. Death does not instantaneously and automatically transfer us into the consummation. The connection with our former life is first of all expressed in what in the language of the Christian faith is called "the judgment." There can be no deep and joyful awareness of the renewal without an equally deep sense of obstruction. The radical renewal does not im*media*-tely follow upon our earthly life, but it is mediated by the judgment that bridges the chasm. Only in the way of an exposure that puts us utterly to shame can we, as people with an *earlier* existence and with an earlier existence in which we were *different,* receive the renewal as God's marvelous gift.

But if that is so, we can hardly stop at this negative mediation. In the judgment we are shown how great the distance that separates us from the goal and which must still be bridged is. Will that distance suddenly, as if by magic, be bridged by a re-creative act of God? Or is there on the other side of death something like purification and maturing? Will we on the other side be required to lose ourselves in still more and new processes of death, in order to become completely ourselves relative to God? On this point we can do nothing else than ask questions. But these are questions that must be raised if we are serious about the tie between life here and beyond. If renewal here is no magical metamorphosis—and nowhere in creation do we observe such a discontinuous transformation—then we may not and should not expect it for the future. What awaits us beyond death may rather prove to be a continuing road, be it on a higher level and with the goal more clearly in view.

Taking this idea into consideration may also keep us from seeing the consummation first of all as a fulfillment of our own earthly desires. It is not a matter of safety, but of sanctity. Only through radical surgery are we made ready for a world in which God is all in all and in which he, as our God, satisfies all the desires he has created in us.

There is thus a goal which in virtue of God's intention is going to be reached. Its content can be variously described. In the New Testament and in church history we find many descriptions: "vision of God," "eternal rest," "be with Christ," etc. We prefer "conformity with Christ," for the reason set forth in paragraph 43. In the context in which we speak about it here this description has the advantage that it clearly maintains the connection with Christ's earthly work and that of the Spirit. It also has this advantage over "vision" and "rest," that it lacks the overtones of individualism and passivism. For to resemble Christ means that like him we are totally oriented toward God and the neighbor. Therefore this conformity is possible only in a fellowship. Hence the New Testament portrays the consummation as the consummated covenant communion of God in Christ with those who have become conformed to Christ's image; as a banquet, a city, a celebrating multitude. The dimensions of the vision of God and of resting are aspects that are implicitly included. More we cannot say in this context about the great consummation. Whatever more can be said about our eternal future will have to be postponed until, in the final chapter, we can also include history, culture, and nature in our expectations.

It remains yet to refer to the practical import of this belief in consummation. Only the outsider will think that this faith deprives our earthly life of its importance. The opposite is true: this perspective lends an eternal importance to our earthly life. For judgment and consummation tell us how seriously God takes this life and how great a responsibility he has given us in this life. At the same time, this seriousness does not crush us, because he guarantees its consummation. And because this earthly life is no goal but a road, we need not demand and expect everything from it. So the expectation of consummation liberates us *from* our passion for happiness now and *unto* the free service of God and man.

On the method of eschatology which extrapolates from what already happens here and now, see K. Rahner, "The Hermeneutics of Eschatological Assertions," in *Theological Investigations,* IV (E.T. 1966), pp. 323–346; and H. Berkhof, *Well-Founded Hope* (1969), pp. 16–21 and *passim.*

The NT sees a close connection between life on this side and on the other side of the death line: the latter is the consequence, the fruit, and the reward of the first. Note the use of words and images like: prize, crown, fruit, harvest, seed and full-grown plant, sowing and harvesting; see e.g. Matt. 13:24–30; Mark 4:1–9; John 12:24f.; 1 Cor. 15:35–53; Gal. 5:8f. Especially characteristic in this connection is the usage of the concept "wages"; this word was taken over from the Jewish moralism of the time and filled with an opposite content; cf. Matt. 20:1–16. Wages is now no longer the correlate of merit, but of the expectation which grace has awakened in the heart. The faithful suffering here, the struggle and perseverance, will on the other side of the death line prove not to have been in vain, but be fulfilled and crowned by God. There is rewarded what is faithfully professed here.

The concept of judgment is used above in one specific sense, namely as the judgment of the works done by believers in their earthly life; see Rom. 14:10–12; 1 Cor. 3:10–15; 2 Cor. 5:10; Gal. 6:8f. On the judgment in this sense, see L. Mattern, *Das Verständnis des Gerichtes bei Paulus* (1966), esp. pp. 151–193. (Later we shall speak about other meanings.) In Protestant theology, this viewpoint is almost completely pushed aside by the accent on grace. In Roman Catholic piety it is (or used to be) very prominent in connection with the veneration of saints and purgatory. The Roman Catholic Church assumes correctly that believers differ greatly in regard to their progress and fruitfulness. In Roman Catholicism a saint is one who has performed perfect or even supererogatory good works *(opera supererogatoria);* such a person can by his works and intercession plead the cause of weaker believers on earth. We do not know, however, what God's standards are, nor whether even one lives up to them. This doctrine is particularly unacceptable because of its moralistic framework. According to the NT proclamation of judgment, each one is personally responsible for himself and should have the desire to make sure that in the judgment his life proves to have answered as much as possible to God's purpose (cf. Gal. 6:1–10). Such because the coming perfection will link up with the measure of our success and failure in this life. While not making the ethical caliber of our deeds here a condition for salvation, these acts do become extremely important since they co-determine how God will give us his salvation.

So the idea of a judgment according to one's deeds leads of itself to the consideration of a process of purification, called purgatory in the Roman Catholic tradition. For the official doctrine which was defined by Trent, see D 1580 and 1820. The Reformation broke with that doctrine because of its moralistic conception of salvation and its detrimental effect on the practice of piety (indulgences; intercessory prayers and masses for the dead). It imagined a sudden, radical transformation after the judgment, usually without giving it further theological reflection and without connecting it with the struggle for sanctification on earth. Meanwhile Roman Catholic thinking, too, has become much more reserved *MS* 5 devotes one page to it (456f.). Rahner develops the idea of "ripening" *(ausreifen)* in "The Life of the Dead," in *Theological Investigations,* IV (E.T. 1966), pp. 347-354. In his thinking this idea is connected with his earlier-noted, dubious view of death; but that connection does not take away its value. The Roman Catholic appeal to 1 Cor. 3:15 as "proof" for a phase of purification is far-fetched; yet that statement does suggest that Paul thought of more than an abrupt re-creation of man; salvation is accompanied by a painful becoming aware of one's own failures on earth. The difficulties here are more an open question for theological reflection than a subject for back and forth theological denouncement. The matter of making inferences from faith about what lies beyond death is fraught with far too many difficulties. One can state with Bavinck: "After death there is no more sanctification, one enters upon a state of complete sanctity . . . for death is the greatest leap someone can make, a sudden transposition of the believer into Christ's presence, and thereby a complete destruction of the outward man and a complete renewal of the inner man" (*GD* IV, no. 650, under 4). But one can also ask with G. J. Heering: "Does this change instantaneously, when God shows mercy to the repentant soul and takes it to himself? . . . Life is called a training school, but perhaps there is a higher training school above" (*De menselijke ziel,* 1955, pp. 190, 192).

It is striking that in the divergent traditions of the NT the content of the consummation is preferably and very soberly and concentratedly designated being-with-Christ (Luke 23:43; John 14:2f.; 17:24; 2 Cor. 5:8; Phil. 1:23; 1 Thess. 4:14, 17; cf. Rev. 14:13). Next to it, the content is often called seeing God; see pp. 538–539. The image of rest, which has become even more popular, is marginal in the NT (Heb. 4:8–11; Rev. 14:13); nothing suggests that this rest is a blessed idleness. For the pros and cons of the various images and concepts, see H. Berkhof, *A Well-founded Hope,* pp. 53–57.

52. PRAYER

ONE COULD ASK WHY we insert the discussion on prayer here. In any case, the reason is not that we intend it to be the capstone, and much less a kind of appendix, to the chapter on man's renewal. This particular location is certainly not compulsory. The nature of prayer happens to be such that its place in the study of the faith is uncertain and therefore varying. The reflection on prayer would fit in with the doctrine of God, the doctrine of man, preservation, the covenant, the Spirit, the church, or man's personal life. We prefer the last-mentioned possibility because prayer, in most of its form and in much of its content, is a highly personal concern. Yet this placement has its drawbacks too. It could add to the widespread misunderstanding that prayer is the most intensely personal expression of a most intensely personal emotion. That in particular is why—out of a mixture of reluctance and intellectualism—in many books on the faith prayer is only scantily treated. In what now follows we hope to be able to avoid and overcome such misunderstandings.

That prayer can be taken up under so many different headings is because from man's side it is a primary and explicit expression of the covenant relationship. We speak of "a" and not of "the" primary expression because there are more manifestations of which this can be said: the reading of the Bible, participation in the work of the congregation, the use of the means of salvation, service to the neighbor, ethical obedience. What holds for all of these certainly holds for prayer: the place it has is apt to vary in accordance with the person, circumstances, era, culture, or cultural phase. What the one regards as required for the faith, need not be that for the other. One should also bear in mind that prayer is a universal religious phenomenon; the history and psychology of religion can teach us a great deal about that. Prayer as such is not yet a Christian act. Christian prayer is the expression of a specific covenant relationship, the response to a very specific knowledge of God and his deeds and plans.

But these demarcations do not take away the primary importance prayer has in the Christian's fellowship with God. At times other utterances may push prayer to the periphery. But where it disappears, faith itself ceases. For "covenant" means our adoption as sons and daughters who may call God "Father." We are not only objects of redemption. In fact, our redemption also "liberates" us from being objects, and changes us again into true subjects. God does not want us as objects, but as covenant partners, partners who can converse. He desires our conversational input, our spontaneous gratitude, and our free concurrence, but also our patient or impatient questioning; and even our vehement protest is dearer to him than a silent, unconvinced acquiescence (see Job).

But as the input of the partner of *this* God it is a restricted input. For in this covenant the partners are not equal. We are the second partner, redeemed by the great Partner unto partnership. All our actions—personal and creative—are a reaction to his. We follow his action, we follow in his steps. We accept his conditions. Our coming to him is determined by his coming to us. Therefore Christian prayer, notwithstanding its spontaneity and variety, is a speaking that is determined and informed by the One whom we address.

So prayer is the accentuated manifestation of what can be called the vertical dimension of our humanity. That is not the first dimension coming to development. Before a person is ready to listen, give thanks, and pray, he has to do a lot of eating and drinking, and do and experience many other things besides. But once that stage is reached, this vertical dimension proves not only to presume the other dimensions but to embrace them as well. In the posture of prayer, as *homo orans,* our humanity perfects itself. And in that posture of prayer we place life with all its heights and depths and in its full horizontality before the face of God. Prayer is indeed for the most part a personal matter, but it is never a private concern and certainly not just that of a purely inner "soul" that is lifted out of this world. In prayer, our total human existence in all its varied contexts and responsibilities and cares which we have in and for the world expresses itself.

This means that prayer is as extensive as the faith and life itself, and thus has and can have a great variety of content. As a matter of fact, that is already implied in the fact that prayer links up with the manner in which God comes to us. Prayer can thus be, and depending on the situation and circumstances will be: thanksgiving for what God does; adoration for who he is; losing oneself in his incomprehensible love; confession of guilt for my sinfulness and for my offending that love; prayer for faith and forgiveness; prayer for strength in the fight of the faith; outcry because of the lostness of our existence; prayer for help in need; for wisdom to make right decisions; for submission and surrender when we see that our will conflicts with God's. And because the believer does not exist only by and for himself, he cannot intercede for himself alone; together with the church and for the sake of the church he prays for the progress of the proclamation of the gospel and for the upbuilding, unity, and expansion of the church in whatever form. And because the church does not exist by and for itself, but for the sake of the world, the believer and the church pray representatively for a groaning world which does not know what it longingly looks forward to, for an increase in the knowledge of God, for a strengthening of the forces that can mitigate the endless suffering, for conversion or restraint of those who in their folly maintain and promote injustice in the world. And in and beyond that, as the all-inclusive basis and goal, there is the prayer for the renewal of all of existence, for the definitive and total coming of God's Kingdom.

Not only has prayer a variety of content, it also has a variety of forms. We think first of all of the liturgy in the congregational worship service which displays a diversity of types of prayer: the hymn of praise and of thanksgiving, confession of sin, prayer for the illumination of the Spirit, intercessory prayer. The hymns in the services are mainly prayers, ranging from the exuberant adoration of God's excellencies to the anxious prayer for the coming of the Kingdom. Beside the church service there is the prayer group, often spontaneously formed in response to special needs. Furthermore, there is family prayer, a prayer that can be of great significance as the intercession by the smallest unit of society for needs great *and* small, but one which suffers from routine or is abandoned out of an aversion to routine. There is the carefully phrased and regular personal prayer, for instance when getting up in the morning or at retirement at night, but also the "quick prayer" in moments of tension and fear. There is also the prayer—unfortunately suffering from misuse and overuse—at the opening of meetings and gatherings which in some way relate to the cause of the gospel. The forms are as extensive as the faith and life itself.

From what we said both about the content and about the form, it could be inferred that petition is the dominant form of prayer. It is not the only form, however. There is also the prayer of thanksgiving, of adoration, of confession, of surrender. But almost always they turn into petition. That happens in the Bible as well as in our own use of the term "prayer," whereby we think in the first place of asking and pleading. With our definition of prayer as "input" we already anticipated that. We defined that further as "restricted input." That cannot mean, however, a timidity and holding back in our asking, as if we were having an audience with a very important person: precisely in the father-child relationship there may and must also be spontaneity. Before the face of this God we dare to voice our deepest motives and all the shortcomings we sense in our life and in the world. Even the most superstitious who came to Jesus, asking for bread or healing, he did not send away unanswered. On the contrary, in fellowship with him they learned to ask for *more* than they had begun with, and to ask differently: no longer only from the standpoint of their own needs, but much more from the perspective of God's purposes of which their cares were a part. Particularly the disciples learned this new way of asking in a hard training school. But their master, Jesus, was not spared this training school either. The words of his agonizing prayer in Gethsemane: "Yet not what I will, but what thou wilt" (Mark 14:36) are, in our judgment, misunderstood if we hear in them only an acquiescence in the unavoidable that is going to happen. It is a real prayer, of the same nature as the third petition in the Lord's Prayer. Jesus asks of God that his own will and desires be made subordinate to the great goal in which he is of one mind with the Father, namely that the Father's will to save people and to establish his Kingdom be carried out—if necessary through the torture and the agonizing death of Jesus.

How to ask questions is something we must be taught. The disciples realized that when they saw Jesus himself pray; therefore they asked: "Lord, teach us to pray" (Luke 11:1). The answer was the Lord's Prayer (vv. 2–4), which in its very structure teaches us by example. First, with three actually synonymous petitions (a repetition necessary for us, not for God) man through prayer makes God's plans of salvation his own, so that his will submits itself to God's will and becomes one with it. Man's will is not thereby obliterated, however. Where God receives the priority, man's will can for that reason come into its own in the petitions for a decent life in the world and for forgiveness of sins, perseverance, and deliverance on the basis of redemption. This prayer does not use "I" and "me" but "we" and "us," because one who gives God the priority will want the same room for his neighbor as he desires for himself. Moreover, the plurals "we" and "us" are used because the believer always prays as a member of the total body of Christ.

In our petitioning prayer we are on a way in which we simultaneously learn and unlearn. Before the face of God we discover that "we do not know how to pray as we ought." Yet that does not make us speechless or resigned. We come with our own desires, trusting that the Spirit will transform them into conformity with God's will, with the consequence that we are heard in a way that everything works for our good (Romans 8:26–28). Christian prayer does not force, but it is not without effect either. It walks the narrow way between magic and mysticism—whereby, depending on the situation, at times it comes very close to the one or to the other.

We may not conclude the discussion of (petitionary) prayer, however, without going into the questions and doubts of today's believer, who is asked to pray in and out of a religious climate that is characterized by an emphasis on the inner life and on experience. Constantly he is faced with the problem: Does it make sense to ask something from God? The thought that comes to our mind is that our conversation with God is or seems one-sided: we ask, but there is no answer. Yet this doubt is no more than superficial. For we ask, do we not, on the basis of an Answer to our need and guilt that was given long before we asked; moreover, concerning that Answer we trust that the Spirit will apply it to us and others in such a way (giving security, deliverance, increase in faith, wisdom in making decisions, etc.) that it becomes an answer to our questions. Another thought that can paralyze us is that God knows and is able to do everything anyway, even without our asking him. We will speak about that later. In our asking we are plagued much more by the determinism in all that happens: can God change it just like that because we ask for it (for instance, with a so-called incurable disease)? Another difficult problem that bothers us is that concerning man's own freedom and responsibility: can God, because we ask for it, contravene human plans and decisions or change situations (for instance, put an end to famine, injustice, or war)? The more we seem to know about the determinative coherence of things and the more we seem to be able to do as free people, the more uncertain and restricted in content prayer becomes.

These questions have engaged us before; see paragraph 25 under 5 and 6 on determinism and miracle, paragraph 28 on the preservation of the world, and paragraph 46 on hiddenness (especially p. 451). Here the following should be said: Believing in God as creator, preserver, and renewer implies that we believe in a world which is simultaneously reliable and open. The whole course of nature (evolution) and history is full of surprise happenings which, though explainable afterward, were unpredictable beforehand. What we call the rule of natural law, the eye of faith sees as the instrument by which God maintains the world. And free and mature man is God's counter-player who achieves a growing mastery over nature, without however being able to manipulate his creator; who on the contrary and for his own good is regularly compelled to go in other directions than he had projected. God respects his own laws and the counter-player he created for himself. Hence he does not violently suspend them either. In our prayers we respect what he respects and thus do not ask contrary to it. Yet we know how open this world is and of the Spirit's desire to make use of that. And precisely the fact that we are called to pray proves how much God respects and wants to involve our freedom, not only to rule the world but also to talk over with him its direction and course. That shows that there is a surprising scope for our petitioning initiative in our walk with God, because much of what may appear humanly impossible is possible with him. In that association with God we also learn to see regularly anew what we must ask and what we may not ask.

But can God not do that alone, without our asking him? Indeed, and often he will have to. Yet as a Father he desires to do things in consultation with his mature children. He desires a church that lays before him the changes and breakthroughs which, from her earthly point of view, she deems necessary for the coming of the Kingdom. But one who does not believe does not ask. And he who does not ask sees no answers. One who believes and asks gets to see many answers, and he will accept whatever is not granted as an answer of higher wisdom.

In the study of the faith prayer is a neglected theme. There are of course exceptions. Calvin devotes a chapter of no less than twenty-five paragraphs to it (*Inst* III,xx). But in S and H the subject is not mentioned at all. And of the fifty-two disputations of the Leyden *Synopsis purioris theologiae* (1625) none deals with prayer. Schleiermacher does consider it, under the heading: "Prayer in the Name of Jesus" (*CF* pars. 146f.). In Bavinck prayer is not a separate theme; he mentions it only in passing in the discussion of God's counsel. Althaus and Weber are hardly better. In Trillhaas the word is not even found in the subject index. Slightly better is Prenter (*Creation and Redemption,* pp. 484ff.). Brunner has a separate chapter (24) on it with the heading "Theology of Prayer" (pp. 324–335). Tillich in *ST* speaks about prayer more incidentally, though with some frequency. The place Ebeling assigns to prayer as that in which the knowledge of God can be found (*Dogmatik,* I, par. 9) is remarkable and unusual; but later he mentions prayer only incidentally. Thielicke in *The Evangelical Faith,* III, devotes only a little more than seven (fine) pages to prayer (pp. 83–89). Barth, more than anyone else, has made prayer a dogmatic theme. In the *CD* it is four times intentionally addressed: first in connection with providence (III,3, par. 49,4), next in connection with ethics (III,4, par. 53,3), then as a subdivision of "The Order of the Community" (IV,2, pp. 704ff.), and finally as part of the ministry to the world (IV,3, pp. 882–884). But outside those sections, too, Barth often refers to prayer on account of the fact that we can never have God's gifts (knowledge of God, conversion, etc.) at our disposal.

Where prayer is neglected, it could be a sign (though this is not absolutely certain) that either man's freedom or God's power is underrated; the first is the case in predestinarian-marked Reformed Scholasticism, the second in 19th-century modernism and 20th-century Existentialism. Prayer becomes an integral theme only in a study of the faith which follows the structure of the covenant.

We may not forget the wealth of more meditative literature on prayer which contains systematic reflections. Moreover, there are also some fine dogmatic monographs on prayer: A. de Quervain, *Das Gebet* (1948), and K. H. Miskotte, *De weg van het gebed* (1962).

Friedrich Heiler has written the classical work on the religious phenomenology of prayer: *Das Gebet* (1918; E.T. 1932). The enormous variety in prayer which he describes exhibits on the one hand the great structural similarities and on the other hand how much the nature of prayer is determined by the nature of the god(s) to which it is directed.

In church history, too, the different religious experiences are reflected in the different types of prayer; see *RGG* II, *s.v. Gebet V.* An enormous and, as we see it, unfortunate influence on Christian prayer has for hundreds of years been that of Thomas a Kempis' *Imitation of Christ;* it bolstered the idea that true prayer is a purely private matter. Standing unrelated alongside of it were the liturgical forms of prayer. In Protestant churches the free pulpit prayer often became the private province of the preacher. Only in recent decades is there developing an "ecumenical" type of corporate prayer in the worship service that avoids both fixedness and total open-endedness.

Secularization, particularly since the mid-20th century, has caused a crisis in the conception of prayer. Existentialism and the feeling of autonomy have estranged many from the dialogue nature of prayer; moreover, one cannot see how on the basis of prayer God could make changes in the course of the world. In this respect one easily (over)reacts against all sorts of pious practices in which prayer is very much an uncritical venting of private wishes. Especially J. A. T. Robinson, *Honest to God* (1963), ch. 5, pp. 99–104 (a "non-religious" understanding of prayer), has made many consciously aware of this crisis. At the moment, prayer for many is little else than man's purifying realization of his own motives before the face of God. That is certainly an important element. Prayer, however, is a meeting and not a monologue. By contrast, in revival movements and Pentecostalism prayer is often experienced as a genuine encounter with God, but in that experience there lies the danger that one manipulates God to satisfy his own desires. Narrow is the path that runs between monologue and magic. On prayer as the expression of "dialogische Existenz" (dialogical existence) see H. Ott, *Der persönliche Gott* (1969), ch. XII.

Is the essence of prayer petition? According to Brunner, "For Christian faith, however, prayer is not in the first instance supplication, but praise, worship and thanksgiving" (*Dg* III, p. 335). Diametrically opposite stands M. Kähler's statement: "The Pharisee thanks, the tax collector asks," and more careful is Barth's conception, "While prayer is a matter of worship and penitence, it is not so in the first instance. In the first instance, it is an asking, a seeking and a knocking directed towards God; a wishing, a desiring and a requesting presented to God" (*CD* III,3, p. 268). While it is not an either-or matter, the prayer of adoration naturally becomes a prayer of petition (cf. Phil. 4:6 and the Lord's Prayer). However grateful we may be, our needs are always greater than what we possess; only in the consummation will there be no more asking (John 16:23).

The nature of such prayer we learn perhaps best from the Psalms. For the reflection on that nature, however, we find help especially in the NT. There it is clear that all true prayer has its focus in the coming of the Kingdom (Matt. 6:9;

Luke 18:1–8). Included, however, in such prayer is the Spirit's involving us in this coming (Luke 11:13), and that implies that we may apply the prayer of petition to our whole life; compare Matt. 7:11 with Luke 11:13, furthermore Matt. 6:5–8; 7:7–11; see also Luke 11:1–13, and the strong assertion in Matt. 19:27–29 which very directly links the ultimate hope and the penultimate expectations. But the Kingdom, the Spirit, and the forgiveness of sins remain the center of this wide circle; therefore such praying "in Jesus' name" is always certain to be heard (John 16:23f.). Such prayer can take it that relative to the penultimate expectations there are unanswered prayers, without falling into despair (Jesus in Gethsemane, Paul with his thorn in the flesh, 2 Cor. 12:1–9). The person who has let go of himself is in a position to ask for himself and for others, trusting that the Spirit will present these prayers in agreement with God's purposes (Rom. 8:26). Theoretically it seems very difficult to keep all these considerations together and to weigh them against each other. But in the act of prayer in which we meet God, that is different. In the encounter in prayer, humility and boldness, quiet surrender and eager expectation naturally go together.

But then, finally and once more, all our questions resolve themselves into one final question: What is the effect of prayer? Does it accomplish something with God? One who is convinced of the genuineness and the decisive nature of the covenant encounter has no doubt that God reacts to his partner—more than we dared pray for or could imagine. One who puts himself outside this partnership has no ground for this belief. One who gets inside it has no more ground for doubt. Read the magnificent pages of Barth (*CD* III,3, pp. 284–288).

The Renewal of the World

53. THE PLACE OF THE WORLD IN THE FAITH

THE CHRISTIAN FAITH is person-oriented. The important thing is the conversion and renewal of people. Faith as such is a personal matter. Yet it is not personalistic. For the person is only himself within and by virtue of a community, a totality of people and structures. That wider totality which makes one really a person we call "world." It is a big and vague term and therefore can also have other meanings. It can stand for all mankind living today, or the totality of mankind and nature. In the New Testament it is frequently used to denote all non-believers who do not know or who reject the gospel. But in this chapter we use "world" as the designation of the totality of the contexts and structures within which human existence takes place. We could also use the word "society," were it not for the fact that it is often limited to the societal structures exclusive of politics (the state) and culture. The term "culture" is also related to "world," but it is often used only for the higher expressions of culture such as art, literature, philosophy, and the like. Therefore we opt for the broader term "world." In doing so, we hope to guard against the vagueness inherent in this word.

It could be defended that faith actually has nothing to do with the world. This view is so widespread that theology textbooks hardly ever devote special attention to this theme. Yet that is a fatal mistake. The God who created man, created him as a human being in the world, and therefore he also created the world. The important thing is man, but precisely for that reason the world is important as well. Man and world are the two sides of *one* reality. They are not reducible to each other but can only define each other. For that reason Christian conceptions of creation, of renewal, and of consummation are bound to remain abstract, unless the world is included in the consideration. Particularly the doctrine of renewal has suffered from this neglect. On the one hand it reduces it to a study of man who is detached from his world and therefore is all too often unreal, not a real creature of real flesh and blood; on the other hand, by its silence about the world it suggests that this world is irrelevant for the faith, either because it is capable of saving itself or because it is unsaveably lost. Neither can be true. If it is God's desire to renew man, it must also be his desire to renew the world. Else he would renew only half a man.

In the Bible, therefore, the renewal of the world is a distinct theme: in the Pentateuchal laws and Israel's theocracy based on it, in the prophetic messages and judgments concerning social and international problems, in Jesus' words and deeds in which he condemns the rich and defends the cause of the poor, in Paul's thoughts on Christ's lordship over the powers, in the admonitions in the epistles on the relationship of Jews and Greeks, the strong and weak, the rich and the poor, citizens and government, master and slave, husband and wife, parents and children.

It is really inexplicable that this bearing which the gospel has upon the structures of society has found no echo in the study of the faith. In our judgment this is due to a combination of reasons: the belief in fixed creation ordinances, the respect for the government (Romans 13) and for the order it has established and upholds, the fact that the New Testament shows far less interest in the structures than the Old, the Spirit's work which seems to be predominantly of a personal, even "inner" nature. The awareness that not only man but also the world can and must be renewed becomes alive again whenever upheavals in society shock the church into the awareness of this aspect of the message entrusted to her. Presumably the church would not need such an admonition since that admonition is already contained in her own message. Historically, however, things have seldom been like that. It so happens that God instructs the church as much by what happens in the world as vice versa. Worse, the church has often too late or insufficiently taken the lesson to heart. It took the church a century and a half to learn the lesson of the French Revolution. Meanwhile, the Industrial Revolution has for a long time already clamored for more and further-reaching structural changes, changes which the churches are willing to face only reluctantly or hesitantly—with the exception of some prophetic visionaries. More recently there has been added to that the growing awareness of the gap between the developed and underdeveloped countries. So far the rich countries hardly appreciate what it takes to narrow this gap. As a consequence, we who live in the twentieth century can no longer, not in our study of the faith either, avoid the question concerning the world and its renewal. But once more, not because theology would have an obligation to deal with pressing problems; very much, however, because these problems remind her of a dimension of the faith which has too long been neglected.

This last statement might sound unfair if we would not distinguish between dogmatics and ethics. Christian social ethics, at least in recent decades, displays a great interest in societal structures and their change. That constitutes an appeal to the church and the believer as concerns their *act*-ual responsibility. The outlook of dogmatics is different; it inquires as to the ground and possibility of such acting insofar as these are grounded in God's acts, his promises and faithfulness. Without such an inquiry Christian ethics remains hanging in mid-air. But we enter here upon an unfamiliar and difficult area. As in the previous chapter, we remain within the orbit of pneumatology. The question this time is: is there a promise that the Spirit who renews people will similarly renew their world? In principle we already answered this question in the affirmative; the Spirit does not do half a job. On further reflection, however, we are faced with great difficulties. People can believe, repent, mend their ways, and try to lead a new life. Structures cannot do that. That consideration has led, and still leads, many Christians to think that the change and the renewal of the world can come about only as the work of renewed people. That is why this change is not dealt with in dogmatics but only under ethics. But that is an unwarranted separation. If renewed man is driven to work for the renewal of structures, this is not a personal hobby but a mandate of the Spirit. The Spirit, however, is not only working through believers in his structure-renewing work. For it is evident that that is to a large extent the work of people other than believers. The renewal of the world is thus not a direct fruit of the renewal of people, but it follows its own ways. Whether those ways are ways of the Spirit can neither be affirmed nor denied beforehand.

In order to be able to make responsible statements in this area, we start with a not yet proven thesis: the renewing work of the Spirit in the world exhibits an analogy to his work in man. Analogy denotes similarity and difference. Speaking of man's renewal we used concepts like sanctification, freedom, love, dying and rising again, struggle and progress. We start from the assumption that if the Spirit works in the *world,* there are bound to be analogies of these concepts. For the world is the institutional manifestation and extension of what man himself is. Structures, too, can be sanctified by God, that is, be made serviceable. They can promote or obstruct freedom and love. Also within the structures the battle rages between egotism and love. And also in this area, in fact precisely here, the concepts of progressing and even progress are central.

With these considerations we venture to give to this chapter a design and arrangement analogous to that of the previous chapter. We shall then wait and see how far we can get with it. We begin with the sanctification of the world (paragraph 54). Next there is the question in which sense, from the perspective of sanctification, one can speak of evolution and progress (paragraph 55). In the third place we put the question how we are to conceive of the Spirit's victory in the future (paragraph 56).

The reserve on the part of faith and in the study of the faith with regard to the possibilities of the renewal of the world is to a large extent due to the nature of the gospel itself. It directs itself, after all, to persons, and in the masses of those who do not believe (the *gōyîm* in the OT, the *kosmos* or *aiōn houtos* in the NT) it sees the combination of the opposition to God and Christ, something which also very much dominates the structures of society. In the NT, which also on this point was accorded decisive authority by the church, this reserve is far greater yet than in the OT; the small and soon persecuted minority of Christians had no voice whatever in the Roman empire (which, moreover, did not know of our system of democracy) in respect of the rules which governed life in society and state. Hence we find little in the NT on the relationship of the Spirit to the world and no designs at all for the sanctification of the world.

On closer examination, however, the conclusion that the theme "world" plays only a marginal role in the Bible is untenable. In the larger type above we mentioned the parts of the OT and NT in which it is clearly an important subject. For the OT we think in the first place of the extensive legislation in the Torah. The various compilations of laws it contains are as many starts toward what we usually call a "theocracy," a type of societal life whose ethical and cultic dimensions were governed by what God had in mind for his people. Many of its regulations had their parallel in the laws of the surrounding nations, particularly Babylon (notably the Code of Hammurabi), and it is not always easy to tell whether there is a difference, and if so, whether this is to be theologically or sociologically explained. But in Israel these laws receive a new context, the context of the covenant and of the theocracy that goes with it. Of some of these laws it is clear that they are closely connected with the character of Israel's God. We mention two. In Deut. 17:14–20 the theocratic king is strictly subjected to God's law and dispossessed of all Oriental sacral glory; he is no more than the first among equals who has to guard himself against too much power, pleasure, and wealth. It is clear how much this picture has influenced Israel's history and even more her historiography and prophecy. As a second example we mention the precepts concerning the sabbatical year and (in P also) the Year of Jubilee (Ex. 23:10f.; Lev. 25; Deut. 15:1–18), which are based on the assumption that man's property is a loan from God and that impoverishment and large landownership are to be prevented; the concept of the Year of Jubilee is a "policy on income" that is based on this starting-point, and it constitutes a *tertium* between communism and capitalism. In the practice of life little came of that. But this ideal hangs closely together with the character of the God with whom Israel entered into a covenant; hence the hard-hitting denunciation by Israel's prophets of the opposite practice (1 Kings 21; Isa. 5:8; Mic. 2:2). For an overview of the connection between the faith in Yahweh and the socio-economic ethic see C. van Leeuwen, *Le développement du sens social en Israel* (1954). As such the social and political designs in the OT have no direct authority for us. Yet it is most significant that they are there and that they have this form. Further investigation would likely show that much of it can also be of significance for the Christian church, whether by way of inspiration or criticism.

Beside the theocracy, prophecy is to be mentioned. They are each other's extension. The prophets always annexed further areas of life and brought God's will to bear upon them: Amos was the first to do this for societal life, Isaiah the first for foreign politics, Deutero-Isaiah for the nations of the world. For the prophets personal conversion implied at the same time a transformation of the rules governing societal life.

In the NT these things seem less prominent, because there Israel was no longer an independent state, because the leaders of what was left of the theocracy crucified Jesus, because the church moved beyond the confines of the Jewish people, and because the church was a powerless and soon-persecuted minority. But Jesus in his preaching continued the prophetic censure of man's social and economic behavior. He turned intentionally to the poor, the despised, and the needy; and for him that was not a philanthropic side interest, but it was integral to his message of grace. This is particularly clear from Luke (1:51–53; 3:10–14; 4:18f.; 5:20, 25; 10:25–37; 12:13–21, 33f., 42ff.; 16:19–31; 18:18–27; 19:1–10). We who do not live in such a feudal society cannot imagine how revolutionary that must have sounded, except by putting this message in a worldwide ethical context: the rich fool and the wicked servant in Luke 12, the rich man in Luke 16, Zacchaeus, and the rich young man are *now* the industrialized and prosperous nations who leave others in their poverty and who must repent of that. The difference in type of society between then and now has thus contributed to the failure of later Christianity to sufficiently appreciate the global aspect of the renewal.

In the NT it is Paul who has conceptually captured this global aspect of salvation, particularly in his doctrine of the powers. That teaching, too, has been so much interpreted in terms of what was then its context (it was thought that Paul referred to a genre of angels) that its abiding thrust and permanent relevance were lost sight of. In the next paragraphs we will say more about this. In addition we must mention the so-called domestic instructions (Eph. 6:1–9; Col. 3:18–4:1; 1 Pet. 2:11–3:7) which are a first design of a Christian social ethic, aiming at the permeation and transformation by Christian love of the current standards for conduct. All that may seem little, but it is much if we consider how easy and how excusable it would have been if the NT would not have come to it at all. Hence one might have expected that in a more favorable political climate these thoughts would have shown great germinative potential.

In the history of the church that expectation has only very partially come true. We pointed already to the obstacles in correctly reading the Bible. The position of being a persecuted minority was an obstacle. But after Constantine the position of being a dominant church proved just as much an obstacle. Such a church easily succumbs to the temptation of gratefully accepting the existing order and exploiting it for its own benefit. And it seemed as if this conformism was fully sanctioned by passages like Rom. 13:1–7 and 1 Pet. 2:13–17.

That is the reason why Christian Europe was for at least a thousand years barren soil in which the seeds of a vision of a world renewed could not germinate. Theology and practice went hand in hand; theological thinking for the most part reflected the conformist practice. Yet there were all sorts of exceptions, both in the history of the church and in the history of theology, which proved that this was indeed the rule. There have been innumerable conflicts between the church and governments. And in the course of Europe's history, many prophetic, protesting, or revolutionary individuals or groups have appealed to the denunciations of the prophets or received their inspiration from the Sermon on the Mount. Speaking about the Netherlands, if her own church history had not shown the same one-sidedness as that of the European national churches, we would now be much more aware of all these things. The theoretical and practical criticism of the society of their time by the early church, the centuries-long battle against usury, the medieval mendicant orders and vows of poverty, the Hussite wars, the activities of Thomas Müntzer, the Anabaptist disturbances, the Spiritualists, and the free church type as it developed in England and later especially in America, all these constitute an impressive and almost uninterrupted piece of ecclesiastical tradition in which the existing order in the world was in no way conformistically accepted.

What holds for the history of the church is also partially true in the history of theology. As a matter of fact, these are continually interwoven. The study of Patristic theology, using a combination of Stoic and biblical ideas, developed the idea of natural law; that meant the designing, in the form of a description of the pre-fall world, of a sort of Christian society governed by the three principles of freedom, equality, and brotherhood. While the Christian may not be a revolutionary, he does have the calling of molding the world as well as he can in conformity with the structure of paradise and of the new Jerusalem. That accounts for the structure of monasticism, the protest against slavery, the prohibition of interest, and the duty to give alms.

It is worthy of note that in the Reformation the doctrine of justification from the outset went hand in hand with the theory and practice of the reform of societal structures. As early as 1520 Luther wrote his program for the reformation of society through the reformation of the church, entitled *To the Christian Nobility of the German Nation.* In that same year Zwingli began his campaign against *Reislaufen* (enlistment in a foreign army). In 1523 he wrote his *Divine and Human Justice.* In Zürich his insights led to social reforms. And Calvin is unthinkable without his strong attempts to reform the city of Geneva and make it into a theocracy. He has even included societal problems in his dogmatics; see the final chapter, *Inst* IV,xx: "Civil government" (state and society are discussed together). The Scottish Confession (1560), ch. 24, and the Belgic Confession (1561), ch. 36, have even included this theme in the official confessions of the church. Calvin's careful thoughts on the right of resistance by the lower magistrates (*Inst* IV,xx,21) have later, contrary to his intention, provided the inspiration for revolutionary theories and practices. Eventually, however, the renewals sought by the Reformers were institutionalized, emasculated, or forgotten, when their churches became settled and prominent and the upholders of the established order in society. The societal-critical spirit was continued in the free churches, who sought to build in the American colonies a society which would be more in conformity with God's will than the one in the Old World.

See on the relation of church and world the classical work of E. Troeltsch, *The Social Teaching of the Christian Churches* (E.T. 1931). Much material can also be found in the five-volume *Cultuurgeschiedenis van het christendom* (1948ff.). On the critical import of Patristic natural law, see also F. Flückiger, *Geschichte des Naturrechtes,* I (1954), esp. ch. VIII.

Dissatisfaction with the rules of society is absent from no period in the history of the church, particularly not from much-maligned Pietism. Already under Francke's leadership in Halle it initiated large diaconal and educational endeavors, in its institutions it created places of refuge for the disadvantaged, and in its conventicles it ignored the differences of class, sex, and material status.

That becomes much clearer yet if we look at the history of missions. On the mission fields, Christians showed a great interest in structural changes and they were often accused by their contemporaries of a lack of respect for the traditional pattern of life. In this regard it should be remembered, however, that missions sought to introduce Western (northern) societal structures which it often regarded as synonymous with Christian structures. That made it possible to do revolutionary work in primitive cultures while remaining conformist in one's own. But there were also endeavors to bring about changes in mentality and institutions within the boundaries of a principial conformism, through extensive and intensive work in the fields of education, the care of the sick, and the care of the poor and disadvantaged; this work sometimes bordered on or even became a critique of the existing structures (T. Chalmers, C. Blumhardt, and others).

Here, however, our concern is the question how and to what extent the theme "world" was taken up by theology. For that we have to make a jump from the Reformation to the second half of the 19th century, at the earliest. For only the arrival of secularism, as the falling apart of the *corpus Christianum,* led to the vision of the world as a power needing anew the confrontation with the gospel. Initially this vision expressed itself only in ethics and hardly at all in dogmatics. An example often mentioned is Richard Rothe (1799–1867), who propounded the view that the moral perfection of mankind should take shape in the state and not in the churches; but that idea was too cultural and too optimistic to be viable in the renewal of the "world." Much more important in this respect was Abraham Kuyper (1837–1920), who tried to attack secularism ideologically and organizationally with a combination of Calvinistic theocracy and modern democracy. He has a great deal of interest in the structures ("spheres of life," "areas of life"). On the two pillars of "common grace" and the "antithesis" he wants to erect, by means of Christian organizations, an independent Christian culture which is to influence general culture, especially in the areas of education, science, politics, and social relationships. See especially *Lectures on Calvinism* (E.T. 1931), *Van de gemeene gratie* (1902–1905), and *Pro Rege* (1911f.).

While Kuyper still thought of the structure problem only in terms of a challenge posed by secularism, this question had arisen already long before that in yet another, quite different form, namely as a result of the Industrial Revolution and the accompanying ruthless capitalism. That made the workers' class aware of the structures, in this sense that they began to see them as hostile, "alienating" powers. Particularly Karl Marx (1818–1883) opened their eyes to that. His conception was so closely connected with materialism and atheism that for a whole century theology discovered no elements in it which would prompt a fresh theological contemplation of the theme "world." Only in recent times do we discover with and through Marx how much of an alienating effect the structures of our world can have with respect to the quality of human life as desired by God. As a result of that discovery, the theme "world" now presses itself upon our attention as never before. It is even difficult to indicate precisely what the difference between Marx and the gospel is on this point. For Marx, too, was concerned with man and his happiness and with trying to make the structures serve that purpose. For Marx, however, man is especially the object and victim of the structures. It is not clear whether according to him man is only freed from this bondage through the process of history or whether man is also a subject of the structures and thus able himself to make the leap from the realm of determinism to that of freedom. In any case, in his younger years Marx also stated: "The materialistic doctrine that men are products of circumstances and upbringing, and that, therefore, changed men are products of other circumstances and changed upbringing, forgets that it is men that change circumstances and that the educator himself needs education" (*Theses on Feuerbach*, 1846, from the 3rd thesis).

A third element, next to secularism and Marxism, that has made us very much aware of the problem of the world is our dynamic outlook caused by evolutionistic thinking. Unlike previous generations, who saw the structures as static and unchangeable entities, we experience them much more as separate moments in an evolutionary process and as things that are inherently changeable. For us the doctrine of "natural law" has lost most of its usefulness. Everything can be quite different, too, from what it is now. That involves a challenge to theologians to broaden the belief in man's changeability (sanctification) so that it includes the sanctification of the world as well. Yet in spite of all that, in present-day dogmatics the problematic of the world is hardly discussed. There are, however, all kinds of preliminary attempts which eventually should also lead to a change in the traditional designs of the study of the faith.

Barth has dealt with the problem of structure using the analogy of the sanctification of man and the church. See *Church and State* (E.T. 1939) and *Christengemeinde und Bürgergemeinde* (1946). But not much of that is found in his dogmatics; also, *CD* IV,3 remains within the confines of witness and apostolate. This is not true of the posthumously published fragments of his ethics, *The Christian Life* (E.T. 1981). On the "powers" see esp. par. 78, "The Lordless Powers."

Also important in this connection is A. A. van Ruler, who incorporated the Calvinistic theocracy into a theology in which the Kingdom and the Spirit are central, and the Kingdom is also conceived of as a political order. Therefore he opposed "personalism," which arose in 1945 and which, in his opinion, misjudged the significance of institutions and structures. But in his thinking the problem of structure stands only in the context of secularism, and for his solution he reverts to concepts like "theocracy," "Christianization," and a "God-honoring state." The sanctification of the structures is thus kept within narrow and conservative confines. As a characteristic example, see his art. "Theocratie en tolerantie," in *Theologisch werk,* I (1969), pp. 191–215.

In Western theology particularly J. Moltmann, under the influence of the neo-Marxist Ernst Bloch, has probed the problem of structure theologically. See his *Theology of Hope* (E.T. 1967), ch. 5, and *The Crucified God* (E.T. 1974), ch. 8. A Lutheran perspective is offered by H. Thielicke, *The Evangelical Faith,* II (E.T. 1979), par. 17.4. H.-J. Kraus in his *Systematische Theologie,* esp. IV, pars. 210–220 (but more in an ethical context), also shows much interest in these questions.

Besides these approaches, derived especially from Western secularization, Latin-American liberation theology, which has its source in the structures of exploitation on that continent, has made its appearance since 1970. Here the structural question is very much the central focus of theology, because structural liberation becomes almost identical with salvation. The classical first liberation theologian G. Gutiérrez, *A Theology of Liberation* (E.T. 1973), radically carries forward lines from the encyclical *Gaudium et Spes* (1965); for an overview of later developments see R. Gibellini, ed., *Frontiers of Theology in Latin America* (1975). This form of theology is often contrasted with the "academic" theology of the north. It is, however, strongly influenced by Moltmann, an influence that later became mutual. For the differences, which are first of all situational in character, see par. 10 and par. 56, small type.

54. THE SANCTIFICATION OF THE WORLD

IN THE STUDY OF THE FAITH sanctification indicates the manner in which God's holy love motivates man's thinking and acting. In that strict sense the word is not applicable to the societal and other structures of the world. Structures cannot be motivated. They channel and combine human activities. For that reason they can greatly hamper by stymieing or killing the sanctifying forces. (Example: an employer seeks to create the best possible working conditions for his employees, but is frustrated in his attempts by the profit motive and the competition inherent in the present economic system.) The structures can help by providing the necessary channels for sanctified activities; and by compelling people, who in themselves are slow or unwilling to help, to do good deeds. (Example: many laws compel us to part with some of our money for the benefit of the community as a whole, the care of the poor, the invalids, etc.) It could be objected that good deeds without good motives are not really good. Deeds, however, apart from having a motive which is either good or not, also have an effect which is either good or not. Christianly speaking, the second is as important as the first: God not only desires to live in the heart but also in the world. He desires societal forms that provide the best possible channels for the forces of his holy love, and which counteract as much as possible the forces of lethargy, egotism, and indifference toward him and the neighbor.

From the foregoing it is clear what we mean by "sanctified structures." The object is forms of government, legislation, forms of discussion and arbitration, written and unwritten rules for dealing with one another, relationships of the sexes and the generations, employers and employees, well-to-do and poor people, associations and countries, etc., which as much as possible allow the transmission or at least room for the purposes of God's holy love. We speak here emphatically of holy love, as a reminder that this sanctification, no more than personal sanctification, agrees with our natural aspirations. A normless permissive-pluralistic society (suppose such a society were possible) is hereby as much excluded as a theocratic dictatorship.

Here the question from the previous paragraph returns with greater urgency, how and whether the renewing work of the Spirit has a bearing on these societal forms. We must distinguish a threefold relation of the Spirit to the structures:

1. The Spirit (God himself in his relationship to the world) also works in the creation and preservation of the world. Man is not forsaken of God. Otherwise he would live in a complete hell. But everywhere in the world, in living memory, the structures in which they live have forced people in spite of their egotism and lethargy to work together, and so in their actions to love their neighbor as themselves. Indeed, man's egotism has regularly stymied those structures; but the reverse is equally true (see also p. 220). People create somewhat sanctified structures, and those structures force people to conduct themselves in a somewhat sanctified manner.

2. Tying in with and deepening, correcting, and extending that work, the Spirit works through sanctified people as instruments of love. Such people are not only interested in what is socially useful and possible, but their first concern is what is normative. They give themselves to the task of enabling the structures to accomplish more deeds of love, but also wherever possible (but how impossible that often is! see pp. 219f.) try to transform them so that they allow more scope and greater effectiveness to these deeds.

3. The societo-critical notions thus introduced by the Spirit can, in conjunction with what is mentioned under 1, persuade many who apart from this special operation of the Spirit know themselves responsible for the preservation and betterment of the world. Just as believers, such people can become bearers of this objective sanctifying work of the Spirit. Conversely, believers can be delinquent in the area of structural sanctification, because their mentality and situation keep their eyes closed to specific, often pressing problem areas.

We thus arrive at the same conclusion as in the preceding paragraph: "The renewal of the world is not a direct fruit of the renewal of people, but follows its own ways." Yet these, too, are ways of the Spirit. Christ as the head of the church has also been made the head of all mankind. Conformity to his image is not only intended for individuals, but for mankind in its totality and thus also for the mode of its communal life. Therefore the Spirit also directs himself to that second aspect.

The application of the concept of sanctification to the societal structures is not something new, only unusual. The author who goes the furthest in this respect is A. W. Kist, *Antwoord aan de machten*, ch. X. The concept can evoke rapturous and utopian expectations that are in conflict with the Christian faith. Brunner writes: "Christians cannot 'sanctify' the world, that is humanity, in such a manner as they sanctify themselves" (*Dg* III, p. 315). Mankind, however, taken in the sense of rules and relationships ordering the community, possesses a greater capacity for sanctification than mankind in the sense of persons who make up the community. On the manner of the Spirit's operation in the general preservation of the world (point 1), see par. 28. In addition to the literature cited there, see on the relation of points 1 and 2 also A. Kuyper, *Van de gemeene gratie,* esp. Vol. III (1905), and *Pro Rege,* Vol. III (1912). For the (Reformed) discussion of the value of "law-resembling" works of unbelievers, see J. Douma, *Algemene genade* (1966). To the best of my knowledge W. Rauschenbusch is the only person who discusses the sanctification of the structures in a systematic theology. See his *A Theology for the Social Gospel* (1917), ch. XI, where he takes up the question under the title "The Salvation of the Super-Personal Forces" (but salvation in his thinking nearly coincides with democratization).

The manner in which the structures of preservation are transformed in the covenantal fellowship and in sanctification can be learned especially from the OT, more particularly from the legislation, the cult, the feasts, and the kingship. In the NT, Paul's doctrine of the powers *(exousiai, stoicheia)* is conspicuous. These powers are part of the preservation of the world (Gal. 4:1–3; Col. 1:16), but in Christ's sphere of operation they are changed as to their character; they are dethroned as the ultimate powers, and henceforth have a kind of right to exist only as instruments of God's love (Rom. 8:38f.; Eph. 1:10, 20f.; Col. 1:20). According to Eph. 3:10, the church has its own function in respect of these powers: by her existence as a reconciled community of Jews and Gentiles (see 2:11–3:7) she is the proclamation of a God-willed type of life over which the powers have no control. We may say that Paul's doctrine of the powers is the only form in which the problem of structures is intentionally taken up in the Bible. That is done in such a way that Paul's problematic and proclamation can be applied to our contemporary problems with a minimum of connecting hermeneutical links. See H. Berkhof, *Christ and the Powers* (E.T. 1962, 1977), and especially A. W. Kist, *Antwoord aan de machten,* chs. III–VIII.

At the moment there is a great difference of opinion as to how the Spirit's relationship to the structures must be thought of. As Van Ruler sees it, the Spirit in his work of "Christianization" reaches primarily backward, restoring the order of creation by means of a theocratic order in Calvin's sense (structural acknowledgment of God's sovereignty). According to Moltmann, the Spirit prepares the way toward the future and creates an "exodus-church" which tries to transcend the established order in the direction of that future. These contrary points of view can of course lead to contrary political visions and actions. Our conception differs from Van Ruler's protological approach to the problem of structure and from Moltmann's eschatological approach in that it is christological-pneumatological, one which starts neither at the beginning nor at the end, but in the "middle," after the analogy of personal sanctification.

Like everything else so far, these are statements of faith. Such statements are unverifiable by general experience. Yet in a way the statements made here are experientially more verifiable than most others. For the gospel has entered the world and in certain parts it has for centuries had the opportunity to influence cultures and structures. We think of course in the first place of Europe along with North America. Since the time that Christendom (after Constantine) also began to make its impact on the structures of society, "Europe" has deviated more and more from "the general human pattern" (Jan Romein). That process started only slowly. Not all deviations have come at once. Rather, we get the impression of a uniformly accelerated movement. The two earliest conspicuous elements are the care of the sick and the poor, and the rejection of the divine nature of the power of the state. Already under the Roman empire these marks set the Christians apart from the common pattern of behavior. As part of it, Christianity also had a view of man that deviated from the Greco-Roman conception; it expressed itself in the value Christians put on humility, self-denial, and service. And on account of that, labor and responsibility receive a strong emphasis. Moreover, viewed in this light, the principial equality of all men becomes much more conspicuous than in earlier cultures. Room is made for the development of the care of the individual and for the idea of social justice. Beside the care of the disadvantaged and the desacralization of the established order, the third basic element to be mentioned is the dedeification of nature, making room not only for the study of nature, but also for an increasingly more drastic domination of nature. And all that happens in the context of an awareness that mankind goes through a history in which it is on the way to a better future, a future which is at once promise and mandate. The notions of love, matter-of-factness, and a goal-oriented history have made this culture dynamic, emancipative, and expansive. It aims at the development of all of life and the humanization of man's existence. This exerts a strong missionary impact on other parts of the world. The other nations like to adopt the same rules, so that they may enjoy the same fruits of freedom, equality, and prosperity.

Meanwhile, in the accelerated post-Enlightenment forms, this process has become increasingly secularized and detached from its Christian roots. On that see par. 55. At the same time it has been transported to other continents through the ambivalent covenant between mission and evangelism *and* imperialism. Especially in the younger black nations in Africa the Christian churches have become conscious of their obligation and opportunity to be a structural influence on the society to which they belong. There surprising indigenous "contextualizations" of the social and political dimensions of the gospel happen. Beside it superficially Christianized Latin-America with its numerous "foundation-groups" is busy discovering those same dimensions, and it is rising up against the inhuman structures. In both continents the structural questions occupy center stage in the Christian witness, and so much so that Europe and North America are beginning to lose their leadership function.

The forms of structural sanctification we discussed here are, of course, not found in the Bible. They are situational applications of the contents of the Bible. Yet not only in the OT but also and precisely in the NT the universal power of the exalted Christ is depicted in such suprapersonal terms that the expectations it evokes and the later applications do not stand in strange juxtaposition. We think of Matt.

28:18; Eph. 1:20–23; Col. 1:15–20; 2:15; Rev. 1:5. The passage on the salt of the earth (Matt. 5:13) and the parables of the mustard seed and the leaven (Matt. 13:31–33) also suggest an extent and penetration of the gospel far beyond the limits of the circle of believers.

We mentioned Emperor Constantine in connection with the christianization of Europe. Nowadays that is often done and for the most part negatively. However, his aim was not a Christian dictatorship, and his dethronement of the Roman ideology of the state has had many beneficial consequences. In the large type we alluded to the book of Jan Romein, *Aera van Europa. De europese geschiedenis als afwijking van het algemeen menselijk patroon* (1954). For Christian views on this phenomenon see K. H. Miskotte, "Het geestesmerk van de europese mens" (1949), in *Grensgebied* (1954), pp. 9–51; H. Berkhof, *Christ the Meaning of History* (E.T. 1966), ch. 5; A. T. van Leeuwen, *Christianity in World History* (1964); and H. van der Linde, *De oecumene in een planetaire wereld* (1967), ch. 5.

55. PROGRESS AND STRUGGLE

WE USE TWO WORDS HERE that derive from the sphere of personal sanctification (see paragraph 50). The question whether analogically these can be applied to structural sanctification is not hard to answer. The history of the sanctification of community structures, as this first happened in Europe, later also in America and now in a great part of the world, and still occurs, is a history of struggle and progress. The progress in that history is so conspicuous that it is precisely in this context that the concept of "progress" has arisen. First we shall consider the theological significance of that progress (a), and then we shall show how this progress entails great negative effects that cause an inner-cultural conflict which is analogous to the struggle between the old and the new man in the believer (b). This happens in an irreversible history whose finish we are unable to see, but within which we on the one hand can observe an accelerated intensification of the conflict and on the other hand can expect it.

a. Progress

It is clear that in and by way of Europe, culture has increasingly faster moved away from the general human pattern, and that in several essential respects this has meant an enormous development of the human personality and of mutual relationships. Or more correctly: the relationships were changed and as a result man could more freely develop himself. What took place was progressive correction and transformation of those relationships, giving to ever more groups and classes the opportunity to realize steadily more of the potential of their personal and social existence. To mention only a few of those structural changes which have been product and factor in this process of development: equality before the law, the separation of the executive and judicial branches of the government, compulsory education, universal franchise, freedom of religion, communal care for the physically and mentally handicapped, insurance, freedom of the press. These and many other provisions, unknown in earlier cultures, have built a society which, though far from perfect, offers comparatively the best chances for freedom from fear, hunger, poverty, and remaining underdeveloped.

All the examples mentioned here are from the latest period, not older than the French Revolution. That could give the impression that what we call the sanctification of the structures is much rather a product of secularism than of the Christian faith. On the truth in that remark we say more under b. Here we have to refer to what we noted in the previous paragraph. The most remarkable fruits in this everywhere accelerated process are only from recent times. But the fertilization of the soil and the growth of the tree have been the decisive factors; and these required a process of centuries. Many postulates of our present culture are of Christian origin. The Christian faith should be able to recognize its fruits. Under b we shall inquire why Christians have often nevertheless had difficulty with that recognition.

Here we raise the principial question whether the Christian church should not only recognize but also acknowledge these fruits. Can this progress indeed be regarded as an analogy of personal sanctification? We answer that question affirmatively, because we observe here a progress to a greater respect for the fellow human being, more room for his creative potential, deliberate care of the weak and disadvantaged; also greater freedom for every "honest" conviction and by implication for the Christian community, proclamation, and service. We see here a widespread application of the ideas of service, love of the neighbor, the spirit of sacrifice, and responsibility. These are accompanied by an element which is no less recognized and acknowledged by the Christian faith: the permanent *dis*-satisfaction with what has been achieved, the restless striving toward improvement, the "bad conscience" which may well be the most striking Christian legacy which distinguishes Western culture from others.

There is thus indeed progress. And that will continue in Europe and outside it, even if Christianity would be no more than a moderate impetus in this process. The latter is a likely possibility; the Christian faith convinces only a minority, while structural sanctification convinces people worldwide. Many regard it as a result or even the highest achievement of the evolutionary process within the human race.

But having said all this, we must point just as emphatically to the limits of progress, and we do not have in mind accidental historical limits, but such as are inherent in the very concept of progress. We point to three such limits: (a) While the concept is applicable to the physical sciences, technology, jurisprudence, and social relationships, it is not applicable to art, the human ethos, love, empathy, and religion. No one will assert that in these areas we have "come further" than, for example, the Greeks or even the primitive people. (b) It is not applicable either to the great powers that demarcate the provisionality of existence: illness, sorrow, and death. Structural progress can do something to make it more bearable, to push it back or put it off, but it cannot abolish it. Due to a and b one cannot speak of progress in the sense of happiness, even though all the striving for progress is aimed at greater human happiness. (c) A third boundary which limits progress is the fact of sin. If within the renewed structures man himself remains unrenewed, these structures, fortunately, can restrain the effects of sin; but the opposite, the hampering of structural renewal by sin, can also happen. All too often the wrongs of the past persist, only with new methods or other people. Much belief in progress leads to great disillusion, because one has the feeling that only the signs have been altered while everything else remains the same. Here we see something of the battle between Spirit and "flesh" in the area of structure; it is a battle in which Christians will have to be involved realistically and persistently, knowing that while they are unable to expel sin, they may nevertheless participate in God's plan. For all stifled progress brings fresh tensions, leading to explosions that are to be regarded as divine judgments for which we are responsible, and which can only be reversed or mitigated by acts of self-sacrificial service. In this sense personal sanctification also entails a challenge to structural sanctification.

b. Struggle

Nevertheless in this context struggle means something altogether different, something which so far we have not mentioned. The fact is that the emancipation process that leads to progress not only rests on struggle and makes headway through struggle, but this process itself elicits its own unique kind of struggle. Structural sanctification without personal holiness has a double effect on man: it develops and uproots. For the man who is being emancipated is the man who was created in God's image, while at the same time he is the man who refuses to obey the calling inherent in that creation in God's image, wanting to be autonomous himself. That means that, despite *and* due to the structural renewals, a world is being built which has no structural room for the priority of God, conversion, and salvation. There are times in which this does not seem to matter, either ecclesiastically or culturally. But sooner or later this second basic decision on which our culture is being built, that of its own autonomy, makes itself clearly and painfully felt (beside the Christian decision, that of the renewal); it does this in individual and collective consumeristic egotism, in the brutal manner in which man acts not as the manager but as the master of creation, in the loss of meaning and the failure to give meaning to existence, leading to boredom and so to the search for powers which claim man for their ideology and purposes. The Christian churches could already predict the alienation which results from it from the growing dechristianization, and even more from their own impotence to get across to modern man the vertical dimension of existence.

Sanctification and secularization progress together. With his sanctification of society the Spirit evokes an ambiguous and internally contradictory world, a society which is busy cutting down the gospel tree from which it is picking the fruits. That was bound to happen. The Spirit who kindles the struggle in the believer, as "at once saint and sinner," does the same in culture. The Christian church cannot possibly reject that culture; it is flesh of her flesh. But she cannot feel at home in it either. Whatever real or apparent freedom may be left to the church in it, with trepidation she anticipates the final outcome of this everywhere accelerated emancipation movement. That is the deepest reason why so many Christians have often initially resisted progress in humanity and emancipation, a progress which on further reflection they should have welcomed—and which indeed they or their children eventually did. Their opposition was premature and wrongly directed. But the eventual outcome is that the way which as such is right brings unrenewed man further estrangement from God and from himself; and that means that it brings the Christian church suffering and isolation, and the struggle against apostasy and indifference. The progress initiated by the Spirit leads to a sifting of the spirits, and is not only liberating but just as much disclosing and enslaving in its effects.

c. Intensification

We anticipated this concept already by speaking of "an everywhere uniformly accelerated movement." This is essential for a culture imbued by the Spirit with a sense of history, future, and purposefulness. Through science and technology this drive for progress has become deeply ingrained in the infrastructure of our world. As a result we find ourselves caught up with our whole existence in an increasingly stronger and swifter current. In view of the ambiguous character of our culture it is a big question what this escalation will lead to. There are all kinds of possibilities: a "brave new world," a third world war unleashed by the robbed and deprived countries, a nuclear war between ideological blocs, a world dictatorship based on an anti-Christian ideology. That would be the stranding or the direct downfall of the experiment called Europe. But it also imaginable that the human race, shocked by these perspectives, will wrestle itself free from the alienating forces and look for renewal by going back to the evangelical root of its culture. At this point we call to mind the double image of the future of the earth as this is developed in the biblical expectation of the future: on the one hand a universal and voluntary acceptance of the evangelical structural rules as the only hope of saving a viable human existence, a "thousand-year kingdom," on the other hand an anti-Christian world dictatorship—in such a way that both elicit and delimit each other, eventually to make room for the total rule of God. This double image of the future cannot be dismissed as apocalyptic and mythological. It is integral to the Christian faith, which knows both of the human decision that was made in the execution of Jesus and of the divine decision that was made in his resurrection. In our history this double decision spreads, expands, and intensifies. Our history leads to and ends in a deadlock of two powers which evoke, delimit, and cannot conquer each other.

In the NT, the lines we have drawn here seem absent due to the *Naherwartung* (imminent expectation). Yet on a closer look such is not the case. There is, first of all, a strong emphasis on the dual effect that goes out from Jesus during his life and afterward in the worldwide proclamation of the gospel (see among others Matt. 10:34; 13:24–30 [the parable of the wheat and the weeds growing up together]; Luke 2:34; John 9:39; 2 Cor. 2:16). These and similar statements are explanations of an event: Jesus was murdered by the people; and yet there gathers around him a new and steadily growing community; but that is accompanied by persecutions, and the large majority of his people continue to reject him. That also sheds light on the (longer or shorter) future of history. Looking at history from the point of view of double effect and intensification must already have been part of the early kerygma, as is evident from 2 Thess. For this vision on history see 2 Thess. 2:1–12; cf. H. Ridderbos, *Paul* (E.T. 1975), pp. 512–528.

The concept of progress, often uncritically accepted in 19th-century modernism, was for a long time just as uncritically rejected by orthodoxy. Roman Catholic theology with its positive evaluation of natural life quickly and maximally absorbed it under the inspiration of P. Teilhard de Chardin, who combined evolutionistic thinking about nature with a mystically colored faith. This association itself was soon rather generally rejected as being too harmonistic. But a theological assessment and integration of the idea of progress were taken up by many, first and foremost in Roman Catholic theology, and later in Protestant theology. Nowhere can this concept be used directly and integrally. But in Roman Catholic theology it is easier to apply it as a framework, its ambivalence notwithstanding. Typical is the Constitution *Gaudium et spes* (1965) of Vatican II, which in par. 2 contains the characteristic sentence: ". . . a world concerning which Christians believe that out of love it was created and is upheld by the Creator; that though it has come under the power of sin, it has been set free by the death on the cross and the resurrection of Christ, who thereby broke the power of the evil one, in order that it may be transformed *(transformetur)* in agreement with God's saving purposes and reach its ultimate consummation *(consum-*

mationem)." And more carefully in par. 39: "Thus, though earthly progress *(progressus terrenus)* is to be carefully distinguished from the growth of the kingdom of God, yet such progress is closely associated with God's kingdom, insofar as it can contribute to a better ordering of human society. For those values of human dignity, of brotherly fellowship and freedom, all these noble fruits of our nature and our effort, we shall, after we have spread them *(propagaverimus)* over the earth in the spirit of the Lord and according to his commandment, find back later, purified from every taint, illuminated and transformed *(illuminata et transfigurata).*"

Such high-sounding notes are not heard in the study report of Faith and Order, *God in Nature and History* (1967); here the ambivalence is much more emphasized, though here, too, the background is evolutionary thinking. Typically modern-Protestant is G. C. van Niftrik, *De vooruitgang der mensheid* (1966); he sees both the cross and the resurrection "etched out" over mankind; for the most part he sees only "fragmentary" and "aphoristic" signs of the coming kingdom, but in the final chapter (ch. X: "De menselijkheid") he goes much further: "That history, through failures and defeats, is on the way to the Kingdom . . . to the very climax of humanity" (p. 264). "Progress? The word is so inadequate, so filled to the brim with unchristian notions. But we are progressing; we are on the way toward becoming people in the fullest sense" (p. 265). See also H. Berkhof, *Christ the Meaning of History,* pp. 169–178. Read the subject dealt with here also in relation to the doctrine of creation (see par. 25, sub 8, 9, and 10). For the Christian presuppositions of the idea of progress, see R. Nisbet, *History of the Idea of Progress* (1979).

A theological conception of progress will have to go together with a theological conception of secularism. That conception has been developed by F. Gogarten in *Despair and Hope for Our Time* (E.T. 1970), where he views secularism especially as the fruit of man's coming of age and the depersonalization of life as a result of Christ's coming. This line, with many historical illustrations, is updated by A. T. van Leeuwen, *Christianity in World History* (1964). Later Gogarten himself emphasized much more the negative tendency in secularism (without God autonomous man falls back into a new slavery), especially in his posthumous *Die Frage nach Gott* (1968). The greatest influence has come from D. Bonhoeffer with his *Letters and Papers from Prison* (posthumously, 1951), in which at first sight an autonomous and mature life *(etsi Deus non daretur)* seems to be greeted as a liberation, but in which this is nevertheless seen as a life wherein God can only be present as One who is powerless and rejected (letter of July 16, 1944). This negative aspect (secularism as rebellion against reality as it is) governs A. Loen, *Secularization: Science without God?* (E.T. 1967). A total rejection of secularism is found in F. de Graaff, *Het europese nihilisme* (1956), and W. Aalders, *Schepping of geschiedenis* (1969). For a more detailed treatment of the ambivalence of development and uprooting see H. Berkhof, *Christ the Meaning of History,* ch. 5, and "De theologie tussen Cassandra en Hananja" (1972), now in *Bruggen en bruggehoofden* (1981), pp. 107–121. A good earlier example of this ambivalent thinking on secularism is A. Kuyper; for a summary see *Pro Rege,* III (1912), pp. 342–353. But the deepest thinking on the Christian ferment *and* on the godlessness of European culture comes from Nietzsche, whose analysis and formulation of the problematic may be regarded as a contrasting correlate of the biblical, and which still have not been assimilated by theology.

The concept of intensification has so far hardly been utilized in theology. What the OT and NT offer in this respect is normally brushed off as "apocalyptic." Meanwhile the concept does infiltrate the analysis and philosophy of culture: "We may now be in the time of the most rapid change in the whole evolution of the human race, either past or to come. . . . The world has now become too dangerous for anything less than Utopia" (a frequently quoted statement from the American biophysicist J. R. Platt). In the Christian world this view and sense of life has, since the reports of the Club of Rome and the escalating nuclear armament, taken on apocalyptic forms, nourished by such biblical statements as 2 Pet. 3:5–13. That kind of perception can be legitimate, provided it does not lead to a spectator's attitude but to the ethical consequence of vv. 11 and 14.

We regard the images of the antichrist and the millennial kingdom as essential for the belief in a genuine relationship between the crucified and risen Christ and the world. They are not in the least chance moments in the NT; see H. Berkhof, *Christ the Meaning of History*, chs. 6 and 7. Granted this, one may differ on the precise extent to which these enormous images are authoritative for us when they are projected on the screen of the future. I would speak with greater reserve now than I did in the above book. Hence in the large type I have indicated only the coherence of these images with the whole of the Christian confession on history.

56. AMBIVALENCE AND VICTORY

WE HAVE OBSERVED HOW THE SPIRIT of Christ endeavors to put his stamp on our reality in two ways: first in personal sanctification, in which through death and resurrection he seeks to conform us to the image of Christ (paragraphs 47–50), and then in structural sanctification, in which he offers a paradigm and prophecy of the world as God intends it in Christ (paragraphs 54f.). But in both cases we noticed that there is a limit to this work of renewal: as regards personal sanctification, in this life we get no further than a small beginning of obedience. And structural sanctification elicits in unredeemed man precisely the opposite of the Spirit's intention, with the result that Christ not only celebrates an incidental and provisional resurrection in the sanctification of the world, but what is even worse, is continually crucified afresh in our world in the secularism evoked by that sanctification.

That we believe in God, in Christ, and in the Spirit means that we believe that the renewal is capable of overcoming this double boundary. In paragraph 51 we saw how the boundary of death, our personal death, is by the Spirit made into a ferment in the process of renewal. We cannot speak in the same manner about the boundary of the world. Here the boundary of the renewal does not consist in a dying off and a dying out of the human race (at least we are in no position to make faith statements about that), but in an intensification that leads to the deadlock of an intensified and insuperable ambivalence of Spirit-power and counter-power. That is induced by the decisive mystery of history: Jesus crucified *and* risen. In that way, and down to that boundary, his fate is going to be reflected worldwide in the fate of the world.

How can this dialectic ever be overcome? If we believe that Jesus' resurrection abolished his crucifixion and death, then we believe that, analogically, that is also going to happen worldwide in history. There is thus indeed an analogy with man's personal death. In the ultimate tension of sanctification and secularization the world ends up in the deadlock of its own contradiction.

The world is heading for the crisis of a stalemate between its two opposing trends. Only God is able to deliver the world from this crisis by causing what is possible with him to triumph in this dilemma. By raising Christ, he caused the resurrection power that was in Christ to triumph. God raised precisely him to justify him on account of the work the Son had accomplished in the name of the Father. The leap was at once a consequence and a crowning reward.

By way of analogy we may conceive of the future of the world as a leap-event from God's side to free the forces his Spirit is activating in the world. Therefore Paul could compare the condition of the world with pregnancy and the pain of labor (Romans 8:22). The leap does not break the continuity; on the contrary, it saves it. Neither the world itself nor the work of the Spirit can give that continuity. A break, a discontinuity is necessary, but this discontinuity is to serve and stands in the framework of the continuity.

Just as with man's personal future expectation, here again we run into the concept of judgment, wherein continuity and discontinuity coincide. In the judgment (Gk. *krisis;* literally: division) the great sifting and purification take place. We have no other way to speak about this than in images, yet we cannot be silent about it. The judgment expresses the connection with history as well as the divine turn toward the future. In the judgment the deformed and derailed world is judged, straightened out, in such a way that all foreign elements are cast off and God's holy love begins to permeate all relationships. God not only becomes all in all (persons), but also all in everything (structures); therefore all that is loveless and self-sufficient will be put down and what is helpless and despised will be exalted. Through and out of this judgment the world arises renewed as an "earth in which righteousness dwells."

We live *after* the provisional leap in Jesus' resurrection, but *before* the definitive leap of our world that is guaranteed in it. That puts a limit to our thought and imagination, and even more to our actions. Can we cooperate in the coming of the Kingdom? What the Spirit works in us cannot redeem the world from its ambivalence. However, through that work we can and do heighten the ambivalence and hasten the great polarization in the ripening of wheat and weeds. In that sense we are directly co-workers in the coming of the Kingdom. But that is also what those people are who unwittingly and unwillingly use the building blocks of sanctification for the construction of an autonomous culture in which there is no room for Christ. Thus the concept of cooperation is also ambivalent. Decisive much rather is the concept of choice. The important thing is that we help the ripening of that which in the great harvest can be harvested as wheat.

For centuries the Bible has been read as if it teaches that the renewal of the world is entirely discontinuous, as a break with this world and history. Closer investigation shows, however, that even in the most discontinuous statements, the background and framework is always the continuity. As concerns the OT, this requires no further argument. But the NT, too, does not speak of destruction but of a renewal of the world we know. Not this world itself, but the "form (Gk. *schēma*) of this world is passing away" (1 Cor. 7:31). Even the apocalyptic-sounding passage 2 Pet. 3:5–13, which speaks of a (purifying) world conflagration, says at the same time: "and the earth with all that is in it will be laid bare" (v. 10). And though at the end of Revelation the concern is indeed a heavenly Jerusalem, it is one that comes down from God onto a new earth (21:1f.) and into which are brought the cultural treasures of history (21:24, 26). In the other NT passages dealing with the relation of this world to the one to come, namely the Synoptic apocalypse (Mark 13 and parallels), 1 Cor. 15:23–30, and 2 Thess. 2, it is entirely clear that the coming world will be the renewal and consummation of this one. See H. Berkhof, *Christ the Meaning of History,* pp. 180–184 and 188–192.

Partly as a reaction against a centuries-old one-sidedness, in most recent theology eschatology is directly tied in with the problematic and development of this world. This theology likes to create the impression that the forces of sanctification will eventually overcome the counter-forces and establish on earth the Kingdom of peace and righteousness, the Kingdom of *shalom.* The leap which in the Bible is just as important as the continuity is passed over in these treatises. That element is regarded as too "dualistic." After *Gaudium et spes* (1965) this tendency can be found in much Roman Catholic thinking (Thomistic: *gratiam naturam perficit!*), and after H. Cox, *The Secular City* (1965), and R. Alves, *A Theology of Human Hope* (1969), in many Protestant thinkers (mostly semi-Marxist). But a purely continuous expectation can neither be biblically founded, nor be shown to be historically and actually true. For the sharp discontinuity between history and consummation in the Bible, see W. Jaeschke, *Die Suche nach den eschatologischen Wurzeln der Geschichtsphilosophie* (1976), pp. 99–217. For a fierce discussion, among others about these questions, between European and liberation theology, see J. Míguez Bonino, *Theologie van verdrukten* (1974), ch. 7, and J. Moltmann, "An Open Letter" in *Christianity and Crisis* (March 29, 1976). For an overview of the standpoints and a plea for a "cooperative model" in the framework of the covenant, see W. van Bruggen, *Futurum en eschaton* (1983).

The concept of judgment has more than one connotation in the Bible. In relation to the world as a whole it means something else than in connection with the subject of par. 50 (the judgment on the works of believers). Here we are to think especially of the OT conception (which also forms the background for the NT conceptions): the derivatives of the root *š-p-ṭ* refer to "judging" in the sense of righting things, and "judgment" in the sense of a setting-straight of distorted relationships. The relationships in the world are not at all in harmony with the intention of the holy love. In the great leap of the world they will be radically set straight. In that context "judgment" means as much as a revolution: the selfish mighty rulers will be dethroned and the oppressed, the "poor," the "humble" will finally be allowed to breathe and be themselves. See e.g. Ps. 72; 75:8; Isa. 11:4; Luke 1:51ff.; 6:20–26; 16:19–31; Jas. 5:1–11. With that connotation judgment is primarily glad tidings; the coming judge is the one who will set things straight, the savior who will bring about in the world the long-awaited structural righteousness. For more on this see H. Berkhof, *Well-Founded Hope* (E.T. 1969), pp. 43–47.

All Things New

57. CHRIST, THE SPIRIT, AND THE FUTURE

IN PARAGRAPH 56 WE POINTED OUT that the gap which separates our world from the world to come, and which can only be overcome by a leap from God's side, puts a boundary to our contemplation of the future. In that sense the future is a limiting concept for Christian thought. The failure to respect this limit leads to fantastic or simply shortsighted pronouncements that are only idle speculation.

Nevertheless the future is a limiting concept of an absolutely unusual character. Paradoxically one could call it a "central limiting concept." We still live on this side of the gap that separates us from the great future, yet we live here from realities pointing to the future on the other side of the gap, and which are "pro-visional" relative to that future in such a way that at least they open up a dim vista on that future. The future involves the two complementary realities of Christ and the Spirit. Christ: that is, Jesus, who in the way of obedience unto death by virtue of the leap of resurrection-through-raising reached the goal God has in mind for humanity. As the glorified one he lives and works in perfect harmony with the Father. This mode of existence is unimaginable to us, but the witnesses of his resurrection, like the apostle Paul on the road to Damascus, caught a glimpse of it and therefore in images dared to stammer about the great renewal. And the Spirit, who as a new leap becomes available from Christ, is the great pioneer of that future, because everywhere in the world he orients people to Christ's new sonship. Both Christ and the Spirit find their ultimate justification in the future. And both are anticipations of that future. Together they constitute a narrow track in a world which is still everywhere marked by provisionality and guilt. But along that track both give a taste of the powers of the life to come: reconciliation, love, communion, justice, peace, happiness, wholeness. We who follow that track look ahead as those not-knowing and yet-knowing. "We are God's children now; it does not yet appear what we shall be, but we know that when he [Christ] appears we shall be like him" (1 John 3:2).

Therefore there is only one language in which we can make statements about the future, namely that of the image, symbolic language. On the one hand imagery is derived from this world which we know, while on the other hand it reaches beyond it. It joins knowing and not-yet-knowing, continuity and discontinuity. Therefore we speak of the future as a wedding, a meal, a city with streets of gold, a feast. Of course we know very well that the future will be something quite different and much more. But on account of Christ and the Spirit we dare to say that the future must lie in that direction and will inspire similar feelings of happiness and ecstasy. This imagery on the one hand infinitely magnifies what is uplifting and gladdening in this world, and on the other hand completely expels other elements which are just as much part of our world, elements such as sorrow, confusion, and sin.

In general the biblical images speak for themselves. To some of them we shall come back later. Here we point specifically to the image of the return of Christ. That image denotes that someday Christ will be revealed in our experiential world as its secret and foundation, and that that revelation will not happen as the unfolding of immanent forces, but as a new encounter-event in which mankind will meet on its way as its liberators the Son and in him the Father. "The Spirit and the Bride say, 'Come!'" (Revelation 22:17). For proceeding from Christ the Spirit works toward that future. And the church is the communion which knows of that future; though not yet possessing it, she is destined for it.

Eschatology becomes speculation or fantasy if it does not "extrapolatingly" start from experiences of God which we acquire in our world and history. See K. Rahner, "The Hermeneutics of Eschatological Assertions," in *Theological Investigations,* IV (E.T. 1966), pp. 323–346; and H. Berkhof, *Well-Founded Hope* (E.T. 1969), pp. 16–21 and *passim.* In par. 51, in our discussion of the consummation of man's personal life, our thinking was also along these lines. See also *MS* 5, ch. 8,1.

An eschatology of the world and mankind was unknown before and outside Israel. People spoke of a cycle, a movement of the waves, a steady worsening of the world, a senseless course, or a coming world conflagration. The question how and why there emerged in Israel an expectation of the future as the expectation of salvation has received widely varying answers as the subject was studied. There has, however, come about a consensus (see the biblical theologies of the OT) which can be formulated as follows: Israel's cumulative experiences with Yahweh in history, especially the deliverance from Egypt, the settlement in Canaan, victory over their enemies, and the rise to national greatness under David and Solomon, resulted in the conviction that with this God they were on the way to a future in which he in and from Israel would set up a perfect and everlasting kingdom of peace. Because Yahweh was an historical God, he necessarily became an eschatological God. This biblical-theological insight thus confirms the correctness of the method of extrapolation in the study of the faith. At surprising turns in history (e.g. the return from exile) this expectation of salvation even became *Naherwartung* (imminent expectation). But due to the sins of the people this expectation was regularly anew put far into the future. Yet it did not disappear; history had given rise to expectations which no amount of disappointment could eradicate.

In the NT, eschatology exhibits similar structures. John the Baptist and Jesus made their appearance in a climate charged with eschatological expectations. Neither satisfied those expectations. But as a result of Jesus' ministry and resurrection there arose in the first church a new and absolute certainty concerning the future, accompanied by the positive expectancy that this future would come very soon, since it was the direct consequence of the life, death, and resurrection of Jesus. In the Synoptic Gospels Jesus' ministry is the prelude of the Kingdom that is at hand; in Paul the eschaton is the consequence of Jesus' death and resurrection; in both explications the future is the extrapolation of the present. When the eschaton failed to come the perspective changed. In John all the emphasis is put on the life eternal which is already present here and now in the Spirit; in the Epistle to the Hebrews, in contrast, it is on the not-yet, on the pilgrimage of God's people, with Christ as the pioneer and the perfecter of the faith (that is, of the hope) leading the way. These differences in accentuation notwithstanding, the tensional unity of present and future is kept intact, with the second through extrapolation being derived from the first. Especially in Paul this relation of Christ, the Spirit, and the future is clear (Rom. 5:5; 8:11, 23; 15:13; 1 Cor. 6:14; 1 Cor. 15:12-22; 2 Cor. 4:14; 1 Thess. 4:14; 5:10; 2 Thess. 2:16). It is striking how in the NT the future is regularly indicated in terms which in another context are used to denote the appearance of Christ or the work of the Spirit; e.g. "eternal life" (cf. Matt. 19:6; John 3:36; 5:24; Gal. 6:8), "being raised" and "resurrection" (cf. Acts 4:2; 1 Cor. 15:12–22; Eph. 5:14), "revelation" (*apokalypsis;* cf. Luke 2:32; Rom. 8:19; Eph. 1:17), "appearing" (*epiphaneia;* cf. 2 Tim. 4:8; Tit. 2:13), "day" (cf. Matt. 25:13; John 8:56; 2 Cor. 6:2), "hour" (namely of decision, *kairos;* cf. Mark 1:15; Rom. 13:11; 1 Pet. 1:5).

Only since the previous century has the study of the faith increasingly begun to develop eschatology from the present fact and experience of grace. In the school of Barth, eschatology has been entirely based on Christology; see Weber, *Gl* II, ch. XI, and especially W. Kreck, *Die Zukunft des Gekommenen* (1961). The role of the Spirit as the One who makes us taste the powers of the age to come usually fails to receive the necessary attention beside the christological accent. A remarkable attempt to widen the christological method pneumatologically is the eschatology of A. König, *Jesus Christus die eschatos* (1970) with its tripartition: "Jesus Christus bereik die eschaton vir ons" (ch. 4), "in ons" (ch. 5), "met ons" (ch. 6) ("Jesus Christ reaches the eschaton for us, in us, with us").

Meanwhile this method should not make us forget the leap that is necessary to extend this christological-pneumatological line into the eschatological. Extrapolation and discontinuity are to be taken together. In the most recent designs of eschatological thinking the second threatens to get lost (see the small-print section of par. 56). But in another sense such was already the case in Barth, for whom Christ was so much the one and all of revelation (the forty days between resurrection and ascension as the real time of revelation, the fullness of time) that he can think of the future only as the disclosure of what is already christologically present: one day the world will become manifest as it now already is in virtue of God's coming in Christ. See *CD* I,2, par. 14,1 and III,2, par. 47,1. Rather suddenly several voices have taken issue with that viewpoint, especially due to the influence of E. Bloch, *Das Prinzip Hoffnung* (1959). See J. Moltmann, *Theology of Hope* (E.T. 1967); G. Sauter, *Zukunft und Verheissung* (1965), and U. Hedinger, *Hoffnung zwischen Kreuz und Reich* (1968). In all these thinkers the methodological movement is not from the center (Christ) to the future, but vice versa: extrapolation turns into utopia. Thus the leap-character of the future is so much more recognized. The relation to the center (esp. Jesus' resurrection) is not denied, but this center is entirely thought of as signifying *promissio.* For a discussion of these contrasting methods see W.-D. Marsch, ed., *Diskussion über die "Theologie der Hoffnung" von Jürgen Moltmann* (1967). It is remarkable, though understandable, that in a utopistic eschatology the future itself becomes little more than a formal principle, which in turn formalistically narrows the center. The opposite method, which deduces the future from Christ and the Spirit, a method particularly used by Paul, results in a speaking about the future which, though modest, is nevertheless much more substantial. But within this extrapolation of salvation and thus continuity of salvation, the leap element has to find its place. That is not difficult once we realize that the continuity does not lie in history itself, but in God who has regularly used leaps to assure the continuity of his work in history. Interesting are the reflections on the relation between "evolution" and "shock" in K. Schilder, *Wat is de hemel?* (1935), ch. V.

With the approach to the future offered here, we reject a number of other approaches: Fundamentalism (which combines and harmonizes biblical texts, and presents the result as direct information), evolutionism (which expects a golden age as the outcome of immanent developments), futurism (which does the same but in a much shorter time, viewing the future in terms of an extrapolation from technological developments), and of course Existentialism (which considers it enough to know the meaning of Christ and the Spirit for us here and now). The line we follow here is pointedly and succinctly formulated in the Heidelberg Catechism (Q. and A. 58), which answers the question: "What comfort do you derive from the article of 'life everlasting'?" with: "That, since I now feel in my heart the beginning of eternal joy, after this life I shall possess perfect bliss. . . ."

Finally, we should still refer to Van Ruler, whose method contrasts both with the method which takes its starting-point in the center and with that which starts at the end. He perceives the eschaton strictly from the perspective of the beginning as a recovery of the order of creation. Not only is Christ an interim which is necessary only on account of sin; the same is true of the Spirit. "The Son . . . stops being Messiah; he just leaves things in their saved state; so that in the joy of their existence they praise God and the Lamb forever. So also the Spirit. When the flesh has been done away, the outpouring and the indwelling will be undone. When the eternal light of the realm of glory arises over the whole creation, the illumination of the Spirit (in his outpouring and indwelling!) is extinguished" (*De vervulling van de wet,* 1947, p. 149). Cf. also *Theologisch werk,* I (1969), chs. VII and VIII; II (1971), ch. XI; IV (1972), ch. VIII. According to this viewpoint, since Christ and the Spirit do not themselves represent the future in the present and we possess no knowledge of our own about God's good creation, eschatology is bound to remain abstract. At times, however, Van Ruler suddenly moves along different lines, e.g. *De vervulling van de wet,* IV, ch. XI, pp. 109f.

The confession of a christological extrapolation, joined with that of a leap, is especially expressed in the idea of the return of Christ. The aspect "re-" (again) is, however, not often found in the NT. *Parousia* simply means "coming." It refers to the public, definitive, triumphal coming. For that reason it is seldom called a re-turn or coming-again (only indirectly in John 14:3; Acts 1:11; Heb. 9:28), because that would presuppose the existence of a vacuum between the then and what is to come later. Christ, however, remains present in the Spirit. That is how he moves with his church in a hidden manner toward his public coming. A remarkable passage in this respect is John 16:16–22, where there is a blending of the coming in the resurrection, in the Spirit, and in the *parousia*. There is a constant coming and going, which is compared to the pains of childbirth (v. 21). In a combination of continuity and leap, Christ and the Spirit move toward the future. See on this Barth, *CD* IV,3, par. 69,4. For a recent overview of the eschatological questions and answers, see H. Vorgrimler, *Hoffnung auf Vollendung* (1980).

58. INDIVIDUALS, MANKIND, AND THE FUTURE

CHRIST AND THE SPIRIT are instrumental in preparing individuals as well as mankind as a whole for the leap to come. The question now is, in view of the work of Christ and the Spirit for man and society, what we may expect at and beyond that boundary. We must begin by acknowledging that we deal here with two totally different boundaries: for individuals the boundary of death, for mankind the boundary of a world ending in a deadlock. This duality is disturbing to our thinking. But logically and biblically it is unavoidable. We have a personal life and at the same time contribute to the advance of history. These two dimensions cannot be reduced to one. If we think of the consummation entirely in terms of mankind and world history, then no place is left for the perfection of the billions of human lives that came to an end before the advent of this new age of salvation. Considering the purport of the whole of redemptive revelation and in particular Jesus' resurrection as promise and guarantee to us, this conception is an unacceptable reduction of the expectation. But that is no less the case if we abstract individual salvation from the salvation of society. No one is set free if all are not set free. For the Christian faith, the individual person, mankind, and the whole of society constitute an indivisible unity. Thus the expectation of their renewal is also indivisible.

But then we face again the problem of the duality; for long before mankind crosses the boundary to its future, the great majority of people will have crossed the death line. Will their personal consummation then have to wait till the time of the consummation of the world? In answer to that question there has been developed the doctrine—or rather, the variant doctrines—of the so-called intermediate state. The taproot of this thinking was the centuries-long concentration on the salvation of the individual soul and the age-old belief in the distinction between a mortal body and an immortal soul. The idea was that the soul of the believer at death ascends into the presence of God (heaven), eternally to "rejoice there before the throne." The consummation of mankind, which would give a new bodily existence as well, could hardly add anything essential to the salvation already received. This thinking is entirely in terms of an individual soul and of space (earth-heaven): not the process of history is being redeemed, but man is redeemed out of it. The question how God will achieve his purpose for the world is thereby reduced to insignificance. This, too, is untenable. Others, in order to make a distinction between salvation after death as the lesser and the consummation of mankind as the greater, think of the intermediate state as a time of waiting or of purification, or even as a sleep in which the consciousness of time is suspended. Though all such conceptions can appeal to biblical ideas, they are on the one hand mutually exclusive, and on the other hand start from the common conviction that life on the other side of the death line proceeds similarly within time as it does here. Existence on the other side is thus entirely conceived of as a continued existence in time. We who live on this side have no other conceptual categories. We should realize, however, that we are ignorant of what "time" means beyond the leap. Thus it makes no sense either to say that beyond the two boundaries we come into (the one) "eternity." For eternity as God's sphere is not intended for us. Time is an integral aspect of the good creation, and thus also of our human existence. What this may mean in the great consummation will be discussed in the final paragraph. We are in no position to make meaningful statements about an in-between time or an intermediate state (except for this statement—and that is decisive—that beyond the death line we shall never and nowhere fall out of the hand of our faithful Covenant-partner. He remains the same on both sides of the boundary).

The OT is concerned almost exclusively with the future of Israel and of humanity, though in a later phase it also makes some statements about what awaits believers after death (Ps. 16:9–11; 49:16; 73:25f.); that both coincide is suggested in Isa. 26:19 and Dan. 12:2f. The NT is concerned with the future of mankind, but no less with the destiny of the individual believer. On account of the *Naherwartung*, the initial feeling was that for many followers of Jesus they would coincide (Luke 9:27; 1 Cor. 15:51f.; 1 Thess. 4:13–17), but this conviction soon disappeared. Very often the dead are said to "sleep" or to "have fallen asleep" (*koimasthai, kekoimēkenai,* John 11:11; 1 Cor. 15:6, 18, 20, 51; 1 Thess. 4:13–15); sometimes they longingly await the consummation (Rev. 6:9–11); sometimes they seem to taste that already now (Heb. 12:22f.; Rev. 7; 14:1–5, 13); in any case they are "with Christ" (John 14:2f.; 2 Cor. 5:8; Phil. 1:23; 1 Thess. 4:14, 17). All these designations have been made into theories in the history of theology. In view of the speculative character of these theories, more recently the idea of a complete non-existence of the dead prior to the great resurrection has also been defended (Van der Leeuw, Althaus, and others). See for literature G. C. Berkouwer, *The Return of Christ* (E.T. 1972), ch. 2; H. Berkhof, *Well-Founded Hope,* pp. 69ff., and H. Ott, *AG* art. 48. After a time when interest in it had been waning, there is again a great interest in the so-called individual eschatology as something that belongs to the essence of the faith. See par. 51, pp. 488ff., and the literature mentioned there. See also W. Aalders, *Schepping of geschiedenis* (1969), who for the sake of the individual expectation of heaven has entirely dropped the line of earth and humanity.

To believe that those who have fallen asleep are, in whatever manner, in the hand of the Father of Jesus Christ may seem a minimum, but it is the maximum. The diverse NT statements and images are no more than approximations of that. As such they offer no material for a theological doctrine, but belong to the language which faith may properly use as it seeks to picture what lies beyond. Accidents occur only where that distinction is not recognized.

The concept or image used from the outset by the Christian faith to capture the conjoined character of the future of the individual and of mankind is that of the resurrection of the dead. It combines several ideas, all of which are integral to the Christian expectation of the future. (a) It indicates the direct connection between Jesus' resurrection and our coming liberation and renewal. (b) It also indicates the relation with what the Spirit does to us in this life, his act of bringing about a new creation by causing man to be born again. (c) But it expresses likewise the discontinuity with everything previously achieved: it is a break and a new miracle when we arise to a new life out of the ambiguity and death of this earthly existence; no reserves of our own, for instance an "immortal soul," but only God guarantees this change. (d) Even so this image expresses the continuity with our earthly existence: it is and remains we ourselves who arise, even though on this side of the boundary we are unable to show or formulate that continuity. It is not another human being that is brought into existence, it is this human being that is changed. (e) At the same time "resurrection" expresses the totality of the renewal. In contrast with the immortality of the soul whereby only a part of man continues to live, the resurrection expresses that man perishes as a totality and is saved as a totality. Saved man is no ghost; he also possesses a renewed physical existence by which he can open himself to others and communicate with others, and this makes possible the existence of associations and structures and consequently the end as well as the resurrection of the *world*. (f) The word "resurrection" is thus the epitome of our confession that our human existence will neither be cast off nor eternalized. It will be renewed after the analogy of Jesus, who out of our old existence arose to a new life. Thus we do not reach our destination by escaping vertically, nor by continuing to run horizontally. All of man's and mankind's existence is saved, preserved, and made fruitful in the way of a radical renewal.

Ad a: It is significant, precisely because of the strange reversal of the argumentation, how in 1 Cor. 15:12–22 Paul makes the connection between Christ's resurrection and the future of mankind; see esp. v. 12: according to the apostle, if there should not be a resurrection, it would prove that Christ himself did not rise (cf. Acts 4:2).

Ad b: For the work of the Spirit, which after all is only a start, a "down payment" *(arrabōn),* the NT avoids the word "resurrection"; cf. Rom. 8:23 and 2 Tim. 2:18. Yet its confession sometimes comes very close to it; see Rom. 6:4; 2 Cor. 5:17; Col. 2:11; 3:1; Eph. 2:5f.; cf. Eph. 5:14.

Ad a and b: The christological and the pneumatological foundation of the expectation are mentioned jointly in Rom. 8:11 and 1 Pet. 1:3.

Ad c and d: See the small type in par. 51.

Ad e: The appearances of Jesus in a new bodily existence, together with the empty grave, have from the very beginning protected the Christian faith from conceiving of the eschaton as the soul's escape from matter. See Phil. 3:21. This existence is saved inwardly *and* outwardly, spiritually *and* materially. Hence the bold expression in the Apostles' Creed: "I believe in the resurrection *of the flesh*" *(sarkos anastasin, carnis resurrectionem).* It could, however, create the misunderstanding that our *sarx* would be eternalized in its material, fragile, and corruptible nature. As regards that aspect, it is done away with in the resurrection. This discontinuity, so strongly underlined by Paul (1 Cor. 15:44, 50), does not sufficiently come out in the expression "resurrection of the flesh" (Dutch: *des vlezes;* the standard English reading is: "of the body"). Yet the emphasis on the discontinuity is all the more necessary because we can say even less about the material dimension of the resurrection than about the psychical and the social. We know nothing about the "what." We only confess the "that." But that is something terrific; for owing to that we can also with a loving hope defend and promote the material well-being of existence.

But now it is high time to consider that our probing of the future expectation, however extensive (mankind), has nevertheless moved only along a narrow track. We were preoccupied with the future of believers, as the completion, by way of a leap, of that which Christ and the Spirit have worked in them in this life. But what are we to think of the innumerable others who have lived their lives outside this covenant relationship? We know, of course, that we cannot tell who belongs to which group, because on the one hand there are many nominal believers, while on the other hand God is able to establish fellowship with people outside the covenantal path of Israel and Christ along which we have come to know him. That, however, does not change the fact that on earth God has never reached and will never reach innumerable people with his covenantal will, a small minority because they refused that encounter, the great majority because that encounter never came to them.

What future expectation is there for non-believers? It is a pressing and difficult question, because the Christian faith holds two seemingly or actually mutually exclusive convictions: on the one hand that covenantal history, however narrow its swath through time and space, is meant to be a blessing and redemption for all men; on the other hand that this blessing and redemption remain unfruitful if men do not accept them in faith and obedience.

When finally the big leap into the realm of freedom and love takes place, it will become manifest that numberless human lives on earth were not headed for that. Here for the third time we come upon the concept of judgment. That concept, after all, expresses at once the continuity and discontinuity between this world and that to come. It says that the distance between these two worlds is determined by our responsibility and our guilt. As concerns the believer, we encountered the judgment as a sifting of his works (paragraph 51); as concerns mankind, as a revolutionary setting-straight of the structures and relationships (paragraph 56). Now it concerns the coming exposure of all of human life that was lived outside the covenant relationship.

But therein too—contrary to the tradition of the church and the study of the faith—we shall have to make clear distinctions.

First of all we need to realize that the structural redemption of mankind needs as its reverse the redemption of innumerable people. When God abolishes the oppressive structures, this means salvation for the oppressed. Millions of people—the outlawed, the victims of discrimination, the persecuted, the trampled upon, and the martyred—were in this life never able to answer to God's purpose, not because of their own sin, but due to the sins of others. If God has in mind to banish sin and to resist sinners, the judgment upon the oppressors must imply the deliverance of their victims. Else it would be meaningless. The Bible is full of that expectation. Most of the time we have overlooked that in our reading of the Bible. Yet how could we stand it in a world which offers such unequal opportunities, a world which is drenched in injustice, if we could not also expect this from God?

That judgment will also be for those who, without knowing of this God or at least without feeling themselves motivated by him, showed justice to the oppressed and so acted in accordance with God's purposes. That same judgment which spells deliverance for the oppressed, implies justification for the merciful. They will receive mercy, as surely as God is faithful to himself.

But what will the judgment mean for those who are unaware of these things, a group which always constitutes the great majority of humanity? They go along, do what is expected of them, avoid adventure and sacrifice, and for themselves and their family and friends try to get out of life what they can. Must not the judgment become for them a terrible revelation of the alienation in which they have lived? But to what extent are they at fault and to what extent was it their fate? We do not know how

God judges. We do know that we may not acquiesce in all the alienation around us. And of God we know that he does not divide people into categories as we are accustomed to, but that he searches and exposes each person with his holy love.

The Bible speaks much about the terror of the judgment, but almost exclusively it concerns God's enemies. They are the people who resist his ways of election and love. They are the enemies who begrudge Israel her (of course undeserved) place in the light, it is disobedient Israel that rejects and kills the Son, it is a Christianity which under cover of God's name persists in her worldly practices and so crucifies her Lord all over again, it is all who knowingly and willingly oppose the proclamation and realization of his holy love in the world. Who are the ones who do that "knowingly and willingly"? We cannot point them out. The judgment will reveal it. For them the judgment will mean total condemnation and total shame: the disclosure not only of an alienated but of a forfeited existence.

And for all these people who differ so much and are of so many different kinds, the judgment will mean that they will be judged in accordance with the light they had received.

In the OT the "day of Yahweh" at first meant the judgment upon the enemies of God and of his people Israel. But since Amos it became clear that Israel and Judah, too, would be condemned as being enemies of Yahweh (Amos 1:2; 5:18–20). Only for a "remnant" will there be escape. To that remnant belong the poor, the miserable, the lowly (Isa. 11:1–5; Zeph. 3:12, etc.). They are found not only in Israel but also outside her (Isa. 11:10; 19:19–25; Jon.; Mic. 3:3, etc.).

In the NT it is expected that the great division will cut right through Israel and the nations, even right through Christ's church itself (the latter esp. in Matt.; see 7:21–23; 18:21–35; 25:1–30). In the judgment the lines of this earthly life are extended; and yet or for that reason the judgment will mean dismay for the one and surprise for the other.

It is remarkable that the NT contains little or no intentional reflection on the question that occupies us here. That is mainly because these writers were not concerned with reflection but were interested in action: by their preaching they seek to save people from the judgment to come (2 Cor. 5:11a, 20f.). Even so, most of the groups we listed are rather clearly recognizable in the NT in their relation to the judgment: the oppressed (Luke 4:18; 6:20–26; 16:19–32; Jas. 5:1–6), the merciful (Matt. 25:31–46; Luke 10:25–37; Rom. 2:14–16), the disobedient in the church (Matt. 7:21–23; 18:21–35; 25:1–30), and the adversaries outside (2 Thess. 1:6–10). Sometimes the NT speaks of a gradation in the judgment, depending on the measure of awareness and knowledge (Luke 10:10–15; 11:29–32). And in Rom. 8:19–23, where "creation" *(ktisis)* refers exclusively or primarily to unredeemed humanity, the church is seen as the people who are aware that they are the firstfruits of the creation (v. 23; cf. Jas. 1:18), after whom and together with whom will be saved all who now groan under "the sufferings of this present time" (v. 18) and who unconsciously yearn for that future toward which the church already now consciously lives.

The churches and the study of the faith have not made use of the distinctions made here. As a rule they simply divided people into believers and unbelievers, without considering that this "un-" comprises a great variety of attitudes. The Roman Catholic Church, owing to its broad substructure of "nature" (to which belong "all people of good will") and its doctrine of purgatory, was able to inject a touch of flexibility. The churches of the Reformation must do without that. The ease with which many orthodox Christians used to and still designate at least 95 percent of the human race (for one should also take into account the many centuries before the beginning of missionary activity) as lost betrays much thoughtlessness and harshness. Fortunately, secularism and the intense contact with non-Christian worlds compel to a deeper and more careful consideration of this matter. But so far little of that is noticeable in the study of the faith. See the literature in the next section.

Naturally the question must now arise whether this judgment, and particularly the condemnation in this judgment, will be made to last forever. The situation of condemnation is called "hell" in the New Testament. Man ends up in the "outer darkness" because in his earthly life he chose against the light and for the darkness; the lines are now extended. The "weeping and gnashing of teeth" express the fruitless dwelling upon wasted opportunities. The question from the previous section (what future expectation is there for non-believers?), applied to a segment of the non-believers, now becomes: is hell forever?

The New Testament writings, which nowhere specifically discuss this question, suggest more than one answer, and that has resulted in a diversity of views in the Christian churches. But in official ecclesiastical doctrine the dominant idea is that hell is eternal. A few biblical passages state that clearly. And the decision for or against Christ carries an eternal weight, does it not? Yet there has always been a reluctance to engage in a deeper probing of this frightening conviction. For the implication is that one will have to assume that the absolute God-forsakenness forever retains a place in a renewed creation. Hence, according to some, the condemnation in the judgment is to be understood as a total annihilation. Another idea is that there may be a chance for conversion in the hereafter. And still others believe that one day all who have been created in God's image will be re-created in Christ's image; this is the belief in universal atonement *(apokatastasis)*.

In the study of the faith, owing to its nature and methodology, the first answer we are compelled to give is: we do not know. Ours is the duty to call people to conversion in this life; and what God does with them in eternity is not our business. Many like to say: that is something we leave confidently up to God who is at once the greatest justice and the highest love. But this answer, in itself correct, implies more than that we do not know. The word "confidence" and the doublet of justice and love are already indicative of a more positive answer. And, indeed, the decision is determined by the manner in which we see justice and mercy, holiness and love, wrath and forgiveness, blend in God. Relative to that we refer to pp. 132–134. There we left open the question that concerns us here. But since then we have had a closer look at the justice and the love that existed in Israel and in Christ. We know that the covenant means that God's faithfulness ever and again does battle with man's unfaithfulness. What ultimately will be forced to yield: divine faithfulness or human unfaithfulness? Paul raised that question with respect to Israel, as the trial grounds of God's relationship to man; and he ends with the confession: "God has consigned all men to disobedience, that he may have mercy upon all" (Romans 11:32). These considerations compel us, not to detract from the gravity of the human "no" against God and its consequences, but to think just a little more of the divine "yes" to recalcitrant humans. God is serious about the responsibility of our decision, but he is even more serious about the responsibility of his love. The darkness of rejection and God-forsakenness cannot and may not be argued away, but no more can and may it be eternalized. For God's sake we hope that hell will be a form of purification.

Above we have discussed four views concerning the eternal destiny of those who resist God. The thought that they will simply be destroyed (annihilation) does not seem to do justice to God's love nor to the seriousness of our decision. Biblical terms—taken literally—that seem to support this view are "perdition," "to be lost," "eternal death," and especially Rev. 20:14. These words, however, precisely presuppose a continuing existence. Moreover, annihilation amounts to a defeat of God's love, though hidden by an act of force. The idea of an opportunity for conversion after death and judgment seeks support in 1 Pet. 3:19f., a much-disputed passage; the sentiment of a "second chance" may be psychologically appealing; it is, however, pious fantasy, and does not resolve the problem that engages us here. The thought that mankind will be forever separated into two groups, though generally accepted in the churches, has against it that the language about hell as a place of weeping and gnashing of teeth is found especially in Matthew (8:12; 13:42, 50; 22:13; 24:51; 25:30), while he also speaks three times (18:8; 25:41, 46) about an "eternal" fire or punishment; furthermore, Paul speaks only once of "eternal destruction" for the persecutors of the church (1 Thess. 2:16; cf. 2 Thess. 1:9). Apparently a concentration on an eternal punishment in hell does not belong to the core of the kerygma. Juxtaposed to these statements, a number of others occur in Paul which so explicitly open up a future of salvation for "all" (usually *pantes;* in Rom. 5:15, 19 *hoi polloi*) that they cannot be harmonized with the ones just mentioned: namely Rom. 5:12–21; 11:25, 30–32, 36; 1 Cor. 15:22, 28; Eph. 1:10; Phil. 2:11; 1 Tim. 2:4; 4:10; 1 John 2:2. In our judgment, the first series of statements is to be understood in terms of a conflict situation: they are all directed against Israel which is throwing away her salvation by her enmity against her Messiah and his church. The setting of the second series is the Hellenistic churches, to whom it must have been a continual question and concern what would happen in eternity to their unbelieving family and neighbors (see also 1 Cor. 15:29); they may rest in the assurance that salvation in Christ extends as far as the lostness in Adam (1 Cor. 15:22).

We should not exegetically tamper with both these series, attempting to reduce the first to the second, or, what is usually done, the second to the first (see the forced exegeses of e.g. Augustine and Calvin). Hermeneutically we are to do justice to both, to the first as expressing the consciousness of the importance of decision *(Entscheidungsbewusstsein),* to the second as expressing the consciousness of the importance of election (*Erwählungsbewusstsein,* Althaus). We should not set them beside each other but the one after the other, as surely as the last word is not left to man's decision but to God's eternal purpose. Unless we would assume with Calvin that according to this purpose certain people are created for eternal damnation *(Inst* III,xxiii). But in that case the deepest character of God is not saving love, but threatening ambiguity; and that is a consequence Calvin and his followers have always shied away from.

The *apokatastasis* doctrine, from the time it was propounded by Origen (someday, through a process of purification, all souls will return to God, *De principiis* II.10, III.6), has had a long line of adherents, among the Greek fathers, in medieval heretics, in sub-movements of the Reformation, in Pietism, in such diverse men as Oetinger, Schleiermacher, F. D. Maurice, C. Blumhardt, etc. In the Netherlands it has been passionately defended by P. Kohnstamm in *De heilige* (1931), pp. 390–403. But the motives of the protagonists often vary widely. Barth, too, is to be counted among the supporters because of his belief in the predominance of grace, which controls all of his thinking; only he refuses (like Maurice) to draw the ultimate consequence, for fear of making grace into a system. See *CD* II,2, p. 417 and IV,3, pp. 470f. See further on this subject P. Althaus, *Die letzten Dinge* (since the 4th printing of 1933), ch. V; Ott, *AG* art. 50; H. Berkhof, *Well-Founded Hope,* pp. 104–106; and H. Küng, *Eternal Life?* (E.T. 1984), the cautious discussion "Hell—Eternal" (ch. VI, 7).

59. ETERNAL LIFE

First we raised the question how we can gain access to statements about the future (paragraph 57); next, how we are to conceive of the leap into that future (paragraph 58); now we are ready to ask what expectations we can have about the life that awaits us on the other side of that leap. When people have gone through the resurrection, when the structures have been made new, when the judgment has had its purifying effect—what then? We are accustomed to call that eternal life. But can we conceive anything at all about it that is not just the product of our fantasy and desires? Fortunately such is not impossible. What we know about God's work along the path of Israel, of Christ, and of the Spirit can guide and correct our thoughts. But even then, does not eternal life lie an eternity ahead of us on that path? Is that still something we can conceptually grasp? Should not the dogmatician here yield to the poet? It is true, imagery is the language that comes closest to what eternity is, together with the language of music. Hence the best verbalizations of eternal life are found in Bach and Handel and in a number of church songs and

Christian hymns. In comparison, the conceptual language of dogmatics is bound to be always meager and dry. Nevertheless in that language, too, we should try to say something about eternal life; if only because the concept may not now suddenly fall silent. In the awareness that it will always fall far short of what it attempts to describe, it ought to keep up its own mode of praise, however inferior and defective, to the end.

On the basis of everything we have seen of God in his course through history and in the hearts of men, a series of elements can be mentioned that are integral to the totally renewed existence we may expect. In the following enumeration we include at the same time the expansion of what we have already stated about eternal life on pp. 491f., an expansion made possible by the concept of "world."

1. It will be the total removal of sin. It will be expelled because love will govern existence in all its relationships and to its remotest parts.

2. It will be the abolition of what is provisional. The new world will be fully permeated with the light of God. Our old world which is still so far away from its Creator is full of dark shadows, natural catastrophes, sickness, and death. The new world will live so close to its source of light that the shadows will have fled and everything is bathed in light; it is a world unimaginable to us, free from pain, sadness, and mourning.

3. Eternal life will also mean that the bond with God is no longer wrapped in veils. In the earthliness of our existence this bond is present everywhere only in concealment and brokenness, in the form of the relativity of our experiential world, and hence subject to doubt and unbelief (see paragraph 9). In eternal life, God will be fully present and knowable in the reality he has made. In contrast to this present existence of hearing and believing, we may then speak of "seeing God," and our drive for ever more knowledge and greater love will have been satisfied. This designation of eternal life, which is a favorite in the Bible and in church history, of course, does not mean a spectator relationship. The point it wants to make is that it is the immediate presence of God and the concomitant certainty and joy that will mark this consummated relationship to God. And of course, the consummated communion is much more than just vision. It is also loving, praising, and service.

4. Eternal life will be the perfected oneness with all other human beings (German: *Mitmenschlichkeit*). In this life God has placed us within a community of people and constantly pointed us to our fellowman. In the great future, the love to God and to fellowman will be absolutely one. There will be no salvation which is only a private concern, simply because such would be self-contradictory.

5. Eternal life will be the perfected society, in which all relationships will be channels of the interaction of love between God and man and among men themselves, without threat or discrimination, without fear or hatred.

6. Then man will reach his destiny in the absolute unity of freedom and love which God has in mind for man (see paragraph 26) and for which the Spirit now trains us in our sanctification (see paragraph 48).

7. Christ will have the central place amid this renewed mankind. For he is the root and the firstfruits of this divinely intended humanity. We will be conformed to his image. He is the forerunner who pulls us along. Because of his work and standing around him as the firstfruits, we shall at last reach our destiny, at last be fully sons and daughters of God ourselves.

8. Finally, looking to what lies ahead, we may hope that what we call "nature" will share in this future. For on the one hand it belongs to the conditions making human existence possible (first of all as concerns our bodily nature), and on the other hand God has his own purpose with nature. It, too, now shares in the shadows, in the being-yet-far-from-God. It is a threat to itself and a threat to man. Furthermore, man threatens and violates nature, and in doing so threatens himself. Moreover, nature and its relationship to man are still unredeemed. Regularly, however, God has also given it a part in his redeeming course through the world. We do not expect a realm of pure spirits but one of real people, which will be a harmonious part and the crown of a larger and healed world.

Reading the delightful vision of Rev. 21:1–22:4 it is striking how in the form of imagery it contains all the above-mentioned elements: 1 in 21:27; 2 in 21:4; 3 in 21:3, 22f.; 22:4; 4–6 in 21:10–21; 7 in 21:9, 22f.; 22:3; 8 in 21:1; 22:1f.

Ad 3: The concept of the vision of God as man's final destiny has a biblical basis (Ex. 33:18–23; Num. 6:24–26; Ps. 27:8; 63:3; Matt. 5:8; 1 Cor. 13:12; 2 Cor. 3:18; Heb. 12:14; Rev. 22:4); only as a result of the questionable combination with the Platonic conception of *theasthai* and *theōria* in a number of fathers since Justin and Clement has it evolved into the medieval doctrine of the *visio Dei beatifica* (*Summa contra gentiles,* III, c. 37, 47–63, and *ST* Supp. q. 92). This outgrowth has everywhere maintained itself in the study of the faith and in Christian piety, leading to a view on the future on the part of many which is too individualistic, vertical, passive, and consumptive. See on this theme K. E. Kirk, *The Vision of God* (1934); K. Schilder, *Wat is de hemel?* (1935), ch. VI,4; V. Lossky, *Vision de Dieu* (1962); G. C. Berkouwer, *The Return of Christ* (E.T. 1972), ch. 12.

Ad 7: On the place of Christ in that future the ideas vary. Will we then still be dependent on his mediation? According to Van Ruler, who sees Christ as belonging integrally to the interim of reconciliation, Christ's humanity will cease to exist in the eschaton; see *De vervulling van de wet* (1947), esp. pp. 90–94. A critique of his thinking is found in Berkouwer, *The Return of Christ,* pp. 430–439. The opposite of Van Ruler's view is that of A. Hulsbosch in *De schepping Gods* (1963), ch. XI: "Also after this life Christ remains the place where we encounter God" (p. 179), because in him according to his humanity dwells the perfect love of the Father and vice versa; therefore the vision of God will be eternally mediated through him. As we see it, both views are extremes that lack a basis in biblical statements or in the totality of the structure of the faith. In our judgment, we shall be in the presence of the Father neither without Christ nor via Christ, but together with him as "the firstborn among many brethren" and therefore around him as the center.

Ad 8: Here we spoke less positively than on the preceding points. For while we know the mode of God's concern for man, we do not know the mode of his concern for nature. With W. Künneth, *The Theology of the Resurrection* (E.T. 1965), one can proceed from the resurrection of Jesus in the direction of a more or less speculative theology of nature (esp. pp. 161–179), but also with P. Teilhard de Chardin, *Oeuvres*, V (1959), pp. 401–403, understand matter as the womb, the matrix, which will have served its purpose when the spiritual life has managed to fully free itself from it. The latter, however, appears to us not to be in line with the way in which biblical thinking consistently combines body and soul, matter and spirit, nature and history. Hence the final sentence of point 8.

The above statements about eternal life are carefully formulated. They are based on the one hand on the principle of exclusion (no sin, provisionality, and concealment), on the other hand on the principle of extrapolation (perfected humanity, communion, love, etc.). But thereby we have not yet indicated what the communal factor in all these elements is, which distinguishes them collectively and separately from what they were before the great leap. It might well be asked whether that is something that can be put into words. Or is that aspect comprehended in the "eternal" of "eternal life"? Eternal is not only "endless"; it is a qualitative concept. But which quality does it express? The New Testament has one basic word that helps us along here: *glory*. In the Old Testament this word (Heb. *kāḇôḏ*) denotes exclusively God's sphere of life. In the New Testament (Gk. *doxa*) it is also used to denote Jesus' sphere of life and especially Jesus as the exalted Christ. And proceeding from him, it now becomes the designation for the sphere of life of redeemed humanity in the great future. What this means is that we will then be fully drawn into the divine sphere of life.

To sense the full implication of that, we have to go back to the often-used term "covenant." It expresses the union of God and man. Up to the present day this is something that takes place only with the greatest of difficulties. In the life of most people God is almost nothing, in the life of several something, in the life of some much, only in Christ is he everything; God is not yet "all in all." From the intimate oneness of the Father and the Son we can tell what God's covenant purpose is. Our expectation of the future is that, on account of Christ and following after him, we shall share in God's sphere of life. That is a staggering and unimaginable perspective. He created us at a great distance from him, where his light can shine only refractedly and indirectly, darkened by heavy shadows. Moreover, we have not followed that light, but chosen to follow our own ways. But God keeps calling and drawing us. And one day his purposes will triumph in our life. Then we will be glorified because he will be glorified in us. Then the distance of our original createdness and all our sinful wanderings away from God will have been overcome, and we shall be at home with the Lord. What we call "mysticism" is only a distantly dim reflection of it. Then the distance between God and us falls away. But we do not become lost in God. We are not wiped out; on the contrary, at last we become ourselves, because of the unity and distance of love and partnership. For the house of this Father has many rooms. But this being-at-home in the sphere of God has the effect of elevating everything we have mentioned in the eight points far beyond all human imagination; analogy and extrapolation will also become useless, so unimaginably great is the future which God holds for us.

Everything will share in that glorification. This includes whatever we may then call "nature": the earth, this minute planet on which God started this grand experiment; and time and space, without which human existence is unthinkable. Space does not become the unbounded free space of God, but it will border on it, be open toward it, and thereby be unimaginably enlarged. And time is not turned into the eternity of God, yet past–present–future will not be dissociated and ebb away, but constitute an unimaginable togetherness as a paradigm of eternity. This is all we can stammeringly say about it. One thing is certain: the questions which we now ask about eternal life, since we can now only think in the categories of our limited space and time, will then appear childish and pointless.

Pseudo-Dionysius the Areopagite (ca. 500) introduced into the doctrine of the knowledge of God the distinction of the three ways: *via causalitatis, via eminentiae,* and *via negationis.* This distinction is so closely related to the assumption of a natural knowledge of God that it is of little use to us. Yet in eschatology the distinction turns out to be useful. We derive our knowledge about the future on the one hand from extending the operational modes of Christ and the Spirit *(via causalitatis)* and extrapolating this toward the consummation *(via eminentiae).* But on the other hand, due to the boundary imposed upon our thinking by the eschatological leap, we find ourselves again and again compelled to reach for the *via negationis.* While keeping the three *viae* together as much as possible, we are aware that with the ultimate perspective, that on "glory," we say something which as to its essence can in the final analysis only be described *per negationem:* that which here and now we are not, "what no eye has seen, nor ear heard, nor the heart of man conceived."

Doxa (and *doxazein*) are used christologically in the NT, especially in reference to Christ after his "glorification" (John 1:14; 2:11; 7:39; 13:31f.; 17:1, 5; 2 Cor. 4:6; 1 Pet. 1:11, 21; 1 Tim. 3:16), occasionally pneumatologically (John 17:10; 2 Cor. 3:8–10, 18), but in particular eschatologically (Rom. 5:2; 8:18, 21, 30; 1 Cor. 15:43; 2 Cor. 3:18; Phil. 3:21; Col. 3:4; 1 Pet. 5:1, 4; Heb. 2:10; Rev. 21:11, 23). Parallel with this eschatological use of *doxa* is that of *pneuma* and *pneumatikos* (in 1 Cor. 15:44–49), as well as the daring expression: *theias koinōnoi physeōs* (2 Pet. 1:4).

This last text reminds us of the Eastern church with its concept of "deification" *(theiōsis, theopoiēsis)*, inspired by the famous words of Athanasius in *De incarnatione*, c. 54: "He became man that we might be made divine" *(autos gar enēnthrōpēsen, hina hēmeis theopoiēthōmen)*. That could create misunderstanding as if it meant an identification with God, whereas the intention is to express the glorification. The desire to avoid the term does not mean that one has to oppose it. For its significance see A. van Haarlem, *Incarnatie en verlossing bij Athanasius* (1961), esp. pp. 84–87 and 137–143. The same holds true for the Roman Catholic preference for the term "elevation" *(elevatio)*. To be sure, Protestantism has decisively rejected this concept on account of its relation with the nature-grace dualism, which involves a two-layer view of creation and an underestimation of the seriousness of sin; see for that B. Wentsel, *Natuur en genade* (1970). But besides being rescue and restoration (that first of all), salvation is also elevation; and if anywhere, the term has its rightful place in eschatology as the parallel of "glorification."

Usually eschatology is silent on the subject of the elevation of the category of space. What could we say about it anyway? Yet, as we see it, the one above-formulated sentence is justified. That sentence is also necessary to rid us of unnecessary doubts on the one hand, and unnecessary speculations about the question how one day the earth will be able to contain those myriads of people on the other. Heaven will be united with the earth, enclosing it and removing its boundaries. Barth has developed a kind of theology of space in connection with the omnipresence of God; see *CD* II,1, pp. 461–490.

In contrast with its treatment of space, eschatology has dealt at great length with time and the relation of time and eternity. Yet one does not really get any further than what we have formulated above. And one who does get "further" will either endlessly prolong time or have it absorbed by a timeless eternity. See H. Berkhof, *Well-Founded Hope*, pp. 27–32 and the literature on p. 102; furthermore, E. Brunner, *Eternal Hope* (E.T. 1954), pp. 42–57 and 130–135.

Two questions remain. We cannot think of eternal life without inquiring about the relation between that life and the totality of our earthly history. And we cannot think of eternal life without inquiring prospectively about the nature of this life as history. First, then, the question concerning the relation between earthly history and eternal life. In the foregoing it has been repeatedly asserted that God's work in Christ and the Spirit is foundational for the coming renewal. But what are we to say of all the struggles as well as the results of social and cultural life? Do these contribute anything to the coming consummation? If already in our treatment of the earthly work of salvation we had to bear in mind that our speaking is on this side of the great eschatological leap, how much more should we do this when we consider the input of human achievements, sinful and ambiguous as they always are. Even so, though by way of a leap with radical consequences, the new world will be born out of this world; it will not be another, a new world, but this old world renewed. It will rise up out of the great crisis toward which this world is heading. See on that paragraph 56. Its birth is thus not wholly disjoined from the technological and cultural achievements and from the progress of the sanctifying forces in this world. But this "not wholly disjoined" can have more than one interpretation. We can say that our culture provides the scaffolding for the coming structure, a scaffolding that will later be torn down again. It is also possible, however, to view our culture as providing the building materials for the coming kingdom. We can speak of a "germ" that is going to sprout, a "content" that is going to be brought into that future. But, more moderately, we can also speak of "preparation," or still more moderately of "witness," "sign," "likeness." We may certainly not expect less than is expressed in these last terms, as surely as this world is going to be renewed. Perhaps we may hope for more. What is certain is that one day the relation between this entire cultural development and eternity will be disclosed and shown to be meaningful. But we are not able to look beyond the great leap. It is wonderful enough to know that all the true, the good, and the beautiful we receive and achieve in our cultural development is a distant foretaste of the fullness of life and the world which God has in store for us.

The Bible, not only in its OT eschatology but also in the NT, speaks quite matter of factly about the continuation of culture and human society in the city of God. But these images are matched by no less vivid images of the destruction of the present world. Compare Rev. 21:2 (the new Jerusalem descends out of heaven) and 21:24, 26 (the cultural treasures of the nations are brought into it).

The study of the faith must include this dual imagery in its conceptualization. Seventeenth-century Lutheran orthodoxy was inclined to think of the future following the destruction of this world in terms of a new creation *(nova creatio);* see S pars. 66f., and P. Althaus, *Die letzten Dinge* (since the 4th edition, 1933), pp. 353–360. Reformed orthodoxy generally thought in terms of a re-creation (*recreatio*) and therefore assumed a strong continuity. See e.g. Bavinck, *GD* IV, pp. 797–803, and A. Kuyper, *Van de gemeene gratie,* I (1902), pp. 454–494. As we see it, one should speak neither of a new creation nor of re-creation, but rather of a transformation. That term gives expression to the fact that all of cultural development will prove to be meaningful in the light of eternity. But that is the limit of what can be said about eternity.

What faith can imagine may and must go further than what the study of the faith can do. Religious imagination is more than idle fantasy; like the magnet of a compass, it searches for the direction in which eternity is to be found. So Barth may hope that there he can listen to Mozart's music, another that technology will produce new and greater wonders, a third that there he will be able to enter into discussion with the philosophers of all ages. All of them will find out that they were more right than they could have imagined here.

And then the second question: are we to think of eternal life as a history? It cannot possibly be a history similar to what we know of earthly history. With us history is a succession of generations which rise, shine, and decline, and it is characterized by perishableness and death. But does this mean that eternal life as such is history-less? That is how it is often presented in the Christian tradition, as a never ending, stationary movement or as an everlasting holiday. The last two centuries we have experienced how much historical development, goal-orientedness, and future planning are integral to humanity, making for acceleration and tension without which we cannot imagine human life; therefore the picture of an unchanging eternity must appear boring, even abhorrent to us. But that picture cannot be right. Time will not be swallowed up in a rigid eternity. Life will be elevated above the contrast of being and becoming. The tension inherent in the triad of past–present–future will not be abolished, leaving only a present. Moreover, glorified time will have in it the dimension of the future. We shall be at our destination without becoming static and be dynamic without want. There love will rule, a love which embraces faith and hope and which is forever active. The historicity *(Geschichtlichkeit)* of our existence will then not be abolished, but glorified. We may speak of eternal rest or eternal joy, provided we speak likewise of eternal activity and service. May we also speak of a progression in knowledge and deeds that will go on forever? We are used to calling that which lies beyond the great leap "the end of the world" or "the end of time." It is better to avoid those expressions. When God has lifted his human creature out of this provisional and alienated form of life and brought him home into his very presence, then, at last, life really begins.

Schleiermacher could conceive of eternal life only as "a sudden and unvarying possession of the highest, or as a gradual ascent to the highest" (*CF* par. 163). The first, however, he regarded as unthinkable, the second he did not think possible without imperfection and dissatisfaction. His conclusion is: "Thus the problem remains unsolved." In our opinion, a combination of the two in a new synthesis is not unthinkable, and not even altogether unimaginable; examples of such a simultaneous possessing and progressing would be the marriage bond or the involvement one can have in one's occupation.

It is not sufficiently noted that the NT does not cater to a static conception of eternal life. The man who in his earthly life has made the most of his pounds is given much greater responsibilities in eternal life (Luke 19:11–27). In this respect the term "rule" *(basileuein)*, through and with Christ, as characteristic of eternal life, is particularly significant (Rom. 5:17; 2 Tim. 2:12; Rev. 3:21; 5:10; cf. Luke 19:17 and 19 and 1 Cor. 4:8). As we see it, this goes back to the position of rule and stewardship which man is assigned in Gen. 1:26–28; eternal life will not mean the end of that position, but rather its real beginning.

In more static times or in periods when life was hard and full of toil and sorrow, Christian piety showed much more interest in other NT images, like "rest" and "sabbath." Not without ground, for eternal life means also that man can breathe again and relax. In times like ours it is also necessary to include the other aspect in our thinking and imagination. As concerns dogmatics, see Bavinck, *GD* IV, no. 580, and especially P. Althaus, *Die letzten Dinge,* pp. 332–337 and his formulation on pp. 363f. that the future consists "not in a stark having-become, but in the living actuality of an eternal becoming, in this way, that God calls us to an inexhaustible knowing and giving shape. The present joy over achievements, the noble joy of knowing and of shaping, is a foretaste, a promise of the joy we will experience in such kinds of work." Althaus speaks only of unfolding (p. 335); he refuses to speak of progress and development. But this distinction, it seems to us, is artificial, in general as well as in the context of his argument. Continuing to think about this, we can ask whether the future of mankind is not to be conceived of in terms of continuing progress, just as in par. 51 we suggested that of the lot of the individual beyond death (in an "intermediate state"?). For we are unable to think of the individual apart from the human world as a whole. Could it be that for the human race as a whole there might be an almost endless moving toward the goal of our life, a progressing in which we are called and being qualified to meet constantly new challenges and to overcome? Who can tell?

Here, too, we wish to point out the independent significance of faith's imaginative ability, next to that of the study of the faith. The sufferer and the toiler need have no qualms about picturing eternal life as undisturbed rest, while the dynamic person may equally as fully expect that there he will be able to realize suppressed or undeveloped potentials and reach for ever wider horizons. God is inexhaustible; and the closer we live to him, the more life will reveal itself to us in all its inexhaustibility. "We hope ever to be receiving more and more from God, and to learn from Him, because He is good, and possesses boundless riches, a kingdom without end, and instruction that can never be exhausted" (Irenaeus, *AH* II, 28,3).

Indexes

PRINCIPAL SUBJECTS

NAMES

SCRIPTURE REFERENCES

Genesis

Exodus

Luke

John

Acts

Romans

1 Corinthians

2 Corinthians

Galatians

Ephesians

Philippians

Colossians

1 Thessalonians